31.95

TOYOTA | CAMRY
2002-06 REPAIR MANUAL

CHILTON'S

Covers U.S. and Canadian models of Toyota Camry, Avalon and Lexus ES 300/330 models - 2002 through 2006 and Toyota Solara - 2002 through 2008

Does not include information specific to the 2005 and later 3.5L V6 engine

by Jay Storer

CHILTON *Automotive Books*

PUBLISHED BY **HAYNES NORTH AMERICA, Inc.**

Manufactured in USA
©2005, 2009, 2012 Haynes North America, Inc.
ISBN-13: 978-1-62092-028-2
Library of Congress Control Number: 2012953809

Haynes Publishing Group
Sparkford Nr Yeovil
Somerset BA22 7JJ England

Haynes North America, Inc
861 Lawrence Drive
Newbury Park
California 91320 USA

ABCDE
FGHIJ
KLMNO

11Q2

Contents

INTRODUCTORY PAGES

About this manual – 0-5
Introduction – 0-5
Vehicle identification numbers – 0-6
Buying parts – 0-7
Maintenance techniques, tools and
 working facilities – 0-7
Booster battery (jump) starting – 0-15

Jacking and towing – 0-16
Automotive chemicals and lubricants – 0-17
Conversion factors – 0-18
Fraction/decimal/millimeter
 equivalents – 0-19
Safety first! – 0-20
Troubleshooting – 0-21

1   TUNE-UP AND ROUTINE MAINTENANCE – 1-1

2   FOUR-CYLINDER ENGINE – 2A-1
V6 ENGINE – 2B-1
GENERAL ENGINE OVERHAUL PROCEDURES – 2C-1

3   COOLING, HEATING AND AIR CONDITIONING SYSTEMS – 3-1

4   FUEL AND EXHAUST SYSTEMS – 4-1

5   ENGINE ELECTRICAL SYSTEMS – 5-1

6   EMISSIONS AND ENGINE CONTROL SYSTEMS – 6-1

MANUAL TRANSAXLE – 7A-1
AUTOMATIC TRANSAXLE – 7B-1

7

CLUTCH AND DRIVEAXLES – 8-1

8

BRAKES – 9-1

9

SUSPENSION AND STEERING SYSTEMS – 10-1

10

BODY – 11-1

11

CHASSIS ELECTRICAL SYSTEM – 12-1
WIRING DIAGRAMS – 12-22

12

GLOSSARY – GL-1

GLOSSARY

MASTER INDEX – IND-1

MASTER INDEX

Mechanic and writer with a 2004 Camry

ACKNOWLEDGEMENTS

The technical writer who contributed to this project was Len Taylor. Wiring diagrams provided exclusively for the publisher by Valley Forge Technical Information Services.

About this manual

ITS PURPOSE

The purpose of this manual is to help you get the best value from your vehicle. It can do so in several ways. It can help you decide what work must be done, even if you choose to have it done by a dealer service department or a repair shop; it provides information and procedures for routine maintenance and servicing; and it offers diagnostic and repair procedures to follow when trouble occurs.

We hope you use the manual to tackle the work yourself. For many simpler jobs, doing it yourself may be quicker than arranging an appointment to get the vehicle into a shop and making the trips to leave it and pick it up. More importantly, a lot of money can be saved by avoiding the expense the shop must pass on to you to cover its labor and overhead costs. An added benefit is the sense of satisfaction and accomplishment that you feel after doing the job yourself.

USING THE MANUAL

The manual is divided into Chapters. Each Chapter is divided into numbered Sections. Each Section consists of consecutively numbered paragraphs.

At the beginning of each numbered Section you will be referred to any illustrations which apply to the procedures in that Section. The reference numbers used in illustration captions pinpoint the pertinent Section and the Step within that Section. That is, illustration 3.2 means the illustration refers to Section 3 and Step (or paragraph) 2 within that Section.

Procedures, once described in the text, are not normally repeated. When it's necessary to refer to another Chapter, the reference will be given as Chapter and Section number. Cross references given without use of the word "Chapter" apply to Sections and/or paragraphs in the same Chapter. For example, "see Section 8" means in the same Chapter.

References to the left or right side of the vehicle assume you are sitting in the driver's seat, facing forward.

Even though we have prepared this manual with extreme care, neither the publisher nor the author can accept responsibility for any errors in, or omissions from, the information given.

➡NOTE

A *Note* provides information necessary to properly complete a procedure or information which will make the procedure easier to understand.

✷✷ CAUTION

A *Caution* provides a special procedure or special steps which must be taken while completing the procedure where the Caution is found. Not heeding a Caution can result in damage to the assembly being worked on.

✷✷ WARNING

A *Warning* provides a special procedure or special steps which must be taken while completing the procedure where the Warning is found. Not heeding a Warning can result in personal injury.

Introduction

This manual covers the Toyota Camry and Lexus ES 300, Solara and Avalon models. The Camry, Lexus ES 300 and Avalon are four-door sedans, while the Solara model is available in 2-door coupe or convertible body styles.

The transversely mounted inline four-cylinder and V6 engines used in these models are equipped with electronic port fuel injection.

The engine drives the front wheels through either a five-speed manual or a four- or five-speed automatic transaxle via independent driveaxles.

Independent suspension, featuring coil spring/strut damper units, is used on all four wheels. The power-assisted rack and pinion steering unit is mounted behind the engine.

The brakes are disc-type at the front with either drum or discs at the rear, depending on model, with power assist standard. Anti-lock brakes (ABS) are available on all models.

VEHICLE IDENTIFICATION NUMBERS

Modifications are a continuing and unpublicized process in vehicle manufacturing. Since spare parts manuals and lists are compiled on a numerical basis, the individual vehicle numbers are essential to correctly identify the component required.

VEHICLE IDENTIFICATION NUMBER (VIN)

This very important identification number is stamped on a plate attached to the dashboard inside the windshield on the driver's side of the vehicle (see illustration). It can also be found on the certification label located on the driver's side door post. The VIN also appears on the Vehicle Certificate of Title and Registration. It contains information such as where and when the vehicle was manufactured, the model year and the body style.

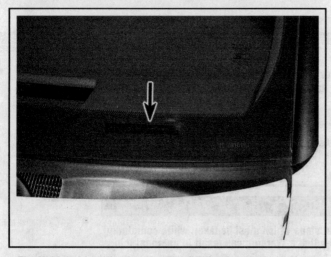

The Vehicle Identification Number (VIN) is located on a plate (arrow) on top of the dash (visible through the windshield)

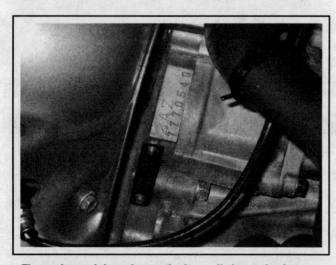

The engine serial number on the four-cylinder engine is located on the rear of the block below the cylinder head

CERTIFICATION LABEL

The certification label is attached to the end of the driver's door post (see illustration). The plate contains the name of the manufacturer, the month and year of production, the Gross Vehicle Weight Rating (GVWR), the Gross Axle Weight Rating (GAWR) and the certification statement.

ENGINE IDENTIFICATION NUMBERS

The engine serial number can be found in a variety of locations, depending on engine type (see illustrations). The Camry and Camry Solara models can be equipped with either the 2AZ-FE four-cylinder or the 1MZ-FE V6. The Avalon and Lexus ES 300/330 models are available in the covered years only with the 1MZ-FE and 3MZ-FE V6 engines.

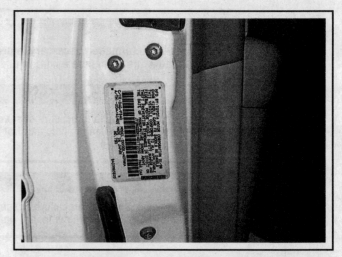

The vehicle certification label is located at the rear of the driver's door

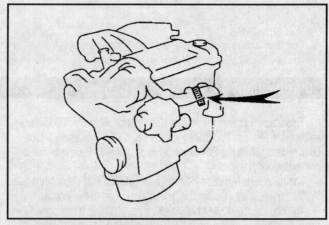

The V6 engine serial number is located on the front side of the block, adjacent to the transaxle

Buying parts

Replacement parts are available from many sources, which generally fall into one of two categories - authorized dealer parts departments and independent retail auto parts stores. Our advice concerning these parts is as follows:

Retail auto parts stores: Good auto parts stores will stock frequently needed components which wear out relatively fast, such as clutch components, exhaust systems, brake parts, tune-up parts, etc. These stores often supply new or reconditioned parts on an exchange basis, which can save a considerable amount of money. Discount auto parts stores are often very good places to buy materials and parts needed for general vehicle maintenance such as oil, grease, filters, spark plugs, belts, touch-up paint, bulbs, etc. They also usually sell tools and general accessories, have convenient hours, charge lower prices and can often be found not far from home.

Authorized dealer parts department: This is the best source for parts which are unique to the vehicle and not generally available elsewhere (such as major engine parts, transmission parts, trim pieces, etc.).

Warranty information: If the vehicle is still covered under warranty, be sure that any replacement parts purchased - regardless of the source - do not invalidate the warranty!

To be sure of obtaining the correct parts, have engine and chassis numbers available and, if possible, take the old parts along for positive identification.

Maintenance techniques, tools and working facilities

MAINTENANCE TECHNIQUES

There are a number of techniques involved in maintenance and repair that will be referred to throughout this manual. Application of these techniques will enable the home mechanic to be more efficient, better organized and capable of performing the various tasks properly, which will ensure that the repair job is thorough and complete.

Fasteners

Fasteners are nuts, bolts, studs and screws used to hold two or more parts together. There are a few things to keep in mind when working with fasteners. Almost all of them use a locking device of some type, either a lockwasher, locknut, locking tab or thread adhesive. All threaded fasteners should be clean and straight, with undamaged threads and undamaged corners on the hex head where the wrench fits. Develop the habit of replacing all damaged nuts and bolts with new ones. Special locknuts with nylon or fiber inserts can only be used once. If they are removed, they lose their locking ability and must be replaced with new ones.

Rusted nuts and bolts should be treated with a penetrating fluid to ease removal and prevent breakage. Some mechanics use turpentine in a spout-type oil can, which works quite well. After applying the rust penetrant, let it work for a few minutes before trying to loosen the nut

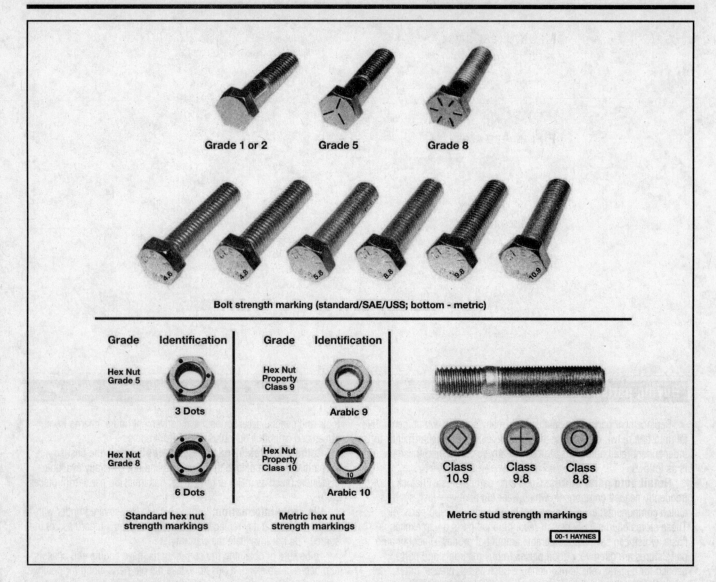

Grade 1 or 2   Grade 5   Grade 8

Bolt strength marking (standard/SAE/USS; bottom - metric)

Grade	Identification		Grade	Identification
Hex Nut Grade 5	3 Dots		Hex Nut Property Class 9	Arabic 9
Hex Nut Grade 8	6 Dots		Hex Nut Property Class 10	Arabic 10

Standard hex nut strength markings   Metric hex nut strength markings

Class 10.9   Class 9.8   Class 8.8

Metric stud strength markings

00-1 HAYNES

or bolt. Badly rusted fasteners may have to be chiseled or sawed off or removed with a special nut breaker, available at tool stores.

If a bolt or stud breaks off in an assembly, it can be drilled and removed with a special tool commonly available for this purpose. Most automotive machine shops can perform this task, as well as other repair procedures, such as the repair of threaded holes that have been stripped out.

Flat washers and lockwashers, when removed from an assembly, should always be replaced exactly as removed. Replace any damaged washers with new ones. Never use a lockwasher on any soft metal surface (such as aluminum), thin sheet metal or plastic.

Fastener sizes

For a number of reasons, automobile manufacturers are making wider and wider use of metric fasteners. Therefore, it is important to be able to tell the difference between standard (sometimes called U.S. or SAE) and metric hardware, since they cannot be interchanged.

All bolts, whether standard or metric, are sized according to diameter, thread pitch and length. For example, a standard 1/2 - 13 x 1 bolt is 1/2 inch in diameter, has 13 threads per inch and is 1 inch long. An M12 - 1.75 x 25 metric bolt is 12 mm in diameter, has a thread pitch of 1.75 mm (the distance between threads) and is 25 mm long. The two bolts are nearly identical, and easily confused, but they are not interchangeable.

In addition to the differences in diameter, thread pitch and length, metric and standard bolts can also be distinguished by examining the bolt heads. To begin with, the distance across the flats on a standard bolt head is measured in inches, while the same dimension on a metric bolt is sized in millimeters (the same is true for nuts). As a result, a standard wrench should not be used on a metric bolt and a metric wrench should not be used on a standard bolt. Also, most standard bolts have slashes radiating out from the center of the head to denote the grade or strength of the bolt, which is an indication of the amount of torque that can be applied to it. The greater the number of slashes, the greater the strength of the bolt. Grades 0 through 5 are commonly used on automobiles. Metric bolts have a property class (grade) number, rather than a slash, molded into their heads to indicate bolt strength. In this case, the higher the number, the stronger the bolt. Property class numbers 8.8, 9.8 and 10.9 are commonly used on automobiles.

Strength markings can also be used to distinguish standard hex nuts from metric hex nuts. Many standard nuts have dots stamped into one side, while metric nuts are marked with a number. The greater the number of dots, or the higher the number, the greater the strength of the nut.

Metric studs are also marked on their ends according to property class (grade). Larger studs are numbered (the same as metric bolts), while smaller studs carry a geometric code to denote grade.

Metric thread sizes

	Ft-lbs	Nm
M-6	6 to 9	9 to 12
M-8	14 to 21	19 to 28
M-10	28 to 40	38 to 54
M-12	50 to 71	68 to 96
M-14	80 to 140	109 to 154

Pipe thread sizes

	Ft-lbs	Nm
1/8	5 to 8	7 to 10
1/4	12 to 18	17 to 24
3/8	22 to 33	30 to 44
1/2	25 to 35	34 to 47

U.S. thread sizes

	Ft-lbs	Nm
1/4 - 20	6 to 9	9 to 12
5/16 - 18	12 to 18	17 to 24
5/16 - 24	14 to 20	19 to 27
3/8 - 16	22 to 32	30 to 43
3/8 - 24	27 to 38	37 to 51
7/16 - 14	40 to 55	55 to 74
7/16 - 20	40 to 60	55 to 81
1/2 - 13	55 to 80	75 to 108

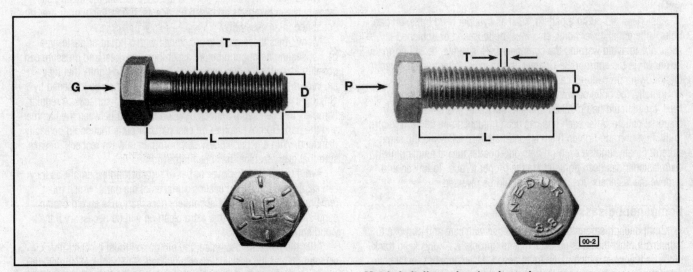

Standard (SAE and USS) bolt dimensions/grade marks

G   Grade marks (bolt strength)
L   Length (in inches)
T   Thread pitch (number of threads per inch)
D   Nominal diameter (in inches)

Metric bolt dimensions/grade marks

P   Property class (bolt strength)
L   Length (in millimeters)
T   Thread pitch (distance between threads in millimeters)
D   Diameter

It should be noted that many fasteners, especially Grades 0 through 2, have no distinguishing marks on them. When such is the case, the only way to determine whether it is standard or metric is to measure the thread pitch or compare it to a known fastener of the same size.

Standard fasteners are often referred to as SAE, as opposed to metric. However, it should be noted that SAE technically refers to a non-metric fine thread fastener only. Coarse thread non-metric fasteners are referred to as USS sizes.

Since fasteners of the same size (both standard and metric) may have different strength ratings, be sure to reinstall any bolts, studs or nuts removed from your vehicle in their original locations. Also, when replacing a fastener with a new one, make sure that the new one has a strength rating equal to or greater than the original.

Tightening sequences and procedures

Most threaded fasteners should be tightened to a specific torque value (torque is the twisting force applied to a threaded component such as a nut or bolt). Overtightening the fastener can weaken it and cause it to break, while undertightening can cause it to eventually come loose. Bolts, screws and studs, depending on the material they are made of and their thread diameters, have specific torque values, many of which are noted in the Specifications at the end of each Chapter. Be sure to follow the torque recommendations closely. For fasteners not assigned a specific torque, a general torque value chart is presented here as a guide. These torque values are for dry (unlubricated) fasteners threaded into steel or cast iron (not aluminum). As was previously mentioned, the size and grade of a fastener determine the amount of torque that can

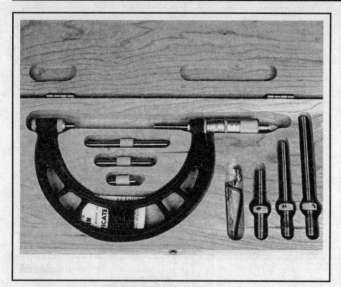

Micrometer set

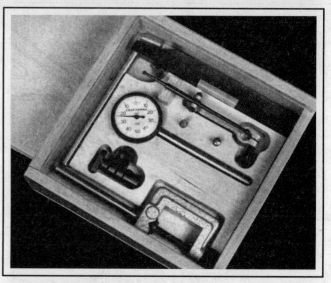

Dial indicator set

safely be applied to it. The figures listed here are approximate for Grade 2 and Grade 3 fasteners. Higher grades can tolerate higher torque values.

Fasteners laid out in a pattern, such as cylinder head bolts, oil pan bolts, differential cover bolts, etc., must be loosened or tightened in sequence to avoid warping the component. This sequence will normally be shown in the appropriate Chapter. If a specific pattern is not given, the following procedures can be used to prevent warping.

Initially, the bolts or nuts should be assembled finger-tight only. Next, they should be tightened one full turn each, in a criss-cross or diagonal pattern. After each one has been tightened one full turn, return to the first one and tighten them all one-half turn, following the same pattern. Finally, tighten each of them one-quarter turn at a time until each fastener has been tightened to the proper torque. To loosen and remove the fasteners, the procedure would be reversed.

Component disassembly

Component disassembly should be done with care and purpose to help ensure that the parts go back together properly. Always keep track of the sequence in which parts are removed. Make note of special characteristics or marks on parts that can be installed more than one way, such as a grooved thrust washer on a shaft. It is a good idea to lay the disassembled parts out on a clean surface in the order that they were removed. It may also be helpful to make sketches or take instant photos of components before removal.

When removing fasteners from a component, keep track of their locations. Sometimes threading a bolt back in a part, or putting the washers and nut back on a stud, can prevent mix-ups later. If nuts and bolts cannot be returned to their original locations, they should be kept in a compartmented box or a series of small boxes. A cupcake or muffin tin is ideal for this purpose, since each cavity can hold the bolts and nuts from a particular area (i.e. oil pan bolts, valve cover bolts, engine mount bolts, etc.). A pan of this type is especially helpful when working on assemblies with very small parts, such as the carburetor, alternator, valve train or interior dash and trim pieces. The cavities can be marked with paint or tape to identify the contents.

Whenever wiring looms, harnesses or connectors are separated, it is a good idea to identify the two halves with numbered pieces of masking tape so they can be easily reconnected.

Gasket sealing surfaces

Throughout any vehicle, gaskets are used to seal the mating surfaces between two parts and keep lubricants, fluids, vacuum or pressure contained in an assembly.

Many times these gaskets are coated with a liquid or paste-type gasket sealing compound before assembly. Age, heat and pressure can sometimes cause the two parts to stick together so tightly that they are very difficult to separate. Often, the assembly can be loosened by striking it with a soft-face hammer near the mating surfaces. A regular hammer can be used if a block of wood is placed between the hammer and the part. Do not hammer on cast parts or parts that could be easily damaged. With any particularly stubborn part, always recheck to make sure that every fastener has been removed.

Avoid using a screwdriver or bar to pry apart an assembly, as they can easily mar the gasket sealing surfaces of the parts, which must remain smooth. If prying is absolutely necessary, use an old broom handle, but keep in mind that extra clean up will be necessary if the wood splinters.

After the parts are separated, the old gasket must be carefully scraped off and the gasket surfaces cleaned. Stubborn gasket material can be soaked with rust penetrant or treated with a special chemical to soften it so it can be easily scraped off.

✳✳ CAUTION:

Never use gasket removal solutions or caustic chemicals on plastic or other composite components.

A scraper can be fashioned from a piece of copper tubing by flattening and sharpening one end. Copper is recommended because it is usually softer than the surfaces to be scraped, which reduces the chance of gouging the part. Some gaskets can be removed with a wire brush, but regardless of the method used, the mating surfaces must be left clean and smooth. If for some reason the gasket surface is gouged, then a gasket sealer thick enough to fill scratches will have to be used during reassembly of the components. For most applications, a non-drying (or semi-drying) gasket sealer should be used.

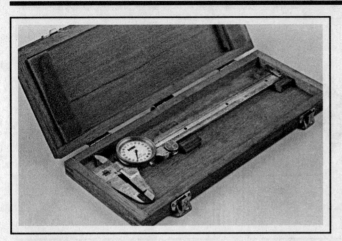

Dial caliper

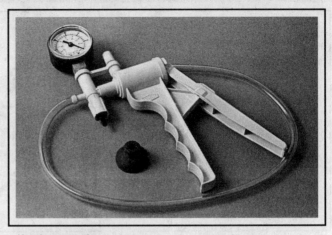

Hand-operated vacuum pump

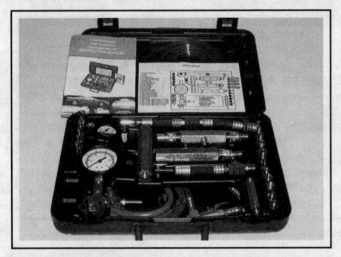

Fuel pressure gauge set

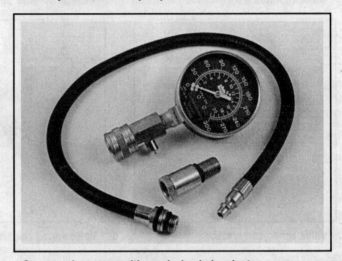

Compression gauge with spark plug hole adapter

Hose removal tips

✳✳ WARNING:

If the vehicle is equipped with air conditioning, do not disconnect any of the A/C hoses without first having the system depressurized by a dealer service department or a service station.

Hose removal precautions closely parallel gasket removal precautions. Avoid scratching or gouging the surface that the hose mates against or the connection may leak. This is especially true for radiator hoses. Because of various chemical reactions, the rubber in hoses can bond itself to the metal spigot that the hose fits over. To remove a hose, first loosen the hose clamps that secure it to the spigot. Then, with slip-joint pliers, grab the hose at the clamp and rotate it around the spigot. Work it back and forth until it is completely free, then pull it off. Silicone or other lubricants will ease removal if they can be applied between the hose and the outside of the spigot. Apply the same lubricant to the inside of the hose and the outside of the spigot to simplify installation.

As a last resort (and if the hose is to be replaced with a new one anyway), the rubber can be slit with a knife and the hose peeled from the spigot. If this must be done, be careful that the metal connection is not damaged.

If a hose clamp is broken or damaged, do not reuse it. Wire-type clamps usually weaken with age, so it is a good idea to replace them with screw-type clamps whenever a hose is removed.

TOOLS

A selection of good tools is a basic requirement for anyone who plans to maintain and repair his or her own vehicle. For the owner who has few tools, the initial investment might seem high, but when compared to the spiraling costs of professional auto maintenance and repair, it is a wise one.

To help the owner decide which tools are needed to perform the tasks detailed in this manual, the following tool lists are offered: *Maintenance and minor repair, Repair/overhaul and Special.*

The newcomer to practical mechanics should start off with the *maintenance and minor repair* tool kit, which is adequate for the simpler jobs performed on a vehicle. Then, as confidence and experience grow, the owner can tackle more difficult tasks, buying additional tools as they are needed. Eventually the basic kit will be expanded into the *repair and overhaul* tool set. Over a period of time, the experienced do-it-yourselfer will assemble a tool set complete enough for most repair and overhaul procedures and will add tools from the special category when it is felt that the expense is justified by the frequency of use.

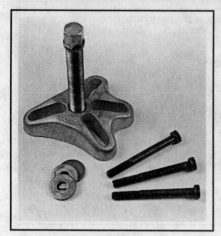

Damper/steering wheel puller

General purpose puller

Hydraulic lifter removal tool

Valve spring compressor

Valve spring compressor

Ridge reamer

Maintenance and minor repair tool kit

The tools in this list should be considered the minimum required for performance of routine maintenance, servicing and minor repair work. We recommend the purchase of combination wrenches (box-end and open-end combined in one wrench). While more expensive than open end wrenches, they offer the advantages of both types of wrench.

Combination wrench set (1/4-inch to 1 inch or 6 mm to 19 mm)
Adjustable wrench, 8 inch
Spark plug wrench with rubber insert
Spark plug gap adjusting tool
Feeler gauge set
Brake bleeder wrench
Standard screwdriver (5/16-inch x 6 inch)
Phillips screwdriver (No. 2 x 6 inch)
Combination pliers - 6 inch
Hacksaw and assortment of blades
Tire pressure gauge
Grease gun
Oil can
Fine emery cloth
Wire brush
Battery post and cable cleaning tool
Oil filter wrench
Funnel (medium size)
Safety goggles
Jackstands (2)
Drain pan

➡**Note: If basic tune-ups are going to be part of routine maintenance, it will be necessary to purchase a good quality stroboscopic timing light and combination tachometer/dwell meter. Although they are included in the list of special tools, it is mentioned here because they are absolutely necessary for tuning most vehicles properly.**

Repair and overhaul tool set

These tools are essential for anyone who plans to perform major repairs and are in addition to those in the maintenance and minor repair tool kit. Included is a comprehensive set of sockets which, though expensive, are invaluable because of their versatility, especially when various extensions and drives are available. We recommend the 1/2-inch drive over the 3/8-inch drive. Although the larger drive is bulky and more expensive, it has the capacity of accepting a very wide range of large sockets. Ideally, however, the mechanic should have a 3/8-inch drive set and a 1/2-inch drive set.

Socket set(s)
Reversible ratchet
Extension - 10 inch
Universal joint
Torque wrench (same size drive as sockets)
Ball peen hammer - 8 ounce
Soft-face hammer (plastic/rubber)
Standard screwdriver (1/4-inch x 6 inch)
Standard screwdriver (stubby - 5/16-inch)
Phillips screwdriver (No. 3 x 8 inch)
Phillips screwdriver (stubby - No. 2)

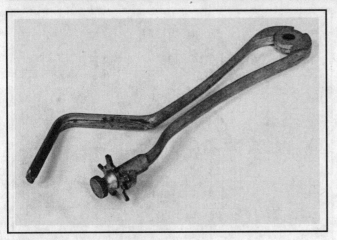

Piston ring groove cleaning tool

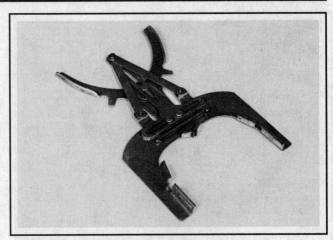

Ring removal/installation tool

Ring compressor

Cylinder hone

Brake hold-down spring tool

Pliers - vise grip
Pliers - lineman's
Pliers - needle nose
Pliers - snap-ring (internal and external)
Cold chisel - 1/2-inch
Scribe
Scraper (made from flattened copper tubing)
Centerpunch
Pin punches (1/16, 1/8, 3/16-inch)
Steel rule/straightedge - 12 inch
Allen wrench set (1/8 to 3/8-inch or 4 mm to 10 mm)
A selection of files
Wire brush (large)
Jackstands (second set)
Jack (scissor or hydraulic type)

➡**Note: Another tool which is often useful is an electric drill with a chuck capacity of 3/8-inch and a set of good quality drill bits.**

Special tools

The tools in this list include those which are not used regularly, are expensive to buy, or which need to be used in accordance with their manufacturer's instructions. Unless these tools will be used frequently, it is not very economical to purchase many of them. A consideration would be to split the cost and use between yourself and a friend or friends. In addition, most of these tools can be obtained from a tool rental shop on a temporary basis.

This list primarily contains only those tools and instruments widely available to the public, and not those special tools produced by the vehicle manufacturer for distribution to dealer service departments. Occasionally, references to the manufacturer's special tools are included in the text of this manual. Generally, an alternative method of doing the job without the special tool is offered. However, sometimes there is no alternative to their use. Where this is the case, and the tool cannot be purchased or borrowed, the work should be turned over to the dealer service department or an automotive repair shop.

Valve spring compressor
Piston ring groove cleaning tool
Piston ring compressor
Piston ring installation tool
Cylinder compression gauge
Cylinder ridge reamer
Cylinder surfacing hone
Cylinder bore gauge
Micrometers and/or dial calipers
Hydraulic lifter removal tool
Balljoint separator
Universal-type puller
Impact screwdriver
Dial indicator set
Stroboscopic timing light (inductive pick-up)
Hand operated vacuum/pressure pump
Tachometer/dwell meter
Universal electrical multimeter

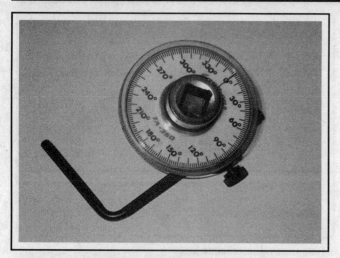

Torque angle gauge

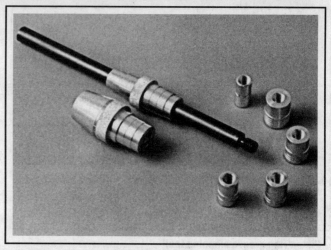

Clutch plate alignment tool

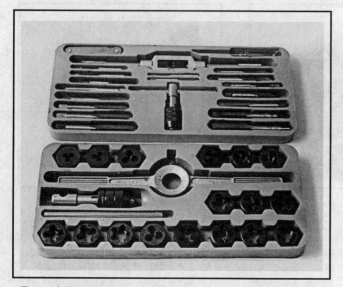

Tap and die set

Cable hoist
Brake spring removal and installation tools
Floor jack

Buying tools

For the do-it-yourselfer who is just starting to get involved in vehicle maintenance and repair, there are a number of options available when purchasing tools. If maintenance and minor repair is the extent of the work to be done, the purchase of individual tools is satisfactory. If, on the other hand, extensive work is planned, it would be a good idea to purchase a modest tool set from one of the large retail chain stores. A set can usually be bought at a substantial savings over the individual tool prices, and they often come with a tool box. As additional tools are needed, add-on sets, individual tools and a larger tool box can be purchased to expand the tool selection. Building a tool set gradually allows the cost of the tools to be spread over a longer period of time and gives the mechanic the freedom to choose only those tools that will actually be used.

Tool stores will often be the only source of some of the special tools that are needed, but regardless of where tools are bought, try to avoid cheap ones, especially when buying screwdrivers and sockets, because they won't last very long. The expense involved in replacing cheap tools will eventually be greater than the initial cost of quality tools.

Care and maintenance of tools

Good tools are expensive, so it makes sense to treat them with respect. Keep them clean and in usable condition and store them properly when not in use. Always wipe off any dirt, grease or metal chips before putting them away. Never leave tools lying around in the work area. Upon completion of a job, always check closely under the hood for tools that may have been left there so they won't get lost during a test drive.

Some tools, such as screwdrivers, pliers, wrenches and sockets, can be hung on a panel mounted on the garage or workshop wall, while others should be kept in a tool box or tray. Measuring instruments, gauges, meters, etc. must be carefully stored where they cannot be damaged by weather or impact from other tools.

When tools are used with care and stored properly, they will last a very long time. Even with the best of care, though, tools will wear out if used frequently. When a tool is damaged or worn out, replace it. Subsequent jobs will be safer and more enjoyable if you do.

HOW TO REPAIR DAMAGED THREADS

Sometimes, the internal threads of a nut or bolt hole can become stripped, usually from overtightening. Stripping threads is an all-too-common occurrence, especially when working with aluminum parts, because aluminum is so soft that it easily strips out.

Usually, external or internal threads are only partially stripped. After they've been cleaned up with a tap or die, they'll still work. Sometimes, however, threads are badly damaged. When this happens, you've got three choices:

1) *Drill and tap the hole to the next suitable oversize and install a larger diameter bolt, screw or stud.*
2) *Drill and tap the hole to accept a threaded plug, then drill and tap the plug to the original screw size. You can also buy a plug already threaded to the original size. Then you simply drill a hole to the specified size, then run the threaded plug into the hole with a bolt and jam nut. Once the plug is fully seated, remove the jam nut and bolt.*

3) *The third method uses a patented thread repair kit like Heli-Coil or Slimsert. These easy-to-use kits are designed to repair damaged threads in straight-through holes and blind holes. Both are available as kits which can handle a variety of sizes and thread patterns. Drill the hole, then tap it with the special included tap. Install the Heli-Coil and the hole is back to its original diameter and thread pitch.*

Regardless of which method you use, be sure to proceed calmly and carefully. A little impatience or carelessness during one of these relatively simple procedures can ruin your whole day's work and cost you a bundle if you wreck an expensive part.

WORKING FACILITIES

Not to be overlooked when discussing tools is the workshop. If anything more than routine maintenance is to be carried out, some sort of suitable work area is essential.

It is understood, and appreciated, that many home mechanics do not have a good workshop or garage available, and end up removing an engine or doing major repairs outside. It is recommended, however, that the overhaul or repair be completed under the cover of a roof.

A clean, flat workbench or table of comfortable working height is an absolute necessity. The workbench should be equipped with a vise that has a jaw opening of at least four inches.

As mentioned previously, some clean, dry storage space is also required for tools, as well as the lubricants, fluids, cleaning solvents, etc. which soon become necessary.

Sometimes waste oil and fluids, drained from the engine or cooling system during normal maintenance or repairs, present a disposal problem. To avoid pouring them on the ground or into a sewage system, pour the used fluids into large containers, seal them with caps and take them to an authorized disposal site or recycling center. Plastic jugs, such as old antifreeze containers, are ideal for this purpose.

Always keep a supply of old newspapers and clean rags available. Old towels are excellent for mopping up spills. Many mechanics use rolls of paper towels for most work because they are readily available and disposable. To help keep the area under the vehicle clean, a large cardboard box can be cut open and flattened to protect the garage or shop floor.

Whenever working over a painted surface, such as when leaning over a fender to service something under the hood, always cover it with an old blanket or bedspread to protect the finish. Vinyl covered pads, made especially for this purpose, are available at auto parts stores.

Booster battery (jump) starting

Observe these precautions when using a booster battery to start a vehicle:

a) *Before connecting the booster battery, make sure the ignition switch is in the Off position.*

b) *Turn off the lights, heater and other electrical loads.*

c) *Your eyes should be shielded. Safety goggles are a good idea.*

d) *Make sure the booster battery is the same voltage as the dead one in the vehicle.*

e) *The two vehicles MUST NOT TOUCH each other!*

f) *Make sure the transaxle is in Neutral (manual) or Park (automatic).*

g) *If the booster battery is not a maintenance-free type, remove the vent caps and lay a cloth over the vent holes.*

Connect the red jumper cable to the positive (+) terminals of each battery (see illustration).

Connect one end of the black jumper cable to the negative (-) terminal of the booster battery. The other end of this cable should be connected to a good ground on the vehicle to be started, such as a bolt or bracket on the body.

Start the engine using the booster battery, then, with the engine running at idle speed, disconnect the jumper cables in the reverse order of connection.

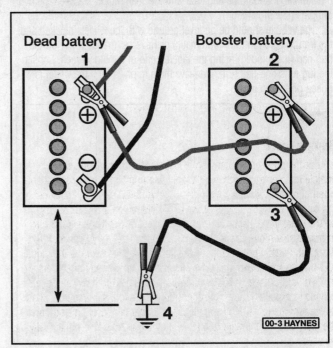

Make the booster battery cable connections in the numerical order shown (note that the negative cable of the booster battery is NOT attached to the negative terminal of the dead battery)

Jacking and towing

JACKING

The jack supplied with the vehicle should only be used for raising the vehicle for changing a tire or placing jackstands under the frame.

❋❋ WARNING:

Never crawl under the vehicle or start the engine when the jack is being used as the only means of support.

All vehicles are supplied with a scissors-type jack. When jacking the vehicle, it should be engaged with the seam notch, between the two dimples (see illustration).

The vehicle should be on level ground with the wheels blocked and the transmission in Park (automatic) or Reverse (manual). Pry off the hub cap (if equipped) using the tapered end of the lug wrench. Loosen the lug nuts one-half turn and leave them in place until the wheel is raised off the ground.

The jack fits over the rocker panel flange, between the two notches (there are two jacking points on each side of the vehicle)

Place the jack under the side of the vehicle in the indicated position. Use the supplied wrench to turn the jackscrew clockwise until the wheel is raised off the ground. Remove the lug nuts, pull off the wheel and replace it with the spare.

With the beveled side in, replace the lug nuts and tighten them until snug. Lower the vehicle by turning the jackscrew counterclockwise. Remove the jack and tighten the nuts in a diagonal pattern to the torque listed in the Chapter 1 Specifications. If a torque wrench is not available, have the torque checked by a service station as soon as possible. Replace the hubcap by placing it in position and using the heel of your hand or a rubber mallet to seat it.

TOWING

Manual transmission-equipped vehicles can be towed with all four wheels on the ground. Automatic transmission-equipped models should only be towed with all four wheels on the ground if speeds do not exceed 35 mph and the distance is not over 50 miles, otherwise transmission damage can result.

Towing equipment specifically designed for this purpose should be used and should be attached to the main structural members of the vehicle, not the bumper or brackets.

Safety is a major consideration when towing and all applicable state and local laws must be obeyed. A safety chain system must be used for all towing.

While towing, the parking brake should be released and the transmission should be in Neutral. The steering must be unlocked (ignition switch in the Off position). Remember that power steering and power brakes will not work with the engine off.

TRACTION CONTROL

On models equipped with Traction-Control system, push in the TRAC switch (on the dashboard or floor console, depending on model) anytime the vehicle is on a "rolling road" tester such as a speedometer test machine or chassis dynamometer. The TRAC OFF indicator light should illuminate when the system is turned off.

Automotive chemicals and lubricants

A number of automotive chemicals and lubricants are available for use during vehicle maintenance and repair. They include a wide variety of products ranging from cleaning solvents and degreasers to lubricants and protective sprays for rubber, plastic and vinyl.

CLEANERS

Carburetor cleaner and choke cleaner is a strong solvent for gum, varnish and carbon. Most carburetor cleaners leave a dry-type lubricant film which will not harden or gum up. Because of this film it is not recommended for use on electrical components.

Brake system cleaner is used to remove brake dust, grease and brake fluid from the brake system, where clean surfaces are absolutely necessary. It leaves no residue and often eliminates brake squeal caused by contaminants.

Electrical cleaner removes oxidation, corrosion and carbon deposits from electrical contacts, restoring full current flow. It can also be used to clean spark plugs, carburetor jets, voltage regulators and other parts where an oil-free surface is desired.

Demoisturants remove water and moisture from electrical components such as alternators, voltage regulators, electrical connectors and fuse blocks. They are non-conductive and non-corrosive.

Degreasers are heavy-duty solvents used to remove grease from the outside of the engine and from chassis components. They can be sprayed or brushed on and, depending on the type, are rinsed off either with water or solvent.

LUBRICANTS

Motor oil is the lubricant formulated for use in engines. It normally contains a wide variety of additives to prevent corrosion and reduce foaming and wear. Motor oil comes in various weights (viscosity ratings) from 0 to 50. The recommended weight of the oil depends on the season, temperature and the demands on the engine. Light oil is used in cold climates and under light load conditions. Heavy oil is used in hot climates and where high loads are encountered. Multi-viscosity oils are designed to have characteristics of both light and heavy oils and are available in a number of weights from 0W-20 to 20W-50.

Gear oil is designed to be used in differentials, manual transmissions and other areas where high-temperature lubrication is required.

Chassis and wheel bearing grease is a heavy grease used where increased loads and friction are encountered, such as for wheel bearings, ball-joints, tie-rod ends and universal joints.

High-temperature wheel bearing grease is designed to withstand the extreme temperatures encountered by wheel bearings in disc brake equipped vehicles. It usually contains molybdenum disulfide (moly), which is a dry-type lubricant.

White grease is a heavy grease for metal-to-metal applications where water is a problem. White grease stays soft under both low and high temperatures (usually from -100 to +190-degrees F), and will not wash off or dilute in the presence of water.

Assembly lube is a special extreme pressure lubricant, usually containing moly, used to lubricate high-load parts (such as main and rod bearings and cam lobes) for initial start-up of a new engine. The assembly lube lubricates the parts without being squeezed out or washed away until the engine oiling system begins to function.

Silicone lubricants are used to protect rubber, plastic, vinyl and nylon parts.

Graphite lubricants are used where oils cannot be used due to contamination problems, such as in locks. The dry graphite will lubricate metal parts while remaining uncontaminated by dirt, water, oil or acids. It is electrically conductive and will not foul electrical contacts in locks such as the ignition switch.

Moly penetrants loosen and lubricate frozen, rusted and corroded fasteners and prevent future rusting or freezing.

Heat-sink grease is a special electrically non-conductive grease that is used for mounting electronic ignition modules where it is essential that heat is transferred away from the module.

SEALANTS

RTV sealant is one of the most widely used gasket compounds. Made from silicone, RTV is air curing, it seals, bonds, waterproofs, fills surface irregularities, remains flexible, doesn't shrink, is relatively easy to remove, and is used as a supplementary sealer with almost all low and medium temperature gaskets.

Anaerobic sealant is much like RTV in that it can be used either to seal gaskets or to form gaskets by itself. It remains flexible, is solvent resistant and fills surface imperfections. The difference between an anaerobic sealant and an RTV-type sealant is in the curing. RTV cures when exposed to air, while an anaerobic sealant cures only in the absence of air. This means that an anaerobic sealant cures only after the assembly of parts, sealing them together.

Thread and pipe sealant is used for sealing hydraulic and pneumatic fittings and vacuum lines. It is usually made from a Teflon compound, and comes in a spray, a paint-on liquid and as a wrap-around tape.

CHEMICALS

Anti-seize compound prevents seizing, galling, cold welding, rust and corrosion in fasteners. High-temperature anti-seize, usually made with copper and graphite lubricants, is used for exhaust system and exhaust manifold bolts.

Anaerobic locking compounds are used to keep fasteners from vibrating or working loose and cure only after installation, in the absence of air. Medium strength locking compound is used for small nuts, bolts and screws that may be removed later. High-strength locking compound is for large nuts, bolts and studs which aren't removed on a regular basis.

Oil additives range from viscosity index improvers to chemical treatments that claim to reduce internal engine friction. It should be noted that most oil manufacturers caution against using additives with their oils.

Gas additives perform several functions, depending on their chemical makeup. They usually contain solvents that help dissolve gum and varnish that build up on carburetor, fuel injection and intake parts. They also serve to break down carbon deposits that form on the inside surfaces of the combustion chambers. Some additives contain upper cylinder lubricants for valves and piston rings, and others contain chemicals to remove condensation from the gas tank.

MISCELLANEOUS

Brake fluid is specially formulated hydraulic fluid that can withstand the heat and pressure encountered in brake systems. Care must be taken so this fluid does not come in contact with painted surfaces or plastics. An opened container should always be resealed to prevent contamination by water or dirt.

Weatherstrip adhesive is used to bond weatherstripping around doors, windows and trunk lids. It is sometimes used to attach trim pieces.

Undercoating is a petroleum-based, tar-like substance that is designed to protect metal surfaces on the underside of the vehicle from corrosion. It also acts as a sound-deadening agent by insulating the bottom of the vehicle.

Waxes and polishes are used to help protect painted and plated surfaces from the weather. Different types of paint may require the use of different types of wax and polish. Some polishes utilize a chemical or abrasive cleaner to help remove the top layer of oxidized (dull) paint on older vehicles. In recent years many non-wax polishes that contain a wide variety of chemicals such as polymers and silicones have been introduced. These non-wax polishes are usually easier to apply and last longer than conventional waxes and polishes.

CONVERSION FACTORS

LENGTH (distance)

Inches (in)	X	25.4	= Millimeters (mm)	X	0.0394 = Inches (in)
Feet (ft)	X	0.305	= Meters (m)	X	3.281 = Feet (ft)
Miles	X	1.609	= Kilometers (km)	X	0.621 = Miles

VOLUME (capacity)

Cubic inches (cu in; in^3)	X	16.387	= Cubic centimeters (cc; cm^3)	X	0.061 = Cubic inches (cu in; in^3)
Imperial pints (Imp pt)	X	0.568	= Liters (l)	X	1.76 = Imperial pints (Imp pt)
Imperial quarts (Imp qt)	X	1.137	= Liters (l)	X	0.88 = Imperial quarts (Imp qt)
Imperial quarts (Imp qt)	X	1.201	= US quarts (US qt)	X	0.833 = Imperial quarts (Imp qt)
US quarts (US qt)	X	0.946	= Liters (l)	X	1.057 = US quarts (US qt)
Imperial gallons (Imp gal)	X	4.546	= Liters (l)	X	0.22 = Imperial gallons (Imp gal)
Imperial gallons (Imp gal)	X	1.201	= US gallons (US gal)	X	0.833 = Imperial gallons (Imp gal)
US gallons (US gal)	X	3.785	= Liters (l)	X	0.264 = US gallons (US gal)

MASS (weight)

Ounces (oz)	X	28.35	= Grams (g)	X	0.035 = Ounces (oz)
Pounds (lb)	X	0.454	= Kilograms (kg)	X	2.205 = Pounds (lb)

FORCE

Ounces-force (ozf; oz)	X	0.278	= Newtons (N)	X	3.6 = Ounces-force (ozf; oz)
Pounds-force (lbf; lb)	X	4.448	= Newtons (N)	X	0.225 = Pounds-force (lbf; lb)
Newtons (N)	X	0.1	= Kilograms-force (kgf; kg)	X	9.81 = Newtons (N)

PRESSURE

Pounds-force per square inch (psi; lbf/in^2; lb/in^2)	X	0.070	= Kilograms-force per square centimeter (kgf/cm^2; kg/cm^2)	X	14.223 = Pounds-force per square inch (psi; lbf/in^2; lb/in^2)
Pounds-force per square inch (psi; lbf/in^2; lb/in^2)	X	0.068	= Atmospheres (atm)	X	14.696 = Pounds-force per square inch (psi; lbf/in^2; lb/in^2)
Pounds-force per square inch (psi; lbf/in^2; lb/in^2)	X	0.069	= Bars	X	14.5 = Pounds-force per square inch (psi; lbf/in^2; lb/in^2)
Pounds-force per square inch (psi; lbf/in^2; lb/in^2)	X	6.895	= Kilopascals (kPa)	X	0.145 = Pounds-force per square inch (psi; lbf/in^2; lb/in^2)
Kilopascals (kPa)	X	0.01	= Kilograms-force per square centimeter (kgf/cm^2; kg/cm^2)	X	98.1 = Kilopascals (kPa)

TORQUE (moment of force)

Pounds-force inches (lbf in; lb in)	X	1.152	= Kilograms-force centimeter (kgf cm; kg cm)	X	0.868 = Pounds-force inches (lbf in; lb in)
Pounds-force inches (lbf in; lb in)	X	0.113	= Newton meters (Nm)	X	8.85 = Pounds-force inches (lbf in; lb in)
Pounds-force inches (lbf in; lb in)	X	0.083	= Pounds-force feet (lbf ft; lb ft)	X	12 = Pounds-force inches (lbf in; lb in)
Pounds-force feet (lbf ft; lb ft)	X	0.138	= Kilograms-force meters (kgf m; kg m)	X	7.233 = Pounds-force feet (lbf ft; lb ft)
Pounds-force feet (lbf ft; lb ft)	X	1.356	= Newton meters (Nm)	X	0.738 = Pounds-force feet (lbf ft; lb ft)
Newton meters (Nm)	X	0.102	= Kilograms-force meters (kgf m; kg m)	X	9.804 = Newton meters (Nm)

VACUUM

Inches mercury (in. Hg)	X	3.377	= Kilopascals (kPa)	X	0.2961 = Inches mercury
Inches mercury (in. Hg)	X	25.4	= Millimeters mercury (mm Hg)	X	0.0394 = Inches mercury

POWER

Horsepower (hp)	X	745.7	= Watts (W)	X	0.0013 = Horsepower (hp)

VELOCITY (speed)

Miles per hour (miles/hr; mph)	X	1.609	= Kilometers per hour (km/hr; kph)	X	0.621 = Miles per hour (miles/hr; mph)

FUEL CONSUMPTION *

Miles per gallon, Imperial (mpg)	X	0.354	= Kilometers per liter (km/l)	X	2.825 = Miles per gallon, Imperial (mpg)
Miles per gallon, US (mpg)	X	0.425	= Kilometers per liter (km/l)	X	2.352 = Miles per gallon, US (mpg)

TEMPERATURE

Degrees Fahrenheit = (°C x 1.8) + 32   Degrees Celsius (Degrees Centigrade; °C) = (°F - 32) x 0.56

*It is common practice to convert from miles per gallon (mpg) to liters/100 kilometers (l/100km), where mpg (Imperial) x l/100 km = 282 and mpg (US) x l/100 km = 235

FRACTION/DECIMAL/MILLIMETER EQUIVALENTS

DECIMALS to MILLIMETERS

Decimal	mm	Decimal	mm
0.001	0.0254	0.500	12.7000
0.002	0.0508	0.510	12.9540
0.003	0.0762	0.520	13.2080
0.004	0.1016	0.530	13.4620
0.005	0.1270	0.540	13.7160
0.006	0.1524	0.550	13.9700
0.007	0.1778	0.560	14.2240
0.008	0.2032	0.570	14.4780
0.009	0.2286	0.580	14.7320
		0.590	14.9860
0.010	0.2540		
0.020	0.5080		
0.030	0.7620		
0.040	1.0160	0.600	15.2400
0.050	1.2700	0.610	15.4940
0.060	1.5240	0.620	15.7480
0.070	1.7780	0.630	16.0020
0.080	2.0320	0.640	16.2560
0.090	2.2860	0.650	16.5100
		0.660	16.7640
0.100	2.5400	0.670	17.0180
0.110	2.7940	0.680	17.2720
0.120	3.0480	0.690	17.5260
0.130	3.3020		
0.140	3.5560		
0.150	3.8100	0.700	17.7800
0.160	4.0640	0.710	18.0340
0.170	4.3180	0.720	18.2880
0.180	4.5720	0.730	18.5420
0.190	4.8260	0.740	18.7960
		0.750	19.0500
0.200	5.0800	0.760	19.3040
0.210	5.3340	0.770	19.5580
0.220	5.5880	0.780	19.8120
0.230	5.8420	0.790	20.0660
0.240	6.0960		
0.250	6.3500		
0.260	6.6040		
0.270	6.8580	0.800	20.3200
0.280	7.1120	0.810	20.5740
0.290	7.3660	0.820	21.8280
		0.830	21.0820
0.300	7.6200	0.840	21.3360
0.310	7.8740	0.850	21.5900
0.320	8.1280	0.860	21.8440
0.330	8.3820	0.870	22.0980
0.340	8.6360	0.880	22.3520
0.350	8.8900	0.890	22.6060
0.360	9.1440		
0.370	9.3980		
0.380	9.6520		
0.390	9.9060	0.900	22.8600
0.400	10.1600	0.910	23.1140
0.410	10.4140	0.920	23.3680
0.420	10.6680	0.930	23.6220
0.430	10.9220	0.940	23.8760
0.440	11.1760	0.950	24.1300
0.450	11.4300	0.960	24.3840
0.460	11.6840	0.970	24.6380
0.470	11.9380	0.980	24.8920
0.480	12.1920	0.990	25.1460
0.490	12.4460	1.000	25.4000

FRACTIONS to DECIMALS to MILLIMETERS

Fraction	Decimal	mm	Fraction	Decimal	mm
1/64	0.0156	0.3969	33/64	0.5156	13.0969
1/32	0.0312	0.7938	17/32	0.5312	13.4938
3/64	0.0469	1.1906	35/64	0.5469	13.8906
1/16	0.0625	1.5875	9/16	0.5625	14.2875
5/64	0.0781	1.9844	37/64	0.5781	14.6844
3/32	0.0938	2.3812	19/32	0.5938	15.0812
7/64	0.1094	2.7781	39/64	0.6094	15.4781
1/8	0.1250	3.1750	5/8	0.6250	15.8750
9/64	0.1406	3.5719	41/64	0.6406	16.2719
5/32	0.1562	3.9688	21/32	0.6562	16.6688
11/64	0.1719	4.3656	43/64	0.6719	17.0656
3/16	0.1875	4.7625	11/16	0.6875	17.4625
13/64	0.2031	5.1594	45/64	0.7031	17.8594
7/32	0.2188	5.5562	23/32	0.7188	18.2562
15/64	0.2344	5.9531	47/64	0.7344	18.6531
1/4	0.2500	6.3500	3/4	0.7500	19.0500
17/64	0.2656	6.7469	49/64	0.7656	19.4469
9/32	0.2812	7.1438	25/32	0.7812	19.8438
19/64	0.2969	7.5406	51/64	0.7969	20.2406
5/16	0.3125	7.9375	13/16	0.8125	20.6375
21/64	0.3281	8.3344	53/64	0.8281	21.0344
11/32	0.3438	8.7312	27/32	0.8438	21.4312
23/64	0.3594	9.1281	55/64	0.8594	21.8281
3/8	0.3750	9.5250	7/8	0.8750	22.2250
25/64	0.3906	9.9219	57/64	0.8906	22.6219
13/32	0.4062	10.3188	29/32	0.9062	23.0188
27/64	0.4219	10.7156	59/64	0.9219	23.4156
7/16	0.4375	11.1125	15/16	0.9375	23.8125
29/64	0.4531	11.5094	61/64	0.9531	24.2094
15/32	0.4688	11.9062	31/32	0.9688	24.6062
31/64	0.4844	12.3031	63/64	0.9844	25.0031
1/2	0.5000	12.7000	1	1.0000	25.4000

Regardless of how enthusiastic you may be about getting on with the job at hand, take the time to ensure that your safety is not jeopardized. A moment's lack of attention can result in an accident, as can failure to observe certain simple safety precautions. The possibility of an accident will always exist, and the following points should not be considered a comprehensive list of all dangers. Rather, they are intended to make you aware of the risks and to encourage a safety conscious approach to all work you carry out on your vehicle.

ESSENTIAL DOS AND DON'TS

DON'T rely on a jack when working under the vehicle. Always use approved jackstands to support the weight of the vehicle and place them under the recommended lift or support points.

DON'T attempt to loosen extremely tight fasteners (i.e. wheel lug nuts) while the vehicle is on a jack - it may fall.

DON'T start the engine without first making sure that the transmission is in Neutral (or Park where applicable) and the parking brake is set.

DON'T remove the radiator cap from a hot cooling system - let it cool or cover it with a cloth and release the pressure gradually.

DON'T attempt to drain the engine oil until you are sure it has cooled to the point that it will not burn you.

DON'T touch any part of the engine or exhaust system until it has cooled sufficiently to avoid burns.

DON'T siphon toxic liquids such as gasoline, antifreeze and brake fluid by mouth, or allow them to remain on your skin.

DON'T inhale brake lining dust - it is potentially hazardous (see Asbestos below).

DON'T allow spilled oil or grease to remain on the floor - wipe it up before someone slips on it.

DON'T use loose fitting wrenches or other tools which may slip and cause injury.

DON'T push on wrenches when loosening or tightening nuts or bolts. Always try to pull the wrench toward you. If the situation calls for pushing the wrench away, push with an open hand to avoid scraped knuckles if the wrench should slip.

DON'T attempt to lift a heavy component alone - get someone to help you.

DON'T rush or take unsafe shortcuts to finish a job.

DON'T allow children or animals in or around the vehicle while you are working on it.

DO wear eye protection when using power tools such as a drill, sander, bench grinder, etc. and when working under a vehicle.

DO keep loose clothing and long hair well out of the way of moving parts.

DO make sure that any hoist used has a safe working load rating adequate for the job.

DO get someone to check on you periodically when working alone on a vehicle.

DO carry out work in a logical sequence and make sure that everything is correctly assembled and tightened.

DO keep chemicals and fluids tightly capped and out of the reach of children and pets.

DO remember that your vehicle's safety affects that of yourself and others. If in doubt on any point, get professional advice.

STEERING, SUSPENSION AND BRAKES

These systems are essential to driving safety, so make sure you have a qualified shop or individual check your work. Also, compressed suspension springs can cause injury if released suddenly - be sure to use a spring compressor.

AIRBAGS

Airbags are explosive devices that can CAUSE injury if they deploy while you're working on the vehicle. Follow the manufacturer's instructions to disable the airbag whenever you're working in the vicinity of airbag components.

ASBESTOS

Certain friction, insulating, sealing, and other products - such as brake linings, brake bands, clutch linings, torque converters, gaskets, etc. - may contain asbestos or other hazardous friction material. Extreme care must be taken to avoid inhalation of dust from such products, since it is hazardous to health. If in doubt, assume that they do contain asbestos.

FIRE

Remember at all times that gasoline is highly flammable. Never smoke or have any kind of open flame around when working on a vehicle. But the risk does not end there. A spark caused by an electrical short circuit, by two metal surfaces contacting each other, or even by static electricity built up in your body under certain conditions, can ignite gasoline vapors, which in a confined space are highly explosive. Do not, under any circumstances, use gasoline for cleaning parts. Use an approved safety solvent.

Always disconnect the battery ground (-) cable at the battery before working on any part of the fuel system or electrical system. Never risk spilling fuel on a hot engine or exhaust component. It is strongly recommended that a fire extinguisher suitable for use on fuel and electrical fires be kept handy in the garage or workshop at all times. Never try to extinguish a fuel or electrical fire with water.

FUMES

Certain fumes are highly toxic and can quickly cause unconsciousness and even death if inhaled to any extent. Gasoline vapor falls into this category, as do the vapors from some cleaning solvents. Any draining or pouring of such volatile fluids should be done in a well ventilated area.

When using cleaning fluids and solvents, read the instructions on the container carefully. Never use materials from unmarked containers.

Never run the engine in an enclosed space, such as a garage. Exhaust fumes contain carbon monoxide, which is extremely poisonous. If you need to run the engine, always do so in the open air, or at least have the rear of the vehicle outside the work area.

THE BATTERY

Never create a spark or allow a bare light bulb near a battery. They normally give off a certain amount of hydrogen gas, which is highly explosive.

Always disconnect the battery ground (-) cable at the battery before working on the fuel or electrical systems.

If possible, loosen the filler caps or cover when charging the battery from an external source (this does not apply to sealed or maintenance-free batteries). Do not charge at an excessive rate or the battery may burst.

Take care when adding water to a non maintenance-free battery and when carrying a battery. The electrolyte, even when diluted, is very corrosive and should not be allowed to contact clothing or skin.

Always wear eye protection when cleaning the battery to prevent the caustic deposits from entering your eyes.

HOUSEHOLD CURRENT

When using an electric power tool, inspection light, etc., which operates on household current, always make sure that the tool is correctly connected to its plug and that, where necessary, it is properly grounded. Do not use such items in damp conditions and, again, do not create a spark or apply excessive heat in the vicinity of fuel or fuel vapor.

SECONDARY IGNITION SYSTEM VOLTAGE

A severe electric shock can result from touching certain parts of the ignition system (such as the spark plug wires) when the engine is running or being cranked, particularly if components are damp or the insulation is defective. In the case of an electronic ignition system, the secondary system voltage is much higher and could prove fatal.

HYDROFLUORIC ACID

This extremely corrosive acid is formed when certain types of synthetic rubber, found in some O-rings, oil seals, fuel hoses, etc. are exposed to temperatures above 750-degrees F (400-degrees C). The rubber changes into a charred or sticky substance containing the acid. *Once formed, the acid remains dangerous for years. If it gets onto the skin, it may be necessary to amputate the limb concerned.*

When dealing with a vehicle which has suffered a fire, or with components salvaged from such a vehicle, wear protective gloves and discard them after use.

Troubleshooting

CONTENTS

Section   Symptom

Engine

CHECK ENGINE light - See Chapter 6
1   Engine will not rotate when attempting to start
2   Engine rotates but will not start
3   Engine hard to start when cold
4   Engine hard to start when hot
5   Starter motor noisy or excessively rough in engagement
6   Engine starts but stops immediately
7   Oil puddle under engine
8   Engine lopes while idling or idles erratically
9   Engine misses at idle speed
10   Engine misses throughout driving speed range
11   Engine stumbles on acceleration
12   Engine surges while holding accelerator steady
13   Engine stalls
14   Engine lacks power
15   Engine backfires
16   Pinging or knocking engine sounds during acceleration or uphill
17   Engine runs with oil pressure light on
18   Engine continues to run after switching off

Engine electrical system

19   Battery will not hold a charge
20   Alternator light fails to go out
21   Alternator light fails to come on when key is turned on

Fuel system

22   Excessive fuel consumption
23   Fuel leakage and/or fuel odor

Cooling system

24   Overheating
25   Overcooling
26   External coolant leakage
27   Internal coolant leakage
28   Coolant loss
29   Poor coolant circulation

Clutch

30   Pedal travels to floor - no pressure or very little resistance
31   Fluid in area of master cylinder dust cover and on pedal
32   Fluid on release cylinder
33   Pedal feels spongy when depressed
34   Unable to select gears
35   Clutch slips (engine speed increases with no increase in vehicle speed)
36   Grabbing (chattering) as clutch is engaged
37   Transaxle rattling (clicking)
39   Clutch pedal stays on floor
38   Noise in clutch area
40   High pedal effort

Manual transaxle

41   Knocking noise at low speeds
42   Noise most pronounced when turning

43   Clunk on acceleration or deceleration
44   Clicking noise in turns
45   Vibration
46   Noisy in neutral with engine running
47   Noisy in one particular gear
48   Noisy in all gears
49   Slips out of gear
50   Leaks lubricant
51   Locked in gear

Automatic transaxle

52   Fluid leakage
53   Transaxle fluid brown or has burned smell
54   General shift mechanism problems
55   Transaxle will not downshift with accelerator pedal pressed to the floor
56   Engine will start in gears other than Park or Neutral
57   Transaxle slips, shifts roughly, is noisy or has no drive in forward or reverse gears

Driveaxles

58   Clicking noise in turns
59   Shudder or vibration during acceleration
60   Vibration at highway speeds

Brakes

61   Vehicle pulls to one side during braking
62   Noise (high-pitched squeal when the brakes are applied)
63   Brake roughness or chatter (pedal pulsates)
64   Excessive pedal effort required to stop vehicle
65   Excessive brake pedal travel
66   Dragging brakes
67   Grabbing or uneven braking action
68   Brake pedal feels spongy when depressed
69   Brake pedal travels to the floor with little resistance
70   Parking brake does not hold

Suspension and steering systems

71   Vehicle pulls to one side
72   Abnormal or excessive tire wear
73   Wheel makes a thumping noise
74   Shimmy, shake or vibration
75   Hard steering
76   Poor returnability of steering to center
77   Abnormal noise at the front end
78   Wander or poor steering stability
79   Erratic steering when braking
80   Excessive pitching and/or rolling around corners or during braking
81   Suspension bottoms
82   Cupped tires
83   Excessive tire wear on outside edge
84   Excessive tire wear on inside edge
85   Tire tread worn in one place
86   Excessive play or looseness in steering system
87   Rattling or clicking noise in steering gear

This section provides an easy reference guide to the more common problems which may occur during the operation of your vehicle. These problems and their possible causes are grouped under headings denoting various components or systems, such as Engine, Cooling system, etc. They also refer you to the chapter and/or section which deals with the problem.

Remember that successful troubleshooting is not a mysterious art practiced only by professional mechanics. It is simply the result of the right knowledge combined with an intelligent, systematic approach to the problem. Always work by a process of elimination, starting with the simplest solution and working through to the most complex - and never overlook the obvious. Anyone can run the gas tank dry or leave the lights on overnight, so don't assume that you are exempt from such oversights.

Finally, always establish a clear idea of why a problem has occurred and take steps to ensure that it doesn't happen again. If the electrical system fails because of a poor connection, check the other connections in the system to make sure that they don't fail as well. If a particular fuse continues to blow, find out why - don't just replace one fuse after another. Remember, failure of a small component can often be indicative of potential failure or incorrect functioning of a more important component or system.

ENGINE

1 Engine will not rotate when attempting to start

1   Battery terminal connections loose or corroded (Chapter 1).
2   Battery discharged or faulty (Chapter 1).
3   Automatic transaxle not completely engaged in Park (Chapter 7) or clutch not completely depressed (Chapter 8).
4   Broken, loose or disconnected wiring in the starting circuit (Chapters 5 and 12).
5   Starter motor pinion jammed in flywheel ring gear (Chapter 5).
6   Starter solenoid faulty (Chapter 5).
7   Starter motor faulty (Chapter 5).
8   Ignition switch faulty (Chapter 12).
9   Starter pinion or flywheel teeth worn or broken (Chapter 5).

2 Engine rotates but will not start

1   Fuel tank empty.
2   Battery discharged (engine rotates slowly) (Chapter 5).
3   Battery terminal connections loose or corroded (Chapter 1).
4   Leaking fuel injector(s), faulty fuel pump, pressure regulator, etc. (Chapter 4).
5   Fuel not reaching fuel rail (Chapter 4).
6   Ignition system problem (Chapter 5).
7   Worn, faulty or incorrectly gapped spark plugs (Chapter 1).
8   Faulty camshaft or crankshaft position sensor (Chapter 6).

3 Engine hard to start when cold

1   Battery discharged or low (Chapter 1).
2   Malfunctioning fuel system (Chapter 4).
3   Injector(s) leaking (Chapter 4).
4   Faulty coolant temperature sensor (Chapter 6).

4 Engine hard to start when hot

1   Air filter clogged (Chapter 1).
2   Fuel not reaching the fuel injection system (Chapter 4).
3   Corroded battery connections, especially ground (Chapter 1).

5 Starter motor noisy or excessively rough in engagement

1   Pinion or flywheel gear teeth worn or broken (Chapter 5).
2   Starter motor mounting bolts loose or missing (Chapter 5).

6 Engine starts but stops immediately

1   Loose or faulty electrical connections at coil(s) or alternator (Chapter 5).
2   Insufficient fuel reaching the fuel injector(s) (Chapters 1 and 4).
3   Vacuum leak at the gasket between the intake manifold/plenum and throttle body (Chapters 1 and 4).

7 Oil puddle under engine

1   Oil pan gasket and/or oil pan drain bolt washer leaking (Chapter 2).
2   Oil pressure sending unit leaking (Chapter 2).
3   Valve covers leaking (Chapter 2).
4   Engine oil seals leaking (Chapter 2).
5   Oil pump housing leaking (Chapter 2).

8 Engine lopes while idling or idles erratically

1   Vacuum leakage (Chapters 2 and 4).
2   Air filter clogged (Chapter 1).
3   Fuel pump not delivering sufficient fuel to the fuel injection system (Chapter 4).
4   Leaking head gasket (Chapter 2).
5   Timing belt or chain and/or sprockets worn (Chapter 2).
6   Camshaft lobes worn (Chapter 2).

9 Engine misses at idle speed

1   Spark plugs worn or not gapped properly (Chapter 1).
2   Vacuum leaks (Chapter 1).
3   Fault in engine management system (Chapter 6).
4   Uneven or low compression (Chapter 2).

10 Engine misses throughout driving speed range

1   Fuel filter clogged and/or impurities in the fuel system (Chapter 1).
2   Faulty injector(s) (Chapter 4).
3   Faulty or incorrectly gapped spark plugs (Chapter 1).
4   Faulty ignition coil(s) (Chapter 5).
5   Fault in engine management system (Chapter 6).
6   Faulty emission system components (Chapter 6).
7   Low or uneven cylinder compression pressures (Chapter 2).
8   Faulty ignition system (Chapter 5).
9   Vacuum leak in intake manifold/plenum, air control valve or vacuum hoses (Chapter 4).

11 Engine stumbles on acceleration

1 Spark plugs fouled (Chapter 1).
2 Fuel injection system faulty (Chapter 4).
3 Fuel filter clogged (Chapter 4).
4 Fault in engine management system (Chapter 6).
5 Intake manifold or plenum air leak (Chapters 2 and 4).

12 Engine surges while holding accelerator steady

1 Intake air leak (Chapter 4).
2 Fuel pump faulty (Chapter 4).
3 Defective PCM or information sensor (Chapter 6).

13 Engine stalls

1 Idle speed incorrect (Chapter 1).
2 Fuel filter clogged and/or water and impurities in the fuel system (Chapter 4).
3 Ignition system problem (Chapter 5).
4 Faulty emissions system components (Chapter 6).
5 Faulty or incorrectly gapped spark plugs (Chapter 1).
6 Vacuum leak in the fuel injection system, intake manifold or vacuum hoses (Chapters 2 and 4).
7 Valve clearances incorrectly set (Chapter 1).

14 Engine lacks power

1 Fault in engine management system (Chapter 6).
2 Faulty or incorrectly gapped spark plugs (Chapter 1).
3 Fuel injection system malfunction (Chapter 4).
4 Faulty coil(s) (Chapter 5).
5 Brakes dragging (Chapter 9).
6 Automatic transaxle fluid level incorrect (Chapter 1).
7 Clutch slipping (Chapter 8).
8 Fuel filter clogged and/or impurities in the fuel system (Chapters 4).
9 Emissions control systems not functioning properly (Chapter 6).
10 Low or uneven cylinder compression pressures (Chapter 2).
11 Obstructed exhaust system (Chapter 4).

15 Engine backfires

1 Emission control system not functioning properly (Chapter 6).
2 Fault in engine management system (Chapter 6).
3 Faulty secondary ignition system (cracked spark plug insulator or ignition coil) (Chapters 1 and 5).
4 Fuel injection system malfunction (Chapter 4).
5 Vacuum leak at fuel injector(s), intake manifold, air control valve or vacuum hoses (Chapters 2 and 4).
6 Valve clearances incorrectly set and/or valves sticking (Chapter 1).

16 Pinging or knocking engine sounds during acceleration or uphill

1 Incorrect grade of fuel.
2 Fault in engine management system (Chapter 6).

3 Fuel injection system faulty (Chapter 4).
4 Improper or damaged spark plugs or wires (Chapter 1).
5 Vacuum leak (Chapters 2 and 4).
6 Defective knock sensor (Chapter 6).

17 Engine runs with oil pressure light on

1 Low oil level (Chapter 1).
2 Faulty oil pressure sender (Chapter 2).
3 Worn engine bearings and/or oil pump (Chapter 2).

18 Engine continues to run after switching off

1 Idle speed too high (Chapter 1).
2 Excessive engine operating temperature (Chapter 3).
3 Fault in engine management system (Chapter 6).

ENGINE ELECTRICAL SYSTEM

19 Battery will not hold a charge

1 Drivebelt defective or not adjusted properly (Chapter 1).
2 Battery electrolyte level low (Chapter 1).
3 Battery terminals loose or corroded (Chapter 1).
4 Alternator not charging properly (Chapter 5).
5 Loose, broken or faulty wiring in the charging circuit (Chapter 5).
6 Internally defective battery (Chapters 1 and 5).

20 Alternator light fails to go out

1 Faulty alternator or charging circuit (Chapter 5).
2 Alternator drivebelt or tensioner defective (Chapter 1).
3 Alternator voltage regulator inoperative (Chapter 5).

21 Alternator light fails to come on when key is turned on

1 Warning light bulb defective (Chapter 12).
2 Fault in the printed circuit, dash wiring or bulb holder (Chapter 12).

FUEL SYSTEM

22 Excessive fuel consumption

1 Dirty or clogged air filter element (Chapter 1).
2 Fault in engine management system (Chapter 6).
3 Emissions systems not functioning properly (Chapter 6).
4 Fuel injection system not functioning properly (Chapter 4).
5 Low tire pressure or incorrect tire size (Chapter 1).

23   Fuel leakage and/or fuel odor

1   Leaking fuel line (Chapters 1 and 4).
2   Tank overfilled.
3   Evaporative canister filter clogged (Chapters 1 and 6).
4   Fuel injection system not functioning properly (Chapter 4).

COOLING SYSTEM

24   Overheating

1   Insufficient coolant in system (Chapter 1).
2   Water pump defective (Chapter 3).
3   Radiator core blocked or grille restricted (Chapter 3).
4   Thermostat faulty (Chapter 3).
5   Electric coolant fan blades broken or cracked (Chapter 3).
6   Radiator cap not maintaining proper pressure (Chapter 3).
7   Fault in engine management system (Chapter 6).

25   Overcooling

1   Faulty thermostat (Chapter 3).
2   Temperature gauge defective.

26   External coolant leakage

1   Deteriorated/damaged hoses; loose clamps (Chapters 1 and 3).
2   Water pump defective (Chapter 3).
3   Leakage from radiator core or coolant reservoir bottle (Chapter 3).
4   Engine drain or water jacket core plugs leaking.
5   Too much coolant in the system (Chapter 1).

27   Internal coolant leakage

1   Leaking cylinder head gasket (Chapter 2).
2   Cracked cylinder bore or cylinder head (Chapter 2).

28   Coolant loss

1   Coolant boiling away because of overheating (Chapter 3).
2   Internal or external leakage (Chapter 3).
3   Faulty radiator cap (Chapter 3).

29   Poor coolant circulation

1   Inoperative water pump (Chapter 3).
2   Restriction in cooling system (Chapters 1 and 3).
3   Water pump drivebelt defective/out of adjustment (Chapter 1).
4   Thermostat sticking (Chapter 3).

CLUTCH

30   Pedal travels to floor - no pressure or very little resistance

1   Master or release cylinder faulty (Chapter 8).
2   Hose/pipe burst or leaking (Chapter 8).

3   Connections leaking (Chapter 8).
4   No fluid in reservoir (Chapter 8).
5   If fluid level in reservoir rises as pedal is depressed, master cylinder center valve seal is faulty (Chapter 8).
6   If there is fluid on dust seal at master cylinder, piston primary seal is leaking (Chapter 8).
7   Broken release bearing or fork (Chapter 8).

31   Fluid in area of master cylinder dust cover and on pedal

Rear seal failure in master cylinder (Chapter 8).

32   Fluid on release cylinder

Release cylinder plunger seal faulty (Chapter 8).

33   Pedal feels spongy when depressed

Air in system (Chapter 8).

34   Unable to select gears

1   Faulty transaxle (Chapter 7).
2   Faulty clutch disc (Chapter 8).
3   Release lever and bearing not assembled properly (Chapter 8).
4   Faulty pressure plate (Chapter 8).
5   Pressure plate-to-flywheel bolts loose (Chapter 8).

35   Clutch slips (engine speed increases with no increase in vehicle speed)

1   Clutch plate worn (Chapter 8).
2   Clutch plate is oil soaked by leaking rear main seal (Chapters 2 and 8).
3   Clutch plate not seated. It may take 30 or 40 normal starts for a new one to seat.
4   Warped pressure plate or flywheel (Chapter 8).
5   Weak diaphragm spring (Chapter 8).
6   Clutch plate overheated. Allow to cool.

36   Grabbing (chattering) as clutch is engaged

1   Oil on clutch plate lining, burned or glazed facings (Chapter 8).
2   Worn or loose engine or transaxle mounts (Chapters 2 and 7).
3   Worn splines on clutch plate hub (Chapter 8).
4   Warped pressure plate or flywheel (Chapter 8).
5   Burned or smeared resin on flywheel or pressure plate (Chapter 8).

37   Transaxle rattling (clicking)

1   Release lever loose (Chapter 8).
2   Clutch plate damper spring failure (Chapter 8).

38   Noise in clutch area

1   Faulty release bearing (Chapter 8).
2   Loose pressure plate bolts.

39   Clutch pedal stays on floor

1   Clutch master cylinder piston binding in bore (Chapter 8).
2   Broken release bearing or fork (Chapter 8).

40   High pedal effort

1   Piston binding in bore (Chapter 8).
2   Pressure plate faulty (Chapter 8).
3   Incorrect size master or release cylinder (Chapter 8).

MANUAL TRANSAXLE

41   Knocking noise at low speeds

1   Worn driveaxle constant velocity (CV) joints (Chapter 8).
2   Worn side gear shaft counterbore in differential case (Chapter 7A).*

42   Noise most pronounced when turning

Differential gear noise (Chapter 7A).*

43   Clunk on acceleration or deceleration

1   Loose engine or transaxle mounts (Chapters 2 and 7A).
2   Worn differential pinion shaft in case.*
3   Worn side gear shaft counterbore in differential case (Chapter 7A).*
4   Worn or damaged driveaxle inner CV joints (Chapter 8).

44   Clicking noise in turns

Worn or damaged outer CV joint (Chapter 8).

45   Vibration

1   Rough wheel bearing (Chapter 10).
2   Damaged driveaxle (Chapter 8).
3   Out of round tires (Chapter 1).
4   Tire out of balance (Chapters 1 and 10).
5   Worn CV joint (Chapter 8).

46   Noisy in neutral with engine running

1   Damaged input gear bearing (Chapter 7A).*
2   Damaged clutch release bearing (Chapter 8).

47   Noisy in one particular gear

1   Damaged or worn constant mesh gears (Chapter 7A).*
2   Damaged fourth speed gear or output gear (Chapter 7A).*
3   Worn or damaged reverse idler gear or idler bushing (Chapter 7A).*

48   Noisy in all gears

1   Insufficient lubricant (Chapters 1 and 7A).
2   Damaged or worn bearings (Chapter 7A).*
3   Worn or damaged input gear shaft and/or output gear shaft (Chapter 7A).*
4   Worn or damaged reverse idler gear or idler bushing (Chapter 7A).*

49   Slips out of gear

1   Worn or improperly adjusted cables(s) (Chapter 7A).
2   Shift linkage does not work freely, binds (Chapter 7A).
3   Input gear bearing retainer broken or loose (Chapter 7A).*
4   Dirt between clutch cover and engine housing (Chapter 7A).
5   Worn shift fork (Chapter 7A).*

50   Leaks lubricant

1   Drriveaxle seals worn (Chapter 7B).
2   Excessive amount of lubricant in transaxle (Chapters 1 and 7A).
3   Loose or broken input gear shaft bearing retainer (Chapter 7A).*
4   Input gear bearing retainer O-ring and/or lip seal damaged (Chapter 7A).*

51   Locked in gear

Lock pin or interlock pin missing (Chapter 7A).*

* Although the corrective action necessary to remedy the symptoms described is beyond the scope of this manual, the above information should be helpful in isolating the cause of the condition so that the owner can communicate clearly with a professional mechanic.

AUTOMATIC TRANSAXLE

➡**Note: Due to the complexity of the automatic transaxle, it is difficult for the home mechanic to properly diagnose and service this component. For problems other than the following, the vehicle should be taken to a dealer or transmission shop.**

52   Fluid leakage

1   Automatic transaxle fluid is a deep red color. Fluid leaks should not be confused with engine oil, which can easily be blown onto the transaxle by air flow.
2   To pinpoint a leak, first remove all built-up dirt and grime from the transaxle housing with degreasing agents and/or steam cleaning. Then drive the vehicle at low speeds so air flow will not blow the leak far from its source. Raise the vehicle and determine where the leak is coming from. Common areas of leakage are:

   a)   Pan (Chapters 1 and 7)
   b)   Dipstick tube (Chapters 1 and 7)
   c)   Transaxle oil lines (Chapter 7)
   d)   Speed sensor (Chapter 7)
   e)   Differential drain plug (Chapters 1 and 7B)

53 Transaxle fluid brown or has a burned smell

Transaxle fluid overheated (Chapter 1).

54 General shift mechanism problems

1   Chapter 7, Part B, deals with checking and adjusting the shift cable on automatic transaxles. Common problems which may be attributed to poorly adjusted cable are:

a) Engine starting in gears other than Park or Neutral.
b) Indicator on shifter pointing to a gear other than the one actually being used.
c) Vehicle moves when in Park.

2   Refer to Chapter 7B for the shift cable adjustment procedure.

55 Transaxle will not downshift with accelerator pedal pressed to the floor

Since these transmissions are electronically controlled, check for any diagnostic trouble codes stored in the PCM. The actual repair will most likely have to be performed by a qualified repair shop with the proper equipment.

56 Engine will start in gears other than Park or Neutral

Park/Neutral Position switch malfunctioning (Chapter 7B).

57 Transaxle slips, shifts roughly, is noisy or has no drive in forward or reverse gears

There are many probable causes for the above problems, but the home mechanic should be concerned with only one possibility - fluid level. Before taking the vehicle to a repair shop, check the level and condition of the fluid as described in Chapter 1. Correct the fluid level as necessary or change the fluid and filter if needed. If the problem persists, have a professional diagnose the cause.

DRIVEAXLES

58 Clicking noise in turns

Worn or damaged outboard CV joint (Chapter 8).

59 Shudder or vibration during acceleration

1   Excessive toe-in (Chapter 10).
2   Worn or damaged inboard or outboard CV joints (Chapter 8).
3   Sticking inboard CV joint assembly (Chapter 8).

60 Vibration at highway speeds

1   Out of balance front wheels and/or tires (Chapters 1 and 10).
2   Out of round tires (Chapters 1 and 10).
3   Worn CV joint(s) (Chapter 8).

BRAKES

→Note: Before assuming that a brake problem exists, make sure that:

a) The tires are in good condition and properly inflated (Chapter 1).
b) The front end alignment is correct (Chapter 10).
c) The vehicle is not loaded with weight in an unequal manner.

61 Vehicle pulls to one side during braking

1   Incorrect tire pressures (Chapter 1).
2   Front end out of alignment (have the front end aligned).
3   Front, or rear, tires not matched to one another.
4   Restricted brake lines or hoses (Chap-ter 9).
5   Malfunctioning drum brake or caliper assembly (Chapter 9).
6   Loose suspension parts (Chapter 10).
7   Excessive wear of brake shoe or pad material or disc/drum on one side.

62 Noise (high-pitched squeal when the brakes are applied)

Front and/or rear disc brake pads worn out. The noise comes from the wear sensor rubbing against the disc (does not apply to all vehicles). Replace pads with new ones immediately (Chapter 9).

63 Brake roughness or chatter (pedal pulsates)

1   Excessive lateral runout (Chapter 9).
2   Uneven pad wear (Chapter 9).
3   Defective disc (Chapter 9).

64 Excessive brake pedal effort required to stop vehicle

1   Malfunctioning power brake booster (Chapter 9).
2   Partial system failure (Chapter 9).
3   Excessively worn pads or shoes (Chapter 9).
4   Piston in caliper or wheel cylinder stuck or sluggish (Chapter 9).
5   Brake pads or shoes contaminated with oil, grease or brake fluid (Chapter 9).
6   New pads or shoes installed and not yet seated. It will take a while for the new material to seat against the disc or drum.

65 Excessive brake pedal travel

1   Partial brake system failure (Chapter 9).
2   Insufficient fluid in master cylinder (Chapters 1 and 9).
3   Air trapped in system (Chapters 1 and 9).

66 Dragging brakes

1   Incorrect adjustment of brake light switch (Chapter 9).
2   Master cylinder pistons not returning correctly (Chapter 9).
3   Restricted brakes lines or hoses (Chapters 1 and 9).
4   Incorrect parking brake adjustment (Chapter 9).

67   Grabbing or uneven braking action

Contaminated lining material (Chapter 9).

68   Brake pedal feels spongy when depressed

1   Air in hydraulic lines (Chapter 9).
2   Master cylinder mounting nuts loose (Chapter 9).
3   Master cylinder defective (Chapter 9).

69   Brake pedal travels to the floor with little resistance

1   Little or no fluid in the master cylinder reservoir caused by leaking caliper piston(s) (Chapter 9).
2   Loose, damaged or disconnected brake lines (Chapter 9).

70   Parking brake does not hold

Parking brake linkage improperly adjusted (Chapters 1 and 9).

SUSPENSION AND STEERING SYSTEMS

➡Note: Before attempting to diagnose the suspension and steering systems, perform the following preliminary checks:

a) Tires for wrong pressure and uneven wear.
b) Steering universal joints from the column to the rack and pinion for loose connectors or wear.
c) Front and rear suspension and the rack and pinion assembly for loose or damaged parts.
d) Out-of-round or out-of-balance tires, bent rims and loose and/or rough wheel bearings.

71   Vehicle pulls to one side

1   Mismatched or uneven tires (Chapter 10).
2   Broken or sagging springs (Chapter 10).
3   Wheel alignment (Chapter 10).
4   Front brake dragging (Chapter 9).

72   Abnormal or excessive tire wear

1   Wheel alignment (Chapter 10).
2   Sagging or broken springs (Chapter 10).
3   Tire out of balance (Chapter 10).
4   Worn strut damper (Chapter 10).
5   Overloaded vehicle.
6   Tires not rotated regularly.

73   Wheel makes a thumping noise

1   Blister or bump on tire (Chapter 10).
2   Improper strut damper action (Chapter 10).

74   Shimmy, shake or vibration

1   Tire or wheel out-of-balance or out-of-round (Chapter 10).
2   Loose or worn wheel bearings (Chapters 1, 8 and 10).
3   Worn tie-rod ends (Chapter 10).
4   Worn lower balljoints (Chapters 1 and 10).
5   Excessive wheel runout (Chapter 10).
6   Blister or bump on tire (Chapter 10).

75   Hard steering

1   Lack of lubrication at balljoints, tie-rod ends and rack and pinion assembly (Chapter 10).
2   Front wheel alignment (Chapter 10).
3   Low tire pressure(s) (Chapters 1 and 10).

76   Poor returnability of steering to center

1   Lack of lubrication at balljoints and tie-rod ends (Chapter 10).
2   Binding in balljoints (Chapter 10).
3   Binding in steering column (Chapter 10).
4   Lack of lubricant in steering gear assembly (Chapter 10).
5   Front wheel alignment (Chapter 10).

77   Abnormal noise at the front end

1   Lack of lubrication at balljoints and tie-rod ends (Chapters 1 and 10).
2   Damaged strut mounting (Chapter 10).
3   Worn control arm bushings or tie-rod ends (Chapter 10).
4   Loose stabilizer bar or worn bushing (Chapter 10).
5   Loose wheel nuts (Chapters 1 and 10).
6   Loose suspension bolts (Chapter 10)

78   Wander or poor steering stability

1   Mismatched or uneven tires (Chapter 10).
2   Lack of lubrication at balljoints and tie-rod ends (Chapters 1 and 10).
3   Worn strut assemblies (Chapter 10).
4   Loose stabilizer bar (Chapter 10).
5   Broken or sagging springs (Chapter 10).
6   Wheels out of alignment (Chapter 10).

79   Erratic steering when braking

1   Wheel bearings worn (Chapter 10).
2   Broken or sagging springs (Chapter 10).
3   Defective brake caliper (Chapter 9).
4   Warped rotors or drums (Chapter 9).

80   Excessive pitching and/or rolling around corners or during braking

1   Loose stabilizer bar (Chapter 10).
2   Worn strut dampers or mountings (Chapter 10).
3   Broken or sagging springs (Chapter 10).
4   Overloaded vehicle.

81   Suspension bottoms

1   Overloaded vehicle.
2   Worn strut dampers (Chapter 10).
3   Incorrect, broken or sagging springs (Chapter 10).

82   Cupped tires

1   Front wheel or rear wheel alignment (Chapter 10).
2   Worn strut dampers (Chapter 10).
3   Wheel bearings worn (Chapter 10).
4   Excessive tire or wheel runout (Chapter 10).
5   Worn balljoints (Chapter 10).

83   Excessive tire wear on outside edge

1   Inflation pressures incorrect (Chapter 1).
2   Excessive speed in turns.
3   Front end alignment incorrect (excessive toe-in). Have professionally aligned.
4   Suspension arm bent (Chapter 10).

84   Excessive tire wear on inside edge

1   Inflation pressures incorrect (Chapter 1).

2   Front end alignment incorrect (toe-out). Have professionally aligned.
3   Loose or damaged steering components (Chapter 10).

85   Tire tread worn in one place

1   Tires out of balance.
2   Damaged or buckled wheel. Inspect and replace if necessary.
3   Defective tire (Chapter 1).

86   Excessive play or looseness in steering system

1   Wheel bearing(s) worn (Chapter 10).
2   Tie-rod end loose (Chapter 10).
3   Steering gear loose (Chapter 10).
4   Worn or loose steering intermediate shaft (Chapter 10).

87   Rattling or clicking noise in steering gear

1   Steering gear loose (Chapter 10).
2   Steering gear defective.

Section

1 Maintenance schedule
2 Introduction
3 Tune-up general information
4 Fluid level checks
5 Tire and tire pressure checks
6 Power steering fluid level check
7 Automatic transaxle fluid level check
8 Engine oil and oil filter change
9 Windshield wiper blade inspection and replacement
10 Battery check, maintenance and charging
11 Underhood hose check and replacement
12 Cooling system check
13 Tire rotation
14 Brake check
15 Steering, suspension and driveaxle boot check
16 Exhaust system check
17 Air filter replacement
18 Fuel system check
19 Automatic transaxle differential lubricant level check
20 Manual transaxle lubricant level check
21 Interior ventilation filter replacement
22 Clutch/brake pedal freeplay, height check and adjustment
23 Fuel tank cap gasket inspection and replacement
24 Positive Crankcase Ventilation (PCV) valve check and replacement
25 Evaporative emissions control system check
26 Automatic transaxle/differential fluid change
27 Manual transaxle lubricant change
28 Chassis and body fastener check
29 Drivebelt check, adjustment and replacement
30 Valve clearance check and adjustment
31 Cooling system servicing (draining, flushing and refilling)
32 Spark plug check and replacement

Reference to other Chapters

CHECK ENGINE light on - See Chapter 6

1

TUNE-UP AND ROUTINE MAINTENANCE

Typical four-cylinder engine compartment layout

1	Brake master cylinder reservoir	6	Engine oil dipstick	11	Main fuse/relay box
2	Air filter housing	7	Radiator hose	12	Engine cover (remove for access to spark plugs)
3	Battery	8	Windshield washer fluid reservoir		
4	Automatic transaxle fluid dipstick	9	Engine coolant reservoir	13	Radiator cap
5	Engine oil filler cap	10	Power steering fluid reservoir	14	Upper control rod and bracket

Typical V6 engine compartment layout

1	Brake master cylinder reservoir	6	Cooling system pressure cap	11	Power steering fluid reservoir
2	Air filter housing	7	Engine oil dipstick	12	Engine cover (remove for access to spark plugs)
3	Battery	8	Radiator hose		
4	Automatic transaxle fluid dipstick	9	Windshield washer fluid reservoir	13	Main fuse/relay box
5	Engine oil filler cap	10	Engine coolant reservoir		

Typical front underside components

1	Engine oil drain plug (four-cylinder engine shown)	6	Exhaust pipe
2	Front brake calipers	7	Inner driveaxle boots
3	Outer driveaxle boots	8	Brake hoses
4	Balljoints	9	Engine oil filter
5	Automatic transaxle drain plug		

Typical rear underside components

1	Brake drums	3	Fuel tank	5	Parking brake cables
2	Shock and spring assembly	4	Exhaust pipe	6	Muffler

1 Toyota Camry and Lexus ES 300/330, Avalon and Solara Maintenance Schedule

The maintenance intervals in this manual are provided with the assumption that you, not the dealer, will be doing the work. These are the minimum maintenance intervals recommended by the factory for vehicles that are driven daily. If you wish to keep your vehicle in peak condition at all times, you may wish to perform some of these procedures even more often. Because frequent maintenance enhances the efficiency, performance and resale value of your car, we encourage you to do so. If you drive in dusty areas, tow a trailer, idle or drive at low speeds for extended periods or drive for short distances (less than four miles) in below freezing temperatures, shorter intervals are also recommended.

When your vehicle is new, it should be serviced by a factory authorized dealer service department to protect the factory warranty. In many cases, the initial maintenance check is done at no cost to the owner.

EVERY 250 MILES OR WEEKLY, WHICHEVER COMES FIRST

Check the engine oil level (Section 4)
Check the engine coolant level (Section 4)
Check the windshield washer fluid level (Section 4)
Check the brake and clutch fluid levels (Section 4)
Check the tires and tire pressures (Section 5)

EVERY 5000 MILES OR 6 MONTHS, WHICHEVER COMES FIRST

All items listed above plus:

Check the power steering fluid level (Section 6)
Check the automatic transaxle fluid level (Section 7)
Change the engine oil and oil filter (Section 8)
Inspect and replace if necessary the windshield wiper blades (Section 9)
Check and service the battery (Section 10)
Inspect and replace if necessary all underhood hoses (Section 11)
Check the cooling system (Section 12)
Rotate the tires (Section 13)
Inspect the brake system (Section 14)

EVERY 15,000 MILES OR 18 MONTHS, WHICHEVER COMES FIRST

All items listed above plus:

Inspect the suspension, steering components and driveaxle boots (Section 15)*
Inspect the exhaust system (Section 16)
Check and adjust if necessary the engine drivebelts (Section 29) (after the initial 60,000-mile or 72-month check)

EVERY 30,000 MILES OR 36 MONTHS, WHICHEVER COMES FIRST

All items listed above plus:

Replace the air filter (Section 17)*
Inspect the fuel system (Section 18)

Check the automatic transaxle differential lubricant level (Avalon and 2002 through 2004 Solara V6 models) (Section 19)
Check the manual transaxle lubricant level (Section 20)**
Replace interior ventilation filter (Section 21)
Check the clutch pedal for proper freeplay and height (Section 22)
Inspect the evaporative emissions control system (Section 25)
Check and tighten critical chassis and body fasteners (Section 28)*

EVERY 50,000 MILES OR 60 MONTHS, WHICHEVER COMES FIRST

Service the cooling system (drain, flush and refill) (Section 31) (after the initial 100,000-mile or 120-month service)
Change the automatic transaxle/differential fluid (Section 26)**

EVERY 60,000 MILES OR 72 MONTHS, WHICHEVER COMES FIRST

All items listed above plus:

Replace the fuel tank cap gasket (Section 23)
Check and replace if necessary the PCV valve (Section 24)
Check and adjust if necessary the engine drivebelts (Section 29)
Inspect and if necessary adjust the valve clearance (Section 30)
Every 90,000 miles or 108 months, whichever comes first
Replace the timing belt (V6 engines only) (Chapter 2B)

100,000 MILES OR 120 MONTHS, WHICHEVER COMES FIRST - THEREAFTER EVERY 50,000 MILES OR 60 MONTHS, WHICHEVER COMES FIRST

Service the cooling system (drain, flush and refill) (Section 31)

EVERY 120,000 MILES OR 144 MONTHS, WHICHEVER COMES FIRST

Replace the spark plugs (except CA, NY, MA, ME and VT four-cylinder PZEV models) (Section 32)

EVERY 150,000 MILES

Replace the spark plugs on CA, NY, MA, ME and VT four-cylinder PZEV models (Section 32)

* This item is affected by "severe" operating conditions as described below. If your vehicle is operated under "severe" conditions, inspect all maintenance indicated with an asterisk (*) at 5000 mile/6 month intervals and perform maintenance or replace parts as necessary. Severe conditions are indicated if you mainly operate your vehicle under one or more of the following conditions:

Operating in dusty areas
Idling for extended periods and/or low speed operation
Operating when outside temperatures remain below freezing and when most trips are less than 4 miles

** If used for trailer towing, change the automatic transaxle/differential fluid or manual transaxle lubricant every 30,000 miles (Section 26 or Section 27)

2 Introduction

This Chapter is designed to help the home mechanic maintain his vehicle for peak performance, economy, safety and long life.

Included is a master maintenance schedule, followed by sections dealing specifically with each item on the schedule. Visual checks, adjustments, component replacement and other helpful items are included. Refer to the accompanying illustrations of the engine compartment and the underside of the vehicle for the location of various components.

Servicing your vehicle in accordance with the mileage/time maintenance schedule and the following Sections will provide it with a planned maintenance program that should result in a long and reliable service life. This is a comprehensive plan, so maintaining some items but not others at the specified service intervals won't produce the same results.

As you service your vehicle, you will discover that many of the procedures can - and should - be grouped together because of the nature of the particular procedure you're performing or because of the close proximity of two otherwise unrelated components to one another.

For example, if the vehicle is raised for any reason, you should inspect the exhaust, suspension, steering and fuel systems while you're under the vehicle. When you're rotating the tires, it makes good sense to check the brakes and wheel bearings since the wheels are already removed.

Finally, let's suppose you have to borrow or rent a torque wrench. Even if you only need to tighten the spark plugs, you might as well check the torque of as many critical fasteners as time allows.

The first step of this maintenance program is to prepare yourself before the actual work begins. Read through all sections pertinent to the procedures you're planning to do, then make a list of and gather together all the parts and tools you will need to do the job. If it looks as if you might run into problems during a particular segment of some procedure, seek advice from your local parts man or dealer service department.

3 Tune-up general information

The term *tune-up* is used in this manual to represent a combination of individual operations rather than one specific procedure.

If, from the time the vehicle is new, the routine maintenance schedule is followed closely and frequent checks are made of fluid levels and high wear items, as suggested throughout this manual, the engine will be kept in relatively good running condition and the need for additional work will be minimized.

More likely than not, however, there will be times when the engine is running poorly due to lack of regular maintenance. This is even more likely if a used vehicle, which has not received regular and frequent maintenance checks, is purchased. In such cases, an engine tune-up will be needed outside of the regular routine maintenance intervals.

The first step in any tune-up or engine diagnosis to help correct a poor running engine would be a cylinder compression check. A check of the engine compression (Chapter 2 Part C) will give valuable information regarding the overall performance of many internal components and should be used as a basis for tune-up and repair procedures. If, for instance, a compression check indicates serious internal engine wear, a conventional tune-up will not help the running condition of the engine and would be a waste of time and money. Also in Chapter 2, Part C is information on checking engine vacuum, which also gives information on the engine's state-of-tune and condition.

The following series of operations are those most often needed to bring a generally poor-running engine back into a proper state of tune.

MINOR TUNE-UP

Check all engine related fluids (Section 4)
Clean, inspect and test the battery (Section 10)
Check all underhood hoses (Section 12)
Check the cooling system (Section 13)
Check the air filter (Section 17)
Check and adjust the drivebelts (Section 29)

MAJOR TUNE-UP

All items listed under Minor tune-up, plus . . .

Replace the air filter (Section 17)
Check the fuel system (Section 18)
Replace the spark plugs (Section 32)
Check the charging system (Chapter 5)

4 Fluid level checks (every 250 miles or weekly)

1 Fluids are an essential part of the lubrication, cooling, brake, clutch and other systems. Because these fluids gradually become depleted and/or contaminated during normal operation of the vehicle, they must be periodically replenished. See *Recommended lubricants* and *fluids* and *Capacities* at the end of this Chapter before adding fluid to any of the following components.

➡**Note: The vehicle must be on level ground before fluid levels can be checked.**

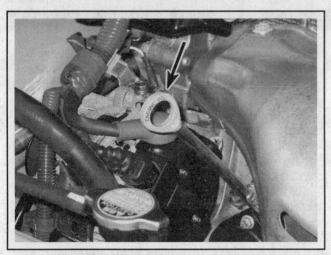

4.2 The engine oil dipstick is mounted on the front (radiator) side of the engine

ENGINE OIL

▶ **Refer to illustrations 4.2, 4.4 and 4.6**

2   The engine oil level is checked with a dipstick located at the front side of the engine (see illustration). The dipstick extends through a metal tube from which it protrudes down into the engine oil pan.

3   The oil level should be checked before the vehicle has been driven, or about 5 minutes after the engine has been shut off. If the oil is checked immediately after driving the vehicle, some of the oil will remain in the upper engine components, producing an inaccurate reading on the dipstick.

4   Pull the dipstick from the tube and wipe all the oil from the end with a clean rag or paper towel. Insert the clean dipstick all the way back into its metal tube and pull it out again. Observe the oil at the end of the dipstick. At its highest point, the level should be between the L and F marks (see illustration).

5   It takes one quart of oil to raise the level from the L mark to the F mark on the dipstick. Do not allow the level to drop below the L mark

4.6 The threaded oil filler cap is located on the valve cover - to prevent dirt from contaminating the engine, always make sure the area around this opening is clean before removing the cap

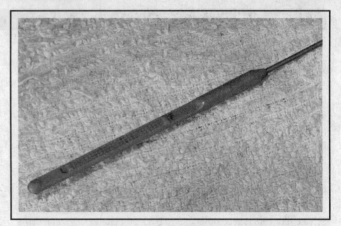

4.4 The oil level should be at or near the F mark on the dipstick - if it isn't, add enough oil to bring the level to or near the F mark (it takes one quart to raise the level from the L to F mark)

or oil starvation may cause engine damage. Conversely, overfilling the engine (adding oil above the F mark) may cause oil-fouled spark plugs, oil leaks or oil seal failures.

6   Remove the threaded cap from the valve cover to add oil (see illustration). Use a funnel to prevent spills. After adding the oil, install the filler cap hand tight. Start the engine and look carefully for any small leaks around the oil filter or drain plug. Stop the engine and check the oil level again after it has had sufficient time to drain from the upper block and cylinder head galleys.

7   Checking the oil level is an important preventive maintenance step. A continually dropping oil level indicates oil leakage through damaged seals, from loose connections, or past worn rings or valve guides. If the oil looks milky in color or has water droplets in it, a cylinder head gasket may be blown. The engine should be checked immediately. The condition of the oil should also be checked. Each time you check the oil level, slide your thumb and index finger up the dipstick before wiping off the oil. If you see small dirt or metal particles clinging to the dipstick, the oil should be changed (see Section 8).

ENGINE COOLANT

▶ **Refer to illustration 4.8**

✳✳ WARNING:

Do not allow antifreeze to come in contact with your skin or painted surfaces of the vehicle. Flush contaminated areas immediately with plenty of water. Don't store new coolant or leave old coolant lying around where it's accessible to children or pets – they're attracted by its sweet smell. Ingestion of even a small amount of coolant can be fatal! Wipe up garage floor and drip pan spills immediately. Keep antifreeze containers covered and repair cooling system leaks as soon as they're noticed.

8   All models covered by this manual are equipped with a coolant recovery system. The coolant reservoir is located in the front corner of the engine compartment and is connected by a hose to the base of the coolant filler cap (see illustration). If the coolant heats up during engine operation, coolant can escape through the pressurized filler cap and connecting hose into the reservoir. As the engine cools, the coolant is

4.8 Make sure the coolant level is between the Full and Low lines - if it's below the Low line, add a sufficient quantity of the specified mixture of antifreeze and water

4.14 The windshield washer fluid reservoir is located at the right front corner of the engine compartment - fluid can be added after flipping up the cap

4.16 The brake fluid should be kept between the Min and Max marks on the reservoir - turn and lift up the cap to add fluid

automatically drawn back into the cooling system to maintain the correct level.

9   The coolant level should be checked regularly. It must be between the Full and Low lines on the tank. The level will vary with the temperature of the engine. When the engine is cold, the coolant level should be at or slightly above the Low mark on the tank. Once the engine has warmed up, the level should be at or near the Full mark. If it isn't, allow the fluid in the tank to cool, then remove the cap from the reservoir and add coolant to bring the level up to the Full line. Use only ethylene/glycol type coolant and water in the mixture ratio recommended by your owner's manual. Do not use supplemental inhibitors or additives. If only a small amount of coolant is required to bring the system up to the proper level, water can be used. However, repeated additions of water will dilute the recommended antifreeze and water solution. In order to maintain the proper ratio of antifreeze and water, it is advisable to top up the coolant level with the correct mixture. Refer to your owner's manual for the recommended ratio.

10 If the coolant level drops within a short time after replenishment, there may be a leak in the system. Inspect the radiator, hoses, engine coolant filler cap, drain plugs, air bleeder plugs and water pump. If no leak is evident, have the radiator cap pressure tested.

❋❋ WARNING:

Never remove the radiator pressure cap when the engine is running or has just been shut down, because the cooling system is hot. Escaping steam and scalding liquid could cause serious injury.

11 If it is necessary to open the radiator cap, wait until the system has cooled completely, then wrap a thick cloth around the cap and turn it to the first stop. If any steam escapes, wait until the system has cooled further, then remove the cap.

12 When checking the coolant level, always note its condition. It should be relatively clear. If it is brown or rust colored, the system should be drained, flushed and refilled. Even if the coolant appears to be normal, the corrosion inhibitors wear out with use, so it must be replaced at the specified intervals.

,13 Do not allow antifreeze to come in contact with your skin or painted surfaces of the vehicle. Flush contacted areas immediately with plenty of water.

WINDSHIELD WASHER FLUID

▶ **Refer to illustration 4.14**

14 Fluid for the windshield washer system is stored in a plastic reservoir which is located at the right front corner of the engine compartment (see illustration). In milder climates, plain water can be used to top up the reservoir, but the reservoir should be kept no more than two-thirds full to allow for expansion should the water freeze. In colder climates, the use of a specially designed windshield washer fluid, available at your dealer and any auto parts store, will help lower the freezing point of the fluid. Mix the solution with water in accordance with the manufacturer's directions on the container. Do not use regular antifreeze. It will damage the vehicle's paint.

BRAKE AND CLUTCH FLUID

▶ **Refer to illustration 4.16**

15 The brake master cylinder is mounted on the front of the power booster unit in the engine compartment. The clutch cylinder, used with a manual transaxle, is located next to the master cylinder.

16 To check the fluid level of the brake master cylinder reservoir, simply look at the MAX and MIN marks on the reservoir (see illustration). To check the fluid level of the clutch master cylinder reservoir, note whether the fluid level is even with the maximum level line. The level should be within the specified distance from the maximum fill line for both reservoirs.

17 If the level is low for either reservoir, wipe the top of the reservoir cover with a clean rag to prevent contamination of the brake or clutch system before lifting the cover.

18 Add only the specified brake fluid to the brake or clutch reservoir (refer to *Recommended lubricants and fluids* at the end of this chapter or to your owner's manual). Mixing different types of brake fluid can damage the system. Fill the brake master cylinder reservoir only to the dotted line - this brings the fluid to the correct level when you put the cover back on.

✳✳ WARNING:

Use caution when filling either reservoir - brake fluid can harm your eyes and damage painted surfaces. Do not use brake fluid that has been opened for more than one year or has been left open. Brake fluid absorbs moisture from the air. Excess moisture can cause a dangerous loss of braking.

19 While the reservoir cap is removed, inspect the master cylinder reservoir for contamination. If deposits, dirt particles or water droplets are present, the system should be drained and refilled (see Chapter 8 for clutch reservoir or Chapter 9 for brake reservoir).

20 After filling the reservoir to the proper level, make sure the lid is properly seated to prevent fluid leakage and/or system pressure loss.

21 The brake fluid in the master cylinder will drop slightly as the brake pads at each wheel wear down during normal operation. If the master cylinder requires repeated replenishing to keep it at the proper level, this is an indication of leakage in the brake system, which should be corrected immediately. Check all brake lines and connections, along with the wheel cylinders and booster (see Section 16 for more information).

22 If, upon checking the master cylinder fluid level, you discover one or both reservoirs empty or nearly empty, the brake system should be bled (see Chapter 9).

5 Tire and tire pressure checks (every 250 miles or weekly)

▶ **Refer to illustrations 5.2, 5.3, 5.4a, 5.4b and 5.8**

1 Periodic inspection of the tires may spare you from the inconvenience of being stranded with a flat tire. It can also provide you with vital information regarding possible problems in the steering and suspension systems before major damage occurs.

2 Normal tread wear can be monitored with a simple, inexpensive device known as a tread depth indicator (see illustration). When the tread depth reaches the specified minimum, replace the tire(s).

3 Note any abnormal tread wear (see illustration). Tread pattern irregularities such as cupping, flat spots and more wear on one side than the other are indications of front end alignment and/or balance problems. If any of these conditions are noted, take the vehicle to a tire shop or service station to correct the problem.

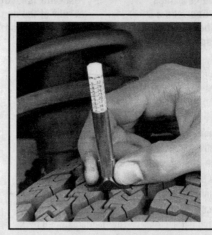

5.2 Use a tire tread depth gauge to monitor tire wear - they are available at auto parts stores and service stations and cost very little

UNDERINFLATION

CUPPING

Cupping may be caused by:
- Underinflation and/or mechanical irregularities such as out-of-balance condition of wheel and/or tire, and bent or damaged wheel.
- Loose or worn steering tie-rod or steering idler arm.
- Loose, damaged or worn front suspension parts.

OVERINFLATION

INCORRECT TOE-IN OR EXTREME CAMBER

FEATHERING DUE TO MISALIGNMENT

5.3 This chart will help you determine the condition of the tires, the probable cause(s) of abnormal wear and the corrective action necessary

5.4a If a tire looses air on a steady basis, check the valve core first to make sure it's snug (a special inexpensive wrench is commonly available at auto parts stores)

5.4b If the valve core is tight, raise the corner of the vehicle with the low tire and spray a soapy water solution onto the tread as the tire is turned slowly - leaks will cause small bubbles to appear

4   Look closely for cuts, punctures and embedded nails or tacks. Sometimes a tire will hold its air pressure for a short time or leak down very slowly even after a nail has embedded itself into the tread. If a slow leak persists, check the valve stem core to make sure it is tight (see illustration). Examine the tread for an object that may have embedded itself into the tire or for a "plug" that may have begun to leak (radial tire punctures are repaired with a plug that is fitted in a puncture). If a puncture is suspected, it can be easily verified by spraying a solution of soapy water onto the puncture area (see illustration). The soapy solution will bubble if there is a leak. Unless the puncture is inordinately large, a tire shop or gas station can usually repair the punctured tire.

5   Carefully inspect the inner sidewall of each tire for evidence of brake fluid leakage. If you see any, inspect the brakes immediately.

6   Correct tire air pressure adds miles to the lifespan of the tires, improves mileage and enhances overall ride quality. Tire pressure cannot be accurately estimated by looking at a tire, particularly if it is a radial. A tire pressure gauge is therefore essential. Keep an accurate gauge in the glovebox. The pressure gauges fitted to the nozzles of air hoses at gas stations are often inaccurate.

7   Always check tire pressure when the tires are cold. "Cold," in this case, means the vehicle has not been driven over a mile in the three hours preceding a tire pressure check. A pressure rise of four to eight pounds is not uncommon once the tires are warm.

8   Unscrew the valve cap protruding from the wheel or hubcap and push the gauge firmly onto the valve (see illustration). Note the reading on the gauge and compare this figure to the recommended tire pressure shown on the tire placard in the glovebox. Be sure to reinstall the valve

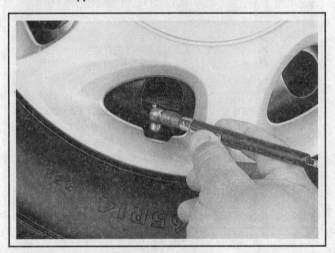

5.8 To extend the life of the tires, check the air pressure at least once a week with an accurate gauge (don't forget the spare)

cap to keep dirt and moisture out of the valve stem mechanism. Check all four tires and, if necessary, add enough air to bring them up to the recommended pressure levels.

9   Don't forget to keep the spare tire inflated to the specified pressure (consult your owner's manual). Note that the air pressure specified for a compact spare is significantly higher than the pressure of the regular tires.

6   Power steering fluid level check (every 5000 miles or 6 months)

▶ Refer to illustration 6.4

1   Unlike manual steering, the power steering system relies on fluid which may, over a period of time, require replenishing.

2   The fluid reservoir for the power steering pump is located on the right (passenger side) inner fender panel near the front of the engine.

3   For the check, the front wheels should be pointed straight ahead and the engine should be off.

6.4 The power steering fluid reservoir is located on the right side of the engine compartment - the reservoir is translucent so the fluid level can be checked either hot or cold without removing the cap

4   The reservoir is translucent plastic and the fluid level can be checked visually (see illustration).

5   If additional fluid is required, pour the specified type directly into the reservoir, using a funnel to prevent spills.

6   If the reservoir requires frequent fluid additions, all power steering hoses, hose connections, the power steering pump and the rack and pinion assembly should be carefully checked for leaks.

7   Automatic transaxle fluid level check (every 5000 miles or 6 months)

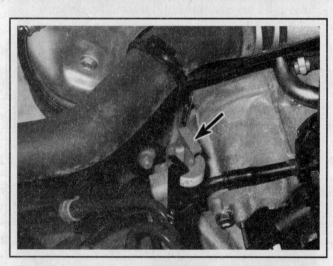

7.4a The automatic transaxle dipstick is located next to the battery

▶ **Refer to illustrations 7.4a and 7.4b**

1   The level of the automatic transaxle fluid should be carefully maintained. Low fluid level can lead to slipping or loss of drive, while overfilling can cause foaming, loss of fluid and transaxle damage.

2   The transaxle fluid level should only be checked when the transaxle is hot (at its normal operating temperature). If the vehicle has just been driven over 10 miles (15 miles in a frigid climate), and the fluid temperature is 160 to 175-degrees F, the transaxle is hot.

✳✳ CAUTION:

If the vehicle has just been driven for a long time at high speed or in city traffic in hot weather, or if it has been pulling a trailer, an accurate fluid level reading cannot be obtained. Allow the fluid to cool down for about 30 minutes.

3   If the vehicle has not just been driven, park the vehicle on level ground, set the parking brake and start the engine. While the engine is idling, depress the brake pedal and move the selector lever through all the gear ranges, beginning and ending in Park.

4   With the engine still idling, remove the dipstick from its tube (see illustration). Check the level of the fluid on the dipstick (see illustration) and note its condition.

5   Wipe the fluid from the dipstick with a clean rag and reinsert it back into the filler tube until the cap seats.

6   Pull the dipstick out again and note the fluid level. If the transaxle is cold, the level should be in the COLD or COOL range on the dipstick. If it is hot, the fluid level should be in the HOT range. If the level is at the low side of either range, add the specified automatic transaxle fluid through the dipstick tube with a funnel.

7   Add just enough of the recommended fluid to fill the transaxle to the proper level. It takes about one pint to raise the level from the low mark to the high mark when the fluid is hot, so add the fluid a little at a time and keep checking the level until it is correct.

8   The condition of the fluid should also be checked along with the level. If the fluid at the end of the dipstick is black or a dark reddish brown color, or if it emits a burned smell, the fluid should be changed (see Section 27). If you are in doubt about the condition of the fluid, purchase some new fluid and compare the two for color and smell.

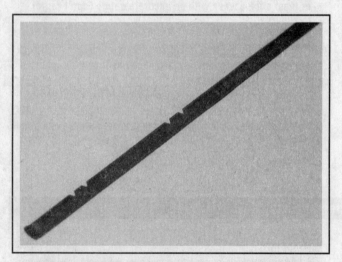

7.4b If the automatic transaxle fluid is cold, the level should be between the lower two notches; if it's at normal operating temperature, the level should be between the upper notches on the dipstick

8   Engine oil and oil filter change (every 5000 miles or 6 months)

▶ **Refer to illustrations 8.2, 8.7, 8.13a, 8.13b, and 8.15**

1   Frequent oil changes are the best preventive maintenance the home mechanic can give the engine, because aging oil becomes diluted and contaminated, which leads to premature engine wear.

2   Make sure that you have all the necessary tools before you begin this procedure (see illustration). You should also have plenty of rags or newspapers handy for mopping up any spills.

3   Access to the underside of the vehicle is greatly improved if the vehicle can be lifted on a hoist, driven onto ramps or supported by jack stands.

❋ **WARNING:**

Do not work under a vehicle which is supported only by a bumper, hydraulic or scissors-type jack.

4   If this is your first oil change, get under the vehicle and familiarize yourself with the location of the oil drain plug. The engine and exhaust components will be warm during the actual work, so try to anticipate any potential problems before the engine and accessories are hot.

5   Park the vehicle on a level spot. Start the engine and allow it to reach its normal operating temperature (the needle on the temperature gauge should be at least above the bottom mark). Warm oil and sludge will flow out more easily. Turn off the engine when it's warmed up. Remove the filler cap.

6   Raise the vehicle and support it securely on jack stands.

❋ **WARNING:**

To avoid personal injury, never get beneath a vehicle when it is supported by only by a jack. The jack provided with your vehicle is designed solely for raising the vehicle to remove and replace the wheels. Always use jack stands to support the vehicle when it becomes necessary to place your body underneath the vehicle.

7   Being careful not to touch the hot exhaust components, place the drain pan under the drain plug in the bottom of the pan and remove the plug (see illustration). You may want to wear gloves while unscrewing the plug the final few turns if the engine is really hot.

8   Allow the old oil to drain into the pan. It may be necessary to move the pan farther under the engine as the oil flow slows to a trickle. Inspect the old oil for the presence of metal shavings and chips.

9   After all the oil has drained, wipe off the drain plug with a clean rag. Even minute metal particles clinging to the plug would immediately contaminate the new oil.

10   Clean the area around the drain plug opening, reinstall the plug and tighten it securely, but do not strip the threads.

11   Move the drain pan into position under the oil filter.

12   Remove all tools, rags, etc. from under the vehicle, being careful not to spill the oil in the drain pan, then lower the vehicle.

13   Loosen the oil filter (see illustrations) by turning it counterclockwise with an oil filter wrench. Once the filter is loose, use your hands to unscrew it from the block. Just as the filter is detached from the block, immediately tilt the open end up to prevent the oil inside the filter from spilling out.

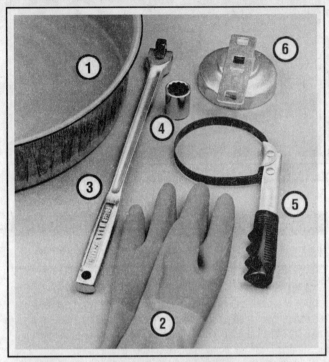

8.2   These tools are required when changing the engine oil and filter

1   *Drain pan* - It should be fairly shallow in depth, but wide to prevent spills

2   *Rubber gloves* - When removing the drain plug and filter, you will get oil on your hands (the gloves will prevent burns)

3   *Breaker bar* - Sometimes the oil drain plug is tight, and a long breaker bar is needed to loosen it

4   *Socket* - To be used with the breaker bar or a ratchet (must be the correct size to fit the drain plug)

5   *Filter wrench* - This is a metal band-type wrench, which requires clearance around the filter to be effective

6   *Filter wrench* - This type fits on the bottom of the filter and can be turned with a ratchet or breaker bar (different-size wrenches are available for different types of filters)

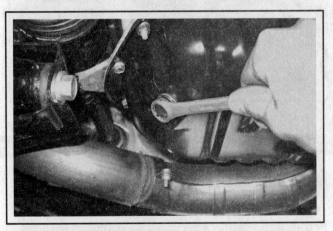

8.7   Use the proper size box-end wrench or socket to remove the oil drain plug without rounding off the corners

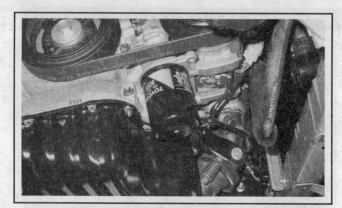

8.13a Location of the oil filter on four-cylinder models

8.13b On V6 models, the oil filter is mounted on the side of the engine block, so it's a good idea to pack rags around it before removal to minimize the mess - since it is usually on very tight, you'll need a special wrench for removal - DO NOT use the wrench to tighten the new filter

WARNING:

The engine exhaust manifold may still be hot, so be careful.

14 With a clean rag, wipe off the mounting surface on the block. If a residue of old oil is allowed to remain, it will smoke when the block is heated up. It will also prevent the new filter from seating properly. Also make sure that the none of the old gasket remains stuck to the mounting surface. It can be removed with a scraper if necessary.

15 Compare the old filter with the new one to make sure they are the same type. Smear some engine oil on the rubber gasket of the new filter and screw it into place (see illustration). Because overtightening the filter will damage the gasket, do not use a filter wrench to tighten the filter. Tighten it by hand until the gasket contacts the seating surface. Then seat the filter by giving it an additional 3/4-turn.

16 Add new oil to the engine through the oil filler cap in the valve cover. Use a funnel to prevent oil from spilling onto the top of the

8.15 Lubricate the oil filter gasket with clean engine oil before installing the filter on the engine

engine. Pour three quarts of fresh oil into the engine. Wait a few minutes to allow the oil to drain into the pan, then check the level on the oil dipstick (see Section 4 if necessary). If the oil level is at or near the F mark, install the filler cap hand tight, start the engine and allow the new oil to circulate.

17 Allow the engine to run for about a minute. While the engine is running, look under the vehicle and check for leaks at the oil pan drain plug and around the oil filter. If either is leaking, stop the engine and tighten the plug or filter slightly.

18 Wait a few minutes to allow the oil to trickle down into the pan, then recheck the level on the dipstick and, if necessary, add enough oil to bring the level to the F mark.

19 During the first few trips after an oil change, make it a point to check frequently for leaks and proper oil level.

20 The old oil drained from the engine cannot be reused in its present state and should be disposed of. Check with your local auto parts store, disposal facility or environmental agency to see if they will accept the oil for recycling. After the oil has cooled it can be drained into a container (capped plastic jugs, topped bottles, milk cartons, etc.) for transport to one of these disposal sites. Don't dispose of the oil by pouring it on the ground or down a drain!

21 Reset the engine oil replacement reminder light, turn the ignition key to the "ACC" position or "LOCK" position with the odometer reading shown.

22 Turn the ignition key to the "ON" position while holding down the trip meter reset button.

23 Hold down the knob for at least 5 seconds. The odometer indicates "000000" and the light goes off. If the system fails to reset, the light will continue flashing.

9   Windshield wiper blade inspection and replacement (every 5000 miles or 6 months)

▶ **Refer to illustrations 9.5, 9.6, 9.7 and 9.8**

1   The windshield wiper and blade assembly should be inspected periodically for damage, loose components and cracked or worn blade elements.

2   Road film can build up on the wiper blades and affect their effi-

ciency, so they should be washed regularly with a mild detergent solution.

3   The action of the wiping mechanism can loosen bolts, nuts and fasteners, so they should be checked and tightened, as necessary, at the same time the wiper blades are checked.

4   If the wiper blade elements are cracked, worn or warped, or no

9.5 Push the tab to release the wiper blade frame assembly from the wiper arm

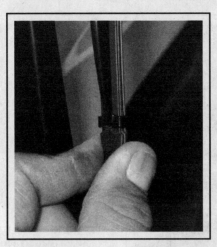

9.6 Squeeze the end of the wiper element and pull it straight out of the frame

9.7 Insert the end without the cutout into the frame

longer clean adequately, they should be replaced with new ones.

5   Lift the arm assembly away from the glass, then push the tab to release the wiper blade frame assembly from the wiper arm (see illustration).

6   Squeeze the end of the wiper element and pull it out of the frame (see illustration).

7   Insert the end of the new element without cutouts into the end of the frame (see illustration).

8   Work the rubber along the slot in the blade frame until the cutouts are locked into place by the wiper frame claw (see illustration).

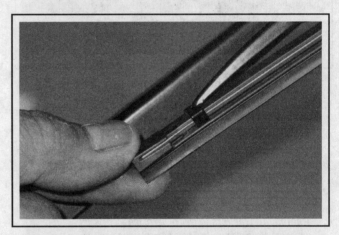

9.8 Slide the element into place until the cutouts seat into the locking claw

10 Battery check, maintenance and charging (every 5000 miles or 6 months)

▶ **Refer to illustrations 10.1, 10.7a, 10.7b, 10.8a, 10.8b and 10.13**

❊❊ WARNING:

Certain precautions must be followed when checking and servicing the battery. Hydrogen gas, which is highly flammable, is always present in the battery cells, so keep lighted tobacco and all other open flames and sparks away from the battery. The electrolyte inside the battery is actually dilute sulfuric acid, which will cause injury if splashed on your skin or in your eyes. It will also ruin clothes and painted surfaces. When removing the battery cables, always detach the negative cable first and hook it up last!

CHECK

1   A routine preventive maintenance program for the battery in your vehicle is the only way to ensure quick and reliable starts. But before performing any battery maintenance, make sure that you have the proper equipment necessary to work safely around the battery (see illustration on next page).

2   There are also several precautions that should be taken whenever battery maintenance is performed. Before servicing the battery, always turn the engine and all accessories off and disconnect the cable from the negative terminal of the battery.

3   The battery produces hydrogen gas, which is both flammable and explosive. Never create a spark, smoke or light a match around the battery. Always charge the battery in a ventilated area.

4   Electrolyte contains poisonous and corrosive sulfuric acid. Do not allow it to get in your eyes, on your skin or your clothes. Never ingest it. Wear protective safety glasses when working near the battery. Keep children away from the battery.

5   Note the external condition of the battery. If the positive terminal and cable clamp on your vehicle's battery is equipped with a rubber protector, make sure that it's not torn or damaged. It should completely cover the terminal. Look for any corroded or loose connections, cracks in the case or cover, or loose hold-down clamps. Also check the entire length of each cable for cracks and frayed conductors.

6   Some models with sealed batteries have a battery condition indi-

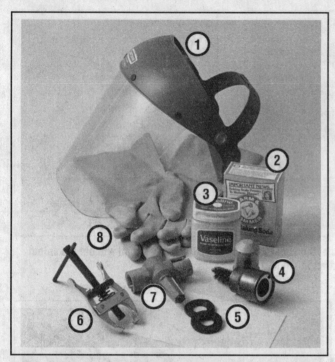

10.1 Tools and materials required for battery maintenance

1 *Face shield/safety goggles* - When removing corrosion with a brush, the acidic particles can easily fly up into your eyes
2 *Baking soda* - A solution of baking soda and water can be used to neutralize corrosion
3 *Petroleum jelly* - A layer of this on the battery posts will help prevent corrosion
4 *Battery post/cable cleaner* - This wire brush cleaning tool will remove all traces of corrosion from the battery posts and cable clamps
5 *Treated felt washers* - Placing one of these on each post, directly under the cable clamps, will help prevent corrosion
6 *Puller* - Sometimes the cable clamps are very difficult to pull off the posts, even after the nut/bolt has been completely loosened. This tool pulls the clamp straight up and off the post without damage
7 *Battery post/cable cleaner* - Here is another cleaning tool which is a slightly different version of Number 4 above, but it does the same thing
8 *Rubber gloves* - Another safety item to consider when servicing the battery; remember that's acid inside the battery!

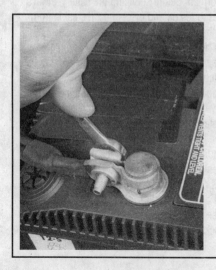

10.7b Loosen the battery cable clamp bolt with a wrench - sometimes special battery pliers are required for this procedure if corrosion has deteriorated the hex nut - always remove the negative cable first and reconnect it last!

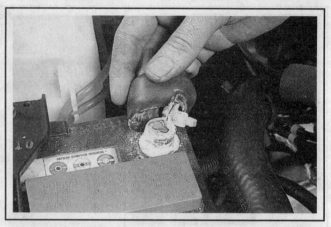

10.7a Battery terminal corrosion usually appears as light, fluffy powder

cator on top of the battery. Compare the color showing in the window to the condition color chart on the battery. You may catch a low-charge battery condition before it strands you on the roadside. If the color indicates a low state of charge, charge the battery and examine the charging system (see Chapter 5 and this Section).

MAINTENANCE

7 If corrosion, which looks like white, fluffy deposits (see illustration) is evident, particularly around the terminals, the battery should be removed for cleaning. Loosen the cable clamp bolts with a wrench, being careful to remove the negative cable first, and slide them off the terminals (see illustration). Then disconnect the hold-down clamp bolt and nut, remove the clamp and lift the battery from the engine compartment.

8 Clean the cable clamps thoroughly with a battery brush or a terminal cleaner and a solution of warm water and baking soda. Wash the terminals and the top of the battery case with the same solution but make sure that the solution doesn't get into the battery. When cleaning the cables, terminals and battery top, wear safety goggles and rubber gloves to prevent any solution from coming in contact with your eyes or

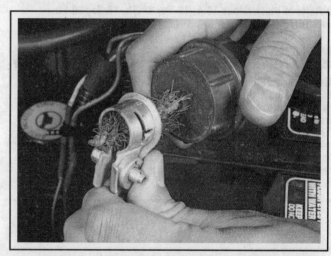

10.8a When cleaning the cable clamps, all corrosion must be removed (the inside of the clamp is tapered to match the taper on the post, so don't remove too much material)

10.8b Regardless of the type of tool used on the battery posts, a clean, shiny surface should be the result

10.13 Make sure the battery hold-down nuts are tight

hands. Wear old clothes too - even diluted, sulfuric acid splashed onto clothes will burn holes in them. If the terminals have been extensively corroded, clean them up with a terminal cleaner (see illustrations). Thoroughly wash all cleaned areas with plain water.

9   Whenever the battery is removed for cleaning or charging, inspect the battery carrier before reinstalling the battery in the engine compartment. If the carrier is dirty or covered with corrosion, clean it in the same solution of warm water and baking soda. Inspect the metal brackets which support the carrier to make sure that they are not covered with corrosion. If they are, wash them off. If corrosion is extensive, sand the brackets down to bare metal and spray them with a zinc-based primer (available in spray cans at auto paint and body supply stores).

10 Reinstall the battery back into the engine compartment. Make sure that no parts or wires are laying on the carrier during installation of the battery. Information on removing and installing the battery can be found in Chapter 5. Information on jump starting can be found at the front of this manual.

11 Install a pair of specially-treated felt washers around the terminals (available at auto parts stores), then coat the terminals and the cable clamps with petroleum jelly or grease to prevent further corrosion. Install the cable clamps and tighten the nuts, being careful to install the negative cable last.

12 Install the hold-down clamp and nuts. Tighten the nuts only enough to hold the battery firmly in place. Overtightening these nuts can crack the battery case.

13 Make sure that the battery tray is in good condition and the hold-down clamp bolts are tight (see illustration). If the battery is removed from the tray, make sure no parts remain in the bottom of the tray when the battery is reinstalled. When reinstalling the hold-down clamp bolts, do not overtighten them.

CHARGING

✳✳ WARNING:

When batteries are being charged, hydrogen gas, which is very explosive and flammable, is produced. Do not smoke or allow open flames near a charging or a recently charged battery. Wear eye protection when near the battery during charging. Also, make sure the charger is unplugged before connecting or disconnecting the battery from the charger.

14 Slow-rate charging is the best way to restore a battery that's discharged to the point where it will not start the engine. It's also a good way to maintain the battery charge in a vehicle that's only driven a few miles between starts. Maintaining the battery charge is particularly important in the winter when the battery must work harder to start the engine and electrical accessories that drain the battery are in greater use.

15 It's best to use a one or two-amp battery charger (sometimes called a "trickle" charger). They are the safest and put the least strain on the battery. They are also the least expensive. For a faster charge, you can use a higher amvperage charger, but don't use one rated more than 1/10th the amp/hour rating of the battery. Rapid boost charges that claim to restore the power of the battery in one to two hours are hardest on the battery and can damage batteries not in good condition. This type of charging should only be used in emergency situations.

16 The average time necessary to charge a battery should be listed in the instructions that come with the charger. As a general rule, a trickle charger will charge a battery in 12 to 16 hours.

11 Underhood hose check and replacement (every 5000 miles or 6 months)

❋❋ CAUTION:

Replacement of air conditioning hoses must be left to a dealer service department or air conditioning shop that has the equipment to depressurize the system safely. Never remove air conditioning components or hoses until the system has been evacuated and the refrigerant recovered by a dealer service department or air-conditioning shop.

GENERAL

1　High temperatures in the engine compartment can cause the deterioration of the rubber and plastic hoses used for engine, accessory and emission systems operation. Periodic inspection should be made for cracks, loose clamps, material hardening and leaks.

2　Information specific to the cooling system hoses can be found in Section 12.

3　Some, but not all, hoses are secured to the fittings with clamps. Where clamps are used, check to be sure they haven't lost their tension, allowing the hose to leak. If clamps aren't used, make sure the hose has not expanded and/or hardened where it slips over the fitting, allowing it to leak.

VACUUM HOSES

4　It's quite common for vacuum hoses, especially those in the emissions system, to be color coded or identified by colored stripes molded into them. Various systems require hoses with different wall thickness, collapse resistance and temperature resistance. When replacing hoses, be sure the new ones are made of the same material.

5　Often the only effective way to check a hose is to remove it completely from the vehicle. If more than one hose is removed, be sure to label the hoses and fittings to ensure correct installation.

6　When checking vacuum hoses, be sure to include any plastic T-fittings in the check. Inspect the fittings for cracks and the hose where it fits over the fitting for distortion, which could cause leakage.

7　A small piece of vacuum hose (1/4-inch inside diameter) can be used as a stethoscope to detect vacuum leaks. Hold one end of the hose to your ear and probe around vacuum hoses and fittings, listening for the "hissing" sound characteristic of a vacuum leak.

❋❋ WARNING:

When probing with the vacuum hose stethoscope, be very careful not to come into contact with moving engine components such as the drivebelts, cooling fan, etc.

FUEL HOSE

❋❋ WARNING:

There are certain precautions which must be taken when inspecting or servicing fuel system components. Work in a well ventilated area and do not allow open flames (cigarettes, appliance pilot lights, etc.) or bare light bulbs near the work area. Mop up any spills immediately and do not store fuel soaked rags where they could ignite.

8　Check all rubber fuel lines for deterioration and chafing. Check especially for cracks in areas where the hose bends and just before fittings, such as where a hose attaches to the fuel filter.

9　High quality fuel line should be used for fuel line replacement. Never, under any circumstances, use unreinforced vacuum line, clear plastic tubing or water hose for fuel lines.

10　Spring-type clamps are commonly used on fuel lines. These clamps often lose their tension over a period of time, and can be "sprung" during removal. Replace all spring-type clamps with screw clamps whenever a hose is replaced.

METAL LINES

11　Sections of metal line are often used for fuel line between the fuel pump and fuel injection unit. Check carefully to be sure the line has not been bent or crimped and that cracks have not started in the line.

12　If a section of metal fuel line must be replaced, only seamless steel tubing should be used, since copper and aluminum tubing don't have the strength necessary to withstand normal engine vibration.

13　Check the metal brake lines where they enter the master cylinder and brake proportioning unit (if used) for cracks in the lines or loose fittings. Any sign of brake fluid leakage calls for an immediate thorough inspection of the brake system.

12 Cooling system check (every 5000 miles or 6 months)

◆ **Refer to illustration 12.4**

1　Many major engine failures can be attributed to a faulty cooling system. If the vehicle is equipped with an automatic transaxle, the cooling system also cools the transaxle fluid and thus plays an important role in prolonging transaxle life.

2　The cooling system should be checked with the engine cold. Do this before the vehicle is driven for the day or after the engine has been shut off for at least three hours.

❋❋ WARNING:

Never remove the radiator pressure cap when the engine is running or has just been shut down, because the cooling system is hot. Escaping steam and scalding liquid could cause serious injury.

3　Remove the radiator pressure cap by turning it to the left until it reaches a stop. If you hear a hissing sound (indicating there is still pressure in the system), wait until it stops. Now press down on the cap

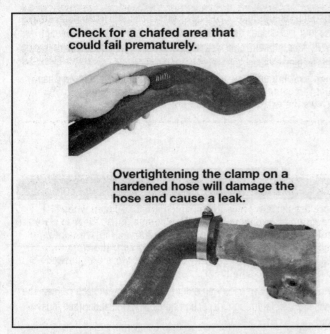

Check for a chafed area that could fail prematurely.

Check for a soft area indicating the hose has deteriorated inside.

Overtightening the clamp on a hardened hose will damage the hose and cause a leak.

Check each hose for swelling and oil-soaked ends. Cracks and breaks can be located by squeezing the hose.

12.4 Hoses, like drivebelts, have a habit of failing at the worst possible time - to prevent the inconvenience of a blown radiator or heater hose, inspect them carefully as shown here

with the palm of your hand and continue turning to the left until the cap can be removed. Thoroughly clean the cap, inside and out, with clean water. Also clean the filler neck on the radiator. All traces of corrosion should be removed. The coolant inside the radiator should be relatively transparent. If it's rust colored, the system should be drained and refilled (see Section 31). If the coolant level isn't up to the top, add additional antifreeze/coolant mixture (see Section 4).

4 Carefully check the large upper and lower radiator hoses along with the smaller diameter heater hoses which run from the engine to the bulkhead. Inspect each hose along its entire length, replacing any hose which is cracked, swollen or shows signs of deterioration. Cracks may become more apparent if the hose is squeezed (see illustration). Regardless of condition, it's a good idea to replace hoses with new

ones every two years.

5 Make sure that all hose connections are tight. A leak in the cooling system will usually show up as white or rust colored deposits on the areas adjoining the leak. If wire-type clamps are used at the ends of the hoses, it may be a good idea to replace them with more secure screw-type clamps.

6 Use compressed air or a soft brush to remove bugs, leaves, etc. from the front of the radiator or air conditioning condenser. Be careful not to damage the delicate cooling fins or cut yourself on them.

7 Every other inspection, or at the first indication of cooling system problems, have the cap and system pressure tested. If you don't have a pressure tester, most gas stations and garages will do this for a minimal charge.

13 Tire rotation (every 5000 miles or 6 months)

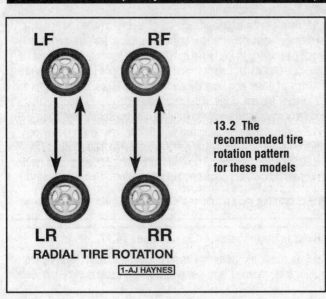

13.2 The recommended tire rotation pattern for these models

RADIAL TIRE ROTATION

1-AJ HAYNES

▶ **Refer to illustration 13.2**

1 The tires should be rotated at the specified intervals and whenever uneven wear is noticed. Since the vehicle will be raised and the tires removed anyway, check the brakes (see Section 14) at this time.

2 Radial tires must be rotated in a specific pattern (see illustration). Most models are equipped with non-directional tires, but some sport models may be equipped with directional tires, which have a specific rotational pattern. When choosing replacement tires, examine the sidewalls. Directional tires have arrows on the sidewall that indicate the direction they must turn, and a set of these tires includes two left-side tires and two right-side tires. The left and right side tires must not be rotated to the other side.

3 Refer to the information in *Jacking and towing* at the front of this

manual for the proper procedures to follow when raising the vehicle and changing a tire. If the brakes are to be checked, do not apply the parking brake as stated. Make sure the tires are blocked to prevent the vehicle from rolling.

4 Preferably, the entire vehicle should be raised at the same time. This can be done on a hoist or by jacking up each corner and then lowering the vehicle onto jack stands placed under the frame rails. Always use four jack stands and make sure the vehicle is firmly supported.

5 After rotation, check and adjust the tire pressures as necessary and be sure to check the wheel lug nut torque.

6 For further information on the wheels and tires, refer to Chapter 10.

14 Brake check (every 5,000 miles or 6 months)

✳ WARNING:

Dust created by the brake system is harmful to your health. Never blow it out with compressed air and don't inhale any of it. An approved filtering mask should be worn when working on the brakes. Do not, under any circumstances, use petroleum-based solvents to clean brake parts. Use brake system cleaner only!

➡ **Note: For detailed photographs of the brake system, refer to Chapter 9.**

1 In addition to the specified intervals, the brakes should be inspected every time the wheels are removed or whenever a defect is suspected. Any of the following symptoms could indicate a potential brake system defect: The vehicle pulls to one side when the brake pedal is depressed; the brakes make squealing or dragging noises when applied; brake travel is excessive; the pedal pulsates; brake fluid leaks, usually onto the inside of the tire or wheel.

2 The disc brake pads have built-in wear indicators which should make a high pitched squealing or scraping noise when they are worn to the replacement point. When you hear this noise, replace the pads immediately or expensive damage to the discs can result.

3 Loosen the wheel nuts.

4 Raise the vehicle and place it securely on jack stands.

5 Remove the wheels (see *Jacking and towing* at the front of this book, or your owner's manual, if necessary).

14.6 You'll find an inspection hole like this in each caliper through which you can view the inner and outer brake pad lining

DISC BRAKES

➧ **Refer to illustration 14.6**

6 There are two pads - an outer and an inner - in each caliper. The pads are visible through inspection holes in each caliper (see illustration).

7 Check the pad thickness by looking at each end of the caliper and through the inspection hole in the caliper body. If the lining material is less than the thickness listed in this Chapter's Specifications, replace the pads.

➡ **Note: Keep in mind that the lining material is riveted or bonded to a metal backing plate and the metal portion is not included in this measurement.**

8 If it is difficult to determine the exact thickness of the remaining pad material by the above method, or if you are at all concerned about the condition of the pads, remove the caliper(s), then remove the pads from the calipers for further inspection (refer to Chapter 9).

9 Once the pads are removed from the calipers, clean them with brake cleaner and remeasure them with a small steel pocket ruler or a vernier caliper.

10 Measure the disc thickness with a micrometer to make sure that it still has service life remaining. If any disc is thinner than the specified minimum thickness, replace it (refer to Chapter 9). Even if the disc has service life remaining, check its condition. Look for scoring, gouging and burned spots. If these conditions exist, remove the disc and have it resurfaced (see Chapter 9).

11 Before installing the wheels, check all brake lines and hoses for damage, wear, deformation, cracks, corrosion, leakage, bends and twists, particularly in the vicinity of the rubber hoses at the calipers. Check the clamps for tightness and the connections for leakage. Make sure that all hoses and lines are clear of sharp edges, moving parts and the exhaust system. If any of the above conditions are noted, repair, reroute or replace the lines and/or fittings as necessary (see Chapter 9).

12 Some models are equipped with disc brakes on the rear wheels which incorporate a drum-type parking brake into the rear discs. The inspection procedure for the parking brake lining is the same as for the rear drum brake lining described below.

REAR DRUM BRAKES

➧ **Refer to illustrations 14.13, 14.15 and 14.17**

13 To check the brake shoe lining thickness without removing the brake drums, remove the rubber plug from the backing plate and use a

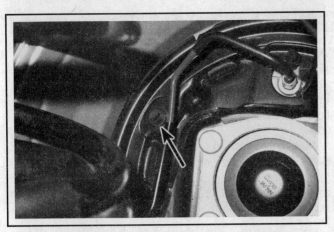

14.13 A quick check of the remaining drum brake shoe lining material can be made by removing the rubber plug in the backing plate and looking through the inspection hole

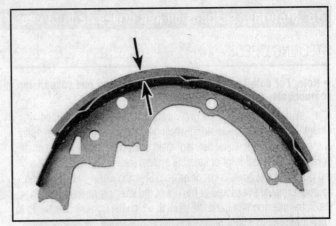

14.15 If the lining is bonded to the brake shoe, measure the lining thickness from the outer surface to the metal shoe, as shown here; if the lining is riveted to the shoe, measure from the lining outer surface to the rivet head

flashlight to inspect the linings (see illustration). For a more thorough brake inspection, follow the procedure below.

14 Refer to Chapter 9 and remove the rear brake drums.

※※ WARNING:

Brake dust produced by lining wear and deposited on brake components is hazardous to your health. DO NOT blow it out with compressed air and DO NOT inhale it!

15 Note the thickness of the lining material on the rear brake shoes (see illustration) and look for signs of contamination by brake fluid and grease. If the lining material is within 1/16-inch of the recessed rivets or metal shoes, replace the brake shoes with new ones. The shoes should also be replaced if they are cracked, glazed (shiny lining surfaces) or contaminated with brake fluid or grease. See Chapter 9 for the replacement procedure.

16 Check the shoe return and hold-down springs and the adjusting mechanism to make sure they're fitted correctly and in good condition. Deteriorated or distorted springs, if not replaced, could allow the linings to drag and wear prematurely.

17 Check the wheel cylinders for leakage by carefully peeling back the rubber boots (see illustration). If brake fluid is noted behind the boots, the wheel cylinders must be replaced (see Chapter 9).

18 Check the drums for cracks, score marks, deep scratches and hard spots, which will appear as small discolored areas. If imperfections cannot be removed with emery cloth, the drums must be resurfaced by an automotive machine shop (see Chapter 9 for more detailed information).

19 Refer to Chapter 9 and install the brake drums.

20 Install the wheels and snug the wheel nuts finger tight.

21 Remove the jack stands and lower the vehicle.

22 Tighten the wheel nuts to the torque listed in this Chapter's Specifications.

BRAKE BOOSTER CHECK

23 Sit in the driver's seat and perform the following sequence of tests.

24 With the brake fully depressed, start the engine - the pedal should move down a little when the engine starts.

14.17 Carefully peel back the wheel cylinder boot and check for leaking fluid indicating that the cylinder must be replaced or rebuilt

25 With the engine running, depress the brake pedal several times - the travel distance should not change.

26 Depress the brake, stop the engine and hold the pedal in for about 30 seconds - the pedal should neither sink nor rise.

27 Restart the engine, run it for about a minute and turn it off. Then firmly depress the brake several times - the pedal travel should decrease with each application.

28 If your brakes do not operate as described above when the preceding tests are performed, the brake booster is either in need of repair or has failed. Refer to Chapter 9 for the removal procedure.

PARKING BRAKE

29 Slowly pull up on the parking brake handle or push down on the parking brake pedal and count the number of clicks you hear until the handle is up (or the pedal down) as far as it will go. The adjustment is correct if you hear the specified number of clicks. If you hear more or fewer clicks, it's time to adjust the parking brake (refer to Chapter 9).

30 An alternative method of checking the parking brake is to park the vehicle on a steep hill with the parking brake set and the transaxle in Neutral. If the parking brake cannot prevent the vehicle from rolling, it is in need of adjustment (see Chapter 9).

15 Steering, suspension and driveaxle boot check (every 15,000 miles or 18 months)

STEERING CHECK

➡**Note: For detailed illustrations of the steering and suspension components, refer to Chapter 10.**

1 With the vehicle on the ground and the front wheels pointed straight ahead, rock the steering wheel gently back and forth. If freeplay is excessive, a front wheel bearing, main shaft yoke, intermediate shaft yoke, lower arm balljoint or steering system joint is worn or the steering gear is out of adjustment or broken. Steering wheel freeplay is the amount of travel (measured at the rim of the steering wheel) between the initial steering input and the point at which the front wheels begin to turn (indicated by slight resistance). Refer to Chapter 10 for the appropriate repair procedure.

2 Other symptoms, such as excessive vehicle body movement over rough roads, swaying (leaning) around corners and binding as the steering wheel is turned, may indicate faulty steering and/or suspension components.

SUSPENSION CHECK

▸ **Refer to illustrations 15.7 and 15.8**

3 Check the shock absorbers by pushing down and releasing the

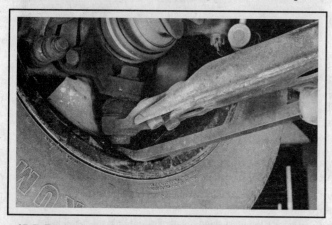

15.7 To check the balljoints attempt to move the lower arm up and down with a prybar to make sure here is no play in the balljoint (if there is, replace it)

15.8 Push on the balljoint boot to check for tears and grease leaks

vehicle several times at each corner. If the vehicle does not come back to a level position within one or two bounces, the shocks/struts are worn and must be replaced. When bouncing the vehicle up and down, listen for squeaks and noises from the suspension components. Additional information on suspension components can be found in Chapter 10.

4 Raise the vehicle with a floor jack and support it securely on jack stands. See *Jacking and towing* at the front of this book for the proper jacking points.

5 Check the tires for irregular wear patterns and proper inflation. See Section 5 in this Chapter for information regarding tire wear and Chapter 10 for the wheel bearing replacement procedures.

6 Inspect the universal joint between the steering shaft and the steering gear housing. Check the steering gear housing for lubricant leakage or oozing. Make sure that the dust seals and boots are not damaged and that the boot clamps are not loose. Check the steering linkage for looseness or damage. Check the track rod ends for excessive play. Look for loose bolts, broken or disconnected parts and deteriorated rubber bushings on all suspension and steering components. While an assistant turns the steering wheel from side to side, check the steering components for free movement, chafing and binding. If the steering components do not seem to be reacting with the movement of the steering wheel, try to determine where the slack is located.

7 Check the balljoints for wear by placing a wood block under each tire. Lower the jack until there is about half a load on the coil spring and place jack stands under the subframe. Make sure that the front wheels are in a straight forward position and block the wheel with chocks. Try to move each lower arm up and down with a prybar (see illustration) to ensure that its balljoint has no play. If any balljoint does have play, replace it. See Chapter 10 for the front balljoint replacement procedure.

8 Inspect the balljoint boots for damage and leaking grease (see illustration). Replace the balljoints with new ones if they are damaged (see Chapter 10).

DRIVEAXLE BOOT CHECK

▸ **Refer to illustration 15.10**

9 The driveaxle boots are very important because they prevent dirt,

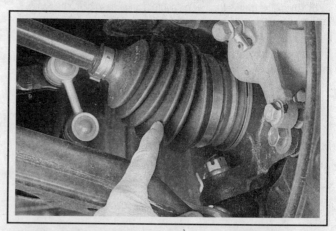

15.10 Flex the driveaxle boots by hand to check for tears, cracks and leaking grease

water and foreign material from entering and damaging the constant velocity (CV) joints. Oil and grease can cause the boot material to deteriorate prematurely, so it's a good idea to wash the boots with soap and water.

10 Inspect the boots for tears and cracks as well as loose clamps (see illustration). If there is any evidence of cracks or leaking lubricant, they must be replaced as described in Chapter 8.

16 Exhaust system check (every 15,000 miles or 18 months)

♦ **Refer to illustration 16.2**

1 With the engine cold (at least three hours after the vehicle has been driven), check the complete exhaust system from its starting point at the engine to the end of the tailpipe. This should be done on a hoist where unrestricted access is available.

2 Check the pipes and connections for evidence of leaks, severe corrosion or damage. Make sure that all brackets and hangers are in good condition and tight (see illustration).

3 At the same time, inspect the underside of the body for holes, corrosion, open seams, etc. which may allow exhaust gases to enter the passenger compartment. Seal all body openings with silicone or body putty.

4 Rattles and other noises can often be traced to the exhaust system, especially the mounts and hangers. Try to move the pipes, silencer and catalytic converter. If the components can come in contact with the body or suspension parts, secure the exhaust system with new mounts.

5 Check the running condition of the engine by inspecting inside the end of the tailpipe. The exhaust deposits here are an indication of engine state-of-tune. If the pipe is black and sooty or coated with white

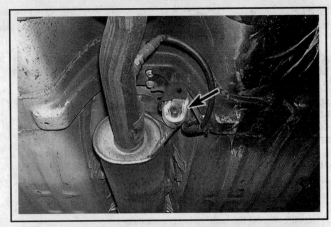

16.2 Check the exhaust system for damage, or worn rubber hangers (arrow)

deposits, the engine is in need of a tune-up, including a thorough fuel system inspection.

17 Air filter replacement (every 30,000 miles or 36 months)

♦ **Refer to illustrations 17.1 and 17.2**

1 The air filter is located inside a housing at the left (driver's) side of the engine compartment. To remove the air filter, unscrew the bolts retaining the two halves of the air filter housing (see illustration).

2 Lift the cover up and remove the air filter element (see illustration).

3 Inspect the outer surface of the filter element. If it is dirty, replace

it. If it is only moderately dusty, it can be reused by blowing it clean from the back to the front surface with compressed air.

❋❋ WARNING:

Always wear eye protection when using compressed air!

Because it is a pleated paper type filter, it cannot be washed or oiled. If it cannot be cleaned satisfactorily with compressed air, discard and replace it.

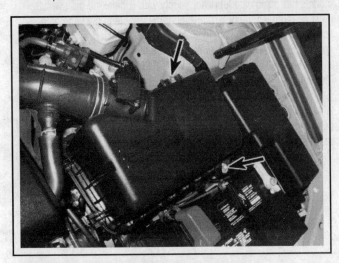

17.1 Unscrew the two bolts securing the air filter housing cover

17.2 Lift the cover up and remove the filter

✳✳ CAUTION:

Never drive the vehicle with the air filter removed. Excessive engine wear could result and backfiring could even cause a fire under the hood.

4   Installation is the reverse of removal. Make sure the hinge tabs on the housing cover engage properly with the lower part of the housing.

18 Fuel system check (every 30,000 miles or 36 months)

✳✳ WARNING:

Certain precautions should be observed when inspecting or servicing the fuel system components. Work in a well ventilated area and do not allow open flames (cigarettes, appliance pilot lights, etc.) near the work area. Mop up spills immediately and do not store fuel-soaked rags where they could ignite. It is a good idea to keep a dry chemical (Class B) fire extinguisher near the work area any time the fuel system is being serviced.

1   If you smell fuel while driving or after the vehicle has been sitting in the sun, inspect the fuel system immediately.

2   Remove the fuel filler cap and inspect if for damage and corrosion. The gasket should have an unbroken sealing imprint. If the gasket is damaged or corroded, remove it and install a new one (see Section 23).

3   Inspect the fuel feed and return lines for cracks. Make sure that the threaded flare nut type connectors which secure the metal fuel lines to the fuel injection system and the banjo bolts which secure the banjo fittings to the in-line fuel filter are tight.

4   Since some components of the fuel system - the fuel tank and part of the fuel feed and return lines, for example - are underneath the vehicle, they can be inspected more easily with the vehicle raised on a hoist. If that's not possible, raise the vehicle and support it securely on jack stands.

5   With the vehicle raised and safely supported, inspect the fuel tank and filler neck for punctures, cracks and other damage. The connection between the filler neck and the tank is particularly critical. Sometimes a rubber filler neck will leak because of loose clamps or deteriorated rubber. These are problems a home mechanic can usually rectify.

✳✳ WARNING:

Do not, under any circumstances, try to repair a fuel tank (except rubber components). A welding torch or any open flame can easily cause fuel vapors inside the tank to explode.

6   Carefully check all rubber hoses and metal lines leading away from the fuel tank. Check for loose connections, deteriorated hoses, crimped lines and other damage. Carefully inspect the lines from the tank to the fuel injection system. Repair or replace damaged sections as necessary (see Chapter 4).

19 Automatic transaxle differential lubricant level check (some Avalon and Solara models) (every 30,000 miles or 36 months)

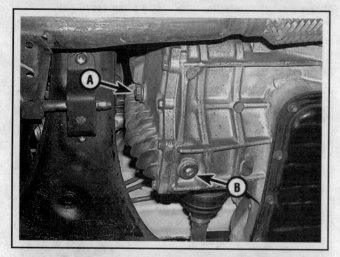

19.2 The automatic transaxle differential check/fill plug (A) is located on the rear of the transaxle - (B) is the drain plug (typical)

▶ **Refer to illustration 19.2**

1   The automatic transaxle differential on some Avalon and Solara models has a separate lubricant supply with a check/fill plug which must be removed to check the level. If the vehicle is raised to gain access to the plug, be sure to support it safely on jack stands - DO NOT crawl under the vehicle when it's supported only by the jack.

2   Remove the check/fill plug from the front of the transaxle (see illustration).

3   Use your little finger as a dipstick to make sure the lubricant level is even with the bottom of the plug hole. If not, use a syringe or a gear oil pump to add the recommended lubricant (see this Chapter's Specifications) until it just starts to run out of the opening.

4   Install the plug and tighten it securely.

20 Manual transaxle lubricant level check (every 30,000 miles or 36 months)

▶ **Refer to illustration 20.1**

1   The manual transaxle does not have a dipstick. To check the fluid level, raise the vehicle and support it securely on jack stands. On the lower front side of the transaxle housing, you will see a plug (see illustration). Remove it. If the lubricant level is correct, it should be up to the lower edge of the hole.

2   If the transaxle needs more lubricant (if the level is not up to the hole), use a syringe or a gear oil pump to add more. Stop filling the transaxle when the lubricant begins to run out the hole.

3   Install the plug and tighten it securely. Drive the vehicle a short distance, then check for leaks.

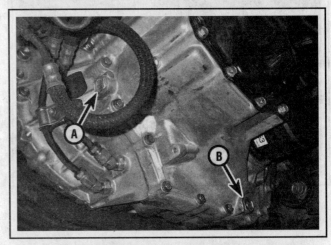

20.1 Remove the filler plug to check the manual transaxle lubricant level - the level should be at the bottom of the hole

A   Check/fill plug   B   Drain plug

21 Interior ventilation filter replacement (every 30,000 miles or 36 months)

▶ **Refer to illustration 21.3**

1   There is an air filter in the blower housing that cleans the air before it enters the passenger's compartment.

2   To remove the air filter, remove the glove box (see Chapter 11).

3   Depress the filter cover mounting tabs (see illustration).

4   Lift the cover up and remove the air filter element.

5   Installation is the reverse of removal.

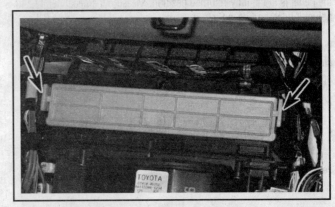

21.3 Ventilation filter mounting tabs

22 Clutch/brake pedal height and freeplay - check and adjustment (every 30,000 miles or 36 months)

PEDAL HEIGHT

▶ **Refer to illustrations 22.1 and 22.2**

1   The height of the clutch and brake pedal is the distance the pedal sits off the floor (see illustration). If the pedal height is not within Specifications, it must be adjusted.

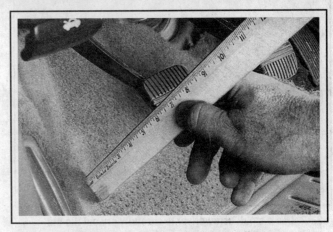

22.1 To check the pedal height, measure the distance between the natural resting place of the pedal and the floor

22.2 Loosen the pedal pushrod locknut, then adjust the pushrod to achieve proper pedal height

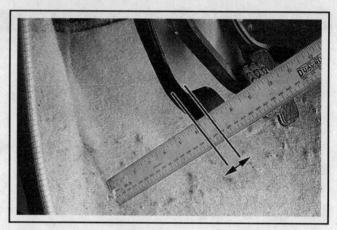

22.5 Pedal freeplay is the distance between the natural resting point of the pedal to the point at which resistance is felt

2   To adjust the clutch pedal, loosen the locknut and back the pushrod out for clearance. Turn the pushrod to adjust the pedal height in the middle of the specified range, then retighten the locknut (see illustration).

3   At the brake pedal, loosen the locknut on the brake switch and retract the switch. Before measuring the brake pedal height, make sure the pedal is in the fully-returned position. Measure the pedal height and adjust if necessary (see Step 2).

4   Adjust the brake pedal switch by turning it clockwise until the switch body just contacts the pedal arm, then rotate it counter-clockwise to gain the specified clearance at the end of this Chapter and tighten the switch locknut.

PEDAL FREEPLAY

▶ **Refer to illustration 22.5**

5   The freeplay is the pedal slack, or the distance the pedal can be depressed before it begins to have any effect on the clutch or brake

system (see illustration). If the pedal freeplay is not within the specified range, it must be adjusted.

6   To adjust the pedal freeplay, loosen the locknut on the clutch pushrod. Then back out the pushrod to adjust the freeplay to the specified range, then retighten the locknut.

7   Before adjusting brake pedal freeplay, depress the brake pedal several times (with the engine off). Measure the freeplay and adjust if necessary. Loosen the locknut on the pushrod, then back off the pushrod to adjust the pedal freeplay to the specified range and retighten the locknut.

BRAKE PEDAL RESERVE DISTANCE

8   With the parking brake released and the engine running, depress the pedal with normal braking effort and have an assistant measure the distance from the center of the pedal pad to the floor. If the distance is less than specified, refer to Chapter 9 and troubleshoot the brake system.

23 Fuel tank cap gasket inspection and replacement (every 30,000 miles or 36 months)

23.2 Use a small screwdriver to carefully pry out the old gasket - take care not to damage the cap

▶ **Refer to illustration 23.2**

1   Remove the tank cap and inspect the rubber gasket for cracks or tears.

2   If replacement is necessary, carefully pry the old gasket out of the recess (see illustration). Be very careful not to damage the sealing surface inside the cap.

3   Work the new gasket into the cap recess.

4   Install the cap, then remove it and make sure the gasket seals all the way around.

24 Positive Crankcase Ventilation (PCV) valve check and replacement (every 30,000 miles or 36 months)

▶ **Refer to illustration 24.4**

1   The PCV valve and hose are located in the valve cover.

2   Disconnect the hose, pull the PCV valve from the cover, then reconnect the hose.

3   With the engine idling at normal operating temperature, place your finger over the valve opening. If there's no vacuum at the valve, check for a plugged hose or valve. Replace any plugged or deteriorated hoses.

4   Turn off the engine. Remove the PCV valve from the hose. Blow through the valve from the valve cover (cylinder head) end (see illustration). If air will not pass through the valve in this direction, replace it with a new one.

5   When purchasing a replacement PCV valve, make sure it's for your particular vehicle and engine size. Compare the old valve with the new one to make sure they're the same.

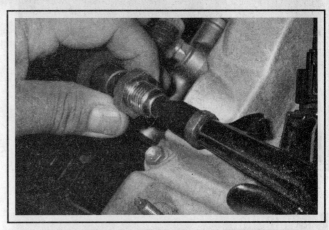

24.4 To check the PCV valve, first attach a clean section of hose to the cylinder head side of the valve and blow through it - air should pass through easily - then blow through the opposite side of the valve and verify that air doesn't pass through it

25 Evaporative emissions control system check (every 30,000 miles or 36 months)

▶ **Refer to illustration 25.2**

1   The function of the evaporative emissions control system is to draw fuel vapors from the fuel tank and fuel system, store them in a charcoal canister and then burn them during normal engine operation.

2   The most common symptom of a fault in the evaporative emissions system is a strong fuel odor in or around the vehicle. If a fuel odor is detected, inspect the charcoal canister. Check the canister and all hoses for damage and deterioration (see illustration).

3   The evaporative emissions control system is explained in more detail in Chapter 6.

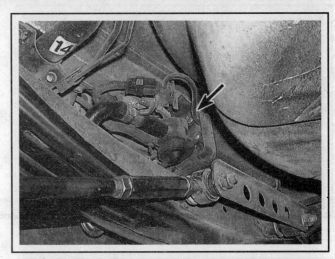

25.2 Check the charcoal canister for damage and the hose connections for cracks and damage; the canister is located at the rear of the vehicle, above the suspension crossmember (typical)

26 Automatic transaxle/differential fluid change (every 50,000 miles or 60 months)

▶ **Refer to illustrations 26.7, 26.8a, 26.8b, 26.9, 26.12 and 26.14**

1   At the specified time intervals, the automatic transaxle and differential fluid should be drained and replaced.

➡**Note: Although the manufacturer doesn't specify it, it is a good idea to clean the transaxle fluid strainer periodically to remove accumulated dirt and metal particles.**

2   Before beginning work, purchase the specified transaxle fluid

(see *Recommended fluids and lubricants* at the end of this Chapter).

3   Other tools necessary for this job include jack stands to support the vehicle in a raised position, a 10 mm hex bit or Allen wrench, a drain pan capable of holding at least eight pints, newspapers and clean rags.

4   The fluid should be drained immediately after the vehicle has been driven. Hot fluid is more effective than cold fluid at removing built up sediment.

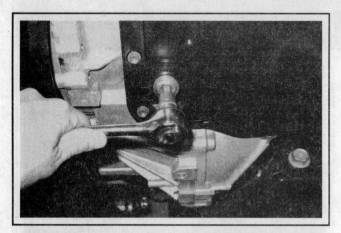

26.7 Remove the automatic transaxle drain plug

26.8a After loosening the front bolts, remove the rear pan bolts and . . .

5   After the vehicle has been driven to warm up the fluid, raise it and place it on jack stands for access to the transaxle and differential drain plugs.

6   Move the necessary equipment under the vehicle, being careful not to touch any of the hot exhaust components.

7   Place the drain pan under the drain plug in the transaxle pan and remove the drain plug (see illustration). Be sure the drain pan is in position, as fluid will come out with some force. Once the fluid is drained, reinstall the drain plug securely. If you aren't going to clean the strainer, proceed to Step 14.

8   To clean the strainer, remove the front transaxle pan bolts, then loosen the rear bolts and carefully pry the pan loose with a screwdriver and allow the remaining fluid to drain (see illustrations). Once the fluid had drained, remove the bolts and lower the pan.

9   Remove the strainer retaining bolts, disconnect the clip (some models) and lower the strainer from the transaxle (see illustration). Be careful when lowering the strainer as it contains residual fluid.

10 Wash the strainer thoroughly in clean transmission fluid.

11 Place the strainer in position, connect the clip (if equipped) and install the bolts. Tighten the bolts to the torque listed in this Chapter's Specifications.

12 Carefully clean the gasket surfaces of the fluid pan, removing all traces of old gasket material. Noting their location, remove the magnets, wash the pan in clean solvent and dry it with compressed air.

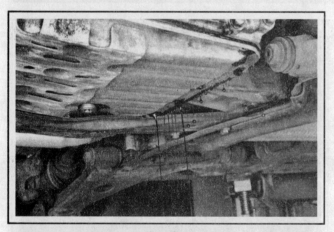

26.8b . . . allow the remaining fluid to drain out

26.9 Remove the strainer bolts and lower the strainer (be careful, there will be some residual fluid)

26.12 Noting their locations, remove the magnets and wash them and the pan in solvent before installing them

Always wear eye protection when using compressed air! Be sure to clean and reinstall the magnets in the pan (see illustration).

13 Install a new gasket, place the fluid pan in position and install the bolts in their original positions. Tighten the bolts to the torque listed in this Chapter's Specifications.

14 Locate the differential drain plug (some Avalon and Solara models). Place the drain pan underneath the plug, remove it with a hex bit or Allen wrench and drain the fluid (see illustration). When the differential fluid has drained, reinstall the plug securely.

15 On models with a separate differential, refer to Section 19 and add new fluid to the differential until it begins to run out of the filler hole (see *Recommended lubricants and fluids* at the end of this Chapter for the specified fluid type and capacity).

Do not overfill. The automatic transaxle and the differential are separate units.

16 Lower the vehicle.

17 With the engine off, add new fluid to the transaxle through the dipstick tube (see *Recommended fluids and lubricants* for the recom-

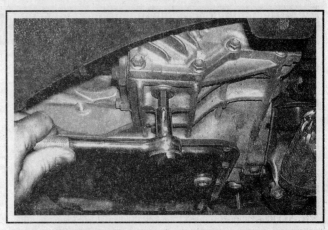

26.14 On some models, also remove the automatic transaxle differential drain plug

mended fluid type and capacity). Use a funnel to prevent spills. It is best to add a little fluid at a time, continually checking the level with the dipstick (see Section 7). Allow the fluid time to drain into the pan.

18 Start the engine and shift the gearchange selector into all positions from P through L, then shift the gearchange into P and apply the parking brake.

19 With the engine idling, check the fluid level. Add fluid up to the Cool level on the dipstick.

27 Manual transaxle lubricant change - when vehicle used for towing (every 30,000 miles or 36 months)

1 The fluid should be drained immediately after the vehicle has been driven. Hot fluid is more effective than cold fluid at removing built up sediment.

2 After the vehicle has been driven to warm up the fluid, raise it and place it on jack stands for access to the drain plug.

3 Remove the drain plug(s) and drain the fluid (see Section 19).

4 Reinstall the drain plug securely.

5 Add new fluid until it begins to run out of the filler hole. See *Recommended lubricants and fluids* for the specified lubricant type.

28 Chassis and body fastener check (every 30,000 miles or 36 months)

▶ **Refer to illustrations 28.1a and 28.1b**

1 Tighten the following fasteners to the torque values listed in this Chapter's Specifications:

a) Front seat mounting bolts.
b) Both front and rear suspension member-to-body mounting bolts and nuts (left and right sides) (see illustrations).

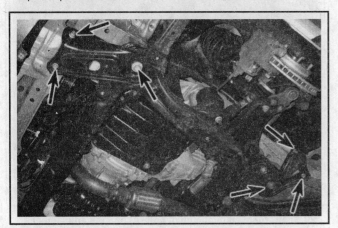

28.1a Periodically check the tightness of the nuts and bolts on each side of the front suspension subframe . . .

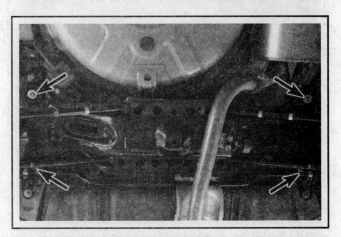

28.1b . . . and rear suspension mounts

29   Drivebelt check, adjustment and replacement (60,000 miles or 72 months and every 15,000 miles and 18 months thereafter)

CHECK

♦ **Refer to illustrations 29.3 and 29.5**

1   The drivebelt(s) are located at the right side of the engine compartment. The good condition and proper adjustment of the belts is critical to the operation of the engine. Because of their composition and the high stresses to which they are subjected, drivebelts stretch and deteriorate as they get older. They must therefore be periodically inspected.

2   On four-cylinder models, one belt drives the alternator, air conditioning and power steering. On V6 models, one belt transmits power from the crankshaft to the alternator and air conditioning, and one belt drives the power steering pump.

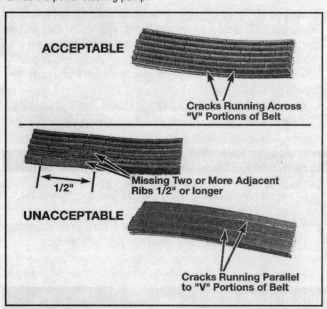

29.3 Check a multi-ribbed belt for signs like these - if the belt looks worn, replace it

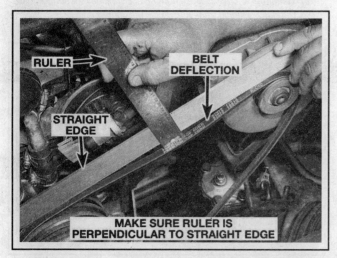

29.5 Measuring drivebelt deflection with a straightedge and ruler

3   With the engine off, open the hood and locate the drivebelts at the right side of the engine compartment. With a flashlight, check each belt for separation of the adhesive rubber on both sides of the core, core separation from the belt side, a severed core, separation of the ribs from the adhesive rubber, cracking or separation of the ribs, and torn or worn ribs or cracks in the inner ridges of the ribs (see illustration). Also check for fraying and glazing, which gives the belt a shiny appearance. Both sides of the belt should be inspected, which means you will have to twist the belt to check the underside. Use your fingers to feel the belt where you can't see it. If any of the above conditions are evident, replace the belt (go to Step 8 or Step 15).

4   To check the tension of each belt in accordance with factory specifications, install either a Nippondenso or Burroughs belt tension gauge on the belt. Measure the tension in accordance with the tool manufacturer's instructions and compare your measurement to the specified drivebelt tension for either a used or new belt.

➡**Note: A "used" belt is defined as any belt which has been operated more than five minutes on the engine; a "new" belt is one that has been used for less than five minutes.**

5   If you don't have either of the above tools, and cannot borrow one, the following rule of thumb method is recommended: Push firmly on the belt with your thumb at a distance halfway between the pulleys and note how far the belt can be pushed (deflected). Measure this deflection with a ruler (see illustration). The belt should deflect 1/4-inch if the distance from pulley center to pulley center is between 7 and 11 inches; the belt should deflect 1/2-inch if the distance from pulley center to pulley center is between 12 and 16 inches.

ADJUSTMENT (V6 ENGINE ONLY)

♦ **Refer to illustration 29.6**

6   If the alternator/air conditioner compressor belt must be adjusted, loosen the alternator pivot bolt located on the front left corner of the block. Loosen the locking bolt and turn the adjusting bolt (see illustration). Measure the belt tension in accordance with one of the above

29.6 After loosening the pivot bolt (A) and the adjustment pinch bolt, turn the adjustment bolt (B) clockwise to tighten the belt, or counterclockwise to loosen the belt

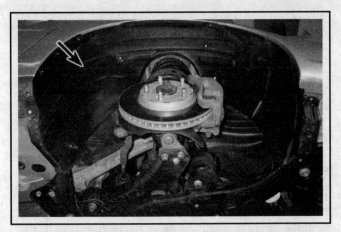

29.9 Locate and remove all the fasteners, then remove the right side fender apron

29.10 Remove the right side engine cover

methods. Repeat this step until the air conditioning compressor drive-belt is adjusted.

7   Adjust the power steering pump belt by loosening the adjustment bolt that secures the pump to the slotted bracket and pivot the pump (away from the engine to tighten the belt, toward it to loosen it). Repeat the procedure until the drivebelt tension is correct and tighten the bolt.

REPLACEMENT

Four-cylinder engine

▶ **Refer to illustrations 29.9 and 29.10**

8   Remove the right front wheel.
9   Remove right side fender apron seal (see illustration).
10 Remove right side engine cover assembly (see illustration).
11 Remove the upper engine control rod and bracket (see the under-hood photo at the beginning of this Chapter).
12 Slowly turn the drivebelt tensioner clockwise and remove the drivebelt from the pulleys.
13 Take the old belts to the parts store in order to make a direct comparison for length, width and design.

14 After replacing the drivebelt, make sure that it fits properly in the ribbed grooves in the pulleys. It is essential that the belt be properly centered.

V6 engine

15 To replace a belt, follow the above procedures for V6 engine drivebelt adjustment, but slip the belt off the crankshaft pulley and remove it. If you are replacing the power steering pump belt, you will have to remove the air conditioning compressor belt first because of the way they are arranged on the crankshaft pulley. Because of this and because belts tend to wear out more or less together, it is a good idea to replace both belts at the same time. Mark each belt and its appropriate pulley groove so the replacement belts can be fitted in their proper positions.
16 Take the old belts to the parts store in order to make a direct comparison for length, width and design.
17 After replacing a drivebelt, make sure that it fits properly in the ribbed grooves in the pulleys. It is essential that the belt be properly centered.
18 Adjust the belt(s) in accordance with the procedure outlined earlier in this Section.

30   Valve clearance check and adjustment (every 60,000 miles or 72 months)

▶ **Refer to illustrations 30.7a, 30.7b, 30.7c, 30.8, 30.9a, 30.9b, 30.10, 30.11a, 30.11b, 30.11c, 30.12, 30.14a and 30.14b**

➡**Note: On V6 models, the following procedure requires the use of a special lifter tool. It is impossible to perform this task without it.**

1   Remove the right-side front fender apron, engine cover and any other components that will interfere with valve cover removal.
2   Remove the ignition coil(s).
3   On V6 models, drain the coolant (see Section 31), remove the radiator hose inlet, air cleaner assembly, upper suspension brace, and any other components that will interfere with valve cover removal.

4   Blow out the spark plug recesses with compressed air, if available, to remove any debris that might fall into the cylinders, then remove the spark plugs (see Section 32)

❄❄ WARNING:

Always wear eye protection when using compressed air!

5   Remove the valve cover(s) (see Chapter 2A or 2B).
6   Refer to Chapter 2A or 2B and position the number 1 piston at TDC on the compression stroke.

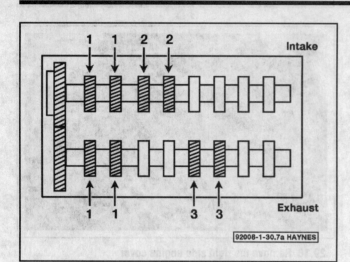

30.7a On four-cylinder engines, when the no. 1 piston is at TDC on the compression stroke, the valve clearance for the no. 1 and no. 3 cylinder exhaust valves and the no. 1 and no. 2 cylinder intake valves can be measured

7 Measure the clearance of the indicated valves with a feeler gauge of the specified thickness (see illustrations). Record the clearance of each valve and note which are out of specification. This information will be used later to determine the required replacement shims or lifters.

8 On four-cylinder engines, turn the crankshaft one complete revolution and realign the timing marks. Measure the remaining valves (see illustration).

9 On V6 engines, turn the crankshaft 2/3-turn (240-degrees) clockwise. Measure the valve clearance on the valves shown (see illustration). Rotate the crankshaft a further 2/3-turn and measure the clearance on the remaining valves (see illustration).

FOUR-CYLINDER MODELS

10 Remove the camshaft(s) for the valve(s) which you intend to adjust (refer to Chapter 2A). Remove and measure each lifter with a micrometer (see illustration). Place each lifter back into its bore in the cylinder head before moving onto the next lifter. Record the measurements for each lifter.

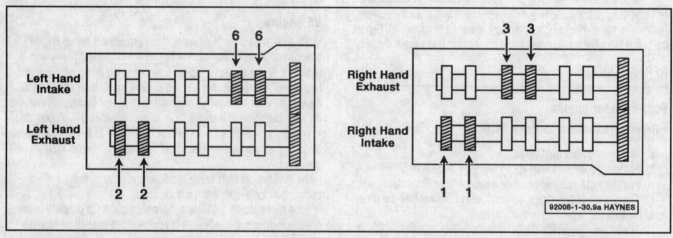

30.7b On the V6 engine, when the no. 1 piston is at TDC on the compression stroke, the clearance of the indicated valves can be measured

30.7c Measure the clearance for each valve with a feeler gauge of the specified thickness - if the clearance is correct, you should feel a slight drag on the gauge as you pull it out

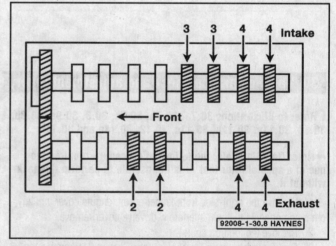

30.8 On four-cylinder engines, when the no. 4 piston is at TDC on the compression stroke, the valve clearance for the no. 2 and no. 4 exhaust valves and the no. 3 and no. 4 intake valves can be measured

V6 MODELS

11 On V6 models, after measuring and recording the clearance of each valve, turn the crankshaft pulley until the camshaft lobe above the first valve which you intend to adjust is pointing upward, away from the shim. Position the notch in the lifter toward the spark plug. Then depress the lifter with the special lifter tools (see illustration). Place the special lifter tool in position as shown, with the longer jaw of the tool gripping the lower edge of the cast lifter boss and the upper, shorter jaw gripping the upper edge of the lifter itself. Depress the lifter by squeezing the handles of the lifter tool together, then hold the lifter down with the smaller tool and remove the larger one. Remove the adjusting shim with a small screwdriver or a pair of tweezers (see illustrations). Note that the wire hook on the end of some lifter tool handles can be used to clamp both handles together to keep the lifter depressed while the shim is removed.

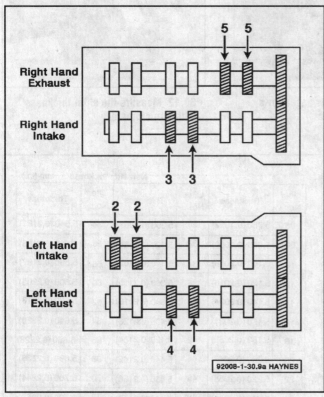

30.9a After the V6 engine has been rotated 240-degrees from TDC for the no. 1 piston, on the compression stroke, measure the clearance of the indicated valves

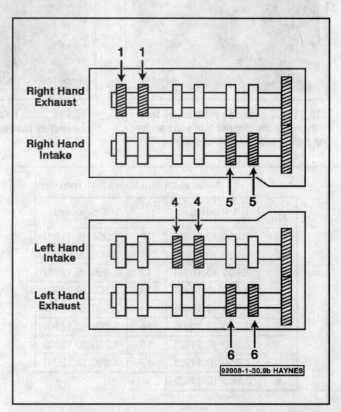

30.9b On the V6 engine, rotate the crankshaft an additional 2/3 of a revolution (240-degrees) and measure the clearance of the remaining valves

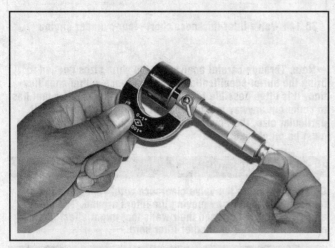

30.10 On four-cylinder models, measure the thickness of the lifter head with a micrometer

30.11a On the V6 engine, install the lifter tool as shown and squeeze the handles together to depress the lifter, then hold the lifter down with the smaller tool so the shim can be removed . . .

30.11b . . . keeping pressure on the lifter with the smaller tool and remove the shim with a small screwdriver . . .

30.11c . . . a pair of tweezers or a magnet as shown here

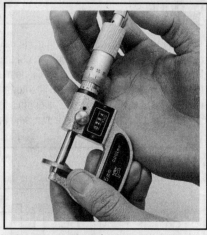

30.12 Measure the shim thickness with a micrometer

Shim No.	Thickness	Shim No.	Thickness
1	2.500 (0.0984)	10	2.950 (0.1161)
2	2.550 (0.1004)	11	3.000 (0.1181)
3	2.600 (0.1024)	12	3.050 (0.1201)
4	2.650 (0.1043)	13	3.100 (0.1220)
5	2.700 (0.1063)	14	3.150 (0.1240)
6	2.750 (0.1083)	15	3.200 (0.1260)
7	2.800 (0.1102)	16	3.250 (0.1280)
8	2.850 (0.1122)	17	3.300 (0.1299)
9	2.900 (0.1142)		

New shim thickness   mm (in.)

30.14a Valve adjusting shim thickness chart - V6 engine

12 Measure the thickness of the shim with a micrometer (see illustration).

ALL MODELS

13 To calculate the correct thickness of a replacement shim or lifter that will place the valve clearance within the specified value, use the following formula:

N = T + (A – V)

Whereas:

T = thickness of the old shim or lifter
A = valve clearance measured
N = thickness of the new shim or lifter
V = desired valve clearance (see this Chapter's Specifications)

14 Select a shim or lifter with a thickness as close as possible to the valve clearance calculated. Shims for V6 models, which are available in 17 sizes in increments of 0.0020-inch (0.050 mm), range in size from 0.0984-inch (2.500 mm) to 0.1299-inch (3.300 mm) (see illustration). Lifters for four-cylinder engines are available in 35 sizes, in increments of 0.0008-inch (0.020 mm), range in size from 0.1992-inch (5.060 mm) to 0.2260 inch (5.740 mm) (see illustration).

Lifter No.	Thickness	Lifter No.	Thickness	Lifter No.	Thickness
06	5.060 (0.1992)	30	5.300 (0.2087)	54	5.540 (0.2181)
08	5.080 (0.2000)	32	5.320 (0.2094)	56	5.560 (0.2189)
10	5.100 (0.2008)	34	5.340 (0.2102)	58	5.580 (0.2197)
12	5.120 (0.2016)	36	5.360 (0.2110)	60	5.600 (0.2205)
14	5.140 (0.2024)	38	5.380 (0.2118)	62	5.620 (0.2213)
16	5.160 (0.2031)	40	5.400 (0.2126)	64	5.640 (0.2220)
18	5.180 (0.2039)	42	5.420 (0.2134)	66	5.660 (0.2228)
20	5.200 (0.2047)	44	5.440 (0.2142)	68	5.680 (0.2236)
22	5.220 (0.2055)	46	5.460 (0.2150)	70	5.700 (0.2244)
24	5.240 (0.2063)	48	5.480 (0.2157)	72	5.720 (0.2252)
26	5.260 (0.2071)	50	5.500 (0.2165)	74	5.740 (0.2260)
28	5.280 (0.2079)	52	5.520 (0.2173)		

New lifter thickness   mm (in.)

30.14b Valve lifter thickness chart - four-cylinder engine

➡Note: Through careful analysis of the shim sizes needed to bring the out-of-specification valve clearance within specification, it is often possible to simply move a shim or lifter that has to come out anyway to another lifter requiring a shim of that particular size, thereby reducing the number of new shims that must be purchased.

✳✳ CAUTION:

Do not try to bring the valve clearance within specification on four-cylinder models by moving the lifters around. The old lifters have wear patterns on their walls that might affect their operation if moved to another lifter bore.

15 On V6 models, place the special lifter tool in position as shown in illustration 30.11a, with the longer jaw of the tool gripping the lower edge of the cast lifter boss and the upper, shorter jaw gripping the

upper edge of the lifter itself, press down the lifter by squeezing the handles of the lifter tool together and install the new adjusting shim (note that the wire hook on the end of one lifter tool handle can be used to clamp the handles together to keep the lifter depressed while the shim is inserted). Measure the clearance with a feeler gauge to make sure that your calculations are correct.

16 Repeat this procedure until all the valves which are out of clearance have been corrected.

17 Installation of the spark plugs, valve cover, camshaft(s), accelerator cable bracket, etc. is the reverse of removal.

18 On four-cylinder models, after the camshafts are reinstalled, check the valve clearances again to be sure they are now within specification.

31 Cooling system servicing (draining, flushing and refilling) (at 100,000 miles or 120 months and every 50,000 miles or 60 months thereafter)

❋❋ WARNING 1:

Wait until the engine is completely cool before beginning this procedure.

❋❋ WARNING 2:

Do not allow engine coolant (antifreeze) to come in contact with your skin or painted surfaces of the vehicle. Rinse off spills immediately with plenty of water. Antifreeze is highly toxic if ingested. Never leave antifreeze laying around in an open container or in puddles on the floor; children and pets are attracted by it's sweet smell and may drink it. Check with local authorities about disposing of used antifreeze. Many communities have collection centers which will see that antifreeze is disposed of safely.

1 Periodically, the cooling system should be drained, flushed and refilled to replenish the antifreeze mixture and prevent formation of rust and corrosion, which can impair the performance of the cooling system and cause engine damage. When the cooling system is serviced, all hoses and the radiator cap should be checked and replaced if necessary.

DRAINING

▶ **Refer to illustrations 31.4 and 31.5**

2 Apply the parking brake and block the wheels. If the vehicle has

just been driven, wait several hours to allow the engine to cool down before beginning this procedure.

3 Once the engine is completely cool, remove the radiator cap.

4 Move a large container under the radiator drain to catch the coolant. Attach a 3/8-inch inner diameter hose to the drain fitting to direct the coolant into the container (some models are already equipped with a hose), then open the drain fitting (a pair of pliers may be required to turn it) (see illustration).

5 After the coolant stops flowing out of the radiator, move the container under the engine block drain plug(s). Loosen the plug(s) and allow the coolant in the block to drain. On four-cylinder models, the block drain plug is on the front side of the engine block. On V6 models, there's one on each side of the block (see illustration).

6 While the coolant is draining, check the condition of the radiator hoses, heater hoses and clamps (refer to Section 12 if necessary).

7 Replace any damaged clamps or hoses (see Chapter 3).

FLUSHING

▶ **Refer to illustration 31.10**

8 Once the system is completely drained, remove the thermostat from the engine (see Chapter 3). Then reinstall the thermostat housing without the thermostat. This will allow the system to be flushed.

9 Reinstall the engine block drain plugs and tighten the radiator drain plug. Turn your heating system controls to Hot, so that the heater core will be flushed at the same time as the rest of the cooling system.

31.4 On most models you will have to remove a splash panel for access to the drain fitting located at the bottom of the radiator

31.5 Engine block drain plug (V6 engine, front cylinder bank)

10 Disconnect the upper radiator hose from the radiator. Place a garden hose in the upper radiator inlet, turn the water on and flush the system until the water runs clear out of the upper radiator hose (see illustration).

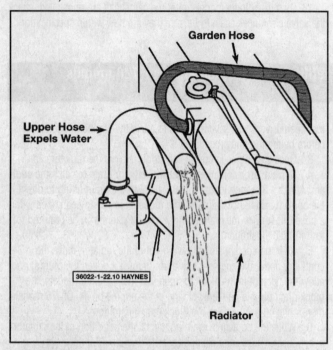

31.10 With the thermostat removed, disconnect the upper radiator hose and flush the radiator and engine block with a garden hose

11 In severe cases of contamination or clogging of the radiator, remove the radiator (see Chapter 3) and have a radiator repair facility clean and repair it if necessary. Many deposits can be removed by the chemical action of a cleaner available at auto parts stores. Follow the procedure outlined in the manufacturer's instructions.

➡ **Note: When the coolant is regularly drained and the system refilled with the correct antifreeze/water mixture, there should be no need to use chemical cleaners or descalers.**

12 After flushing, drain the radiator and remove the block drain plugs once again to drain the water from the system.

REFILLING

13 Close and tighten the radiator drain. Install and tighten the block drain plug.

14 Place the heater temperature control in the maximum heat position.

15 Slowly add new coolant to the radiator until it's full. Add coolant to the reservoir up to the lower mark.

16 Leave the radiator cap off and run the engine in a well-ventilated area until the thermostat opens (coolant will begin flowing through the radiator and the upper radiator hose will become hot).

17 Turn the engine off and let it cool. Add more coolant mixture to bring the level back up to the lip on the radiator filler neck.

18 Squeeze the upper radiator hose to expel air, then add more coolant mixture if necessary. Replace the radiator cap.

19 Start the engine, allow it to reach normal operating temperature and check for leaks.

32 Spark plug check and replacement (every 120,000 miles or 144 months)* OR (every 150,000 miles)**

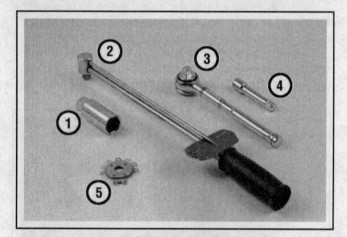

32.1 Tools required for changing spark plugs

1 *Spark plug socket* - This will have special padding inside to protect the spark plug's porcelain insulator
2 *Torque wrench* - Although not mandatory, using this tool is the best way to ensure the plugs are tightened properly
3 *Ratchet* - Standard hand tool to fit the spark plug socket
4 *Extension* - Depending on model and accessories, you may need special extensions and universal joints to reach one or more of the plugs
5 *Spark plug gap gauge* - This gauge for checking the gap comes in a variety of styles. Make sure the gap for your engine is included

* Except CA, NY, MA, ME and VT four-cylinder PZEV models
** CA, NY, MA, ME and VT four-cylinder PZEV models

▶ **Refer to illustrations 32.1, 32.4, 32.6a, 32.6b, 32.9, 32.10, 32.11a and 32.11b**

1 Spark plug replacement requires a spark plug socket that fits onto a ratchet. This socket is lined with a rubber grommet to protect the porcelain insulator of the spark plug and to hold the plug while you insert it into the spark plug hole. You will also need a wire-type feeler gauge to check and adjust the spark plug gap and a torque wrench to tighten the new plugs to the specified torque (see illustration).

2 If you are replacing the plugs, purchase the new plugs, adjust them to the proper gap and then replace each plug one at a time.

32.4 Spark plug manufacturers recommend using a wire-type gauge when checking the gap - if the wire does not slide between the electrodes with a slight drag, spark plug replacement is required

32.6a On four-cylinder engines, remove the retaining bolt (A), disconnect the electrical connector (B) and detach the individual coils to reach the front spark plugs

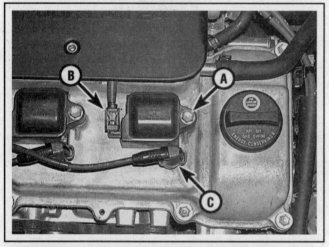

32.6b On V6 engines, remove the retaining bolt (A), disconnect the electrical connector (B) and detach the individual coils to reach the front spark plugs - earlier models have spark plug wires (C) that lead to the rear bank spark plugs

32.9 Because they are deeply recessed, the proper spark plug socket and an extension will be required when removing or installing the spark plugs

➡Note: The manufacturer specifies that only iridium-tipped spaRk plugs be used on these models. When buying new spark plugs, it's essential that you obtain the correct plugs for your specific vehicle. This information can be found in the Specifications Section at the end of this Chapter, on the Vehicle Emissions Control Information (VECI) label located on the underside of the hood or in the owner's manual. If these sources specify different plugs, purchase the spark plug type specified on the VECI label because that information is provided specifically for your engine.

3   Inspect each of the new plugs for defects. If there are any signs of cracks in the porcelain insulator of a plug, don't use it.

4   Note: Do not adjust the gap on iridium spark plugs. Using a gapping tool on them could damage the iridium plating on the electrodes. These spark plugs are pre-gapped by the manufacturer.

Check the gap by inserting the wire gauge of the proper thickness between the electrodes at the tip of the plug (see illustration). The gap

between the electrodes should be identical to that listed in this Chapter's Specifications or on the VECI label. If the gap is incorrect, replace the spark plug.

5   Remove the engine cover(s) and disconnect any hoses or components that would interfere with access and move them out of the way.

6   Remove the bolts and detach each ignition coil assembly from the spark plugs (see illustrations).

7   To prevent the possibility of mixing up of ignition coil assemblies, work on one spark plug at a time.

8   If compressed air is available, blow any dirt or foreign material away from the spark plug area before proceeding (a common bicycle pump will also work).

❋❋ WARNING:

Always wear eye protection when using compressed air!

9   Remove the spark plug (see illustration).

A normally worn spark plug should have light tan or gray deposits on the firing tip.

A carbon fouled plug, identified by soft, sooty, black deposits, may indicate an improperly tuned vehicle. Check the air cleaner, ignition components and engine control system.

An oil fouled spark plug indicates an engine with worn piston rings and/or bad valve seals allowing excessive oil to enter the chamber.

This spark plug has been left in the engine too long, as evidenced by the extreme gap. Plugs with such an extreme gap can cause misfiring and stumbling accompanied by a noticeable lack of power.

A physically damaged spark plug may be evidence of severe detonation in that cylinder. Watch that cylinder carefully between services, as a continued detonation will not only damage the plug, but could also damage the engine.

A bridged or almost bridged spark plug, identified by a build-up between the electrodes caused by excessive carbon or oil build-up on the plug.

32.10 Inspect the spark plug to determine engine running conditions

10 Whether you are replacing the plugs at this time or intend to re-use the old plugs, compare each old spark plug with those shown in this chart to determine the overall running condition of the engine.

11 Apply a small amount of anti-seize compound to the spark plug threads (see illustration). It's often difficult to insert spark plugs into their holes without cross-threading them. To avoid this possibility, fit a short piece of rubber hose over the end of the spark plug (see illustra-

tion). The flexible hose acts as a universal joint to help align the plug with the spark plug hole. Should the plug begin to cross-thread, the hose will slip on the spark plug, preventing thread damage. Tighten the plug to the torque listed in this Chapter's Specifications.

12 Attach the ignition coil assembly to the new spark plug.

13 Follow the above procedure for the remaining spark plugs, replacing them one at a time to prevent mixing up the spark plug wires.

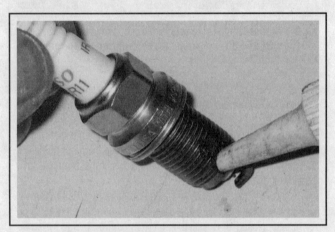
32.11a A light coat of anti-seize compound applied to the threads of the spark plugs will keep the threads in the cylinder head from being damaged the next time the plugs are removed

32.11b A section of rubber hose will aid in getting the spark plug threads started

Specifications

Recommended lubricants and fluids

➡**Note: Listed here are manufacturer recommendations at the time this manual was written. Manufacturers occasionally upgrade their fluid and lubricant specifications, so check with your auto parts store for current recommendations.**

Engine oil type	API GF-4 "certified for gasoline engines"
Viscosity	SAE 5W-30
Fuel	
2002 through 2006	
Four-cylinder engine	Unleaded fuel, 87 octane or higher
V6 engines	Unleaded fuel, 91 octane or higher
2007 and later	Unleaded fuel, 87 octane or higher
Coolant	Toyota Genuine Long Life Coolant or equivalent
Automatic transaxle/differential fluid type	
2002 through 2006	Toyota ATF Type T-IV automatic transmission fluid
2007 and later	
Four cylinder engine	Toyota ATF Type T-IV automatic transmission fluid
V6 engines	Toyota ATF Type WS automatic transmission fluid
Manual transaxle lubricant type	API GL-4 or GL-5 75W-90 gear oil
Brake fluid type	DOT 3 brake fluid
Clutch fluid type	DOT 3 brake fluid
Power steering system fluid	Dexron III automatic transmission fluid

Capacities (approximate)

Engine oil (including filter)	
Four-cylinder engine	4.0 qts.
V6 engine	5.0 qts.
Coolant	
Four-cylinder engine	6.6 qts.
V6 engine	9.7 qts.
Transaxle	
Automatic	
Four-cylinder engine	
All except 2004 (drain and refill)	3.7 qts.
2004 (drain and refill)	4.1 qts.
V6 engine (drain and refill)	3.7 qts.
Manual	2.6 qts.

Ignition system

Spark plug
  Type
    Camry and Avalon   BKR6ES-11
    Solara
      2002 and 2003 models   BKR6ES-11
      2004 models   1FR6T11
      2005 and later models   1FR6A11
    ES300 (2002 and 2003)   BKR6ES-11
    ES330 (2004 and later)   BKR6ES
  Gap   0.043 inch
Engine firing order
  Four-cylinder engine   1-3-4-2
  V6 engine   1-2-3-4-5-6

Cylinder numbering - four-cylinder engine

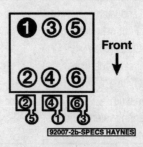

Cylinder numbering and coil terminal locations - early V6 engine
➡Note: Later models use one coil for each spark plug

Valve clearance (engine cold)

Four cylinder engine
  2002 through 2006 models
    Intake   0.008 to 0.011 inch (0.19 to 0.29 mm)
    Exhaust   0.012 to 0.016 inch (0.30 to 0.40 mm)
  2007 and later models
    Intake   0.007 to 0.011 inch (0.19 to 0.29 mm)
    Exhaust   0.015 to 0.019 inch (0.38 to 0.48 mm)
V6 engine
  Intake   0.006 to 0.010 inch (0.15 to 0.25 mm)
  Exhaust   0.010 to 0.014 inch (0.25 to 0.35 mm)

Cooling system

Thermostat rating
  Starts to open   176 to 183-degrees F
  Fully open   203-degrees F

Accessory drivebelt tension - V6 engine only (with Burroughs or Nippondenso tension gauge)

Air conditioning
  New belt   139 to 192 lbs
  Used belt   66 to 110 lbs
Alternator
  New belt   170 to 180 lbs
  Used belt   95 to 135 lbs

Power steering pump
    New belt   154 to 176 lbs
    Used belt   77 to 110 lbs

Clutch

Clutch pedal freeplay   0.197 to 0.591 inch
Pedal height   6.260 to 6.654 inches
Pushrod play at pedal top   0.039 to 0.197 inch

Brakes

Disc brake pad lining thickness (minimum)   1/8 inch
Drum brake shoe lining thickness (minimum)   1/16 inch
Brake pedal
    Freeplay   0.04 to 0.24 inch
    Free height   5.673 to 6.067 inches
    Brake light switch clearance   0.20 to 0.098 inch
    Pedal reserve height
        2002 through 2006 models   2.5 inches
        2007 and later models
            Without Vehicle Stability Control (VSC) 2.7 inches
            With Vehicle Stability Control (VSC)   3.1 inches
Parking brake adjustment
    Cable adjustment
        Hand lever type   3 to 6 clicks to firm apply
        Foot pedal type   6 to 9 clicks to firm apply
    Shoe adjustment (rear disc brakes)   Back off 8 notches from shoe contact

Suspension and steering

Steering wheel freeplay limit   1-3/16 inches
Balljoint allowable movement   0.0 inch

Torque specifications   Ft-lbs (unless otherwise indicated)

➡**Note: One foot-pound (ft-lb) of torque is equivalent to 12 inch-pounds (in-lbs) of torque. Torque values below approximately 15 ft-lbs are expressed in inch-pounds, since most foot-pound torque wrenches are not accurate at these smaller values.**

Automatic transaxle
    Pan bolts   69 in-lbs
    Strainer bolts   96 in-lbs
    Drain plug   36
Drivebelt tensioner mounting bolt/nut
    (four cylinder engine)   See Chapter 2A
Manual transaxle drain and filler plugs   36
Chassis and body
    Front seat mounting bolts   27
    Front suspension subframe-to-body nuts/bolts   See Chapter 7A
    Rear suspension crossmember-to-body
        nuts/bolts   See Chapter 10

Torque specifications (continued)	**Ft-lbs (unless otherwise indicated)**
Spark plugs	
Four-cylinder engine	168 in-lbs
V6 engine	
2002 and 2003	156 in-lbs
2004 and later	19
Wheel lug nuts	76
Rear suspension mount bolts/nuts	41
Subframe mounting bolts	See Chapter 7A
Oil pan drain plug	
Four cylinder engine	18
V6 engine	33

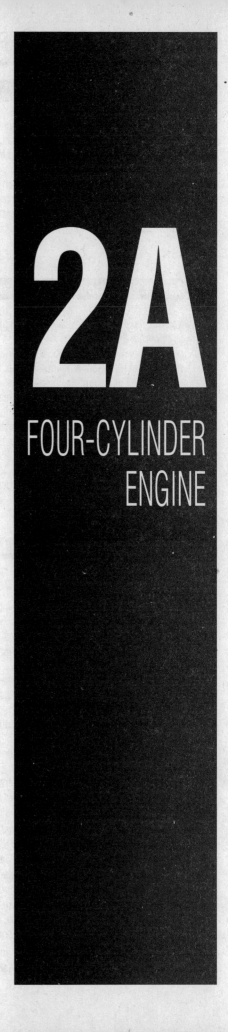

2A
FOUR-CYLINDER ENGINE

Section

1   General information
2   Repair operations possible with the engine in the vehicle
3   Top Dead Center (TDC) for number one piston - locating
4   Valve cover - removal and installation
5   Variable Valve Timing (VVT) system - description
6   Timing chain and sprockets - removal, inspection and installation
7   Camshafts and lifters - removal, inspection and installation
8   Intake manifold - removal and installation
9   Exhaust manifold - removal and installation
10 Cylinder head - removal and installation
11 Crankshaft pulley/vibration damper - removal and installation
12 Crankshaft front oil seal - replacement
13 Oil pan - removal and installation
14 Oil pump - removal and installation
15 Flywheel/driveplate - removal and installation
16 Rear main oil seal - replacement
17 Powertrain mounts - check and replacement
18 Engine balancer assembly - removal and installation

Reference to other Chapters

CHECK ENGINE light on - See Chapter 6
Cylinder compression check - See Chapter 2C
Drivebelt - check, adjustment and replacement - See Chapter 1
Engine - removal and installation - See Chapter 2C
Engine oil and filter change - See Chapter 1
Engine overhaul - general information - See Chapter 2C
Spark plug replacement - See Chapter 1
Water pump - removal and installation - See Chapter 3

1 General information

This Part of Chapter 2 is devoted to in-vehicle repair procedures for the 2AZ-FE four-cylinder engine. All information concerning engine removal, installation and overhaul can be found in Part C of this Chapter.

The following repair procedures are based on the assumption that the engine is installed in the vehicle. If the engine has been removed from the vehicle and mounted on a stand, many of the steps outlined in this Part of Chapter 2 will not apply. The Specifications included in this Part of Chapter 2 apply only to the in-vehicle procedures contained in this Part.

This engine incorporates an aluminum cylinder block with a lower crankcase to strengthen the lower half of the block. The cylinder head utilizes dual overhead camshafts (DOHC) with four valves per cylinder. The camshafts are driven from a single timing chain off the crankshaft, and a Variable Valve Timing (VVT) system is incorporated on the intake camshaft to increase horsepower and decrease emissions.

2 Repair operations possible with the engine in the vehicle

Many major repair operations can be accomplished without removing the engine from the vehicle.

Clean the engine compartment and the exterior of the engine with some type of degreaser before any work is done. It will make the job easier and help keep dirt out of the internal areas of the engine.

Depending on the components involved, it may be helpful to remove the hood to improve access to the engine as repairs are performed (refer to Chapter 11 if necessary). Cover the fenders to prevent damage to the paint. Special pads are available, but an old bedspread or blanket will also work.

If vacuum, exhaust, oil or coolant leaks develop, indicating a need for gasket or seal replacement, the repairs can generally be made with the engine in the vehicle. The intake and exhaust manifold gaskets, oil pan gasket, crankshaft oil seals and cylinder head gasket are all accessible with the engine in place.

Exterior engine components, such as the intake and exhaust manifolds, the oil pan, the oil pump, the water pump, the starter motor, the alternator and the fuel system components can be removed for repair with the engine in place.

Since the cylinder head can be removed without pulling the engine, camshaft and valve component servicing can also be accomplished with the engine in the vehicle. Replacement of the timing chain and sprockets is also possible with the engine in the vehicle.

3 Top Dead Center (TDC) for number one piston - locating

▶ Refer to illustrations 3.5 and 3.8

1 Top Dead Center (TDC) is the highest point in the cylinder that each piston reaches as it travels up the cylinder bore. Each piston reaches TDC on the compression stroke and again on the exhaust stroke, but TDC generally refers to piston position on the compression stroke.

2 Positioning the piston(s) at TDC is an essential part of many procedures such as valve adjustment and camshaft and timing chain/sprocket removal.

3 Before beginning this procedure, be sure to place the transmission in Neutral and apply the parking brake or block the rear wheels. Also, disable the ignition system by disconnecting the primary electrical connectors at the ignition coils (see Chapter 5).

4 In order to bring any piston to TDC, the crankshaft must be turned using one of the methods outlined below. When looking at the front of the engine, normal crankshaft rotation is clockwise.

   a) The preferred method is to turn the crankshaft with a socket and ratchet attached to the bolt threaded into the front of the crankshaft. Turn the bolt in a clockwise direction.

   b) If an assistant is available to turn the ignition switch to the Start position in short bursts, you can get the piston close to TDC without a remote starter switch. Make sure your assistant is out of the vehicle, away from the ignition switch, then use a socket and ratchet as described in Paragraph (a) to complete the procedure.

5 Remove the spark plugs (see Chapter 1) and install a compression gauge in the number one spark plug hole (see illustration). It

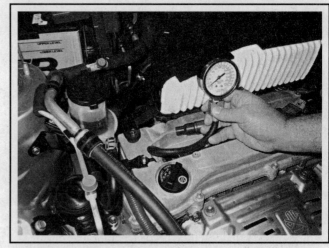

3.5 A compression gauge can be used in the number one plug hole to assist in finding TDC

should be a gauge with a screw-in fitting and a hose at least six inches long.

6 Rotate the crankshaft using one of the methods described above while observing for pressure on the compression gauge. The moment the gauge shows pressure indicates that the number one cylinder has begun the compression stroke.

7 Once the compression stroke has begun, TDC for the compres-

sion stroke is reached by bringing the piston to the top of the cylinder.

8   Continue turning the crankshaft until the notch in the crankshaft damper is aligned with the "TDC" or the "0" mark on the timing chain cover (see illustration). At this point, the number one cylinder is at TDC on the compression stroke. If the marks are aligned but there was no compression, the piston was on the exhaust stroke; continue rotating the crankshaft 360-degrees (1-turn).

➡**Note: If a compression gauge is not available, you can simply place a blunt object over the spark plug hole and listen for compression as the engine is rotated. Once compression at the No.1 spark plug hole is noted the remainder of the Step is the same.**

9   After the number one piston has been positioned at TDC on the compression stroke, TDC for any of the remaining cylinders can be located by turning the crankshaft 180 degrees and following the firing order (refer to the Specifications). Rotating the engine 180 degrees past TDC #1 will put the engine at TDC compression for cylinder #3.

3.8 Align the notch in the damper with the "0" mark on the timing chain cover

Valve cover - removal and installation

REMOVAL

▶ **Refer to illustrations 4.1 and 4.4**

1   Disconnect the cable from the negative terminal of the battery (see Chapter 5, Section 1). Remove the engine cover (see illustration).
2   Disconnect the electrical connectors from the ignition coils, remove the nuts securing the wiring harness to the valve cover and position the ignition coil wiring harness aside. Then remove the ignition coil pack from each of the spark plugs (see Chapter 5).
3   Detach the PCV hoses from the valve cover.
4   Remove the valve cover mounting bolts and nuts, then detach the valve cover and gasket from the cylinder head (see illustration). If the valve cover is stuck to the cylinder head, bump the end with a wood block and a hammer to jar it loose. If that doesn't work, try to slip a flexible putty knife between the cylinder head and valve cover to break the seal.

CAUTION:

Don't pry at the valve cover-to-cylinder head joint or damage to the sealing surfaces may occur, leading to oil leaks after the valve cover is reinstalled.

4.1 Remove the nuts and the engine cover

INSTALLATION

▶ **Refer to illustrations 4.5 and 4.6**

5   Remove the valve cover gasket from the valve cover and clean the mating surfaces with lacquer thinner or acetone. Install a new rubber

4.4 Valve cover fastener locations

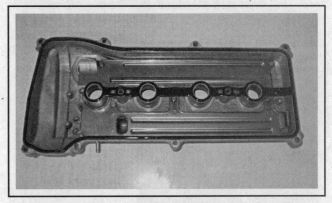

4.5 The valve cover gasket and the spark plug tube seals are incorporated into a single rubber O-ring-like seal - press the gasket evenly into the grooves around the underside of the valve cover and the spark plug openings

4.6 Apply sealant at the timing chain cover-to-cylinder head joint before installing the valve cover

gasket, pressing it evenly into the grooves around the underside of the valve cover.

➡**Note: Make sure the spark plug tube seals are in place on the underside of the valve cover before reinstalling it (see illustration).**

The mating surfaces of the timing chain cover, the cylinder head and valve cover must be perfectly clean when the valve cover is installed. If there's residue or oil on the mating surfaces when the valve cover is installed, oil leaks may develop.

6   Apply RTV sealant at the timing chain cover-to-cylinder head joint, then install the valve cover and fasteners (see illustration).

7   Tighten the nuts/bolts to the torque listed in this Chapter's Specifications in three or four equal steps.

8   Reinstall the remaining parts, run the engine and check for oil leaks.

5   Variable Valve Timing (VVT) system - description

▶ **Refer to illustrations 5.2a and 5.2b**

1   The VVT system varies intake camshaft timing by directing oil pressure to advance or retard the intake camshaft sprocket/actuator assembly. Changing the intake camshaft timing during certain engine conditions increases engine power output, fuel economy and reduces emissions.

2   System components include the Powertrain Control Module (PCM), the VVT oil control valve (OCV) and the intake camshaft sprocket/actuator assembly (see illustrations).

3   The PCM uses inputs from the following sensors to turn the oil control valve ON or OFF:

a) *Vehicle Speed Sensor (VSS)*
b) *Throttle Position Sensor (TPS)*
c) *Mass Airflow (MAF) sensor*
d) *Engine Coolant Temperature (ECT) sensor*

4   Once the VVT oil control valve is actuated by the PCM it directs the specified amount of oil pressure from the engine to advance or retard the intake camshaft sprocket/actuator assembly.

5   The intake camshaft sprocket/actuator assembly is equipped with an inner hub that is attached to the camshaft. The inner hub consists of a series of fixed vanes that use oil pressure as a wedge against the

vanes to rotate the camshaft. The higher the oil pressure (or flow) the more the actuator assembly will rotate, thereby advancing or retarding the camshaft.

6   When oil is applied to the advance side of the vanes, the actuator can advance the camshaft up to 21 degrees in a clockwise direction. When oil is applied to the retard side of the vanes, the actuator will start to rotate the camshaft counterclockwise back to 0 degrees which is the normal position of the actuator during engine operation under no load or at idle. The PCM can also send a signal to the oil control valve to stop oil flow to both (advance and retard) passages to hold camshaft advance in its current position.

7   Under light engine loads, the VVT system will retard the camshaft timing to decrease valve overlap and stabilize engine output. Under medium engine loads, the VVT system will advance the camshaft timing to increase valve overlap, thereby increasing fuel economy and decreasing exhaust emissions. Under heavy engine loads at low RPM, the VVT system will advance the camshaft timing to help close the intake valve faster, which improves low to midrange torque. Under heavy engine loads at high RPM, the VVT system will retard the camshaft timing to slow the closing of the intake valve to improve engine horsepower.

5.2a The Variable Valve Timing (VVT) oil control valve is located at the right (passenger's) end of the cylinder head

5.2b The intake camshaft actuator assembly is only visible with the valve cover removed

6   Timing chain and sprockets - removal, inspection and installation

❊ WARNING:

Wait until the engine is completely cool before beginning this procedure.

➡ **Note: Special tools are required for this procedure. Read through the entire procedure and acquire the necessary tools and equipment before beginning work.**

REMOVAL

◆ **Refer to illustrations 6.7, 6.11, 6.13a, 6.13b, 6.14a, 6.14b, 6.14c, 6.14d, 6.15 and 6.16**

❊ CAUTION:

The timing system is complex. Severe engine damage will occur if you make any mistakes. Do not attempt this procedure unless you are highly experienced with this type of repair. If you are at all unsure of your abilities, consult an expert. Double-check all your work and be sure everything is correct before you attempt to start the engine.

1   Detach the cable from the negative terminal of the battery (see Chapter 5, Section 1).

2   Remove the drivebelt (see Chapter 1) and the alternator (see Chapter 5).

3   Remove the valve cover (see Section 4) and the ABS actuator if equipped (see Chapter 9).

4   With the parking brake applied and the rear wheels blocked, loosen the right front wheel lug nuts, then raise the front of the vehicle and support it securely on jackstands. Remove the right front wheel and the right splash shield from the wheelwell.

5   Drain the cooling system (see Chapter 1).

6   While the coolant is draining, refer to Chapter 10 and remove the power steering pump from the engine without disconnecting the fluid lines. Tie the power steering pump to the body with a piece of wire and position it out of the way. Refer to Chapter 4 and disconnect the front exhaust pipe from the manifold-converter.

7   Position the number one piston at TDC on the compression stroke (see Section 3). Visually confirm the engine is at TDC on the compression stroke by verifying that the timing mark on the crankshaft pulley/vibration damper is aligned with the "0" mark on the timing chain cover and the camshaft sprocket marks are aligned with the marks at the camshaft front bearing caps (see illustration 3.8 and the accompanying illustration).

➡ **Note: There are two sets of marks on the camshaft sprockets. The marks that align at TDC are for TDC reference only; the other two marks are used to align the sprockets with the timing chain during installation.**

8   Remove the crankshaft pulley/vibration damper, being careful not to rotate the engine from TDC (see Section 11). If the engine rotates off TDC during this step, reposition the engine back to TDC before proceeding. The engine should be left at TDC for the No. 1 piston during this entire procedure.

9   Support the engine from above, using an engine support fixture (available at rental yards).

10 Remove the passenger side engine mount (see Section 17).

11 Remove the drivebelt tensioner and the crankshaft position sensor from the timing chain cover (see illustration). Also remove the bolt securing the crankshaft position sensor wiring harness to the timing chain cover.

12 Remove the oil pan (see Section 13).

13 Detach the main wiring harness junction and remove the timing chain tensioner from the rear side of the timing chain cover (see illustrations).

14 Remove the timing chain cover fasteners and pry the cover off the engine (see illustrations).

6.7 Verify the engine is at TDC by observing the position of the camshaft sprocket marks (lower arrows) - they must be aligned with the marks on the camshaft bearing caps (upper arrows)

6.11 Drivebelt tensioner mounting bolts

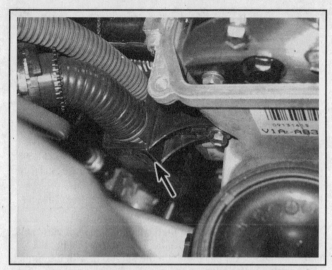

6.13a Remove the two bolts securing the main harness to the timing chain cover and position the harness aside

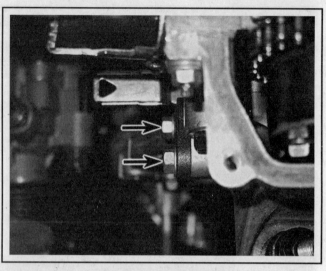

6.13b Timing chain tensioner mounting nuts

6.14a Timing chain cover upper fasteners

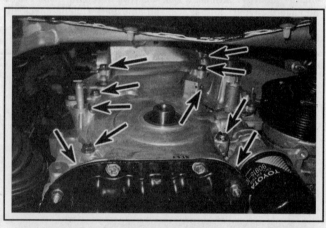

6.14b Timing chain cover lower fasteners - make a note of the fastener sizes, locations and lengths as you're removing them, as they must be installed back in their original positions

6.14c It will be necessary to remove the timing chain cover studs . . .

6.14d . . . before prying the timing chain cover off the engine

6.15 Slide the crankshaft position sensor reluctor ring off the crankshaft - note the "F" mark on the front (it must be facing outward upon installation)

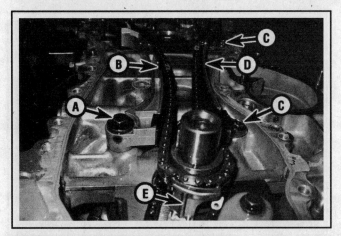

6.16 Timing chain guide mounting details

- A Pivot bolt
- B Tensioner pivot arm/chain guide
- C Stationary chain guide mounting bolts
- D Stationary chain guide
- E Lower timing chain guide

15 Slide the crankshaft position sensor reluctor ring off the crankshaft (see illustration).

16 Remove the timing chain tensioner pivot arm/chain guide and the lower chain guide (see illustration).

17 Lift the timing chain off the camshaft sprockets and remove the timing chain and the crankshaft sprocket as an assembly from the engine. The crankshaft sprocket should slip off the crankshaft by hand. If not, use several flat bladed screwdrivers to evenly pry the sprocket off the crankshaft.

➡**Note: If you intend to reuse the timing chain, use white paint or chalk to make a mark indicating the front of the chain. If a used timing chain is reinstalled with the wear pattern in the opposite direction, noise and increased wear may occur.**

18 Remove the stationary timing chain guide (see illustration 6.16).

19 To remove the camshaft sprockets, loosen the bolts while holding the lug on the camshaft with a wrench, on the hex portion of the camshaft only. Note the identification marks on the camshaft sprockets before removal, then remove the bolts. Pull on the sprockets by hand until they slip off the dowels. If necessary, use a small puller, with the legs inserted in the relief holes, to pull the sprockets off.

➡**Note: These models are equipped with variable valve timing, which consists of an actuator assembly attached to the intake camshaft sprocket. When removing the intake camshaft sprocket on these models only loosen and remove the center bolt, which fastens the sprocket to the camshaft. Do not loosen the outer four bolts that secure the actuator to the sprocket.**

INSPECTION

▶ **Refer to illustrations 6.20a, 6.20b and 6.21**

20 Visually inspect all parts for wear and damage. Check the timing chain for loose pins, cracks, worn rollers and side plates. Check the sprockets for hook-shaped, chipped and broken teeth. Also check the timing chain for stretching and the diameter of the timing sprockets for wear with the chain assembled on the sprockets. Timing chain stretch is measured by checking the length of the chain between 8 links (16 pins) at 3 or more places (selected randomly) around the chain - if chain

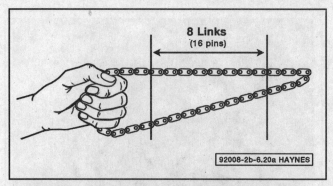

6.20a Timing chain stretch is measured by checking the length of the chain between 8 links (16 pins) at three or more places around the chain

6.20b Wrap the chain around each of the timing sprockets and measure the diameter of the sprockets across the chain rollers - if the measurement is less than the minimum sprocket diameter, the chain and the timing sprockets must be replaced

stretch exceeds the specifications between any 8 links, the chain must be replaced (see illustration). Be sure to measure across the chain rollers when checking the sprocket diameter and to measure chain stretch at three or more places around the chain. Maximum chain elongation and minimum sprocket diameter (with chain) should not exceed the amount listed in this Chapter's Specifications (see illustration). Replace the timing chain and sprockets as a set if the engine has high mileage or fails inspection.

21 Check the chain guides for excessive wear (see illustration). Replace the chain guides if scoring or wear exceeds the amount listed in this Chapter's Specifications. Note that some scoring of the timing chain guide shoes is normal. If excessive wear is indicated, it will also be necessary to inspect the chain guide oil hole on the front of the block for clogging (see illustration 14.5). The oil pump is driven by a second chain driven from the crankshaft sprocket. If the timing chain is to be replaced, replace the oil pump drive chain at the same time (see Section 14).

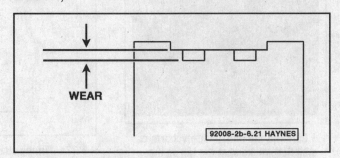

6.21 Timing chain guide wear is measured from the top of the chain contact surface to the bottom of the wear grooves

6.27 Loop the timing chain around the crankshaft sprocket (crankshaft keyway straight up) and align the No.1 colored link with the mark on the crankshaft sprocket, then install the chain and crankshaft sprocket as an assembly on the engine and install the lower chain guide

INSTALLATION

▶ Refer to illustrations 6.27, 6.28, 6.29, 6.32a, 6.32b, 6.34, 6.35, 6.37 and 6.39

✲✲ CAUTION:

Before starting the engine, carefully rotate the crankshaft by hand through at least two full revolutions (use a socket and breaker bar on the crankshaft pulley center bolt). If you feel any resistance, STOP! There is something wrong - most likely, valves are contacting the pistons. You must find the problem before proceeding. Check your work and see if any updated repair information is available.

22 Remove all traces of old sealant from the timing chain cover and the mating surfaces of the engine block and cylinder head.

6.28 Loop the timing chain up over the exhaust camshaft and around the intake camshaft, while aligning the remaining two colored links with the marks on the camshaft sprockets

23 Make sure the camshafts are positioned with the dowel pins at the top in the 12 o'clock position, then install both camshaft sprockets in their original locations by aligning the dowel pin hole on the rear of the sprockets with dowel pin on the camshaft. Apply medium strength thread locking compound to the camshaft sprocket bolt threads and make sure the washers are in place. Hold the camshaft from turning as described in Step 19 and tighten the bolts to the torque listed in this Chapter's Specifications.

24 Rotate the camshafts as necessary to align the TDC marks on the camshaft sprockets (see illustration 6.7).

25 If the crankshaft has been rotated off TDC during this procedure, it will be necessary to rotate the crankshaft until the keyway is pointing straight up in the 12 o'clock position with the centerline of the cylinder bores.

26 Install the stationary timing chain guide (see illustration 6.16).

27 Loop the timing chain around the crankshaft sprocket and align the No.1 colored link (gold or orange) with the mark on the crankshaft sprocket. Install the chain and crankshaft sprocket as an assembly on the engine, then install the lower timing chain guide (see illustration).

6.29 After the tensioner pivot arm is installed, make sure the tab on the pivot arm can't move past the stopper on the cylinder head

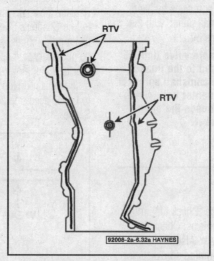

6.32a Timing chain cover sealant application details

6.32b Apply a bead of sealant on each side of the parting line between the cylinder head and the engine block

6.34 Raise the ratchet pawl and push the plunger inward until the hook on the tensioner body can be engaged with the pin on the plunger to lock the plunger in place

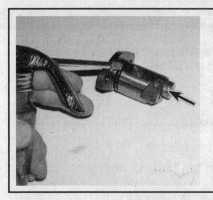

6.35 Apply a small amount of oil to the tensioner O-ring and insert the tensioner into the timing chain cover with the hook facing upward

➡️**Note: There are three colored links on the timing chain. The No.1 colored link is the link farthest away from the two colored links that are closest together.**

28 Slip the timing chain into the lip of the stationary timing chain guide and over the exhaust camshaft sprocket, then around the intake camshaft sprocket making sure to align the remaining two colored links with the marks on the camshaft sprockets (see illustration). Make sure to remove all slack from the right side of the chain when doing so.

29 Use one hand to remove the slack from the left side of the chain and install the timing chain tensioner pivot arm/chain guide. Tighten the pivot bolt to torque listed in this Chapter's Specifications. After installation, make sure the tab on the pivot arm can't move past the stopper on the cylinder head (see illustration).

30 Reconfirm that the number one piston is still at TDC on the compression stroke and that the timing marks on the crankshaft and camshaft sprockets are aligned with the colored links on the chain.

31 Install the crankshaft position sensor reluctor ring with the "F" mark facing outward.

32 Apply a bead of RTV sealant to the timing chain cover sealing surfaces, where the two central bolts go and around the perimeter of the cover's flange (see illustration). Place the timing chain cover in position on the engine and install the bolts in their original locations.

33 Tighten the bolts evenly in several steps to the torque listed in this Chapter's Specifications (see illustration). Be sure to follow the sealant manufacturer's recommendations for assembly and sealant curing times.

34 Reload and lock the timing chain tensioner to its "zero" position as follows:

a) Raise the ratchet pawl and push the plunger inward until it bot-

toms out (see illustration).
b) Engage the hook on the tensioner body with the pin on the tensioner plunger to lock the plunger in place.

35 Lubricate the tensioner O-ring with a small amount of oil and install the tensioner into the timing chain cover with the hook facing up (see illustration).

36 Install the crankshaft pulley/vibration damper (see Section 11).

37 Rotate the engine counterclockwise slightly to set the chain tension. As the engine is rotated, the hook on the tensioner body should release itself from the pin on the plunger and allow the plunger to spring out and apply tension to the timing chain (see illustration). If the plunger does not spring outward and apply tension to the timing chain, press downward on the pivot arm and release the hook with a screwdriver.

38 Rotate the engine clockwise several turns and reposition the number one piston at TDC on the compression stroke (see Section 3). Visually confirm that the timing mark on the crankshaft pulley/vibration damper is aligned with the "0" mark on the timing chain cover and the camshaft sprocket marks are aligned and parallel with the top of the timing chain cover as shown in illustration 6.7.

39 Tighten the timing chain cover fasteners to the torque listed in this Chapter's Specifications (see illustration). The remainder of the installation is the reverse of removal.

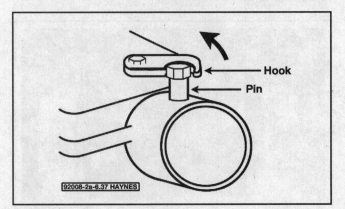

6.37 Rotate the engine counterclockwise to disengage the hook from the plunger pin on the tensioner, then rotate it clockwise and confirm that the plunger has extended outward against the pivot arm/chain guide

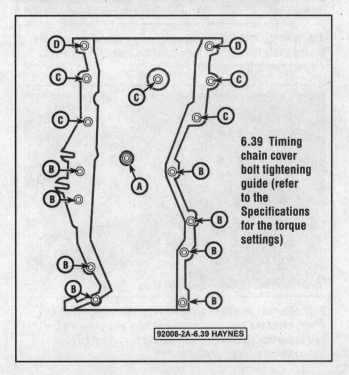

6.39 Timing chain cover bolt tightening guide (refer to the Specifications for the torque settings)

7 Camshafts and lifters - removal, inspection and installation

➡Note: The camshafts should always be thoroughly inspected before installation and camshaft endplay should always be checked prior to camshaft removal (see Step 13).

REMOVAL

▸ Refer to illustrations 7.4, 7.7, 7.8, 7.11a and 7.11b

1 Disconnect the cable from the negative terminal of the battery (see Chapter 5, Section 1).

2 Remove the valve cover (see Section 4).

3 Refer to Section 3 and place the engine on TDC for number 1 cylinder. Visually confirm the engine is at TDC on the compression stroke by verifying that the timing mark on the crankshaft pulley/vibration damper is aligned with the "0" mark on the timing chain cover and the camshaft sprocket TDC marks are aligned and parallel with the top of the timing chain cover (see illustrations 3.8 and 6.7).

4 With the TDC marks aligned, apply a dab of paint to the timing chain links where they meet the upper timing marks on the camshaft sprockets (see illustration).

7.4 With the TDC marks aligned, apply a dab of paint to the timing chain links where they meet the upper timing marks on the camshaft sprockets

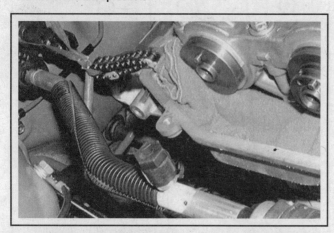

7.7 With the camshaft sprockets removed, hang the timing chain out of the way with a piece of wire and place a shop rag in the timing chain cover opening to prevent foreign objects from falling into the engine

➡Note: There are two sets of marks on the camshaft sprockets. The marks that align at TDC are for TDC reference only, the other two marks are used to align the sprockets with the timing chain during installation.

5 Using a large wrench (on the hex portion of the camshaft only) to hold the camshaft from turning, loosen the camshaft sprocket bolts several turns. If the camshaft sprockets have rotated during the bolt loosening process, rotate the engine clockwise until the "TDC" marks on the cam sprockets are realigned.

6 Remove the timing chain tensioner from the timing cover (see illustrations 6.13a and 6.13b) and the camshaft position sensor from the cylinder head (see Chapter 6).

7 Remove the camshaft sprocket retaining bolts. Disengage the timing chain from the sprockets and remove the camshaft sprockets from the engine. Make sure to note that the Variable Valve Timing (VVT) actuator is installed on the intake (rear) camshaft. After removing the sprockets, hang the timing chain up with a piece of wire and attach it to an object on the firewall (see illustration). This will prevent the timing chain from falling into the engine as the remaining steps in this procedure are performed. Also place a rag into the opening of the timing chain cover to prevent any foreign objects from falling into the engine.

8 Verify the markings on the camshaft bearing caps. The caps should be marked from 1 to 5 with an "I" or an "E" mark on the cap indicating whether they're for the intake or exhaust camshaft (see illustration).

9 Loosen the camshaft bearing caps in two or three steps, in the reverse order of the tightening sequence (see illustration 7.22).

❋❋ CAUTION:

Keep the caps in order. They must go back in the same location they were removed from.

10 Detach the bearing caps, then remove the camshaft(s) from the cylinder head. Mark the camshaft(s) "Intake" or "Exhaust" to avoid mixing them up.

➡Note: When looking at the engine from the front of the vehicle, the forward facing cam is the exhaust camshaft and the cam nearest the firewall is the intake camshaft. It is very important that the camshafts are returned to their original locations during installation.

7.8 The camshaft bearing caps are numbered and have an arrow that should face the timing chain end of the engine

7.11a Mark the lifters (I for intake, E for exhaust, and number their location) and remove them with a magnetic retrieval tool

11 Remove the lifters from the cylinder head, keeping them in order with their respective valve and cylinder (see illustrations).

※ CAUTION:

Keep the lifters in order. They must go back in the position from which they were removed.

12 Inspect the camshafts, camshaft bearings and lifters as described below. Also inspect the camshaft sprockets for wear on the teeth. Inspect the chains for cracks or excessive wear of the rollers, and for stretching (see Section 7). If any of the components show signs of excessive wear they must be replaced.

INSPECTION

▶ **Refer to illustrations 7.13, 7.14, 7.15, 7.16, 7.18 and 7.19**

13 Before the camshafts are removed from the engine, check the camshaft endplay by placing a dial indicator with the stem in line with the camshaft and touching the snout (see illustration). Push the camshaft all the way to the rear and zero the dial indicator. Next, pry the camshaft to the front as far as possible and check the reading on the dial indicator. The distance it moves is the endplay. If the endplay

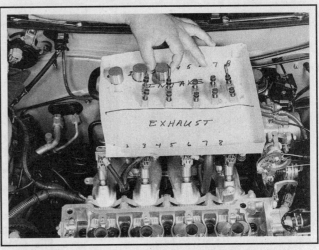

7.11b Mark up a cardboard box to store the lifters and bearing caps in order

for the intake camshaft is greater than the Specifications listed in this Chapter, check the thrust surfaces of the No.1 journal bearing for wear. If the thrust surface is worn, the bearings must be replaced. If the endplay for the exhaust camshaft is greater than the Specifications listed in this Chapter, the camshaft or the cylinder head (or both) may need to be replaced.

14 With the camshafts removed, visually check the camshaft bearing surfaces in the cylinder head for pitting, score marks, galling and abnormal wear (see illustration). If the bearing surfaces are damaged, the cylinder head or the No.1 journal bearings of the intake camshaft may have to be replaced. If so, it will be necessary to replace them with the same size as originally installed.

➡ **Note: The size markings are located on the machined surface of the cylinder head near the no. 1 journals, and the corresponding marks are located on the back sides of the bearing shells.**

15 Measure the outside diameter of each camshaft bearing journal and record your measurements (see illustration). Compare them to the journal outside diameter specified in this Chapter, then measure the inside diameter of each corresponding camshaft bearing and record the

7.13 Mount a dial indicator as shown to measure camshaft endplay - pry the camshaft forward and back and read the endplay on the dial

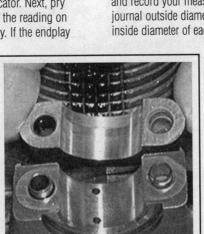

7.14 Inspect the No.2 through No.5 cam bearing surfaces in the cylinder head for pits, score marks and abnormal wear - if wear or damage is noted, the cylinder head must be replaced

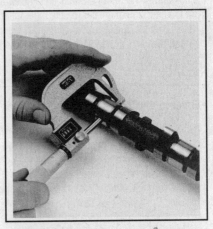

7.15 Measure each journal diameter with a micrometer - if any journal measures less than the specified limit, replace the camshaft

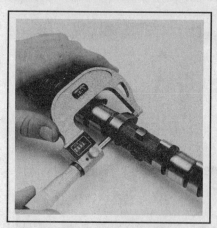

7.16 Measure the lobe heights on each camshaft - if any lobe height is less than the specified allowable minimum, replace that camshaft

7.18 Wipe off the oil and inspect each lifter for wear and scuffing

7.19 Measure the outside diameter of each lifter and the inside diameter of each lifter bore to determine the oil clearance measurement

measurements. Subtract each cam journal outside diameter from its respective cam bearing bore inside diameter to determine the oil clearance for each bearing. Compare the results to the specified journal-to-bearing clearance. If any of the measurements fall outside the standard specified wear limits in this Chapter, either the camshaft or the cylinder head, or both, must be replaced.

➡**Note: If precision measuring tools are not available, Plastigage may be used to determine the bearing journal oil clearance.**

16 Using a micrometer, measure the height of each camshaft lobe (see illustration). Compare your measurements with this Chapter's Specifications. If the height for any one lobe is less than the specified minimum, replace the camshaft.

17 Check the camshaft runout by placing the camshaft back into the cylinder head and set up a dial indicator on the center journal. Zero the dial indicator. Turn the camshaft slowly and note the dial indicator readings. Runout should not exceed 0.0012 inch (0.03 mm). If the measured runout exceeds the specified runout, replace the camshaft.

18 Inspect each lifter for scuffing and score marks (see illustration).

19 Measure the outside diameter of each lifter (see illustration) and the corresponding lifter bore inside diameter. Subtract the lifter diameter from the lifter bore diameter to determine the oil clearance. Compare it to this Chapter's Specifications. If the oil clearance is excessive, a new cylinder head and/or new lifters will be required.

INSTALLATION

◆ **Refer to illustration 7.22**

20 If the No.1 journal bearings for the intake camshaft were removed or replaced, install them into the cylinder head and the bearing cap now. Apply moly-based engine assembly lubricant to the camshaft lobes and journals and install the camshaft into the cylinder head with the No.1 cylinder camshaft lobes pointing outward away from each other, and the dowel pins facing upward. If the old camshafts are being used, make sure they're installed in the exact location from which they came.

21 Install the bearing caps and bolts and tighten them hand tight.

22 Tighten the bearing cap bolts in several equal steps, to the torque listed in this Chapter's Specifications, using the proper tightening sequence (see illustration).

23 Engage the camshaft sprocket teeth with the timing chain links so that the match marks made during removal align with the upper timing marks on the sprockets, then position the sprockets over the dowels on the camshaft hubs and install the camshaft sprocket bolts finger tight. At this point the mark on the crankshaft pulley should be aligned with the "0" mark on the timing chain cover, the camshaft sprocket TDC marks should be aligned and parallel with the top of the timing chain cover and the timing chain match marks should be aligned with the upper timing sprocket marks with all of the slack in the chain positioned towards the tensioner side of the engine (see illustration 7.4).

24 Double check that the timing sprockets are returned to the proper camshaft and tighten the camshaft sprocket bolts to the torque listed in this Chapter's Specifications.

25 Install the timing chain tensioner as described in Section 6, Steps 34 and 35.

26 The remainder of installation is the reverse of removal.

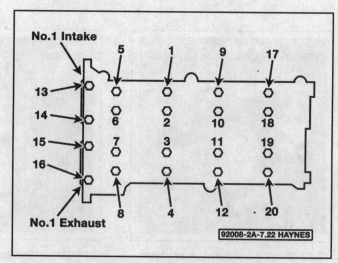

7.22 Camshaft bearing cap bolt TIGHTENING sequence

8 Intake manifold - removal and installation

✲✲ WARNING:

Wait until the engine is completely cool before beginning this procedure.

REMOVAL

▶ **Refer to illustrations 8.4, 8.5 and 8.6**

1 Relieve the fuel system pressure (see Chapter 4), then disconnect the negative cable from the battery (see Chapter 5, Section 1).

2 Remove the air intake duct and resonator (see Chapter 4). Then remove the cowl cover and vent tray (see Chapter 11). On models with performance suspension, remove the brace between the shock towers.

3 Remove the fuel rail and injectors as an assembly. Disconnect the electronic throttle motor connector and remove the throttle body (see Chapter 4).

4 Label and detach the PCV and vacuum hoses connected to the rear of the intake manifold (see illustration).

5 Raise the vehicle and support it securely on jackstands. Working below the vehicle, remove the manifold lower mounting bolts (see illustration).

6 Working from above, remove the intake manifold upper mounting nuts and bolts. Remove the manifold, the gasket and the manifold insulator from the engine (see illustration).

INSTALLATION

▶ **Refer to illustration 8.8**

7 Clean the mating surfaces of the intake manifold and the cylinder head mounting surface with lacquer thinner or acetone. If the gasket shows signs of leaking, check the manifold for warpage with a straight edge. If the manifold is warped it must be replaced.

8 Press a new gasket into the grooves on the intake manifold (see illustration). Install the manifold and gasket over the studs on the cylinder head.

9 Tighten the manifold-to-cylinder head nuts/bolts in three or four equal steps to the torque listed in this Chapter's Specifications. Work from the top bolts down to avoid warping the manifold.

10 Install the remaining parts in the reverse order of removal. Check

8.4 Label and disconnect the vacuum hoses (A) and the wire harness retainers (B) from the intake manifold

8.5 Intake manifold lower fastener locations

the coolant level, adding as necessary (see Chapter 1).

11 Before starting the engine, check the throttle linkage for smooth operation.

12 Run the engine and check for coolant and vacuum leaks.

13 Road test the vehicle and check for proper operation of all accessories, including the cruise control system, if equipped.

8.6 Intake manifold upper fastener locations

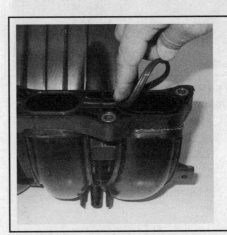

8.8 Press the gasket into the groove on the intake manifold

9 Exhaust manifold - removal and installation

☀☀ WARNING:

The engine must be completely cool before beginning this procedure.

REMOVAL

◆ Refer to illustrations 9.3, 9.5 and 9.6

1 Disconnect the negative cable from the battery (see Chapter 5, Section 1).

2 Raise the front of the vehicle and support it securely on jackstands. Working below the vehicle, remove the lower splash shields.

3 Apply penetrating oil to the bolts and springs retaining the exhaust pipe to the manifold. After the bolts have soaked, remove the bolts retaining the exhaust pipe to the manifold. Separate the front exhaust pipe from the manifold, being careful not to damage the oxygen sensor (see illustration).

4 Unbolt the lower exhaust manifold braces and remove them from the engine. Also disconnect the oxygen sensor connectors.

5 Working in the engine compartment, remove the upper heat shield from the manifold (see illustration).

6 Remove the nuts/bolts and detach the manifold and gasket (see illustration).

INSTALLATION

7 Use a scraper to remove all traces of old gasket material and carbon deposits from the manifold and cylinder head mating surfaces. If the gasket shows signs of leaking, check the manifold for warpage with a straight edge. If the manifold is warped it must be replaced.

8 Position a new gasket over the cylinder head studs, noting any directional marks or arrows on the gasket that may be present.

9 Install the manifold and thread the mounting nuts into place.

10 Working from the center out, tighten the nuts/bolts to the torque listed in this Chapter's Specifications in three or four equal steps.

11 Reinstall the remaining parts in the reverse order of removal.

12 Run the engine and check for exhaust leaks.

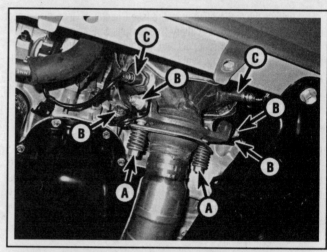

9.3 Working below the vehicle, remove the exhaust pipe-to-manifold mounting bolts (A) and lower the front exhaust pipe. Be careful not to damage the oxygen sensor (C) - (B) indicates the mounting bolts for the exhaust manifold lower brace

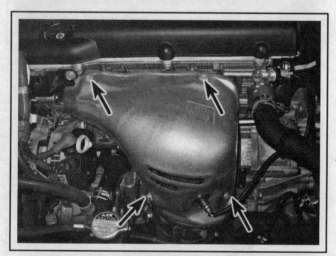

9.5 Working from the engine compartment, remove the upper heat shield mounting bolts . . .

9.6 . . . and the exhaust manifold retaining nuts, then pull the manifold off the studs on the cylinder head and remove from above

10 Cylinder head - removal and installation

REMOVAL

1 Relieve the fuel system pressure (see Chapter 4), then disconnect the cable from the negative terminal of the battery (see Chapter 5, Section 1).

2 Drain the engine coolant (see Chapter 1).

3 Remove the drivebelt and the alternator (see Chapter 5).

4 Remove the valve cover (see Section 4).

5 Remove the throttle body, fuel injectors and fuel rail (see Chapter 4).

6 Remove the intake manifold (see Section 8).

7 Remove the exhaust manifold (see Section 9).

8 Remove the timing chain and camshaft sprockets (see Section 6).

9 Remove the camshafts and lifters (see Section 7).

10 Remove the variable valve timing control valve (see illustration 5.2a).

11 Label and remove the coolant hoses and electrical connections from the cylinder head.

12 Using a 10 mm hex-head socket bit and a breaker bar, loosen the cylinder head bolts in 1/4-turn increments until they can be removed by hand. Loosen the cylinder head bolts in the reverse order of the recommended tightening sequence (see illustration 10.24) to avoid warping or cracking the cylinder head.

13 Lift the cylinder head off the engine block. If it's stuck, very carefully pry up at the transaxle end, beyond the gasket surface.

14 Remove any remaining external components from the cylinder head to allow for thorough cleaning and inspection.

INSTALLATION

▶ **Refer to illustration 10.24**

15 The mating surfaces of the cylinder head and block must be perfectly clean when the cylinder head is installed.

16 Use a gasket scraper to remove all traces of carbon and old gasket material, then clean the mating surfaces with lacquer thinner or acetone. If there's oil on the mating surfaces when the cylinder head is installed, the gasket may not seal correctly and leaks could develop. When working on the block, stuff the cylinders with clean shop rags to keep out debris. Use a vacuum cleaner to remove material that falls into the cylinders.

17 Check the block and cylinder head mating surfaces for nicks, deep scratches and other damage. If damage is slight, it can be removed with a file; if it's excessive, machining may be the only alternative.

18 Use a tap of the correct size to chase the threads in the cylinder head bolt holes, then clean the holes with compressed air - make sure that nothing remains in the holes.

19 Using a wire brush, clean the threads on each bolt to remove corrosion and restore the threads. Dirt, corrosion, sealant and damaged threads will affect torque readings.

20 Install the components that were removed from the cylinder head.

21 Position the new gasket over the dowel pins in the block, with the "lot number" identification UP. Then apply RTV sealant to the areas at the end of the cylinder head gasket as shown in illustration 6.32b.

22 Carefully set the cylinder head on the block without disturbing the gasket.

23 Before installing the cylinder head bolts, apply a small amount of clean engine oil to the threads and under the bolt heads.

24 Install the bolts and their washers in their original locations and tighten them finger tight. Following the recommended sequence, tighten the bolts to the torque listed in this Chapter's Specifications (see illustration). Step 2 of the tightening sequence requires each bolt to be tightened an additional 90-degrees. If you don't have an angle-torque attachment for your torque wrench, simply apply a paint mark at one edge of each cylinder head bolt and tighten the bolt until that mark is 90-degrees (1/4-turn) from where you started.

25 The remaining installation steps are the reverse of removal.

26 Check and adjust the valves as necessary (see Chapter 1).

27 Change the engine oil and filter (see Chapter 1).

28 Refill the cooling system (see Chapter 1), run the engine and check for leaks.

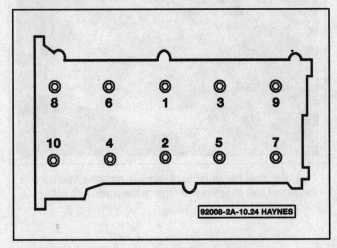

10.24 Cylinder head bolt TIGHTENING sequence

11 Crankshaft pulley/vibration damper - removal and installation

▶ Refer to illustrations 11.4, 11.5 and 11.6

1 Detach the cable from the negative terminal of the battery (see Chapter 5).

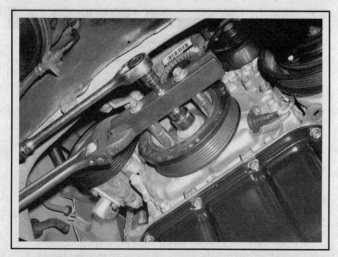

11.4 A puller base and several spacers can be mounted to the center hub of the pulley to keep the crankshaft from turning as the pulley retaining bolt is loosened - install the socket over the crankshaft bolt head before installing the puller, then insert the extension through the center hole of the puller

11.5 Reinstall the puller back onto the crankshaft pulley with the center bolt attached and remove the crankshaft pulley

2 Remove the drivebelt (see Chapter 1). Unbolt the bracket from the engine movement control rod (see Section 17).

3 With the parking brake applied and the shifter in Park (automatic) or in gear (manual), loosen the lug nuts from the right front wheel, then raise the front of the vehicle and support it securely on jackstands. Remove the right front wheel and the right splash shield from the wheelwell.

4 Remove the bolt from the front of the crankshaft. A breaker bar will probably be necessary, since the bolt is very tight (see illustration).

5 Using a puller that bolts to the crankshaft hub, remove the crankshaft pulley from the crankshaft (see illustration).

➡ **Note: Depending on the type of puller you have, it may be necessary to support the engine from above; remove the right side engine mount and lower the engine to gain sufficient clearance to use the puller.**

✳✳ **CAUTION:**

Do not use a jaw-type puller - it will damage the pulley/damper assembly.

6 To install the crankshaft pulley, slide the pulley onto the crankshaft as far as it will slide on, then use a vibration damper installation tool to press the pulley onto the crankshaft. Note that the slot (keyway) in the hub must be aligned with the Woodruff key in the end of the crankshaft (see illustration) and that the crankshaft bolt can also be used to press the crankshaft pulley into position.

7 Tighten the crankshaft bolt to the torque listed in this Chapter's Specifications.

8 The remaining installation steps are the reverse of removal.

11.6 Align the keyway in the crankshaft pulley hub with the Woodruff key in the crankshaft

12 Crankshaft front oil seal - replacement

▶ Refer to illustrations 12.2, 12.3 and 12.4

1 Remove the crankshaft pulley (see Section 11).

2 Note how the seal is installed - the new one must be installed to the same depth and facing the same way. Carefully pry the oil seal out

of the cover with a seal puller or a large screwdriver (see illustration). Be very careful not to distort the cover or scratch the crankshaft! Wrap electrician's tape around the tip of the screwdriver to avoid damage to the crankshaft.

3 Apply clean engine oil or multi-purpose grease to the outer edge

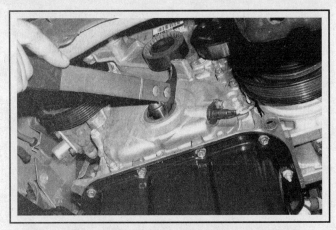

12.2 Carefully pry the old seal out of the timing chain cover - don't damage the crankshaft in the process

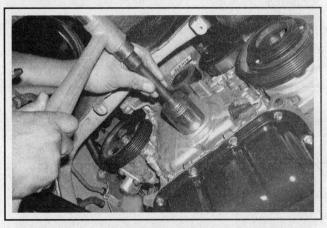

12.3 Drive the new seal into place with a seal driver or a large socket and hammer

of the new seal, then install it in the cover with the lip (spring side) facing IN. Drive the seal into place with a seal driver or a large socket and a hammer (see illustration). Make sure the seal enters the bore squarely and stop when the front face is at the proper depth.

4   Check the surface on the pulley hub that the oil seal rides on. If the surface has been grooved from long-time contact with the seal, a press-on sleeve may be available to renew the sealing surface (see illustration). This sleeve is pressed into place with a hammer and a block of wood and is commonly available at auto parts stores for various applications.

5   Lubricate the pulley hub with clean engine oil and reinstall the crankshaft pulley (see Section 11).

6   Install the crankshaft pulley retaining bolt and tighten it to the torque listed in this Chapter's Specifications.

7   The remainder of installation is the reverse of the removal.

12.4 If the sealing surface of the pulley hub has a wear groove from contact with the seal, repair sleeves are available at most auto parts stores

13 Oil pan - removal and installation

REMOVAL

▶ **Refer to illustrations 13.6a and 13.6b**

1   Disconnect the cable from the negative terminal of the battery (see Chapter 5).

2   Set the parking brake and block the rear wheels.

3   Raise the front of the vehicle and support it securely on jackstands.

4   Remove the two plastic splash shields under the engine, if equipped.

5   Drain the engine oil and remove the oil filter (see Chapter 1). Remove the oil dipstick.

6   Remove the bolts and detach the oil pan. If it's stuck, pry it loose

13.6a Oil pan mounting bolts

13.6b Pry the oil pan loose with a screwdriver or putty knife - be careful not to damage the mating surfaces of the pan and block or oil leaks may develop

very carefully with a small screwdriver or putty knife (see illustrations). Don't damage the mating surfaces of the pan and block or oil leaks could develop.

INSTALLATION

7   Use a scraper to remove all traces of old sealant from the block and oil pan. Clean the mating surfaces with lacquer thinner or acetone.

8   Make sure the threaded bolt holes in the block are clean.

9   Check the oil pan flange for distortion, particularly around the bolt holes. Remove any nicks or burrs as necessary.

10   Inspect the oil pump pick-up tube assembly for cracks and a blocked strainer. If the pick-up was removed, clean it thoroughly and install it now, using a new gasket. Tighten the nuts/bolts to the torque listed in this Chapter's Specifications.

11   Apply a 3/16-inch wide bead of RTV sealant to the mating surface of the oil pan, following the groove but going to the inside where the bolt holes are located.

12   Carefully position the oil pan on the engine block and install the oil pan-to-engine block bolts loosely.

13   Working from the center out, tighten the oil pan-to-engine block bolts to the torque listed in this Chapter's Specifications in three or four steps.

14   The remainder of installation is the reverse of removal.

➡ **Note: Be sure follow the sealant manufacturer's recommendations for assembly and sealant curing times.**

15   Run the engine and check for oil pressure and leaks.

14   Oil pump - removal and installation

14.2a Rotate the engine 90-degrees counterclockwise (from TDC) and set the crankshaft key to the left horizontal position (A), then remove the oil pump drive chain tensioner and bolt (B)

REMOVAL

▶ **Refer to illustrations 14.2a, 14.2b, 14.3, 14.5a and 14.5b**

1   Refer to Section 6, Steps 1 through 17 and remove the timing chain and the crankshaft sprocket.

2   Remove the oil pump drive chain and sprockets (see illustrations).

3   Remove the three bolts and detach the oil pump body from the engine (see illustration). You may have to pry carefully between the front of the block and the pump body with a screwdriver to remove it.

4   Use a scraper to remove all traces of sealant and old gasket material from the pump body and engine block, then clean the mating surfaces with lacquer thinner or acetone.

5   Inspect the oil pump and chain for wear and damage. If the oil pump shows signs of wear or you're in doubt about its condition it is simply best to replace it. The oil pump drive chain and tensioner, however, can be inspected as follows. Oil pump drive chain stretch is measured by checking the length of the chain between 4 links (8 pins) at 3 or more places (selected randomly) around the chain - if chain

14.2b Using a screwdriver to lock the lower gear in place, loosen the retaining bolt and remove the drive chain and lower gear and from the engine

14.3 Oil pump mounting bolts

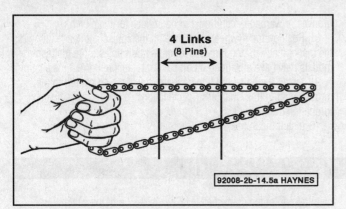

14.5a Oil pump drive chain stretch is measured by checking the length of the chain between 4 links (8 pins) at three or more places around the chain

14.5b Check that the oil jet is free of debris - a blockage here will lead to an excessively worn timing chain, oil pump drive chain and guides

stretch exceeds the specifications between any 4 links, the chain must be replaced (see illustration). Wrap the chain around each of the oil pump drive sprockets and measure the diameter of the sprockets across the chain rollers (see illustration 6.20b) - if the measurement is less than the minimum sprocket diameter, the chain and the sprockets must be replaced. Oil pump chain guide wear is measured from the top of the chain contact surface to the bottom of the wear grooves (see illustration 6.21). Also check the oil jet for blockage (see illustration).

INSTALLATION

⬦ **Refer to illustration 14.9**

6   Lubricate the pump cavity by pouring a small amount of clean engine oil into the inlet side of the oil pump and turning the drive gear shaft.

7   Position the oil pump and a new gasket against the block and install the mounting bolts.

8   Tighten the bolts to the torque listed in this Chapter's Specifications in several steps. Follow a criss-cross pattern to avoid warping the body.

9   With the crankshaft key still set in the left horizontal position and the flat on the oil pump drive shaft facing upward, install the drive chain and sprockets so that the colored links on the chain align with the alignment marks on the drive gears (see illustration).

10   Tighten the lower drive sprocket retaining bolt to the torque listed

14.9 Install the oil pump drive chain with the colored links aligned with the marks on the sprockets

in this Chapter's Specifications.

11   Reinstall the remaining parts in the reverse order of removal.

12   Add oil to the proper level, start the engine and check for oil pressure and leaks.

15 Flywheel/driveplate - removal and installation

REMOVAL

1   Disconnect the cable from the negative terminal of the battery (see Chapter 5, Section 1).

➡ **Note: For purposes of description, a flywheel is a solid plate used with manual transaxle vehicles, while a driveplate is a thinner disc of steel, often with holes in it, used with automatic transaxles.**

2   Remove the transaxle (see Chapter 7A or 7B).

3   Remove the pressure plate and disc on manual transaxle vehicles (see Chapter 8).

4   Using a center-punch or paint, apply alignment marks on the

crankshaft flange and flywheel/driveplate to ensure correct alignment on installation.

5   Remove the bolts retaining the flywheel/driveplate to the crankshaft. Use a flywheel/driveplate holding tool (available at auto parts stores) or wedge a screwdriver or prybar through one of the holes in the driveplate to keep it from turning while you loosen the bolts.

6   Remove the flywheel/driveplate, taking note of spacers used and on which side of the flywheel/driveplate they were installed.

❋❋ CAUTION:

The flywheel is fairly heavy and the edges of the ring-gear teeth are often sharp, so use gloves when removing the flywheel.

INSTALLATION

7   Clean the flywheel to remove grease and oil. Inspect the surface for cracks, rivet grooves, burned areas and score marks. On driveplates, look for cracks. Light scoring on the flywheel friction surface can be cleaned up with emery paper. Lay a metal straightedge across the flywheel to check for warpage. Machine work will be required to remove grooves or warpage, restoring a good surface for the clutch.

8   Position the flywheel/driveplate on the crankshaft flange, aligning the marks made during removal. Align the bolt holes; note that some models' may have a staggered bolt pattern to ensure correct installation.

9   Install the bolts and tighten them in a crossing pattern to the torque listed in this Chapter's Specifications. Work up to the final torque in several steps.

10 Install the transaxle (see Chapter 7).

16 Rear main oil seal - replacement

1   Remove the transmission (see Chapter 7A or 7B).

2   Remove the flywheel/driveplate (see Section 15).

3   Pry the oil seal from the rear of the engine with a screwdriver. Be careful not to nick or scratch the crankshaft or the seal bore. Be sure to note how far it's recessed into the bore before removal so the new seal can be installed to the same depth. Thoroughly clean the seal bore in the block with a shop towel. Remove all traces of oil and dirt.

4   Lubricate the outside diameter of the seal and install the seal over the end of the crankshaft. Make sure the lip of the seal points toward the engine. Preferably, a seal installation tool (available at most auto parts store) is needed to press the new seal back into place. If the proper seal installation tool is unavailable, use a large socket, section of pipe or a blunt tool and carefully drive the new seal squarely into the seal bore and flush with the edge of the engine block.

5   Install the flywheel/driveplate (see Section 15).

6   Install the transmission (see Chapter 7A or 7B).

17 Powertrain mounts - check and replacement

1   Powertrain mounts seldom require attention, but broken or deteriorated mounts should be replaced immediately or the added strain placed on driveline components may cause damage or wear.

CHECK

2   During the check, the engine (or transaxle) must be raised slightly to remove the weight from the mounts.

3   Raise the vehicle and support it securely on jackstands, then remove the splash shields under the engine and position a jack under the engine oil pan. Place a large block of wood between the jack and the oil pan, then carefully raise the engine just enough to take the weight off the mounts. Do not position the wood block under the oil drain plug.

> ❄️ **WARNING:**
>
> **DO NOT place any part of your body under the engine when it is supported only by a jack!**

4   Check the mounts to see if the rubber is cracked, hardened or separated from the bushing in the center of the mount.

5   Check for relative movement between the mount plates and the engine or frame, (use a large screwdriver or pry bar to attempt to move the mounts). If movement is noted, lower the engine and tighten the mount fasteners.

6   Rubber preservative should be applied to the mounts to slow deterioration.

REPLACEMENT

7   Disconnect the negative battery cable from the battery, then raise the vehicle and support it securely on jackstands, if not already done. Support the engine as described in Step 3.

➡️ **Note:** If several mounts need replacement, only replace one at a time and tighten them as you go. Do not remove all the mounts at once.

Passenger's side (right-hand) engine mount

▶ **Refer to illustration 17.8**

8   Working below the vehicle, remove the nuts securing the mount to the upper and lower brackets (see illustration).

9   Remove the bolts securing the mount to the frame, then raise the transaxle enough to allow removal of the mount.

10 Installation is the reverse of the removal. Use thread-locking compound on the bolts and be sure to tighten them securely.

Driver's side (left-hand) transaxle mount

11 Working below the vehicle, remove the nut securing the mount to the upper and lower brackets (see illustration 17.8).

12 Remove the bolts securing the mount to the frame, then raise the engine enough to allow removal of the mount.

13 Installation is the reverse of the removal. Use thread-locking compound on the bolts and be sure to tighten them securely.

17.8 Right-hand powertrain mount nuts (A) and bolts (B) (under the covers)

Front engine mount

14 Working below the vehicle, remove the nut securing the engine bracket to the mount.

15 Remove the bolts securing the mount to the frame, then raise the engine enough to allow removal of the mount.

16 Installation is the reverse of the removal. Use thread-locking compound on the bolts and be sure to tighten them securely.

Rear engine mount

17 Working below the vehicle, remove the nut securing the engine bracket to the mount.

18 Remove the bolts securing the mount to the frame, then raise the engine enough to allow removal of the mount.

19 Installation is the reverse of the removal. Use thread-locking compound on the bolts and be sure to tighten them securely.

Engine movement control rod

20 Working in the engine compartment, remove the bolts securing the engine movement control rod and its bracket (see illustration 8.9 in Chapter 2B).

21 Installation is the reverse of the removal. Use thread-locking compound on the bolts and be sure to tighten them securely.

---

18 Engine balancer assembly - removal and installation

♦ **Refer to illustrations 18.6, 18.7, 18.8, 18.9 and 18.10**

➡**Note: It is recommended to remove the engine to perform this procedure (see Chapter 2C). Additionally, it is important to note that in the following procedure, the orientation of the components and timing marks are shown with the engine inverted (as if mounted on an engine stand).**

1 Disconnect the negative battery cable (see Chapter 5).

2 Remove the oil pan and the oil pump (see Sections 13 and 14).

3 Remove the balance shaft housing bolts, in the order opposite that of the tightening sequence (see illustration 18.10).

4 Remove the balance shafts.

5 Remove the balance shaft bearing shells from the housing and the lower crankcase and install new ones. Lubricate the bearing faces with engine assembly lube.

6 Turn the driven gear of balance shaft no. 1 counterclockwise until it hits its stop. Make sure the matchmarks on the no. 1 driven gear and the no. 2 driven gear are in alignment (see illustration).

7 Turn the crankshaft so the balance shaft drive gear timing mark on the crankshaft is approximately 16-degrees before the 12 o'clock position (see illustration).

8 Mesh the gears of the balance shafts, aligning the matchmarks (see illustration).

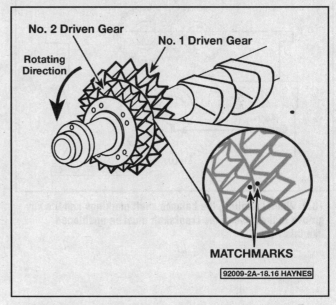

18.6 Align the matchmarks of the driven gears on the No. 1 balance shaft

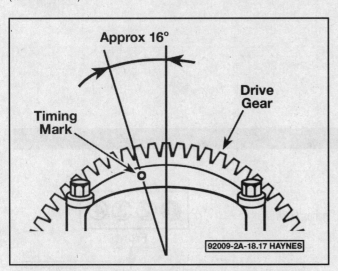

18.7 The timing mark on the balance shaft drive gear must be approximately 16-degrees before the 12 o'clock position (engine shown inverted)

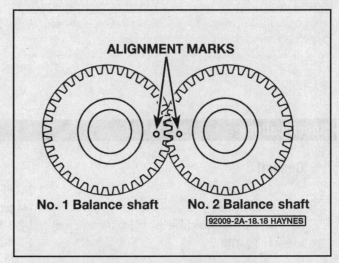

18.8 Mesh the gears of the balance shafts with the marks in alignment

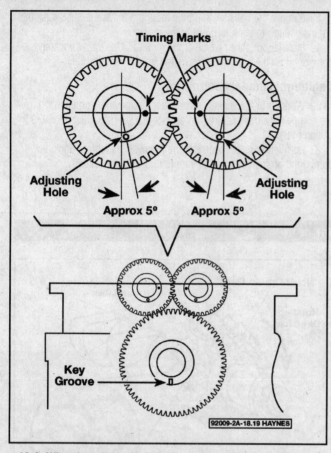

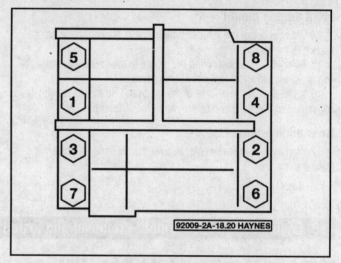

18.10 Balance shaft housing bolt tightening sequence

9 Install the balance shafts in the crankcase with the timing marks and adjusting holes aligned as shown (see illustration).

10 Install the balance shaft housing and tighten the bolts, in sequence (see illustration), to the torque listed in this Chapter's Specifications.

18.9 When installed, the balance shaft markings and the key groove in the nose of the crankshaft must be positioned like this

Specifications

General

Engine designation	2AZ-FE
Displacement	144 cubic inches (2.36 liters)
Cylinder numbers (drivebelt end-to-transaxle end)	1-2-3-4
Firing order	1-3-4-2

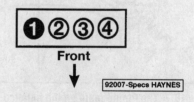

Cylinder numbering

Cylinder head

Warpage limit   0.0031 inch

Timing chain

Timing chain sprocket wear limit
    Camshaft sprocket(s) (w/chain)   3.831 inches
    Crankshaft sprocket (w/chain)   2.031 inches
Timing chain stretch limit
    8 links (16 pins)   4.827 inches
Timing chain guide wear limit   0.039 inch

Camshaft and lifters

Journal diameter
    No. 1 journal   1.4162 to 1.4167 inches
    All others   0.9040 to 0.9045 inch
Bearing oil clearance
    No.1 journal
        Intake
            Mark 1 size   0.0015 to 0.0028 inch
            Mark 2 and mark 3 sizes   0.0015 to 0.0031 inch
        Exhaust   0.0016 to 0.0031 inch
    All others   0.0001 to 0.0024 inch
Runout limit   0.0012 inch
Thrust clearance (endplay)
    Intake   0.0016 to 0.0037 inch
    Exhaust   0.0032 to 0.0053 inch
Lobe height
    2002 through 2006 models
        Intake and exhaust   1.8305 to 1.8345 inches
        Service limit (minimum)   1.8262 inches
    2007 and later models
        Intake   1.8624 to 1.8664 inches
        Exhaust   1.8135 to 1.8174 inches
        Service limit (minimum)
            Intake   1.8581 inches
            Exhaust   1.8092 inches
Valve lifter
    Diameter   1.2191 to 1.2195 inches
    Bore diameter   1.2208 to 1.2215 inches
Lifter oil clearance
    Standard   0.0013 to 0.0023 inch
    Service limit   0.0031 inch

Oil pump

Drive chain sprocket wear limit (diameter w/chain)   1.898 inches
Drive chain stretch limit
    4 links (8 pins)   2.063 inches
Drive chain guide wear limit   0.020 inch

Torque specifications	Ft-lbs (unless otherwise indicated)

➡**Note: One foot-pound (ft-lb) of torque is equivalent to 12 inch-pounds (in-lbs) of torque. Torque values below approximately 15 ft-lbs are expressed in inch-pounds, since most foot-pound torque wrenches are not accurate at these smaller values.**

Camshaft bearing cap bolts	
Journal No.1 (intake and exhaust)	22
All others	80 in-lbs
Camshaft sprocket bolts	40
Crankshaft pulley/vibration damper bolt	125
Cylinder head bolts (in sequence; see illustration 10.24)	
2002 through 2006 models	
Step 1	58
Step 2	Tighten an additional 90 degrees
2007 and later models	
Step 1	52
Step 2	Tighten an additional 90 degrees
Drivebelt tensioner mounting bolt/nut	44
Engine balancer assembly	
Step 1	16
Step 2	Tighten an additional 90-degrees
Exhaust manifold nuts/bolts	27
Exhaust manifold brace bolts	32
Exhaust manifold heat shield bolts	108 in-lbs
Exhaust pipe to manifold-converter nuts	46
Flywheel/driveplate bolts	
Manual transaxle	96
Automatic transaxle	72
Intake manifold nuts/bolts	22
Lower crankcase-to-engine block bolts	24
Oil pump bolts	168 in-lbs
Oil pump drive chain tensioner	108 in-lbs
Oil pump sprocket bolt	20
Oil pan bolts	80 in-lbs
Timing chain guide bolts (stationary)	80 in-lbs
Timing chain tensioner pivot arm bolt	168 in-lbs
Timing chain cover bolts (see illustration 6.39)	
2002 through 2006 models	
Bolt A	80 in-lbs
Bolts B	15
Bolts C	32
Nut D	80 in-lbs
2007 and later models	
Bolt A	80 in-lbs
Bolts B	18
Bolts C	41
Nut D	80 in-lbs
Timing chain tensioner nuts	80 in-lbs
Valve cover	96 in-lbs

2B
V6 ENGINE

Section

1 General information
2 Repair operations possible with the engine in the vehicle
3 Top Dead Center (TDC) for number one piston - locating
4 Variable Valve Timing (VVT) system - description, check and component replacement
5 Valve covers - removal and installation
6 Intake manifold - removal and installation
7 Exhaust manifolds - removal and installation
8 Timing belt and sprockets - removal, inspection and installation
9 Oil seals - replacement
10 Camshafts and lifters - removal, inspection and installation
11 Cylinder heads - removal and installation
12 Oil pan - removal and installation
13 Oil pump - removal, inspection and installation
14 Flywheel/driveplate - removal and installation
15 Rear main oil seal - replacement
16 Powertrain mounts - check and replacement

Reference to other Chapters

CHECK ENGINE light on - See Chapter 6
Cylinder compression check - See Chapter 2C
Drivebelt check, adjustment and replacement - See Chapter 1
Engine oil and filter change - See Chapter 1
Engine overhaul - general information - See Chapter 2C
Engine - removal and installation - See Chapter 2C
Spark plug replacement - See Chapter 1
Water pump - removal and installation - See Chapter 3

1 General information

The models covered by this manual are available with the 3.0L 1MZ-FE V6 engine or the 3MZ-FE, which is virtually the same engine as the 1MZ-FE but with a larger displacement of 3.3L. The design is a DOHC (dual overhead cam) with four valves per cylinder (24 in all), an aluminum engine block, distributorless ignition, and two-piece oil pan.

This Part of Chapter 2 is devoted to in-vehicle repair procedures for the V6 engine. Information concerning engine removal and installation and engine overhaul can be found in Part C of this Chapter.

The following repair procedures are based on the assumption that the engine is installed in the vehicle. If the engine has been removed from the vehicle and mounted on a stand, many of the steps outlined in this Part of Chapter 2 will not apply.

2 Repair operations possible with the engine in the vehicle

Many major repair operations can be accomplished without removing the engine from the vehicle.

Clean the engine compartment and the exterior of the engine with some type of degreaser before any work is done. It will make the job easier and help keep dirt out of the internal areas of the engine.

Depending on the components involved, it may be helpful to remove the hood to improve access to the engine as repairs are performed (refer to Chapter 11 if necessary). Cover the fenders to prevent damage to the paint. Special pads are available, but an old bedspread or blanket will also work.

If vacuum, exhaust, oil or coolant leaks develop, indicating a need for gasket or seal replacement, the repairs can generally be made with the engine in the vehicle. The intake and exhaust manifold gaskets, oil pan gasket, crankshaft oil seals and cylinder head gaskets are all accessible with the engine in place.

Exterior engine components, such as the intake and exhaust manifolds, the oil pan, the oil pump, the water pump, the starter motor, the alternator, and the fuel system components can be removed for repair with the engine in place.

Since the cylinder heads can be removed without pulling the engine, valve component servicing can also be accomplished with the engine in the vehicle. Replacement of the camshafts, timing belt and pulleys is also possible with the engine in the vehicle.

3 Top Dead Center (TDC) for number one piston - locating

▶ **Refer to illustrations 3.5 and 3.6**

1   Top Dead Center (TDC) is the highest point in the cylinder that each piston reaches as it travels up the cylinder bore. Each piston reaches TDC on the compression stroke and again on the exhaust stroke, but TDC generally refers to piston position on the compression stroke.

2   Positioning the piston(s) at TDC is an essential part of many procedures such as valve timing, camshaft and timing belt/pulley removal and distributor removal.

3   Before beginning this procedure, be sure to place the transaxle in Neutral and apply the parking brake or block the rear wheels. Disable the fuel system by removing the C/OPN relay from the underhood fuse/relay box.

4   In order to bring any piston to TDC, the crankshaft must be turned using one of the methods outlined below. When looking at the front of the engine, normal crankshaft rotation is clockwise.

a) The preferred method is to turn the crankshaft clockwise with a socket and ratchet attached to the bolt threaded into the front of the crankshaft.

b) A remote starter switch, which may save some time, can also be used. Follow the instructions included with the switch. Once the piston is close to TDC, use a socket and ratchet as described in the previous paragraph.

c) If an assistant is available to turn the ignition switch to the Strt position in short bursts, you can get the piston close to TDC without a remote starter switch. Make sure your assistant is out of the vehicle, away from the ignition switch, then use a socket and ratchet as described in Paragraph (a) to complete the procedure.

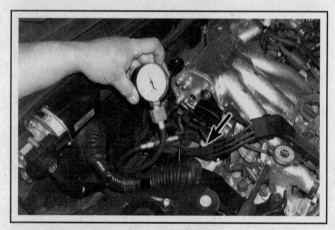

3.5 A compression gauge can be used in the number one plug hole to assist in finding TDC on V6 engines

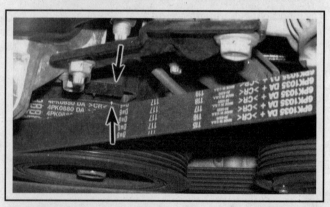

3.6 Turn the crankshaft until the notch in the pulley aligns with the zero on the timing plate

5   Remove the spark plug and install a compression pressure gauge in the number one spark plug hole. It should be a gauge with a screw-in fitting and a hose at least six inches long (see illustration).

6   Rotate the crankshaft using one of the methods described above while observing the compression gauge. When TDC for the compression stroke of number one cylinder is reached, compression pressure will show on the gauge as the marks are beginning to line up on the crankshaft pulley (see illustration). If you go past the marks, release the gauge pressure and rotate the crankshaft around two more revolutions.

➡Note: The most positive method for finding TDC on the V6 engine is to examine the crankshaft timing marks and camshaft sprocket timing marks (see Section 8).

---

4   Variable Valve Timing (VVT) system - description, check and component replacement

DESCRIPTION

▶ Refer to illustration 4.4

➡Note: The following procedures apply to the oil control valve, oil filter or intake camshaft sprocket/actuator on either cylinder head.

1   The VVT system varies intake camshaft timing by directing oil pressure to advance or retard the intake camshaft sprocket/actuator assembly. Changing the intake camshaft timing during certain engine conditions increases engine torque and fuel economy and reduces emissions.

2   System components include the Powertrain Control Module (PCM), an oil control valve (OCV) in each cylinder head, an oil filter for each OCV and an intake camshaft sprocket/actuator assembly.

3   The PCM uses inputs from the vehicle speed sensor (VSS), the throttle position sensor (TPS), the mass air flow (MAF) sensor and the engine coolant temperature (ECT) sensor to turn the oil control valve ON or OFF.

4   When the OCV is energized by the PCM, it directs a specified amount of oil pressure from the engine to advance or retard the intake camshaft sprocket/actuator assembly (see illustration).

5   The intake camshaft sprocket/actuator assembly is equipped with an inner hub that is attached to the camshaft. The inner hub consists of a series of fixed vanes that use oil pressure as a wedge against the vanes to rotate the camshaft. The higher the oil pressure, the greater the amount of actuator rotation and, therefore, the amount of camshaft advance or retard. How does greater oil pressure advance or retard the cam? By directing the oil to the advance or retard side of the fixed vanes.

6   When oil is applied to the advance side of the vanes, the actuator can advance the camshaft up to 21 degrees in a clockwise direction. When oil is applied to the retard side of the vanes, the actuator will start to rotate the camshaft counterclockwise back to 0 degrees, which is the normal position of the actuator during engine operation under no load or at idle. The PCM can also send a signal to the oil control valve to stop oil flow to both (advance and retard) passages to hold camshaft advance in its current position.

7   Under light engine loads, the VVT system retards the camshaft timing to decrease valve overlap and stabilize engine output. Under medium engine loads, the VVT system advances the camshaft timing to increase valve overlap, thereby increasing fuel economy and decreasing exhaust emissions. Under heavy engine loads at low RPM, the VVT system advances the camshaft timing to help close the intake valve faster, which improves low to midrange torque. Under heavy engine loads at high RPM, the VVT system retards the camshaft timing to slow the closing of the intake valve to improve engine horsepower.

COMPONENT REPLACEMENT

➡Note 1: A problem in the VVT oil control valve circuit will set a diagnostic trouble code and turn on the Check Engine light on the dash. Refer to Chapter 6 for accessing trouble codes.

➡Note 2: Most problems in the VVT system originate from the oil control valve(s) and filter(s). Regular engine oil and filter changes are necessary for trouble-free operation of the OCVs.

➡Note 3: Some checks and inspections of the VVT system require removal of the valve cover and the intake camshaft.

Oil control valve (OCV) filter

▶ Refer to illustration 4.8

8   A clogged OCV filter screen is often the cause of VVT system problems. Remove the OCV filter from the rear of the cylinder head and then inspect the filter for clogging. Clean the filter if necessary and reinstall it using a new O-ring. Make sure that the big end of the filter faces toward the head (see illustration). Be sure to tighten the filter plug to the torque listed in this Chapter's Specifications.

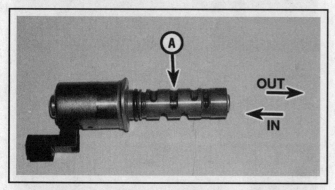

4.4 When voltage is applied, the OCV plunger (A), which you can see through the slots in the housing, should move out; when voltage is cut, the plunger should move in

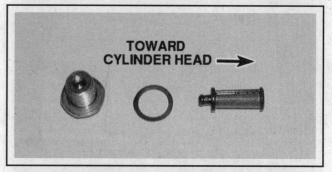

4.8 If you suspect a problem with the VVT system, inspect the OCV filter for obstructions; when you install the filter, use a new O-ring and make sure that the big end of the filter faces toward the head

Oil control valve (OCV)

9　To replace the OCV, remove the hold-down bolt and pull the OCV out of the cylinder head. There is one valve at the rear (transaxle end) of each cylinder head. Use a new O-ring when installing the new OCV. Be sure to tighten the OCV hold-down bolt to the torque listed in this Chapter's Specifications.

Camshaft sprocket/actuator assembly

10　Remove the valve cover (see Section 5), the timing belt (see Section 8) and the intake camshaft (see Section 10).

➡**Note: Do NOT remove the exhaust camshaft or sprocket from the engine.**

11　Mount the camshaft in a bench vise. Secure the camshaft in the vise by clamping up the hexagonal nut part of the cam.

✳✳ CAUTION:

Be careful not to damage the camshaft or any of the cam lobes or journals.

12　Verify that the sprocket/actuator will not rotate from the locked position. The locked position is a neutral position in which the actuator is placed during idle and no load conditions, and anytime that the VVT system is not activated by the PCM.

13　Using brake system cleaner, remove all traces of oil from the front cam journals and the VVT oil control orifices. Apply vinyl tape over all the oil control orifices except the advance side oil port.

14　Apply 14 psi of air pressure to the advance side oil port and try to rotate the actuator assembly by hand. The actuator should rotate freely, with no obvious binding, for about 30-degrees in the advance angle direction from the locked position.

➡**Note: It is critical to have an air tight seal between the air gun nozzle and the advance oil port hole, because if air leaks out at the air nozzle, or at any of the other oil control orifices, the lock pin in the actuator won't be forced out of its locating hole. If leakage occurs, apply a little more air pressure to the advance side oil port to force the lock pin from the locating hole.**

15　If the actuator does not rotate freely as described, replace the intake camshaft sprocket/actuator assembly.

16　To replace the sprocket/actuator assembly, put the camshaft in a bench vise and remove the 46mm nut by turning it clockwise (the nut is reverse-threaded).

17　Remove the sprocket/actuator assembly. If it's hard to pull off the camshaft, tap it lightly with a plastic-tip hammer.

✳✳ CAUTION:

Do NOT try to disassemble the sprocket/actuator assembly - it's NOT rebuildable.

18　Lubricate the sprocket/actuator seating surface on the camshaft with clean engine oil. Before installing the sprocket/actuator assembly, make sure that the lock pin (in the camshaft) and lock pin groove (inside the sprocket/actuator) are aligned. Install the sprocket/actuator assembly. Using a NEW sprocket/actuator assembly retaining nut, tighten the retaining nut to the torque listed in this Chapter's Specifications (don't forget, it's reverse-threaded).

19　Install the intake camshaft (see Section 10), the timing belt (see Section 8) and the valve cover (see Section 5).

5　Valve covers - removal and installation

REMOVAL

◆ **Refer to illustrations 5.2, 5.3, 5.4a, 5.4b and 5.5**

1　Disconnect the negative cable from the battery (see Chapter 5, Section 1).

2　Remove the V-bank cover. If you're removing the rear (firewall side) cover, remove the intake plenum assembly (see Section 6).

3　Remove the coil connectors, coils or spark plug wires, as applicable (see illustration).

4　Detach the engine wiring harness from the left side of the engine, the number 3 timing belt cover, the rear of the engine and right-hand

5.2　Remove the oil filler cap, then the three fasteners to remove the V-bank cover

5.3　Disconnect the harness from the ignition coils, remove the mounting bolts and pull the coils from the valve cover

5.4a Remove two nuts and disconnect the left-hand engine harness . . .

5.4b . . . disconnect the wire clips at the timing belt cover and the five bolts retaining the right-hand harness, then move the harness away from the rear valve cover

side (see illustrations).

5   Remove the retaining nuts and sealing washers, then detach the cover(s) (see illustration). If the cover is stuck to the head, bump the end with a wood block and a hammer to jar it loose. If that doesn't work, try to slip a flexible putty knife between the head and cover to break the seal.

✳✳ CAUTION:

Don't pry at the cover-to-head joint or damage to the sealing surfaces may occur, leading to oil leaks after the cover is reinstalled.

INSTALLATION

◆ **Refer to illustration 5.8**

6   The mating surfaces of the cylinder head and cover must be clean when the cover is installed. Use a gasket scraper to remove all traces of sealant and old gasket material, then clean the mating surfaces with lacquer thinner or acetone. If there's residue or oil on the mating surfaces when the cover is installed, oil leaks may develop.

7   Install new spark plug tube seals.

8   Apply RTV sealant to the gasket/seal joints at the front and rear camshaft-to-head mounts and install the valve cover with a new gasket (see illustration).

9   Tighten the nuts to the torque listed in this Chapter's Specifications in three or four equal steps.

10 Reinstall the remaining parts, run the engine and check for oil leaks.

5.5 Remove the bolts and sealing washers and remove the valve cover

5.8 Apply RTV sealant to the areas indicated and install the cover with a new gasket

6   Intake manifold - removal and installation

REMOVAL

1   Relieve the fuel system pressure, then disconnect the negative cable from the battery (see Chapter 5, Section 1).

Upper intake plenum

▶ **Refer to illustrations 6.7 and 6.8**

2   Drain the coolant into a clean container (see Chapter 1).
3   Remove the V-bank cover (see illustration 5.2).
4   Remove the air cleaner assembly (see Chapter 4).
5   Disconnect the electrical connectors, vacuum and coolant bypass hoses from the throttle body, then disconnect the throttle motor connector (see Chapter 4). The throttle body can remain attached to the intake plenum unless it is being removed for cleaning or gasket service.
6   On models with performance suspension, remove the front sus-

pension brace between the two shock towers.
7   Unbolt the two intake plenum braces at the firewall side of the rear cylinder head (see illustrations).
8   Remove the bolts and nuts holding the plenum to the lower intake manifold and lift the plenum off (see illustration).

Lower intake manifold

▶ **Refer to illustrations 6.10, 6.11 and 6.12**

9   Disconnect the electrical connectors from the fuel injectors.

➡**Note: The intake manifold can be removed with the injectors and fuel rails in place or removed, depending on the work to be done.**

10 Disconnect the air assist and heater hoses at the left end of the intake manifold (see illustration). Also detach the fuel line from the fuel rail (see Chapter 4).
11 Remove the nine mounting bolts and two nuts, then detach the manifold from the engine (see illustration). If it's stuck, don't pry between the gasket mating surfaces or damage may result.

6.8 Remove the bolts (A) and nuts (B), then remove the intake plenum (typical shown)

6.7 Unbolt the two intake plenum braces

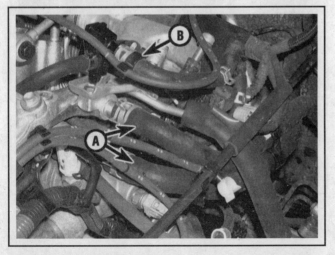

6.10 Detach the heater hoses (A) and the air assist hose (B)

6.11 Remove the bolts and nuts, then remove the lower intake manifold - numbers indicate tightening sequence for reassembly

12 There is a water transfer hose (see illustration) that is exposed only when the intake manifold is removed. Because of the difficulty in getting at this hose for replacement, we recommend that it be replaced with a new hose if the intake manifold is removed for other work.

INSTALLATION

13 Use a scraper to remove all traces of old gasket material and sealant from the manifold and cylinder heads, then clean the mating surfaces with lacquer thinner or acetone.

14 Install new gaskets, then position the manifold on the engine. Make sure the gaskets haven't shifted, then install the nuts/bolts.

15 Tighten the nuts/bolts, in three or four equal steps, to the torque listed in this Chapter's Specifications. Tighten the bolts in the sequence shown in illustration 6.11.

16 Install the remaining parts in the reverse order of removal. Use a new gasket between the intake manifold and the plenum.

17 Refill the cooling system. Run the engine and check for fuel, vacuum and coolant leaks.

6.12 This water transfer hose should be replaced whenever the intake manifold is off for other repairs

7 Exhaust manifolds - removal and installation

♦ **Refer to illustrations 7.5 and 7.6**

❋❋ **WARNING:**

The engine must be completely cool before beginning this procedure.

1 Disconnect the negative cable from the battery (see Chapter 5, Section 1).

2 Spray penetrating oil on the exhaust manifold fasteners and allow it to soak in.

3 Remove the heated oxygen sensors from the front and rear manifolds.

4 Remove the EGR pipe from the rear exhaust manifold and cylinder head (see Chapter 6).

5 Remove the nuts retaining the exhaust pipes to the front and rear exhaust manifolds (see illustration). On the front manifold, remove the two bolts securing the manifold support bracket.

6 Disconnect the electrical connector from the oxygen sensor at each manifold. Remove the bolts and the heat shield over the exhaust manifolds (see illustration).

7 Unbolt the exhaust manifolds from the cylinder heads, working from the ends toward the middle, and slip them off the mounting studs.

8 Carefully inspect the manifolds and fasteners for cracks and damage.

9 Use a scraper to remove all traces of old gasket material and carbon deposits from the manifolds and cylinder head mating surfaces. If the gasket was leaking, check the manifolds for warpage on the cylinder head mounting surface by placing a straightedge over the surface and trying to insert a feeler gauge. If the clearance exceeds the limit listed in this Chapter's Specifications, have the manifold resurfaced at an automotive machine shop.

10 Position new gaskets over the cylinder head studs.

11 Install the manifolds and thread the mounting nuts into place.

12 Working from the center out, tighten the nuts to the torque listed in this Chapter's Specifications in three or four equal steps.

13 Reinstall the remaining parts in the reverse order of removal. Use new gaskets when connecting the exhaust pipes.

14 Run the engine and check for exhaust leaks.

7.5 Remove the two nuts at the exhaust pipe/manifold joint - typical front pipe shown, rear similar

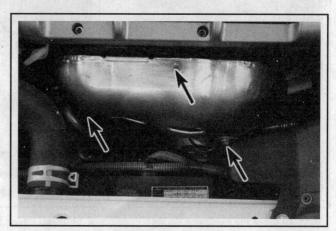

7.6 Remove the exhaust heat shield bolts

8   Timing belt and sprockets - removal, inspection and installation

REMOVAL

▶ **Refer to illustrations 8.9, 8.11, 8.12, 8.15, 8.18 and 8.22**

✳✳ CAUTION:

The timing system is complex. Severe engine damage will occur if you make any mistakes. Do not attempt this procedure unless you are highly experienced with this type of repair. If you are at all unsure of your abilities, consult an expert. Double-check all your work and be sure everything is correct before you attempt to start the engine.

1   Disconnect the cable from the negative terminal of the battery (see Chapter 5).

2   Remove the coolant overflow tank and windshield washer tank (see Chapter 3).

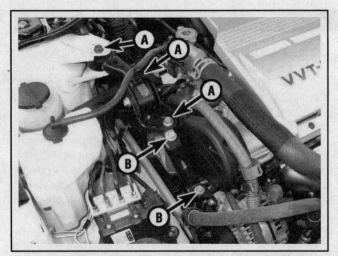

8.9 Remove the movement-control rod bolts (A) and the engine movement control rod, then remove the bolts (B) and the engine mounting brace

3   On models so equipped, remove the four nuts and the front suspension upper brace from the strut towers.

4   Remove the drivebelts from the alternator and power steering pump (see Chapter 1).

5   Loosen the lug nuts on the right front wheel, but don't remove them yet.

6   Raise the front of the vehicle and support it securely on jackstands. Apply the parking brake and block the rear wheels. Remove the right front wheel.

7   Remove the right front inner fender apron (see Chapter 11).

8   Position the number one cylinder at TDC (see Section 3).

9   Support the engine with a jack from below and remove the engine movement control rod and its bracket on the engine (see illustration). Place a wood block on the jack head and do not place the jack directly under the oil pan drain plug.

10   Remove the spark plugs (see Chapter 1).

11   Remove the upper (no. 2) timing belt cover and gasket (see illustration).

➡**Note: Unclip the wiring harness above the cover and push it back enough to remove the belt cover.**

12   Check to see if there are installation marks on the timing belt - if you intend to re-use the belt and the marks have been obscured, make new ones (see illustration).

13   Make sure the camshaft pulley timing marks are properly aligned.

14   Rotate the crankshaft pulley counterclockwise 60 degrees BTDC.

✳✳ CAUTION:

The engine pistons must be moved from the TDC number 1 position where they will not accidentally contact the valves when the timing belt tension has been released and the timing belt removed.

➡**Note: The crankshaft pulley bolt must be installed and tightened enough to be able to rotate the engine in a counterclockwise direction.**

15   Remove the timing belt tensioner (see illustration). Be sure to remove the rubber boot as well; it may stick in the tensioner recess.

8.11 Remove the number 2 timing belt cover

8.12 If you intend to re-use the belt and the original installation marks are obscured or missing, make new ones

8.15 Remove the two bolts and detach the timing belt tensioner

8.18 If the camshaft sprockets are damaged, or the cams are to be removed, hold the hex portion of the camshaft with a wrench while removing the sprocket bolt

✳✳ CAUTION:

Loosen the bolts a little at a time, alternating from side-to-side until the tensioner pressure is off.

16 Relieve the tension between the rear (right-hand) and front (left-hand) camshaft sprockets by turning the rear sprocket slightly clockwise.

✳✳ CAUTION:

Don't turn the sprocket any more than is necessary to provide enough slack to allow you to slip the belt off the sprockets.

17 Remove the timing belt from the camshaft sprockets.

18 The camshaft sprockets can be removed at this point, if they are worn or damaged. Remove the valve cover(s) (see Section 5) and hold the camshaft with a wrench on the cast-in hex while loosening the sprocket bolt (see illustration). Remove the bolt and detach the sprocket.

19 Remove the upper (no. 2) idler pulley.

20 Remove the crankshaft (drivebelt) pulley bolt. Wedge a large screwdriver into the flywheel/driveplate ring gear teeth or against a converter bolt to keep the engine from turning, or use a two-pin spanner to hold the pulley. Use a breaker bar and socket to loosen the pulley bolt.

21 When the crankshaft pulley bolt is loosened, the TDC position of the crankshaft may be disturbed. Check and align again, if necessary.

➡**Note: The crankshaft timing belt sprocket has a TDC alignment mark that lines up with a mark on the oil pump housing, making it easy to check the TDC alignment even after the crankshaft pulley and lower timing belt cover are removed.**

22 Once the pulley bolt is loosened, use a puller pushing against the pulley bolt. When the pulley comes loose, remove the tool and the bolt, and remove the pulley by hand (see illustration).

23 Remove the lower (no. 1) timing belt cover and gasket.

24 Slip the timing belt guide off the crankshaft.

25 If you're re-using the belt, check for a mark on the belt adjacent to the drilled mark on the crankshaft sprocket. If the original mark is gone, make a new one, then slip the belt off the sprocket.

26 Using an Allen wrench, remove the no. 1 idler pulley and plate washer. It is located at the belt end of the engine, just above the crank-

8.22 After loosening the crankshaft pulley with a puller, it will come off by hand

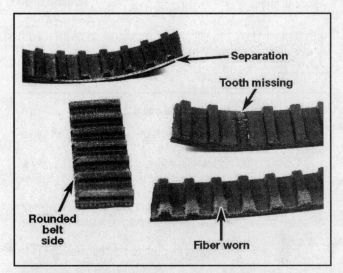

8.28 Check the timing belt for cracked or missing teeth - if the belt is cracked or worn, also check the pulleys for nicks or burrs - wear on one side of the belt indicates pulley misalignment problems

shaft sprocket, to the left of the engine's centerline.

27 If it's worn or damaged, or if you're replacing the crankshaft front oil seal, the crankshaft sprocket can now be removed. If it won't come off by hand, a steering wheel type puller may be needed to remove the sprocket. Be careful not to damage the crankshaft sensor portion of the

8.30 Check the tensioner for signs of leakage and test for leakdown by forcing it against an immovable object

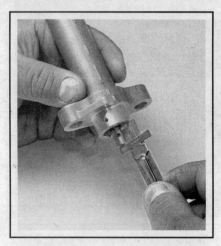

8.31 Measure the tensioner pushrod protrusion and compare it to the Specifications

8.34 Align the marks on thecrankshaft timing sprocket with the marks on the oil pump case (A), and install the sprocket retainer (B) and bolt

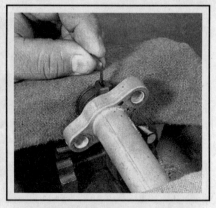

8.49 Restrain the tensioner pushrod by compressing the unit in a vise and inserting a pin approximately 0.060-inch (1.5 mm) in diameter - make sure the rubber boot is in place

sprocket during the removal process. If necessary, remove the lower sprocket retainer (see illustration 8.34).

INSPECTION

▶ **Refer to illustrations 8.28, 8.30 and 8.31**

28 Check the belt for the presence of oil or dirt, and inspect for visible defects (see illustration).

29 Check the belt tensioner for visible oil leakage. If there's only a faint trace of oil on the pushrod side, the tensioner seal is in satisfactory condition.

30 Hold the tensioner in both hands and push it forcefully against an immovable object (see illustration). If the pushrod moves, replace the tensioner.

31 Measure the protrusion of the pushrod from the housing end (see illustration). Compare your measurement to this Chapter's Specifications. If the protrusion is not as specified, replace the tensioner.

32 Check that the idler pulleys turn smoothly.

INSTALLATION

▶ **Refer to illustrations 8.34 and 8.49**

⁜ **CAUTION:**

Before starting the engine, carefully rotate the crankshaft by hand through at least two full revolutions (use a socket and breaker bar on the crankshaft pulley center bolt). If you feel any resistance, STOP! There is something wrong - most likely, valves are contacting the pistons. You must find the problem before proceeding. Check your work and see if any updated repair information is available.

33 Remove all dirt, oil and grease from the timing belt area at the front of the engine.

34 Align the crankshaft timing sprocket keyway with the crankshaft key and install the sprocket with the flange side up against the engine. Be careful not to damage the crankshaft sensor portion of the crankshaft sprocket. Check the alignment of the TDC marks on the sprocket and the oil pump housing, and reinstall the retainer and bolt (see illustration). Rotate the engine 60 degrees counterclockwise.

35 Apply thread-locking compound to the first two or three threads on the lower (no. 1) idler pulley bolt, then position the idler pulley and washer and install the bolt. Tighten the bolt to the torque listed in this Chapter's Specifications.

36 Install the timing belt, starting at the crankshaft sprocket. If you're re-using the original belt, align the marks on the belt with the marks on the sprockets and covers. Install the belt over the lower (no. 1) idler and water pump pulleys.

37 Slip the belt guide over the end of the crankshaft with the cupped side facing out.

38 Install the lower (no. 1) timing belt cover and gasket.

39 Slip the crankshaft (drivebelt) pulley onto the crankshaft, aligning the pulley keyway with the crankshaft key. Install the bolt and tighten it to the torque listed in this Chapter's Specifications. Prevent the crankshaft from turning by using the method described in Step 20.

40 Install the upper (no. 2) idler pulley. Tighten the bolt to the torque listed in this Chapter's Specifications. Make sure the pulley turns smoothly.

41 Install the front camshaft sprocket (if it was removed) on the camshaft with the flange side facing OUT. Align the pin hole in the sprocket with the pin in the end of the camshaft.

42 Install the sprocket-retaining bolt and tighten it to the torque listed in this Chapter's Specifications. Use the method described in Step 18 to keep the camshaft from turning.

43 Turn the crankshaft sprocket back to TDC (see illustration 8.34). If you're re-using the original belt, the installation mark should line up as it did in Step 13. If not, change the position of the timing belt on the crankshaft sprocket. The mark on the front (left-hand) camshaft sprocket should be at the top (12 o'clock position), aligned with the mark on the rear (no. 3) timing cover.

44 The rear (right-hand) camshaft knock-pin hole should be at the top (12 o'clock position). If necessary, remove the valve cover and turn the camshaft slightly with a wrench to align the sprocket with the mark on the rear (no. 3) cover.

45 Install the rear (right-hand) camshaft sprocket (if it was removed) on the camshaft with the flange side facing IN. Align the pin hole in the sprocket with the knock pin in the end of the camshaft.

46 Install the retaining bolt and tighten it to the torque listed in this Chapter's Specifications. Use the method described in Step 18 to keep the camshaft from turning. Be sure the timing mark is still aligned with the rear (no. 3) cover.

47 Turn the front (left-hand) camshaft sprocket clockwise slightly (about one tooth) with a pin spanner. If the special tool isn't available, grip the hex on the camshaft with a wrench and turn it (see illustration 8.18). If you're re-using the original belt, align the installation mark with the camshaft timing mark. Slip the belt onto the sprocket, then turn the camshaft counterclockwise, back to its original position. There should now be slight tension on the belt.

48 Slip the belt onto the rear sprocket. If you're re-using the original belt, align the installation marks.

49 Using a press or vise, slowly compress the timing belt tensioner pushrod (see illustration). Insert a metal pin, drill bit or Allen wrench through the holes in the pushrod and housing. Release the pressure from the press or vise.

50 Install the timing belt tensioner and tighten the bolts to the torque listed in this Chapter's Specifications. Remove the retaining pin.

51 Using a socket and breaker bar on the crankshaft pulley bolt, turn the crankshaft slowly (clockwise) through two complete revolutions (720-degrees). Recheck the timing marks (see illustration 3.6).

❈ **CAUTION:**

If the timing marks are not aligned exactly as shown, repeat the timing belt installation procedure. DO NOT start the engine until you're absolutely certain that the timing belt is installed correctly. Serious and costly engine damage could occur if the belt is installed wrong.

52 Reinstall the engine movement control rod's mounting bracket.

53 Install the upper (no. 2) timing belt cover and gasket.

54 Install the engine movement control rod and braces and tighten the bolts securely.

55 Reinstall the remaining parts in the reverse order of removal.

9 Oil seals - replacement

CRANKSHAFT OIL SEAL

1 Remove the timing belt and crankshaft timing belt sprocket (see Section 8).

2 Note how far the seal is recessed in the bore, then cut away the seal lip with a razor knife.

3 Carefully pry the seal out of the engine with a screwdriver or seal removal tool. If you use a screwdriver, wrap tape around the tip - don't scratch the housing bore or damage the crankshaft (if the crankshaft is damaged, the new seal will end up leaking).

4 Clean the bore in the engine and coat the outer edge of the new seal with engine oil or multi-purpose grease. Apply the same grease to the seal lip.

5 Using a seal driver or a socket with an outside diameter slightly smaller than the outside diameter of the seal, carefully drive the new seal into place with a hammer. Make sure it's installed squarely and driven in to the same depth as the original. Check the seal after installation to make sure the spring didn't pop out of place.

6 Reinstall the crankshaft timing sprocket and timing belt (see Section 8). Be careful not to scratch the crankshaft sensor portion of the sprocket.

7 Run the engine and check for oil leaks at the front seal.

CAMSHAFT OIL SEALS

8 Remove the timing belt and camshaft sprocket(s) (see Section 8).

9 Remove the bolts and detach the rear (no. 3) timing belt cover.

10 Note how far the seal is seated in the bore, then carefully pry it out with a screwdriver. Wrap the screwdriver tip with tape - don't scratch the bore or damage the camshaft (if the camshaft is damaged, the new seal will end up leaking).

11 Clean the bore and coat the outer edge of the new seal with engine oil or multi-purpose grease. Apply multi-purpose grease to the seal lip.

12 Using a seal driver or a socket with an outside diameter slightly smaller than the outside diameter of the seal, carefully drive the new seal into place with a hammer. Make sure it's installed squarely and driven in to the same depth as the original.

13 Reinstall the rear timing belt cover and tighten the bolts.

14 Reinstall the camshaft sprocket(s) and timing belt (see Section 8).

15 Run the engine and check for oil leaks at the camshaft seal.

10 Camshafts and lifters - removal, inspection and installation

➡**Note: Before beginning this procedure, obtain two 6 x 1.0 mm bolts 16 to 20 mm long. They will be referred to as service bolts in the text.**

REMOVAL

▶ **Refer to illustrations 10.3, 10.10, 10.12, 10.13 and 10.14**

1 Position the engine at TDC (see Section 3), then remove the valve covers (see Section 5), the timing belt and the camshaft sprocket (see Section 8).

2 The following steps apply to the removal of each of the four camshafts. On each head, the exhaust camshaft subgear is secured first, the intake cam removed, then the exhaust camshaft is removed.

3 Make sure the cam timing marks on the drive and driven gears are in alignment (see illustration).

10.3 Align the timing marks on the backside of the camshaft gears (typical markings)

10.10 Mark up a cardboard box to store the lifters/shims and camshaft bearing caps - use a separate box for each set to avoid mix-ups and mark the FRONT, INTAKE and EXHAUST orientation

10.12 With the hex portion of the camshaft held in a vise, use a two-pin spanner to remove the tension from the subgear and remove the service bolt, then release the subgear

10.13 Remove the snap-ring with a pair of snap-ring pliers

➡Note: On the right (rear) cylinder head, align the two dots on the intake camshaft gear with the two dots on the exhaust camshaft gear. On the left (front) cylinder head, align the one dot on the intake camshaft gear with the one dot on the exhaust camshaft gear.

4   Secure the exhaust camshaft sub-gear to the driven gear with a service bolt installed in the threaded hole (see illustration 10.12).

❋❋ CAUTION:

Since the camshaft thrust clearance is minimal, the camshafts must be held level as they are being removed. If they aren't, the portion of the cylinder head next to the cam gears may crack or be damaged by the gear leverage. Before lifting a camshaft out of the head, make certain that the torsional spring force of the sub-gear has been eliminated by the service bolt.

5   Loosen the intake camshaft bearing cap bolts in 1/4-turn increments until they can be removed by hand. Start with the outer caps and work inward.

6   Remove the bearing caps and gently lift out the intake camshaft. Be sure to keep it level.

7   Loosen the exhaust camshaft bearing cap bolts in 1/4-turn increments until they can be removed by hand. Start with the outer caps and work inward.

8   Remove the exhaust camshaft bearing caps and oil seal and gently lift out the exhaust camshaft. Be sure to keep it level.

9   Repeat the steps for the other cylinder head.

10   Store the bearing caps in the correct order.

➡Note: If necessary, the valve lifters and shims can now be removed with a magnetic tool. Be sure to store them separately so they can be reinstalled in their original locations (see illustration).

11   To disassemble an exhaust camshaft gear, mount the cam in a vise with the jaws gripping the large hex on the shaft.

12   Install a second service bolt in the unthreaded hole in the camshaft sub-gear. Using a screwdriver positioned against the service bolt just installed, rotate the sub-gear clockwise and remove the first service bolt. The second bolt isn't needed if you have a two-pin spanner (see illustration).

13   Remove the sub-gear snap-ring (see illustration).

14   The wave washer, sub-gear and camshaft gear spring can now be removed from the exhaust camshaft (see illustration). Be sure to keep

10.14 Remove the wave washer (1), the camshaft subgear (2) and the gear spring (3) - exhaust camshaft shown

the parts from the rear cylinder head cams separate from the front cylinder head parts. The front of the intake camshaft has the VVT assembly, which is secured to the camshaft with a large nut. To remove the VVT assembly, hold the hex portion of the camshaft in a vise and user a breaker bar and 46mm socket.

➡Note: The nut is a left-hand thread. Do NOT remove the nut or the VVT assembly unless either the camshaft or VVT assembly is to be replaced.

INSPECTION

15   Refer to Chapter 2, Part A for camshaft, lifter and related component inspection procedures. Be sure to use the Specifications in this Part of Chapter 2 for the V6 engines.

INSTALLATION

16   Reassemble the exhaust camshaft gear(s) by installing the camshaft gear spring, sub-gear, wave washer and snap-ring.

17   Mount the camshaft in a padded vise.

18   Insert a service bolt into the unthreaded hole in the camshaft subgear. Using a screwdriver, align the holes of the camshaft driven gear and sub-gear by turning the camshaft sub-gear clockwise. Install a second service bolt in the threaded hole, tightening it to clamp the

gears together. Remove the service bolt from the unthreaded hole. Repeat the procedure for the other exhaust camshaft.

19 Apply moly-base grease or engine assembly lube to the lifters, then install them in their original locations in the cylinder heads. Make sure the valve adjustment shims are in place in the lifters, and that all lifters are installed in their original bores.

20 Apply camshaft installation lubricant to the exhaust camshaft lobes, bearing journals and gear thrust faces.

21 Set the exhaust camshaft in place in the cylinder head with the timing mark on the subgear facing the center of the head.

22 Apply a thin coat of RTV sealant to the outer edges of the front bearing cap-to-cylinder head mating surfaces.

23 Install the bearing caps in numerical order with the arrows pointing toward the timing belt end of the engine.

24 Tighten the bearing cap bolts in 1/4-turn increments to the torque listed in this Chapter's Specifications. Start with the center cap and work your way out to the ends.

25 Refer to Section 9 and install a new camshaft oil seal.

26 Apply camshaft installation lubricant to the intake camshaft lobes, bearing journals and gear thrust faces. If the VVT assembly was removed from the intake camshaft, install it with its groove aligned with the pin on the camshaft. Oil the threads and install a new nut and torque to this Chapter's specifications.

27 Set the intake camshaft in place in the cylinder head, with the timing mark aligned with the exhaust camshaft timing mark (see illus-tration 10.3).

➡Note: On the right (rear) cylinder head, align the two dots on the intake camshaft gear with the two dots on the exhaust camshaft gear. On the left (front) cylinder head, align the one dot on the intake camshaft gear with the one dot on the exhaust camshaft gear.

28 Install the bearing caps in numerical order with the arrows pointing toward the front (timing belt end) of the engine.

29 Tighten the bearing cap bolts in 1/4-turn increments to the torque listed in this Chapter's Specifications. Start with the center cap and work your way out to the ends.

30 Remove the service bolt from the exhaust camshaft subgear.

31 Reinstall the timing belt rear cover, the camshaft sprockets and the timing belt (see Section 8). Before installation, inspect the gasket on the timing belt rear cover. If there is minor damage, repair it with RTV. If there are large sections missing, scrape off the old gasket and install a new one.

32 Reinstall the remaining components in the reverse order of removal.

33 Before reinstalling the valve covers, apply RTV sealant in the areas indicated (see illustration 5.8). Clean the rubber half-circle plugs for the back of the heads and reinstall with new RTV sealant.

34 The remainder of the installation is the reverse of the disassembly sequence.

35 Run the engine, then check for leaks and proper operation.

11 Cylinder heads - removal and installation

❄❄ WARNING:

Wait until the engine is completely cool before beginning this procedure.

REMOVAL

◆ Refer to illustrations 11.8 and 11.11

1 Disconnect the negative cable from the battery (see Chapter 5, Section 1).

2 Drain the cooling system, including the block (see Chapter 1).

3 Remove the air intake plenum and intake manifold (see Section 6).

4 Remove the exhaust manifold(s) (see Section 7).

5 Remove the alternator (see Chapter 5). Refer to Chapter 10 and unbolt and set aside the power steering pump.

6 Remove the timing belt, camshaft sprockets and upper idler pulley (see Section 8).

➡Note: If the timing belt is not being replaced at the time the heads are removed, the timing belt and lower timing belt cover don't have to be completely removed. Follow the Steps in Section 8, marking the belt location at the lower cover at TDC, and removing the belt only from the camshaft sprockets and idler pulley.

7 Remove the bolts holding the number 3 timing belt cover.

8 Disconnect the coolant sensor connectors and remove the water transfer casting (see illustration).

9 Remove the camshaft(s) from the head(s) you intend to remove (see Section 10). Disconnect the electrical connectors from the VVT sensors and the timing oil control valve (see Section 4).

10 Remove the bolts at the rear of the cylinder heads and move the

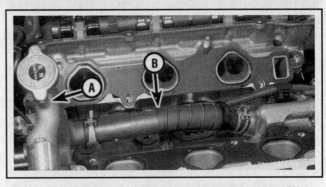

11.8 Remove the bolts and the coolant transfer casting (A) - the transfer hose (B) should be replaced whenever the intake manifold is removed

engine wiring harnesses away from the heads.

11 Using an 8 mm hex bit or Allen wrench, remove the recessed head bolts (one in each head) (see illustration).

11.11 Remove the recessed bolt with an 8 mm hex bit socket

11.20 Be sure the new head gaskets are positioned right side up (check all holes and coolant passages for correct alignment) and over the block dowels

12 Using a 12-point socket, loosen the rest of the cylinder head bolts in 1/4-turn increments until they can be removed by hand, along with their hardened washers. Follow the reverse order of the recommended tightening sequence (see illustration 11.23).

13 Lift the cylinder head off the engine block. If the head is stuck, place a wood block against it and strike the wood with a hammer.

✳✳ CAUTION:

Don't pry between the head and block. The gasket surfaces may be damaged and leaks could result.

14 Repeat the procedure for the other head.

INSTALLATION

▶ **Refer to illustrations 11.20 and 11.23**

15 The mating surfaces of the cylinder heads and block must be perfectly clean when the heads are installed.

16 Use a gasket scraper to remove all traces of carbon and old gasket material, then clean the mating surfaces with lacquer thinner or acetone. If there's oil on the mating surfaces when the head is installed, the gasket may not seal correctly and leaks could develop. When working on the block, stuff the cylinders with clean shop rags to keep out debris. Use a vacuum cleaner to remove material that falls into the cylinders.

17 Check the block and head mating surfaces for nicks, deep scratches and other damage. If damage is slight, it can be removed with a file; if it's excessive, machining may be the only alternative.

18 Use a tap of the correct size to chase the threads in the cylinder head bolt holes, then clean the holes with compressed air - make sure that nothing remains in the holes.

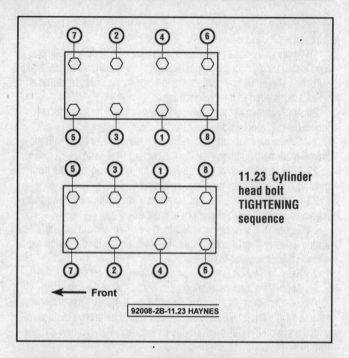

11.23 Cylinder head bolt TIGHTENING sequence

◀— **Front**

92008-2B-11.23 HAYNES

✳✳ WARNING:

Wear eye protection when using compressed air!

19 Mount each bolt in a vise and run a die down the threads to remove corrosion and restore the threads. Dirt, corrosion, sealant and damaged threads will affect torque readings.

20 Position the new gaskets over the dowel pins in the block (see illustration).

21 Carefully set the head on the block without disturbing the gasket.

22 Before installing the head bolts, apply a small amount of clean engine oil to the threads.

23 Install the bolts in their original locations and tighten them finger tight. Following the recommended sequence, tighten the bolts to the torque listed in this Chapter's Specifications (see illustration). Don't tighten the recessed bolt at this time.

24 Mark the front of each bolt head with paint. You can also mark the socket you are using. Place the socket over the 12-point bolt so that you can observe the mark.

25 Following the same sequence, tighten each 12-point bolt an additional 1/4-turn (90-degrees) (see illustration 11.23).

26 Tighten the recessed bolt to the torque listed in this Chapter's Specifications.

27 Repeat the entire procedure to install the other cylinder head.

28 The remaining installation steps are the reverse of removal.

29 Refill the cooling system, change the oil and filter (see Chapter 1), run the engine and check for leaks.

12 Oil pan - removal and installation

REMOVAL

♦ **Refer to illustrations 12.7, 12.8 and 12.9**

1 Remove the hood (see Chapter 11).
2 Disconnect the negative cable from the battery (see Chapter 5, Section 1).
3 Raise the vehicle and support it securely on jackstands.
4 Remove the engine splash shields.
5 Drain the engine oil and remove the oil filter. The oil pan on the V6 engine is a two-part assembly, with an aluminum casting attached to the block and transaxle, and a lower stamped-steel pan section at the bottom.
6 Disconnect the front exhaust pipe from the catalytic converter, the two bolts and the support bracket, and the nuts holding the pipe to the front and rear exhaust manifolds (see Chapter 4 and Section 6).
7 Remove the flywheel housing cover (see illustration).
8 Remove the two bolts holding the aluminum oil pan section to the transaxle (see illustration).
9 Remove the ten bolts and two nuts securing the steel oil pan section, and detach the steel pan (see illustration). If it's stuck, pry it loose very carefully with a small screwdriver or putty knife. Don't damage the mating surfaces of the pan or oil leaks could develop.
10 Remove the oil pump strainer/pickup (see illustration 13.4).
11 Remove the bolts securing the aluminum oil pan section to the block.

➡**Note: Some bolts are within the area formerly covered by the steel pan.**

12 Remove the oil pan baffle plate, if equipped.

INSTALLATION

♦ **Refer to illustration 12.18**

13 Use a scraper to remove all traces of old sealant from the block and oil pan. Clean the mating surfaces with lacquer thinner or acetone.
14 Make sure the threaded bolt holes in the block are clean.
15 Check the flange of the steel pan section for distortion, particularly around the bolt holes. If necessary, place the pan on a wood block and use a hammer to flatten and restore the gasket surface.

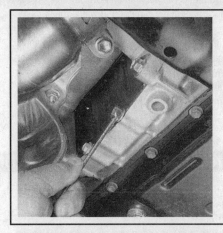

12.7 Remove two bolts and the flywheel housing cover

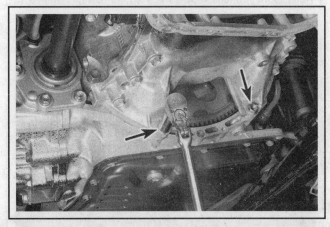

12.8 Remove the two bolts securing the aluminum upper pan to the transaxle

16 If the baffle had been removed, reinstall it now.
17 Clean the mating surfaces of the engine block and aluminum pan section, being careful not to gouge the soft metal, which could lead to leaks.
18 Apply a 4 mm wide bead of RTV sealant to the aluminum pan section (see illustration).

12.9 Remove the steel section of the oil pan

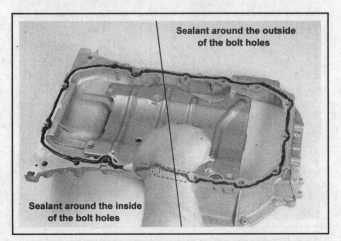

Sealant around the outside of the bolt holes

Sealant around the inside of the bolt holes

12.18 Apply the bead of RTV sealant around the perimeter of the aluminum pan section as shown

19 Install the aluminum pan section within five minutes and uniformly tighten the bolts to the torque listed in this Chapter's Specifications in several passes. Work from the center out towards the ends of the pan.

20 Inspect the oil pump pick-up/strainer assembly for cracks and a blocked strainer. If the pick-up was removed, clean it with solvent or thinner and install it now, using a new gasket (see Section 13). Tighten the fasteners to the torque listed in this Chapter's Specifications.

21 Apply a 3 to 4 mm wide bead of RTV sealant to the flange of the steel oil pan section.

➡️**Note: The steel pan section must be installed within five minutes once the sealant has been applied.**

22 Carefully position the steel pan on the aluminum section and install the bolts. Working from the center out, tighten them to the torque listed in this Chapter's Specifications in three or four steps.

23 The remainder of installation is the reverse of removal. Allow the sealant to set for at least two hours before adding new oil and a new oil filter.

24 Run the engine and check for oil pressure and leaks.

13 Oil pump - removal, inspection and installation

REMOVAL

▶ **Refer to illustrations 13.4, 13.7, 13.8, 13.9, 13.11 and 13.12**

1 Remove the oil pan (see Section 12).

2 Remove the timing belt (see Section 8) and lower timing belt idler pulley.

3 Remove the crankshaft sprocket (see Section 8). Place a jack under the engine. Remove the mounting nuts for the engine insulator and raise the engine, then remove the insulator.

4 Remove the oil pick-up tube (see illustration).

5 Remove the alternator and its bracket (see Chapter 5).

6 Unbolt the air conditioning compressor and set it aside without disconnecting the refrigerant lines.

7 Remove the compressor bracket (see illustration).

8 Remove the power steering pump adjusting bar and pry the pump away from the oil pump body (see illustration).

9 Remove the lower timing belt idler pulley (see illustration).

10 Remove the bolts and detach the oil pump from the engine. You may have to pry carefully between the front main bearing cap and the

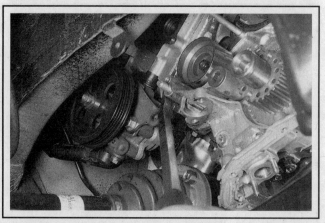

13.4 The oil pick-up tube is held in place with three fasteners

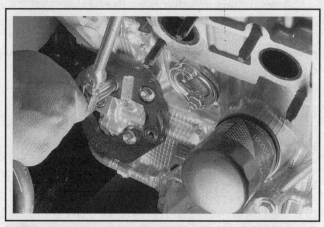

13.7 Unbolt the air conditioning compressor bracket from the block

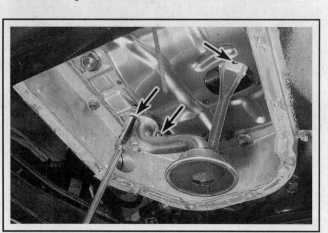

13.8 Remove the power steering pump adjuster bar and pry the pump away from the oil pump body

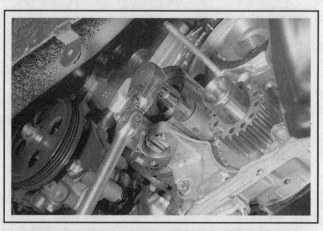

13.9 Using a 10 mm hex bit or Allen wrench, remove the lower timing belt idler pulley stud

13.11 Remove the oil pressure relief plug, spring and valve

13.12 Use a large Phillips screwdriver or bit to remove the screws retaining the pump cover

pump body with a screwdriver.

11 Remove the O-ring. Remove the oil pressure relief valve snap-ring, retainer, spring and valve (see illustration).

※※ WARNING:

The spring is tightly compressed - be careful and wear eye protection.

12 Use a large Phillips screwdriver to remove the screws retaining the body cover to the rear of the oil pump (see illustration).

13 Lift the cover off and remove the pump rotors.

14 Use a scraper to remove all traces of sealant and old gasket material from the pump body and engine block, then clean the mating surfaces with lacquer thinner or acetone.

INSPECTION

▶ **Refer to illustrations 13.17a, 13.17b and 13.17c**

15 Clean all components with solvent, then inspect them for wear and damage.

16 Check the oil pressure relief valve sliding surface and valve spring. If either the spring or the valve is damaged, they must be replaced as a set.

17 Check the clearance of the following components with a feeler

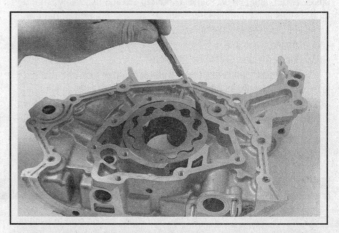

13.17a Measure the driven rotor-to-body clearance with a feeler gauge

gauge and compare the measurements to this Chapter's Specifications (see illustrations):

a) Driven rotor-to-oil pump body clearance
b) Rotor side clearance
c) Rotor tip clearance

13.17b Measure the rotor side clearance with a precision straightedge and feeler gauge

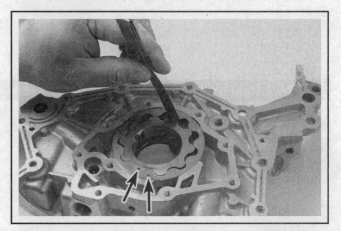

13.17c Measure the rotor tip clearance with a feeler gauge - note the rotor marks are facing out (when the pump body cover is installed, the marks will be against the cover)

INSTALLATION

▶ **Refer to illustration 13.26**

18 Pry the old crankshaft seal out with a screwdriver.

19 Apply multi-purpose grease or engine oil to the outer edge of the new seal and carefully drive it into place with a seal driver and a hammer. Also apply multi-purpose grease to the seal lip.

20 Place the drive and driven rotors into the pump body with the marks facing out (see illustration 13.17c).

21 Pack the pump cavity with petroleum jelly and install the cover. Tighten the screws securely following a criss-cross pattern.

22 Lubricate the oil pressure relief valve with engine oil and install the valve components in the pump body.

23 Use acetone or lacquer thinner and a clean rag to remove all traces of oil from the gasket surfaces.

24 Apply a 2 to 3 mm wide bead of anaerobic sealant to the oil pump. Avoid using an excessive amount of sealant, especially around oil passages and bolt holes. Assembly must be completed within five minutes of sealant application, otherwise the material must be removed and reapplied.

25 Position a new O-ring on the block.

26 Engage the spline teeth on the oil pump drive rotor with the large teeth on the crankshaft and slide the pump into place (see illustration).

27 Install the oil pump mounting bolts in their original locations and tighten them to the torque listed in this Chapter's Specifications in a

13.26 Be sure to install a new O-ring on the block, and align the drive rotor and the crankshaft as the oil pump is installed

criss-cross pattern.

28 Using a new gasket, install the oil pick-up tube and tighten the fasteners to the torque listed in this Chapter's Specifications.

29 Reinstall the remaining parts in the reverse order of removal.

30 Add oil, start the engine and check for oil leaks.

31 Recheck the engine oil level.

4 Flywheel/driveplate - removal and installation

Refer to Chapter 2, Part A for this procedure, but be sure to use the torque specifications in this Part of Chapter 2 for the V6 engine.

On V6 engines, there are two spacers used in driveplate mounting, one between the crankshaft flange and the driveplate, the other between the rear face of the driveplate and the driveplate mounting bolts. When removing the driveplate, mark the spacers and reinstall them in the same positions and facing the same way as originally installed.

15 Rear main oil seal - replacement

Refer to Chapter 2, Part A for this procedure, but note that the V6 engine doesn't have a gasket between the seal retainer and the engine block. Instead, apply a 2 to 3 mm wide bead of anaerobic sealant to the retainer flange before attaching the retainer to the block. Also, be sure to use the torque specifications in this Part of Chapter 2 for the V6 engine.

6 Powertrain mounts - check and replacement

1 Refer to Chapter 2, Part A, but note that the V6 engine mounts are slightly different in ways that don't significantly affect the check and replacement procedures.

2 The basic arrangement and construction of the three engine mounts is very similar to the four-cylinder model, except that the engine movement control rod assembly has two stays, one mounted on either side of the bracket on the engine (see illustration 8.9).

Specifications

General

Engine designations	1MZ-FE and 3MZ-FE
Displacement	
1MZ-FE	183 cubic inches (3.0 liters)
3MZ-FE	202 cubic inches (3.3 liters)
Cylinder numbers (timing belt end-to-transaxle end)	
Right (firewall) side	1-3-5
Left (radiator) side	2-4-6
Firing order	1-2-3-4-5-6

Cylinder numbering and coil terminal locations (early models have three coils on the front cylinder bank and spark plug wires running from them to the rear cylinder bank; later models have one individual coil per cylinder)

Cylinder head

Warpage limits	
Cylinder head	0.0039 inch
Intake manifold	0.0031 inch
Exhaust manifolds	0.0196 inch

Camshaft and related components

Valve clearance (engine cold)	
Intake	0.006 to 0.010 inch
Exhaust	0.010 to 0.014 inch
Bearing journal diameter	
Intake	1.0614 to 1.0620 inches
Exhaust	1.0613 to 1.0620 inches
Bearing oil clearance	
Standard	
Intake #4 and #5	0.0010 to 0.0022 inch
All others	0.0010 to 0.0024 inch
Service limit	0.0039 inch
Lobe height	
2002 through 2004 models	
Intake	
Standard	1.6579 to 1.6618 inches
Service limit (minimum)	1.6520 inches
Exhaust	
Standard	1.6520 to 1.6559 inches
Service limit (minimum)	1.6461 inches
2005 and later models	
Intake	1.6921 to 1.7020 inches
Exhaust	1.6874 to 1.6972 inches
Service limit (minimum)	Not available
Thrust clearance (endplay)	
Standard	
2002 models	0.0016 to 0.0035 inch
Later models	0.0016 to 0.0047 inch
Service limit	0.0047 inch
Runout limit (total indicator reading)	0.0024 inch

Camshaft and related components (continued)

Camshaft gear backlash
    Standard   0.0008 to 0.0079 inch
    Service limit   0.0188 inch
Timing belt tensioner protrusion   0.394 to 0.425 inch
Lifters
    Outside diameter   1.2191 to 1.2195 inches
    Bore diameter   1.2205 to 1.2211 inches
    Lifter-to-bore (oil) clearance
        Standard   0.0009 to 0.0020 inch
        Service limit   0.0028 inch

Oil pump

Driven rotor-to-pump body clearance
    Standard   0.0050 to 0.0064 inch
    Service limit   0.0118 inch
Rotor tip clearance
    Standard   0.0043 to 0.0094 inch
    Service limit   0.0138 inch
Rotor side clearance
    Standard   0.0012 to 0.0035 inch
    Service limit   0.0059 inch

Torque specifications   Ft-lbs (unless otherwise indicated)

➡ **Note: One foot-pound (ft-lb) of torque is equivalent to 12 inch-pounds (in-lbs) of torque. Torque values below approximately 15 ft-lbs are expressed in inch-pounds, since most foot-pound torque wrenches are not accurate at these smaller values.**

Air conditioning compressor bracket mounting bolts	19
Intake manifold bolts/nuts	132 in-lbs
Intake plenum bolts/nuts	32
Intake plenum brace bolts	168 in-lbs
Exhaust manifold nuts	36
Crankshaft pulley bolt	159
Timing belt cover bolts (no. 3)	76 in-lbs
Idler pulley bolts	
No. 1 (to block)	25
No. 2 (to bracket)	32
Timing belt tensioner bolts	20
Camshaft pulley bolts	92
Camshaft bearing cap bolts	144 in-lbs
Cylinder head bolts (12-point)	
Step 1	40
Step 2	Tighten an additional 90-degrees (1/4-turn)
Cylinder head bolt (recessed)	168 in-lbs
Oil pan bolts	
Aluminum section	
10 mm bolt head	71 in-lbs
12 mm bolt head	15
14 mm bolt head	27
Steel section	71 in-lbs

Torque specifications (continued)   Ft-lbs (unless otherwise indicated)

➡Note: One foot-pound (ft-lb) of torque is equivalent to 12 inch-pounds (in-lbs) of torque. Torque values below approximately 15 ft-lbs are expressed in inch-pounds, since most foot-pound torque wrenches are not accurate at these smaller values.

Oil pump mounting bolts	
10 mm bolt head	71 in-lbs
12 mm bolt head	15
14 mm bolt head	32
Oil pick-up tube mounting bolts	69 in-lbs
Flywheel/driveplate bolts*	61
Rear crankshaft oil seal retainer mounting bolts	69 in-lbs
Shock tower brace nuts	59
Valve cover nuts	71 in-lbs
Variable Valve Timing (VVT) system	
Oil control valve filter plug	33
Oil control valve hold-down bolt	71 in-lbs
Camshaft sprocket/actuator assembly retaining nut	**111
Engine mounts	
Engine movement control rod mounting bolts	47
Front engine mount	
To engine	64
To frame	38
Right engine mount	
To bracket	70
To frame	64
Left (transaxle) mount insulator nut	70

*   Apply thread locking compound to the threads prior to installation

** Reverse-threaded.

Notes

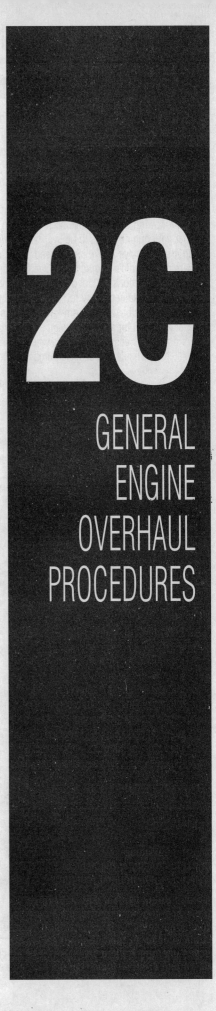

2C

GENERAL
ENGINE
OVERHAUL
PROCEDURES

Section

1 General information - engine overhaul
2 Oil pressure check
3 Cylinder compression check
4 Vacuum gauge diagnostic checks
5 Engine rebuilding alternatives
6 Engine removal - methods and precautions
7 Engine - removal and installation
8 Engine overhaul - disassembly sequence
9 Pistons and connecting rods - removal and installation
10 Crankshaft - removal and installation
11 Engine overhaul - reassembly sequence
12 Initial start-up and break-in after overhaul

Reference to other Chapters

Oil pan - removal and installation - See Chapter 2B

Oil pump - removal and installation - See Chapter 2B

1 General information - engine overhaul

▶ **Refer to illustrations 1.1, 1.2, 1.3, 1.4, 1.5 and 1.6**

Included in this portion of Chapter 2 are general information and diagnostic testing procedures for determining the overall mechanical condition of your engine.

The information ranges from advice concerning preparation for an overhaul and the purchase of replacement parts and/or components to detailed, step-by-step procedures covering removal and installation.

The following Sections have been written to help you determine whether your engine needs to be overhauled and how to remove and install it once you've determined it needs to be rebuilt. For information concerning in-vehicle engine repair, see Chapter 2A or 2B.

The Specifications included in this Part are general in nature and include only those necessary for testing the oil pressure, checking the engine compression, and bottom-end torque specifications. Refer to Chapter 2A or 2B for additional engine Specifications.

It's not always easy to determine when, or if, an engine should be completely overhauled, because a number of factors must be considered.

High mileage is not necessarily an indication that an overhaul is needed, while low mileage doesn't preclude the need for an overhaul. Frequency of servicing is probably the most important consideration. An engine that's had regular and frequent oil and filter changes, as well as other required maintenance, will most likely give many thousands of miles of reliable service. Conversely, a neglected engine may require an overhaul very early in its service life.

Excessive oil consumption is an indication that piston rings, valve seals and/or valve guides are in need of attention. Make sure that oil leaks aren't responsible before deciding that the rings and/or guides are bad. Perform a cylinder compression check to determine the extent of the work required (see Section 3). Also check the vacuum readings under various conditions (see Section 4).

Check the oil pressure with a gauge installed in place of the oil pressure sending unit and compare it to this Chapter's Specifications (see Section 2). If it's extremely low, the bearings and/or oil pump are probably worn out.

Loss of power, rough running, knocking or metallic engine noises, excessive valve train noise and high fuel consumption rates may also point to the need for an overhaul, especially if they're all present at the same time. If a complete tune-up doesn't remedy the situation, major mechanical work is the only solution.

An engine overhaul involves restoring the internal parts to the specifications of a new engine. During an overhaul, the piston rings are replaced and the cylinder walls are reconditioned (rebored and/or honed) (see illustrations 1.1 and 1.2). If a rebore is done by an automotive machine shop, new oversize pistons will also be installed. The main bearings, connecting rod bearings and camshaft bearings are generally replaced with new ones and, if necessary, the crankshaft may be reground to restore the journals (see illustration 1.3). Generally, the

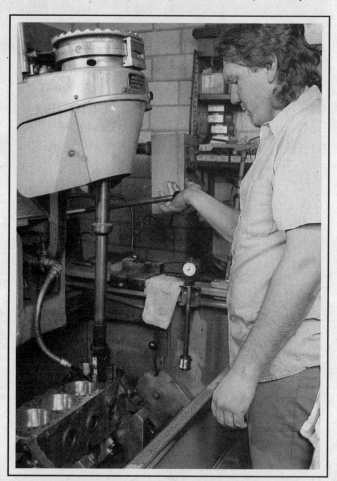

1.1 An engine block being bored - an engine rebuilder will use special machinery to recondition the cylinder bores

1.2 If the cylinders are bored, the machine shop will normally hone the engine on a machine like this

valves are serviced as well, since they're usually in less-than-perfect condition at this point. While the engine is being overhauled, other components, such as the distributor, starter and alternator, can be rebuilt as well. The end result should be a like-new engine that will give many trouble-free miles.

➡**Note: Critical cooling system components such as the hoses, drivebelts, thermostat and water pump should be replaced with new parts when an engine is overhauled. The radiator should be checked carefully to ensure that it isn't clogged or leaking (see Chapter 3). If you purchase a rebuilt engine or short block, some rebuilders will not warranty their engines unless the radiator has been professionally flushed. Also, we don't recommend overhauling the oil pump - always install a new one when an engine is rebuilt.**

Overhauling the internal components on today's engines is a difficult and time-consuming task which requires a significant amount of specialty tools and is best left to a professional engine rebuilder (see illustrations 1.4, 1.5 and 1.6). A competent engine rebuilder will handle the inspection of your old parts and offer advice concerning the reconditioning or replacement of the original engine. Never purchase parts or have machine work done on other components until the block has been thoroughly inspected by a professional machine shop. As a general rule, time is the primary cost of an overhaul, especially since the vehicle may be tied up for a minimum of two weeks or more. Be aware that some engine builders only have the capability to rebuild the

1.3 A crankshaft having a main bearing journal ground

engine you bring them while other rebuilders have a large inventory of rebuilt exchange engines in stock. Also be aware that many machine shops could take as much as two weeks time to completely rebuild your engine depending on shop workload. Sometimes it makes more sense to simply exchange your engine for another engine that's already rebuilt to save time.

1.4 A machinist checks for a bent connecting rod, using specialized equipment

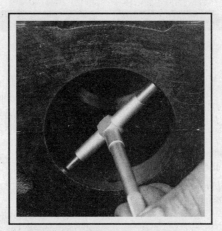

1.5 A bore gauge being used to check the main bearing bore

1.6 Uneven piston wear like this indicates a bent connecting rod

2 Oil pressure check

▶ **Refer to illustrations 2.2a, 2.2b and 2.3**

1   Low engine oil pressure can be a sign of an engine in need of rebuilding. A "low oil pressure" indicator (often called an "idiot light") is not a test of the oiling system. Such indicators only come on when the oil pressure is dangerously low. Even a factory oil pressure gauge in the instrument panel is only a relative indication, although much better for driver information than a warning light. A better test is with a mechanical (not electrical) oil pressure gauge.

2   Locate the oil pressure indicator sending unit on the engine block (see illustrations).

2.2a On four-cylinder models, the oil-pressure sending unit is located at the end of the cylinder head on the driver's side

2.2b On V6 models, the oil pressure sending unit is located at the front of the engine, above the crankshaft position sensor

2.3 The oil pressure can be checked by removing the sending unit and installing a pressure gauge in its place

3   Unscrew and remove the oil pressure sending unit and then screw in the hose for your oil pressure gauge (see illustration). If necessary, install an adapter fitting. Use Teflon tape or thread sealant on the threads of the adapter and/or the fitting on the end of your gauge's hose.

4   Connect an accurate tachometer to the engine, according to the tachometer manufacturer's instructions.

5   Check the oil pressure with the engine running (normal operating temperature) at the specified engine speed, and compare it to this Chapter's Specifications. If it's extremely low, the bearings and/or oil pump are probably worn out.

3   Cylinder compression check

Refer to illustration 3.6

1   A compression check will tell you what mechanical condition the upper end of your engine (pistons, rings, valves, head gaskets) is in. Specifically, it can tell you if the compression is down due to leakage caused by worn piston rings, defective valves and seats or a blown head gasket.

→**Note: The engine must be at normal operating temperature and the battery must be fully charged for this check.**

2   Begin by cleaning the area around the spark plugs before you remove them (compressed air should be used, if available). The idea is to prevent dirt from getting into the cylinders as the compression check is being done.

3   Remove all of the spark plugs from the engine (see Chapter 1).

4   Block the throttle wide open.

5   Disable the ignition system by disconnecting the electrical connectors from the igniter/ignition coil assemblies (see Chapter 5). The fuel pump circuit should also be disabled by removing the circuit opening relay (C/OPN) from the fuse/relay center in the engine compartment (see Chapter 4).

6   Install a compression gauge in the spark plug hole (see illustration).

7   Crank the engine over at least seven compression strokes and watch the gauge. The compression should build up quickly in a healthy engine. Low compression on the first stroke, followed by gradually increasing pressure on successive strokes, indicates worn piston rings. A low compression reading on the first stroke, which doesn't build up during successive strokes, indicates leaking valves or a blown head gasket (a cracked head could also be the cause). Deposits on the undersides of the valve heads can also cause low compression. Record the highest gauge reading obtained.

8   Repeat the procedure for the remaining cylinders and compare the results to this Chapter's Specifications.

9   Add some engine oil (about three squirts from a plunger-type oil can) to each cylinder, through the spark plug hole, and repeat the test.

10 If the compression increases after the oil is added, the piston rings are definitely worn. If the compression doesn't increase significantly, the leakage is occurring at the valves or head gasket. Leakage past the valves may be caused by burned valve seats and/or faces or warped, cracked or bent valves.

11 If two adjacent cylinders have equally low compression, there's a strong possibility that the head gasket between them is blown. The appearance of coolant in the combustion chambers or the crankcase would verify this condition.

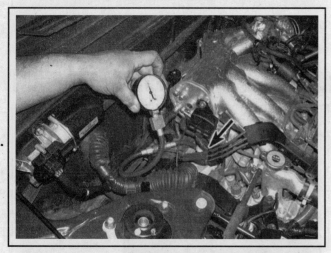

3.6 Use a compression gauge with a threaded fitting for the spark plug hole, not the type that requires hand pressure to maintain the seal - be sure to open the throttle valve as far as possible during the test

12 If one cylinder is slightly lower than the others, and the engine has a slightly rough idle, a worn lobe on the camshaft could be the cause.

13 If the compression is unusually high, the combustion chambers are probably coated with carbon deposits. If that's the case, the cylinder head(s) should be removed and decarbonized.

14 If compression is way down or varies greatly between cylinders, it would be a good idea to have a leak-down test performed by an automotive repair shop. This test will pinpoint exactly where the leakage is occurring and how severe it is.

4 Vacuum gauge diagnostic checks

♦ Refer to illustrations 4.4 and 4.6

1 A vacuum gauge provides inexpensive but valuable information about what is going on in the engine. You can check for worn rings or cylinder walls, leaking head or intake manifold gaskets, incorrect carburetor adjustments, restricted exhaust, stuck or burned valves, weak valve springs, improper ignition or valve timing and ignition problems.

2 Unfortunately, vacuum gauge readings are easy to misinterpret, so they should be used in conjunction with other tests to confirm the diagnosis.

3 Both the absolute readings and the rate of needle movement are important for accurate interpretation. Most gauges measure vacuum in inches of mercury (in-Hg). The following references to vacuum assume the diagnosis is being performed at sea level. As elevation increases (or atmospheric pressure decreases), the reading will decrease. For every 1,000 foot increase in elevation above approximately 2000 feet, the gauge readings will decrease about one inch of mercury.

4.4 A simple vacuum gauge can be handy in diagnosing engine condition and performance

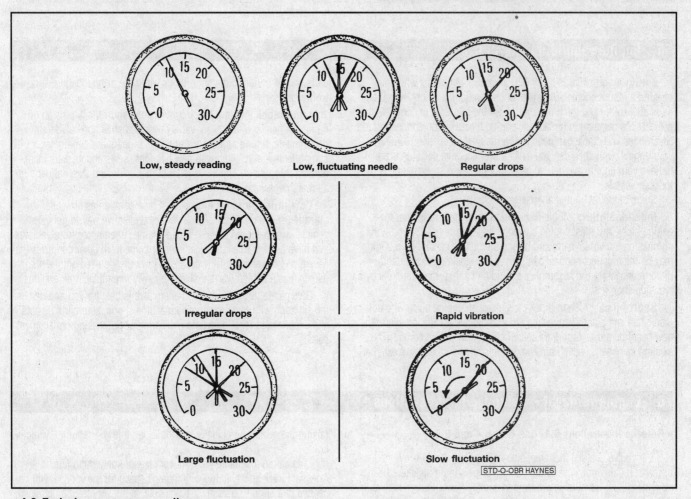

4.6 Typical vacuum gauge readings

4   Connect the vacuum gauge directly to the intake manifold vacuum, not to ported (throttle body) vacuum (see illustration). Be sure no hoses are left disconnected during the test or false readings will result.

5   Before you begin the test, allow the engine to warm up completely. Block the wheels and set the parking brake. With the transmission in Park, start the engine and allow it to run at normal idle speed.

❋❋ WARNING:

Keep your hands and the vacuum gauge clear of the fans.

6   Read the vacuum gauge; an average, healthy engine should normally produce about 17 to 22 in-Hg with a fairly steady needle (see illustration). Refer to the following vacuum gauge readings and what they indicate about the engine's condition:

7   A low steady reading usually indicates a leaking gasket between the intake manifold and cylinder head(s) or throttle body, a leaky vacuum hose, late ignition timing or incorrect camshaft timing. Check ignition timing with a timing light and eliminate all other possible causes, utilizing the tests provided in this Chapter before you remove the timing chain cover to check the timing marks.

8   If the reading is three to eight inches below normal and it fluctuates at that low reading, suspect an intake manifold gasket leak at an intake port or a faulty fuel injector.

9   If the needle has regular drops of about two-to-four inches at a steady rate, the valves are probably leaking. Perform a compression check or leak-down test to confirm this.

10 An irregular drop or down-flick of the needle can be caused by a sticking valve or an ignition misfire. Perform a compression check or leak-down test and read the spark plugs.

11 A rapid vibration of about four in-Hg vibration at idle combined with exhaust smoke indicates worn valve guides. Perform a leak-down test to confirm this. If the rapid vibration occurs with an increase in engine speed, check for a leaking intake manifold gasket or head gasket, weak valve springs, burned valves or ignition misfire.

12 A slight fluctuation, say one inch up and down, may mean ignition problems. Check all the usual tune-up items and, if necessary, run the engine on an ignition analyzer.

13 If there is a large fluctuation, perform a compression or leak-down test to look for a weak or dead cylinder or a blown head gasket.

14 If the needle moves slowly through a wide range, check for a clogged PCV system, incorrect idle fuel mixture, throttle body or intake manifold gasket leaks.

15 Check for a slow return after revving the engine by quickly snapping the throttle open until the engine reaches about 2,500 rpm and let it shut. Normally the reading should drop to near zero, rise above normal idle reading (about 5 in-Hg over) and then return to the previous idle reading. If the vacuum returns slowly and doesn't peak when the throttle is snapped shut, the rings may be worn. If there is a long delay, look for a restricted exhaust system (often the muffler or catalytic converter). An easy way to check this is to temporarily disconnect the exhaust ahead of the suspected part and redo the test.

5   Engine rebuilding alternatives

The do-it-yourselfer is faced with a number of options when purchasing a rebuilt engine. The major considerations are cost, warranty, parts availability and the time required for the rebuilder to complete the project. The decision to replace the engine block, piston/connecting rod assemblies and crankshaft depends on the final inspection results of your engine. Only then can you make a cost effective decision whether to have your engine overhauled or simply purchase an exchange engine for your vehicle.

Some of the rebuilding alternatives include:

Individual parts - If the inspection procedures reveal that the engine block and most engine components are in reusable condition, purchasing individual parts and having a rebuilder rebuild your engine may be the most economical alternative. The block, crankshaft and piston/connecting rod assemblies should all be inspected carefully by a machine shop first.

Short block - A short block consists of an engine block with a crankshaft and piston/connecting rod assemblies already installed. All new bearings are incorporated and all clearances will be correct. The existing camshafts, valve train components, cylinder head and external parts can be bolted to the short block with little or no machine shop work necessary.

Long block - A long block consists of a short block plus an oil pump, oil pan, cylinder head, valve cover, camshaft and valve train components, timing sprockets and chain or gears and timing cover. All components are installed with new bearings, seals and gaskets incorporated throughout. The installation of manifolds and external parts is all that's necessary.

Low mileage used engines - Some companies now offer low mileage used engines which is a very cost effective way to get your vehicle up and running again. These engines often come from vehicles that have been in totaled in accidents or come from other countries that have a higher vehicle turn over rate. A low mileage used engine also usually has a similar warranty like the newly remanufactured engines.

Give careful thought to which alternative is best for you and discuss the situation with local automotive machine shops, auto parts dealers and experienced rebuilders before ordering or purchasing replacement parts.

6   Engine removal - methods and precautions

▶ **Refer to illustrations 6.1, 6.2, 6.3, 6.4 and 6.5**

If you've decided that an engine must be removed for overhaul or major repair work, several preliminary steps should be taken. Read all removal and installation procedures carefully prior to committing this job. Some engines are removed by lowering to the floor and then raising the vehicle sufficiently to slide it out; this will require a vehicle hoist.

Locating a suitable place to work is extremely important. Adequate work space, along with storage space for the vehicle, will be needed. If a shop or garage isn't available, at the very least a flat, level, clean work surface made of concrete or asphalt is required.

6.1 After tightly wrapping water-vulnerable components, use a spray cleaner on everything, with particular concentration on the greasiest areas, usually around the valve cover and lower edges of the block. If one section dries out, apply more cleaner

6.2 Depending on how dirty the engine is, let the cleaner soak in according to the directions and then hose off the grime and cleaner. Get the rinse water down into every area you can get at; then dry important components with a hair dryer or paper towels

Cleaning the engine compartment and engine before beginning the removal procedure will help keep tools clean and organized (see illustrations 6.1 and 6.2).

An engine hoist or A-frame will also be necessary. Make sure the equipment is rated in excess of the combined weight of the engine and transmission. Safety is of primary importance, considering the potential hazards involved in lifting the engine out of the vehicle.

If you're a novice at engine removal, get at least one helper. One person cannot easily do all the things you need to do to lift a big heavy

6.4 Get an engine stand sturdy enough to firmly support the engine while you're working on it. Stay away from three-wheeled models: they have a tendency to tip over more easily, so get a four-wheeled unit

6.3 Get an engine hoist that's strong enough to easily lift your engine in and out of the engine compartment; an adapter, like the one shown here (arrow), can be used to change the angle of the engine as it's being removed or installed

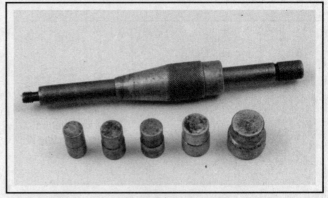

6.5 A clutch alignment tool is necessary if you plan to install a rebuilt engine mated to a manual transmission

engine out of the engine compartment. Also helpful is to seek advice and assistance from someone who's experienced in engine removal.

Plan the operation ahead of time. Arrange for or obtain all of the tools and equipment you'll need prior to beginning the job (see illustrations 6.3, 6.4 and 6.5). some of the equipment necessary to perform engine removal and installation safely and with relative ease are (in addition to an engine hoist) a heavy duty floor jack, complete sets of wrenches and sockets as described in the front of this manual, wooden blocks, plenty of rags and cleaning solvent for mopping up spilled oil, coolant and gasoline. If the hoist must be rented, make sure that you arrange for it in advance and have everything disconnected and/or removed before bringing the hoist home. This will save you money and time.

Plan for the vehicle to be out of use for quite a while. A machine shop can do the work that is beyond the scope of the home mechanic. Machine shops often have a busy schedule, so before removing the engine, consult the shop for an estimate of how long it will take to rebuild or repair the components that may need work.

7 Engine - removal and installation

→Note 1: **Engine removal on these vehicles is a difficult job, especially for the do-it-yourself mechanic working at home. Because of the vehicle's design, the manufacturer states that the engine and transaxle have to be removed as a unit from the bottom of the vehicle, not the top. With a floor jack and jackstands, the vehicle can't be raised high enough or supported safely enough for the engine/transaxle assembly to slide out from underneath. The manufacturer recommends that removal of the engine/transaxle assembly only be performed with the use of a frame-contact type vehicle hoist.**

→Note 2: **Keep in mind that during this procedure you'll have to adjust the height of the vehicle with the vehicle hoist to perform certain operations.**

REMOVAL

▶ **Refer to illustration 7.13**

1 Park the vehicle on a frame-contact type vehicle hoist, then engage the arms of the hoist with the jacking points of the vehicle. Raise the hoist arms until they contact the vehicle, but not so much that the wheels come off the ground.

2 Relieve the fuel system pressure (see Chapter 4).

3 Remove the battery and battery tray (see Chapter 5).

4 Remove the air filter housing and air intake duct (see Chapter 4).

5 Disconnect the accelerator cable(s) from the throttle body (see Chapter 4).

6 Disconnect the cruise control cable from the throttle body, if equipped.

7 Disconnect the shift cable(s) from the transaxle (see Chapter 7A or 7B).

8 If you're working on a model with a manual transaxle, remove the clutch release cylinder (see Chapter 8).

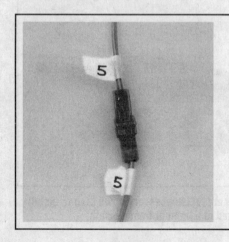

7.13 Label both ends of each wire or hose before disconnecting it

9 Remove the alternator (see Chapter 5).

10 Remove the air conditioning compressor without disconnecting the refrigerant lines (see Chapter 3). Tie the compressor out of the way (but not to the subframe).

11 Disconnect the intermediate shaft from the steering gear (see Chapter 10).

12 Disconnect the fuel feed hose from the rigid line on the left (driver's) side of the engine compartment (four-cylinder models) or from the fuel filter (V6 models) (see Chapter 4). Plug the line and fitting.

13 Clearly label and disconnect all vacuum lines, emissions hoses, electrical connectors and ground straps connecting the engine and transaxle to the vehicle. Masking tape and/or a touch up paint applicator work well for marking items (see illustration). Take instant photos or sketch the locations of components and brackets, if necessary.

14 Using a suction gun, remove as much fluid from the power steering fluid reservoir as possible. Detach the power steering hose from the return line.

15 Remove the engine movement control rod (see Chapter 2A). Also remove its mounting bracket from the cylinder head.

16 Working inside the vehicle, unplug the electrical connectors from the Powertrain Control Module (see Chapter 6). Disconnect any other electrical connectors attached to the harness leading to the PCM, then dislodge the grommet and pass the wiring harness through the firewall.

17 Loosen the front wheel lug nuts and the driveaxle/hub nuts (see Chapter 8). Raise the vehicle on the hoist and remove the front wheels.

18 Remove the under-vehicle splash shield. Also remove the inner fender liners and fender apron seals (see Chapter 11).

19 Disconnect the stabilizer bar links from the stabilizer bar and the tie-rod ends from the steering knuckles (see Chapter 10).

20 Remove the driveaxles (see Chapter 8).

21 Drain the engine coolant (see Chapter 1).

22 Drain the engine oil (see Chapter 1).

23 Drain the transaxle lubricant or fluid (see Chapter 1).

24 If you're working on a model with an automatic transaxle, remove the driveplate-to-torque converter bolts (see Chapter 7B). Also disconnect the fluid cooler hoses from the radiator.

25 Disconnect the fluid lines from the power steering pump. Also detach the pressure and return lines from the power steering gear.

26 Unbolt the exhaust pipe(s) from the exhaust manifold(s) (see Chapter 2A or 2B), then remove the front portion of the exhaust system (see Chapter 4).

27 Lower the vehicle and disconnect the radiator hoses and heater hoses from the engine.

28 Support the engine/transaxle assembly from above with a hoist. Attach the hoist chain to the lifting brackets. If no lifting brackets or hooks are present, lifting hooks may be available from your local auto parts store or dealer parts department. If not, you will have to fasten the

chains to some substantial parts of the engine - ones that are strong enough to take the weight, but in locations that will provide good balance. If you're attaching a chain to a stud on the engine, or are using a bolt passing through the chain and into a threaded hole, place a washer between the nut or bolt head and the chain and tighten the nut or bolt securely.

❖ WARNING:

Do not place any part of your body under the engine/transaxle when it's supported only by a hoist or other lifting device.

29 Take up the slack until there is slight tension on the hoist. Position the chain on the hoist so it balances the engine and the transaxle level with the vehicle.

Note 1: Depending on the design of the engine hoist, it may be helpful to position the hoist from the side of the vehicle, so that when the engine/transaxle assembly is lowered, it will fit between the legs of the hoist.

Note 2: The sling or chain must be long enough to allow the engine hoist to lower the engine/transaxle assembly to the ground, without letting the hoist arm contact the vehicle.

30 Support the subframe with a pair of floor jacks. Recheck to be sure that there aren't any hoses or wiring between the subframe and the vehicle. Unbolt the powertrain mounts from the subframe, then remove the subframe mounting bolts (see illustration 5.31 in Chapter 7A), lower it to the floor, then remove it out from underneath the vehicle.

❖ WARNING:

This can be tricky, depending on the design of the engine hoist, but it is imperative that the subframe be supported securely before its mounting bolts are removed.

31 Recheck to be sure nothing is still connecting the engine or transaxle to the vehicle. Disconnect and label anything still remaining.

32 Lower the engine/transaxle assembly. Once the engine/transaxle assembly is on the floor, disconnect the engine lifting hoist and raise the vehicle until it clears the engine/transaxle assembly.

33 Reconnect the chain or sling to support the engine and transaxle.

34 Raise the engine/transaxle assembly, then support the engine with blocks of wood or another floor jack, while leaving the sling or chain attached. Support the transaxle with another floor jack, preferably one with a transaxle jack head adapter. At this point the transaxle can be unbolted and removed from the engine. Be very careful to ensure that the components are supported securely so they won't topple off their supports during disconnection.

35 Reconnect the lifting chain to the engine, then raise the engine and attach it to an engine stand.

INSTALLATION

36 Installation is the reverse of removal, noting the following points:

a) *Check the engine/transaxle mounts. If they're worn or damaged, replace them.*

b) *Attach the transaxle to the engine following the procedure described in Chapter 7.*

c) *When installing the subframe, tighten the subframe mounting bolts to the torque listed in Chapter 7A Specifications.*

d) *Tighten the driveaxle/hub nuts to the torque listed in the Chapter 8 Specifications. Tighten all steering and suspension fasteners to the torque listed in the Chapter 10 Specifications. Tighten the wheel lug nuts to the torque listed in the Chapter 1 Specifications.*

e) *Refill the engine coolant, oil, power steering and transaxle fluids (see Chapter 1).*

f) *Reconnect the battery (see Chapter 5, Section 1).*

g) *Run the engine and check for proper operation and leaks. Shut off the engine and recheck fluid levels.*

---

8 Engine overhaul - disassembly sequence

1 It's much easier to remove the external components if it's mounted on a portable engine stand. A stand can often be rented quite cheaply from an equipment rental yard. Before the engine is mounted on a stand, the flywheel/driveplate should be removed from the engine.

2 If a stand isn't available, it's possible to remove the external engine components with it blocked up on the floor. Be extra careful not to tip or drop the engine when working without a stand.

3 If you're going to obtain a rebuilt engine, all external components must come off first, to be transferred to the replacement engine. These components include:

Clutch and flywheel (models with manual transaxle)
Driveplate (models with automatic transaxle)
Ignition system components
Emissions-related components
Engine mounts and mount brackets
Fuel injection components

Intake/exhaust manifolds
Oil filter
Thermostat and housing assembly
Water pump

Note: When removing the external components from the engine, pay close attention to details that may be helpful or important during installation. Note the installed position of gaskets, seals, spacers, pins, brackets, washers, bolts and other small items.

4 If you're going to obtain a short block (assembled engine block, crankshaft, pistons and connecting rods), then you should remove the timing belt, cylinder head, oil pan, oil pump pick-up tube, oil pump and water pump from your engine so that you can turn in your old short block to the rebuilder as a core. See *Engine rebuilding alternatives* for additional information regarding the different possibilities to be considered.

9 Pistons and connecting rods - removal and installation

REMOVAL

▶ **Refer to illustrations 9.1, 9.3 and 9.4**

➡**Note: Prior to removing the piston/connecting rod assemblies, remove the cylinder head, upper (aluminum) oil pan section and oil pan (see Chapter 2A or 2B).**

1   Use your fingernail to feel if a ridge has formed at the upper limit of ring travel (about 1/4-inch down from the top of each cylinder). If carbon deposits or cylinder wear have produced ridges, they must be completely removed with a special tool (see illustration). Follow the manufacturer's instructions provided with the tool. Failure to remove the ridges before attempting to remove the piston/connecting rod assemblies may result in piston breakage.

2   After the cylinder ridges have been removed, turn the engine so the crankshaft is facing up.

3   Before the main bearing cap assembly and connecting rods are removed, check the connecting rod endplay with feeler gauges. Slide them between the first connecting rod and the crankshaft throw until the play is removed (see illustration). Repeat this procedure for each connecting rod. The endplay is equal to the thickness of the feeler

gauge(s). Check with an automotive machine shop for the endplay service limit. If the play exceeds the service limit, new connecting rods will be required. If new rods (or a new crankshaft) are installed, the endplay may fall under the minimum allowable clearance. If it does, the rods will have to be machined to restore it. If necessary, consult an automotive machine shop for advice.

4   Check the connecting rods and caps for identification marks (see illustration). If they aren't plainly marked, use a small center-punch to make the appropriate number of indentations on each rod and cap (1, 2, 3, etc., depending on the cylinder they're associated with).

5   Loosen each of the connecting rod cap bolts 1/2-turn at a time until they can be removed by hand. Remove the number one connecting rod cap and bearing insert. Don't drop the bearing insert out of the cap.

6   Remove the bearing insert and push the connecting rod/piston assembly out through the top of the engine. Use a wooden or plastic hammer handle to push on the upper bearing surface in the connecting rod.

7   If resistance is felt, double-check to make sure that all of the ridge was removed from the cylinder.

8   Repeat the procedure for the remaining cylinders.

➡**Note: If the connecting rod caps are secured by bolts (instead of nuts), discard the old rod cap bolts. Use new bolts when reassembling the engine.**

9   After removal, reassemble the connecting rod caps and bearing inserts in their respective connecting rods and install the cap bolts finger tight. Leaving the old bearing inserts in place until reassembly will help prevent the connecting rod bearing surfaces from being accidentally nicked or gouged.

10 The pistons and connecting rods are now ready for inspection and overhaul at an automotive machine shop.

PISTON RING INSTALLATION

▶ **Refer to illustrations 9.13, 9.14, 9.15, 9.19a, 9.19b and 9.22**

11 Before installing the new piston rings, the ring end gaps must be checked. It's assumed that the piston ring side clearance has been checked and verified correct.

➡**Note: Pistons and rods can only be installed after the crankshaft has been installed (see Section 10).**

9.1 Before you try to remove the pistons, use a ridge reamer to remove the raised material (ridge) from the top of the cylinders

9.3 Checking the connecting rod endplay (side clearance)

9.4 If the connecting rods and caps are not marked, use a center punch or numbered impression stamps to mark the caps to the rods by cylinder number - do not confuse the markings shown here with rod numbers; these are bearing size identifications

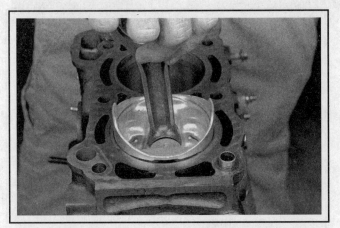

9.13 Install the piston ring into the cylinder then push it down into position using a piston so the ring will be square in the cylinder

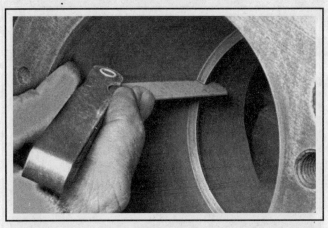

9.14 With the ring square in the cylinder, measure the ring end gap with a feeler gauge

12 Lay out the piston/connecting rod assemblies and the new ring sets so the ring sets will be matched with the same piston and cylinder during the end gap measurement and engine assembly.

13 Insert the top (number one) ring into the first cylinder and square it up with the cylinder walls by pushing it in with the top of the piston (see illustration). The ring should be near the bottom of the cylinder, at the lower limit of ring travel.

14 To measure the end gap, slip feeler gauges between the ends of the ring until a gauge equal to the gap width is found (see illustration). The feeler gauge should slide between the ring ends with a slight amount of drag. Check with an automotive machine shop for the correct end gap for your engine. If the gap is larger or smaller than specified, double-check to make sure you have the correct rings before proceeding.

15 If the gap is too small, it must be enlarged or the ring ends may come in contact with each other during engine operation, which can cause serious damage to the engine. The end gap can be increased by filing the ring ends very carefully with a fine file. Mount the file in a vise equipped with soft jaws, slip the ring over the file with the ends contacting the file face and slowly move the ring to remove material from the ends. When performing this operation, file only by pushing the ring from the outside end of the file towards the vise (see illustration).

16 Excess end gap isn't critical unless it's greater than approximately 0.040-inch. Again, double-check to make sure you have the correct ring type and that you are referencing the correct section and category of specifications.

17 Repeat the procedure for each ring that will be installed in the first cylinder and for each ring in the remaining cylinders. Remember to keep rings, pistons and cylinders matched up.

18 Once the ring end gaps have been checked/corrected, the rings can be installed on the pistons.

19 The oil control ring (lowest one on the piston) is usually installed first. It's composed of three separate components. Slip the spacer/expander into the groove (see illustration). If an anti-rotation tang is used, make sure it's inserted into the drilled hole in the ring groove. Next, install the upper side rail in the same manner (see illustration). Don't use a piston ring installation tool on the oil ring side rails, as they may be damaged. Instead, place one end of the side rail into the groove between the spacer/expander and the ring land, hold it firmly in place and slide a finger around the piston while pushing the rail into the groove. Finally, install the lower side rail.

20 After the three oil ring components have been installed, check to make sure that both the upper and lower side rails can be rotated smoothly inside the ring grooves.

9.15 If the ring end gap is too small, clamp a file in a vise as shown and file the piston ring ends - be sure to file the ends squarely and finish by removing all raised material or burrs with a fine stone

9.19a Installing the spacer/expander in the oil ring groove

9.19b DO NOT use a piston ring installation tool when installing the oil control side rails

9.22 Use a piston ring installation tool to install the number 2 and the number 1 (top) rings - be sure the directional mark on the piston ring(s) is facing toward the top of the piston

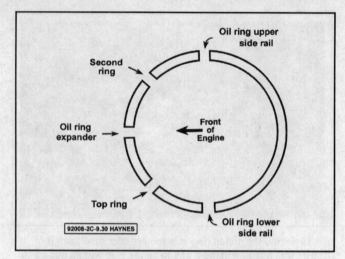

9.30 Position the piston ring end gaps as shown

21 The number two (middle) ring is installed next. It's usually stamped with a mark that must face up, toward the top of the piston. Do not mix up the top and middle rings, as they have different cross-sections.

➡**Note: Always follow the instructions printed on the ring package or box - different manufacturers may require different approaches.**

22 Use a piston ring installation tool and make sure the identification mark is facing the top of the piston, then slip the ring into the middle groove on the piston (see illustration). Don't expand the ring any more than necessary to slide it over the piston.

23 Install the number one (top) ring in the same manner. Make sure the mark is facing up. Be careful not to confuse the number one and number two rings.

24 Repeat the procedure for the remaining pistons and rings.

INSTALLATION

25 Before installing the piston/connecting rod assemblies, the cylinder walls must be perfectly clean, the top edge of each cylinder bore must be chamfered, and the crankshaft must be in place.

26 Remove the cap from the end of the number one connecting rod (refer to the marks made during removal).

27 Remove the original bearing inserts and wipe the bearing surfaces of the connecting rod and cap with a clean, lint-free cloth. They must be kept spotlessly clean.

Connecting rod bearing oil clearance check

▶ **Refer to illustrations 9.30, 9.35, 9.37 and 9.41**

28 Clean the back side of the new upper bearing insert, then lay it in place in the connecting rod. Make sure the tab on the bearing fits into the recess in the rod. Don't hammer the bearing insert into place and be very careful not to nick or gouge the bearing face. Don't lubricate the bearing at this time.

29 Clean the back side of the other bearing insert and install it in the rod cap. Again, make sure the tab on the bearing fits into the recess in the cap, and don't apply any lubricant. It's critically important that the mating surfaces of the bearing and connecting rod are perfectly clean and oil free when they're assembled.

30 Position the piston ring gaps around the piston as shown (see illustration).

31 Lubricate the piston and rings with clean engine oil and attach a piston ring compressor to the piston. Leave the skirt protruding about 1/4-inch to guide the piston into the cylinder. The rings must be compressed until they're flush with the piston.

32 Rotate the crankshaft until the number one connecting rod journal is at BDC (bottom dead center) and apply a liberal coat of engine oil to the cylinder walls.

33 With the mark (dot, arrow or letter R or L) on top of the piston facing the front (timing belt end) of the engine, gently insert the piston/connecting rod assembly into the number one cylinder bore and rest the bottom edge of the ring compressor on the engine block.

➡**Note: The connecting rod also has a mark on it that must face the correct direction. On all models, the marks on the connecting rods face the front (timing belt or chain) of the engine.**

34 Tap the top edge of the ring compressor to make sure it's contacting the block around its entire circumference.

35 Gently tap on the top of the piston with the end of a wooden or plastic hammer handle (see illustration) while guiding the end of the connecting rod into place on the crankshaft journal. The piston rings may try to pop out of the ring compressor just before entering the cylinder bore, so keep some downward pressure on the ring compres-

9.35 Use a plastic or wooden hammer handle to push the piston into the cylinder

9.37 Place Plastigage on each connecting rod bearing journal parallel to the crankshaft centerline

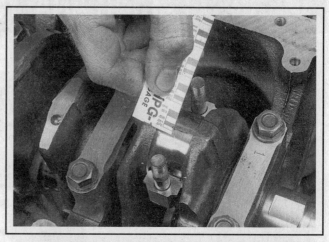

9.41 Use the scale on the Plastigage package to determine the bearing oil clearance - be sure to measure the widest part of the Plastigage and use the correct scale; it comes with both standard and metric scales

sor. Work slowly, and if any resistance is felt as the piston enters the cylinder, stop immediately. Find out what's hanging up and fix it before proceeding. Do not, for any reason, force the piston into the cylinder - you might break a ring and/or the piston.

36 Once the piston/connecting rod assembly is installed, the connecting rod bearing oil clearance must be checked before the rod cap is permanently installed.

37 Cut a piece of the appropriate size Plastigage slightly shorter than the width of the connecting rod bearing and lay it in place on the number one connecting rod journal, parallel with the journal axis (see illustration).

38 Clean the connecting rod cap bearing face and install the rod cap. Make sure the mating mark on the cap is on the same side as the mark on the connecting rod.

39 Install the old rod bolts, at this time, and tighten them to the torque listed in this Chapter's Specifications in two steps.

➡**Note: Use a thin-wall socket to avoid erroneous torque readings that can result if the socket is wedged between the rod cap and the bolt. If the socket tends to wedge itself between the fastener and the cap, lift up on it slightly until it no longer contacts the cap. DO NOT rotate the crankshaft at any time during this operation.**

40 Remove the fasteners and detach the rod cap, being very careful not to disturb the Plastigage. Discard the cap bolts at this time as they cannot be reused.

❊❊ CAUTION:

You MUST use new connecting rod bolts.

41 Compare the width of the crushed Plastigage to the scale printed on the Plastigage envelope to obtain the oil clearance (see illustration). The connecting rod oil clearance is usually about 0.001 to 0.002 inch. Consult an automotive machine shop for the clearance specified for the rod bearings on your engine.

42 If the clearance is not as specified, the bearing inserts may be the wrong size (which means different ones will be required). Before deciding that different inserts are needed, make sure that no dirt or oil was between the bearing inserts and the connecting rod or cap when the clearance was measured. Also, recheck the journal diameter. If the Plastigage was wider at one end than the other, the journal may be tapered.

If the clearance still exceeds the limit specified, the bearing will have to be replaced with an undersize bearing.

❊❊ CAUTION:

When installing a new crankshaft always use a standard size bearing.

Final installation

43 Carefully scrape all traces of the Plastigage material off the rod journal and/or bearing face. Be very careful not to scratch the bearing - use your fingernail or the edge of a plastic card.

44 Make sure the bearing faces are perfectly clean, then apply a uniform layer of clean moly-base grease or engine assembly lube to both of them. You'll have to push the piston into the cylinder to expose the face of the bearing insert in the connecting rod.

45 Slide the connecting rod back into place on the journal, install the rod cap, install the new bolts and tighten them to the torque listed in this Chapter's Specifications in two steps.

46 Repeat the entire procedure for the remaining pistons/connecting rods.

47 The important points to remember are:

a) *Keep the back sides of the bearing inserts and the insides of the connecting rods and caps perfectly clean when assembling them.*

b) *Make sure you have the correct piston/rod assembly for each cylinder.*

c) *The mark on the piston must face the front (timing belt end) of the engine.*

d) *Lubricate the cylinder walls liberally with clean oil.*

e) *Lubricate the bearing faces when installing the rod caps after the oil clearance has been checked.*

48 After all the piston/connecting rod assemblies have been correctly installed, rotate the crankshaft a number of times by hand to check for any obvious binding.

49 As a final step, check the connecting rod endplay again. If it was correct before disassembly and the original crankshaft and rods were reinstalled, it should still be correct. If new rods or a new crankshaft were installed, the endplay may be inadequate. If so, the rods will have to be removed and taken to an automotive machine shop for resizing.

ENGINE BEARING ANALYSIS

Debris

Babbitt bearing embedded with debris from machinings

Microscopic detail of debris

Microscopic detail of gouges

Overplated copper alloy bearing gouged by cast iron debris

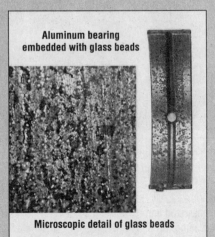

Aluminum bearing embedded with glass beads

Microscopic detail of glass beads

Damaged lining caused by dirt left on the bearing back

Misassembly

Result of a lower half assembled as an upper - blocking the oil flow

Excessive oil clearance is indicated by a short contact arc

Polished and oil-stained backs are a result of a poor fit in the housing bore

Result of a wrong, reversed, or shifted cap

Overloading

Damage from excessive idling which resulted in an oil film unable to support the load imposed

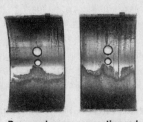

Damaged upper connecting rod bearings caused by engine lugging; the lower main bearings (not shown) were similarly affected

The damage shown in these upper and lower connecting rod bearings was caused by engine operation at a higher-than-rated speed under load

Misalignment

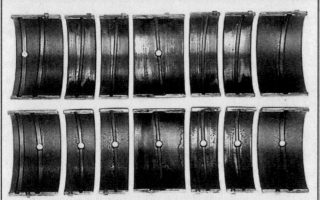

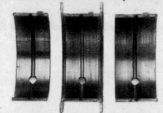

A poorly finished crankshaft caused the equally spaced scoring shown

A tapered housing bore caused the damage along one edge of this pair

A warped crankshaft caused this pattern of severe wear in the center, diminishing toward the ends

A bent connecting rod led to the damage in the "V" pattern

Corrosion

Microscopic detail of corrosion

Corrosion is an acid attack on the bearing lining generally caused by inadequate maintenance, extremely hot or cold operation, or inferior oils or fuels

Lubrication

Result of dry start: The bearings on the left, farthest from the oil pump, show more damage

Microscopic detail of cavitation

Example of cavitation - a surface erosion caused by pressure changes in the oil film

Result of a low oil supply or oil starvation

Severe wear as a result of inadequate oil clearance

Damage from excessive thrust or insufficient axial clearance

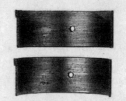

Bearing affected by oil dilution caused by excessive blow-by or a rich mixture

10 Crankshaft - removal and installation

REMOVAL

♦ **Refer to illustrations 10.1 and 10.3**

➡**Note 1:** The crankshaft can be removed only after the engine has been removed from the vehicle. It's assumed that the flywheel or driveplate, crankshaft pulley, timing belt, oil pan, oil pump body, oil filter and piston/connecting rod assemblies have already been removed. On V6 engines, the rear main oil seal retainer must be unbolted and separated from the block before proceeding with crankshaft removal.

➡**Note 2:** V6 engines have main caps that are retained by four bolts each, plus side bolts (one on each side) that pass through the block and bear against the installed main caps.

1   Before the crankshaft is removed, measure the endplay. Mount a dial indicator with the indicator in line with the crankshaft and touching the end of the crankshaft (see illustration).

2   Pry the crankshaft all the way to the rear and zero the dial indicator. Next, pry the crankshaft to the front as far as possible and check the reading on the dial indicator. The distance traveled is the endplay. A typical crankshaft endplay will fall between 0.003 to 0.010-inch. If it's greater than that, check the crankshaft thrust surfaces for wear after it's removed. If no wear is evident, new main bearings should correct the endplay.

3   If a dial indicator isn't available, feeler gauges can be used. Gen-

10.1 Checking crankshaft endplay with a dial indicator

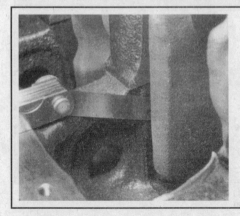

10.3 Checking crankshaft endplay with feeler gauges at the thrust bearing journal

tly pry the crankshaft all the way to the front of the engine. Slip feeler gauges between the crankshaft and the front face of the thrust bearing or washer to determine the clearance (see illustration).

4   Loosen the main bearing cap bolts 1/4-turn at a time each, until they can be removed by hand. On V6 engines, remove the side bolts first (in sequence), then the inner bolts (see illustrations 10.19a, 10.19b and 10.19c).

5   Gently tap the main bearing caps with a soft-face hammer. Pull the main bearing cap straight up and off the cylinder block. Try not to drop the bearing inserts if they come out with the cap.

6   Carefully lift the crankshaft out of the engine. It may be a good idea to have an assistant available, since the crankshaft is quite heavy and awkward to handle. With the bearing inserts in place inside the engine block and main bearing caps, reinstall the main bearing caps onto the engine block and tighten the bolts finger tight. Make sure you install the main bearing cap(s) with the arrow facing the front end of the engine.

INSTALLATION

7   Crankshaft installation is the first step in engine reassembly. It's assumed at this point that the engine block and crankshaft have been cleaned, inspected and repaired or reconditioned.

8   Position the engine block with the bottom facing up.

9   Remove the mounting bolts and lift off the main bearing cap(s).

10 If they're still in place, remove the original bearing inserts from the block and from the main bearing caps. Wipe the bearing surfaces of the block and main bearing caps with a clean, lint-free cloth. They must be kept spotlessly clean. This is critical for determining the correct bearing oil clearance.

MAIN BEARING OIL CLEARANCE CHECK

♦ **Refer to illustrations 10.17, 10.19a, 10.19b, 10.19c and 10.21**

11 Without mixing them up, clean the back sides of the new upper main bearing inserts (with grooves and oil holes) and lay one in each main bearing saddle in the block. Each upper bearing has an oil groove and oil hole in it.

❈❈ CAUTION:

The oil holes in the block must line up with the oil holes in the upper bearing inserts.

If you're working on a V6 engine, the thrust bearings (washers) must be installed in the number two cap and saddle. On four-cylinder engines, the thrust bearings (washers) must be installed in the number three (center) cap. Install the thrust bearings with the oil grooves facing out. Install the thrust washers with the grooved side facing out. Install the thrust washers so that one set is located in the block and the other set is with the main bearing cap. Clean the back sides of the lower main bearing inserts (without grooves) and lay them in the corresponding caps. Make sure the tab on the bearing insert fits into the recess in the block or main bearing cap.

10.17 Place the Plastigage onto the crankshaft bearing journal as shown

✳✳ CAUTION:

Do not hammer the bearing insert into place and don't nick or gouge the bearing faces. DO NOT apply any lubrication at this time.

12 Clean the faces of the bearing inserts in the block and the crankshaft main bearing journals with a clean, lint-free cloth.

13 Check or clean the oil holes in the crankshaft, as any dirt here can go only one way - straight through the new bearings.

14 Once you're certain the crankshaft is clean, carefully lay it in position in the cylinder block.

15 Before the crankshaft can be permanently installed, the main bearing oil clearance must be checked.

16 Cut several strips of the appropriate size of Plastigage (they must be slightly shorter than the width of the main bearing journal).

17 Place one piece on each crankshaft main bearing journal, parallel with the journal axis (see illustration).

18 Clean the faces of the bearing inserts in the main bearing caps. Hold the bearing inserts in place and install the caps onto the crank-

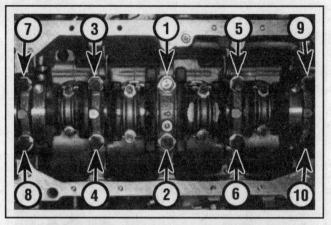

10.19a Main bearing cap bolt tightening sequence (four-cylinder models)

shaft and cylinder block. DO NOT disturb the Plastigage. Make sure you install the main bearing cap with the arrow facing the front of the engine.

19 Apply clean engine oil to all bolt threads prior to installation, then install all bolts finger-tight.

➡**Note: Use the old bolts at this time. New bolts must be used during final crankshaft installation.**

Tighten main bearing cap bolts in the sequence shown (see illustrations) progressing in two steps, to the torque listed in this Chapter's Specifications. DO NOT rotate the crankshaft at any time during this operation.

20 Remove the bolts in the reverse order of the tightening sequence and carefully lift the main bearing cap straight up and off the block. Do not disturb the Plastigage or rotate the crankshaft. If the main bearing cap is difficult to remove, tap it gently from side-to-side with a soft-face hammer to loosen it.

21 Compare the width of the crushed Plastigage on each journal to the scale printed on the Plastigage envelope to determine the main bearing oil clearance (see illustration). A typical main bearing oil clear-

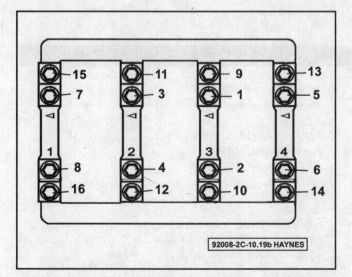

10.19b Main bearing cap bolt tightening sequence (V6 models)

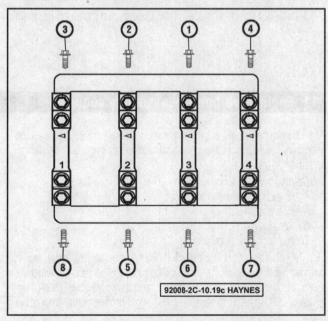

10.19c V6 main cap side-bolt tightening sequence

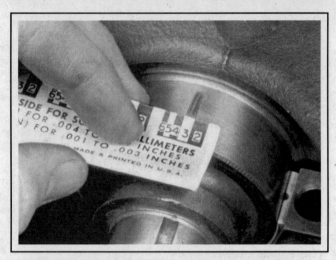

10.21 Use the scale on the Plastigage package to determine the bearing oil clearance - be sure to measure the widest part of the Plastigage and use the correct scale; it comes with both standard and metric scales

ance should fall between 0.0015 to 0.0023-inch. Check with an automotive machine shop for the clearance specified for your engine.

22 If the clearance is not as specified, the bearing inserts may be the wrong size (which means different ones will be required). Before deciding if different inserts are needed, make sure that no dirt or oil was between the bearing inserts and the cap or block when the clearance was measured. If the Plastigage was wider at one end than the other, the crankshaft journal may be tapered. If the clearance still exceeds the limit specified, the bearing insert(s) will have to be replaced with an undersize bearing insert(s).

❊❊ CAUTION:

When installing a new crankshaft always install a standard bearing insert set.

23 Carefully scrape all traces of the Plastigage material off the main

bearing journals and/or the bearing insert faces. Be sure to remove all residue from the oil holes. Use your fingernail or the edge of a plastic card - don't nick or scratch the bearing faces.

FINAL INSTALLATION

24 Carefully lift the crankshaft out of the cylinder block.
25 Clean the bearing insert faces in the cylinder block, then apply a thin, uniform layer of moly-base grease or engine assembly lube to each of the bearing surfaces. Be sure to coat the thrust faces as well as the journal face of the thrust bearing.
26 Make sure the crankshaft journals are clean, then lay the crankshaft back in place in the cylinder block.
27 Clean the bearing insert faces and then apply the same lubricant to them.
28 Hold the bearing inserts in place and install the main bearing caps on the crankshaft and cylinder block. Tap the bearing caps into place with a brass punch or a soft-face hammer.
29 Using NEW main bearing cap bolts, apply clean engine oil to the bolt threads, wipe off any excess oil and then install the bolts finger-tight.
30 Tighten the main bearing cap bolts in the indicated sequence (see illustration 10.19a or 10.19b), to 10 or 12 foot-pounds.
31 Push the crankshaft forward using a screwdriver or prybar to seat the thrust bearing. Once the crankshaft is pushed fully forward to seat the thrust bearing, leave the screwdriver in position so that force stays on the crankshaft until after all main bearing cap bolts have been tightened.
32 Tighten the main bearing cap bolts in two steps in the indicated sequence (see illustration 10.19a or 10.19b) and to the torque and angle listed in this Chapter's Specifications. On V6 engines, tighten the main cap side-bolts last (see illustration 10.19c).
33 Recheck crankshaft endplay with a feeler gauge or a dial indicator. The endplay should be correct if the crankshaft thrust faces aren't worn or damaged and if new bearings have been installed.
34 Rotate the crankshaft a number of times by hand to check for any obvious binding. It should rotate with a running torque of 50 in-lbs or less. If the running torque is too high, correct the problem at this time.
35 Install a new rear main oil seal (see Chapter 2A or 2B).

11 Engine overhaul - reassembly sequence

1 Before beginning engine reassembly, make sure you have all the necessary new parts, gaskets and seals as well as the following items on hand:

Common hand tools
A 1/2-inch drive torque wrench
New engine oil
Gasket sealant
Thread locking compound

2 If you obtained a short block it will be necessary to install the cylinder head, the oil pump and pick-up tube, the oil pan, the water pump, the timing belt and timing cover, and the valve cover (see Chapter 2A or 2B). In order to save time and avoid problems, the external

components must be installed in the following general order:

Thermostat and housing cover
Water pump
Intake and exhaust manifolds
Fuel injection components
Emission control components
Spark plugs
Ignition coils
Oil filter
Engine mounts and mount brackets
Flywheel and clutch (manual transaxle)
Driveplate (automatic transaxle)

12 Initial start-up and break-in after overhaul

1 Once the engine has been installed in the vehicle, double-check the engine oil and coolant levels.

2 With the spark plugs out of the engine and the ignition system and fuel pump disabled (remove the C/OPN relay from the underhood fuse/relay box to disable the fuel pump), crank the engine until oil pressure registers on the gauge or the light goes out.

3 Install the spark plugs, hook up the plug wires and/or ignition coils and restore the ignition system and fuel pump functions.

4 Start the engine. It may take a few moments for the fuel system to build up pressure, but the engine should start without a great deal of effort.

5 After the engine starts, it should be allowed to warm up to normal operating temperature. While the engine is warming up, make a thorough check for fuel, oil and coolant leaks.

6 Shut the engine off and recheck the engine oil and coolant levels.

7 Drive the vehicle to an area with minimum traffic, accelerate from 30 to 50 mph, then allow the vehicle to slow to 30 mph with the throttle closed. Repeat the procedure 10 or 12 times. This will load the piston rings and cause them to seat properly against the cylinder walls. Check again for oil and coolant leaks.

8 Drive the vehicle gently for the first 500 miles (no sustained high speeds) and keep a constant check on the oil level. It is not unusual for an engine to use oil during the break-in period.

9 At approximately 500 to 600 miles, change the oil and filter.

10 For the next few hundred miles, drive the vehicle normally. Do not pamper it or abuse it.

11 After 2000 miles, change the oil and filter again and consider the engine broken in.

GLOSSARY

B

Backlash - The amount of play between two parts. Usually refers to how much one gear can be moved back and forth without moving gear with which it's meshed.

Bearing Caps - The caps held in place by nuts or bolts which, in turn, hold the bearing surface. This space is for lubricating oil to enter.

Bearing clearance - The amount of space left between shaft and bearing surface. This space is for lubricating oil to enter.

Bearing crush - The additional height which is purposely manufactured into each bearing half to ensure complete contact of the bearing back with the housing bore when the engine is assembled.

Bearing knock - The noise created by movement of a part in a loose or worn bearing.

Blueprinting - Dismantling an engine and reassembling it to EXACT specifications.

Bore - An engine cylinder, or any cylindrical hole; also used to describe the process of enlarging or accurately refinishing a hole with a cutting tool, as to bore an engine cylinder. The bore size is the diameter of the hole.

Boring - Renewing the cylinders by cutting them out to a specified size. A boring bar is used to make the cut.

Bottom end - A term which refers collectively to the engine block, crankshaft, main bearings and the big ends of the connecting rods.

Break-in - The period of operation between installation of new or rebuilt parts and time in which parts are worn to the correct fit. Driving at reduced and varying speed for a specified mileage to permit parts to wear to the correct fit.

Bushing - A one-piece sleeve placed in a bore to serve as a bearing surface for shaft, piston pin, etc. Usually replaceable.

C

Camshaft - The shaft in the engine, on which a series of lobes are located for operating the valve mechanisms. The camshaft is driven by gears or sprockets and a timing chain. Usually referred to simply as the cam.

Carbon - Hard, or soft, black deposits found in combustion chamber, on plugs, under rings, on and under valve heads.

Cast iron - An alloy of iron and more than two percent carbon, used for engine blocks and heads because it's relatively inexpensive and easy to mold into complex shapes.

Chamfer - To bevel across (or a bevel on) the sharp edge of an object.

Chase - To repair damaged threads with a tap or die.

Combustion chamber - The space between the piston and the cylinder head, with the piston at top dead center, in which air-fuel mixture is burned.

Compression ratio - The relationship between cylinder volume (clearance volume) when the piston is at top dead center and cylinder volume when the piston is at bottom dead center.

Connecting rod - The rod that connects the crank on the crankshaft with the piston. Sometimes called a con rod.

Connecting rod cap - The part of the connecting rod assembly that attaches the rod to the crankpin.

Core plug - Soft metal plug used to plug the casting holes for the coolant passages in the block.

Crankcase - The lower part of the engine in which the crankshaft rotates; includes the lower section of the cylinder block and the oil pan.

Crank kit - A reground or reconditioned crankshaft and new main and connecting rod bearings.

Crankpin - The part of a crankshaft to which a connecting rod is attached.

Crankshaft - The main rotating member, or shaft, running the length of the crankcase, with offset throws to which the connecting rods are attached; changes the reciprocating motion of the pistons into rotating motion.

Cylinder sleeve - A replaceable sleeve, or liner, pressed into the cylinder block to form the cylinder bore.

D

Deburring - Removing the burrs (rough edges or areas) from a bearing.

Deglazer - A tool, rotated by an electric motor, used to remove glaze from cylinder walls so a new set of rings will seat.

E

Endplay - The amount of lengthwise movement between two parts. As applied to a crankshaft, the distance that the crankshaft can move forward and back in the cylinder block.

F

Face - A machinist's term that refers to removing metal from the end of a shaft or the face of a larger part, such as a flywheel.

Fatigue - A breakdown of material through a large number of loading and unloading cycles. The first signs are cracks followed shortly by breaks. •

Feeler gauge - A thin strip of hardened steel, ground to an exact thickness, used to check clearances between parts.

Free height - The unloaded length or height of a spring.

Freeplay - The looseness in a linkage, or an assembly of parts, between the initial application of force and actual movement. Usually perceived as slop or slight delay.

Freeze plug - See Core plug.

G

Gallery - A large passage in the block that forms a reservoir for engine oil pressure.

Glaze - The very smooth, glassy finish that develops on cylinder walls while an engine is in service.

H

Heli-Coil - A rethreading device used when threads are worn or damaged. The device is installed in a retapped hole to reduce the thread size to the original size.

I

Installed height - The spring's measured length or height, as installed on the cylinder head. Installed height is measured from the spring seat to the underside of the spring retainer.

J

Journal - The surface of a rotating shaft which turns in a bearing.

K

Keeper - The split lock that holds the valve spring retainer in position on the valve stem.

Key - A small piece of metal inserted into matching grooves machined into two parts fitted together - such as a gear pressed onto a shaft - which prevents slippage between the two parts.

Knock - The heavy metallic engine sound, produced in the combustion chamber as a result of abnormal combustion - usually detonation. Knock is usually caused by a loose or worn bearing. Also referred to as detonation, pinging and spark knock. Connecting rod or main bearing knocks are created by too much oil clearance or insufficient lubrication.

L

Lands - The portions of metal between the piston ring grooves.

Lapping the valves - Grinding a valve face and its seat together with lapping compound.

Lash - The amount of free motion in a gear train, between gears, or in a mechanical assembly, that occurs before movement can begin. Usually refers to the lash in a valve train.

Lifter - The part that rides against the cam to transfer motion to the rest of the valve train.

M

Machining - The process of using a machine to remove metal from a metal part.

Main bearings - The plain, or babbitt, bearings that support the crankshaft.

Main bearing caps - The cast iron caps, bolted to the bottom of the block, that support the main bearings.

O

O.D. - Outside diameter.

Oil gallery - A pipe or drilled passageway in the engine used to carry engine oil from one area to another.

Oil ring - The lower ring, or rings, of a piston; designed to prevent excessive amounts of oil from working up the cylinder walls and into the combustion chamber. Also called an oil-control ring.

Oil seal - A seal which keeps oil from leaking out of a compartment. Usually refers to a dynamic seal around a rotating shaft or other moving part.

O-ring - A type of sealing ring made of a special rubberlike material; in use, the O-ring is compressed into a groove to provide the sealing action.

Overhaul - To completely disassemble a unit, clean and inspect all parts, reassemble it with the original or new parts and make all adjustments necessary for proper operation.

P

Pilot bearing - A small bearing installed in the center of the flywheel (or the rear end of the crankshaft) to support the front end of the input shaft of the transmission.

Pip mark - A little dot or indentation which indicates the top side of a compression ring.

Piston - The cylindrical part, attached to the connecting rod, that moves up and down in the cylinder as the crankshaft rotates. When the fuel charge is fired, the piston transfers the force of the explosion to the connecting rod, then to the crankshaft.

Piston pin (or wrist pin) - The cylindrical and usually hollow steel pin that passes through the piston. The piston pin fastens the piston to the upper end of the connecting rod.

Piston ring - The split ring fitted to the groove in a piston. The ring contacts the sides of the ring groove and also rubs against the cylinder wall, thus sealing space between piston and wall. There are two types of rings: Compression rings seal the compression pressure in the combustion chamber; oil rings scrape excessive oil off the cylinder wall.

Piston ring groove - The slots or grooves cut in piston heads to hold piston rings in position.

Piston skirt - The portion of the piston below the rings and the piston pin hole.

Plastigage - A thin strip of plastic thread, available in different sizes, used for measuring clearances. For example, a strip of plastigage is laid across a bearing journal and mashed as parts are assembled. Then parts are disassembled and the width of the strip is measured to determine clearance between journal and bearing. Commonly used to measure crankshaft main-bearing and connecting rod bearing clearances.

Press-fit - A tight fit between two parts that requires pressure to force the parts together. Also referred to as drive, or force, fit.

Prussian blue - A blue pigment; in solution, useful in determining the area of contact between two surfaces. Prussian blue is commonly used to determine the width and location of the contact area between the valve face and the valve seat.

R

Race (bearing) - The inner or outer ring that provides a contact surface for balls or rollers in bearing.

Ream - To size, enlarge or smooth a hole by using a round cutting tool with fluted edges.

Ring job - The process of reconditioning the cylinders and installing new rings.

Runout - Wobble. The amount a shaft rotates out-of-true.

S

Saddle - The upper main bearing seat.

Scored - Scratched or grooved, as a cylinder wall may be scored by abrasive particles moved up and down by the piston rings.

Scuffing - A type of wear in which there's a transfer of material between parts moving against each other; shows up as pits or grooves in the mating surfaces.

Seat - The surface upon which another part rests or seats. For example, the valve seat is the matched surface upon which the valve face rests. Also used to refer to wearing into a good fit; for example, piston rings seat after a few miles of driving.

Short block - An engine block complete with crankshaft and piston and, usually, camshaft assemblies.

Static balance - The balance of an object while it's stationary.

Step - The wear on the lower portion of a ring land caused by excessive side and back-clearance. The height of the step indicates the ring's extra side clearance and the length of the step projecting from the back wall of the groove represents the ring's back clearance.

Stroke - The distance the piston moves when traveling from top dead center to bottom dead center, or from bottom dead center to top dead center.

Stud - A metal rod with threads on both ends.

T

Tang - A lip on the end of a plain bearing used to align the bearing during assembly.

Tap - To cut threads in a hole. Also refers to the fluted tool used to cut threads.

Taper - A gradual reduction in the width of a shaft or hole; in an engine cylinder, taper usually takes the form of uneven wear, more pronounced at the top than at the bottom.

Throws - The offset portions of the crankshaft to which the connecting rods are affixed.

Thrust bearing - The main bearing that has thrust faces to prevent excessive end-play, or forward and backward movement of the crankshaft.

Thrust washer - A bronze or hardened steel washer placed between two moving parts. The washer prevents longitudinal movement and provides a bearing surface for thrust surfaces of parts.

Tolerance - The amount of variation permitted from an exact size of measurement. Actual amount from smallest acceptable dimension to largest acceptable dimension.

U

Umbrella - An oil deflector placed near the valve tip to throw oil from the valve stem area.

Undercut - A machined groove below the normal surface.

Undersize bearings - Smaller diameter bearings used with re-ground crankshaft journals.

V

Valve grinding - Refacing a valve in a valve-refacing machine.

Valve train - The valve-operating mechanism of an engine; includes all components from the camshaft to the valve.

Vibration damper - A cylindrical weight attached to the front of the crankshaft to minimize torsional vibration (the twist-untwist actions of the crankshaft caused by the cylinder firing impulses). Also called a harmonic balancer.

W

Water jacket - The spaces around the cylinders, between the inner and outer shells of the cylinder block or head, through which coolant circulates.

Web - A supporting structure across a cavity.

Woodruff key - A key with a radiused backside (viewed from the side).

Specifications

General

Displacement

2AZ-FE four-cylinder	144 cubic inches (2.36 liters)
1MZ-FE V6	183 cubic inches (3.0 liters)
3MZ-FE V6	202 cubic inches (3.3 liters)

Cylinder compression pressure

Four-cylinder	198 psi
V6	213 psi
Minimum compression pressure (all models)	142 psi
Variation between cylinders (all models)	14 psi

Oil pressure (all models)

At curb idle	4.3 psi or more
At 3000 rpm	36 to 78 psi

Torque specifications *   Ft-lbs (unless otherwise indicated)

Four-cylinder models

Connecting rod bearing cap bolts

Step 1	18
Step 2	Tighten an additional 90-degrees (1/4-turn)

Main bearing cap bolts

Step 1	15
Step 2	30
Step 3	Tighten an additional 90-degrees (1/4-turn)

V6 models

Connecting rod bearing cap bolts

Step 1	18
Step 2	Tighten an additional 90-degrees (1/4-turn)

Main bearing cap bolts

Step 1 (12-point bolts)	16
Step 2 (12-point bolts)	Tighten an additional 90-degrees (1/4-turn)
Step 3 (six-point bolts)	20

*Refer to Chapter 2, Part A or B for additional torque specifications

Section

1 General information
2 Antifreeze - general information
3 Thermostat - check and replacement
4 Engine cooling fans - removal and installation
5 Radiator and coolant reservoir - removal and installation
6 Water pump - check
7 Water pump - removal and installation
8 Coolant temperature sending unit - replacement
9 Blower motor - removal and installation
10 Heater and air conditioning control assembly - removal and installation
11 Heater core - removal and installation
12 Air conditioning and heating system - check and maintenance
13 Air conditioning receiver/drier - removal and installation
14 Air conditioning compressor - removal and installation
15 Air conditioning condenser - removal and installation

Reference to other Chapters

CHECK ENGINE light - See Chapter 6
Coolant level check - See Chapter 1
Cooling system check - See Chapter 1
Cooling system servicing (draining, flushing and refilling) - See Chapter 1
Drivebelt check, adjustment and replacement - See Chapter 1
Underhood hose check and replacement - See Chapter 1

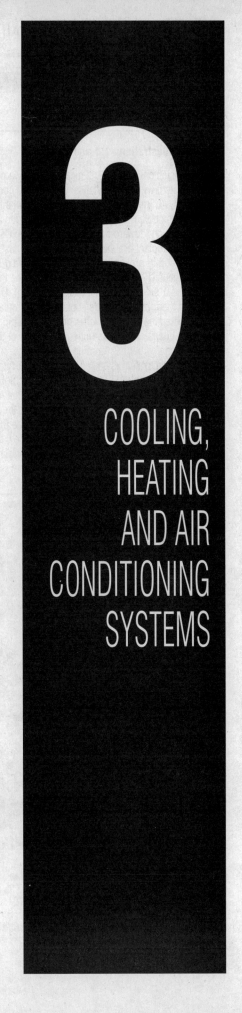

3

COOLING,
HEATING
AND AIR
CONDITIONING
SYSTEMS

ENGINE COOLING SYSTEM

▶ **Refer to illustrations 1.1 and 1.2**

All vehicles covered by this manual employ a pressurized engine cooling system with thermostatically controlled coolant circulation (see illustration). An impeller type water pump mounted on the front of the block pumps coolant through the engine. The coolant flows around each cylinder and toward the rear of the engine. Cast-in coolant passages direct coolant around the intake and exhaust ports, near the spark plug areas and in proximity to the exhaust valve guides.

A wax pellet-type thermostat is located in the thermostat housing near the front of the engine (see illustration). During warm up, the closed thermostat prevents coolant from circulating through the radiator. When the engine reaches normal operating temperature, the thermostat opens and allows hot coolant to travel through the radiator, where it is cooled before returning to the engine.

The cooling system is sealed by a pressure-type radiator cap. This raises the boiling point of the coolant, and the higher boiling point of the coolant increases the cooling efficiency of the radiator. If the system pressure exceeds the cap pressure relief value, the excess pressure in the system forces the spring-loaded valve inside the cap off its seat and allows the coolant to escape through the overflow tube into a coolant reservoir. When the system cools, the excess coolant is automatically drawn from the reservoir back into the radiator.

The coolant reservoir serves as both the point at which fresh coolant is added to the cooling system to maintain the proper fluid level and as a holding tank for overheated coolant.

This type of cooling system is known as a closed design because coolant that escapes past the pressure cap is saved and reused.

HEATING SYSTEM

The heating system consists of a blower fan and heater core located within the heater box, the inlet and outlet hoses connecting the heater core to the engine cooling system and the heater/air conditioning control head on the dashboard. Hot engine coolant is circulated through the heater core. When the heater mode is activated, a flap door opens to expose the heater box to the passenger compartment. A fan switch on the control head activates the blower motor, which forces air through the core, heating the air.

AIR CONDITIONING SYSTEM

The air conditioning system consists of a condenser mounted in front of the radiator, an evaporator mounted adjacent to the heater core under the dashboard, a compressor mounted on the engine, a receiver-drier which contains a high pressure relief valve and the plumbing connecting all of the above.

A blower fan forces the warmer air of the passenger compartment

1.1 Typical cooling system component locations (four-cylinder shown, V6 similar)

1	*Radiator cap*	*3*	*Upper radiator hose*	*5*	*Water pump*
2	*Cooling fans*	*4*	*Thermostat*	*6*	*Coolant recovery tank*

through the evaporator core (sort of a radiator-in-reverse), transferring the heat from the air to the refrigerant. The liquid refrigerant boils off into low-pressure vapor, taking the heat with it when it leaves the evaporator. The compressor keeps refrigerant circulating through the system, pumping the warmed coolant through the condenser where it is cooled and then circulated back to the evaporator.

Some models are equipped with an optional Automatic Air Conditioning system. With this system, you select the desired interior temperature with a knob on the controls, similar to setting the temperature on a home heating/cooling thermostat, and the system automatically adds the right blend of cool or warm air to maintain this temperature. The system has sensors that detect both the interior and outside temperature.

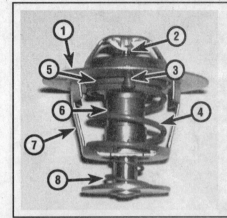

1.2 A typical thermostat

1   Flange
2   Piston
3   Jiggle valve
4   Main coil spring
5   Valve seat
6   Valve
7   Frame
8   Secondary coil spring

2   Antifreeze - general information

▶ Refer to illustration 2.4

❄ WARNING:

Do not allow antifreeze to come in contact with your skin or painted surfaces of the vehicle. Rinse off spills immediately with plenty of water. Antifreeze is highly toxic if ingested. Never leave antifreeze lying around in an open container or in puddles on the floor; children and pets are attracted by its sweet smell and may drink it. Check with local authorities on disposing of used antifreeze. Many communities have collection centers that will see that antifreeze is disposed of safely. Never dump used antifreeze on the ground or into drains.

➡Note: Non-Toxic coolant is available at local auto parts stores. Although the coolant is non-toxic when fresh, proper disposal of used coolant is still required.

The cooling system should be filled with a water/ethylene-glycol based antifreeze solution, which will prevent freezing down to at least -20 degrees F, or lower if local climate requires it. It also provides protection against corrosion and increases the coolant boiling point.

The cooling system should be drained, flushed and refilled at least every other year (see Chapter 1). The use of antifreeze solutions for periods of longer than two years is likely to cause damage and encourage the formation of rust and scale in the system. If your tap water is "hard," i.e. contains a lot of dissolved minerals, use distilled water with the antifreeze.

2.4 An inexpensive hydrometer can be used to test the condition of your coolant

Before adding antifreeze to the system, check all hose connections, because antifreeze tends to leak through very minute openings. Engines do not normally consume coolant. Therefore, if the level goes down, find the cause and correct it.

The exact mixture of antifreeze-to-water that you should use depends on the relative weather conditions. The mixture should contain at least 50 percent antifreeze, but should never contain more than 70-percent antifreeze. Consult the mixture ratio chart on the antifreeze container before adding coolant. Hydrometers are available at most auto parts stores to test the ratio of antifreeze to water (see illustration). Use antifreeze which meets the vehicle manufacturer's specifications.

3   Thermostat - check and replacement

❄ WARNING:

Do not attempt to remove the radiator cap, coolant or thermostat until the engine has cooled completely.

GENERAL CHECK

1   Before assuming the thermostat is responsible for a cooling system problem, check the coolant level (see Chapter 1), drivebelt tension (see Chapter 1) and temperature gauge (or light) operation.

2   If the engine takes a long time to warm up (as indicated by the temperature gauge or heater operation), the thermostat is probably

stuck open. Replace the thermostat with a new one.

3   If the engine runs hot, use your hand to check the temperature of the lower radiator hose. If the hose is not hot, but the engine is, the thermostat is probably stuck in the closed position, preventing the coolant inside the engine from escaping to the radiator. Replace the thermostat.

❄ CAUTION:

Do not drive the vehicle without a thermostat. The computer may stay in open loop and emissions and fuel economy will suffer.

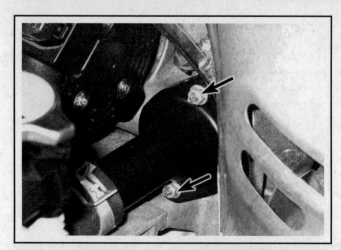

3.12 The thermostat cover on four-cylinder models is located between the alternator and the exhaust manifold

3.13a With the air cleaner cover removed, remove the nuts (arrows indicate two of three) on the back of the V6 engine and move the harness for access to the thermostat cover bolts

4 If the lower radiator hose is hot, it means that the coolant is flowing and the thermostat is open. Consult the Troubleshooting Section at the front of this manual for further diagnosis.

THERMOSTAT TEST

5 A more thorough test of the thermostat can only be made when it is removed from the vehicle (see below). If the thermostat remains in the open position at room temperature, it is faulty and must be replaced.

6 To test it fully, suspend the (closed) thermostat on a length of string or wire in a container of cold water, with a thermometer (cooking type that reads beyond 212-degrees F). A clear Pyrex cooking container is easiest to use.

7 Heat the water on a stove while observing the temperature and the thermostat. Neither should contact the sides of the container.

8 Note the temperature when the thermostat begins to open and when it is fully open. Compare the temperatures to the Specifications in this Chapter. The number stamped into the thermostat is generally the fully-open temperature. Some manufacturers provide Specifications for the beginning-to-open temperature, the fully-open temperature, and sometimes the amount the valve should open.

9 If the thermostat doesn't open and close as specified, or sticks in any position, replace it.

REPLACEMENT

▶ Refer to illustrations 3.12, 3.13a, 3.13b, 3.14 and 3.16

10 Disconnect the negative cable from the battery (see Chapter 5, Section 1).

11 Drain the coolant from the radiator (see Chapter 1). Disconnect the radiator hose from the thermostat housing or water inlet pipe.

12 On four-cylinder models remove the water inlet pipe from the thermostat housing (located on the back of the water pump housing) (see illustration).

13 On V6 models, unbolt the water inlet pipe and remove the pipe and O-ring (see illustrations).

14 Remove the fasteners and electrical connectors from the thermostat housing and detach the housing from the engine (see illustration). Be prepared for some coolant to spill as the gasket seal is broken.

➡Note: Access on V6 engines is easier with the air cleaner cover and hose removed.

15 Remove the thermostat, noting the direction in which it was

3.13b On V6 models, unbolt the water inlet pipe (arrow) from the cylinder head and remove it from the thermostat housing

3.14 The V6 thermostat housing is at the back of the intake manifold, above the transaxle - remove the hoses, wiring plugs and the three nuts

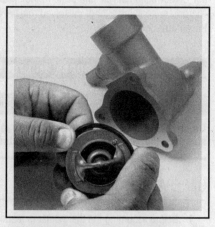

3.16 The thermostat gasket fits around the edge of the thermostat like a grooved sealing ring

installed in the housing, and thoroughly clean the sealing surfaces.

16 Fit a new gasket onto the thermostat (see illustration). Make sure it is evenly fitted all the way around.

17 Install the thermostat and housing, positioning the jiggle pin at the highest point.

18 Tighten the housing fasteners to the torque listed in this Chapter's Specifications and reinstall the remaining components in the reverse order of removal. On V6 models, use a new O-ring on the water inlet pipe and lubricate the O-ring with soapy water.

19 Refill the cooling system and on V6 models, bleed the air from the system (see Chapter 1). Run the engine and check for leaks and proper operation.

4 Engine cooling fans - removal and installation

▸ **Refer to illustrations 4.4, 4.5 and 4.6**

❉❉ **WARNING:**

Do not start this procedure until the engine is completely cool. Do not allow antifreeze to come in contact with your skin or painted surfaces of the vehicle. Rinse off spills immediately with plenty of water. Antifreeze is highly toxic if ingested. Never leave antifreeze lying around in an open container or in puddles on the floor; children and pets are attracted by its sweet smell and may drink it. Check with local authorities on disposing of used antifreeze. Many communities have collection centers, which will see that antifreeze is disposed of safely. Never dump used antifreeze on the ground or into drains.

1 Disconnect the negative battery cable (see Chapter 5, Section 1). Drain the cooling system (see Chapter 1), then detach the upper radiator hose from the radiator.

2 Disconnect the electrical connector at the fan motor.

3 Remove the two bolts and the air inlet duct.

4 Unbolt the fan/shroud from the radiator and lift it from the vehicle (see illustration).

5 Hold the fan blades and remove the fan retaining nut (see illustration).

6 Unbolt the fan motor from the shroud (see illustration).

7 Installation is the reverse of removal. Refill the cooling system (see Chapter 1).

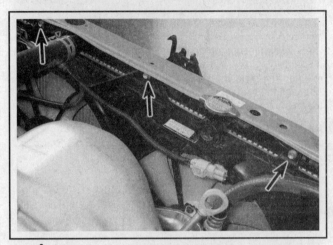

4.4 Unbolt the fan and shroud and remove the assembly from the radiator - arrows indicate the upper bolts at each fan; there are more at the bottom of the shroud

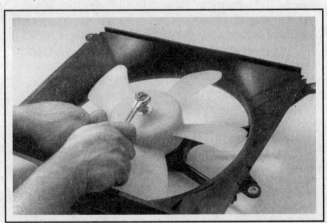

4.5 Remove the fan from the motor

4.6 Remove the screws and separate the motor from the shroud

5 Radiator and coolant reservoir - removal and installation

❉❉ **WARNING:**

Do not start this procedure until the engine is completely cool. Do not allow antifreeze to come in contact with your skin or painted surfaces of the vehicle. Rinse off spills immediately with plenty of water. Antifreeze is highly toxic if ingested. Never leave antifreeze lying around in an open container or in puddles on the floor; children and pets are attracted by its sweet smell and may drink it. Check with local authorities on disposing of used antifreeze. Many communities have collection centers, which will see that antifreeze is disposed of safely. Never dump used antifreeze on the ground or into drains.

5.5 Radiator support mounting bolts

➡Note: Non-toxic coolant is available at local auto parts stores. Although the coolant is non-toxic when fresh, proper disposal of used coolant is still required.

RADIATOR

Removal

▶ **Refer to illustrations 5.5 and 5.6**

1 Disconnect the negative battery cable (see Chapter 5, Section 1).
2 Drain the coolant into a container (see Chapter 1).
3 Detach the upper and lower radiator hoses from the radiator.
4 Disconnect the reservoir hose from the radiator filler neck.
5 Remove the cooling fans (see Section 4). At the radiator support, remove the horns (see Chapter 12) and the hood latch (see Chapter 11), then remove the bolts securing the support to the body (see illustration).
6 If equipped with an automatic transaxle, disconnect the cooler lines from the radiator (see illustration). Place a drip pan to catch the

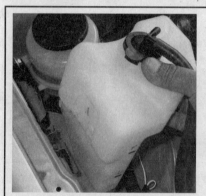

5.14 Pull the coolant reservoir up and out of its bracket to remove it

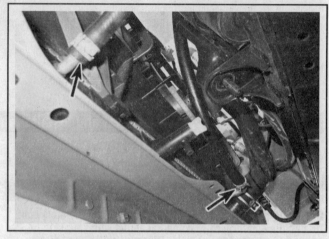

5.6 Detach the automatic transaxle cooler lines, if equipped

fluid and cap the fittings.
7 Lift out the radiator. Be aware of dripping fluids and the sharp fins.
8 With the radiator removed, it can be inspected for leaks, damage and internal blockage. If in need of repairs, have a professional radiator shop perform the work, as special techniques are required.
9 Bugs and dirt can be cleaned from the radiator with compressed air and a soft brush. Don't bend the cooling fins as this is done.

❄❄ **WARNING:**

Wear eye protection.

Installation

10 Installation is the reverse of the removal procedure. Be sure the rubber mounts are in place.
11 After installation, fill the cooling system with the proper mixture of antifreeze and water. Refer to Chapter 1 if necessary.
12 Start the engine and check for leaks. Allow the engine to reach normal operating temperature, indicated by the upper radiator hose becoming hot. Recheck the coolant level and add more if required.
13 On automatic transmission equipped models, check and add fluid as needed (see Chapter 1).

COOLANT RESERVOIR

▶ **Refer to illustration 5.14**

14 On most models, the coolant reservoir simply pulls up and out of the bracket on the fenderwell (see illustration).
15 Pour the coolant into a container. Wash out and inspect the reservoir for cracks and chafing. Replace it if damaged.
16 Installation is the reverse of removal.

6 Water pump - check

1 A failure in the water pump can cause serious engine damage due to overheating.
2 With the engine running and warmed to normal operating temperature, squeeze the upper radiator hose. If the water pump is working properly, a pressure surge should be felt as the hose is released.

❄❄ **WARNING:**

Keep hands away from fan blades!

3 Water pumps are equipped with weep or vent holes. If a failure

occurs in the pump seal, coolant will leak from this hole. In most cases it will be necessary to use a flashlight to find the hole on the water pump by looking through the space behind the pulley just below the water pump shaft. A slight gray discoloration around the weep hole is normal, while dark brown stains indicate a problem.

4   If the water pump shaft bearings fail there may be a howling sound at the front of the engine while it is running. Bearing wear can be felt if the water pump pulley is rocked up and down. Do not mistake drivebelt slippage, which causes a squealing sound, for water pump failure. Spray automotive drivebelt dressing on the belts to eliminate the belt as a possible cause of the noise.

7   Water pump - removal and installation

❄❄ WARNING:

Do not start this procedure until the engine is completely cool. Do not allow antifreeze to come in contact with your skin or painted surfaces of the vehicle. Rinse off spills immediately with plenty of water. Antifreeze is highly toxic if ingested. Never leave antifreeze lying around in an open container or in puddles on the floor; children and pets are attracted by its sweet smell and may drink it. Check with local authorities on disposing of used antifreeze. Many communities have collection centers, which will see that antifreeze is disposed of safely. Never dump used antifreeze on the ground or into drains.

➡Note: Non-toxic coolant is available at local auto parts stores. Although the coolant is non-toxic when fresh, proper disposal of used coolant is still required.

FOUR-CYLINDER ENGINE

♦ Refer to illustrations 7.4 and 7.5

1   Disconnect the negative battery cable (see Chapter 5, Section 1) and drain the cooling system (see Chapter 1).

2   Refer to Chapter 2A and remove the engine movement control rod and its bracket, then the #2 engine stay and bracket.

3   Remove the drivebelt (see Chapter 1) and the alternator (see Chapter 5).

4   Remove the water pump pulley, using a strap wrench or pin spanner wrench to hold the pulley while you loosen the bolts (see illustration).

5   Remove the four bolts and two nuts and pry the water pump off (see illustration). If necessary, tap the pump loose with a soft-face hammer.

6   To install, clean the water pump and block of any old gasket material or sealant, then clean with lacquer thinner.

7   Apply a new bead of sealant and install the water pump. Install the water pump bolts and nuts and tighten them to the torque listed in

7.4 Using a pin spanner to hold the water pump pulley, remove the pulley mounting bolts

this Chapter's Specifications within five minutes.

8   Install the remaining parts in the reverse order of removal.

9   Refill the cooling system (see Chapter 1), run the engine and check for leaks and proper operation.

V6 ENGINE

♦ Refer to illustrations 7.12, 7.13 and 7.15

10 Disconnect the negative battery cable (see Chapter 5, Section 1) and drain the cooling system (see Chapter 1).

11 Remove the timing belt and camshaft sprockets (see Chapter 2B).

12 Remove the bolt retaining the water inlet pipe to the alternator adjuster and remove the water inlet pipe and thermostat (see Section 3). Remove the number 3 timing belt cover (see illustration).

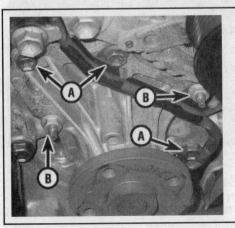

7.5 The four-cylinder water pump is retained by four bolts (A, one lower bolt not seen in this photo) and two nuts (B)

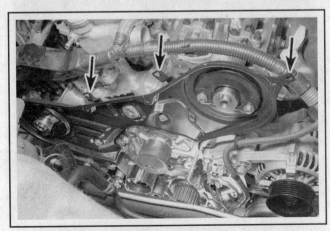

7.12 Release the three wiring harness clips, pull the harness back and remove the number three timing belt cover

7.13 V6 water pumps have two long studs - at least one must be removed with a small wrench to allow water pump removal

7.15 On V6 models, a new metal/rubber gasket is used when installing the water pump

13 Remove the water pump retaining bolts/nuts and separate the pump from the engine.

➡**Note: On some models there are two long studs (some engines may have bolts) that hold the engine mounting bracket and the water pump. The studs have a small hex-head that is used to remove the stud (see illustration). If it is stuck, remove the stud with locking pliers and replace the stud with a new bolt of the same length. At least one of these long studs must be removed to allow the water pump to be removed.**

14 Thoroughly clean all sealing surfaces, removing all traces of old gaskets, sealer and O-rings. Remove any traces of oil with acetone or lacquer thinner and a clean rag.

15 These models use a metal and rubber gasket (see illustration).

16 Reinstall the pump and the remaining parts in the reverse order of removal. Tighten the water pump bolts/nuts in several steps to the torque listed in this Chapter's Specifications.

17 Refill the cooling system (see Chapter 1) and run the engine, checking for leaks and proper operation.

8   Coolant temperature sending unit - replacement

▶ Refer to illustrations 8.2a and 8.2b

✳✳ WARNING:

Do not start this procedure until the engine is completely cool. Do not allow antifreeze to come in contact with your skin or painted surfaces of the vehicle. Rinse off spills immediately with plenty of water. Antifreeze is highly toxic if ingested. Never leave antifreeze lying around in an open container or in puddles on the floor; children and pets are attracted by its sweet smell and may drink it. Check with local authorities on disposing of used antifreeze. Many communities have collection centers which will see that antifreeze is disposed of safely. Never dump used antifreeze on the ground or into drains.

➡**Note: Non-toxic coolant is available at local auto parts stores. Although the coolant is non-toxic when fresh, proper disposal of used coolant is still required.**

1   Drain the coolant (see Chapter 1).

8.2a On four-cylinder models the Engine Coolant Temperature (ECT) sensor also functions as the coolant temperature sending unit - it's located on the left (driver's) end of the cylinder head

8.2b The coolant temperature sending unit no. 2 on V6 engines is located in the water outlet at the passenger's side of the engine - use a deep socket to remove it (sensor no. 1 is threaded into the lower tank of the radiator)

2   Disconnect the electrical connector from the sending unit (see illustrations).

3   Using a deep socket or a wrench, remove the sending unit.

4   Install the new unit and tighten it securely. Do not use thread

sealer as it may electrically insulate the sending unit.

5   Reconnect the electrical connector, refill the cooling system and check for coolant leakage and proper gauge function.

9   Blower motor - removal and installation

▶ **Refer to illustration 9.4 and 9.5**

> ✳✳ **WARNING:**
>
> **The models covered by this manual are equipped with Supplemental Restraint systems (SRS), more commonly known as airbags. Always disarm the airbag system before working in the vicinity of any airbag system component to avoid the possibility of accidental deployment of the airbag, which could cause personal injury (see Chapter 12).**

1   Disconnect the negative cable from the battery (see Chapter 5, Section 1).

2   The blower unit is located in the passenger compartment above the right front footwell.

3   Remove the glove compartment liner, the glove compartment door and the right lower dash panel (see Chapter 11).

4   To remove the blower, remove the blower unit retaining screws and lower the unit from the housing (see illustration).

5   If the motor is being replaced, transfer the fan to the new motor prior to installation (see illustration).

6   Installation is the reverse of removal. Check for proper operation.

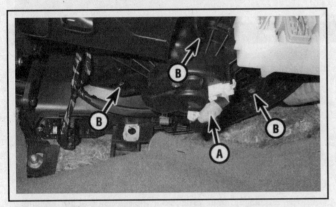

9.4 Blower motor location

A   Blower motor connector   *B   Blower motor mounting screws*

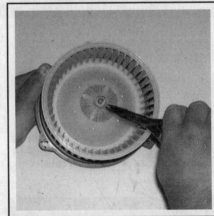

9.5 Use pliers to release and remove the clip, then lift the blower fan off the motor shaft

10   Heater and air conditioning control assembly - removal and installation

▶ **Refer to illustrations 10.2 and 10.4**

> ✳✳ **WARNING:**
>
> **The models covered by this manual are equipped with Supplemental Restraint systems (SRS), more commonly known as airbags. Always disarm the airbag system before working in the vicinity of any airbag system component to avoid the possibility of accidental deployment of the airbag, which could cause personal injury (see Chapter 12).**

1   Disconnect the negative cable from the battery (see Chapter 5, Section 1).

2   Reach behind the instrument panel and release the two large clips securing each side of the control assembly, but wear gloves as the clips may be sharp. If you use a wide-bladed plastic trim tool, the panel can be released from the front, working slowly and carefully (see illustration).

3   On Lexus models, remove the center trim panel, then remove the screws holding the control panel to the audio unit.

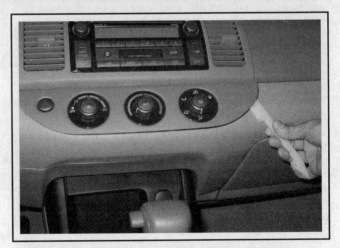

10.2 Carefully use a trim tool at each side of the control panel to release it from the dash clips

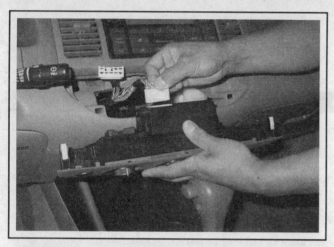

10.4 Disconnect the electrical connectors from the control assembly (Camry model shown)

4   Pull the control out slightly. Disconnect the electrical connectors and cable, if equipped (see illustration).

5   Installation is the reverse of the removal procedure.

6   Run the engine and check for proper functioning of the heater (and air conditioning, if equipped). If any of the switches (including the hazard warning switch that is in the heat/AC control panel) are faulty, the assembly must be replaced as a unit. The trim cover can be separated from the black control housing and reused on a new control assembly.

11 Heater core - removal and installation

▶ Refer to illustrations 11.6, 11.7, 11.8, 11.9, 11.10a, 11.10b, 11.11a, 11.11b, 11.12, 11.13, 11.14 and 11.15

✳ WARNING 1:

The models covered by this manual are equipped with Supplemental Restraint systems (SRS), more commonly known as airbags. Always disarm the airbag system before working in the vicinity of any airbag system component to avoid the possibility of accidental deployment of the airbag, which could cause personal injury (see Chapter 12).

✳ WARNING 2:

Do not allow antifreeze to come in contact with your skin or painted surfaces of the vehicle. Rinse off spills immediately with plenty of water. Antifreeze is highly toxic if ingested. Never leave antifreeze lying around in an open container or in puddles on the floor; children and pets are attracted by its sweet smell and may drink it. Check with local authorities on disposing of used antifreeze. Many communities have collection centers which will see that antifreeze is disposed of safely. Never dump used antifreeze on the ground or into drains.

➡Note 1: Non-toxic coolant is available at local auto parts stores. Although the coolant is non-toxic when fresh, proper disposal of used coolant is still required.

➡Note 2: Removal of the heater core is a difficult procedure for the home mechanic. There are numerous fasteners involved, some of which can be difficult to access, and we recommend that you have considerable mechanical experience before performing a heater core replacement.

1   Take the vehicle to a dealer service department or automotive air conditioning shop and have the air conditioning system discharged and the refrigerant recovered.

2   Disconnect the negative battery cable from the battery (see Chapter 5, Section 1).

3   Refer to Chapter 1 and drain the cooling system.

4   The factory procedure for removal of the heater core involves removal of the heater/evaporator housing, which requires complete removal of the instrument panel and cross-cowl support tube. The procedure in the following Steps is an easier method that involves just moving the box enough to replace the heater core. It still requires removal of the instrument panel, however.

5   Refer to Chapter 11 and remove the floor console and instrument panel cover.

6   Pull back the carpeting around the heater core/evaporator housing, which is supported on each side by brackets from the floor. Remove the bolts and other fasteners at the right side of the housing (see illustration).

7   Remove the bolts and other fasteners at the left housing support (see illustration).

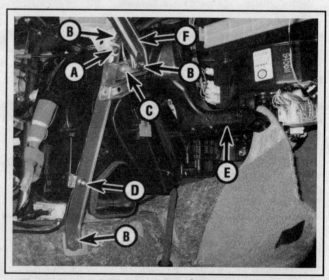

11:6 Remove the right-side support brackets for the heater core housing

A Nut	D Antenna retaining nut
B Support bracket bolts	E Floor air duct
C Ground wire	F Upper support bracket

11.7 At the left side, remove the harness fasteners (A), the ground wire bolt (B), and the support mounting bolts and nut (C)

11.8 Pull up the defroster ducting, then release the clips securing the harness to the cross-cowl tube (harness seen here just in front of the duct)

8   Release the two retaining clips and pull up on the central defroster duct to separate it from the heater core housing (see illustration).

9   The cross-cowl support tube will be unbolted but not removed, saving the trouble of disconnecting many electrical connectors. Remove the right-hand mounting bolts and the four bolts securing the heater box and blower box to the firewall (see illustration).

10 At the left end of the cross-cowl support tube, the two far-left mounting bolts (near the door pillar) need only be loosened, not removed. Two cross-cowl tube bolts must be removed at the firewall and the brake pedal assembly. At the right side, pull the tube rearward three or four inches (see illustrations).

11 From the engine side of the firewall, disconnect the refrigerant lines to the evaporator, then twist the coolant hoses off the heater core tubes (see illustrations). If the hoses are stuck, cut the hoses off and cut the remaining hose from the metal heater core tubes.

11.9 Remove the two bolts at the right side of the cross-cowl support tube (A) and remove the heater core box and blower housing mounting bolts (B)

11.10a Remove the cross-cowl tube retaining bolts at the firewall (A), and the brake pedal assembly (B)

11.10b At the right side of the cross-cowl support tube, pull the tube rearward until the bracket (A) rests on the firewall brace (B)

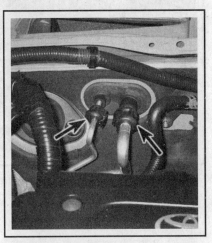

11.11a Disconnect the two refrigerant lines at the firewall, using a special tool

11.11b The A/C line clamp tool has two prongs that fit into the clamps for removal (shown off-vehicle for clarity)

11.12 Pull the housing away from the firewall until the heater core tubes clear the holes through the firewall

12 From inside the vehicle, carefully pull the heater core housing/blower case assembled toward the rear of the vehicle, until the heater core tubes clear the firewall (see illustration).

13 Remove the retaining clips securing the heater core to the side of the housing (see illustration).

14 To prevent damage to the carpet from spilled coolant, it is best to cover the carpet area around the heater core with an old blanket or towels on the floor. Slide the heater core and its tubes out to the left from the housing (see illustration).

➡Note: Tuck the throttle pedal down and under the carpeting for clearance.

15 Installation is the reverse order of removal. Use new O-rings to seal the evaporator refrigerant connections. Make sure all of the cross-cowl support tube mounting fasteners are tightened before installing the instrument panel pad (see illustration).

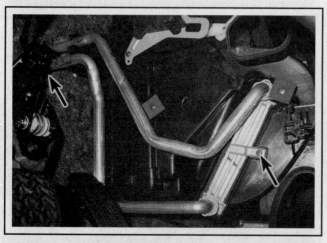

11.13 Near the firewall, release the clip, and at the housing remove the screw on the retaining strap

11.14 Carefully slide the heater core from the housing

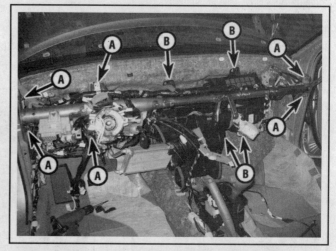

11.15 During installation, make sure all the fasteners are tight for the cowl support tube (A) and the heater/blower housings (B)

12 Air conditioning and heating system - check and maintenance

AIR CONDITIONING SYSTEM

✳ WARNING:

The air conditioning system is under high pressure. Do not loosen any hose fittings or remove any components until the system has been discharged. Air conditioning refrigerant must be properly discharged into an EPA-approved recovery/recycling unit by a dealer service department or an automotive air conditioning repair facility. Always wear eye protection when disconnecting air conditioning system fittings.

1 The following maintenance checks should be performed on a regular basis to ensure that the air conditioner continues to operate at peak efficiency.

a) *Inspect the condition of the compressor drivebelt. If it is worn or deteriorated, replace it (see Chapter 1).*

b) *Check the drivebelt tension and, if necessary, adjust it (see Chapter 1).*

c) *Inspect the system hoses. Look for cracks, bubbles, hardening and deterioration. Inspect the hoses and all fittings for oil bubbles or seepage. If there is any evidence of wear, damage or leakage, replace the hose(s).*

d) *Inspect the condenser fins for leaves, bugs and any other foreign material that may have embedded itself in the fins. Use a "fin comb" or compressed air to remove debris from the condenser.*

e) *Make sure the system has the correct refrigerant charge.*

2 It's a good idea to operate the system for about ten minutes at least once a month. This is particularly important during the winter months because long term non-use can cause hardening, and subsequent failure, of the seals.

3 Because of the complexity of the air conditioning system and the special equipment necessary to service it, in-depth troubleshooting and repairs are beyond the scope of this manual. However, simple component replacement procedures are provided in this Chapter.

4 The most common cause of poor cooling is simply a low system refrigerant charge. If a noticeable drop in system cooling ability occurs, one on the following quick checks will help you determine whether the refrigerant level is low.

CHECK

▶ **Refer to illustration 12.8**

5 Warm the engine up to normal operating temperature.

6 Place the air conditioning temperature selector at the coldest setting and put the blower at the highest setting. Open the doors (to make sure the air conditioning system doesn't cycle off as soon as it cools the passenger compartment).

7 After the system reaches operating temperature, feel the two pipes connected to the evaporator at the firewall.

8 The pipe (thinner tubing) leading from the condenser outlet to the evaporator should be cold, and the evaporator outlet line (the thicker tubing that leads back to the compressor) should be slightly colder (3 to 10 degrees F). If the evaporator outlet is considerably warmer than the inlet, the system needs a charge.

9 Insert a thermometer in the center air distribution duct (see illustration) while operating the air conditioning system - the temperature of

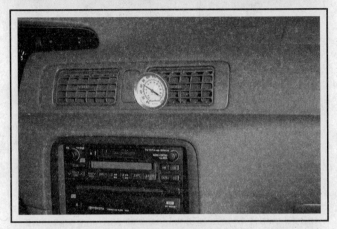

12.8 Place an accurate thermometer in the center dash vent, turn the air conditioning on and check the output temperature

the output air should be 35 to 40 degrees F below the ambient air temperature (down to approximately 40 degrees F). If the ambient (outside) air temperature is very high, say 110-degrees F, the duct air temperature may be as high as 60 degrees F, but generally the air conditioning is 35 to 40 degrees F cooler than the ambient air. If the air isn't as cold as it used to be, the system probably needs a charge. Further inspection or testing of the system is beyond the scope of the home mechanic and should be left to a professional.

ADDING REFRIGERANT

▶ **Refer to illustrations 12.10 and 12.13**

➡**Note: All models covered by this manual use refrigerant R-134a. When recharging or replacing air conditioning components, use only refrigerant, refrigerant oil and seals compatible with this system. The seals and compressor oil used with older, conventional R-12 refrigerant are not compatible with the components in this system.**

10 Buy an automotive charging kit at an auto parts store. A charging kit includes a 12-ounce can of R-134a refrigerant, a tap valve and a short section of hose that can be attached between the tap valve and the system low side service valve (see illustration).

11 Connect the charging kit by following the manufacturer's instructions.

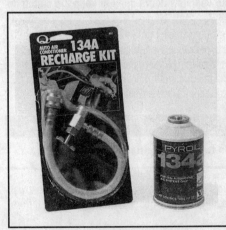

12.10 A basic charging kit for R-134a systems is available at most auto parts stores - it must say R-134a (not R-12) and so must the can of refrigerant

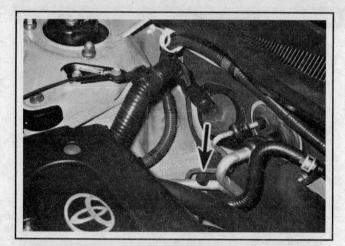

12.13 Add R-134a only to the low side port - the procedure is easier if you wrap the can with a warm, wet towel to prevent icing

12 Back off the valve handle on the charging kit and screw the kit onto the refrigerant can, making sure first that the O-ring or rubber seal inside the threaded portion of the kit is in place.

❊❊ **WARNING:**

Wear protective eyewear when dealing with pressurized refrigerant cans.

13 Remove the dust cap from the low-side charging port and attach the quick-connect fitting on the kit hose (see illustration).

❊ **WARNING:**

DO NOT hook the charging kit hose to the system high side! The fittings on the charging kit are designed to fit only on the low side of the system.

14 Warm the engine to normal operating temperature and turn on the air conditioning. Keep the charging kit hose away from the fan and other moving parts. In some cases, if the refrigerant charge is low enough, the air-conditioning system pressure switch may prevent the compressor from operating.

➡**Note: The charging process requires that the compressor be running. If the clutch cycles off, you can switch the A/C controls to High and leave the vehicle's doors open to keep the clutch on the compressor working.**

15 Turn the valve handle on the kit until the stem pierces the can, then back the handle out to release the refrigerant. You should be able to hear the rush of gas. Add refrigerant to the low side of the system until both the outlet and the evaporator inlet pipe feel about the same temperature. Allow stabilization time between each addition.

❊ **WARNING:**

Never add more than two cans of refrigerant to the system.

The can may tend to frost up, slowing the procedure. Wet a shop towel with hot water and wrap it around the bottom of the can to keep it from frosting.

16 Put your thermometer back in the center register and check that the output air is getting colder.

17 When the can is empty, turn the valve handle to the closed position and release the connection from the low-side port. Replace the dust cap.

18 Remove the charging kit from the can and store the kit for future use with the piercing valve in the UP position, to prevent inadvertently piercing the can on the next use.

HEATING SYSTEMS

▶ **Refer to illustration 12.23**

19 If the air coming out of the heater vents isn't hot, the problem could stem from any of the following causes: .

a) *The thermostat is stuck open, preventing the engine coolant from warming up enough to carry heat to the heater core. Replace the thermostat (see Section 3).*

b) *A heater hose is blocked, preventing the flow of coolant through the heater core. Feel both heater hoses at the firewall. They should be hot. If one of them is cold, there is an obstruction in one of the hoses or in the heater core, or the heater control valve is shut. Detach the hoses and back flush the heater core with a water hose. If the heater core is clear but circulation is impeded, remove the two hoses and flush them out with a garden hose.*

c) *If flushing fails to remove the blockage from the heater core, the core must be replaced (see Section 11).*

20 If the blower motor speed does not correspond to the setting selected on the blower switch, the problem could be a bad fuse, circuit, blower relay, speed switch or blower resistor.

21 If there isn't any air coming out of the vents:

a) *Turn the ignition ON and activate the fan control. Place your ear at the heating/air conditioning register (vent) and listen. Most motors are audible. Can you hear the motor running?*

b) *If you can't (and have already verified that the blower switch and the blower motor resistor are good), the blower motor itself is probably bad (see Section 9).*

22 If the carpet under the heater core is damp, or if antifreeze vapor or steam is coming through the vents, the heater core is leaking. Remove it (see Section 11) and install a new unit (most radiator shops will not repair a leaking heater core).

23 Inspect the drain hose from the heater/evaporator, which exits the body under the floor (see illustration). If there is a humid mist coming from the system ducts, this hose may be plugged with leaves or road debris.

12.23 This drain hose from the heater/air conditioning unit should be kept clear to allow drainage of condensation (shown from under the vehicle)

ELIMINATING AIR CONDITIONING ODORS

▶ **Refer to illustration 12.27**

24 Unpleasant odors that often develop in air conditioning systems are caused by the growth of a fungus, usually on the surface of the evaporator core. The warm, humid environment there is a perfect breeding ground for mildew to develop.

25 The evaporator core on most vehicles is difficult to access, and factory dealerships have a lengthy, expensive process for eliminating the fungus by opening up the evaporator case and using a powerful disinfectant and rinse on the core until the fungus is gone. You can service your own system at home, but it takes something much stronger than basic household germ-killers or deodorizers.

26 Aerosol disinfectants for automotive air-conditioning systems are available in most auto parts stores, but remember when shopping for them that the most effective treatments are also the most expensive. The basic procedure for using these sprays is to start by running the system in the RECIRC mode for ten minutes with the blower on its highest speed. Use the highest heat mode to dry out the system and keep the compressor from engaging by disconnecting the wiring connector at the compressor (see Section 14).

27 The disinfectant can usually comes with a long spray hose. Remove the cabin air filter, point the nozzle inside the hole and spray according to the manufacturer's recommendations (see illustration). Follow the manufacturer's recommendations for the length of spray and waiting time between applications.

28 Once the evaporator has been cleaned, the best way to prevent the mildew from coming back again is to make sure your evaporator housing drain tube is clear (see illustration 12.23) and to run the defrost cycle briefly to dry the evaporator out after a long drive with the air conditioning on.

AUTOMATIC AIR CONDITIONING

29 Solara, Lexus and Avalon models may have an optional Automatic Air Conditioning system to control the temperature inside the vehicle. You set the desired temperature on the control panel and the climate control module (computer) blends the right amount of cooled or heated air to maintain this cabin temperature. The speed of the blower motor in this system is electronically controlled by the microprocessor through a linear controller that replaces the conventional blower motor resistor.

30 Most repairs or diagnostics of the system are beyond the scope of the home mechanic, but there is an on-board diagnostics function in the computer that will display trouble codes relating to the climate-con-

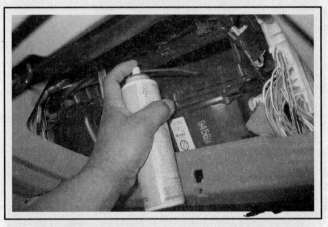

12.27 Remove the cabin air filter, then insert the disinfectant spray nozzle - be sure to support the nozzle so it doesn't get tangled up in the blower fan!

trol system. The codes can indicate what area, if any, is malfunctioning:

    11 Room temperature sensor
    12 Ambient temperature sensor
    13 Evaporator temperature sensor
    14 Water temperature sensor
    21 Solar sensor
    22 Compressor lock sensor
    23 Pressure switch
    31 Air mix damper position
    32 Air inlet damper position
    33 Air outlet damper position
    41 Air mix control servo motor
    42 Air inlet control servo motor
    43 Air outlet control servo motor

31 To begin the self-test function (vehicle interior at normal temperature), push the RECIRC/FR and AUTO buttons at the same time, while turning the ignition key to On. If all is normal with the system, the four indicator lights will come on for one second then go off in sequence.

32 After the indicators display, the computer performs a search for Diagnostic Trouble Codes (DTC's). Any codes will appear on the control head where the temperature setting is usually displayed.

33 After the trouble code check, the system will operate all of the system's actuators at one-second intervals. The test mode can be exited any time by pressing the OFF button, but the computer will keep the codes in memory. If you want to clear the climate control DTC's, pull the fuse marked "ECU-B" from the underhood fuse/relay box and keep it disconnected for at least 10 seconds.

13 Air conditioning receiver/drier - removal and installation

✳✳ WARNING:

The air conditioning system is under high pressure. Do not loosen any hose fittings or remove any components until the system has been discharged. Air conditioning refrigerant must be properly discharged into an EPA-approved recovery/recycling unit by a dealer service department or an automotive air conditioning repair facility. Always wear eye protection when disconnecting air conditioning system fittings.

➡**Note: Some models have a traditional receiver/drier, mounted at the right front of the engine compartment. Models that don't have a separate receiver/drier have one that is built into the side of the condenser.**

1 Have the refrigerant discharged by an air conditioning technician.
2 Disconnect the negative battery cable (see Chapter 5, Section 1).

13.3 After the system has been discharged, remove the Allen plug and pull the drier from the tube on the condenser

RECEIVER/DRIER INTEGRAL WITH CONDENSER

▶ **Refer to illustration 13.3**

3   Using an Allen wrench, detach the end plug (see illustration) and remove the drier from the condenser with a pair of needle-nose pliers.

4   Use new O-rings when installing the new drier and tighten the end plug to the torque listed in this Chapter's Specifications. Be sure to lubricate the O-rings with R-134a compatible refrigerant oil.

5   Installation is the reverse of removal.

SEPARATE RECEIVER/DRIER

▶ **Refer to illustration 13.6**

6   Disconnect the refrigerant lines from the receiver/drier and cap the open fittings to prevent the entry of moisture (see illustration).

13.6 Typical remote-mounted receiver/drier

7   Unscrew the two mounting bolts and remove the receiver/drier.

8   Loosen the clamp bolt and slide the receiver/drier out of the bracket.

9   Install the new receiver/drier by reversing the removal procedure.

10 If a new receiver/drier is being installed, add 20cc (0.71 ounce) of R-134a compatible refrigerant oil to it before connecting the lines.

11 Be sure to install new O-rings on the refrigerant lines, and lubricate them with R-134a compatible refrigerant oil, before connecting the lines.

ALL MODELS

12 Have the system evacuated, charged and leak tested by the shop that discharged it.

14 Air conditioning compressor - removal and installation

▶ **Refer to illustrations 14.4a and 14.4b**

❊❊ WARNING:

The air conditioning system is under high pressure. Do not loosen any hose fittings or remove any components until the system has been discharged. Air conditioning refrigerant must be properly discharged into an EPA-approved recovery/recycling unit by a dealer service department or an automotive air conditioning repair facility. Always wear eye protection when disconnecting air conditioning system fittings.

❊❊ CAUTION:

The receiver/drier should be replaced whenever the compressor is replaced (see Section 13).

1   Have the refrigerant discharged by an automotive air conditioning technician.

2   Disconnect the negative cable from the battery (see Chapter 5, Section 1).

3   Remove the drivebelt from the compressor (see Chapter 1). On V6 models, remove the alternator (see Chapter 5).

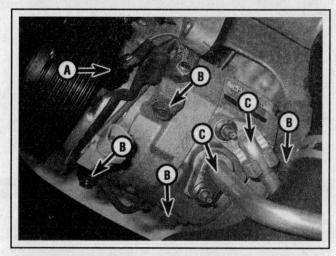

14.4a Compressor details - four-cylinder models (shown with alternator removed)

A Electrical connector   C Refrigerant lines
B Mounting bolts

4   Detach the wiring connector and the refrigerant lines (see illustrations).

5   Unbolt the compressor and lift it from the vehicle.

6   If a new or rebuilt compressor is being installed, follow the directions, which come with it regarding the proper level of oil prior to installation.

7   Installation is the reverse of removal. Replace any O-rings with new ones specifically made for the purpose and lubricate them with refrigerant oil.

8   Have the system evacuated, recharged and leak tested by the shop that discharged it.

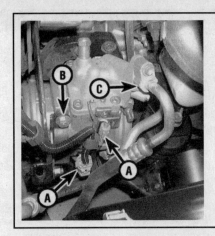

14.4b Compressor details - V6 models (shown with alternator removed)

A   Electrical connectors
B   Mounting bolts (one shown here)
C   Refrigerant lines

15 Air conditioning condenser - removal and installation

▶ **Refer to illustrations 15.4 and 15.5**

❊❊ WARNING:

The air conditioning system is under high pressure. Do not loosen any hose fittings or remove any components until the system has been discharged. Air conditioning refrigerant must be properly discharged into an EPA-approved recovery/recycling unit by a dealer service department or an automotive air conditioning repair facility. Always wear eye protection when disconnecting air conditioning system fittings.

❊❊ CAUTION:

The receiver/drier should be replaced whenever the condenser is replaced.

1   Have the refrigerant discharged by an air conditioning technician.

2   Remove the radiator upper mounts as described in Section 5.

3   On models with a separately mounted receiver/drier, remove the receiver/drier (see Section 13).

4   Disconnect the inlet and outlet fittings (see illustration). Cap the open fittings immediately to keep moisture and dirt out of the system.

5   Remove the mounting nuts/bolts (see illustration). Push the radiator back toward the engine, then push the condenser rearward until it's free of the radiator support and can be pulled up and out of the vehicle.

6   Install the condenser, brackets and bolts, making sure the rubber cushions fit on the mounting points properly.

7   Reconnect the refrigerant lines, using new O-rings where needed.

8   Reinstall the remaining parts in the reverse order of removal.

9   Have the system evacuated, charged and leak tested by the shop that discharged it.

15.4 Remove the bolts holding the refrigerant lines to the right side of the condenser - on some models, the line is clamped to the side of the condenser as well

15.5 Remove the mounting bolt and nut at the condenser bracket on each side (left side shown, right side similar)

Specifications

General

Radiator cap pressure rating	
Four-cylinder engine	10.7 to 14.9 psi
V6 engine	12.1 to 16.4 psi
Thermostat rating	
Opens	176 to 183-degrees F
Fully open	203-degrees F

Torque specifications   Ft-lbs (unless otherwise indicated)

➡Note: One foot-pound (ft-lb) of torque is equivalent to 12 inch-pounds (in-lbs) of torque. Torque values below approximately 15 ft-lbs are expressed in inch-pounds, since most foot-pound torque wrenches are not accurate at these smaller values.

Receiver/drier Allen plug	108 in-lbs
Thermostat housing bolts	
Four-cylinder engine	78 in-lbs
V6 engine	70 in-lbs
Water pump bolts/nuts	
Four-cylinder engine	80 in-lbs
V6 engine	71 in-lbs

Section

1   General information
2   Fuel pressure relief
3   Fuel pump/fuel pressure - check
4   Fuel lines and fittings - general information
5   Fuel pump - removal and installation
6   Fuel pressure regulator - removal and installation
7   Fuel level sending unit - replacement
8   Fuel tank - removal and installation
9   Fuel tank cleaning and repair - general information
10   Air cleaner assembly - removal and installation
11   Electronic fuel injection system - general information
12   Electronic fuel injection system - check
13   Throttle body - check, removal and installation
14   Fuel pulsation damper - replacement
15   Fuel rail and injectors - removal and installation
16   Exhaust system servicing - general information

Reference to other Chapters

Air filter replacement - See Chapter 1
CHECK ENGINE light on - See Chapter 6
Exhaust system check - See Chapter 1
Fuel system check - See Chapter 1
Underhood hose check and replacement - See Chapter 1

4

FUEL AND EXHAUST SYSTEMS

1 General information

♦ **Refer to illustrations 1.1a and 1.1b**

The fuel system consists of a fuel tank, an electric fuel pump (located in the fuel tank), a fuel pressure regulator located next to the fuel pump, an EFI main relay, a fuel pump relay (circuit opening relay), the fuel rail and fuel injectors, an air cleaner assembly and a throttle body unit. All models are equipped with a Sequential Electronic Fuel Injection system (see illustrations).

SEQUENTIAL ELECTRONIC FUEL INJECTION SYSTEM

Sequential Electronic Fuel Injection uses timed impulses to inject the fuel directly into the intake port of each cylinder according to its firing order. The injectors are controlled by the Powertrain Control Module (PCM). The PCM monitors various engine parameters and delivers the exact amount of fuel required into the intake ports. The throttle body serves only to control the amount of air passing into the system. Because each cylinder is equipped with its own injector, much better control of the fuel/air mixture ratio is possible.

FUEL PUMP AND LINES

Fuel is circulated from the fuel tank to the fuel injection system through a metal line running along the underside of the vehicle. An electric fuel pump and fuel level sending unit is located inside the fuel tank along with a fuel pressure regulator. A vapor return system routes all vapors back to the fuel tank through a separate return line.

The fuel pump relay is equipped with a primary and secondary volt-

1.1a Fuel injection components - four-cylinder engine

1	Fuel rail	3	Throttle body
2	Intake manifold	4	Fuel injectors

age circuit. The primary circuit is controlled by the PCM and the secondary circuit is linked directly to the EFI main relay from the ignition switch. With the ignition switch ON (engine not running), the PCM will ground the relay for two seconds. During cranking, the PCM grounds the fuel pump relay as long as the camshaft position sensor sends its position signal (see Chapter 6). If there are no reference pulses, the fuel pump will shut off after two seconds.

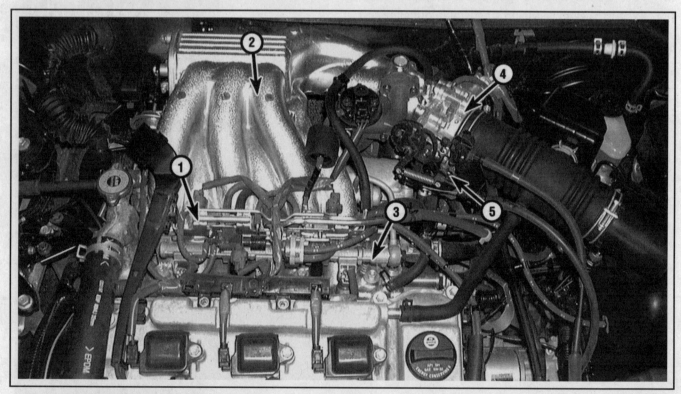

1.1b Fuel injection components - typical V6 engine

1	Fuel injector	3	Fuel rail	5	Idle Air Control (IAC) valve (below throttle body)
2	Air intake plenum	4	Throttle body		

EXHAUST SYSTEM

The exhaust system consists of exhaust manifolds (one on four-cylinder models, two on V6 models), exhaust pipes, catalytic converters, a muffler and a tail pipe. On some California models, two catalytic converters are used, in which case the front catalytic converter is an integral component of the exhaust manifold.

The catalytic converters are an emission control device added to the exhaust system to reduce pollutants. Refer to Chapter 6 for more information regarding the catalytic converters.

2   Fuel pressure relief

▶ Refer to illustration 2.1

※※ WARNING:

Gasoline is extremely flammable, so take extra precautions when you work on any part of the fuel system. Don't smoke or allow open flames or bare light bulbs near the work area, and don't work in a garage where a gas-type appliance (such as a water heater or a clothes dryer) is present. Since gasoline is carcinogenic, wear latex gloves when there's a possibility of being exposed to fuel, and, if you spill any fuel on your skin, rinse it off immediately with soap and water. Mop up any spills immediately and do not store fuel-soaked rags where they could ignite. The fuel system is under constant pressure, so, if any fuel lines are to be disconnected, the fuel pressure in the system must be relieved first. When you perform any kind of work on the fuel system, wear safety glasses and have a Class B type fire extinguisher on hand.

1   Remove the gas cap to release any pressure there. In the underhood fuse/relay panel, remove the relay marked C/OPN (see illustration).

2   Start the engine and allow it to run until it stops, then turn the key Off. Disconnect the cable from the negative terminal of the battery before working on the fuel system (see Chapter 5, Section 1).

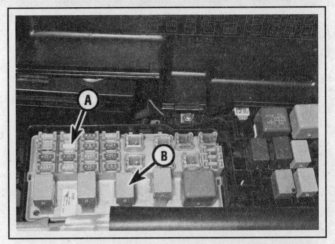

2.1 Location of the EFI fuse (A) and the C/OPN relay (B) - 2004 Camry shown (be sure to check the fuse/relay box cover on your vehicle to verify the locations of these components)

3   The fuel system pressure is now relieved. When you're finished working on the fuel system, reinstall the C/OPN relay, reinstall the gas cap and connect the negative cable to the battery.

3   Fuel pump/fuel pressure - check

※※ WARNING:

Gasoline is extremely flammable, so take extra precautions when you work on any part of the fuel system. See the Warning in Section 2.

GENERAL CHECKS

1   Check that there is adequate fuel in the fuel tank.

2   Verify the fuel pump actually runs. Have an assistant turn the ignition switch to ON - you should hear a brief whirring noise (for approximately two seconds) as the pump comes on and pressurizes the system.

➡Note: The fuel pump is easily heard through the gas tank filler neck.

If there is no response from the fuel pump (makes no sound), check the IGN fuse and the EFI fuse, and the C/OPN and EFI relays (these are located in the engine compartment fuse/relay box). If the fuses and relays are OK, check the wiring back to the fuel pump. If voltage is present at the fuel pump electrical connector for a couple of seconds when the ignition key is turned on, the fuel pump is defective. If no voltage is present, the PCM may be at fault. Have the vehicle checked at a dealer service department or other qualified repair shop.

FUEL PUMP PRESSURE CHECK

▶ Refer to illustrations 3.3a and 3.3b

➡Note: In order to perform the fuel pressure test, you will need to obtain a fuel pressure gauge capable of measuring high fuel pressure and the proper adapter set for the specific fuel injection system.

3   Relieve the fuel system pressure (see Section 2). On Avalon models, disconnect the fuel line at the bottom of the fuel filter to hook up the test gauge. On other models, remove the fuel line from the fuel rail and where this line attaches to a steel line near the master cylinder. A simple special tool is used to separate the quick-connect fittings (see Section 4). The fuel pressure test hose temporarily replaces this factory hose (see illustrations). Make sure the clamps are tight on the hoses.

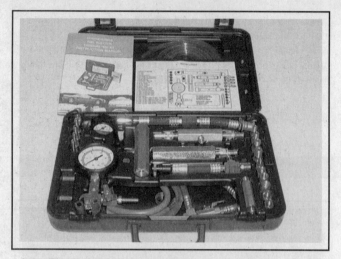

3.3a This fuel pressure testing kit contains all the necessary fittings and adapters, along with the fuel pressure gauge, to test most automotive fuel systems

3.3b Attach the fuel pressure gauge with fuel hose and clamps between the fuel rail and the fuel feed line; turn the ignition key ON and check the fuel pressure

4   Turn all the accessories Off and switch the ignition key On. The fuel pump should run for about two seconds; note the reading on the gauge. After the pump stops running, the pressure should hold steady. After five minutes it should not drop below the minimum listed in this Chapter's Specifications.

5   Start the engine and let it idle at normal operating temperature. The pressure should remain the same. If all the pressure readings are within the limits listed in this Chapter's Specifications, the system is operating properly.

6   If the fuel pressure is not within specifications, check the following:

a) If the pressure is higher than specified, replace the fuel pressure regulator (see Section 6).
b) If the pressure is lower than specified, check the fuel filter and fuel lines from the fuel rail to the fuel tank for restrictions or damage. Check the fuel injectors for leaks. If the pressure is still low, most likely the fuel pressure regulator and/or the fuel pump is defective. In this situation, it is recommended that both the fuel pressure regulator and fuel pump are replaced to prevent any future fuel pressure problems.

7   After the testing is done, relieve the fuel pressure (see Section 2) and remove the fuel pressure gauge.

4   Fuel lines and fittings - general information

✳✳ WARNING:

Gasoline is extremely flammable, so take extra precautions when you work on any part of the fuel system. See the Warning in Section 2.

1   Always relieve the fuel pressure and disconnect the cable from the negative battery terminal before servicing fuel lines or fittings (see Section 2).

2   The fuel line extends from the fuel tank to the engine compartment. The line is secured to the underbody with clip and screw assemblies. This line must be occasionally inspected for leaks, kinks and dents.

3   If evidence of dirt is found in the system or fuel filter during disassembly, the line should be disconnected and blown out. Check the fuel strainer on the fuel gauge sending unit (see Section 5) for damage and deterioration.

STEEL TUBING

4   If replacement of a fuel line or emission line is called for, use welded steel tubing meeting the manufacturer's specifications or its equivalent.

5   Don't use copper or aluminum tubing to replace steel tubing.

These materials cannot withstand normal vehicle vibration.

6   Because fuel lines used on fuel-injected vehicles are under high pressure, they require special consideration.

7   Some fuel lines have threaded fittings with O-rings. Any time the fittings are loosened to service or replace components:

a) Use an open-end wrench on the stationary fitting while loosening and tightening the fitting nuts.
b) Check all O-rings for cuts, cracks and deterioration. Replace any that appear hardened, worn or damaged.
c) If the lines are replaced, always use original equipment parts, or parts that meet the original equipment standards specified in this Section.

FLEXIBLE HOSE

✳✳ WARNING:

Use only original equipment replacement hoses or their equivalent. Others may fail from the high pressures of this system.

8   Don't route fuel hose within four inches of any part of the exhaust system or within ten inches of the catalytic converter. Metal lines and rubber hoses must never be allowed to chafe against the frame. A mini-

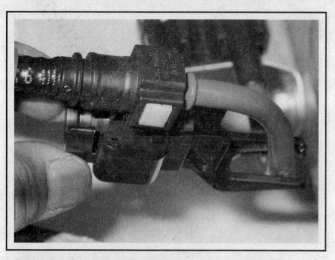

4.12a Pushing in the yellow button on quick-connect fuel connections releases the two halves of the cover over the joint

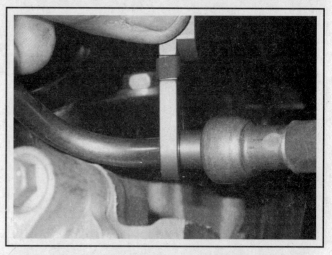

4.12b Push this simple special tool into the fuel connection, push the line toward the tool, then pull the line back to separate the fuel line connection

mum of 1/4-inch clearance must be maintained around a line or hose to prevent contact with the frame.

9   Some models may be equipped with nylon fuel line and quick-connect fittings at the fuel filter and/or fuel pump. The quick-connect fittings cannot be serviced separately. Do not attempt to service these types of fuel lines in the event the retainer tabs or the line becomes damaged. Replace the entire fuel line as an assembly.

REPLACEMENT

▶ **Refer to illustrations 4.12a and 4.12b**

10   In the event of any fuel line damage (metal or flexible lines) it is necessary to replace the damaged lines with factory replacement parts.

Others may fail from the high pressures of this system.

11   Relieve the fuel pressure.

12   Remove all fasteners attaching the lines to the vehicle body. On fuel lines so equipped, detach the clamp(s) that attach the fuel hoses to the metal lines, then pull the hose off the fitting. Twisting the hoses back and forth will allow them to separate more easily. To separate quick-connect fittings, hold the connector with one hand and depress the retaining tabs with the other hand, then separate the connector from the pipe (see illustrations).

13   Installation is the reverse of removal. Be sure to use new O-rings at the threaded fittings (if equipped). On quick-connect fittings, align the retainer locking pawls with the connector grooves. Push the connector onto the pipe until both retaining pawls lock with a clicking sound, then reinstall the covers.

5   Fuel pump - removal and installation

> ❊❊ **WARNING:**
>
> **Gasoline is extremely flammable, so take extra precautions when you work on any part of the fuel system. See the Warning in Section 2.**

REMOVAL

▶ **Refer to illustrations 5.5, 5.8, 5.9a and 5.9b**

1   Relieve the fuel system pressure (see Section 2) and remove the fuel tank cap.

2   Disconnect the cable from the negative terminal of the battery (see Chapter 5, Section 1).

3   Remove the rear seat from inside the passenger compartment (see Chapter 11).

4   Remove the fuel pump/sending unit floor service hole cover.

5   Disconnect the electrical connectors and the fuel line from the top of the fuel pump unit (see illustration).

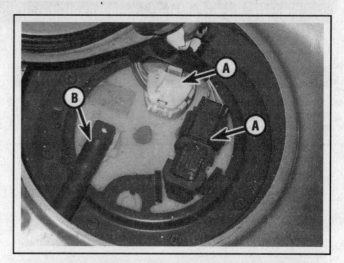

5.5 Disconnect the two electrical connectors (A), pull off the cover and the yellow clip, then withdraw the fuel hose (B)

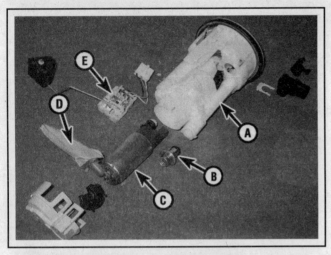

5.8 Exploded view of the fuel pump assembly

A   Fuel tank fuel filter
B   Fuel pressure regulator
C   Fuel pump
D   Sock filter at fuel pump
E   Fuel level sending unit

6   Remove the fuel pump/sending unit retaining bolts.

7   Carefully withdraw the fuel pump/fuel level sending unit assembly from the fuel tank.

8   The components of the fuel pump assembly are modular and all attach to the main housing (see illustration).

9   Remove the plastic support on the bottom of the pump by releasing the clips with a screwdriver, then pull off the rubber isolator, the fuel sock filter clip, then the electrical connector (see illustrations).

10 Withdraw the pump from the housing.

11 Inspect the strainer for contamination. If it is dirty, replace it.

INSTALLATION

12 Reassemble the fuel pump/sending unit in the reverse order of disassembly.

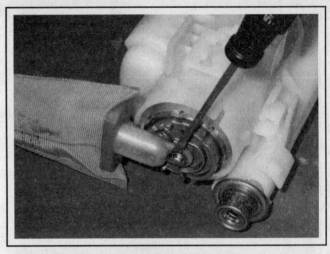

5.9a Carefully use a screwdriver to remove the clip securing the fuel sock filter to the pump

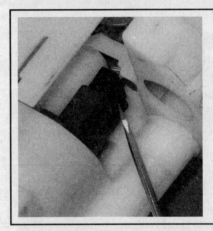

5.9b Release the electrical connector at the top of the fuel pump assembly

13 Install the fuel pump/sending unit assembly in the fuel tank. Connect the fuel line and electrical connectors.

14 The remainder of installation is the reverse of removal.

6   Fuel pressure regulator - removal and installation

♦ **Refer to illustration 6.3**

❊❊ WARNING:

Gasoline is extremely flammable, so take extra precautions when you work on any part of the fuel system. See the Warning in Section 2.

1   Relieve the fuel system pressure (see Section 2), then disconnect the negative battery cable (see Chapter 5, Section 1).

2   Remove the fuel pump (see Section 5).

3   Twist the fuel pressure regulator from the assembly (see illustration).

4   Installation is the reverse of removal. Be sure to install a new O-ring on the fuel pressure regulator.

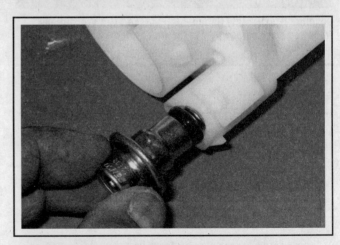

6.3 The fuel pressure regulator is a push-fit in the fuel pump/sending unit assembly, make sure the O-ring comes out with it

7 Fuel level sending unit - replacement

▶ **Refer to illustration 7.4**

❋❋ WARNING:

Gasoline is extremely flammable, so take extra precautions when you work on any part of the fuel system. See the Warning in Section 2.

1 Relieve the fuel system pressure (see Section 2), then disconnect the negative battery cable (see Chapter 5, Section 1). Remove the fuel pump/fuel level sending unit assembly from the fuel tank (see Section 5).

2 Carefully angle the sending unit out of the opening without damaging the fuel level float located at the bottom of the assembly.

3 Disconnect the electrical connector from the sending unit.

4 Pry the sending unit from the retaining clips (see illustration) and separate it from the assembly.

5 Installation is the reverse of removal.

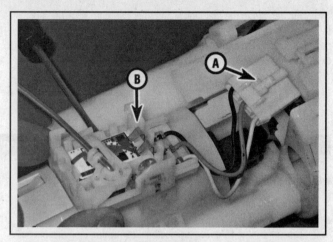

7.4 Disconnect the electrical connector (A) and pry the fuel level sending unit from the clips (B)

8 Fuel tank - removal and installation

▶ **Refer to illustrations 8.7 and 8.8**

❋❋ WARNING:

Gasoline is extremely flammable, so take extra precautions when you work on any part of the fuel system. See the Warning in Section 2.

1 Relieve the fuel system pressure (see Section 2).

2 Remove the fuel filler cap to relieve fuel tank pressure.

3 Detach the cable from the negative terminal of the battery (see Chapter 5).

4 If the tank is full or nearly full, siphon the fuel into an approved container using a siphoning kit (available at most auto parts stores).

❋❋ WARNING:

Do not start the siphoning action by mouth!

5 Raise the vehicle and place it securely on jackstands. Refer to Chapter 9 and disconnect the parking brake cables.

6 Remove the exhaust system from the center exhaust pipe completely to the rear of the vehicle.

7 Disconnect the fuel lines, the vapor return line and the fuel inlet pipe from the fuel tank fittings (see illustration).

➡**Note: Be sure to plug the hoses to prevent leakage and contamination of the fuel system.**

8 Remove the four fasteners securing the exhaust heat shield below the fuel tank (see illustration).

9 Support the fuel tank with a floor jack. Place a sturdy plank between the jack head and the fuel tank to protect the tank.

10 Remove the bolts from the fuel tank retaining straps.

11 Remove the tank from the vehicle.

12 Installation is the reverse of removal.

8.7 Loosen the clamp and disconnect the fuel filler hose from the fuel tank

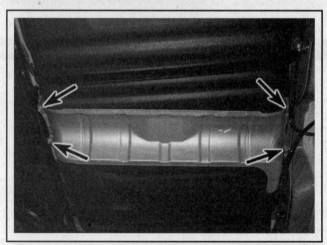

8.8 Remove the four bolts and the exhaust heat shield

9 Fuel tank cleaning and repair - general information

1   Any repairs to the fuel tank or filler neck should be carried out by a professional who has experience in this critical and potentially dangerous work. Even after cleaning and flushing of the fuel system, explosive fumes can remain and ignite during repair of the tank.

2   If the fuel tank is removed from the vehicle, it should not be placed in an area where sparks or open flames could ignite the fumes coming out of the tank. Be especially careful inside garages where a gas-type appliance is located, because it could cause an explosion.

10 Air cleaner assembly - removal and installation

▶ **Refer to illustrations 10.2 and 10.3**

1   Detach the clips, lift up the air cleaner cover and remove the filter element (see Chapter 1).

2   Disconnect the MAF sensor electrical connector, then disconnect the air intake hose from the cover (see illustration).

3   Remove the three bolts and remove the air cleaner assembly from the engine compartment (see illustration).

4   Installation is the reverse of removal.

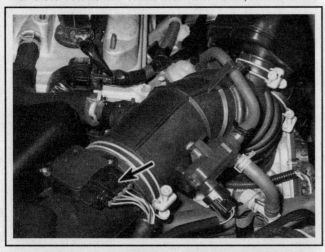

10.2 Disconnect the MAF sensor connector, then remove the clamp to separate the air intake hose from the air cleaner

10.3 Remove the three bolts from the air cleaner assembly and lift the assembly from the compartment

11 Electronic fuel injection system - general information

The Electronic Fuel Injection (EFI) system consists of three sub-systems: air intake, electronic control and fuel delivery. The system uses a Powertrain Control Module (PCM) along with several sensors to determine the proper air/fuel ratio under all operating conditions. Refer to illustrations 1.1a and 1.1b for component locations.

The fuel injection system and the emissions control system are closely linked in function and design. For additional information, refer to Chapter 6.

AIR INTAKE SYSTEM

The air intake system consists of the air cleaner, the air intake ducts, the throttle body, the idle control system and the intake manifold. V6 engines are equipped with an intake manifold (lower) and an intake

air plenum (upper). Four-cylinder engines are equipped with a single intake manifold. Refer to Chapters 2A or 2B for the replacement procedures.

The throttle body is a single barrel, side-draft design. The lower portion of the throttle body is heated by engine coolant to prevent icing in cold weather. A throttle position sensor is attached to the throttle shaft to monitor changes in the throttle opening. All throttle bodies are electronically-controlled. There is no accelerator cable. The idle function is controlled by the electronic throttle control system.

ELECTRONIC CONTROL SYSTEM

The electronic control system, Powertrain Control Module and sensors are described in detail in Chapter 6.

FUEL DELIVERY SYSTEM

The fuel delivery system consists of these components: The fuel pump, fuel pressure regulator, fuel filter, fuel lines, fuel rail and the fuel injectors.

The fuel pump is an electric in-line type. Fuel is drawn through an inlet strainer into the pump, flows through the fuel pressure regulator, passes through the fuel filter and is delivered to the injectors. The fuel pressure regulator maintains a constant fuel pressure to the injectors.

The injectors are solenoid-actuated, constant stroke, pintle types consisting of a solenoid, plunger, needle valve and housing. When current is applied to the solenoid coil, the needle valve raises and pres-

surized fuel fills the injector housing and squirts out the nozzle. The injection quantity is determined by the length of time the valve is open (the length of time during which current is supplied to the solenoid coils). Because it determines opening and closing intervals - which in turn determines the air-fuel mixture ratio - injector timing must be quite accurate.

The EFI main relay, located in the engine compartment relay/fuse box, supplies power to the fuel pump relay (circuit opening relay) from the ignition key. The PCM controls the grounding signal to the fuel pump in response to the starting and camshaft position signals at start-up.

12 Electronic fuel injection system - check

♦ **Refer to illustrations 12.7 and 12.8**

✳ WARNING:

Gasoline is extremely flammable, so take extra precautions when you work on any part of the fuel system. See the Warning in Section 2.

1   Check all electrical connectors, especially ground connections, for the system. Loose connectors and poor grounds can cause many engine control system problems.

2   Verify that the battery is fully charged, because the Powertrain Control Module (PCM) and sensors cannot operate properly without adequate supply voltage.

3   Refer to Chapter 1 and check the air filter element. A dirty or partially blocked filter will reduce performance and economy.

4   Check fuel pump operation (see Section 3). If the fuel pump fuse

is blown, replace it and see if it blows again. If it does, look for a short in the wiring harness to the fuel pump.

5   Inspect the vacuum hoses connected to the intake manifold for damage, deterioration and leakage.

6   Remove the air intake duct from the throttle body and check for dirt, carbon, varnish, or other residue in the throttle body, particularly around the throttle plate. If it's dirty, refer to Chapter 6 and troubleshoot the PCV and EGR systems for the cause of excessive varnish buildup.

7   With the engine running, place an automotive stethoscope against each injector, one at a time, and listen for a clicking sound that indicates operation (see illustration). If you don't have a stethoscope, you can place the tip of a long screwdriver against the injector and listen through the handle.

8   If an injector does not seem to be operating electrically (not clicking), purchase a special injector test light (sometimes called a "noid" light) and install it into the injector wiring harness connector (see illustration). Start the engine and see if the noid light flashes. If it

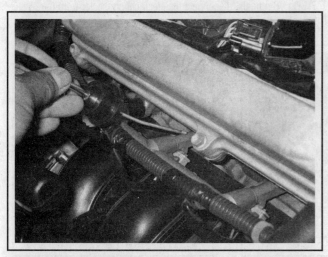

12.7 Use a stethoscope or a screwdriver to determine if the injectors are working properly - they should make a steady clicking sound that rises and falls with engine speed changes

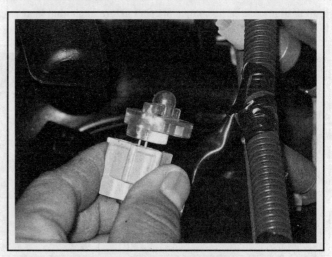

12.8 Install the "noid" light into the fuel injector electrical connector and check to see that it blinks with the engine running

does, the injector is receiving proper voltage. If it doesn't flash, further diagnosis is necessary. You might want to have it checked by a dealership service department or other qualified repair shop.

9   With the engine off and the fuel injector electrical connectors disconnected, measure the resistance of each injector with an ohmmeter. Refer to the Specifications at the end of this Chapter for the correct resistance.

10 Refer to Chapter 6 for other system checks.

13 Throttle body - check, removal and installation

> ❋❋ **WARNING:**
>
> Gasoline is extremely flammable, so take extra precautions when you work on any part of the fuel system. See the Warning in Section 2.

CHECK

▶ Refer to illustration 13.2

1   Verify that the throttle linkage operates smoothly.
2   Remove the air intake duct from the throttle body and check for carbon and residue build-up. If it is dirty, clean it with aerosol carburetor cleaner (make sure the can specifically states that it is safe with oxygen sensor systems and catalytic converters) and a toothbrush (see illustration).

> ❋❋ **CAUTION:**
>
> Do not clean the throttle position sensor (TPS) or Idle Air Control (IAC) valve with the solvent.

REMOVAL AND INSTALLATION

▶ Refer to illustrations 13.4, 13.5 and 13.8

> ❋❋ **WARNING:**
>
> Wait until the engine is completely cool before beginning this procedure.

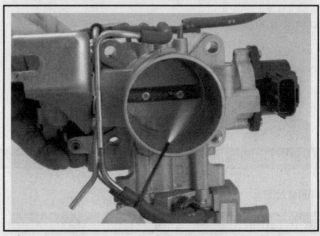

13.2 With the engine off, use aerosol carburetor cleaner (make sure it is safe for use with catalytic converters and oxygen sensors), a toothbrush and a rag to clean the throttle body - open the throttle plate so you can clean behind it

3   Detach the cable from the negative terminal of the battery (see Chapter 5, Section 1).
4   Loosen the hose clamps and remove the air intake duct (see illustration).
5   Disconnect the electrical connector from the throttle body (see illustration).
6   Clearly label, then detach, all vacuum and coolant hoses from the throttle body. Plug the coolant hoses to prevent coolant leakage.
7   On V6 models, disconnect the electrical connector from the Throttle Position Sensor (TPS).

13.4 Loosen the clamp and separate the air intake tube from the throttle body

13.5 Disconnect the electrical connector from the throttle body

13.8 The throttle body on four-cylinder models is retained by four bolts

8 Remove the throttle body mounting nuts/bolts (see illustration).
9 Detach the throttle body and gasket from the intake manifold.
10 Installation of the throttle body is the reverse of removal. Use a new gasket between the throttle body and the intake manifold.

11 Be sure to tighten the throttle body mounting bolts to the torque listed in this Chapter's Specifications.
12 Check the coolant level and add some, if necessary, to bring it to the appropriate level (see Chapter 1).

14 Fuel pulsation damper - replacement

▶ **Refer to illustration 14.4**

1 Relieve the fuel pressure (see Section 2).
2 Refer to Section 4 and disconnect the fuel line connector where it joins the pipe from the fuel pulsation damper at the end of the fuel rail. A special tool is required to disconnect the quick-connect coupling.
3 On V6 models, the pulsation damper is attached to the fuel rail for the rear bank. Simply unscrew the damper from the fuel rail.
4 On four-cylinder models, remove the two damper mounting bolts at the fuel rail (see illustration).
5 Installation is the reverse of removal. Be sure to install a new O-ring on four-cylinder models and a new gasket on V6 models. Tighten the bolts to the torque listed in this Chapter's Specifications.

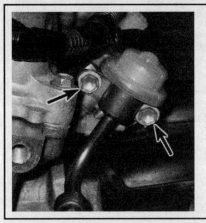

14.4 Remove the two bolts, then separate the pulsation damper from the fuel rail

15 Fuel rail and injectors - removal and installation

WARNING:

Gasoline is extremely flammable, so take extra precautions when you work on any part of the fuel system. See the Warning in Section 2.

REMOVAL

▶ **Refer to illustrations 15.4, 15.7a, 15.7b, 15.8, 15.9 and 15.10**

1 Relieve the fuel pressure (see Section 2).
2 Detach the cable from the negative terminal of the battery (see Chapter 5, Section 1).

3 Remove the PCV hose. On V6 models with performance suspension, remove the bolts and the suspension brace between the two shock towers.
4 On V6 models, remove the assembly that retains the Vacuum Switching Valve (VSV) control solenoids (see illustration). On V6 models, remove the air intake plenum to gain access to the rear (right bank) fuel rail (see Chapter 2B).
5 Disconnect the fuel injector electrical connectors and set the injector wire harness aside.
6 Disconnect the fuel lines from the fuel rail (see Section 4).
➡ **Note: On V6 models, the fuel line is a metal crossover tube connected to the front fuel rail and to the fuel pulsation damper on the rear bank fuel rail.**

7 Remove the fuel rail mounting bolts (see illustrations).

15.4 Remove the two nuts and position the VSV assembly off to the side

15.7a Remove the fuel rail mounting bolts (four-cylinder model shown)

15.7b Location of the fuel rail mounting bolts on V6 models

8   Remove the fuel rail with the fuel injectors attached (see illustration).

9   Remove the fuel injector(s) from the fuel rail (see illustration) and set them aside in a clearly labeled storage container.

10   If you intend to re-use the same injectors, replace the grommets and O-rings (see illustration).

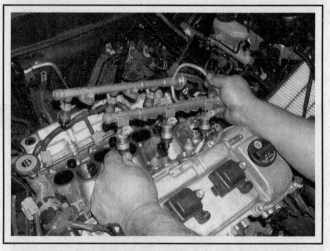

15.8 Carefully lift the fuel rail/injector assembly out of the engine compartment (V6 engine shown)

INSTALLATION

11   Installation of the fuel injectors is the reverse of removal.

12   Tighten the fuel rail mounting bolts to the torque listed in this Chapter's Specifications.

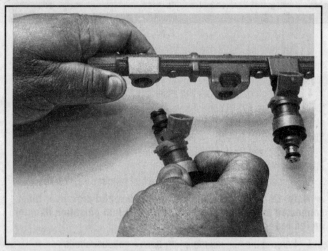

15.9 Simultaneously twist and pull the injector to remove it from the fuel rail

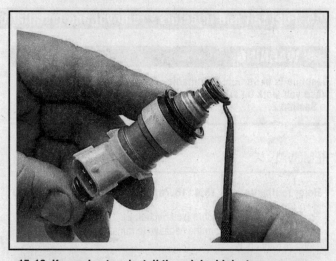

15.10 If you plan to reinstall the original injectors, remove and discard the O-rings and grommets and replace them with new ones

16 Exhaust system servicing - general information

♦ **Refer to illustrations 16.1a, 16.1b, 16.1c and 16.4**

❈❈ WARNING:

Inspection and repair of exhaust system components should be done only after the system components have cooled completely.

1   The exhaust system consists of the exhaust manifold, catalytic converter, the muffler, the tailpipe and all connecting pipes, brackets, hangers and clamps. The exhaust system is attached to the body with mounting brackets and rubber hangers (see illustrations). If any of these parts are damaged or deteriorated, excessive noise and vibration will be transmitted to the body.

2   Conducting regular inspections of the exhaust system will keep it safe and quiet. Look for any damaged or bent parts, open seams, holes, loose connections, excessive corrosion or other defects which could allow exhaust fumes to enter the vehicle. Deteriorated exhaust system components should not be repaired - they should be replaced

16.1a The front exhaust pipe mounts to the engine and to the rear converter with flanges

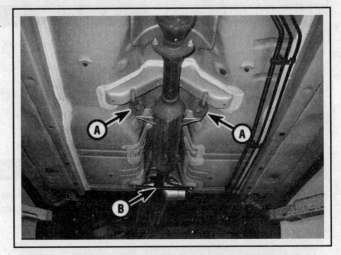

16.1b At the center portion of the exhaust system, there are rubber hangers (A) that should be inspected for cracks - B indicates the floor support brace that must be unbolted to remove the exhaust system

with new parts.

3   If the exhaust system components are extremely corroded or rusted together, they will probably have to be cut from the exhaust system. The convenient way to accomplish this is to have a muffler repair shop remove the corroded sections with a cutting torch. If, however, you want to save money by doing it yourself and you don't have an oxy/acetylene welding outfit with a cutting torch, simply cut off the old components with a hacksaw. If you have compressed air, special pneumatic cutting chisels can also be used. If you do decide to tackle the job at home, be sure to wear eye protection to protect your eyes from metal chips and work gloves to protect your hands.

4   Here are some simple guidelines to apply when repairing the exhaust system:

  a) *Work from the back to the front when removing exhaust system components.*
  b) *Apply penetrating oil to the exhaust system component fasteners to make them easier to remove (see illustration).*

  c) *Use new gaskets, hangers and clamps when installing exhaust system components.*
  d) *Apply anti-seize compound to the threads of all exhaust system fasteners during reassembly. Be sure to allow sufficient clearance between newly installed parts and all points on the underbody to avoid overheating the floor pan and possibly damaging the interior carpet and insulation. Pay particularly close attention to the catalytic converter and its heat shield.*

✳✳ WARNING:

The catalytic converter operates at very high temperatures and takes a long time to cool. Wait until it's completely cool before attempting to remove the converter. Failure to do so could result in serious burns.

16.1c The main muffler mounts at the rear of the vehicle

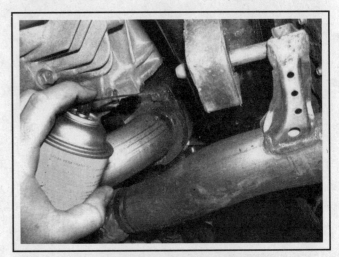

16.4 Lubricate the exhaust system fasteners with penetrating oil before attempting to loosen them

Specifications

Fuel system

Fuel system pressure	44 to 50 psi
Fuel system hold pressure (after five minutes)	21 psi minimum
Fuel injector resistance (approximate)	13.4 to 14.2 ohms

Torque specifications — Ft-lbs (unless otherwise indicated)

➡ **Note: One foot-pound (ft-lb) of torque is equivalent to 12 inch-pounds (in-lbs) of torque. Torque values below approximately 15 ft-lbs are expressed in inch-pounds, since most foot-pound torque wrenches are not accurate at these smaller values.**

Throttle body mounting nuts	
Four-cylinder engines	22
V6 engines	96 in-lbs
Throttle body-to-No. 1 intake air control valve screws	61 in-lbs
Fuel rail mounting bolts	
Four-cylinder models	15
V6 models	84 in-lbs
Fuel pressure regulator mounting screw	17 in-lbs
Fuel pulsation damper	80 in-lbs
In-tank fuel filter/pump assembly	52 in-lbs

Section

1   General information, precautions and battery disconnection
2   Battery - emergency jump starting
3   Battery - check and replacement
4   Battery cables - check and replacement
5   Ignition system - general information and precautions
6   Ignition system - check
7   Ignition coil(s) - replacement
8   Charging system - general information and precautions
9   Charging system - check
10 Alternator - removal and installation
11 Starting system - general information and precautions
12 Starter motor and circuit - check
13 Starter motor - removal and installation

Reference to other Chapters

Battery check, maintenance and charging - See Chapter 1
CHECK ENGINE light - See Chapter 6
Drivebelt check, adjustment and replacement - See Chapter 1
Spark plug replacement - See Chapter 1
Spark plug wire check and replacement - See Chapter 1

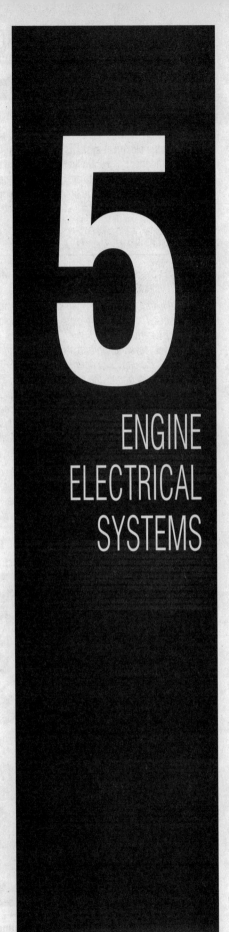

5

ENGINE ELECTRICAL SYSTEMS

1 General information, precautions and battery disconnection

♦ **Refer to illustration 1.1**

The engine electrical systems include all ignition, charging and starting components (see illustration). Because of their engine-related functions, these components are discussed separately from body electrical devices such as the lights, the instruments, etc. (which are included in Chapter 12).

PRECAUTIONS

Always observe the following precautions when working on the electrical system:

a) *Be extremely careful when servicing engine electrical components. They are easily damaged if checked, connected or handled improperly.*

b) *Never leave the ignition switched on for long periods of time when the engine is not running.*

c) *Never disconnect the battery cables while the engine is running.*

d) *Maintain correct polarity when connecting battery cables from another vehicle during jump starting - see the "Booster battery (jump) starting" section at the front of this manual.*

e) *Always disconnect the negative battery cable from the battery before working on the electrical system, but read the following battery disconnection procedure first.*

It's also a good idea to review the safety-related information regarding the engine electrical systems located in the "Safety first!" section at the front of this manual, before beginning any operation included in this Chapter.

BATTERY DISCONNECTION

Several systems on the vehicle require battery power to be available at all times, either to ensure their continued operation (such as the radio, alarm system, power door locks, windows, etc.) or to maintain control unit memories (such as that in the engine management system's Powertrain Control Module [PCM]) which would be lost if the battery were to be disconnected. Therefore, whenever the battery is to be disconnected, first note the following to ensure that there are no unforeseen consequences of this action:

a) *The engine management system's PCM will lose the information stored in its memory when the battery is disconnected. This includes idling and operating values, any fault codes detected and system monitors required for emissions testing. Whenever the battery is disconnected, the computer may require a certain period of time to "re-learn" the operating values.*

b) *On any vehicle with power door locks, it is a wise precaution to remove the key from the ignition and to keep it with you, so that it does not get locked inside if the power door locks should engage accidentally when the battery is reconnected!*

Devices known as "memory-savers" can be used to avoid some of the above problems. Precise details vary according to the device used. Typically, it is plugged into the cigarette lighter and is connected by its own wires to a spare battery; the vehicle's own battery is then disconnected from the electrical system, leaving the "memory-saver" to pass sufficient current to maintain audio unit security codes and PCM memory values, and also to run permanently live circuits such as the clock and radio memory, all the while isolating the battery in the event of a short-circuit occurring while work is carried out.

1.1 Charging and ignition system components - four-cylinder engine

| 1 | *Alternator* | 2 | *Individual ignition coils* | 3 | *Starter* | 4 | *Battery* |

⁑ WARNING 1:

Some of these devices allow a considerable amount of current to pass, which can mean that many of the vehicle's systems are still operational when the main battery is disconnected. If a "memory-saver" is used, ensure that the circuit concerned is actually "dead" before carrying out any work on it!

⁑ WARNING 2:

If work is to be performed around any of the airbag system components, the battery must be disconnected. If a memory-saver device is used, power will be supplied to the airbag and personal injury may result if the airbag is accidentally deployed.

The battery on all vehicles is located in the front left corner of the engine compartment. To disconnect the battery for service procedures requiring power to be cut from the vehicle, loosen the negative cable clamp nut and detach the negative cable from the negative battery post. Isolate the cable end to prevent it from accidentally coming into contact with the battery post.

BATTERY RECONNECTION

The manufacturer states that, after reconnecting the battery, you must:

a) *Enter the anti-theft code for the radio and navigation system (see owner's manual)*
b) *Enter the radio station presets (see owner's manual)*
c) *Reset the clock (see owner's manual)*
d) *Reset the power window control unit (push the DOWN switch and lower the window halfway, then push the UP switch until the window closes and hold the switch for one second)*
e) *Reset the moonroof control unit (push and hold the switch on the TILT UP side until the moonroof tilts all the way up, then tilts down a little automatically)*

2   Battery - emergency jump starting

Refer to the *Booster battery (jump) starting* procedure at the front of this manual.

3   Battery - check and replacement

CHECK

◆ **Refer to illustrations 3.2 and 3.3**

1   Disconnect the negative battery cable, then the positive cable from the battery.

2   Check the battery state of charge. Visually inspect the indicator eye on the top of the battery; if the indicator eye is black in color charge the battery as described in Chapter 1. Next perform an open voltage circuit test using a digital voltmeter (see illustration).

➡**Note: The battery's surface charge must be removed before accurate voltage measurements can be made. Turn On the high beams for ten seconds, then turn them Off, and let the vehicle stand for two minutes.**

With the engine and all accessories Off, touch the negative probe of the voltmeter to the negative terminal of the battery and the positive probe to the positive terminal of the battery. The battery voltage should be at least 12.6 volts. If the battery is less than the specified voltage, charge the battery before proceeding to the next test. Do not proceed with the battery load test unless the battery charge is correct.

3   Perform a battery load test. An accurate check of the battery condition can only be performed with a load tester (available at most auto parts stores). This test evaluates the ability of the battery to operate the starter and other accessories during periods of heavy amperage draw (load). Install a special battery load-testing tool onto the terminals (see illustration). Load test the battery according to the manufacturer's instructions for the particular tool. This tool utilizes a carbon pile to

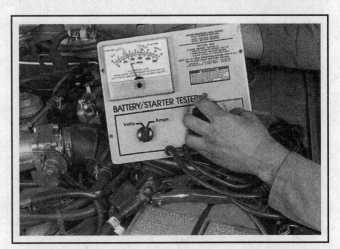

3.2 To test the open circuit voltage of the battery, simply touch the black probe of the voltmeter to the negative terminal and the red probe to the positive terminal of the battery - a fully charged battery should read at least 12.6 volts depending on the outside air temperature

3.3 Some battery load testers are equipped with an ammeter which enables the battery load to be precisely dialed in, as shown - less expensive testers have a load switch and voltmeter only

increase the load demand (amperage draw) on the battery. Maintain the load on the battery for 15 seconds or less and observe that the battery voltage does not drop below 9.6 volts. If the battery condition is weak or defective, the tool will indicate this condition immediately.

➡**Note: Cold temperatures will cause the minimum voltage requirements to drop slightly. Follow the chart given in the manufacturer's instructions to compensate for cold climates. Minimum load voltage for freezing temperatures (32 degrees F) should be approximately 9.1 volts.**

REPLACEMENT

▶ **Refer to illustration 3.5**

4   Disconnect the negative battery cable, then the positive cable from the battery.

5   Remove the battery hold-down clamp (see illustration).

6   Lift out the battery. Be careful - it's heavy.

➡**Note: Battery straps and handlers are available at most auto parts stores for a reasonable price. They make it easier to remove and carry the battery.**

7   While the battery is out, inspect the battery tray for corrosion.

8   If corrosion exists on the battery tray, detach the bolts and remove the tray from the engine compartment. Clean the deposits from

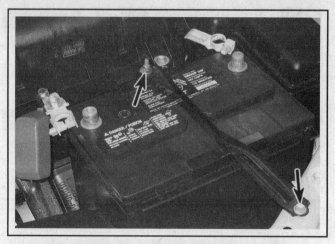

3.5 Remove the nut and bolt and detach the hold-down clamp

the metal to prevent the battery tray from further corrosion.

9   If you are replacing the battery, make sure you get one that's identical, with the same dimensions, amperage rating, cold cranking rating, etc.

10   Installation is the reverse of removal.

4   Battery cables - check and replacement

▶ **Refer to illustrations 4.4a and 4.4b**

1   Periodically inspect the entire length of each battery cable for damage, cracked or burned insulation and corrosion. Poor battery cable connections can cause starting problems and decreased engine performance.

2   Check the cable-to-terminal connections at the ends of the cables for cracks, loose wire strands and corrosion (see Chapter 1). The presence of white, fluffy deposits under the insulation at the cable terminal connection is a sign that the cable is corroded and should be replaced. Check the terminals for distortion, missing mounting bolts and corrosion.

3   When removing the cables, always disconnect the negative cable first and hook it up last or the battery may be shorted by the tool used to loosen the cable clamps. Even if only the positive cable is being replaced, be sure to disconnect the negative cable from the battery first (see Section 1).

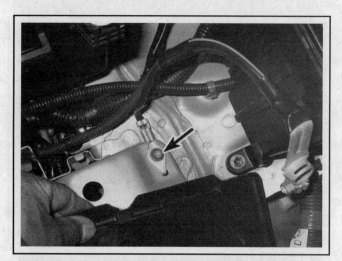

4.4a The negative battery cable is attached to the chassis as well as the engine to ensure a proper ground - remove the battery box for access to the chassis end of the cable

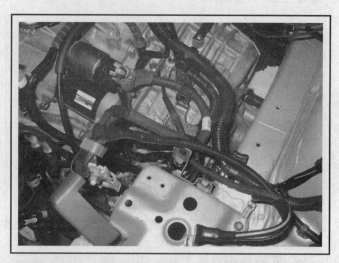

4.4b Note the routing of the cable and replace it as originally installed

4   Disconnect the old cables from the battery, then trace each of them to their opposite ends and detach them from the starter solenoid and ground terminals. Note the routing of each cable to ensure correct installation (see illustrations).

5   If you are replacing either or both of the old cables, take them with you when buying new cables. It is vitally important that you replace the cables with identical parts. Cables have characteristics that make them easy to identify: positive cables are usually red and larger in cross-section; ground cables are usually black and smaller in cross section.

6   Clean the threads of the solenoid or ground connection with a wire brush to remove rust and corrosion. Apply a light coat of battery terminal corrosion inhibitor, or petroleum jelly, to the threads to prevent future corrosion.

7   Attach the cable to the solenoid or ground connection and tighten the mounting nut/bolt securely.

8   Before connecting a new cable to the battery, make sure that it reaches the battery post without having to be stretched.

9   Connect the positive cable first, followed by the negative cable.

5   Ignition system - general information and precautions

1   All models covered by this manual are equipped with a Distributorless Ignition System (DIS). The DIS system includes the camshaft position sensor, a coil/igniter assembly for each cylinder (or pair of cylinders on V6 models), the spark plugs, and the PCM (computer).

2   The coil and igniter are built into one unit and mounted over each cylinder's spark plug on most models. On earlier V6 models, only the front-bank spark plugs have separate coils - the rear-bank plugs are connected to the front-bank coils by wires. The camshaft and crankshaft sensors generate cylinder identification signals that allow the PCM to trigger the correct igniter/coil assembly.

3   The igniter distributes the signal to the coil driver and determines dwell period based on coil primary current flow.

4   The spark on most models is "direct" (cylinder specific) and sequenced to the engine's firing order. Earlier V6 models have a "waste spark" system where each coil fires twice, once for each paired cylinder.

Only earlier V6 models have secondary spark plug wires, since the individual coils on other models mount directly to each spark plug.

5   When working on the ignition system, take the following precautions:

a) *Do not keep the ignition switch on for more than 10 seconds if the engine will not start.*

b) *Always connect a tachometer in accordance with the manufacturer's instructions. Some tachometers may be incompatible with this ignition system. Consult an auto parts counterperson before buying a tachometer for use with this vehicle.*

c) *Never allow the ignition coil terminals to touch ground. Grounding the coil could result in damage to the igniter and/or the ignition coil.*

d) *Do not disconnect the battery when the engine is running.*

6   Ignition system - check

▶ **Refer to illustration 6.2**

✳✳ WARNING:

Because of the high voltage generated by the ignition system, extreme care should be taken whenever an operation is performed involving ignition components. This not only includes the igniter, coil and spark plug wires, but related components such as plug connectors, tachometer and other test equipment as well.

1   Relieve the fuel system pressure (see Chapter 4). Keep the fuel system disabled while performing the ignition system checks.

2   If the engine turns over but won't start, disconnect the ignition coil from any spark plug (see Section 7) and attach it to a calibrated ignition tester (available at most auto parts stores) (see illustration). Make sure the tester is designed for a distributorless ignition system if a universal tester isn't available.

3   Connect the clip on the tester to a bolt or metal bracket on the engine

4   Crank the engine and watch the end of the tester to see if bright blue, well-defined sparks occur.

5   If sparks occur, sufficient voltage is reaching the spark plug to fire it (repeat the check at the remaining spark plug wires to verify that all the ignition coils are functioning). However, the plugs themselves may be fouled, so remove and check them as described in Chapter 1 or install new ones.

6   If no sparks or intermittent sparks occur, check for battery voltage

6.2 To use a calibrated ignition tester, simply connect it to one of the individual coil's boot, clip the tester to a convenient ground and operate the starter with the ignition ON - if there is enough power to fire the plug, sparks will be visible between the electrode tip and the tester body

to the ignition coils. If battery voltage is not present, check the ignition fuse (see Chapter 12).

7   Refer to Chapter 6 and use a code-reading tool to check for Diagnostic Trouble Codes relating to the ignition system, the PCM, or the camshaft and crankshaft position sensors.

7 Ignition coil(s) - replacement

▶ **Refer to illustrations 7.2 and 7.3**

➡**Note: Toyota and Lexus do not publish primary or secondary resistance specifications for the ignition coil/igniter units used on these models. The only way to check them is to substitute a known good unit. But this option isn't feasible for a home mechanic because you can't return electrical components to a parts department once you have purchased them. If you have already eliminated all other possible causes of an ignition malfunction, a defective ignition coil/igniter unit is the likely cause of the problem, but the only way to verify this is to have a dealer substitute a known good unit.**

1 Disconnect the negative cable from the battery (see Section 1). On V6 models, remove the engine cover and, for access to the rear bank coils, remove the intake manifold plenum (see Chapter 2B).

2 Label each electrical connector at the individual coils, then remove the mounting bolts (see illustration). On earlier V6 models, be sure to disconnect the secondary wire as well.

3 Pull each coil straight up and out of the valve cover (see illustration).

4 Installation is the reverse of the removal procedure.

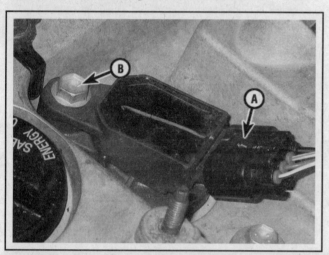

7.2 Disconnect the electrical connector (A) at each coil, then remove the mounting bolt (B)

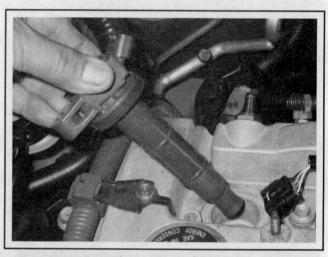

7.3 The individual igniter/coil is also the boot for direct mounting over each spark plug

8 Charging system - general information and precautions

The charging system includes the alternator, an internal voltage regulator, a charge indicator, the battery, a fusible link and the wiring between all the components. The charging system supplies electrical power for the ignition system, the lights, the radio, etc. The alternator is driven by a drivebelt at the front of the engine.

The purpose of the voltage regulator is to limit the alternator's voltage to a preset value. This prevents power surges, circuit overloads, etc., during peak voltage output.

The charging system doesn't ordinarily require periodic maintenance. However, the drivebelt, battery and wires and connections should be inspected at the intervals outlined in Chapter 1.

The dashboard warning light should come on when the ignition key is turned to Start, then should go off immediately. If it remains on, there is a malfunction in the charging system. Some vehicles are also equipped with a voltage gauge. If the voltage gauge indicates abnormally high or low voltage, check the charging system (see Section 9).

Be very careful when making electrical circuit connections to a vehicle equipped with an alternator and note the following:

a) *When reconnecting wires to the alternator from the battery, be sure to note the polarity.*

b) *Before using arc-welding equipment to repair any part of the vehicle, disconnect the wires from the alternator and the battery terminals.*

c) *Never start the engine with a battery charger connected.*

d) *Always disconnect both battery leads before using a battery charger.*

e) *The alternator is driven by an engine drivebelt that could cause serious injury if your hand, hair or clothes become entangled in it with the engine running.*

f) *Because the alternator is connected directly to the battery, it could arc or cause a fire if overloaded or shorted out.*

g) *Wrap a plastic bag over the alternator and secure it with rubber bands before steam cleaning the engine.*

9 Charging system - check

▶ **Refer to illustration 9.3**

1   If a malfunction occurs in the charging circuit, do not immediately assume that the alternator is causing the problem. First, check the following items:

a) *Make sure the battery cable clamps, where they connect to the battery, are clean and tight.*

b) *Test the condition of the battery (see Section 3). If it does not pass all the tests, replace it with a new battery.*

c) *Check the external alternator wiring and connections.*

d) *Check the drivebelt condition and tension (see Chapter 1).*

e) *Check the alternator mounting bolts for tightness.*

f) *Run the engine and check the alternator for abnormal noise.*

g) *Check the fusible links (if equipped) in the engine compartment fuse box (see Chapter 12). If they're burned, determine the cause and repair the circuit.*

h) *Check the charge light on the dash. It should illuminate when the ignition key is turned ON (engine not running). If it does not, check the circuit from the alternator to the charge light on the dash.*

i) *Check all the fuses that are in series with the charging system circuit. The location of these fuses and fusible links may vary from year and model but the designations are generally the same. Refer to the wiring schematics at the end of Chapter 12 for additional information.*

2   With the ignition key off, check the battery voltage with no accessories operating. It should be approximately 12.5 volts. It may be slightly higher if the engine had been operating within the last hour.

3   Connect an ammeter to the charging system following the tool manufacturer's instructions. Start the engine, and check the battery voltage and amperage. It should now be approximately 13.2 to 15.0 volts at 10 amps or less (see illustration).

4   Load the battery by turning on the high beam headlights and the air conditioning (if equipped) and place the blower fan on HIGH. Raise

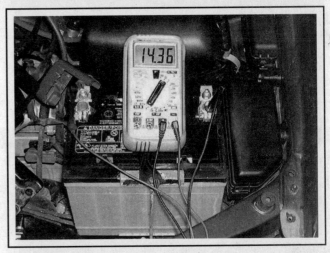

9.3 Connect a voltmeter to the battery terminals and check the battery voltage with the engine Off and again with the engine running

the engine speed to 2,000 rpm and check the voltage and amperage. If the charging system is working properly the voltage should stay above 13.5 volts and the amperage should be 30 amps or more (depending on the condition of the battery - it could be less than 30 amps).

5   If the voltage rises above 15.0 volts in either test, the regulator is defective.

6   If the indicated voltage reading is less than the specified charge voltage, the alternator is probably defective. Have the charging system checked at a dealer service department or other properly equipped repair facility.

➡**Note: Many auto parts stores will bench test an alternator off the vehicle. Refer to your local auto parts store regarding their policy (many stores will perform this service free of charge).**

10 Alternator - removal and installation

REMOVAL

▶ **Refer to illustration 10.4**

1   Detach the cable from the negative terminal of the battery (see Section 1).

2   Remove the drivebelt (see Chapter 1).

3   Detach the electrical connectors from the alternator, and the electrical harness that goes over the alternator.

4   Remove the two bolts and the alternator (see illustration).

5   On V6 models, loosen the alternator adjustment bolt to remove the drivebelt, then remove the two alternator mounting bolts.

INSTALLATION

6   If you are replacing the alternator, take the old alternator with you when purchasing a replacement unit. Make sure that the new/rebuilt unit is identical to the old alternator. Look at the terminals - they should be the same in number, size and locations as the terminals on

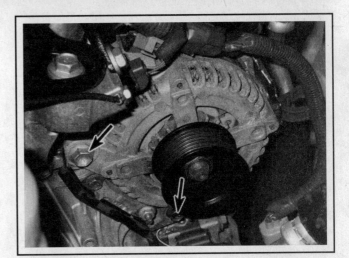

10.4 Alternator mounting bolts (four-cylinder shown, V6 similar)

the old alternator. Finally, look at the identification markings - they will be stamped in the housing or printed on a tag or plaque affixed to the housing. Make sure that these numbers are the same on both alternators.

7   Many new/rebuilt alternators do not have a pulley installed, so you may have to switch the pulley from the old unit to the new/rebuilt one. When buying an alternator, find out the shop's policy regarding

installation of pulleys - some shops will perform this service free of charge.

8   Installation is the reverse of removal.

9   After the alternator is installed, adjust the drivebelt tension (see Chapter 1).

10 Check the charging voltage to verify proper operation of the alternator (see Section 9).

11 Starting system - general information and precautions

The starting system consists of the battery, the starter motor, the starter solenoid and the electrical circuit connecting the components. The solenoid is mounted directly on the starter motor.

The solenoid/starter motor assembly is installed on the upper part of the engine, next to the transaxle bellhousing.

When the ignition key is turned to the START position, the starter solenoid is actuated through the starter control circuit. The starter solenoid then connects the battery to the starter. The battery supplies the electrical energy to the starter motor, which does the actual work of cranking the engine.

The starter motor on a vehicle equipped with a manual transaxle can be operated only when the clutch pedal is depressed; the starter on

a vehicle equipped with an automatic transaxle can be operated only when the transaxle selector lever is in Park or Neutral.

Always observe the following precautions when working on the starting system:

a) *Excessive cranking of the starter motor can overheat it and cause serious damage. Never operate the starter motor for more than 15 seconds at a time without pausing to allow it to cool for at least two minutes.*

b) *The starter is connected directly to the battery and could arc or cause a fire if mishandled, overloaded or short-circuited.*

c) *Always detach the cable from the negative terminal of the battery before working on the starting system.*

12 Starter motor and circuit - check

▶ **Refer to illustrations 12.3 and 12.4**

1   If a malfunction occurs in the starting circuit, do not immediately assume that the starter is causing the problem. First, check the following items:

a) *Make sure the battery cable clamps, where they connect to the battery, are clean and tight.*

b) *Check the condition of the battery cables (see Section 4). Replace any defective battery cables with new parts.*

c) *Test the condition of the battery (see Section 3). If it does not pass all the tests, replace it with a new battery.*

d) *Check the starter solenoid wiring and connections. Refer to the wiring diagrams at the end of Chapter 12.*

e) *Check the starter mounting bolts for tightness.*

f) *Check the fusible links (if equipped) exiting the engine compartment fuse box (see Chapter 12). If they're burned, determine the cause and repair the circuit. Also, check the ignition switch circuit for correct operation (see Chapter 12).*

g) *Check the operation of the Park/Neutral switch (automatic transaxle) or clutch start switch (manual transaxle). Make sure the shift lever is in PARK or NEUTRAL (automatic transaxle) or the clutch pedal is pressed (manual transaxle). Refer to Chapter 7B for the Park/Neutral switch check and adjustment procedure. Refer to Chapter 12 wiring diagrams, if necessary, when performing circuit checks. These systems must operate correctly to provide battery voltage to the ignition solenoid.*

h) *Check the operation of the starter relay. The starter relay is located in the fuse/relay box inside the engine compartment. Refer to Chapter 12 for the testing procedure.*

2   If the starter does not actuate when the ignition switch is turned

to the start position, check for battery voltage to the solenoid. This will determine if the solenoid is receiving the correct voltage signal from the ignition switch. Connect a test light or voltmeter to the starter solenoid positive terminal and while an assistant turns the ignition switch to the start position. If voltage is not available, refer to the wiring diagrams in Chapter 12 and check all the fuses and relays in series with the starting system. If voltage is available but the starter motor does not operate, remove the starter from the engine compartment (see Section 13) and bench test the starter (see Step 4).

3   If the starter turns over slowly, check the starter cranking voltage and the current draw from the battery. This test must be performed with the starter assembly on the engine. Crank the engine over (for 10 seconds or less) and observe the battery voltage. It should not drop below 8.0 volts on manual transaxle models or 8.5 volts on automatic transaxle models. Also, observe the current draw using an amp meter

12.3 To use an inductive ammeter, simply hold the ammeter over the positive or negative cable (whichever is more accessible)

(see illustration). It should not exceed 400 amps or drop below 250 amps. If the starter motor cranking amp values are not within the correct range, replace it with a new unit. There are several conditions that may affect the starter cranking potential. The battery must be in good condition and the battery cold-cranking rating must not be under-rated for the particular application. Be sure to check the battery specifications carefully. The battery terminals and cables must be clean and not corroded. Also, in cases of extreme cold temperatures, make sure the battery and/or engine block is warmed before performing the tests.

4   If the starter is receiving voltage but does not activate, remove and check the starter/solenoid assembly on the bench (see illustration). Most likely the solenoid is defective. In some rare cases, the engine may be seized so be sure to try and rotate the crankshaft pulley (see Chapter 2A or 2B) before proceeding. With the starter/solenoid assembly mounted in a vise on the bench, install one jumper cable from the negative battery terminal to the body of the starter. Install the other jumper cable from the positive battery terminal to the B+ terminal on the starter. Install a starter switch and apply battery voltage to the solenoid S terminal (for 10 seconds or less) and see if the solenoid plunger, shift lever and overrunning clutch extends and rotates the pinion drive. If the pinion drive extends but does not rotate, the solenoid is operating but the starter motor is defective. If there is no movement but the solenoid clicks, the solenoid and/or the starter motor is defective. If the solenoid plunger extends and rotates the pinion drive, the starter/solenoid assembly is working properly.

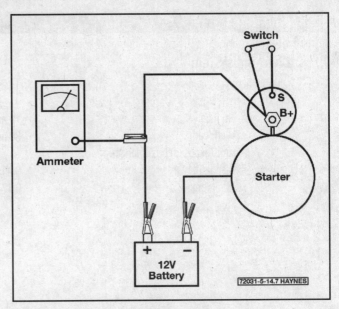

12.4 Starter motor bench testing details

13 Starter motor - removal and installation

▶ **Refer to illustration 13.5**

1   Detach the cable from the negative terminal of the battery (see Section 1).
2   Remove the air cleaner and housing from the engine compartment (see Chapter 4).
3   Disconnect and remove the cruise control actuator from the engine compartment, if equipped.
4   Detach the electrical connectors from the starter/solenoid assembly.
5   Remove the starter motor mounting bolts (see illustration).
6   Remove the bracket from the upper section of the starter/solenoid assembly.
➡**Note: It is necessary to loosen one or two of the bracket bolts to allow the starter/solenoid assembly to partially drop down to gain access to the remaining bracket assembly bolts and hardware.**

7   Installation is the reverse of removal.

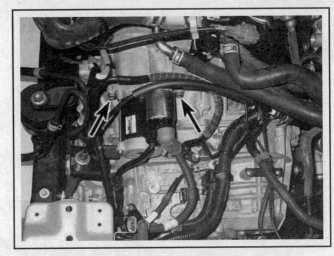

13.5 Starter motor mounting bolts (four-cylinder engine)

Specifications

Charging system

Charging voltage	13.2 to 14.8 volts
Standard amperage	
No load	10 amps or less
With load	30 amps or more
Alternator (exposed) brush length	
Standard	0.413 inch
Minimum	0.177 inch

6

EMISSIONS AND ENGINE CONTROL SYSTEMS

Section

1   General information
2   On-Board Diagnostic (OBD) system and trouble codes
3   Powertrain Control Module (PCM) - removal and installation
4   Throttle Position Sensor (TPS) and throttle control motor - replacement
5   Mass Airflow (MAF) sensor - replacement
6   Engine Coolant Temperature (ECT) sensor - replacement
7   Crankshaft Position (CKP) sensor - replacement
8   Camshaft Position (CMP) sensor - replacement
9   Oxygen sensor and air/fuel sensor - general information and replacement
10 Knock sensor - replacement
11 Vehicle Speed Sensor (VSS) - replacement
12 Positive Crankcase Ventilation (PCV) system
13 Exhaust Gas Recirculation (EGR) system (2002 and 2003 V6 models)
14 Evaporative emissions control (EVAP) system
15 Catalytic converters

1 General information

▶ **Refer to illustrations 1.6a and 1.6b**

To prevent pollution of the atmosphere from incompletely burned and evaporating gases, and to maintain good driveability and fuel economy, a number of emission control systems are incorporated. They include the:

On-Board Diagnostic (OBD-II) system
Electronic Fuel Injection (EFI) system
Exhaust Gas Recirculation (EGR) system (2002-2003 V6 models)
Evaporative Emissions Control (EVAP) system
Positive Crankcase Ventilation (PCV) system
Catalytic converter

The Sections in this Chapter include general descriptions, checking procedures within the scope of the home mechanic and component replacement procedures (when possible) for each of the systems listed above.

Before assuming that an emissions control system is malfunctioning, check the fuel and ignition systems carefully. The diagnosis of some emission control devices requires specialized tools, equipment and training. If checking and servicing become too difficult or if a procedure is beyond your ability, consult a dealer service department or other repair shop. Remember, the most frequent cause of emissions problems is simply a loose or broken wire or vacuum hose, so always check the hose and wiring connections first.

This doesn't mean, however, that emissions control systems are particularly difficult to maintain and repair. You can quickly and easily perform many checks and do most of the regular maintenance at home with common tune-up and hand tools.

➡**Note: Because of a Federally mandated warranty which covers the emissions control system components, check with your dealer about warranty coverage before working on any emissions-related systems. Once the warranty has expired, you may wish to perform some of the component checks and/or replacement procedures in this Chapter to save money.**

Pay close attention to any special precautions outlined in this Chapter. It should be noted that the illustrations of the various systems may not exactly match the system installed on your vehicle because of changes made by the manufacturer during production or from year-to-year.

A Vehicle Emissions Control Information (VECI) label is attached to the underside of the hood (see illustration). This label contains important emissions specifications and adjustment information. Also under the hood, the Vacuum Hose Routing Diagram (see illustration), provides a vacuum hose schematic with emissions components identified. When servicing the engine or emissions systems, the VECI label and the vacuum hose routing diagram in your particular vehicle should always be checked for up-to-date information.

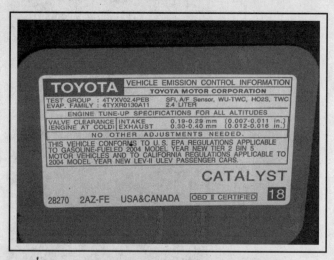

1.6a The Vehicle Emission Control Information (VECI) label contains such essential information as the types of emission control systems installed on the engine and certain tune-up specifications

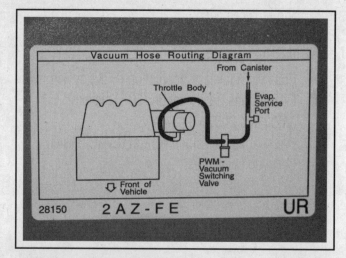

1.6b Vacuum hose routing diagram for a 2004 four-cylinder model

2 On Board Diagnostic (OBD) system and trouble codes

SCAN TOOL INFORMATION

▶ **Refer to illustration 2.2**

1   Hand-held scanners are handy for analyzing the engine management systems used on late-model vehicles. Because extracting the Diagnostic Trouble Codes (DTCs) from an engine management system is now the first step in troubleshooting many computer-controlled systems and components, even the most basic generic scan tools are capable of accessing a computer's DTCs. More powerful scan tools can also perform many of the diagnostics once associated with expensive factory scan tools. If you're planning to obtain a generic scan tool for your vehicle, make sure that it's compatible with the year, make and model of the vehicle(s) on which you plan to use it. Some of the more versatile scan tools accept removable cartridges, each of which contains the diagnostics for a particular manufacturer. An aftermarket

2.2 Scanners like these from Actron and AutoXray are powerful diagnostic aids - they can tell you just about anything you want to know about your engine management system

5 If your vehicle is still under warranty, virtually every fuel, ignition and emission control component in the OBD-II system is covered by a Federally mandated emissions warranty that is longer than the warranty covering the rest of the vehicle. Vehicles sold in California and in some other states have even longer emissions warranties than other states. Read your owner's manual for the terms of the warranty protecting the emission-control systems on your vehicle. It isn't a good idea to "do-it-yourself" at home while the vehicle emission systems are still under warranty because owner-induced damage to the PCM, the sensors and/or the control devices might VOID this warranty. So as long as the emission systems are still under warranty, take the vehicle to a dealer service department if there's a problem.

INFORMATION SENSORS

6 **Oxygen sensors (O2S)** - The O2S generates a voltage signal that varies with the difference between the oxygen content of the exhaust and the oxygen in the surrounding air.

7 **Crankshaft Position (CKP) sensor** - The crankshaft sensor provides information on crankshaft position and the engine speed signal to the PCM.

8 **Camshaft Position (CMP) sensor** - The camshaft sensor produces a signal which the PCM uses to identify number 1 cylinder and to time the sequential fuel injection.

9 **Air/Fuel Sensor** - Some vehicles are equipped with an air/fuel ratio sensor mounted upstream of the catalytic converter. These sensors work similar to the O2 sensors.

10 **Engine Coolant Temperature (ECT) sensor** - The coolant temperature (ECT) sensor monitors engine coolant temperature and sends the PCM a voltage signal that affects PCM control of the fuel mixture, ignition timing, and EGR operation.

11 **Throttle Position Sensor (TPS)** - The TPS senses throttle movement and position, then transmits a voltage signal to the PCM. This signal enables the PCM to determine when the throttle is closed, in a cruise position, or wide open. On these models, the TPS is part of the electronic throttle control on the throttle body.

12 **Mass Airflow (MAF) sensor** - The MAF sensor measures the mass of the intake air by detecting volume and weight of the air from samples passing over the hot wire element.

13 **Vehicle Speed Sensor (VSS)** - The vehicle speed sensor provides information to the PCM to indicate vehicle speed.

14 **Vapor pressure sensor** - The vapor pressure sensor is part of the evaporative emission control system and is used to monitor vapor pressure in the EVAP system. The PCM uses this information to turn on and off the vacuum switching valves (VSV) of the evaporative emission system.

15 **Power Steering Pressure (PSP) switch** - The PSP sensor is used to increase engine idle speed during low-speed vehicle maneuvers.

16 **Transaxle sensors** - In addition to the vehicle speed sensor, the PCM receives input signals from the direct clutch speed sensor.

17 **Accelerator pedal position sensor** - The covered vehicles do not have a throttle cable, but rather a "drive-by-wire" system with an electronically-controlled throttle body. This sensor informs the PCM of the driver's pedal input, which is compared to the operation of the throttle body to check for malfunctions. On most models, there are two of these sensors.

18 **Intake Air Temperature (IAT) sensor** - The PCM uses information from this sensor to control fuel flow, timing, and EGR functions (on V6 models). The IAT sensor is part of the MAF sensor module.

generic scanner should work with any model covered by this manual. But before purchasing a scan tool, contact the manufacturer of the scanner you're planning to buy and verify that it will work properly with the system you want to scan. If you don't plan to purchase a scan tool and don't have access to one, you can have the codes extracted by a dealer service department or by an independent repair shop.

2 With the advent of the Federally mandated emission control system known as On-Board Diagnostics-II (OBD-II), specially designed scanners were developed. Several tool manufacturers have released OBD-II scan tools for the home mechanic (see illustration).

OBD-II SYSTEM GENERAL DESCRIPTION

3 All vehicles covered by this manual are equipped with the OBD-II system. This system consists of the on-board computer, known as the Powertrain Control Module (PCM), and information sensors that monitor various functions of the engine and send a constant stream of data to the PCM during engine operation. Unlike earlier on-board diagnostics systems, the OBD-II system doesn't just monitor everything, store Diagnostic Trouble Codes (DTCs) and illuminate a Check Engine light or Malfunction Indicator Light (MIL) when there's a problem. This warning light was referred to as the "Check Engine" light prior to OBD-II, and many do-it-yourselfers and professional technicians still use this term. However, its name was changed to "Malfunction Indicator Light," or simply "MIL," as part of the Society of Automotive Engineers' standard terminology that was introduced in 1996 to encourage all manufacturers to use the same terms when referring to the same components. So in this manual we will refer to this warning light as the Malfunction Indicator Light, or MIL.

4 The PCM is the brain of the electronically controlled OBD-II system. It receives data from a number of information sensors and switches. Based on the data that it receives from the sensors, the PCM constantly alters engine operating conditions to optimize driveability, performance, emissions and fuel economy. It does so by turning on and off and by controlling various output actuators such as relays, solenoids, valves and other devices. The PCM can only be accessed with an OBD-II scan tool plugged into the 16-pin Data Link Connector (DLC), which is located underneath the driver's end of the dashboard, near the steering column.

OUTPUT ACTUATORS

19 **EFI main relay** - The EFI main relay activates power to the fuel pump relay (circuit opening relay). It is activated by the ignition switch and supplies battery power to the PCM and the EFI system when the switch is in the Start or Run position. Refer to Chapter 4 or your owner's manual for more information on relay location.

20 **Fuel injectors** - The PCM opens the fuel injectors individually in firing order sequence. The PCM also controls the time the injector is open, called the "pulse width." The pulse width of the injector (measured in milliseconds) determines the amount of fuel delivered. For more information on the fuel delivery system and the fuel injectors, including injector replacement, refer to Chapter 4.

21 **Igniter** - The igniter triggers the ignition coil. The igniter is an integral part of each coil.

22 **EVAP Vacuum Switching Valve (VSV)** - The EVAP vacuum switching valve is a solenoid valve, operated by the PCM to purge the fuel vapor canister and route fuel vapor to the intake manifold for combustion. This valve is also called the purge control valve.

OBTAINING TROUBLE CODES

▸ **Refer to illustration 2.24**

23 The PCM will illuminate the CHECK ENGINE light (also called the Malfunction Indicator Light) on the dash if it recognizes a component fault for two consecutive drive cycles. It will continue to set the light until the PCM does not detect any malfunction for three or more consecutive drive cycles.

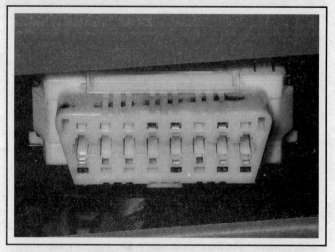

2.24 The 16-pin Data Link Connector (DLC) is located under the left side of the dash

24 The diagnostic codes for the OBD-II system can be extracted from the PCM by plugging a generic OBD-II scan tool (see illustration 2.2) into the PCM's data link connector (see illustration), which is located under the left end of the dash.

25 Plug the scan tool into the 16-pin data link connector (DLC), and then follow the instructions included with the scan tool to extract all the diagnostic codes.

DIAGNOSTIC TROUBLE CODES

Code	Code identification
P0010	Camshaft position A actuator circuit (Bank 1)
P0011	Camshaft position A, timing over-advanced or system performance (Bank 1)
P0012	Camshaft position A, timing over-retarded (Bank 1)
P0016	Crankshaft position/camshaft position correlation (Bank 1, Sensor A)
P0018	Crankshaft position/camshaft position correlation (Bank 2, Sensor A)
P0020	Camshaft position A actuator circuit (Bank 2)
P0021	Camshaft position A, timing over-advanced or system performance (Bank 1)
P0022	Camshaft position A, timing over-retarded (Bank 1)
P0031	Oxygen sensor heater control circuit, low voltage (Bank 1, Sensor 1)
P0032	Oxygen sensor heater control circuit, high voltage (Bank 1, Sensor 1)
P0037	Oxygen sensor heater control circuit, low voltage (Bank 1, Sensor 2)
P0038	Oxygen sensor heater control circuit, high voltage (Bank 1, Sensor 2)
P0051	Oxygen sensor heater control circuit, low voltage (Bank 2, Sensor 1)
P0052	Oxygen sensor heater control circuit, high voltage (Bank 2, Sensor 1)
P0057	Oxygen sensor heater control circuit, low voltage (Bank 2, Sensor 2)
P0058	Oxygen sensor heater control circuit, high voltage (Bank 2, Sensor 2)

Code	Code identification
P0100	Mass Air Flow (MAF) sensor, circuit fault
P0101	Mass Air Flow (MAF) sensor, range or performance problem
P0102	Mass Air Flow (MAF) sensor circuit, low input voltage
P0103	Mass Air Flow (MAF) sensor circuit, high input voltage
P0110	Intake Air Temperature (IAT) sensor (in MAF sensor), circuit fault
P0112	Intake Air Temperature (IAT) sensor circuit, low input voltage
P0113	Intake Air Temperature (IAT) sensor circuit, high input voltage
P0115	Engine Coolant Temperature (ECT) sensor, circuit fault
P0116	Engine Coolant Temperature (ECT) sensor, circuit range or performance problem
P0117	Engine Coolant Temperature (ECT) sensor, low input voltage
P0118	Engine Coolant Temperature (ECT) sensor, high input voltage
P0120	Throttle/Accelerator Pedal Position sensor or circuit fault
P0121	Throttle/Accelerator Pedal Position sensor, circuit range or performance problem
P0122	Throttle/Accelerator Pedal Position sensor A circuit, low voltage input
P0123	Throttle/Accelerator Pedal Position sensor A circuit, high voltage input
P0125	Insufficient coolant temperature for closed-loop fuel control
P0128	Coolant temperature below thermostat regulating temperature
P0136	Oxygen sensor circuit fault (Bank 1, Sensor 2)
P0137	Oxygen sensor circuit, low voltage (Bank 1, Sensor 2)
P0138	Oxygen sensor circuit, high voltage (Bank 1, Sensor 2)
P0141	Oxygen sensor heater or circuit fault (Bank 1, Sensor 2)
P0156	Oxygen sensor circuit malfunction (Bank 2, Sensor 2)
P0157	Oxygen sensor circuit, low voltage (Bank 2, Sensor 2)
P0158	Oxygen sensor circuit, high voltage (Bank 2, Sensor 2)
P0171	Fuel injection system too lean (Bank 1)
P0172	Fuel injection system too rich (Bank 1)
P0174	Fuel injection system lean (Bank 2)
P0175	Fuel injection system rich (Bank 2)
P0220	Throttle/Accelerator Pedal Position sensor B, circuit fault
P0222	Throttle/Accelerator Pedal Position sensor B circuit, low voltage input
P0223	Throttle/Accelerator Pedal Position sensor B circuit, high voltage input
P0300	Random/multiple cylinder misfire detected
P0301	Cylinder No. 1 misfire detected
P0302	Cylinder No. 2 misfire detected
P0303	Cylinder No. 3 misfire detected
P0304	Cylinder No. 4 misfire detected
P0305	Cylinder No. 5 misfire detected
P0306	Cylinder No. 6 misfire detected

DIAGNOSTIC TROUBLE CODES (CONTINUED)

Code	Code identification
P0325	Knock sensor No. 1, circuit fault
P0327	Knock sensor No. 1 circuit, low voltage (Bank 1 or single sensor)
P0328	Knock sensor No. 1 circuit, high voltage (Bank 1 or single sensor)
P0330	Knock sensor no. 2, circuit fault
P0332	Knock sensor No. 2 circuit, low voltage (Bank 2)
P0333	Knock sensor No. 2 circuit, high voltage (Bank 2)
P0335	Crankshaft Position (CKP) sensor A, circuit fault
P0339	Crankshaft Position (CKP) sensor A, circuit intermittent
P0340	Camshaft Position (CMP) sensor A circuit (Bank 1 or single sensor)
P0341	Camshaft Position (CMP) sensor A circuit, range or performance problem (Bank 1 or single sensor)
P0345	Camshaft Position (CMP) sensor A circuit (Bank 2)
P0346	Camshaft Position (CMP) sensor A circuit, range or performance problem (Bank 2)
P0351	Ignition coil 1 primary/secondary circuit
P0352	Ignition coil 2 primary/secondary circuit
P0353	Ignition coil 3 primary/secondary circuit
P0354	Ignition coil 4 primary/secondary circuit
P0355	Ignition coil 5 primary/secondary circuit
P0356	Ignition coil 6 primary/secondary circuit
P0420	Catalyst system efficiency below threshold (Bank 1)
P0430	Catalyst system efficiency below threshold (Bank 2)
P043E	Evaporative Emission Control (EVAP) system, reference orifice clogged
P043F	Evaporative Emission Control (EVAP) system, reference orifice high flow
P0441	Evaporative Emission Control (EVAP) system, incorrect purge flow
P0442	Evaporative Emission Control (EVAP) system, small leak detected
P0446	EVAP canister vent control valve, circuit fault
P0450	EVAP system vapor pressure sensor (fuel tank pressure sensor)
P0451	EVAP system vapor pressure sensor, range or performance problem
P0452	EVAP system vapor pressure sensor, low voltage input
P0453	EVAP system vapor pressure sensor, high voltage input
P0455	Evaporative Emission Control (EVAP) system, big leak detected
P0456	Evaporative Emission Control (EVAP) system, very small leak detected
P0500	Vehicle Speed Sensor (VSS) A, circuit malfunction
P0503	Vehicle Speed Sensor (VSS) A, intermittent, erratic or and/or high voltage
P0504	Brake switch correlation
P0505	Idle control system malfunction
P050A	Cold start idle air system performance

Code	Code identification
P050B	Cold start ignition timing performance
P0560	System voltage
P0604	Internal control module random access memory (RAM) error
P0606	PCM processor exhaust monitoring
P0607	PCM performance
P0617	Starter relay circuit, high voltage
P0630	Vehicle Identification Number (VIN) not programmed or mismatched PCM
P0657	Actuator supply voltage, open circuit
P0705	Transmission Range (TR) sensor circuit malfunction (PRNDL input)
P0710	Transmission fluid temperature sensor A circuit malfunction
P0711	Transmission fluid temperature sensor A performance
P0712	Transmission fluid temperature sensor A circuit, low input voltage
P0713	Transmission fluid temperature sensor A circuit, high input voltage
P0717	Input/turbine speed sensor A circuit, no signal
P0724	Brake switch B circuit, high voltage
P0741	Torque converter clutch (TCC) solenoid performance
P0746	Pressure control solenoid A performance
P0748	Pressure control solenoid A electrical (shift solenoid valve SL1)
P0766	Shift solenoid D performance (shift solenoid valve S4)
P0771	Shift solenoid E performance (shift solenoid valve SR)
P0776	Pressure control solenoid B performance (shift solenoid valve SL2)
P0778	Pressure control solenoid B electrical (shift solenoid valve SL2)
P0793	Intermediate shaft speed sensor circuit A no signal
P0796	Pressure control solenoid C performance (shift solenoid valve SL3)
P0798	Pressure control solenoid C electrical (shift solenoid valve SL3)
P0982	Shift solenoid D control circuit, low voltage
P0983	Shift solenoid D control circuit, high voltage
P0985	Pressure control solenoid E performance (shift solenoid valve SR)
P0986	Pressure control solenoid E electrical (shift solenoid valve SR)

3 Powertrain Control Module (PCM) - removal and installation

▶ Refer to illustration 3.1

✳✳ WARNING:

The models covered by this manual are equipped with Supplemental Restraint systems (SRS), more commonly known as airbags. Always disable the airbag system before working in the vicinity of any airbag system component to avoid the possibility of accidental deployment of the airbag, which could cause personal injury (see Chapter 12).

✳✳ CAUTION:

To avoid electrostatic discharge damage to the PCM, handle the PCM only by its case. Do not touch the electrical terminals during removal and installation. If available, ground yourself to the vehicle with an anti-static ground strap, available at computer supply stores.

➡Note: The manufacturer states that on 2004 and later models, engine performance may be affected after the Powertrain Control Module (PCM) has been removed and reinstalled. Be sure to have the PCM reprogrammed by a dealer service department or other qualified automotive repair facility.

1 The PCM is located inside the passenger compartment behind the glovebox, to the right of the heater blower case (see illustration).
2 Disconnect the cable from the negative battery terminal (see Chapter 5, Section 1).
3 Remove the glovebox (see Chapter 11).
4 Remove the right scuff plate, cowl side trim and the panel below the glove compartment (see Chapter 11).
5 Unplug the electrical connectors from the PCM.

✳✳ CAUTION:

The ignition switch must be turned OFF when pulling out or plugging in the electrical connectors to prevent damage to the PCM.

6 Remove the retaining bolts from the PCM bracket.
7 Carefully remove the PCM.

➡Note: Avoid any static electricity damage to the computer by grounding yourself to the body before touching the PCM and using a special anti-static pad to store the PCM on once it is removed.

8 Installation is the reverse of removal.

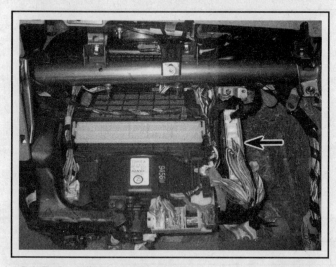

3.1 Typical PCM mounting location

4 Throttle Position Sensor (TPS) and throttle control motor - replacement

▶ Refer to illustration 4.1

1 The Throttle Position Sensor (TPS) on these models is part of the throttle motor assembly (see illustration). Problems with the TPS and/or motor can cause intermittent bursts of fuel from the injectors and an unstable idle because the PCM thinks the throttle is moving. The PCM is constantly comparing the driver's input from the accelerator pedal position sensor to the actual throttle position at the throttle body. A problem with the TPS circuits will set a diagnostic trouble code (see Section 2).

2 The TPS cannot be replaced separately. If there are problems with the throttle control motor or the TPS, the complete throttle body must be replaced (see Chapter 4).

4.1 The TPS and electronic throttle control is the black portion of the throttle body as seen here with the electrical connector

5 Mass Airflow (MAF) sensor - replacement.

▶ **Refer to illustration 5.3**

1 The Mass Airflow (MAF) sensor is located on the air intake duct. The MAF system circuit consists of a platinum hot wire, a thermistor and a control circuit inside a plastic housing. The sensor uses a hot wire sensing element to measure the molecular mass (weight) of air entering the engine. As the throttle opens, increasing volume of air passes over the hot wire, which cools the wire. The MAF sensor circuit is designed to maintain the hot wire at a constant preset temperature by controlling the current flow through the hot wire. So, as the wire cools, the PCM increases the flow of current through the hot wire in order to maintain the wire at a constant temperature. The output voltage signal of the MAF sensor varies in accordance with this current flow. This voltage signal is measured by the PCM, which converts this signal into a digital waveform, calculates the fuel injector pulse width (duration) and turns the injectors on and off accordingly. A problem in the MAF sensor circuit will set a diagnostic trouble code (see Section 2).

2 Make sure the ignition key is in the OFF position.

3 Disconnect the electrical connector from the MAF sensor (see illustration).

4 Remove the two sensor retaining bolts and remove the MAF sensor and O-ring from the air intake duct.

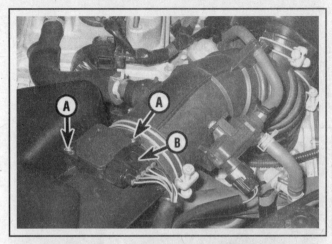

5.3 The MAF sensor is located on the air intake tube - note the two mounting screws (A) and the electrical connector (B)

5 Installation is the reverse of removal. Be sure to install a new O-ring between the MAF sensor and the intake duct.

6 Engine Coolant Temperature (ECT) sensor - replacement

▶ **Refer to illustrations 6.4a and 6.4b**

✳✳ WARNING:

Wait until the engine has cooled completely before beginning this procedure.

1 The Engine Coolant Temperature (ECT) sensor is a thermistor (a resistor which varies the value of its resistance in accordance with temperature changes). The change in the resistance values will directly affect the voltage signal from the sensor to the PCM. As the sensor temperature DECREASES, the resistance values will INCREASE. As the sensor temperature INCREASES, the resistance values will DECREASE. A problem in any of the ECT sensor circuits will set a diagnostic trouble code.

2 Make sure the ignition key is in the OFF position.

3 Drain approximately one gallon of coolant from the cooling system (see Chapter 1).

4 Disconnect the electrical connector and carefully unscrew the sensor (see illustrations).

5 Wrap the threads of the new sensor with Teflon sealing tape to prevent leakage and thread corrosion.

6 Installation is the reverse of removal.

✳✳ CAUTION:

Handle the ECT sensor with care. Damage to this sensor will affect the operation of the entire fuel injection system.

6.4a Location of the ECT sensor at the rear (left, or driver's end) of the cylinder head - four-cylinder engines

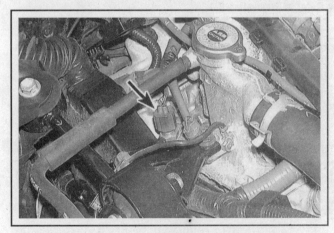

6.4b Location of the Engine Coolant Temperature (ECT) sensor at the front (right, or passenger's end) of the engine - V6 engine

7 Crankshaft Position (CKP) sensor - replacement

▶ **Refer to illustrations 7.4 and 7.5**

1 The Crankshaft Position (CKP) sensor determines the timing for the fuel injection and ignition on each cylinder. The sensor is mounted on the timing chain cover next to the crankshaft pulley. A problem in the sensor circuit will set a diagnostic trouble code (see Section 2).

2 Disconnect the cable from the negative battery terminal (see Chapter 5, Section 1).

3 Working under the vehicle, remove the inner fender shield from the right side of the vehicle (see Chapter 11).

4 Remove the bolt and detach the sensor (see illustration).

5 At the upper part of the timing cover, remove the bolt securing the CKP sensor harness and withdraw the harness and sensor (see illustration).

6 Installation is the reverse of removal.

7.4 The CKP sensor location on the timing cover (four-cylinder shown, V6 similar)

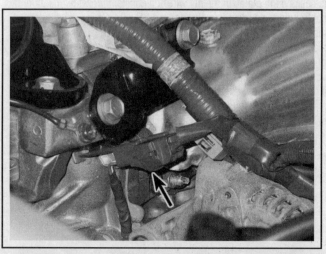

7.5 Disconnect the CKP sensor connector, then take out the harness with the sensor

8 Camshaft Position (CMP) sensor - replacement

▶ **Refer to illustration 8.1**

1 The CMP sensor determines the position of the cylinder for sequential fuel injection signals to each cylinder. The sensor is mounted on the cylinder head near the camshaft sprocket (see illustration). A problem in the sensor circuit will set a diagnostic trouble code (see Section 2).

2 Make sure the ignition key is in the OFF position.

3 Remove the air filter housing (see Chapter 4).

4 Disconnect the harness connector, remove the mounting bolt and remove the CMP sensor from the cylinder head.

5 Installation is the reverse of the removal. Use a new O-ring, lightly coated with engine oil.

8.1 The CMP sensor mounts with one bolt to the cylinder head

9 Oxygen sensor and air/fuel sensor - general information and replacement

GENERAL INFORMATION

▶ **Refer to illustrations 9.2a and 9.2b**

1   All vehicles covered by this manual have On-Board Diagnostics II (OBD-II) engine management systems, which means that they have the ability to verify the accuracy of the basic feedback loop between the oxygen sensor and the PCM. They accomplish this by using an oxygen sensor or air/fuel sensor ahead of the catalytic converter and an oxygen sensor behind the catalytic converter. By sampling the exhaust gas before and after the catalytic converter, the PCM can determine the efficiency of the converter and can even predict when it will fail.

2   The primary (upstream) oxygen sensor is located in the exhaust manifold and the secondary (downstream) oxygen sensor is located behind the catalytic converter (see illustrations). The downstream sensor on all models is a heated oxygen sensor. Some models are equipped with a heated upstream oxygen sensor. The upstream sensor is an air/fuel sensor.

3   Don't confuse oxygen sensors and air/fuel sensors. They're similar in appearance, but they operate differently and have different operating characteristics. Like an oxygen sensor, the air/fuel sensor provides a variable voltage output to the PCM that's proportional to the air/fuel mixture ratio in the exhaust stream. The air/fuel sensor doesn't "switch" back and forth like an oxygen sensor at the 14.7 to 1 stoichiometric threshold. Instead, it alters a PCM-controlled voltage between 3.3 volts (at the positive PCM terminal for the air/fuel sensor) and 3.0 volts (at the negative PCM terminal for the air/fuel sensor) in direct proportion to the amount of oxygen in the exhaust. As the air/fuel mixture in the exhaust becomes leaner, the air/fuel sensor voltage increases (within its operating range of 3.0 to 3.3 volts). Like an oxygen sensor, the air/fuel sensor doesn't operate correctly until it's warmed up. Also, like an oxygen sensor, the air/fuel sensor has a heating element that enables it to warm up quickly.

4   Special care must be taken whenever a sensor is serviced.

 a) *Oxygen sensors and air/fuel sensors have a permanently attached pigtail and electrical connector, which should not be removed from the sensor. Damage to or removal of the pigtail or electrical connector can adversely affect operation of the sensor.*

 b) *Grease, dirt and other contaminants should be kept away from the electrical connector and the louvered end of the sensor.*

 c) *Do not use cleaning solvents of any kind on an oxygen sensor or air/fuel ratio sensor.*

 d) *Do not drop or roughly handle an oxygen sensor or air/fuel ratio sensor.*

 e) *The silicone boot must be installed in the correct position to prevent the boot from being melted and to allow the sensor to operate properly.*

REPLACEMENT

▶ **Refer to illustration 9.8**

➡**Note: Because it is installed in the exhaust manifold or pipe, which contracts when cool, the oxygen sensor may be very difficult to loosen when the engine is cold. Rather than risk damage to the sensor (assuming you are planning to reuse it in another manifold or pipe), start and run the engine for a minute or two, then shut it off. Be careful not to burn yourself during the following procedure.**

5   Disconnect the cable from the negative terminal of the battery.

6   If you're replacing the downstream sensor, raise the vehicle and secure it on jackstands. Access the oxygen sensor harness and then unplug the electrical connector.

7   The upstream sensor can be replaced without raising the vehicle. Unplug the sensor electrical connector.

8   Unscrew the sensor from the exhaust manifold or exhaust pipe (see illustration).

➡**Note: The best tool for removing an oxygen sensor is a special slotted socket, especially if you're planning to reuse a sensor. If you don't have this tool, and you plan to reuse the sensor, be extremely careful when unscrewing the sensor.**

9   Apply anti-seize compound to the threads of the sensor to facilitate future removal. The threads of new sensors should already be coated with this compound, but if you're planning to reuse an old sensor, recoat the threads. Install the sensor and tighten it securely.

10   Reconnect the electrical connector of the pigtail lead to the main wiring harness.

11   Lower the vehicle (if it was raised), test drive the car and verify that no trouble codes have been set.

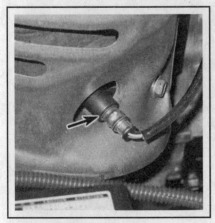

9.2a The upstream sensor is located in the exhaust manifold

9.2b Location of the downstream oxygen sensor connector (A) and sensor (B)

9.8 Use a slotted socket to remove the oxygen sensors

10 Knock sensor - replacement

▶ Refer to illustration 10.5

✳✳ WARNING:

Wait for the engine to cool completely before performing this procedure.

1   The knock control system is designed to reduce spark knock during periods of heavy detonation. This allows the engine to use optimal spark advance to improve driveability. The knock sensor detects abnormal vibration in the engine and produces a voltage output that increases with the severity of the knock. The voltage signal is monitored by the PCM, which retards ignition timing until the detonation ceases. On four-cylinder engines the knock sensor is located on the backside of the engine block, directly below the cylinder head (facing toward the rear of the engine compartment). On V6 engines there are two knock sensors; one for each cylinder bank. They're located underneath the intake manifold.

2   Disconnect the cable from the negative terminal of the battery (see Chapter 5). If you're working on a V6 engine, drain the cooling system (see Chapter 1).

3   If you're working on a four-cylinder engine, pinch off the coolant hoses to the throttle body before removing the intake manifold/throttle body.

4   Remove the intake manifold (see Chapter 2A or 2B).

5   Disconnect the electrical connector and remove the knock sensor (see illustration).

6   If you're going to reuse the old sensor, coat the threads with thread sealant. New sensors are pre-coated with thread sealant, do

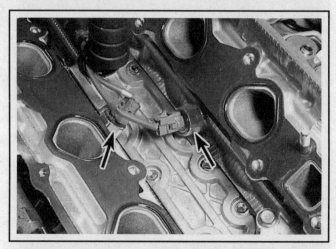

10.5 On V6 engines, the knock sensors are under the intake manifold (on four-cylinder engines the sensor is screwed into the side of the block, below the intake manifold)

not apply any additional sealant or the operation of the sensor may be affected.

7   Install the knock sensor and tighten it securely (approximately 30 ft-lbs). Don't overtighten the sensor or damage may occur. Plug in the electrical connector, refill the cooling system and check for leaks. On 3MZ V6 models, turn the knock sensors so the connector ends are pointed toward the timing belt end of the engine, for ease of harness hookup.

11 Vehicle Speed Sensor (VSS) - replacement

▶ Refer to illustration 11.1

1   The Vehicle Speed Sensor (VSS) (see illustration) is located on top of the transaxle. This sensor is an electronic component that produces a pulsing voltage signal whenever the sensor shaft is rotated. These voltage pulses are monitored by the PCM, which uses this information to help control the fuel and ignition systems and transaxle shifting.

2   Disconnect the electrical connector from the VSS.

3   Remove the VSS from the transaxle.

4   Replace the O-ring.

5   Installation is the reverse of removal.

11.1 The VSS is located on top of the transaxle

12 Positive Crankcase Ventilation (PCV) system

▶ **Refer to illustration 12.1**

1   The Positive Crankcase Ventilation (PCV) system reduces hydrocarbon emissions by scavenging crankcase vapors. It does this by circulating fresh air from the air cleaner through the crankcase, where it mixes with blow-by gases and is then rerouted through a PCV valve to the intake manifold (see illustration).

2   The main components of the PCV system are the PCV valve, a blow-by filter and the vacuum hoses connecting these two components with the engine.

3   To maintain idle quality, the PCV valve restricts the flow when the intake manifold vacuum is high. If abnormal operating conditions (such as piston ring problems) arise, the system is designed to allow excessive amounts of blow-by gases to flow back through the crankcase vent tube into the air cleaner to be consumed by normal combustion.

4   Checking and replacement of the PCV valve is covered in Chapter 1.

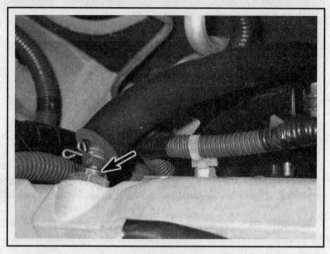

12.1 PCV valve location (four-cylinder model shown)

13 Exhaust Gas Recirculation (EGR) system (2002 and 2003 V6 models)

GENERAL DESCRIPTION

▶ **Refer to illustration 13.2**

1   To reduce oxides of nitrogen (NOx) emissions, some of the exhaust gases are recirculated through the EGR valve to the intake manifold to lower combustion temperatures.

2   The EGR system consists of an EGR valve, an EGR modulator, a vacuum switching valve (VSV) and the vacuum lines to the throttle body (see illustration). The position of the EGR valve is controlled by vacuum, which is controlled by the Powertrain Control Module (PCM).

REPLACEMENT

EGR valve

3   Remove the throttle body (see Chapter 4).

4   Detach the vacuum hose from the EGR valve. Disconnect the EGR pipe, remove the EGR valve mounting bolts and remove the EGR valve

from the intake manifold. Check the valve for sticking and heavy carbon deposits. If the valve is sticking or clogged with deposits, clean or replace it.

5   Installation is the reverse of removal. Be sure to use new gaskets

EGR vacuum modulator and modulator filter

▶ **Refer to illustration 13.7**

6   Clearly label and disconnect the vacuum hoses to the EGR vacuum modulator. Remove the EGR vacuum modulator from its bracket.

7   If you're planning to reuse the old modulator, pull the cover off and check the filters (see illustration). Clean them with compressed air and then reinstall the cover. If the filters cannot be cleaned, replace them or replace the modulator.

8   Installation is the reverse of removal.

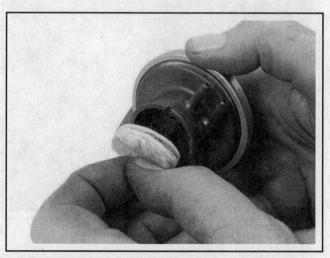

13.7 Remove the cap, pull out the two filters and blow them out with compressed air; make sure the coarse side of the outer filter faces out when reinstalling the filters

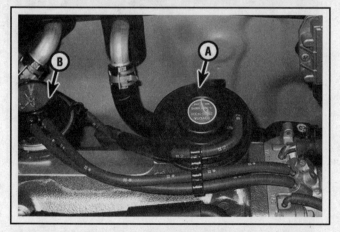

13.2 Typical EGR valve (A) and EGR vacuum modulator (B)

Vacuum switching valve (VSV)

9 Disconnect the negative battery cable (see Chapter 5). Raise the vehicle and place it securely on jackstands.

10 Locate the VSV near the exhaust manifold. Unplug the electrical connector from the VSV. Clearly label and disconnect the vacuum hoses attached to the VSV.

11 Remove the VSV from its mounting bracket. If you have difficulty removing the VSV from the bracket, remove the bracket bolt, remove the entire assembly and separate the VSV from the bracket off the vehicle.

12 Installation is the reverse of removal.

14 Evaporative emissions control (EVAP) system

GENERAL DESCRIPTION

▶ **Refer to illustrations 14.1 and 14.6**

1 The fuel evaporative emissions control (EVAP) system absorbs fuel vapors and, during engine operation, releases them into the engine intake where they mix with the incoming air-fuel mixture. The charcoal canister is mounted behind the fuel tank under the vehicle (see illustration).

2 When the engine is not operating, fuel vapors are transferred from the fuel tank, throttle body and intake manifold to the charcoal canister where they are stored. When the engine is running, the fuel vapors are purged from the canister by the purge control valve. The gasses are consumed in the normal combustion process. The electronic purge control valve is directly controlled by the PCM.

3 The fuel filler cap is fitted with a two-way valve as a safety device. The valve vents fuel vapors to the atmosphere if the EVAP system fails.

4 The EVAP system also incorporates a vapor pressure sensor. This sensor detects abnormal vapor pressure in the system. The vapor pressure sensor is mounted in the fuel pump/sending unit assembly on top of the fuel tank.

5 After the engine has been running and warmed up to a pre-set temperature, the Vacuum Switching Valve (VSV) opens. The VSV (purge control valve) allows intake manifold vacuum to draw the fuel vapors from the canister to the intake manifold, where they are mixed with intake air before being burned with the air/fuel mixture inside the combustion chambers.

6 The fuel tank vapor pressure sensor monitors changes in pressure inside the tank and, when the pressure exceeds a preset threshold, opens the VSV (see illustration), which allows a purge port in the canister to admit fuel tank vapors into the canister.

CHARCOAL CANISTER REPLACEMENT

7 Disconnect the cable from the negative battery terminal (see Chapter 5).

8 Raise the rear of the vehicle and support it securely on jackstands.

9 Unplug all electrical connectors and clearly label and disconnect the vent hoses to the charcoal canister, remove the bolts and separate the canister from the underside of the vehicle.

10 Installation is the reverse of removal.

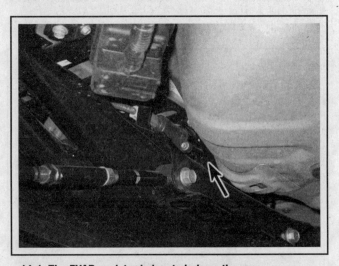

14.1 The EVAP canister is located above the rear crossmember, near the fuel tank

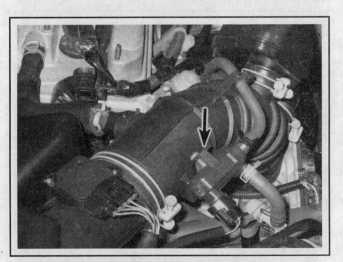

14.6 Location of the EVAP vacuum switching valve (four-cylinder model shown, V6 similar)

15 Catalytic converters

➡**Note 1: Because of a Federally mandated extended warranty which covers emissions-related components such as the catalytic converter, check with a dealer service department before replacing the converter at your own expense.**

➡**Note 2: The front catalytic converter is incorporated into the exhaust manifold. Refer to Chapter 2A or 2B for the exhaust manifold replacement procedure.**

GENERAL DESCRIPTION

1   The catalytic converter is an emission control device added to the exhaust system to reduce pollutants from the exhaust gas stream. There are two types of converters. The conventional oxidation catalyst reduces the levels of hydrocarbon (HC) and carbon monoxide (CO). The three-way catalyst lowers the levels of oxides of nitrogen (NOx) as well as hydrocarbons (HC) and carbon monoxide (CO). These models are equipped only with three-way catalytic converters. On the covered models, the primary catalytic converter is mounted in the engine's exhaust manifold. On V6 engines, there is one in the exhaust manifold for each bank of the engine.

CHECK

2   The test equipment for a catalytic converter is expensive and highly sophisticated. If you suspect that the converter on your vehicle is malfunctioning, take it to a dealer or authorized emissions inspection facility for diagnosis and repair.

3   Whenever the vehicle is raised for servicing of underbody components, check the converter for leaks, corrosion, dents and other dam-age. Check the welds/flange bolts that attach the front and rear ends of the converter to the exhaust system. If damage is discovered, the converter should be replaced.

4   Although catalytic converters don't break too often, they can become plugged. The easiest way to check for a restricted converter is to use a vacuum gauge to diagnose the effect of a blocked exhaust on intake vacuum.

  a) *Connect a vacuum gauge to an intake manifold vacuum source (see Chapter 2C).*
  b) *Warm the engine to operating temperature, place the transaxle in Park (automatic) or Neutral (manual) and apply the parking brake.*
  c) *Note and record the vacuum reading at idle.*
  d) *Quickly open the throttle to near full throttle and release it shut. Note and record the vacuum reading.*
  e) *Perform the test three more times, recording the reading after each test.*
  f) *If the reading after the fourth test is more than one in-Hg lower than the reading recorded at idle, the exhaust system may be restricted (the catalytic converter could be plugged or an exhaust pipe or muffler could be restricted).*

REPLACEMENT

▶ **Refer to illustrations 15.6a and 15.6b**

5   Be sure to spray the nuts on the exhaust flange studs before removing them from the catalytic converter.

6   Remove the nuts and separate the catalytic converter from the exhaust system (see illustrations).

7   Installation is the reverse of removal.

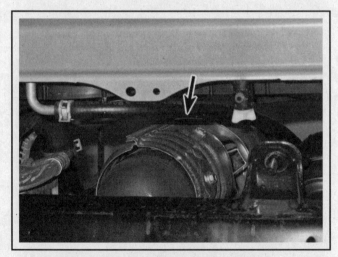

15.6a The primary catalytic converter at the exhaust manifold (four-cylinder, shown from below)

15.6b On most models, the secondary catalytic converter is located near the middle of the exhaust system

Notes

Section

1   General information
2   Shift and select cables - replacement
3   Shift lever assembly - removal and installation
4   Back-up light switch - check and replacement
5   Manual transaxle - removal and installation
6   Manual transaxle overhaul - general information

Reference to other Chapters

Engine mounts - check and replacement - See Chapter 2A or 2B
Manual transaxle lubricant change - See Chapter 1
Manual transaxle lubricant level check - See Chapter 1

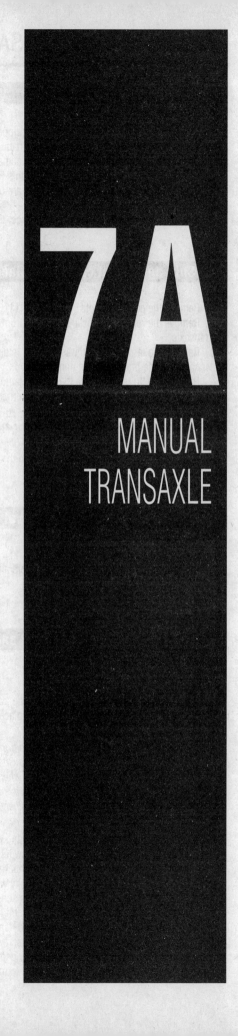

7A

MANUAL TRANSAXLE

1 General information

The vehicles covered by this manual are equipped with either a 5-speed manual or a 4-speed or 5-speed automatic transaxle. The 5-speed transaxle used in the covered models is named the E-351. Information on the manual transaxle is included in this Part of Chapter 7. Service procedures for the automatic transaxle are contained in Chapter 7, Part B.

The manual transaxle is a compact, two-piece, lightweight alumi-num alloy housing containing both the transmission and differential assemblies.

Because of the complexity, unavailability of replacement parts and special tools necessary, internal repair procedures for the manual transaxle are not recommended for the home mechanic. The bulk of information in this Chapter is devoted to removal and installation procedures.

2 Shift and select cables - replacement

1 Remove the center console (see Chapter 11).

2 Remove the retaining clips and washers from the cable ends at the transaxle.

3 Remove the large clips and washers that retain the shift and select cables to the bracket on the transaxle.

4 Remove the bolts that attach the cable retainer, if applicable, to the firewall. Remove the outer retainer and grommet.

➡**Note: On some models it is necessary to remove the heater core/evaporator housing (see Chapter 3) for access to these bolts.**

5 Remove the clips and washers that attach the shift and select cables to the shift lever.

6 Remove the large clip-type cable retainers that attach the cables to the bracket at the forward end of the shift lever base.

7 Remove the inner retainer and grommet from the passenger side of the firewall.

8 Pull the cable(s) out through the firewall.

9 Installation is the reverse of removal. When attaching cables to the front of the shifter assembly, the wider part of the cable end flange should face Up. When attaching the shift cable ends to the shifter with the clips and washers, the toothed edge of the cable eyes should face Up.

3 Shift lever assembly - removal and installation

1 Remove the center console (see Chapter 11).

2 Remove the shift and select cable retainers and disconnect both cables from the shift lever (see Section 2).

3 Remove the retaining bolts and detach the shift lever assembly.

4 Installation is the reverse of removal.

4 Back-up light switch - check and replacement

▶ **Refer to illustration 4.1**

1 The backup light switch is mounted on the transaxle (see illustration). With the ignition key in the On position, place the shift lever in Reverse. The back-up lights should come on.

   a) *If the lights don't come on, check the ignition switch, the GAUGE fuse, the bulbs and the wire harness (see Chapter 12).*

   b) *If the lights remain on all the time, even when the shift lever is not in REVERSE, check the wire harness.*

   c) *If only one light comes on, but not the other, check the bulb for that light and check the harness.*

2 To check the operation of the back-up light switch itself, disconnect the electrical connector and unscrew the switch from the top of the transaxle, then use an ohmmeter to verify that there's continuity when the plunger is depressed, and no continuity when the plunger is released. The back-up light switch and harness connector are located on the side of the transaxle near the starter assembly.

3 If the switch doesn't operate as described, replace it. Disconnect the electrical connector from the switch and unscrew it from the case.

4 Test the new switch before installation by depressing the plunger with an ohmmeter connected across the switch terminals. There should

4.1 The backup light switch is threaded into the top of the transaxle case

be continuity only when the plunger is depressed.

5 Install the new switch and tighten it securely.

5   Manual transaxle - removal and installation

REMOVAL

▶ **Refer to illustration 5.5**

➡**Note: The manufacturer requires the engine and transaxle to be removed as a unit, then separated once they are out of the vehicle (see Chapter 2C for the engine/transaxle removal procedure).**

1   Disconnect the negative cable from the battery and remove the battery (see Chapter 5).

2   Remove the engine and transaxle as a unit (see Chapter 2C).

> ※※ **CAUTION:**
>
> **Do not depress the clutch pedal while the transaxle is removed from the vehicle.**

> ※※ **WARNING:**
>
> **Do not place any part of your body under the transaxle assembly when it's supported only by a hoist or other lifting device.**

3   With the engine and transaxle lowered, support the transaxle with a floor jack. Place a block of wood on the jack head to prevent damage to the transaxle. Safety chains will help steady the transaxle on the jack.

4   Remove the transaxle case protector fasteners and lift the case protector from the transaxle.

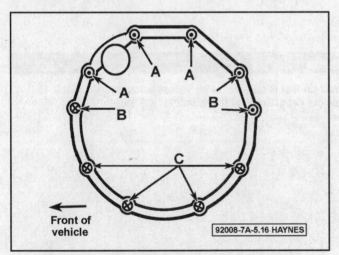

5.5 Manual transaxle mounting bolts (refer to letters for torque specs when installing)

5   Remove the transaxle-to-engine bolts (see illustration).

6   Recheck to be sure nothing is connecting the engine or the transaxle. Disconnect and label anything still remaining.

7   Move the transaxle assembly away from the engine and carefully place the transaxle assembly on the floor onto wood blocks. Leave enough room for a floor jack underneath the transaxle.

8   The clutch components can now be inspected (see Chapter 8). In most cases, new clutch components should be routinely installed whenever the transaxle is removed.

9   Check the engine and transaxle mounts and the engine control rod. If any of these components are worn or damaged, replace them.

INSTALLATION

10 If removed, install the clutch components (see Chapter 8).

11 With the transaxle secured to the jack as on removal, raise it into position and carefully slide it forward, engaging the input shaft with the clutch disc splines. Do not use excessive force to install the transaxle - if the input shaft does not slide into place, readjust the angle of the transaxle so it is level and/or turn the input shaft so the splines engage properly with the clutch.

> ※※ **CAUTION:**
>
> **Do NOT use transaxle-to-engine bolts to force the engine and transaxle into alignment. Doing so could crack or damage major components. If you experience difficulties, have an assistant help you line up the dowel pins on the block with the transaxle. Some wiggling of the engine and/or the transaxle will probably be necessary to secure proper alignment of the two.**

12 Install the transaxle-to-engine bolts and the engine-to-transaxle bolt. Tighten the bolts to the torque listed in this Chapter's Specifications (see illustration 5.5).

13 Install the engine and transaxle unit (see Chapter 2C) and tighten all mounting bolts and nuts securely.

14 Reinstall the remaining components in the reverse order of removal.

15 Tighten the wheel lug nuts to the torque listed in the Chapter 1 Specifications.

16 Add the specified amounts of coolant, oil and transaxle fluid (see Chapter 1).

17 Connect the negative battery cable. Start the engine and check for proper operation and leaks.

18 Shut off the engine and recheck the fluid levels. Road test the vehicle to check for proper transaxle operation and check for leakage.

6   Manual transaxle overhaul - general information

1   Overhauling a manual transaxle is a difficult job for the do-it-yourselfer. It involves the disassembly and reassembly of many small parts. Numerous clearances must be precisely measured and, if necessary, changed with select fit spacers and snap-rings. As a result, if transaxle problems arise, it can be removed and installed by a competent do-it-yourselfer, but overhaul should be left to a transmission repair shop. Rebuilt transaxles may be available - check with your dealer parts department and auto parts stores. At any rate, the time and money

involved in an overhaul is almost sure to exceed the cost of a rebuilt unit.

2   Nevertheless, it's not impossible for an inexperienced mechanic to rebuild a transaxle if the special tools are available and the job is done in a deliberate step-by-step manner so nothing is overlooked.

3   The tools necessary for an overhaul include internal and external snap-ring pliers, a bearing puller, a slide hammer, a set of pin punches, a dial indicator and possibly a hydraulic press. In addition, a large, sturdy workbench and a vise or transaxle stand will be required.

4   During disassembly of the transaxle, make careful notes of how each piece comes off, where it fits in relation to other pieces and what holds it in place.

5   Before taking the transaxle apart for repair, it will help if you have some idea what area of the transaxle is malfunctioning. Certain problems can be closely tied to specific areas in the transaxle, which can make component examination and replacement easier. Refer to the *Troubleshooting* section at the front of this manual for information regarding possible sources of trouble.

Torque specifications	Ft-lbs (unless otherwise indicated)

➡ **Note: One foot-pound (ft-lb) of torque is equivalent to 12 inch-pounds (in-lbs) of torque. Torque values below approximately 15 ft-lbs are expressed in inch-pounds, since most foot-pound torque wrenches are not accurate at these smaller values.**

Back-up light switch	30
Exhaust manifold brace	
Four cylinder models	31
V6 models	168 in-lbs
Power steering gear assembly	134
Shift lever mounting bolts	108 in-lbs
Subframe assembly	
Bolts A	63
Bolts B	24
Bolts C	63
Bolts D	24
Nuts E	24
Stiffener plate	
Left side	27
Right side	29
Transaxle-to-engine bolts (see illustration 5.5)	
Bolts A	47
Bolts B	34
Bolts C	32

7B

AUTOMATIC
TRANSAXLE

Section

1   General information
2   Diagnosis - general
3   Shift cable - adjustment and replacement
4   Throttle Valve (TV) cable (Avalon and Solara models) - adjustment
    and replacement
5   Transmission position switch - replacement and adjustment
6   Shift lock system - description and component replacement
7   Oil seal replacement
8   Automatic transaxle - removal and installation
9   Electronic control system

Reference to other Chapters

Automatic transaxle/differential fluid change - See Chapter 1
Automatic transaxle/differential lubricant level check - See Chapter 1
Automatic transaxle fluid level check - See Chapter 1
CHECK ENGINE light on - See Chapter 6
Engine mounts - check and replacement - See Chapter 2A or 2B

1 General information

There are several models of automatic transaxles on the covered vehicles. Four-cylinder engines have been equipped with the U241-E 4-speed or U151-E five-speed. Models with V6 engines are equipped with the U140-E or U250-E transaxles. Some Lexus models are equipped with a U150-E transaxle. The transaxles vary in oil capacity, bearing and gear size to compensate for the engine horsepower and torque. Information on the automatic transaxle is included in this Part of Chapter 7. Service procedures for the manual transaxle are contained in Chapter 7, Part A.

Due to the complexity of the automatic transaxles covered in this manual and to the specialized equipment necessary to perform most service operations, this Chapter contains only those procedures related to general diagnosis, routine maintenance, adjustment and removal and installation.

If the transaxle requires major repair work, it should be left to a dealer service department or an automotive or transmission shop. You can, however, remove and install the transaxle yourself and save the expense, even if a transmission shop does the repair work.

2 Diagnosis - general

Automatic transaxle malfunctions may be caused by five general conditions:

- a) *Poor engine performance*
- b) *Improper adjustments*
- c) *Hydraulic malfunctions*
- d) *Mechanical malfunctions*
- e) *Malfunctions in the computer or its signal network*

Diagnosis of these problems should always begin with a check of the easily repaired items: fluid level and condition (see Chapter 1), shift linkage adjustment and throttle linkage adjustment. Next, perform a road test to determine if the problem has been corrected or if more diagnosis is necessary. If the problem persists after the preliminary tests and corrections are completed, additional diagnosis should be done by a dealer service department or transmission shop. Refer to the *Troubleshooting* section at the front of this manual for information on symptoms of transaxle problems.

PRELIMINARY CHECKS

1   Drive the vehicle to warm the transaxle to normal operating temperature.

2   Check the fluid level as described in Chapter 1:

- a) *If the fluid level is unusually low, add enough fluid to bring the level within the designated area of the dipstick, then check for external leaks (see below).*
- b) *If the fluid level is abnormally high, drain off the excess, then check the drained fluid for contamination by coolant. The presence of engine coolant in the automatic transaxle fluid indicates that a failure has occurred in the internal radiator walls that separate the coolant from the transaxle fluid (see Chapter 3).*
- c) *If the fluid is foaming, drain it and refill the transaxle, then check for coolant in the fluid, or a high fluid level.*

3   Check the engine idle speed.

➡**Note: If the engine is malfunctioning, do not proceed with the preliminary checks until it has been repaired and runs normally.**

4   Check the throttle valve cable for freedom of movement (Avalon models only). Adjust it if necessary (see Section 4).

➡**Note: The throttle cable may function properly when the engine is shut off and cold, but it may malfunction once the engine is hot. Check it cold and at normal engine operating temperature.**

5   Inspect the shift cable (see Section 3). Make sure that it's properly adjusted and that the linkage operates smoothly.

FLUID LEAK DIAGNOSIS

6   Most fluid leaks are easy to locate visually. Repair usually consists of replacing a seal or gasket. If a leak is difficult to find, the following procedure may help.

7   Identify the fluid. Make sure it's transmission fluid and not engine oil or brake fluid (automatic transmission fluid is a deep red color).

8   Try to pinpoint the source of the leak. Drive the vehicle several miles, then park it over a large sheet of cardboard. After a minute or two, you should be able to locate the leak by determining the source of the fluid dripping onto the cardboard.

9   Make a careful visual inspection of the suspected component and the area immediately around it. Pay particular attention to gasket mating surfaces. A mirror is often helpful for finding leaks in areas that are hard to see.

10 If the leak still cannot be found, clean the suspected area thoroughly with a degreaser or solvent, then dry it.

11 Drive the vehicle for several miles at normal operating temperature and varying speeds. After driving the vehicle, visually inspect the suspected component again.

12 Once the leak has been located, the cause must be determined before it can be properly repaired. If a gasket is replaced but the sealing flange is bent, the new gasket will not stop the leak. The bent flange must be straightened.

13 Before attempting to repair a leak, check to make sure that the following conditions are corrected or they may cause another leak.

➡Note: Some of the following conditions cannot be fixed without highly specialized tools and expertise. Such problems must be referred to a transmission shop or a dealer service department.

Gasket leaks

14 Check the pan periodically. Make sure the bolts are tight, no bolts are missing, the gasket is in good condition and the pan is flat (dents in the pan may indicate damage to the valve body inside).

15 If the pan gasket is leaking, the fluid level or the fluid pressure may be too high, the vent may be plugged, the pan bolts may be too tight, the pan sealing flange may be warped, the sealing surface of the transaxle housing may be damaged, the gasket may be damaged or the transaxle casting may be cracked or porous. If sealant instead of gasket material has been used to form a seal between the pan and the transaxle housing, it may be the wrong sealant.

Seal leaks

16 If a transaxle seal is leaking, the fluid level or pressure may be too high, the vent may be plugged, the seal bore may be damaged, the seal itself may be damaged or improperly fitted, the surface of the shaft protruding through the seal may be damaged or a loose bearing may be causing excessive shaft movement.

17 Make sure the dipstick tube seal is in good condition and the tube is properly seated. Periodically check the area around the speedometer gear or sensor for leakage. If fluid is evident, check the O-ring for damage.

Case leaks

18 If the case itself appears to be leaking, the casting is porous and will have to be repaired or replaced.

19 Make sure the oil cooler hose fittings are tight and in good condition.

Fluid comes out vent pipe or fill tube

20 If this condition occurs, the transaxle is overfilled, there is coolant in the fluid, the case is porous, the dipstick is incorrect, the vent is plugged or the drain-back holes are plugged.

---

3   Shift cable - adjustment and replacement

ADJUSTMENT

♦ **Refer to illustrations 3.3 and 3.4**

1   When the shift lever inside the vehicle is moved from the Neutral position to other positions, it should move smoothly and accurately to each position and the shift indicator should indicate the correct gear position. If the indicator isn't aligned with the correct position, adjust the shift cable as follows:

2   Raise the vehicle and support it securely on jackstands. Remove the splash shields that cover the area between the front of the vehicle and the lower crossmember (see Chapter 11).

3   Loosen the swivel nut on the manual shift lever at the transaxle (see illustration).

4   Move the manual lever down into Park, then return it two notches to the Neutral position (see illustration).

5   Move the shift lever inside the vehicle to the Neutral position.

6   While holding the lever with a slight pressure toward the REVERSE position, tighten the swivel nut securely.

7   Check the operation of the transaxle in each shift lever position (try to start the engine in each gear - the starter should operate in the Park and Neutral positions only).

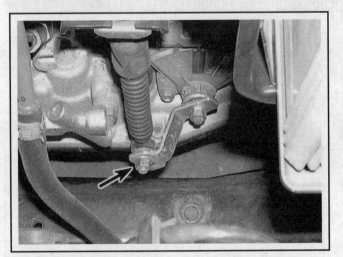

3.3 Before adjusting the shift cable, loosen the swivel nut that connects the shift cable to the manual lever on the transaxle

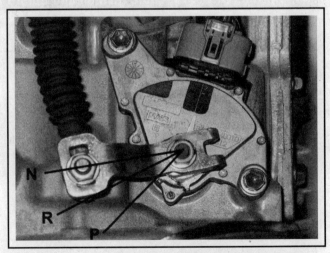

3.4 To adjust the shift cable, push the manual lever all the way DOWN, return it two clicks to the Neutral position, place the shift lever inside the vehicle at the Neutral position and tighten the swivel nut

3.8 To disconnect the shift cable from the transaxle, remove the large C-clip retainer from the bracket on the front of the transaxle

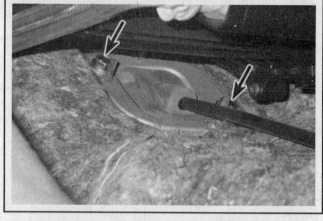

3.10 To detach the cable boot seal from the floor under the heat/AC housing, remove the mounting bolts

REPLACEMENT

▸ **Refer to illustrations 3.8, 3.10 and 3.11**

8 Disconnect the cable from the manual lever (see illustration 3.3) and remove the large C-clip cable retainer (see illustration) from the bracket above the manual lever.

9 Remove the center console (see Chapter 11).

10 Remove the bolts from the cable housing retainer on the floor inside the vehicle (see illustration).

11 Pry off the cable end from the shift housing (see illustration).

12 Disconnect the cable eye from the shift lever pin.

13 Pull the cable through the floor.

14 Installation is the reverse of removal.

15 Be sure to adjust the cable when you're done.

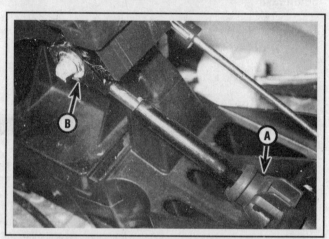

3.11 To detach the shift cable from the shift lever base, twist the flange (A) to release its clips, then pry the cable eye (B) from the shifter pin

---

4 Throttle Valve (TV) cable (Avalon and Solara models) - adjustment and replacement

ADJUSTMENT

▸ **Refer to illustration 4.2**

1 Have an assistant hold the throttle pedal down while you verify that the throttle valve linkage opens all the way.

2 If the linkage does not open all the way, ask your assistant to hold the pedal down while you loosen the adjusting nuts and adjust the cable until the mark or stopper is the specified distance from the boot end (see illustration).

3 Tighten the adjusting nuts securely, recheck the clearance and make sure the link opens all the way when the throttle is depressed.

REPLACEMENT

4 Remove the battery (see Chapter 5), then unbolt the cruise control actuator and set it aside for access to the throttle cable at the transmission.

5 Disconnect the throttle cable end from the throttle body.

6 Remove the transmission position switch (see Section 5) and the valve body behind it on the transmission case.

7 Remove the cable end mounting bolt and the cable from the transmission.

8 Insert the new cable at the transmission and adjust as described in Step 2.

9 The remainder of the installation is the reverse of removal.

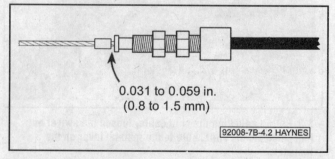

0.031 to 0.059 in.
(0.8 to 1.5 mm)

92008-7B-4.2 HAYNES

4.2 Throttle valve (TV) cable housing-to-stopper gap details

5   Transmission position switch - replacement and adjustment

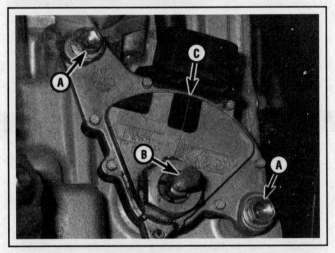

5.4 Remove the manual shift-lever retaining nut

1   The transmission position switch incorporates the Park/Neutral function as well as the backup light switch and transmission gear position information which it sends to the PCM. The Park/Neutral function of the switch prevents the engine from starting in any gear other than Park or Neutral. If the engine starts with the shift lever in any position other than Park or Neutral, adjust the switch. The transmission position switch is also an information sensor for the Electronic Controlled Transaxle (ECT) Electronic Control Unit (ECU). When the shift lever is placed in position, the Park/Neutral position switch sends a voltage signal to the ECU.

REPLACEMENT

▶ **Refer to illustration 5.4**

2   Raise the front of the vehicle and place it securely on jackstands.
3   Disconnect the electrical connector.
4   Remove the manual lever retaining nut and its lock plate (see illustration).

➡**Note: Bend the tabs flat on the lock plate before removing it (if equipped).**

5   Remove the switch retaining bolts (see illustration 5.8).
6   Remove the switch.
7   Installation is the reverse of removal. Be sure to adjust the switch.

ADJUSTMENT

▶ **Refer to illustration 5.8**

8   Loosen the switch retaining bolts and rotate the switch until the groove at the shaft and the neutral basic line on the switch are aligned (see illustration). Hold the switch in this position and tighten the bolts.

➡**Note: The pointer on the sheetmetal lock plate will indicate the alignment of the groove on the shaft with the Neutral line on the body of the switch.**

9   Refer to Section 3 for the cable adjustment procedure.

5.8 Detach the manual lever and remove the switch retaining bolts (A) - the groove on the shaft (B) should align with the Neutral line on the switch (C) when installing the switch

6   Shift lock system - description and component replacement

DESCRIPTION

1   The shift lock system prevents the shift lever from being shifted out of Park until the brake pedal is applied. The system consists of a stop light switch, a key interlock solenoid, a shift lock override button, a shift lock solenoid, and a shift lock control computer that incorporates a switch operated by the shift lever.

COMPONENT REPLACEMENT

▶ **Refer to illustrations 6.3, 6.4 and 6.5**

2   Remove the center console (see Chapter 11).
3   To disconnect the cable, push in the locking tab and separate the cable end (see illustration).
4   Where the cable mounts below the steering column, disconnect the clip (see illustration).

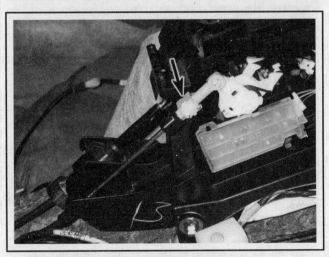

6.3 Disconnect the shift lock cable at the shifter end

6.4 Use a screwdriver to release the clip securing the cable at the front

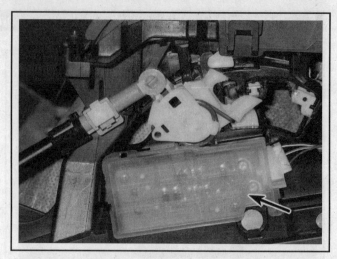

6.5 Shift lock system computer location

5   The shift lock control computer is located at the bottom of the shift lever base on the right side (see illustration). Disconnect the electrical connector and unclip the shift-lock computer from the shifter assembly.

6   The key interlock solenoid is located near the ignition switch (see Chapter 12).

7   Oil seal replacement

1   Fluid leaks frequently occur due to wear of the driveaxle oil seals and/or the speedometer drive gear oil seal and O-rings. Replacement of these seals is relatively easy, since the repairs can usually be performed without removing the transaxle from the vehicle.

DRIVEAXLE SEALS

▸ **Refer to illustrations 7.4 and 7.6**

2   The driveaxle oil seals are located in either sides of the transaxle, where the driveaxle shaft is splined into the differential. If leakage at the seal is suspected, raise the vehicle and support it securely on jackstands. If the seal is leaking, fluid will be found on the side of the transaxle.

3   Remove the driveaxle (see Chapter 8). If you're replacing the right side driveaxle seal, remove the intermediate shaft and the driveaxle assembly as a single unit.

4   Using a screwdriver or prybar, carefully pry the oil seal out of the transaxle bore (see illustration).

5   If the oil seal cannot be removed with a screwdriver or prybar, a special oil seal removal tool (available at auto parts stores) will be required.

6   Using a seal driver or a large deep socket as a drift, install the new oil seal. Drive it into the bore squarely and make sure that it is completely seated (see illustration). Lubricate the lip of the new seal with multi-purpose grease.

7   Install the driveaxle assembly (see Chapter 8). Be careful not to damage the lip of the new seal.

7.4 Carefully pry out the old driveaxle seal with a prybar, screwdriver or a special seal removal tool; make sure you don't gouge or nick the surface of the seal bore

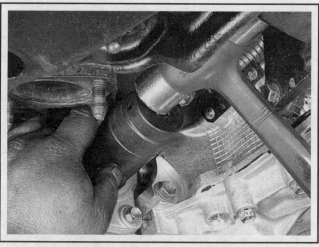

7.6 Drive in the new driveaxle seal with a large socket or a special seal installer

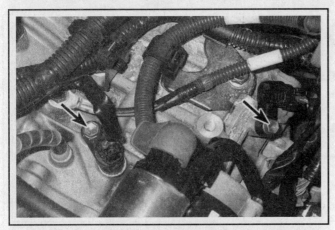

7.10 Remove the O-ring from the speed sensor

7.9 To remove the vehicle speed sensor from the transaxle, disconnect the electrical connector and remove the sensor hold-down bolt (2 sensors shown here)

SPEED SENSORS

▶ **Refer to illustrations 7.9 and 7.10**

8   The vehicle speed sensor and one or two transmission speed sensors (depending on model) are located on the case of the transaxle. Look for lubricant around the sensor housings to determine if an O-ring is leaking.

9   Disconnect the electrical connector from the vehicle or transmission speed sensor and remove it from the transaxle (see illustration).

10   Remove the O-ring (see illustration).

11   Install a new O-ring on the driven gear housing and reinstall the

speedometer driven gear and vehicle speed sensor housing. Tighten the hold-down bolt securely.

DIRECT CLUTCH SPEED SENSOR SEAL (AVALON MODELS)

12   The direct clutch speed sensor seal is located on the transaxle housing. Look for lubricant around the sensor housing to determine if the O-ring is leaking.

13   Disconnect the electrical connector from the direct clutch speed sensor and remove the sensor from the transaxle.

14   Remove the O-ring.

15   Install a new O-ring (coat it with ATF) on the sensor body and reinstall the direct clutch speed sensor. Tighten the hold-down bolt securely.

---

8   Automatic transaxle - removal and installation

➡**Note: The following procedure applies to Avalon and Solara models. The manufacturer states that transaxle removal on Camry and Lexus ES300/330 models requires the engine and transaxle to be removed as a unit, then separated once they are out of the vehicle (see Chapter 2, Part C for the engine/transaxle removal procedure).**

REMOVAL

▶ **Refer to illustrations 8.5, 8.7, 8.11, 8.29, 8.32a and 8.32b**

1   Place protective covers on the fenders and cowl and remove the hood (see Chapter 11).

2   Disconnect the negative cable from the battery (see Chapter 5, Section 1).

3   Remove the battery and the battery tray (see Chapter 5).

4   On V6 models, remove the engine cover.

5   On models equipped with cruise control, unplug the electrical connector for the actuator and remove the actuator (see illustration).

6   Remove the starter (see Chapter 5).

7   Remove the fluid cooler lines from the transaxle (see illustration). Be sure to position a pan below the line connections to catch any residual fluid.

8   Disconnect the transmission position switch electrical connector (see Section 5).

8.5 Location of the cruise control actuator

9   Disconnect the Vehicle Speed Sensor (VSS) connector and, on models so equipped, the direct clutch speed sensor (see Section 7).

10   Disconnect the Throttle Valve (TV) cable from the throttle linkage (see Section 4).

11   Clearly label, then disconnect any vacuum lines, wiring harnesses, electrical connectors, and ground straps connected to the transaxle (see illustration). Masking tape and/or a touch-up paint appli-

8.7 Disconnect the automatic transaxle fluid cooler lines

8.11 Location of the ground strap bolt

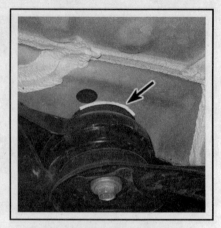

8.29 Paint subframe-to-chassis reference marks to insure correct reassembly

cator works well for marking items. Take instant photos or sketch the locations of components and brackets.

12 Disconnect the shift cable (see Section 3) from the transaxle.

13 Loosen the driveaxle/hub nuts (see Chapter 8).

14 Loosen but do NOT remove the front wheel lug nuts.

15 Remove the transaxle upper mounting bolts.

16 Raise the vehicle and support it securely on jackstands.

17 Secure the engine using an engine support fixture that is fitted above the engine compartment. If an engine support fixture is not available, install an engine hoist and a lifting chain assembly. This will keep the engine stable during the entire transaxle removal procedure.

✸✸ WARNING:

Be sure the engine/transaxle is securely supported by the fixture or hoist. If it is not securely supported, it could fall during the removal procedure, causing injury or death. Remove the front wheels.

18 Remove the manifold brace between the exhaust manifold and the transaxle.

19 Remove the under-vehicle splash shields.

20 Detach the exhaust pipe(s) from the manifold(s) (see Chapter 4). Detach the exhaust pipe from the catalytic converter and separate the pipe from the exhaust system.

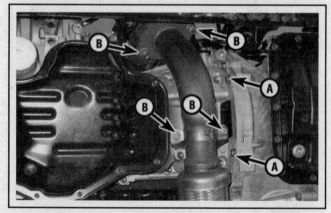

8.32a Remove the torque converter cover mounting bolts (A); exhaust pipe flange and brace bolts are indicated by (B)

➡Note: On some models, it will be necessary to remove the front pipe support brace from the engine (see illustration 8.32a).

21 Drain the transaxle fluid (see Chapter 1).

22 Remove the driveaxles (see Chapter 8).

23 Remove the mounting bolts from the front engine mount (see Chapter 2A or 2B).

24 Remove the left side transaxle mount nuts (see Chapter 2A or 2B).

25 Remove the rear engine mount from the transaxle (see Chapter 2A or 2B).

26 Remove the two stabilizer bar mounting nuts and disconnect the stabilizer bar from the links (see Chapter 10).

27 Remove the four set bolts from the stabilizer bar bracket (see Chapter 10).

28 Use wire to tie the power steering gear to a component above it, then remove the two mounting bolts. The steering gear should remain suspended but out of the way during the transaxle removal procedure.

29 Support the subframe with two floorjacks, then remove the subframe mounting bolts from the chassis (see illustration). The front section of the subframe is attached with two bolts and two nuts while the rear section of the subframe is attached with a combination of six nuts and bolts. Be sure to note exactly the size and location of each nut and bolt to insure correct reassembly.

➡Note: The transaxle should be supported by a transmission jack immediately after the subframe is removed from the vehicle. The transaxle will tilt slightly but should remain steady if the engine is properly secured with the engine support fixture or hoist.

30 Support the transaxle with an approved transmission jack and safety chains. Floor jacks are often not stable enough to support and lower the transaxle from the vehicle.

31 Remove the stiffener plate from the left side and right side of the transaxle, if equipped.

32 Remove the torque converter mounting bolts (see illustrations). Rotate the engine to gain access to each bolt.

33 Remove the transaxle lower mounting bolts.

34 Recheck to be sure nothing is connecting the transaxle to the engine or to the vehicle. Disconnect and label anything still remaining.

35 Separate the transaxle from the engine, then slowly lower the transaxle assembly out of the vehicle. Keep the transaxle level as you're separating it from the engine to prevent damage to the input shaft. It may be necessary to pry the mounts away from the frame brackets.

8.32b Remove the torque converter-to-driveplate bolts - rotate the engine to gain access to the other bolts, also seen clearly here are the lower transaxle-to-engine bolts

❊❊ WARNING:

Do not place any part of your body under the transaxle assembly or engine when it's supported only by a hoist or other lifting device.

36 Move the transaxle assembly away from the vehicle and carefully place the transaxle assembly on the floor onto wood blocks. Leave enough room for a floor jack underneath the transaxle.

37 Check the engine and transaxle mounts and the transaxle shock absorber. If any of these components are worn or damaged, replace them.

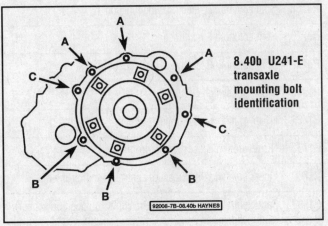

8.40b U241-E transaxle mounting bolt identification

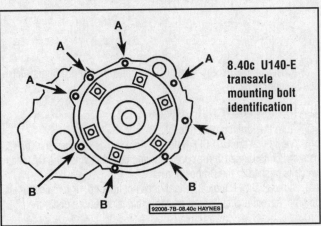

8.40c U140-E transaxle mounting bolt identification

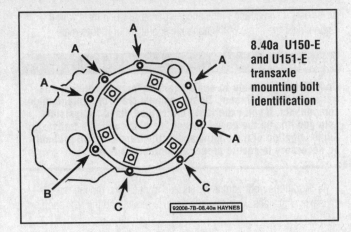

8.40a U150-E and U151-E transaxle mounting bolt identification

INSTALLATION

▶ **Refer to illustrations 8.40a, 8.40b, 8.40c and 8.40d**

38 If removed, install the torque converter on the transaxle input shaft. Make sure the converter hub splines are properly engaged with the splines on the transaxle input shaft.

39 With the transaxle secured to the jack as on removal, and with an assistant holding the torque converter in place, raise the transaxle into position and turn the converter to align the bolt holes in the converter with the bolt holes in the driveplate. Install the converter-to-driveplate bolts.

➡**Note: Install all six bolts before tightening any of them.**

40 Install the transaxle-to-engine bolts and the engine-to-transaxle bolt (see illustrations). Tighten the bolts to the torque listed in this Chapter's Specifications. Do not use excessive force to install the

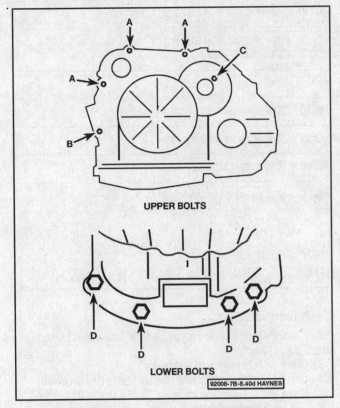

UPPER BOLTS

LOWER BOLTS

8.40d U250-E transaxle mounting bolt identification

transaxle - if something binds and the transaxle won't mate with the engine, alter the angle of the transaxle slightly until it does mate.

✳✳ CAUTION:

Do NOT use transaxle-to-engine bolts to force the engine and transaxle into alignment. Doing so could crack or damage major components. If you experience difficulties, have an assistant help you line up the dowel pins on the block with the transaxle. Some wiggling of the engine and/or the transaxle will probably be necessary to secure proper alignment of the two.

41 Install the right engine mount, the front engine mount, the transaxle shock absorber, the left transaxle mount and the rear engine mount. Install the center bearing support on the rear of the block. Tighten all mounting bolts and nuts securely.

42 Reinstall the remaining components in the reverse order of removal.

43 Remove all jacks and hoists and lower the vehicle. Tighten the wheel nuts to the torque listed in the Chapter 1 Specifications.

44 Add the specified type and amount of transaxle fluid (see Chapter 1).

45 Connect the negative battery cable. Run the engine, cycle the transaxle through the gears, then check the fluid level (see Chapter 1). Check for proper operation and leaks.

46 Road test the vehicle to check for proper transmission operation and check for leakage. Recheck the fluid level.

9 Electronic control system

TROUBLE CODES

1 The electronic control system for the transaxle has some self-diagnostic capabilities. If certain kinds of system malfunctions occur, the PCM stores the appropriate diagnostic trouble code in its memory and the CHECK ENGINE indicator light illuminates to inform the driver.

The diagnostic trouble codes can only be extracted from the PCM using a SCAN tool that can be linked to the On Board Diagnostic (OBD II) computer via the 16-pin diagnostic link. Codes are listed below for reference, but can only be extracted with the correct scan tool connected to the diagnostic connector under the left side of the instrument panel (refer to Chapter 6 for additional information).

Code	Code identification
P0500	Vehicle speed sensor or circuit fault
P0710	Transmission fluid temperature sensor fault
P0711	Transmission fluid temperature sensor, range or performance fault
P0750	Shift solenoid A fault
P0753	Shift solenoid A, electrical malfunction
P0755	Shift solenoid B malfunction
P0758	Shift solenoid B, open or short
P0765	Shift solenoid D malfunction

Code	Code identification
P0768	Shift solenoid D, electrical malfunction
P0770	Shift solenoid E malfunction
P0773	Shift solenoid E, electrical malfunction
P1520	Stop light switch circuit
P1725	NT revolution sensor circuit problem
P1730	NC revolution sensor circuit problem
P1760	Linear solenoid line pressure control, circuit problem
P1780	Park/Neutral Position switch (transmission position sensor) malfunction

OTHER ELECTRONIC CONTROL SYSTEM CHECKS

Preliminary checks

2 Check the fluid level and condition. If the fluid smells burned, replace it (see Chapter 1).

3 Check for fluid leaks (see Section 2).

4 Check and, if necessary, adjust the shift cable (see Section 3).

5 Check and, if necessary, adjust the Throttle Valve (TV) cable on Avalon models only (see Section 4).

6 Check and, if necessary, adjust the transmission position switch (see Section 5).

O/D OFF indicator light check

7 Turn the ignition switch to ON.

8 Verify that the O/D OFF indicator light comes on when the O/D main switch is in the Off (up) position, and goes out when the O/D main switch is pushed to the On position.

9 If the O/D OFF indicator light does not light up, or remains on all the time, have the circuit checked out by a dealer service department.

Torque specifications	Ft-lbs
Back-up light switch	33
Exhaust manifold brace	
Four-cylinder models	31
V6 models	
California models	25
Except California models	15
Subframe assembly	See Chapter 7A
Stiffener plate bolts	34
Transaxle-to-engine bolts	
U150-E and U151-E (see illustration 8.40a)	
Bolts A	47
Bolts B	34
Bolts C	27
U241-E (see illustration 8.40b)	
Bolts A	47
Bolts B	32
Bolts C	34
U140-E (see illustration 8.40c)	
Bolts A	47
Bolts B	32
U250-E (see illustration 8.40d)	
Bolts A	47
Bolts B	34
Bolts C	34
Bolts D	32
Torque converter to driveplate bolts	30

Notes

Section

1   General information
2   Clutch - description and chec
3   Clutch components - removal, inspection and installation
4   Clutch release bearing and lever - removal, inspection and installation
5   Clutch master cylinder - removal and installation
6   Clutch release cylinder and accumulator - removal and installation
7   Clutch hydraulic system - bleeding
8   Clutch start switch - replacement
9   Driveaxles - general information and inspection
10 Driveaxle - removal and installation
11 Driveaxle boot replacement

Reference to other Chapters

Clutch fluid level check - See Chapter 1
Clutch pedal height and freeplay check and adjustment - See Chapter 1
Driveaxle boot check - See Chapter 1
Driveaxle oil seal - replacement - See Chapter 7B
Flywheel - removal and installation - See Chapter 2

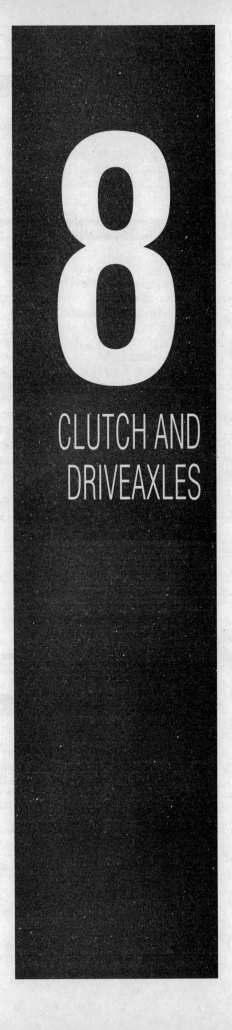

8

CLUTCH AND DRIVEAXLES

1 General information

The information in this Chapter deals with the components from the rear of the engine to the front wheels, except for the transaxle, which is dealt with in Chapter 7A and 7B. For the purposes of this Chapter, these components are grouped into two categories: Clutch and driveaxles. Separate Sections within this Chapter offer general descriptions and checking procedures for both groups.

Since nearly all the procedures covered in this Chapter involve working under the vehicle, make sure it's securely supported on sturdy jackstands or a hoist where the vehicle can be easily raised and lowered.

2 Clutch - description and check

1 All vehicles with a manual transaxle use a single dry plate, diaphragm spring type clutch. The clutch disc has a splined hub that allows it to slide along the splines of the transaxle input shaft. The clutch and pressure plate are held in contact by spring pressure exerted by the diaphragm in the pressure plate.

2 The clutch release system is operated by hydraulic pressure. The hydraulic release system consists of the clutch pedal, a master cylinder and fluid reservoir, the hydraulic line, an accumulator (on V6 models), a release (or slave) cylinder which actuates the clutch release lever and the clutch release (or throw-out) bearing.

3 When pressure is applied to the clutch pedal to release the clutch, hydraulic pressure is exerted against the outer end of the clutch release lever. As the lever pivots, the shaft fingers push against the release bearing. The bearing pushes against the fingers of the diaphragm spring of the pressure plate assembly, which in turn releases the clutch plate.

4 Terminology can be a problem regarding the clutch components because common names have in some cases changed from that used by the manufacturer. For example, the driven plate is also called the clutch plate or disc, the pressure plate assembly is sometimes referred to as the clutch cover, the clutch release bearing is sometimes called a throw-out bearing, and the release cylinder is sometimes called the operating or slave cylinder.

5 Other than replacing components that have obvious damage, some preliminary checks should be performed to diagnose a clutch system failure.

a) The first check should be of the fluid level in the clutch master cylinder (see Chapter 1). If the fluid level is low, add fluid as necessary and inspect the hydraulic clutch system for leaks. If the master cylinder reservoir has run dry, bleed the system (see Section 7) and re-test the clutch operation.

b) To check "clutch spin-down time," run the engine at normal idle speed with the transaxle in Neutral (clutch pedal up - engaged). Disengage the clutch (pedal down), wait several seconds and shift the transaxle into Reverse. No grinding noise should be heard. A grinding noise would most likely indicate a problem in the pressure plate or the clutch disc.

c) To check for complete clutch release, run the engine (with the parking brake applied to prevent movement) and hold the clutch pedal approximately 1/2-inch from the floor. Shift the transaxle between 1st gear and Reverse several times. If the shift is not smooth, component failure is indicated. Check the release cylinder pushrod travel. With the clutch pedal depressed completely the release cylinder pushrod should extend substantially. If it doesn't, check the fluid level in the clutch master cylinder.

d) Visually inspect the clutch pedal bushing at the top of the clutch pedal to make sure there is no sticking or excessive wear.

e) Under the vehicle, check that the clutch release lever is solidly mounted on the ball stud.

3 Clutch components - removal, inspection and installation

�֎ WARNING:

Dust produced by clutch wear and deposited on clutch components is hazardous to your health. DO NOT blow it out with compressed air and DO NOT inhale it. DO NOT use gasoline or petroleum based solvents to remove the dust. Brake system cleaner should be used to flush the dust into a drain pan. After the clutch components are wiped clean with a rag, dispose of the contaminated rags and cleaner in a labeled, covered container.

REMOVAL

▶ **Refer to illustration 3.6**

1 Access to the clutch components is normally accomplished by removing the transaxle, leaving the engine in the vehicle. If, of course, the engine is being removed for major overhaul, then the opportunity should always be taken to check the clutch for wear and replace worn components as necessary. However, the relatively low cost of the clutch components compared to the time and labor involved in gaining access to them warrants their replacement any time the engine or transaxle is removed, unless they are new or in near-perfect condition. The following procedures assume that the engine will stay in place.

2 Remove the release cylinder (see Section 6). Hang it out of the way with a piece of wire - it's not necessary to disconnect the hose.

3 Remove the transaxle from the vehicle (see Chapter 7A). Support the engine while the transaxle is out. Preferably, an engine hoist should be used to support it from above. However, if a jack is used underneath the engine, make sure a piece of wood is used between the jack and oil pan to spread the load.

�֎ CAUTION:

The pick-up for the oil pump is very close to the bottom of the oil pan. If the pan is bent or distorted in any way, engine oil starvation could occur.

3.6 Mark the relationship of the pressure plate to the flywheel (in case you are going to re-use the same pressure plate)

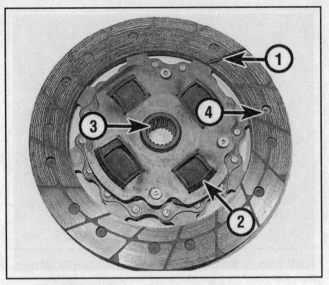

3.10 The clutch disc

1   **Lining** - *this will wear down in use*
2   **Springs or dampers** - *check for cracking and deformation*
3   **Splined hub** - *the splines must not be worn and should slide smoothly on the transaxle input shaft splines*
4   **Rivets** - *these secure the lining and will damage the flywheel or pressure plate if allowed to contact the surfaces*

4   The release fork and release bearing can remain attached to the transaxle for the time being.

5   To support the clutch disc during removal, install a clutch alignment tool through the clutch disc hub.

6   Carefully inspect the flywheel and pressure plate for indexing marks. The marks are usually an X, an O or a white letter. If they cannot be found, scribe marks yourself so the pressure plate and the flywheel will be in the same alignment during installation (see illustration).

7   Slowly loosen the pressure plate-to-flywheel bolts. Work in a diagonal pattern and loosen each bolt a little at a time until all spring pressure is relieved. Then hold the pressure plate securely and completely remove the bolts, followed by the pressure plate and clutch disc.

INSPECTION

♦ **Refer to illustrations 3.10, 3.12a and 3.12b**

8   Ordinarily, when a problem occurs in the clutch, it can be attributed to wear of the clutch driven plate assembly (clutch disc). However, all components should be inspected at this time.

9   Inspect the flywheel for cracks, heat checking, score marks and other damage. If the imperfections are slight, a machine shop can resurface it to make it flat and smooth. Refer to Chapter 2 for the flywheel removal procedure.

10 Inspect the lining on the clutch disc. There should be at least 1/16-inch of lining above the rivet heads. Check for loose rivets, distortion, cracks, broken springs and other obvious damage (see illustration). As mentioned above, ordinarily the clutch disc is replaced as a matter of course, so if in doubt about the condition, replace it with a new one.

11 The release bearing should be replaced along with the clutch disc (see Section 4).

12 Check the machined surface and the diaphragm spring fingers of the pressure plate (see illustrations). If the surface is grooved or otherwise damaged, replace the pressure plate assembly. Also check for obvious damage, distortion, cracking, etc. Light glazing can be removed with emery cloth or sandpaper. If a new pressure plate is indicated, new or factory rebuilt units are available.

INSTALLATION

♦ **Refer to illustration 3.14**

13 Before installation, carefully wipe the flywheel and pressure plate machined surfaces clean. It's important that no oil or grease is on these surfaces or the lining of the clutch disc. Handle these parts only with clean hands.

NORMAL FINGER WEAR

EXCESSIVE WEAR

EXCESSIVE FINGER WEAR

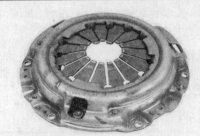

BROKEN OR BENT FINGERS

3.12a Replace the pressure plate if any of these conditions are noted

3.12b Examine the pressure plate friction surface for score marks, cracks and evidence of overheating (blue spots)

3.14 Center the clutch disc in the pressure plate with a clutch alignment tool

14 Position the clutch disc and pressure plate with the clutch held in place with an alignment tool (see illustration). Make sure it's installed properly (most replacement clutch plates will be marked "flywheel side" or something similar - if not marked, install the clutch disc with the damper springs or cushion toward the transaxle).

15 Tighten the pressure plate-to-flywheel bolts only finger-tight, working around the pressure plate.

16 Center the clutch disc by ensuring the alignment tool is through the splined hub and into the recess in the crankshaft. Wiggle the tool up, down or side-to-side as needed to bottom the tool. Tighten the pressure plate-to-flywheel bolts a little at a time, working in a criss-cross pattern to prevent distortion of the cover. After all of the bolts are snug, tighten them to the torque listed in this Chapter's Specifications. Remove the alignment tool.

17 Using high-temperature grease, lubricate the inner groove of the release bearing (see Section 4). Also place grease on the release lever contact areas and the transaxle input-shaft bearing retainer.

18 Install the clutch release bearing (see Section 4).

19 Install the transaxle, release cylinder and all components removed previously, tightening all fasteners to the proper torque specifications.

4 Clutch release bearing and lever - removal, inspection and installation

✳✳ WARNING

Dust produced by clutch wear and deposited on clutch components is hazardous to your health. DO NOT blow it out with compressed air and DO NOT inhale it. DO NOT use gasoline or petroleum-based solvents to remove the dust. Brake system cleaner should be used to flush it into a drain pan. After the clutch components are wiped clean with a rag, dispose of the contaminated rags and cleaner in a labeled, covered container.

REMOVAL

1 Disconnect the negative cable from the battery (see Chapter 5, Section 1).

2 Remove the transaxle (see Chapter 7A).

3 Reach behind the release lever and disengage the lever from the ballstud by pulling on the retention spring, then remove the lever and bearing.

INSPECTION

▶ **Refer to illustration 4.4**

4 Hold the bearing by the outer race and rotate the inner race while applying pressure (see illustration). If the bearing doesn't turn smoothly

4.4 To check the operation of the bearing, hold it by the outer race and rotate the inner race while applying pressure - the bearing should turn smoothly - if it doesn't, replace it

or if it's noisy, replace the bearing/hub assembly with a new one. Wipe the bearing with a clean rag and inspect it for damage, wear and cracks. Don't immerse the bearing in solvent - it's sealed for life and to do so would ruin it. Also check the release lever for cracks and bends.

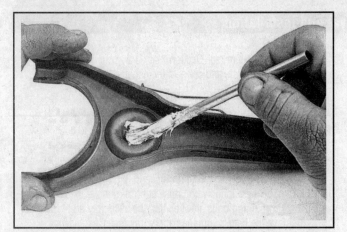

4.6a Using high temperature grease, lubricate the ball stud socket in the back of the release lever . . .

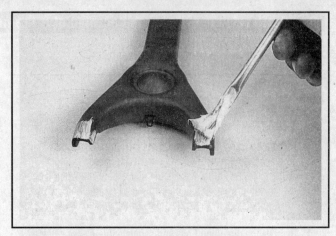

4.6b . . . the lever ends and the depression for the cylinder pushrod

INSTALLATION

▶ **Refer to illustrations 4.6a and 4.6b**

5   Fill the inner groove of the release bearing with high-temperature grease. Also apply a light coat of the same grease to the transaxle input shaft splines and the sleeve of the front bearing retainer.

6   Lubricate the release lever ball socket, lever ends and release cylinder pushrod socket with high-temperature grease (see illustrations).

7   Attach the release bearing to the release lever.

8   Slide the release bearing onto the transaxle input shaft front bearing retainer while passing the end of the release lever through the opening in the clutch housing. Push the clutch release lever onto the ballstud until it's firmly seated.

9   Apply a light coat of high-temperature grease to the face of the release bearing where it contacts the pressure plate diaphragm fingers.

10   The remainder of installation is the reverse of the removal procedure.

---

5   Clutch master cylinder - removal and installation

REMOVAL

▶ **Refer to illustration 5.4**

1   Disconnect the negative cable from the battery (see Chapter 5, Section 1).

2   If you're working on a Camry, refer to Chapter 9 and remove the brake master cylinder and power brake booster.

3   Disconnect the hydraulic line at the clutch master cylinder. If available, use a flare-nut wrench on the fitting, which will prevent the

fitting from being rounded off. Have rags handy as some fluid will be lost as the line is removed.

✳✳ CAUTION:

Don't allow brake fluid to come into contact with paint, as it will damage the finish.

4   Under the dashboard, disconnect the pushrod from the top of the clutch pedal. It's held in place with a clevis pin (see illustration).

5   From under the dash, remove the nuts which secure the master cylinder to the firewall. Remove the master cylinder, again being careful not to spill any of the fluid.

INSTALLATION

6   Position the master cylinder on the firewall, installing the mounting nuts finger-tight.

7   Connect the hydraulic line to the master cylinder, moving the cylinder slightly as necessary to thread the fitting properly into the bore. Don't cross-thread the fitting as it's installed.

8   Tighten the mounting nut to the torque listed in this Chapter's Specifications. Tighten the hydraulic line fitting securely.

9   Connect the pushrod to the clutch pedal.

10   Fill the clutch master cylinder reservoir with brake fluid conforming to DOT 3 specifications and bleed the clutch system (see Section 7).

11   Check the clutch pedal height and freeplay and adjust if necessary, following the procedure in Chapter 1.

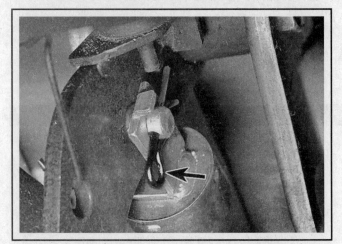

5.4 To release the clutch pushrod from the clutch pedal, remove the clip and clevis pin from the clutch pedal

6   Clutch release cylinder and accumulator - removal and installation

CLUTCH RELEASE CYLINDER

Removal

1   Disconnect the negative cable from the battery (see Chapter 5, Section 1).

2   Raise the vehicle and support it securely on jackstands.

3   To disconnect the hydraulic line from the release cylinder, unscrew the threaded fitting. If available, use a flare-nut wrench on the fitting, which will prevent the fitting from being rounded off. Have a small can and rags handy, as some fluid will be spilled as the line is removed.

4   Remove the mounting bolts and separate the release cylinder from the accumulator bracket.

Installation

5   Connect the hydraulic line to the release cylinder. Install the release cylinder on the bracket, making sure the pushrod is seated in the release fork pocket. Tighten the nuts to the torque listed in this Chapter's Specifications.

6   Tighten the hydraulic line threaded fitting securely.

7   Fill the clutch master cylinder with brake fluid (conforming to DOT 3 specifications).

8   Bleed the system (see Section 7).

9   Lower the vehicle and connect the negative battery cable.

ACCUMULATOR

Removal

10   Disconnect the negative cable from the battery (see Chapter 5, Section 1).

11   Raise the vehicle and support it securely on jackstands.

12   On models equipped with cruise control, remove the cruise control actuator mounting bolts and position the assembly off to the side.

13   Remove the battery and the battery tray (see Chapter 5).

14   Remove the starter (see Chapter 5).

15   Unscrew the hydraulic line fittings from the accumulator and release cylinder, then remove the mounting bolts from the accumulator bracket.

Installation

16   Connect the hydraulic lines to the accumulator, but don't tighten them completely yet. Install the accumulator mounting bolts and tighten them to the torque listed in this Chapter's Specifications. Now tighten the hydraulic line fittings securely.

17   The remainder of installation is the reverse of removal.

7   Clutch hydraulic system - bleeding

1   The hydraulic system should be bled of all air whenever any part of the system has been removed or if the fluid level has been allowed to fall so low that air has been drawn into the master cylinder. The procedure is very similar to bleeding a brake system.

2   Fill the master cylinder with new brake fluid conforming to DOT 3 specifications.

✳ CAUTION:

Do not re-use any of the fluid coming from the system during the bleeding operation or use fluid which has been inside an open container for an extended period of time.

3   Raise the vehicle and place it securely on jackstands to gain access to the release cylinder, which is located on the left side of the clutch housing.

4   Remove the dust cap that fits over the bleeder valve and push a length of plastic hose over the valve. Place the other end of the hose into a clear container with about two inches of brake fluid in it. The hose end must be submerged in the fluid.

5   Have an assistant depress the clutch pedal and hold it. Open the bleeder valve on the release cylinder, allowing fluid to flow through the hose. Close the bleeder valve when fluid stops flowing from the hose. Once closed, have your assistant release the pedal.

6   Continue this process until all air is evacuated from the system, indicated by a full, solid stream of fluid being ejected from the bleeder valve each time and no air bubbles in the hose or container. Keep a close watch on the fluid level inside the clutch master cylinder reservoir; if the level drops too low, air will be sucked back into the system and the process will have to be started all over again.

7   Install the dust cap and lower the vehicle. Check carefully for proper operation before placing the vehicle in normal service.

8   Clutch start switch - replacement

1   Check the pedal height, pedal freeplay and pushrod play (see Chapter 1).

2   Verify that the engine will not start when the clutch pedal is released.

3   Verify that the engine will start when the clutch pedal is depressed all the way.

4   The clutch start switch is located on a bracket forward of the clutch pedal (under the dash).

5   If the switch fails either of the tests, replace it. This is accomplished by removing the nut nearest the plunger end of the switch and unscrewing the switch. Disconnect the wire harness. Installation is the reverse of removal.

6   To adjust the clutch start switch, depress the clutch pedal completely and turn the switch in or out to achieve the spacing of the original switch.

7   Verify that the switch operates properly by performing Steps 2 and 3 again.

9 Driveaxles - general information and inspection

1 Power is transmitted from the transaxle to the wheels through a pair of driveaxles. The inner end of each driveaxle is connected to the transaxle, directly splined to the differential side gears. The outer ends of the driveaxles are splined to the axle hubs and locked in place by a large nut. The left side driveaxle is shorter while the right side driveaxle is longer and equipped with an intermediate shaft that is supported in the middle by a bearing support.

2 The inner ends of the driveaxles are equipped with sliding constant velocity joints, which are capable of both angular and axial motion. Each inner joint assembly consists of either a tripod bearing and a joint tulip (housing) or a ball-and-cage type constant velocity joint in which the joint is free to slide in-and-out as the driveaxle moves up-and-down with the wheel. The joints can be disassembled and cleaned in the event of a boot failure, but if any parts are damaged, the joints must be replaced as a unit (see Section 11).

3 Each outer joint, which consists of ball bearings running between an inner race and an outer race (housing), is capable of angular but not axial movement.

4 The boots should be inspected periodically for damage and leaking lubricant. Torn CV joint boots must be replaced immediately or the joints can be damaged. Boot replacement involves removal of the driveaxle (see Section 10).

➡**Note: Some auto parts stores carry "split" type replacement boots, which can be installed without removing the driveaxle from the vehicle. This is a convenient alternative; however, the driveaxle should be removed and the CV joint disassembled and cleaned to ensure the joint is free from contaminants such as moisture and dirt which will accelerate CV joint wear.**

The most common symptom of worn or damaged CV joints, besides lubricant leaks, is a clicking noise in turns, a clunk when accelerating after coasting and vibration at highway speeds. To check for wear in the CV joints and driveaxle shafts, grasp each axle (one at a time) and rotate it in both directions while holding the CV joint housings, feeling for play indicating worn splines or sloppy CV joints. Also check the driveaxle shafts for cracks, dents and distortion.

10 Driveaxle - removal and installation

REMOVAL

▶ **Refer to illustrations 10.3, 10.4, 10.8, 10.11, 10.13a, 10.13b, 10.13c and 10.14**

➡**Note: Not all of the steps in this procedure apply to all models. Read through the procedure carefully and determine which steps apply to the vehicle being worked on before actually beginning any work.**

1 Disconnect the cable from the negative terminal of the battery (see Chapter 5, Section 1).

2 Set the parking brake.

3 Remove the wheel cover or hub cap. Remove the cotter pin and the bearing nut lock from the driveaxle/hub nut (see illustration).

4 Break loose the driveaxle/hub nut, but don't remove it yet (see illustration).

5 Loosen the front wheel lug nuts, raise the vehicle and support it securely on jackstands. Remove the wheel.

6 Remove any engine splash shields that are in the way. Remove the driveaxle/hub nut.

➡**Note: Toyota recommends removing the entire right driveaxle assembly as a single unit before attempting to disassemble it because, although you could disassemble it, reattaching the outer driveaxle assembly to the intermediate shaft on the vehicle would be extremely difficult.**

7 Disconnect the stabilizer link at the suspension strut and disconnect the tie-rod ends from the knuckle. Remove the nuts and bolt securing the balljoint to the control arm, then pry the control arm down

10.3 Remove the cotter pin and the nut lock

10.4 You'll need a large breaker bar to loosen the driveaxle/hub nut

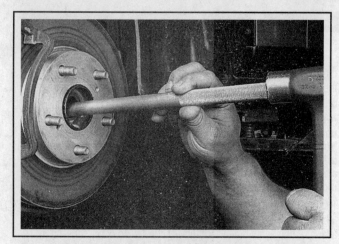

10.8 Using a hammer and a brass punch, sharply strike the end of the driveaxle - it should move noticeably (don't push it in too far, though, only until it's loose)

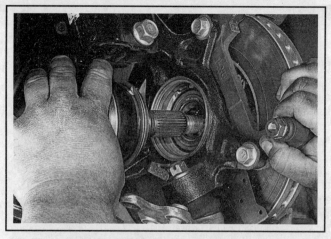

10.11 Pull the steering knuckle out and slide the end of the driveaxle out of the hub. There is a sharp ring around the CV joint just behind the stub axle - wrap a rag around it so you don't cut your hand

to separate the components (see Chapter 10). On models with ABS brakes, disconnect the ABS sensor from the steering knuckle and the ABS harness clamp at the suspension strut.

8   To loosen the driveaxle from the hub splines, tap the end of the driveaxle with a soft-faced hammer or a hammer and a brass punch (see illustration). If the driveaxle is stuck in the hub splines and won't move, it may be necessary to remove the brake disc (see Chapter 9) and push it from the hub with a two-jaw puller.

9   Place a drain pan underneath the transaxle just in case lubricant leaks out.

10 If the transaxle has a case protector (the small plastic cover bolted to the transaxle) over the inner CV joint, remove it.

11 Pull out on the steering knuckle and detach the driveaxle from the hub (see illustration).

12 On right driveaxle assemblies, the intermediate shaft and driveaxle assembly must be removed as a single unit.

13 If you're removing the right driveaxle on any model, remove the center bearing lock bolt (see illustration), remove the snap-ring (see illustration), grasp the intermediate shaft and pull the splined inner end of the shaft out of the differential side gear (see illustration).

14 If you're removing the left driveaxle, carefully pry the inner CV

joint out of the transaxle (see illustration).

15 Should it become necessary to move the vehicle while the driveaxle is out, place a large bolt with two large washers (one on each side of the hub) through the hub and tighten the nut securely.

16 Refer to Chapter 7 for the driveaxle seal replacement procedure.

10.13a To release the intermediate shaft bearing from the bearing support bracket, remove this lock bolt

10.13b To remove the snap-ring from the bearing support bracket, pinch the ends together as shown and pull it out of its groove in the bracket (driveaxle assembly and bearing support bracket removed from the vehicle for clarity)

10.13c To detach the intermediate shaft from the differential side gear, grasp the shaft firmly and pull

INSTALLATION

17 Installation is the reverse of the removal procedure, but with the following additional points:

a) *When installing the left driveaxle or when installing the intermediate shaft on any model, push the driveaxle sharply inward to seat the retaining ring on the inner CV joint in the groove in the differential side gear.*

b) *When installing the right driveaxle/intermediate shaft assembly, be sure to tighten the center bearing lock bolt to the torque listed in this Chapter's Specifications.*

c) *Install the wheel and lug nuts, lower the vehicle and tighten the lug nuts to the torque listed in the Chapter 1 Specifications.*

d) *Tighten the driveaxle/hub nut to the torque listed in this Chapter's Specifications, then install the nut lock and a new cotter pin.*

e) *Check the transaxle lubricant (manual transaxle) or differential lubricant (automatic transaxle) and add, if necessary, to bring it to the proper level (see Chapter 1).*

18 Check the intermediate shaft bearing for smooth operation. If it feels rough or sticky it should be replaced. Take it to a dealer service

10.14 Pry the splined end of the left driveaxle from the transaxle using a screwdriver or crowbar

department or other repair shop, as special tools are needed to perform this job.

11 Driveaxle boot replacement

➡**Note: Complete rebuilt driveaxles are available on an exchange basis, which eliminates much time and work. Check on the cost and availability of parts before disassembling the vehicle.**

1 Remove the driveaxle (see Section 10).

2 Mount the driveaxle in a vise with wood lined jaws (to prevent damage to the axleshaft). Check the CV joint for excessive play in the radial direction, which indicates worn parts. Check for smooth operation throughout the full range of motion for each CV joint. If a boot is torn, the recommended procedure is to disassemble the joint, clean the components and inspect for damage due to loss of lubrication and possible contamination by foreign matter.

DISASSEMBLY

♦ **Refer to illustrations 11.3, 11.4, 11.6 and 11.7**

3 Using diagonal cutters, cut the boot clamps (see illustration),

remove the clamps and discard them.

4 Using a screwdriver, carefully pry up on the edge of the outer boot and push it away from the CV joint. Old and worn boots can be cut off. Pull the inner CV joint boot back from the housing and slide the housing from the tripod (see illustration).

➡**Note: Right side driveaxles are equipped with an intermediate shaft attached to the inner driveaxle housing.**

5 Mark the tripod and axleshaft to ensure that they are reassembled properly.

6 Remove the tripod joint snap-ring with a pair of snap-ring pliers (see illustration).

7 Use a hammer and a brass punch to drive the tripod joint from the driveaxle (see illustration).

➡**Note: The tripod joint must be removed from the driveaxle to be able to slide the inner and outer driveaxle boots over the driveaxle. Do not remove the outer CV joint from the driveaxle.**

8 If you haven't already cut them off, remove both boots.

11.3 Cut the old boot clamps off and discard them

11.4 Remove the boot from the inner CV joint and slide the tripod from the joint housing

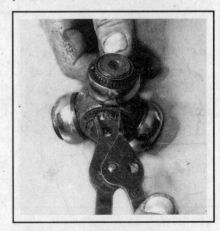

11.6 Remove the snap-ring with a pair of snap-ring pliers

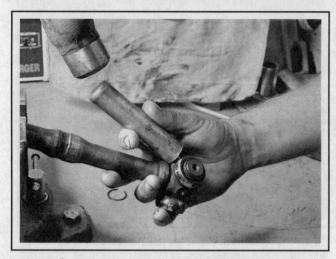

11.7 Drive the tripod joint from the driveaxle with a brass punch and hammer; be careful not to damage the bearing surfaces or the splines on the shaft

11.9a Clean the outer CV joint thoroughly with solvent and, working the joint through its entire range of motion, inspect the bearing surfaces of the balls; if they're worn or damaged, so are the bearing races

11.9b Check the condition of the center support bearing on the intermediate shaft. Make sure it turns freely, quietly and smoothly; if the bearing is hard to turn, is noisy or feels rough, have it replaced by an automotive machine shop (be sure to have a pair of new dust covers installed too)

CHECK

▶ Refer to illustrations 11.9a and 11.9b

9   Thoroughly clean all components, including the outer CV joint assembly, with solvent until the old CV joint grease is completely removed. Inspect the bearing surfaces of the inner tripods and housings for cracks, pitting, scoring and other signs of wear. It's not possible to inspect the bearing surfaces of the inner and outer races of the outer CV joint, but you can at least check the surfaces of the ball bearings themselves (see illustration). If they're in good shape, the races probably are, too; if they're not, neither are the races. If the inner CV joint is worn, you can buy a new inner CV joint and install it on the old axleshaft; if the outer CV joint is worn, you'll have to purchase a new outer CV joint and axleshaft (they're sold pre-assembled). Check the condition of the bearing for the intermediate shaft (see illustration). It should turn freely and smoothly. If it's difficult to turn, or makes a grinding noise when rotated, take the intermediate shaft to an automotive machine shop and have a new bearing installed on the shaft.

11.10a Wrap the splined area of the axleshaft with tape to prevent damage to the boots when removing or installing them

11.10b Install the tripod with the recessed portion of the splines facing the axleshaft, then install a new snap-ring

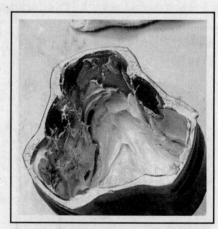

11.10c Place grease at the bottom of the CV joint housing

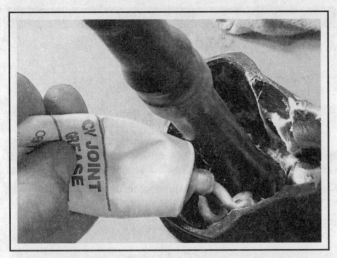

11.10d Install the boot and clamps onto the axleshaft, then insert the tripod into the housing, followed by the rest of the grease

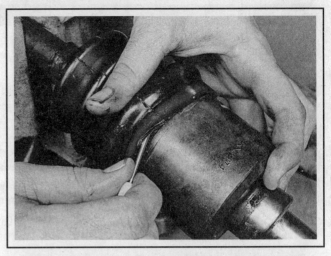

11.12a With the inner CV joint positioned half-way through its in-out travel, equalize the pressure inside the boot by inserting a small, dull screwdriver between the boot and the outer race

REASSEMBLY

▶ **Refer to illustrations 11.10a, 11.10b, 11.10c, 11.10d, 11.12a and 11.12b**

10 Wrap the splines on the inner end of the axleshaft with electrical or duct tape to protect the boots from the sharp edges of the splines (see illustration). Slide the clamps and boots onto the axleshaft, outer boot first, then place the tripod on the shaft and install a new snap-ring. Apply grease to the tripod assembly and inside the housing. Insert the tripod into the housing and pack the remainder of the grease around the tripod (see illustrations). If you're repacking the outer joint, be sure to work the entire tube of CV joint grease (included with the boot kit) into the bearing assembly.

11 Slide the boots into place, making sure the ends of both boots seat in their respective grooves in the axleshaft.

12 Position the inner CV joint mid-way through its range of travel (in/out), then equalize the pressure in the boot and tighten the boot clamps (see illustrations). The driveaxle is now ready for installation (see Section 10).

11.12b You'll need a special boot clamp installation tool like this one to tighten the new clamps; follow the instructions provided by the tool manufacturer

Specifications

Clutch

Fluid type	See Chapter 1
Pedal freeplay	See Chapter 1
Pedal height	See Chapter 1

Torque specifications   Ft-lbs (unless otherwise indicated)

➡**Note: One foot-pound (ft-lb) of torque is equivalent to 12 inch-pounds (in-lbs) of torque. Torque values below approximately 15 ft-lbs are expressed in inch-pounds, since most foot-pound torque wrenches are not accurate at these smaller values.**

Clutch master cylinder mounting nuts	108 in-lbs
Clutch accumulator	
Bracket bolts	108 in-lbs
Bolts at housing	29
Clutch pressure plate-to-flywheel bolts	168 in-lbs
Clutch release cylinder	108 in-lbs
Driveaxle/hub nut	217
Right driveaxle center bearing lock bolt	24
Wheel lug nuts	See Chapter 1

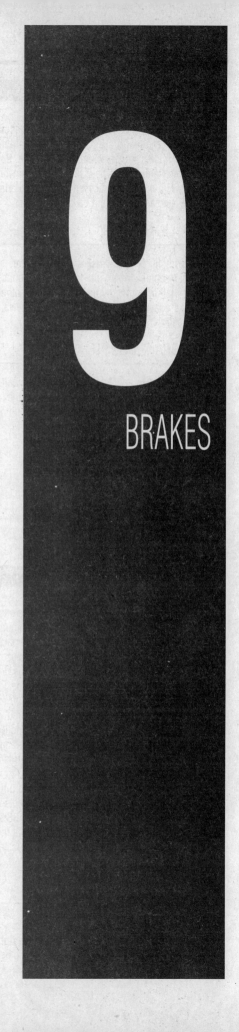

9

BRAKES

Section

1   General information
2   Anti-lock Brake System (ABS) - general information
3   Disc brake pads - replacement
4   Disc brake caliper - removal and installation
5   Brake disc - inspection, removal and installation
6   Drum brake shoes - replacement
7   Wheel cylinder - removal and installation
8   Master cylinder - removal and installation
9   Brake hoses and lines - inspection and replacement
10   Brake hydraulic system - bleeding
11   Power brake booster - check, removal and installation
12   Parking brake shoes (rear disc brakes only) - inspection
     and replacement
13   Parking brake - adjustment
14   Parking brake cables - replacement
15   Brake light switch - removal, installation and adjustment

Reference to other Chapters

Brake check - See Chapter 1
Brake fluid level check - See Chapter 1
Brake pedal - adjustment - See Chapter 1

1 General information

The vehicles covered by this manual are equipped with hydraulically operated front and rear brake systems. The front brakes are disc type and the rear brakes are either drum or disc type. Both the front and rear brakes are self-adjusting. The disc brakes automatically compensate for pad wear, while the drum brakes incorporate an adjustment mechanism that is activated as the parking brake is applied.

HYDRAULIC SYSTEM

The hydraulic system consists of two separate circuits. The master cylinder has separate reservoirs for the two circuits, and, in the event of a leak or failure in one hydraulic circuit, the other circuit will remain operative. A dual proportioning valve on the firewall provides brake balance between the front and rear brakes.

POWER BRAKE BOOSTER

The power brake booster, utilizing engine manifold vacuum and atmospheric pressure to provide assistance to the hydraulically operated brakes, is mounted on the firewall in the engine compartment.

PARKING BRAKE

The parking brake operates the rear brakes only, through cable actuation. It's activated by a lever mounted in the center console (Camry and Solara models) or a pedal mounted on the left side kick panel (Camry LXE, Avalon and Lexus ES 300/330 models).

SERVICE

After completing any operation involving disassembly of any part of the brake system, always test-drive the vehicle to check for proper braking performance before resuming normal driving. When testing the brakes, perform the tests on a clean, dry, flat surface. Conditions other than these can lead to inaccurate test results.

Test the brakes at various speeds with both light and heavy pedal pressure. The vehicle should stop evenly without pulling to one side or the other. Avoid locking the brakes, because this slides the tires and diminishes braking efficiency and control of the vehicle.

Tires, vehicle load and wheel alignment are factors which also affect braking performance.

2 Anti-lock Brake System (ABS) - general information

1   The Anti-lock Brake System (ABS) is designed to maintain vehicle steerabilty, directional stability and optimum deceleration under severe braking conditions and on most road surfaces. It does so by monitoring the rotational speed of each wheel and controlling the brake line pressure to each wheel during braking. This prevents the wheel from locking up. The ABS system is primarily designed to prevent wheel lockup during heavy braking, but the information provided by the wheel speed sensors of the ABS system is shared with several optional systems that use the data to control vehicle handling. EBD (Electronic Brakeforce Distribution) varies the front-to-rear and side-to-side braking balance under different vehicle loads. The Trac system controls only the front (driving) wheels, and is designed to automatically adjust front wheel speed when starting or accelerating on slippery surfaces. The VSC system (Vehicle Stability Control) affects your car's handling during cornering, using information from the ABS sensors and the yaw-rate sensor (which senses the side-to-side tilt of the vehicle). When the stability-control ECU senses oversteer or understeer, it reduces engine power and selectively applies the brakes.

COMPONENTS

Actuator assembly

2   The actuator assembly is mounted in the right front corner of the engine compartment, and consists of an electric hydraulic pump and four solenoid valves.

➡**Note: There are two different manufacturers for the ABS system components; TMMK and TMC. The basic design and component locations are similar, but the configuration of actuator and stability-control ECU differ.**

a) *The electric pump provides hydraulic pressure to charge the reservoirs in the actuator, which supplies pressure to the braking system. The pump and reservoirs are housed in the actuator assembly.*

b) *The solenoid valves modulate brake line pressure during ABS operation. The body contains four valves - one for each wheel.*

Speed sensors

3   These sensors are located at each wheel and generate small electrical pulsations when the toothed sensor rings are turning, sending a signal to the electronic controller indicating wheel rotational speed.

4   The front speed sensors are mounted to the front steering knuckle in close relationship to the toothed sensor rings, which are integral with the front driveaxle outer CV joints.

5   The rear wheel sensors are bolted to the axle carriers. The sensor rings are integral with the rear hub assemblies.

ABS computer

6   The ABS computer is mounted with the actuator and is the brain for the ABS system. The function of the computer is to accept and process information received from the wheel speed sensors to control

the hydraulic line pressure, avoiding wheel lock up. The computer also constantly monitors the system, even under normal driving conditions, to find faults within the system.

DIAGNOSIS AND REPAIR

7   If a problem develops within the system, an "ABS" light will glow on the dashboard. If the dashboard warning light comes on and stays on while the vehicle is in operation, the ABS system requires attention and should be examined for stored trouble codes. Before checking for trouble codes, however, you should perform a few simple checks.

   a)   *Check the brake fluid level in the master cylinder reservoir.*
   b)   *Check that all electrical connectors are securely connected.*
   c)   *Check all the applicable fuses.*

If the above preliminary checks do not rectify the problem, or if any stored trouble codes don't lead you to the problem, the vehicle should be diagnosed and repaired by a dealer service department or other repair shop.

TROUBLE CODE RETRIEVAL

▶ **Refer to illustration 2.10**

8   The ABS system control unit (computer) has a built-in self-diagnosis system which detects malfunctions in the system sensors and alerts the driver by illuminating an ABS warning light in the instrument panel. The computer stores the failure code until the diagnostic system is cleared or malfunction is repaired.

9   The ABS warning light should come on when the ignition switch is placed in the ON position. When the engine is started, the warning light should go out. If the light remains on, the diagnostic system has detected a malfunction or abnormality in the system.

10   The codes for the ABS can be accessed by turning the ignition key to the OFF position (engine not running). Install a jumper wire onto terminals TC and CG of the DLC3 diagnostic link connector and turn the ignition key ON (engine not running) (see illustration). Observe the codes on the ABS warning light.

11   The diagnostic code is the number of flashes indicated on the ABS light. If any malfunction has been detected, the light will blink the

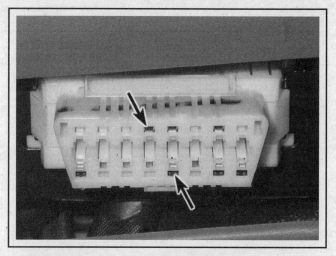

2.10 Using a jumper wire between these terminals on the diagnostic connector allows the ABS light to display trouble codes (the connector is located under the driver's side of the dash)

first digit(s) of the code, pause 1.5 seconds, and then blink the second digit of the code. For example, a code 34 (left rear wheel sensor) will first blink three flashes, pause 1.5 seconds and blink four flashes. If there is more than one code stored in the ECM, the ECM will pause 2.5 seconds before flashing the next code. If the system is operating normally (no malfunctions), the warning light will blink once every 0.5 seconds.

12   The accompanying tables explain the code that will be flashed for each of the malfunctions. The accompanying charts indicate the diagnostic code - in blinks - along with the system, diagnosis and specific areas.

13   After the diagnosis check, clear the trouble codes. First, jump terminals TC and CG on the data link connector. Turn the ignition key ON (engine not running) and clear the codes by depressing the brake pedal eight or more times within five seconds. Remove the jumper wire and reinstall the cap on the data link connector. Check the indicated system or component or take the vehicle to a dealer service department to have the malfunction repaired.

ABS TROUBLE CODES

Code number	Trouble area	Action to take
Code 11 (1 flash, pause, 1 flash)	Open circuit in solenoid relay circuit	Check the solenoid relay and the relay circuit
Code 12 (1 flash, pause, 2 flashes)	Short circuit in solenoid relay circuit	Check the solenoid relay and the relay circuit
Code 13 (1 flash, pause, 3 flashes)	Open circuit in ABS motor relay circuit	Check the pump motor relay and circuit
Code 14 (1 flash, pause, 4 flashes)	Short circuit in ABS motor relay circuit	Check the solenoid relay and the relay circuit
Code 21 (2 flashes, pause, 1 flash)	Problem in right front wheel solenoid circuit	Check the actuator solenoid and circuit

ABS TROUBLE CODES (CONTINUED)

Code number	Trouble area	Action to take
Code 22 (2 flashes, pause, 2 flashes)	Problem in left front wheel solenoid circuit	Check the actuator solenoid and circuit
Code 23 (2 flashes, pause, 3 flashes)	Problem in right rear wheel solenoid circuit	Check the actuator solenoid and circuit
Code 24 (2 flashes, pause, 4 flashes)	Problem in left rear wheel solenoid circuit	Check the actuator solenoid and circuit
Code 25 (2 flashes, pause, 5 flashes)	SMC1 circuit open or shorted	Check the ABS actuator and circuit
Code 26 (2 flashes, pause, 6 flashes)	SMC2 circuit open or shorted	Check the ABS actuator and circuit
Code 27 (2 flashes, pause, 7 flashes)	SRC1 circuit open or shorted	Check the ABS actuator and circuit
Code 28 (2 flashes, pause, 8 flashes)	SRC2 circuit open or shorted	Check the ABS actuator and circuit
Code 31 (3 flashes, pause, 1 flash)	Sensor signal problem - right front wheel	Check the speed sensor, sensor rotors, wire harness and connector of the speed sensor
Code 32 (3 flashes, pause, 2 flashes)	Sensor signal problem - left front wheel	Check the speed sensor, sensor rotors, wire harness and connector of the speed sensor
Code 33 (3 flashes, pause, 3 flashes)	Sensor signal problem - right rear wheel	Check the speed sensor, sensor rotors, wire harness and connector of the speed sensor
Code 34 (3 flashes, pause, 4 flashes)	Sensor signal problem - left rear wheel	Check the speed sensor, sensor rotors, wire harness and connector of the speed sensor
Code 35 (3 flashes, pause, 5 flashes)	Open circuit - right front speed sensor or circuit	Check the speed sensor, wire harness and electrical connector
Code 36 (3 flashes, pause, 6 flashes)	Open circuit - left front speed sensor or circuit	Check the speed sensor, wire harness and electrical connector
Code 37 (3 flashes, pause, 7 flashes)	Speed sensor rotor has incorrect number of teeth	Check for a damaged sensor rotor
Code 38 (3 flashes, pause, 8 flashes)	Open circuit - right rear speed sensor or circuit	Check the speed sensor, wire harness and electrical connector
Code 39 (3 flashes, pause, 9 flashes)	Open circuit - left rear speed sensor or circuit	Check the speed sensor, wire harness and electrical connector
Code 41 (4 flashes, pause, 1 flash)	Abnormally low battery positive voltage	Check the charging system (alternator, battery and voltage regulator) for any problems (see Chapter 5)
Code 43 (4 flashes, pause, 3 flashes)	ABS control system malfunction	Check all wiring and connections associated with the ABS system
Code 44 (4 flashes, pause, 4 flashes)	NE signal circuit open or shorted	Check wiring harness and connectors between ABS ECU and PCM
Code 45 (4 flashes, pause, 5 flashes)	Deceleration sensor malfunction	Check deceleration sensor and wiring harness connectors

Code number	Trouble area	Action to take
Code 46 (4 flashes, pause, 6 flashes)	Master cylinder sensor malfunction	Check master cylinder sensor and wiring harness connectors
Code 49 (4 flashes, pause, 9 flashes)	Open circuit - brake light switch or circuit	Check the brake light switch or circuit
Code 51 (5 flashes, pause, 1 flash)	Pump motor locked	Check the pump motor, relay and battery for shorts or abnormalities
Code 53 (5 flashes, pause, 3 flashes)	PCM communication circuit malfunction	Check wiring harness and connectors between ABS ECU and PCM
Code 58 (5 flashes, pause, 8 flashes)	Open circuit - brake light switch or circuit	Check the brake light switch or circuit
Code 61 (6 flashes, pause, 1 flash)	Engine control system malfunction	Check for engine control system trouble codes (see Chapter 6)
Code 62 (6 flashes, pause, 2 flashes)	Stability control ECU	Check stability control ECU
Light always ON	ECU malfunction	ECU problem

ABS TROUBLE CODES FOR VEHICLES WITH EBD, BA, TRAC AND VSC SYSTEMS

Code number	Trouble area	Action to take
Code 31 (3 flashes, pause, 1 flash)	Steering angle sensor	Check sensor circuit
Code 32 (3 flashes, pause, 2 flashes)	Deceleration sensor	Check the yaw rate sensor and circuit
Code 34 (3 flashes, pause, 1 flash)	Yaw rate sensor malfunction	Check sensor and circuit, check CAN communication circuit
Code 39	Decel sensor off calibration	Check sensor and calibrate zero point
Code 51 (5 flashes, pause, 1 flash)	Engine control system malfunction	Check engine control system
Code 62 (6 flashes, pause, 2 flashes)	CAN communication with yaw rate sensor	Check sensor and harness
Code 63 (6 flashes, pause, 3 flashes)	Steering angle position sensor	Check sensor and wire harness
Code 91 (9 flashes, pause, 1 flash)	Short in ABS motor failsafe relay	Check ABS fuse, cut relay, cut relay circuit and VSC
Code 94 (9 flashes, pause, 4 flashes)	CAN communication malfunction	Check stability control ECU and harness
Code 95 (9 flashes, pause, 5 flashes)	Decel sensor malfunction	Check yaw rate sensor and harness
Code 97 (9 flashes, pause, 7 flashes)	Power supply for yaw rate sensor	Check yaw rate sensor power circuit for proper voltage

3 Disc brake pads - replacement

▶ Refer to illustrations 3.5, 3.6a through 3.6t and 3.7a through 3.7l

✳✳ WARNING:

Disc brake pads must be replaced on both front or rear wheels at the same time - never replace the pads on only one wheel. Also, the dust created by the brake system is harmful to your health. Never blow it out with compressed air and don't inhale any of it. An approved filtering mask should be worn when working on the brakes. Do not, under any circumstances, use petroleum-based solvents to clean brake parts. Use brake system cleaner only!

➡Note 1: This procedure applies to both the front and rear disc brakes.

➡Note 2: The manufacturer recommends replacing the pad shims and wear indicators whenever the pads are replaced.

1   Remove the cap from the brake fluid reservoir.

2   Loosen the wheel lug nuts, raise the front or rear of the vehicle and support it securely on jackstands. Block the wheels at the opposite end.

3   Remove the wheels. Work on one brake assembly at a time, using the assembled brake for reference if necessary.

4   Inspect the brake disc carefully as outlined in Section 5. If

3.5 Before removing the caliper, be sure to depress the piston into its bore in the caliper with a large C-clamp to make room for the new pads

3.6a Always wash the brakes with brake cleaner before disassembling anything

FRONT BRAKE PADS

3.6b To remove the caliper, remove the bolts indicated by the upper and lower arrows (the center arrow points to the brake hose banjo bolt, which shouldn't be unscrewed unless the caliper is being completely removed from the vehicle)

3.6c Remove the caliper . . .

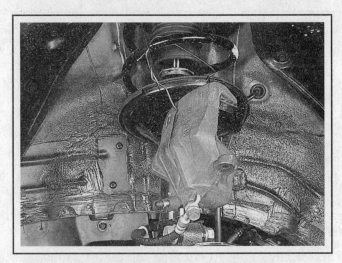

3.6e Remove the upper anti-squeal spring (four-cylinder models only) . . .

3.6d . . . and hang it from the strut coil spring with a piece of wire; do not allow the caliper to hang by the flexible brake hose

tion). As the piston is depressed to the bottom of the caliper bore, the fluid in the master cylinder will rise. Make sure that it doesn't overflow. If necessary, siphon off some of the fluid.

6   If you're replacing the front brake pads, follow the accompanying photos, beginning with illustration 3.6a. Be sure to stay in order and read the caption under each illustration.

7   If you're replacing the rear brake pads, wash the brake assembly (see illustration 3.6a), then follow the accompanying photos beginning with illustration 3.7a. Be sure to stay in order and read the caption under each illustration.

machining is necessary, follow the information in that Section to remove the disc, at which time the pads can be removed as well.

5   Push the piston back into its bore to provide room for the new brake pads. A C-clamp can be used to accomplish this (see illustra-

3.6f . . . and the lower anti-squeal spring (four-cylinder models only)

3.6g Remove the outer shim . . .

3.6h . . . and the inner shim from the outer brake pad

3.6i Remove the outer brake pad

3.6j Remove the outer shim . . .

3.6k . . . and the inner shim from the inner brake pad

3.6l Remove the inner brake pad

3.6m Remove the upper and lower pad support plates; inspect them for damage and replace as necessary (if they're weak or distorted, they should be replaced)

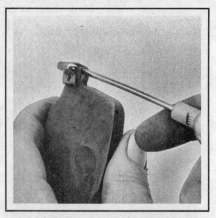

3.6n Pry the wear indicator off the old inner brake pad and transfer it to the new inner pad (if the wear indicator is worn or bent, replace it)

3.6o Install the upper and lower pad support plates, the new inner brake pad and the shims; make sure the ears on the pad are properly engaged with the pad support plates as shown

3.6p Install the outer pad and the shims, engaging the pad with the support plates

3.6q Install the upper and lower anti-squeal springs (four-cylinder models only); make sure both springs are properly engaged with the pads

3.6r Pull out the upper and lower sliding pins and clean them off (if either rubber boot is damaged, remove it by levering the flange of the metal bushing that retains the boot) . . .

3.6s . . . apply a coat of high-temperature grease to the pins and install them

3.6t Install the caliper and tighten the caliper bolts to the torque listed in this Chapter's Specifications

REAR BRAKE PADS

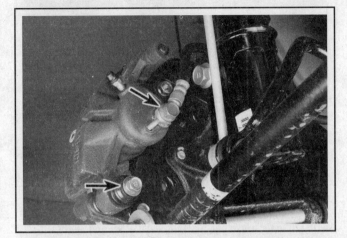

3.7a Remove the caliper retaining bolt (lower arrow); the upper arrow points to the brake hose banjo fitting bolt, which shouldn't be unscrewed unless the caliper is being removed from the vehicle

3.7b Pivot the caliper up and support it in that position

8   When reinstalling the caliper, be sure to tighten the mounting bolts to the torque listed in this Chapter's Specifications. After the job has been completed, firmly depress the brake pedal a few times to bring the pads into contact with the disc. Check the level of the brake fluid, adding some if necessary. Check the operation of the brakes carefully before placing the vehicle into normal service.

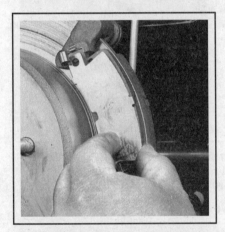

3.7c Remove the outer shim . . .

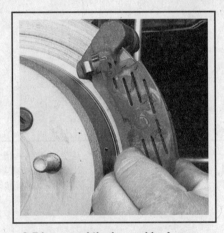

3.7d . . . and the inner shim from the outer brake pad

3.7e Remove the outer brake pad

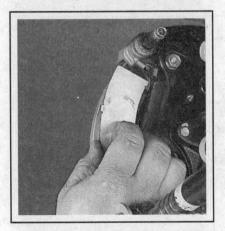

3.7f Remove the outer shim . . .

3.7g . . . and the inner shim from the inner brake pad

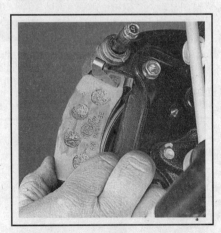

3.7h Remove the inner brake pad

3.7i Remove the pad support plates; inspect them for wear and replace as necessary (the plates should "snap" into place in the torque plate; if they're weak or distorted, replace them)

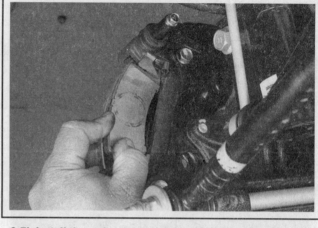

3.7j Install the pad support plates, the inner brake pad and the new shims; make sure both shims are properly engaged with the inner brake pad and with each other and apply anti-squeak brake compound to the backside of the shims

3.7k Install the pad support plates, the outer brake pad and the shims; make sure both shims are properly engaged with the outer brake pad and with each other

3.7l Pivot the caliper down over the new pads. Install the caliper-retaining bolt and tighten it to the torque listed in this Chapter's Specifications

4 Disc brake caliper - removal and installation

✳✳ WARNING:

Dust created by the brake system is harmful to your health. Never blow it out with compressed air and don't inhale any of it. An approved filtering mask should be worn when working on the brakes. Do not, under any circumstances, use petroleum-based solvents to clean brake parts. Use brake system cleaner only!

➡ Note: Always replace the calipers in pairs - never replace just one of them.

REMOVAL

▸ **Refer to illustrations 4.2 and 4.3**

1   Loosen the wheel lug nuts, raise the vehicle and support it securely on jackstands. Remove the wheels.

4.2 Using a piece of rubber hose of the appropriate size, plug the brake line banjo fitting to prevent brake fluid from leaking out and to prevent dirt and moisture from contaminating the fluid in the hose

2 Remove the brake hose banjo bolt and disconnect the hose from the caliper. Plug the hose to keep contaminants out of the brake system and to prevent losing any more brake fluid than is necessary (see illustration).

→**Note: If you're just removing the caliper for access to other components, don't detach the hose.**

3 Remove the caliper mounting bolts (see illustration).

4 Remove the caliper. If necessary, remove the caliper torque plate from the steering knuckle or rear axle carrier (see illustrations 5.2a and 5.2b).

INSTALLATION

5 Install the caliper by reversing the removal procedure. Install new sealing washers on either side of the brake hose banjo fitting. Tighten the caliper mounting bolts (and torque plate bolts, if removed) to the torque listed in this Chapter's Specifications.

6 Bleed the brake system (see Section 10).

7 Install the wheels and lug nuts. Lower the vehicle and tighten the lug nuts to the torque listed in the Chapter 1 Specifications.

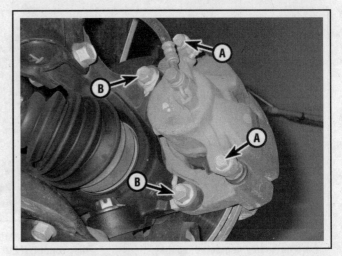

4.3 Front brake caliper details (rear caliper similar)

A *Caliper mounting bolts*
B *Torque plate mounting bolts*

---

5 Brake disc - inspection, removal and installation

INSPECTION

▶ **Refer to illustrations 5.2a, 5.2b, 5.3, 5.4a, 5.4b, 5.5a and 5.5b**

1 Loosen the wheel lug nuts, raise the vehicle and support it securely on jackstands. Remove the wheel and install the lug nuts to hold the disc in place. If the rear brake disc is being worked on, release the parking brake.

2 Remove the brake caliper as outlined in Section 4. It isn't necessary to disconnect the brake hose. After removing the caliper bolts, suspend the caliper out of the way with a piece of wire (see illustration 3.6d). Remove the torque plate mounting bolts and detach the torque plate (see illustrations).

3 Visually inspect the disc surface for score marks and other damage. Light scratches and shallow grooves are normal after use and may not always be detrimental to brake operation, but deep scoring - over 0.039-inch (1.0 mm) - requires disc removal and refinishing by an

5.2a To remove the front caliper torque plate from the steering knuckle, remove these two bolts

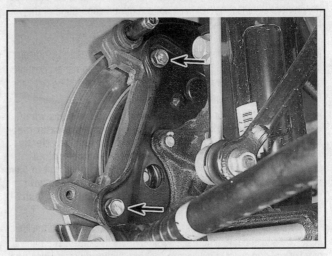

5.2b To remove the rear caliper torque plate from the axle carrier, remove these two bolts

5.3 The brake pads on this vehicle were obviously neglected, as they wore down completely and cut deep grooves into the disc - wear this severe means the disc must be replaced

5.4a Use a dial indicator to check disc runout; if the reading exceeds the maximum allowable runout limit, the disc will have to be machined or replaced

5.4b Using a swirling motion, remove the glaze from the disc surface with sandpaper or emery cloth

5.5a The minimum wear dimension is cast into the back side of the disc (typical)

5.5b Use a micrometer to measure disc thickness

5.6a If the rear disc is difficult to remove, remove this plug . . .

automotive machine shop. Be sure to check both sides of the disc (see illustration). If pulsating has been noticed during application of the brakes, suspect disc runout.

4   To check disc runout, place a dial indicator at a point about 1/2-inch from the outer edge of the disc (see illustration). Set the indicator to zero and turn the disc. The indicator reading should not exceed the specified allowable runout limit. If it does, the disc should be refinished by an automotive machine shop.

➡**Note: Professionals recommend resurfacing the discs whenever the pads are replaced regardless of the dial indicator reading, as this will impart a smooth finish and ensure a perfectly flat surface, eliminating any brake pedal pulsation or other undesirable symptoms. At the very least, if you elect not to have the discs resurfaced, remove the glaze from the surface with sandpaper or emery cloth using a swirling motion (see illustration).**

5   It's absolutely critical that the disc not be machined to a thickness under the specified minimum allowable refinish thickness. The minimum wear (or discard) thickness is cast into the inside of the disc (see illustration). The disc thickness can be checked with a micrometer (see illustration).

5.6b . . . insert a screwdriver through the hole (the hole must be at the 6 o'clock position, because that's where the adjuster is located) and rotate the adjuster

REMOVAL

▶ **Refer to illustrations 5.6a and 5.6b**

6   Remove the lug nuts that were put on to hold the disc in place and slide the disc off the hub. If the rear disc won't come off, it may be interfering with the parking brake shoes; remove the plug (see illustration) and rotate the adjuster to back the parking brake shoes away from the drum surface within the disc (see illustration). Rotate the adjuster wheel in a clockwise direction (as seen from the front of the vehicle) to back off the parking brake shoes.

INSTALLATION

7   Place the disc in position over the threaded studs.
8   Install the torque plate, tightening the bolts to the torque listed in this Chapter's Specifications.
9   Install the caliper, tightening the bolts to the torque listed in this Chapter's Specifications. Bleeding won't be necessary unless the brake hose was disconnected from the caliper.
10   Install the wheel and lug nuts. Lower the vehicle and tighten the lug nuts to the torque listed in the Chapter 1 Specifications. Depress the brake pedal a few times to bring the brake pads into contact with the disc. Check the operation of the brakes carefully before driving the vehicle.

6   Drum brake shoes - replacement

▶ **Refer to illustrations 6.4a through 6.4v and 6.5**

✳ WARNING:

Drum brake shoes must be replaced on both wheels at the same time - never replace the shoes on only one wheel. Also, the dust created by the brake system is harmful to your health. Never blow it out with compressed air and don't inhale any of it. An approved filtering mask should be worn when working on the brakes. Do not, under any circumstances, use petroleum-based solvents to clean brake parts. Use brake system cleaner only!

✳ CAUTION:

Whenever the brake shoes are replaced, the return and hold-down springs should also be replaced. Due to the continuous heating/cooling cycle the springs are subjected to, they lose tension over a period of time and may allow the shoes to drag on the drum and wear at a much faster rate than normal.

1   Loosen the wheel lug nuts, raise the rear of the vehicle and support it securely on jackstands. Block the front wheels to keep the vehicle from rolling.
2   Release the parking brake.

6.4a Mark the relationship of the drum to the hub to insure that the dynamic balance is unaltered

3   Remove the wheel.

➡**Note: All four rear brake shoes must be replaced at the same time, but to avoid mixing up parts, work on only one brake assembly at a time.**

4   Follow the accompanying illustrations for the brake shoe replacement procedure (see illustrations 6.4a through 6.4v). Be sure to stay in order and read the caption under each illustration.

6.4b Before removing anything, clean the brake assembly with brake cleaner and allow it to dry (position a drain pan under the brake to catch the fluid and residue); DO NOT USE COMPRESSED AIR TO BLOW OFF BRAKE DUST!

6.4c Unhook the return spring from the front brake shoe. Use a pair of locking pliers to stretch the spring and pull the end out of the hole in the shoe

6.4d Depress the hold-down spring and turn the retainer 90-degrees, then release it; a pair of pliers will work, but a special hold-down spring removal tool makes the job easier (these inexpensive tools are available at most auto parts stores)

6.4e Remove the front shoe from the backing plate and unhook the anchor spring from the end of the shoe

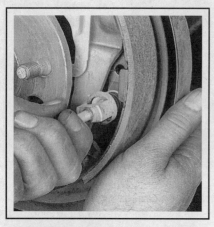

6.4f Remove the hold-down spring from the rear shoe

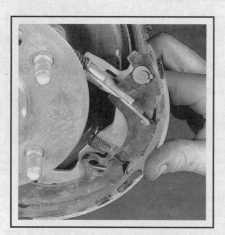

6.4g Remove the rear shoe and adjuster assembly from the backing plate

6.4h Hold the end of the parking brake cable with a pair of pliers and pull it out of the parking brake lever

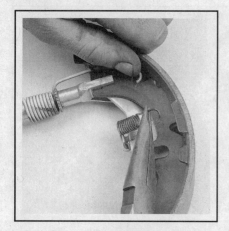

6.4i Remove the adjusting lever spring

6.4j Unhook the return spring from the shoe and slide the adjuster and spring off

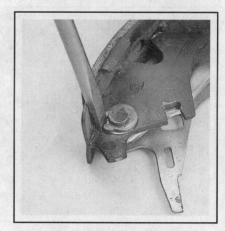

6.4k Pry the C-washer apart and remove it to separate the parking brake lever and adjuster lever from the rear shoe

6.4l Assemble the parking brake lever and adjuster lever to the new rear shoe and crimp the C-washer closed with a pair of pliers (always use a new C-washer)

6.4m Lubricate the moving parts of the adjuster screw with a light coat of high-temperature grease; the screw portion of the adjuster will need to be threaded in further than before to allow the drum to fit over the new shoes

6.4n Install the adjuster assembly on the rear shoe (make sure the end fits properly into the slot in the shoe and hook the spring into the opening in the shoe)

6.4o Install the adjuster lever spring

6.4p Lubricate the brake shoe contact areas with high-temperature grease

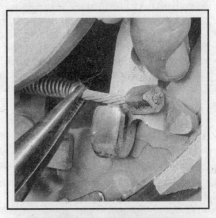

6.4q Pull the parking brake cable spring back and hold it there with a pair of pliers, then place the cable into the hooked end of the parking brake lever

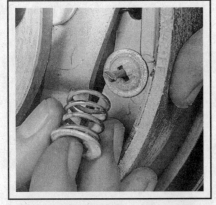

6.4r Place the rear shoe assembly against the backing plate and push the hold-down pin through the shoe. Install the cups (one on each end of the spring) and lock the outer cup to the pin by turning it 90-degrees after the spring has been compressed

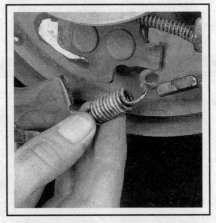

6.4s Connect the anchor spring to the bottom of each shoe and mount the front shoe to the backing plate, then install the hold-down spring and cups

6.4t Using a screwdriver, stretch the return spring into its hole in the front shoe

6.4u Pry the parking brake lever forward and verify that the return spring hasn't come unhooked from the rear shoe

6.4v Wiggle the assembly to make sure it's seated properly against the backing plate

➥**Note: If the brake drum cannot be easily removed, make sure the parking brake is completely released. If the drum still cannot be pulled off, the brake shoes will have to be retracted. This is done by first removing the plug from the backing plate. With the plug removed, push the lever off the adjuster star wheel with a narrow screwdriver while turning the adjuster wheel with another screwdriver, moving the shoes away from the drum. The drum should now come off.**

5   Before reinstalling the drum, it should be checked for cracks, score marks, deep scratches and hard spots, which will appear as small discolored areas. If the hard spots cannot be removed with fine emery cloth or if any of the other conditions listed above exist, the drum must be taken to an automotive machine shop to have it resurfaced.

➥**Note: Professionals recommend resurfacing the drums each time a brake job is done. Resurfacing will eliminate the possibility of out-of-round drums. If the drums are worn so much that they can't be resurfaced without exceeding the maximum allowable diameter (stamped into the drum), then new ones will be required (see illustration). At the very least, if you elect not to have the drums resurfaced, remove the glaze from the surface with emery cloth using a swirling motion.**

6   Install the brake drum on the axle flange.

7   Install the wheel and lug nuts, then lower the vehicle. Tighten the lug nuts to the torque listed in the Chapter 1 Specifications.

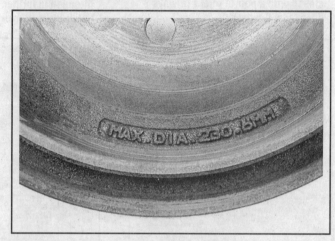

6.5 The maximum drum diameter is cast into the inside of the rear drums (typical)

8   Make a number of forward and reverse stops and operate the parking brake to adjust the brakes until satisfactory pedal action is obtained.

9   Check the operation of the brakes carefully before driving the vehicle.

7   Wheel cylinder - removal and installation

➥**Note: Never replace only one wheel cylinder - always replace both of them at the same time.**

REMOVAL

▶ **Refer to illustration 7.4**

1   Raise the rear of the vehicle and support it securely on jackstands. Block the front wheels to keep the vehicle from rolling.

2   Remove the brake shoe assembly (see Section 6).

3   Remove all dirt and foreign material from around the wheel cylinder.

4   Disconnect the brake line with a flare-nut wrench, if available (see illustration). Don't pull the brake line away from the wheel cylinder.

5   Remove the wheel cylinder mounting bolts.

7.4 To remove the wheel cylinder, unscrew the hydraulic line-to-wheel cylinder threaded fitting, then remove the mounting bolts

6   Detach the wheel cylinder from the brake backing plate and place it on a clean workbench. Immediately plug the brake line to prevent fluid loss and contamination.

INSTALLATION

7   Place the wheel cylinder in position and install the bolts finger tight. Connect the brake line to the cylinder, being careful not to cross-thread the fitting. Tighten the wheel cylinder bolts to the torque listed in this Chapter's Specifications.

8   Tighten the brake line fitting and install the brake shoes and drum.

9   Bleed the brakes (see Section 10). Install the wheel and lug nuts. Lower the vehicle to the ground and tighten the lug nuts to the torque listed in the Chapter 1 Specifications.

10 Check the operation of the brakes carefully before driving the vehicle.

8   Master cylinder - removal and installation

REMOVAL

▶ **Refer to illustration 8.1**

1   Unplug the electrical connector for the brake fluid level warning switch (see illustration).

2   Remove as much fluid as possible from the reservoir with a syringe.

3   Place rags under the fittings and prepare caps or plastic bags to cover the ends of the lines once they're disconnected.

✳✳ CAUTION:

Brake fluid will damage paint. Cover all body parts and be careful not to spill fluid during this procedure.

4   Loosen the fittings at the ends of the brake lines where they enter the master cylinder. To prevent rounding off the flats, use a flare-nut wrench, which wraps around the fitting hex.

5   Pull the brake lines away from the master cylinder and plug the ends to prevent contamination.

6   Remove the nuts attaching the master cylinder to the power booster. Pull the master cylinder off the studs to remove it. Again, be careful not to spill the fluid as this is done.

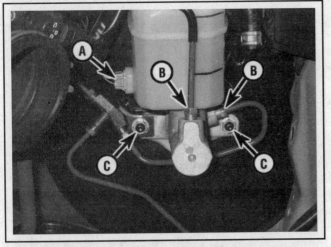

8.1 Master cylinder installation details

A   *Electrical connector*   C   *Mounting nuts*
B   *Brake line fittings*

INSTALLATION

▶ **Refer to illustration 8.8**

7   Bench bleed the new master cylinder before installing it. Because it will be necessary to apply pressure to the master cylinder piston and, at the same time, control flow from the brake line outlets, it is recommended that the master cylinder be mounted in a vise.

8   Attach a pair of master cylinder bleeder tubes to the outlet ports of the master cylinder (see illustration).

9   Fill the reservoir with brake fluid of the recommended type (see Chapter 1).

10 Slowly push the pistons into the master cylinder (a large Phillips screwdriver can be used for this) - air will be expelled from the pressure chambers and into the reservoir. Because the tubes are submerged in fluid, air can't be drawn back into the master cylinder when you release the pistons.

11 Repeat the procedure until no more air bubbles are present.

12 Remove the bleed tubes, one at a time, and install plugs in the open ports to prevent fluid leakage and air from entering. If installing a new master cylinder, adjust the booster pushrod length (see Section 11).

13 Install the reservoir cover, then install the master cylinder over the studs on the power brake booster and tighten the attaching nuts only finger tight at this time.

8.8 The best way to bleed air from the master cylinder before installing it on the vehicle is with a pair of bleed tubes

14 Thread the brake line fittings into the master cylinder. Since the master cylinder is still a bit loose, it can be moved slightly in order for the fittings to thread in easily. Do not strip the threads as the fittings are tightened.

15 Fully tighten the mounting nuts, then the brake line fittings.

16 Fill the master cylinder reservoir with fluid, then bleed the master cylinder and the brake system as described in Section 10. To bleed the cylinder on the vehicle, have an assistant pump the brake pedal several times slowly and then hold the pedal to the floor. Loosen the fitting nut to allow air and fluid to escape. Repeat this procedure on both fittings until the fluid is clear of air bubbles.

> ✳✳ **CAUTION:**
>
> **Have plenty of rags on hand to catch the fluid - brake fluid will ruin painted surfaces.**

17 Test the operation of the brake system carefully before placing the vehicle into normal service.

> ✳✳ **WARNING:**
>
> **Do not operate the vehicle if you are in doubt about the effectiveness of the brake system.**

9 Brake hoses and lines - inspection and replacement

INSPECTION

1 About every six months, with the vehicle raised and supported securely on jackstands, the rubber hoses which connect the steel brake lines with the front and rear brake assemblies should be inspected for cracks, chafing of the outer cover, leaks, blisters and other damage. These are important and vulnerable parts of the brake system and inspection should be complete. A light and mirror will be helpful for a thorough check. If a hose exhibits any of the above conditions, replace it with a new one.

REPLACEMENT

Front brake hose

▶ **Refer to illustrations 9.3 and 9.4**

2 Loosen the wheel lug nuts, raise the vehicle and support it securely on jackstands. Remove the wheel.

3 At the frame bracket, unscrew the brake line fitting from the hose (see illustration). Use a flare-nut wrench to prevent rounding off the corners.

4 Remove the U-clip from the female fitting at the bracket with a pair of pliers (see illustration), then pass the hose through the bracket.

5 At the caliper end of the hose, remove the banjo fitting bolt (see illustration 3.6b), then separate the hose from the caliper. Note that there are two copper sealing washers on either side of the fitting - they should be replaced with new ones during installation.

6 Remove the U-clip from the strut bracket, then feed the hose through the bracket.

7 To install the hose, pass the caliper fitting end through the strut bracket, then connect the fitting to the caliper with the banjo bolt and copper washers. Make sure the locating lug on the fitting is engaged with the hole in the caliper, then tighten the bolt to the torque listed in this Chapter's Specifications.

8 Push the metal support into the strut bracket and install the U-clip. Make sure the hose isn't twisted between the caliper and the strut bracket.

9 Route the hose into the frame bracket, again making sure it isn't twisted, then connect the brake line fitting, starting the threads by hand. Install the clip and E-ring, if equipped, then tighten the fitting securely.

10 Bleed the caliper (see Section 10).

11 Install the wheel and lug nuts, lower the vehicle and tighten the lug nuts to the torque specified in Chapter 1.

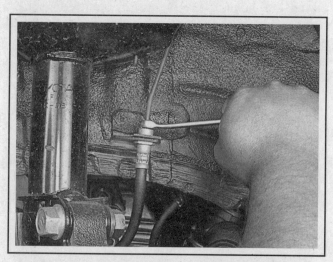

9.3 Unscrew the brake line threaded fitting with a flare-nut wrench to protect the fitting corners from being rounded off

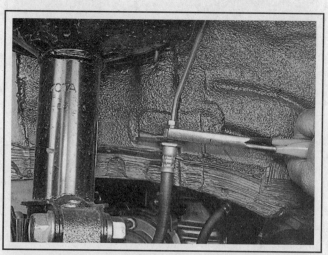

9.4 Remove the brake hose-to-brake line U-clip with a pair of pliers

Rear brake hose

12 Perform Steps 2, 3 and 4, then repeat Steps 3 and 4 at the other end of the hose. Be sure to bleed the wheel cylinder (or caliper) (see Section 10).

Metal brake lines

13 When replacing brake lines, be sure to use the correct parts. Don't use copper tubing for any brake system components. Purchase genuine steel brake lines from a dealer or auto parts store.

14 Prefabricated brake line, with the tube ends already flared and fittings installed, is available at auto parts stores and dealer parts departments.

15 When installing the new line, make sure it's securely supported in the brackets and has plenty of clearance between moving or hot components.

16 After installation, check the master cylinder fluid level and add fluid as necessary. Bleed the brake system (see Section 10) and test the brakes carefully before driving the vehicle in traffic.

10 Brake hydraulic system - bleeding

▶ **Refer to illustration 10.8**

> ※※ **WARNING:**
>
> **Wear eye protection when bleeding the brake system. If the fluid comes in contact with your eyes, immediately rinse them with water and seek medical attention.**

> ※※ **WARNING:**
>
> **On vehicles equipped with the Vehicle Stability Control (VSC) system, a scan tool may be required to activate the ABS hydraulic actuator after bleeding if the pedal feels spongy or the pedal height is not correct. Do not drive the vehicle if the pedal feels spongy or the pedal height is not correct.**

➡ **Note: Bleeding the hydraulic system is necessary to remove any air that manages to find its way into the system when it's been opened during removal and installation of a hose, line, caliper or master cylinder.**

1 You'll probably have to bleed the system at all four brakes if air has entered it due to low fluid level, or if the brake lines have been disconnected at the master cylinder.

2 If a brake line was disconnected only at a wheel, then only that caliper or wheel cylinder must be bled.

3 If a brake line is disconnected at a fitting located between the master cylinder and any of the brakes, that part of the system served by the disconnected line must be bled.

4 Remove any residual vacuum from the brake power booster by applying the brake several times with the engine off.

5 Remove the master cylinder reservoir cover and fill the reservoir with brake fluid. Reinstall the cover.

➡ **Note: Check the fluid level often during the bleeding operation and add fluid as necessary to prevent the fluid level from falling low enough to allow air bubbles into the master cylinder.**

6 Have an assistant on hand, as well as a supply of new brake fluid, a clear container partially filled with clean brake fluid, a length of tubing to fit over the bleeder valve and a wrench to open and close the bleeder valve.

7 Beginning at the right rear wheel, loosen the bleeder valve slightly, then tighten it to a point where it's snug but can still be loosened quickly and easily.

8 Place one end of the tubing over the bleeder valve and submerge the other end in brake fluid in the container (see illustration).

9 Have the assistant depress the brake pedal slowly, then hold the pedal down firmly.

10 While the pedal is held down, open the bleeder valve just enough to allow a flow of fluid to leave the valve. Watch for air bubbles to exit the submerged end of the tube. When the fluid flow slows after a couple of seconds, close the valve and have your assistant release the pedal.

11 Repeat Steps 9 and 10 until no more air is seen leaving the tube, then tighten the bleeder valve and proceed to the left rear wheel, the right front wheel and the left front wheel, in that order, and perform the same procedure. Be sure to check the fluid in the master cylinder reservoir frequently.

12 Never use old brake fluid. It contains moisture that will deteriorate the brake system components.

13 Refill the master cylinder with fluid at the end of the operation.

14 Check the operation of the brakes. The pedal should feel solid when depressed, with no sponginess. If necessary, repeat the entire process.

> ※※ **WARNING:**
>
> **Do not operate the vehicle if you're in doubt about the effectiveness of the brake system.**

10.8 When bleeding the brakes, a hose is connected to the bleeder valve at the caliper or wheel cylinder and then submerged in brake fluid. Air will be seen as bubbles in the tube and container. All air must be expelled before moving to the next wheel

11 Power brake booster - check, removal and installation

OPERATING CHECK

1 Depress the brake pedal several times with the engine off and make sure there's no change in the pedal reserve distance.

2 Depress the pedal and start the engine. If the pedal goes down slightly, operation is normal.

AIRTIGHTNESS CHECK

3 Start the engine and turn it off after one or two minutes. Depress the brake pedal slowly several times. If the pedal depresses less each time, the booster is airtight.

4 Depress the brake pedal while the engine is running, then stop the engine with the pedal depressed. If there's no change in the pedal reserve travel after holding the pedal for 30 seconds, the booster is airtight.

REMOVAL

▶ Refer to illustration 11.11

5 Power brake booster units shouldn't be disassembled. They require special tools not normally found in most automotive repair stations or shops. They're fairly complex and, because of their critical relationship to brake performance, should be replaced with a new or rebuilt one.

6 Remove the brake master cylinder (see Section 8). To provide room for booster removal on Lexus models, the brake line at the front of the master cylinder must be removed, not just disconnected. Disconnect the line at the left-front wheel and remove the line (see illustration 9.3). On Avalon models with Vehicle Stability Control, disconnect the electrical connector at the precharge pump (in front of the master cylinder), disconnect the hoses, remove the three bolts and set the precharge pump aside.

7 Remove the air cleaner assembly (see Chapter 4). On some models it will also be necessary to unbolt the charcoal canister and position it out of the way.

8 Disconnect the vacuum hose from the brake booster. On Lexus models, disconnect the vacuum hose at both ends and remove it from the vehicle. Be careful not to damage the hose when removing it from the booster fitting.

9 Inside the vehicle, remove the driver's kick panel, knee bolster and the knee bolster reinforcement brace (see Chapter 11). On Avalon

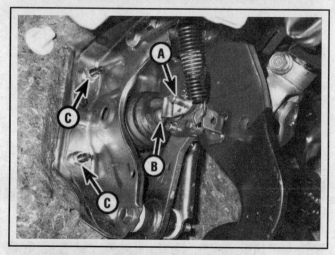

11.11 Power brake booster installation details

A Clevis and pin	C Mounting nuts (two
B Pushrod	shown)

models, remove two screws and the heater duct blocking access to the booster mounting nuts.

10 On some models with cruise control, remove the two nuts and set aside the cruise control ECU for better access to the brake pedal assembly.

11 Locate the clevis which connects the booster pushrod to the top of the brake pedal. Remove the clevis pin-retaining clip with pliers and pull out the pin (see illustration).

12 Remove the four nuts and washers holding the brake booster to the firewall (you may need a light to see them). Slide the booster straight out from the firewall until the studs clear the holes.

INSTALLATION

▶ Refer to illustrations 11.14a, 11.14b, 11.14c and 11.14d

13 Installation procedures are basically the reverse of removal. Tighten the clevis locknut securely and the booster mounting nuts to the torque listed in this Chapter's Specifications.

14 If a new power brake booster unit is being installed, check the

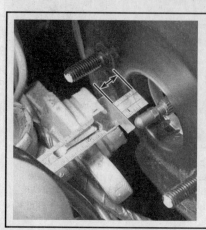

11.14a Measure the distance that the pushrod protrudes from the brake booster at the master cylinder mounting surface (including the gasket)

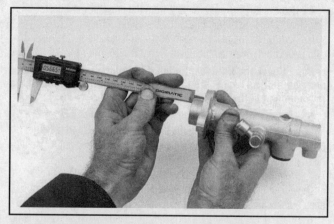

11.14b Measure the distance from the mounting flange to the end of the master cylinder

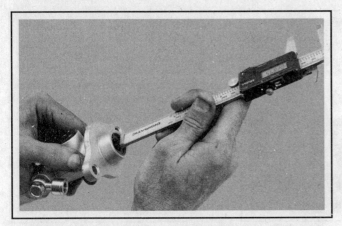

11.14c Measure the distance from the piston pocket to the end of the master cylinder

11.14d To adjust the length of the booster pushrod, hold the serrated portion of the rod with a pair of pliers and turn the adjusting screw in or out, as necessary, to achieve the desired setting

pushrod clearance as follows:

 a) *Measure the distance that the pushrod protrudes from the master cylinder mounting surface on the front of the power brake booster, including the gasket. Write down this measurement (see illustration). This is "dimension A."*
 b) *Measure the distance from the mounting flange to the end of the master cylinder (see illustration). Write down this measurement. This is "dimension B."*
 c) *Measure the distance from the end of the master cylinder to the bottom of the pocket in the piston (see illustration). Write down this measurement. This is "dimension C."*
 d) *Subtract measurement B from measurement C, then subtract*

 measurement A from the difference between B and C. This is the pushrod clearance.
 e) *Compare your calculated pushrod clearance to the pushrod clearance listed in this Chapter's Specifications. If necessary, adjust the pushrod length to achieve the correct clearance (see illustration).*

15 After the final installation of the master cylinder and brake hoses and lines, the brake pedal height and freeplay must be adjusted and the system must be bled. See the appropriate Sections of this Chapter for the procedures.

12 Parking brake shoes (rear disc brakes only) - inspection and replacement

▶ Refer to illustrations 12.4 and 12.5a through 12.5u

❄❄ WARNING 1:

Dust created by the brake system is hazardous to your health. Never blow it out with compressed air and don't inhale any of it. An approved filtering mask should be worn when working on the brakes. Do not, under any circumstances, use petroleum-based solvents to clean brake parts. Use brake system cleaner only!

❄❄ WARNING 2:

Parking brake shoes must be replaced on both wheels at the same time - never replace the shoes on only one wheel!.

1 Remove the brake disc (see Section 5).
2 Inspect the thickness of the lining material on the shoes. If the lining has worn down to 1/32-inch or less, the shoes must be replaced.
3 Remove the hub and bearing assembly (see Chapter 10).

➡Note: It is possible to perform the shoe replacement procedure without removing the hub and bearing assembly, although working room is limited.

4 Wash off the brake parts with brake system cleaner (see illustration).

12.4 Before disassembling it, be sure to wash the parking brake assembly with brake cleaner

5 Follow the accompanying illustrations for the brake shoe replacement procedure (see illustrations 12.5a through 12.5u). Be sure to stay in order and read the caption under each illustration.

12.5a Remove the rear parking brake shoe return spring from the anchor pin . . .

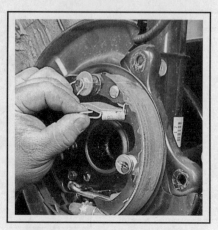

12.5b . . . and unhook it from the rear shoe

12.5c Remove the front parking brake shoe return spring from the anchor pin . . .

6   Install the brake disc. Temporarily thread three of the wheel lug nuts onto the studs to hold the disc in place.

7   Remove the hole plug from the brake disc. Adjust the parking brake shoe clearance by turning the adjuster star wheel with a brake adjusting tool or screwdriver until the shoes contact the disc and the disc can't be turned (see illustrations 5.6a and 5.6b). Back off the adjuster eight notches, then install the hole plug.

8   Install the torque plate (see illustration 5.2b) and brake caliper

12.5d . . . and unhook it from the front shoe

12.5e Remove the rear shoe hold-down spring and pull out the pin

12.5f Remove the shoe strut from between the shoes

12.5g Remove the front shoe hold-down spring and pull out the pin

12.5h Remove the adjuster and the tension spring (the tension spring, which is not visible in this photo, is behind the adjuster and is attached to both shoes)

12.5i Pop the C-washer off the pivot pin on the back of the rear shoe . . .

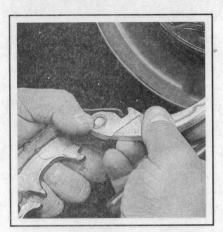

12.5j . . . and pull the parking brake lever off the pivot pin

12.5k Apply a thin coat of high-temperature grease to the contact surfaces of the backing plate

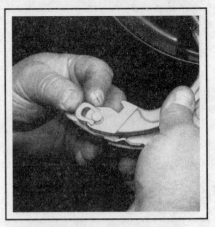

12.5l Slide the parking brake lever onto the pivot pin and install a new C-washer

(see Section 4). Be sure to tighten the bolts to the torque listed in this Chapter's Specifications.

9   Install the wheel and tighten the lug nuts to the torque specified in Chapter 1.

10 If the vehicle is equipped with a parking brake lever, pull up on the lever and count the number of clicks that it travels. It should be between three to six clicks - if it's not, adjust the parking brake as described in the next Section.

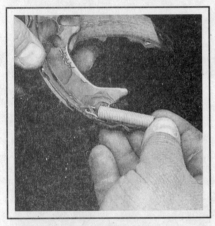

12.5m Attach the tension spring to the back side of the rear shoe . . .

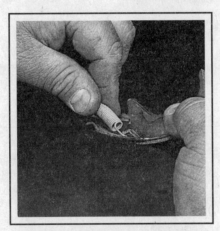

12.5n . . . and to the back side of the front shoe

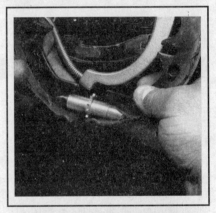

12.5o Flip the shoes around and install the adjuster; make sure both ends of the adjuster are properly engaged with the shoes as shown

12.5p Place the shoes in position and install the strut and spring as shown; make sure the ends of the strut are properly engaged with the shoes as shown

12.5q Install the front shoe return spring . . .

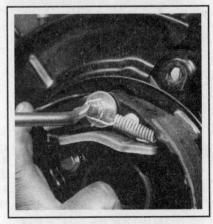

12.5r . . . and the rear shoe return spring

12.5s Install the rear shoe hold-down spring

12.5t . . . and the front shoe hold-down spring

12.5u This is how the parking brake assembly should look when you're done!

11 To bed the shoes to the drum, drive the vehicle at approximately 30 mph on a dry, level road. If the vehicle has a parking brake lever, push in on the parking brake release button and pull up slightly on the lever with about 20 pounds of force; if the vehicle has a pedal-type parking brake system, apply the pedal with about 33 pounds of force. Drive the vehicle with the parking brake applied like this for 1/4-mile. Repeat this procedure two or three times, allowing the brakes to cool between applications.

13 Parking brake - adjustment

LEVER TYPE

▶ **Refer to illustration 13.3**

1 The parking brake lever, when properly adjusted, should travel three to six clicks when a moderate pulling force is applied. If it travels less than three clicks, there's a chance the parking brake might not be releasing completely and might be dragging on the drum or disc. If the lever can be pulled up more than six clicks, the parking brake may not hold adequately on an incline, allowing the car to roll.

2 To gain access to the parking brake cable adjuster, remove the center console (see Chapter 11).

3 Loosen the locknut (the upper nut) while holding the adjusting nut (lower nut) with a wrench (see illustration). Tighten the adjusting nut until the desired travel is attained. Tighten the locknut.

4 Install the console.

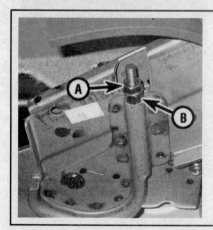

13.3 Parking brake cable locknut (A) and adjuster nut (B) for lever-type parking brake system

PEDAL TYPE

5 Slowly depress the parking brake pedal all the way and count the number of clicks. It should take about six to nine clicks to apply the parking brake. If it travels less than six clicks, there's a chance the parking brake might not be releasing completely and might be dragging on the drum or disc. If it travels more than nine clicks, the parking brake may not hold adequately on an incline, allowing the car to roll. Release the pedal.

6 On Camry LXE and Avalon models, the parking brake adjustment is performed at a turnbuckle located in the console.

➡**Note: On Lexus models, the cable adjustment can be made at the pedal assembly or the turnbuckle in the console.**

7 Remove the console (see Chapter 11).

8 With a small wrench, hold the intermediate cable at the rear of the turnbuckle from turning (the cable has a red mark, which should remain at the top). Loosen the locknut at the rear of the turnbuckle and adjust the turnbuckle by turning it to tighten or loosen the adjustment. Tighten the lock nut after the desired travel is attained.

➡**Note: On Lexus models with VSC, you'll have to remove the yaw rate sensor from the console for access to the adjusting turnbuckle. Disconnect the electrical connector at the sensor, remove the two sensor bracket-to-floor bolts and remove the sensor.**

※ **CAUTION:**

Do not separate the sensor from its bracket; remove them as an assembly only.

9 Install the console.

14 Parking brake cables - replacement

REAR PARKING BRAKE CABLES-TO-EQUALIZER

▶ **Refer to illustrations 14.4, 14.5, 14.6a and 14.6b**

1   Loosen the rear wheel lug nuts, raise the rear of the vehicle and support it securely on jackstands. Block the front wheels. Remove the wheel.

2   Make sure the parking brake is completely released, then remove the brake drum or disc.

3   On models with rear drum brakes, remove the brake shoes and disconnect the cable from the parking brake lever (see Section 6); on models with rear disc brakes, remove the parking brake shoes and disconnect the parking brake lever (see Section 12).

4   Unbolt the cable housing from the backing plate (see illustration).

5   Unbolt all cable brackets (see illustration).

6   Remove the exhaust heat shield for access to the cable clamps (see illustration). Trace the cable forward and locate the cable clamp

(see illustration). Loosen the clamp bolt and slide the cable housing out of the clamp.

7   Disconnect the cable end from the equalizer by aligning the cable with the slot in the top of the equalizer. Slide the cable end out of the hole (see illustration 14.6b).

8   Installation is the reverse of removal.

9   Adjust the parking brake (see Section 13).

PARKING BRAKE LEVER-TO-EQUALIZER CABLE

▶ **Refer to illustration 14.12**

10 Remove the center console (see Chapter 11).

11 With the parking brake cable released, remove the locknut and the adjusting nut (see Section 13) and detach the cable from the lever.

12 Inside the console area, remove the two bolts securing the cable flange to the floor (see illustration). Twist the flange 90-degrees and push it out through the hole in the floorpan.

14.4 To detach either parking brake cable housing from the brake backing plate, remove these two bolts (disc brake backing plate shown, drum brake setup similar)

14.5 This parking brake cable bracket is located near the forward end of the strut rod (but there may be others, depending on the year and model)

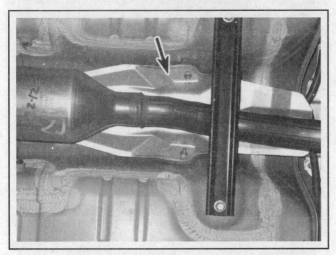

14.6a Remove the bolts and the exhaust heat shield that protects the cables (you may have to drop the exhaust pipe)

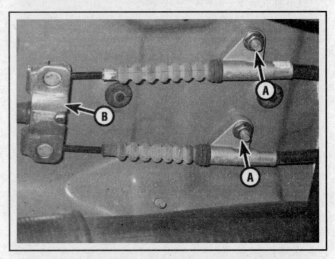

14.6b To release either parking brake cable from its cable clamp, loosen the clamp bolts (A) and slide the cable housing out of the clamp - B indicates the equalizer

13 Installation is the reverse of the removal procedure. Apply a light coat of grease to the portion of the cable end that contacts the equalizer. Adjust the parking brake cable as outlined previously (see Section 13).

PARKING BRAKE PEDAL-TO-INTERMEDIATE LEVER CABLE (PEDAL-TYPE MODELS)

14 Remove the console (see Chapter 11).

15 Refer to Section 13 and remove the two nuts securing the cable to the rear of the turnbuckle. Twist the turnbuckle off the front cable end.

16 Remove the driver's kick panel, knee bolster and knee bolster reinforcement (see Chapter 11) to access the parking brake pedal bracket sub-assembly.

17 Loosen and remove the locknut and adjuster nut on the cable end at the pedal assembly. Using locking pliers, remove the clip securing the cable end to the front of the parking brake pedal assembly and pull the cable out of the assembly.

18 Pull back the carpeting between the pedal assembly and the console area to locate the clamps securing the cable to the floor. Remove the clamps and the cable.

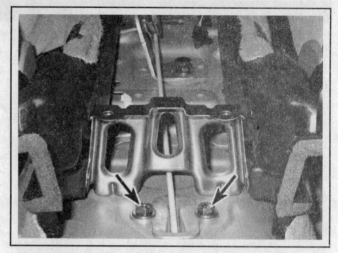

14.12 The cable flange is secured to the floorpan by these two bolts

19 Installation is the reverse of removal. Refer to Section 13 for parking brake adjustment.

REMOVAL AND INSTALLATION

▶ **Refer to illustration 15.1**

1 The brake light switch (see illustration) is located on a bracket at the top of the brake pedal.

2 Disconnect the wiring harness at the brake light switch.

3 Loosen the locknut and unscrew the switch from the pedal bracket.

4 Installation is the reverse of removal.

ADJUSTMENT

▶ **Refer to illustration 15.6**

5 Check and, if necessary, adjust brake pedal height (see Chapter 1).

6 Loosen the switch locknut, adjust the switch so that the distance the plunger protrudes (see illustration) is within the range listed in this Chapter's Specifications. (If you're unable to measure this distance, adjust the plunger so that it lightly contacts the pedal stop.) Tighten the locknut.

7 Plug the electrical connector into the switch and reconnect the battery. Make sure the brake lights come on when the brake pedal is depressed and go off when the pedal is released. If not, repeat the adjustment procedure until the brake lights function properly

8 Check and, if necessary, adjust brake pedal freeplay (see Chapter 1).

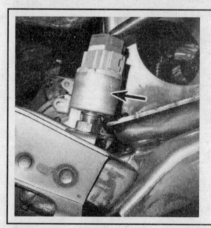

15.1 The brake light switch is located at the top of the brake pedal

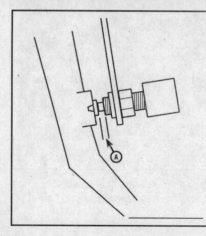

15.6 To adjust the brake light switch, loosen the locknut and rotate the switch until the plunger distance (dimension A) is within the range listed in this Chapter's Specifications, then tighten the locknut

Specifications

General

Brake fluid type	See Chapter 1
Brake pedal specifications	See Chapter 1
Power brake booster pushrod-to-master cylinder piston clearance	0.0 inch
Brake light switch plunger (dimension A)	1/32 to 3/32-inch

Disc brakes

Minimum brake pad thickness	1/8-inch
Disc minimum thickness	Cast into disc
Disc runout limit	
Front	0.0020 inch
Rear	0.0059 inch
Parking brake shoe minimum thickness	1/32-inch

Drum brakes

Brake shoe minimum lining thickness	1/16-inch
Drum maximum diameter	Cast into drum

Torque specifications — Ft-lbs (unless otherwise indicated)

→Note: One foot-pound (ft-lb) of torque is equivalent to 12 inch-pounds (in-lbs) of torque. Torque values below approximately 15 ft-lbs are expressed in inch-pounds, since most foot-pound torque wrenches are not accurate at these smaller values.

Caliper mounting bolts	
Front caliper	25
Rear caliper	
Camry	
TMC manufacture	
Upper bolt	29
Lower bolt	25
TMMK manufacture	32
Solara	
2002 and 2003 models	
All except convertible	168 in-lbs
Convertible	32
2004 and later models	32
Avalon	25
Lexus	
Upper bolt	29
Lower bolt	25
Caliper torque plate bolts	
Front	79
Rear	
Camry	
TMC manufacture	46
TMMK manufacture	34
Solara	
2002 and 2003 models	34
2004 and later models	46
Avalon	34
Lexus	46

Torque specifications (continued)	Ft-lbs (unless otherwise indicated)
Brake hose-to-caliper banjo bolt	22
Wheel cylinder mounting bolts	84 in-lbs
Master cylinder-to-brake booster nuts	108 in-lbs
Power brake booster mounting nuts	108 in-lbs
Wheel lug nuts	See Chapter 1

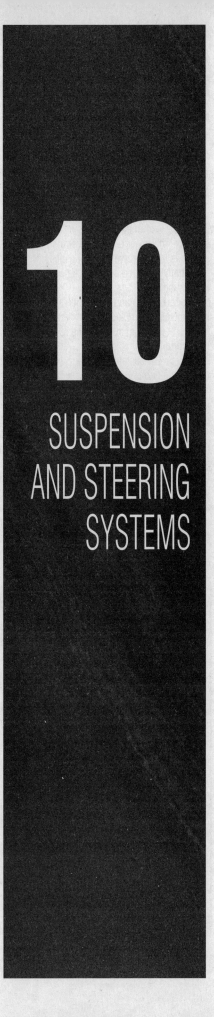

10

SUSPENSION AND STEERING SYSTEMS

Section

1   General information
2   Stabilizer bar and bushings (front) - removal and installation
3   Strut assembly (front) - removal, inspection and installation
4   Strut/coil spring assembly - replacement
5   Control arm - removal, inspection and installation
6   Balljoints - replacement
7   Steering knuckle and hub - removal and installation
8   Hub and bearing assembly (front) - removal and installation
9   Stabilizer bar and bushings (rear) - removal and installation
10   Strut assembly (rear) - removal, inspection and installation
11   Strut rod - removal and installation
12   Suspension arms (rear) - removal and installation
13   Hub and bearing assembly (rear) - removal and installation
14   Rear axle carrier - removal and installation
15   Steering system - general information
16   Steering wheel - removal and installation
17   Tie-rod ends - removal and installation
18   Steering gear boots - replacement
19   Steering gear - removal and installation
20   Power steering pump - removal and installation
21   Power Steering Pressure (PSP) switch - check and replacement
22   Power steering system - bleeding
23   Wheels and tires - general information
24   Wheel alignment - general information

Reference to other Chapters

Power steering fluid level check - See Chapter 1
Steering and suspension check - See Chapter 1
Tire and tire pressure checks - See Chapter 1
Tire rotation - See Chapter 1

1   General information

▶ **Refer to illustrations 1.1 and 1.2**

The front suspension is a MacPherson strut design. The upper end of each strut is attached to the vehicle's body strut support. The lower end of the strut is connected to the upper end of the steering knuckle. The steering knuckle is attached to a balljoint mounted on the outer end of the suspension control arm (see illustration).

The rear suspension also utilizes strut/coil spring assemblies. The upper end of each strut is attached to the vehicle body by a strut support. The lower end of the strut is attached to an axle carrier. The carrier is located by a pair of suspension arms on each side, and a longitudinally mounted strut rod between the body and each knuckle (see illustration).

Lexus ES 300 and 330 models are available with electronic modulated suspension. Electronic modulated suspension allows the driver to control the adjustment of the shock absorber damping depending on road conditions.

The power-assisted rack-and-pinion steering gear, which is located behind the engine/transaxle assembly, is mounted on the engine cradle. The steering gear actuates the tie-rods, which are attached to the steering knuckles. The steering column is designed to collapse in the event of an accident.

Some late models are equipped with the Vehicle Stability Control (VSC) system. This system can be observed in the active mode on the instrument cluster when the SLIP indicator light blinks and the stability control buzzer sounds. The VSC OFF indicator light and the VSC Warning light will illuminate (stay ON) only when the controller detects a failure in the VSC system. The VSC system helps prevent the vehicle from slipping sideways as a result of strong front and rear wheel skid during cornering. The VSC system incorporates the ABS system components as well as the traction control system (TRAC) components.

The Traction Control system helps prevent the drive (front) wheels from slipping when the driver depresses the accelerator pedal excessively during starting from a stop or accelerating on a slippery surface. The stability control module receives information from the wheel speed sensors by way of the CAN communication. The stability controller monitors and regulates the engine rpm's in conjunction with the PCM and brake hydraulic pressure using the ABS hydraulic control unit. The SLIP indicator light blinks when the system is operating. The SLIP indicator light and the VSC warning light will illuminate (stay ON) when a fault is detected in the TRAC system. The TRAC system can be turned off at the switch.

Frequently, when working on the suspension or steering system components, you may come across fasteners that seem impossible to loosen. These fasteners on the underside of the vehicle are continually subjected to water, road grime, mud, etc., and can become rusted or "frozen," making them extremely difficult to remove. In order to unscrew these stubborn fasteners without damaging them (or other components), be sure to use lots of penetrating oil and allow it to soak in for a while. Using a wire brush to clean exposed threads will also ease removal of the nut or bolt and prevent damage to the threads. Sometimes a sharp blow with a hammer and punch will break the bond between nut and bolt threads, but care must be taken to prevent the punch from slipping off the fastener and ruining the threads. Heating the stuck fastener and surrounding area with a torch sometimes helps too, but isn't recommended because of the obvious dangers associated with fire. Long breaker bars and extension, or "cheater," pipes will increase leverage, but never use an extension pipe on a ratchet - the ratcheting mechanism could be damaged. Sometimes tightening the nut or bolt first will help to break it loose. Fasteners that require drastic measures to remove should always be replaced with new ones.

Since most of the procedures dealt with in this Chapter involve

1.1 Front suspension and steering components

1	Steering gear assembly	3	Strut and spring assembly	5	Steering knuckle
2	Control arm	4	Balljoint	6	Tie-rod end

1.2 Rear suspension components

1	Stabilizer bar	3	Strut rod	5	Strut assembly
2	Suspension arm (no. 1)	4	Rear axle carrier	6	Suspension arm (no. 2)

jacking up the vehicle and working underneath it, a good pair of jackstands will be needed. A hydraulic floor jack is the preferred type of jack to lift the vehicle, and it can also be used to support certain components during various operations.

❋❋ WARNING:

Never, under any circumstances, rely on a jack to support the

vehicle while working on it. Whenever any of the suspension or steering fasteners are loosened or removed they must be inspected and, if necessary, replaced with new ones of the same part number or of original equipment quality and design. Torque specifications must be followed for proper reassembly and component retention. Never attempt to heat or straighten any suspension or steering components. Instead, replace any bent or damaged part with a new one.

2 Stabilizer bar and bushings (front) - removal and installation

REMOVAL

▶ **Refer to illustrations 2.4 and 2.5**

1 Loosen the front wheel lug nuts. Raise the front of the vehicle and support it securely on jackstands. Apply the parking brake and block the rear wheels to keep the vehicle from rolling off the stands. Remove the front wheels.

2 Remove the left and right fender apron seals. Each seal is retained by two bolts.

3 Disconnect the left and right tie-rod ends from the steering knuckles (see Section 17).

4 Disconnect the stabilizer bar links from the bar (see illustration). If the ballstud turns with the nut, use an Allen wrench to hold the stud.

2.4 To detach the stabilizer bar link from the bar, remove the lower nut; if you're removing the strut, remove the upper nut

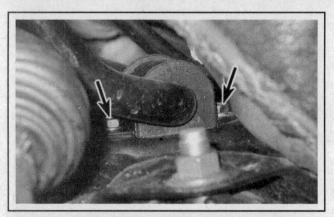

2.5 To detach the stabilizer bar from the subframe, remove these bushing retainer bolts and remove the retainer

5 Detach both stabilizer bar bushing retainers from the subframe (see illustration).

6 Remove the front exhaust pipe (see Chapter 4).

7 Remove the steering gear mounting bolts (see Section 19).

8 Lift the steering gear assembly and remove the stabilizer bar by

working it out through the left wheel housing.

9 While the stabilizer bar is off the vehicle, slide off the retainer bushings and inspect them. If they're cracked, worn or deteriorated, replace them. It's also a good idea to inspect the stabilizer bar link. To check it, flip the balljoint stud side-to-side five or six times as shown, then install the nut. Using an inch-pound torque wrench, turn the nut continuously one turn every two to four seconds and note the torque reading on the fifth turn. It should be about 0.4 to 17 in-lbs. If it isn't, replace the link assembly.

10 Clean the bushing area of the stabilizer bar with a stiff wire brush to remove any rust or dirt.

INSTALLATION

11 Lubricate the inside and outside of the new bushings with vegetable oil (used in cooking) to simplify reassembly.

✳✳ CAUTION:

Don't use petroleum or mineral-based lubricants or brake fluid - they will lead to deterioration of the bushings.

12 Installation is the reverse of removal.

---

3 Strut assembly (front) - removal, inspection and installation

REMOVAL

▶ **Refer to illustrations 3.3, 3.5 and 3.7**

1 Loosen the wheel lug nuts, raise the vehicle and support it securely on jackstands. Remove the wheel. Support the control arm with a floor jack.

2 Disconnect the stabilizer bar link end from the strut (see illustration 2.4).

3 Remove the brake hose bracket and, if equipped, the speed sensor wiring harness from the strut (see illustration).

4 Detach the speed sensor wiring harness from the strut by removing the clamp bracket bolt. On models equipped with electronic modulated suspension, remove the shock absorber cap and disconnect

the shock absorber wiring harness. If the strut is to be disassembled, loosen, but do not remove, the damper shaft (center) nut (this will require a special socket if the vehicle is equipped with electronic modulated suspension; check with your local auto parts store or tool dealer).

5 Remove the strut-to-knuckle nuts (see illustration) and knock the bolts out with a hammer and punch.

6 Separate the strut from the steering knuckle. Be careful not to overextend the inner CV joint. Also, don't let the steering knuckle fall outward, as the brake hose could be damaged.

7 Support the strut and spring assembly with one hand and remove the three strut-to-shock tower nuts (this is only if the strut is going to be disassembled) (see illustration). On models equipped with electronic modulated suspension, loosen but do not remove, the nut in the center of the strut (this is only necessary if the strut is going to be disassembled). Remove the assembly out from the fenderwell.

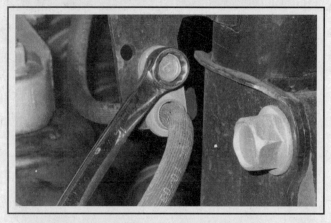

3.3 Detach the brake hose from the strut bracket

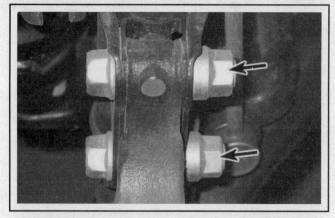

3.5 To disconnect the lower end of the strut from the steering knuckle, remove these two nuts and knock out the bolts with a hammer and punch

➡Note: Some models have a front suspension brace between the tops of the two shock towers that is retained by the same nuts that secure the strut to the body. At the inner stud, there are two spacer washers under the brace that are easy to lose when removing the strut.

INSPECTION

8   Check the strut body for leaking fluid, dents, cracks and other obvious damage that would warrant repair or replacement.

9   Check the coil spring for chips or cracks in the spring coating (this can cause premature spring failure due to corrosion). Inspect the spring seat for cuts, hardness and general deterioration.

10   If any undesirable conditions exist, proceed to the strut disassembly procedure (see Section 4).

INSTALLATION

11   Guide the strut assembly up into the fenderwell and insert the three upper mounting studs through the holes in the shock tower. Once the three studs protrude from the shock tower, install the nuts so the strut won't fall back through. This is most easily accomplished with the help of an assistant, as the strut is quite heavy and awkward.

12   Slide the steering knuckle into the strut flange and insert the two bolts. Install the nuts and tighten them to the torque listed in this Chapter's Specifications.

13   Reattach the brake hose bracket to the strut. If equipped, install the speed sensor wiring harness bracket.

14   Install the wheel and lug nuts, then lower the vehicle and tighten the lug nuts to the torque listed in the Chapter 1 Specifications.

15   Tighten the three upper mounting nuts to the torque listed in this Chapter's Specifications.

3.7 To disconnect the upper end of the strut from the vehicle body, remove these three nuts - do not lose the two spacer washers under the shock tower brace (not all models) at the inner stud

✳✳ WARNING:

Don't remove the large nut in the center

16   If you're working on a model equipped with electronic modulated suspension and the strut had been disassembled, tighten the nut in the center of the strut to the torque listed in this Chapter's Specifications, using a special tool (check with your local auto parts store, dealer parts department or tool dealer regarding tool availability). Connect the electrical connector and install the cap.

4   Strut/coil spring assembly - replacement

1   If the struts or coil springs exhibit the telltale signs of wear (leaking fluid, loss of damping capability, chipped, sagging or cracked coil springs) explore all options before beginning any work. The strut/shock absorber assemblies are not serviceable and must be replaced if a problem develops. However, strut assemblies complete with springs may be available on an exchange basis, which eliminates much time and work. Whichever route you choose to take, check on the cost and availability of parts before disassembling your vehicle.

✳✳ WARNING:

Disassembling a strut is potentially dangerous and utmost attention must be directed to the job, or serious injury may result. Use only a high-quality spring compressor and carefully follow the manufacturer's instructions furnished with the tool. After removing the coil spring from the strut assembly, set it aside in a safe, isolated area.

DISASSEMBLY

▶ **Refer to illustrations 4.3, 4.4, 4.5, 4.6 and 4.7**

2   Remove the strut and spring assembly (see Section 3 [front] or Section 10 [rear]). Mount the strut assembly in a vise. Line the vise jaws with wood or rags to prevent damage to the unit and don't tighten the vise excessively.

4.3 Install the spring compressor in accordance with the tool manufacturer's instructions and compress the spring until all pressure is relieved from the upper spring seat

3   Following the tool manufacturer's instructions, install the spring compressor (which can be obtained at most auto parts stores or equipment yards on a daily rental basis) on the spring and compress it sufficiently to relieve all pressure from the upper spring seat (see illustration). This can be verified by wiggling the spring.

4.4 Remove the damper shaft nut

4.5 Lift the suspension support off the damper shaft

4.6 Remove the spring seat from the damper shaft

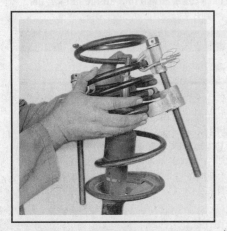

4.7 Remove the compressed spring assembly - keep the ends of the spring pointed away from your body

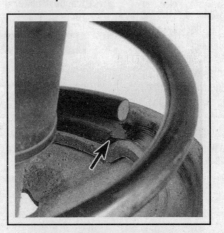

4.11 When installing the spring, make sure the end fits into the recessed portion of the lower seat

4.12 The flats on the damper shaft must match up with the flats in the spring seat

4   Loosen the damper shaft nut (see illustration).
5   Remove the nut and suspension support (see illustration). Inspect the bearing in the suspension support for smooth operation. If it doesn't turn smoothly, replace the suspension support. Check the rubber portion of the suspension support for cracking and general deterioration. If there is any separation of the rubber, replace it.
6   Remove the upper spring seat from the damper shaft (see illustration). Check the spring seat for cracking and hardness; replace it if necessary. Remove the upper insulator from the damper shaft.
7   Carefully lift the compressed spring from the assembly (see illustration) and set it in a safe place.

✳✳ WARNING:

Never place your head near the end of the spring!

8   Slide the rubber bumper off the damper shaft.
9   Check the lower insulator for wear, cracking and hardness and replace it if necessary.

REASSEMBLY

▶ **Refer to illustrations 4.11, 4.12 and 4.14**

10   If the lower insulator is being replaced, set it into position with

4.14 Make sure the arrows on the upper spring seat face toward the outside of the vehicle

the dropped portion seated in the lowest part of the seat. Extend the damper rod to its full length and install the rubber bumper.
11   Carefully place the coil spring onto the lower insulator, with the end of the spring resting in the lowest part of the insulator (see illustration).

12 Install the upper insulator and spring seat, making sure that the flats in the hole in the seat match up with the flats on the damper shaft (see illustration).

13 Align the OUT mark of the spring upper seat with the mark of the upper insulator.

14 If you're working on a front strut, make sure the arrow on the spring seat faces toward the lower bracket, where the steering knuckle fits (see illustration).

15 Install the dust seal and suspension support to the damper shaft.

16 Install the nut and, if you're working on a model without electronic modulated suspension, tighten it to the torque listed in this Chapter's Specifications (on models with electronic modulated suspension, final tightening of this nut is carried out when the strut is installed on the vehicle). Remove the spring compressor tool.

17 Install the strut/spring assembly (see Section 3 [front] or 10 [rear]). If you're working on a model with electronic modulated suspension, tighten the damper shaft nut to the torque listed in this Chapter's Specifications (see Section 3).

---

5 Control arm - removal, inspection and installation

REMOVAL

▶ **Refer to illustrations 5.3a, 5.3b, 5.4 and 5.5**

1   Loosen the wheel lug nuts on the side to be dismantled, raise the front of the vehicle, support it securely on jackstands and remove the wheel.

2   On 2004 and later Toyota and all Lexus models, the transverse engine mount at the subframe interferes with removal of the rear bolts of the control arms. The procedure is difficult and requires the use of an engine lifting hoist or support fixture (refer to Chapter 2 for engine mount removal/installation).

3   Remove the balljoint retaining bolt and nuts (see illustration). Use a prybar to disconnect the balljoint from the control arm (see illustration).

4   Remove the two bolts that attach the front of the control arm to the engine cradle (see illustration).

5   Remove the bolt and nut that attach the rear of the control arm to the engine cradle (see illustration).

6   Remove the control arm.

5.3a Remove these nuts and this bolt to disconnect the control arm from the balljoint

5.3b Separate the control arm from the balljoint with a prybar

5.4 To detach the front end of the control arm from the engine cradle, remove these two bolts

5.5 To detach the rear end of the control arm from the engine cradle, remove this nut and bolt

INSPECTION

7   Make sure the control arm is straight. If it's bent, replace it. Do not attempt to straighten a bent control arm.

8   Inspect the bushings. If they're cracked, torn or worn out, replace the control arm.

INSTALLATION

9   Installation is the reverse of removal. Be sure to tighten all fasteners to the torque listed in this Chapter's Specifications.

10 Install the wheel and lug nuts, lower the vehicle and tighten the lug nuts to the torque listed in the Chapter 1 Specifications.

11 It's a good idea to have the front wheel alignment checked, and if necessary, adjusted after this job has been performed.

6   Balljoints - replacement

1   Loosen the wheel lug nuts, raise the vehicle and support it securely on jackstands. Remove the wheel.

➡**Note: If you're going to remove the balljoint using a puller (as described in Steps 9 through 13), loosen the driveaxle/hub nut before raising the vehicle (see Chapter 8).**

PICKLEFORK METHOD

✳✳ CAUTION:

The following procedure is the quickest way to detach a balljoint from the steering knuckle, but it will very likely damage the balljoint boot. If you want to save the boot, proceed to Step 9.

2   Remove the cotter pin from the balljoint stud and loosen the nut (but don't remove it yet).

3   Separate the balljoint from the steering knuckle with a picklefork-type balljoint separator. Lubricate the rubber boot with grease and work carefully so as not to tear the boot. Remove the balljoint stud nut.

4   Remove the bolt and nuts securing the balljoint to the control arm (see illustration 5.3a). Separate the balljoint from the control arm with a prybar (see illustration 5.3b).

5   To install the balljoint, position it on the steering knuckle and install the nut, but don't tighten it yet.

6   Attach the balljoint to the control arm and install the bolt and nuts, tightening them to the torque listed in this Chapter's Specifications.

7   Tighten the balljoint stud nut to the torque listed in this Chapter's Specifications and install a new cotter pin. If the cotter pin hole doesn't line up with the slots on the nut, tighten the nut additionally until it does line up - don't loosen the nut to insert the cotter pin.

8   Install the wheel and lug nuts. Lower the vehicle and tighten the lug nuts to the torque listed in the Chapter 1 Specifications.

PULLER METHOD

▸ **Refer to illustration 6.12**

9   Separate the control arm from the balljoint (see Section 5).

10 Pull the outer end of the driveaxle from the steering knuckle (see

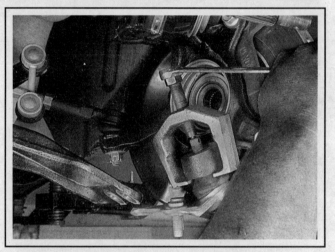

6.12 To separate the balljoint from the steering knuckle, install a small puller and pop the balljoint stud loose

Chapter 8) and suspend the driveaxle with a piece of wire.

11 Remove the cotter pin from the balljoint stud and loosen the nut (but don't remove it yet).

12 Install a small puller (see illustration) and pop the balljoint stud from the steering knuckle.

13 Remove the nut and remove the balljoint.

14 Install the new balljoint into the steering knuckle and tighten the nut to the torque listed in this Chapter's Specifications. Install a new cotter pin. If the cotter pin hole doesn't line up with the slots on the nut, tighten the nut additionally until it does line up - don't loosen the nut to insert the cotter pin.

15 Insert the outer end of the driveaxle through the steering knuckle and install the nut. Tighten it securely, but don't attempt to tighten it completely yet.

16 Connect the balljoint to the lower arm and tighten the fasteners to the torque listed in this Chapter's Specifications.

17 Install the wheel and lug nuts, lower the vehicle and tighten the lug nuts to the torque listed in the Chapter 1 Specifications.

18 Tighten the driveaxle/hub nut to the torque listed in the Chapter 8 Specifications. Install the lock washer and cotter pin.

7 Steering knuckle and hub - removal and installation

❋❋ WARNING:

Dust created by the brake system is harmful to your health. Never blow it out with compressed air and don't inhale any of it. Do not, under any circumstances, use petroleum-based solvents to clean brake parts. Use brake system cleaner only.

REMOVAL

1 Loosen the driveaxle/hub nut (see Chapter 8). Loosen the wheel lug nuts, raise the vehicle and support it securely on jackstands. Remove the wheel.

2 Remove the brake caliper and support it with a piece of wire as described in Chapter 9. Remove the caliper torque plate and separate the brake disc from the hub.

3 Loosen, but do not remove the strut-to-steering knuckle bolts (see illustration 3.5).

4 Separate the tie-rod end from the steering knuckle arm (see Section 17).

5 Remove the balljoint-to-lower arm bolt and nuts (see illustrations 5.3a and 5.3b). The strut-to-knuckle bolts can now be removed.

6 Push the driveaxle from the hub as described in Chapter 8. Support the end of the driveaxle with a piece of wire.

7 Separate the steering knuckle from the strut. If necessary, detach the balljoint from the steering knuckle.

INSTALLATION

8 Guide the knuckle and hub assembly into position, inserting the driveaxle into the hub.

9 Push the knuckle into the strut flange and install the bolts and nuts, but don't tighten them yet.

10 Connect the balljoint to the control arm and install the bolt and nuts (don't tighten them yet).

11 Attach the tie-rod to the steering knuckle arm (see Section 17). Tighten the strut bolt nuts, the balljoint-to-control arm bolt and nuts and the tie-rod nut to the torque values listed in this Chapter's Specifications.

12 Place the brake disc on the hub and install the caliper as outlined in Chapter 9.

13 Install the driveaxle/hub nut and tighten it securely (final tightening will be carried out when the vehicle is lowered).

14 Install the wheel and lug nuts.

15 Lower the vehicle and tighten the lug nuts to the torque listed in the Chapter 1 Specifications. Tighten the driveaxle/hub nut to the torque listed in the Chapter 8 Specifications.

8 Hub and bearing assembly (front) - removal and installation

Due to the special tools and expertise required to press the hub and bearing from the steering knuckle, this job should be left to a professional shop. However, the steering knuckle and hub may be removed and the assembly taken to a dealer service department or other repair shop. See Section 7 for the steering knuckle and hub removal procedure.

9 Stabilizer bar and bushings (rear) - removal and installation

▶ **Refer to illustrations 9.3 and 9.4**

1 Loosen the rear wheel lug nuts. Raise the rear of the vehicle and place it securely on jackstands. Remove the rear wheels.

2 Remove the heat insulator from the exhaust system.

3 Disconnect the stabilizer bar links from the bar (see illustration). If the ballstud turns with the nut, use an Allen wrench to hold the stud.

4 Unbolt the stabilizer bar bushing retainers and the two brackets (at each side) from the body (see illustration).

➡**Note: On Camry Solara convertible models, there is a floor reinforcement subassembly of braces that must be removed to allow stabilizer bar removal.**

5 The stabilizer bar can now be removed from the vehicle. Pull the retainers off the stabilizer bar (if they haven't fallen off already) using a rocking motion.

9.3 To detach the stabilizer bar link from the bar, remove the lower nut; if you're removing the strut, remove the upper nut

6   Check the bushings for wear, hardness, distortion, cracking and other signs of deterioration, replacing them if necessary. Check the stabilizer bar links as described in Section 2, Step 9.

7   Using a wire brush, clean the areas of the bar where the bushings ride. If necessary, use a light coat of vegetable oil to ease bushing and U-bracket installation (don't use petroleum-based products or brake fluid, as these will damage the rubber).

8   Installation is otherwise the reverse of removal. On Solara convertible models, tighten the floor reinforcement brace bolts to 38 ft-lbs.

9.4 Remove the bushing retainer bolts and brackets from both the left and right retainers (left retainer shown)

10 Strut assembly (rear) - removal, inspection and installation

REMOVAL

▶ **Refer to illustrations 10.7 and 10.8**

➡**Note: When removing/replacing any rear suspension arms, loosely tighten all the bolts, move the suspension to its normal ride-height angle and position, then fully tighten the bolts.**

1   Remove the rear seat and package tray trim panel (see Chapter 11).

2   Loosen the rear wheel lug nuts, raise the rear of the vehicle and support it securely on jackstands. Remove the wheel.

3   Remove the flexible hose and ABS speed sensor from the shock absorber, if equipped.

4   Detach the brake hose from the strut (see illustration 3.3). Detach the ABS sensor wire from the strut. On models equipped with electronic modulated suspension, remove the clip and clamp, and disconnect the shock absorber wiring harness.

5   Disconnect the stabilizer bar link from the strut (see illustration 9.3).

6   Support the axle carrier with a floor jack.

7   Loosen the strut-to-axle carrier bolt nuts (see illustration).

8   Remove the three upper strut-to-body mounting nuts (see illustration). On models equipped with electronic modulated suspension, loosen but do not remove the damper shaft (center) nut (see Section 3). Remove the assembly out from the fenderwell.

9   Lower the axle carrier with the jack and remove the two strut-to-axle carrier bolts.

10 Remove the strut assembly.

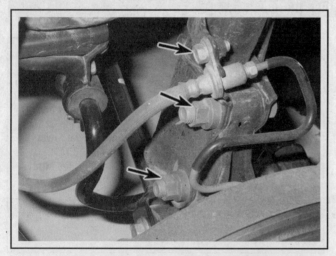

10.7 To disconnect the lower end of the strut from the rear axle carrier, unbolt the brake hose from the strut, then remove these nuts and knock out the bolts (but don't remove the bolts until after the upper strut nuts are removed and the axle carrier is supported by a floor jack)

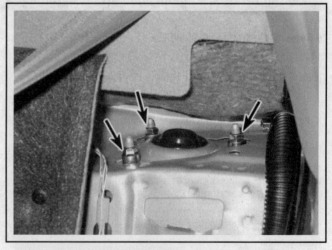

10.8 To disconnect the upper end of the strut from the vehicle, remove these three nuts

INSPECTION

11 Follow the inspection procedures described in Section 3. If you determine that the strut assembly must be disassembled for replacement of the strut or the coil spring, refer to Section 4.

INSTALLATION

12 Maneuver the assembly up into the fenderwell and insert the mounting studs through the holes in the body. Install the nuts, but don't tighten them yet.

13 Push the axle carrier into the strut lower bracket and install the bolts and nuts, tightening them to the torque listed in this Chapter's Specifications.

14 Connect the stabilizer bar link to the strut bracket.

15 Attach the brake hose bracket to the strut. Attach the ABS wire to the strut, if equipped.

16 Install the wheel and lug nuts, lower the vehicle and tighten the lug nuts to the torque listed in the Chapter 1 Specifications.

17 Tighten the three strut upper mounting nuts to the torque listed in this Chapter's Specifications.

18 If you're working on a model equipped with electronic modulated suspension and the strut has been disassembled, tighten the strut center nut to the torque listed in this Chapter's Specifications. Connect the electrical connector.

19 Install the package tray trim and seat.

11 Strut rod - removal and installation

▶ **Refer to illustrations 11.2 and 11.3**

➡ **Note: When removing/replacing any rear suspension arms, loosely tighten all the bolts, move the suspension to its normal ride-height angle and position, then fully tighten the bolts.**

1 Loosen the wheel lug nuts, raise the vehicle and support it securely on jackstands. Remove the wheel.

2 Remove the strut rod-to-axle carrier bolt (see illustration).

3 Remove the strut rod-to-body bracket bolt (see illustration) and detach the rod from the vehicle.

➡ **Note: The parking brake cable bracket may need to be unbolted to allow removal of the strut bolt.**

4 Installation is the reverse of the removal procedure. Be sure to tighten the bolts to the torque listed in this Chapter's Specifications.

11.2 To disconnect the strut rod from the carrier, hold the nut with a wrench and remove the bolt

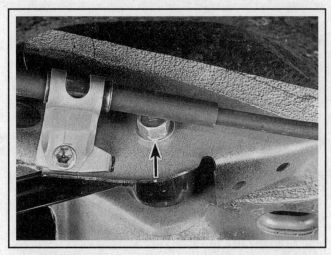

11.3 To disconnect the forward end of the strut rod from the vehicle body, remove this bolt

12 Suspension arms (rear) - removal and installation

REMOVAL

▶ **Refer to illustrations 12.4 and 12.5**

1 Raise the rear of the vehicle and support it securely on jackstands. Block the front wheels.

2 Disconnect the strut rod from the axle carrier (see illustration 11.2).

3 Remove the exhaust center section and tailpipe (see Chapter 4). Remove the rear stabilizer bar (see Section 9).

4 Remove the suspension arm-to-rear axle carrier bolt and nut (see illustration).

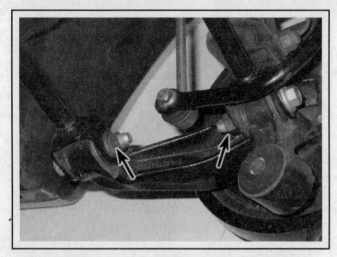

12.4 To disconnect the suspension arms from the carrier, hold the bolt with a wrench and remove the nut (bolts indicated for both #1 and #2 arms).

➡Note: On some models, a single long bolt passes through both suspension arms

5   To access the bolts at the inner ends of the suspension arms, the rear suspension crossmember must be lowered. Position a floor jack under the center of the crossmember, then loosen and remove the crossmember-to-body bolts (see illustration). Lower the rear suspension crossmember with the jack (do not place any part of your body under the suspension while it is supported only by the jack) until the suspension arm bolts are accessible. Remove the bolts.

➡Note: On some models, a single long bolt passes through both suspension arms.

6   Remove the No. 2 (rear) suspension arm.
7   Remove the No. 1 (front) suspension arm.

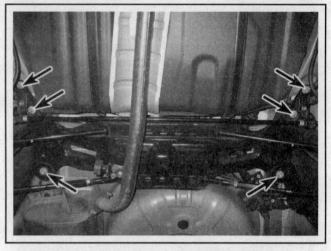

12.5 Rear suspension crossmember mounting bolts

INSTALLATION

➡Note: When installing any rear suspension arms, loosely tighten all the bolts, move the suspension to its normal ride-height angle and position, then fully tighten the bolts.

8   Installation is the reverse of removal. Be sure to tighten all fasteners to the torque listed in this Chapter's Specifications.

➡Note: When reinstalling the suspension arms, the factory paint marks on the arms should face the rear of the vehicle.

9   Install the wheel and lug nuts, then lower the vehicle to the ground. Tighten the wheel lug nuts to the torque listed in the Chapter 1 Specifications.

10 Have the rear wheel alignment checked by a dealer service department or an alignment shop.

13 Hub and bearing assembly (rear) - removal and installation

❋❋ WARNING:

Dust created by the brake system is harmful to your health. Never blow it out with compressed air and don't inhale any of it. Do not, under any circumstances, use petroleum-based solvents to clean brake parts. Use brake system cleaner only.

➡Note: The rear hub and bearing assembly is not serviceable. If found to be defective, it must be replaced as a unit.

REMOVAL

▸ **Refer to illustration 13.3**

1   Loosen the wheel lug nuts, raise the vehicle and support it securely on jackstands. Remove the wheel.
2   Remove the brake drum or disc from the hub (see Chapter 9). If equipped, disconnect the wheel speed sensor.
3   Remove the four hub-to-axle carrier bolts, accessible by turning the hub flange so that the large circular cutout exposes each bolt (see illustration).

13.3 To remove the four bolts that attach the hub and bearing assembly to the rear axle carrier, rotate the hub flange and align one of the holes in the flange with each of the bolts

4   Remove the hub and bearing assembly from its seat, maneuvering it out through the brake assembly.

5   Remove the old O-ring from the hub seat and install a new one. Wheel bearing grease may be used to keep the O-ring in place before installing the hub-and-bearing assembly.

INSTALLATION

6   Position the hub and bearing assembly on the axle carrier and align the holes in the backing plate. Install the bolts. A magnet is useful in guiding the bolts through the hub flange and into position. After all four bolts have been installed, tighten them to the torque listed in this Chapter's Specifications.

7   Install the brake drum, or disc and caliper, and the wheel. Lower the vehicle and tighten the lug nuts to the torque listed in the Chapter 1 Specifications.

14 Rear axle carrier - removal and installation

✳✳ WARNING:

Dust created by the brake system is harmful to your health. Never blow it out with compressed air and don't inhale any of it. Do not, under any circumstances, use petroleum-based solvents to clean brake parts. Use brake system cleaner only.

REMOVAL

1   Loosen the wheel lug nuts, raise the vehicle and support it on jackstands. Block the front wheels and remove the rear wheel.

2   Remove the rear brake drum, or caliper and disc (see Chapter 9). On models with rear drum brakes, disconnect the brake line from the wheel cylinder (see Chapter 9). If the vehicle is equipped with rear disc brakes, don't detach the brake hose from the caliper.

3   On drum brake models, loosen and remove the bolt that retains the flexible hose to the strut.

4   Remove the rear hub and bearing assembly (see Section 13).

5   It isn't necessary to disassemble the brake shoe assembly or disconnect the parking brake cable from the backing plate. On models with rear drum brakes, detach the backing plate and rear brake assembly from the axle carrier; on models with rear disc brakes, detach the backing plate and rear parking brake assembly from the axle carrier. Suspend the backing plate and brake assembly from the coil spring with a piece of wire.

6   Remove the wheel speed sensor from the axle carrier, if equipped.

7   Loosen, but don't remove the strut-to-axle carrier bolts (see illustration 10.7).

8   Detach the strut rod and suspension arms from the axle carrier (see Sections 11 and 12).

9   Remove the loosened strut-to-axle carrier bolts while supporting the carrier so it doesn't fall and detach the axle carrier from the strut bracket.

INSTALLATION

10   Inspect the carrier bushing for cracks, deformation and signs of wear. If it is worn out, take the carrier to a dealer service department or other repair shop to have the old one pressed out and a new one pressed in.

11   Push the axle carrier into the strut bracket, aligning the two bolt holes. Insert the two strut-to-carrier bolts and tighten them to the torque listed in this Chapter's Specifications.

12   Connect the suspension arms to the axle carrier, but don't tighten the nut(s) yet.

13   Connect the strut rod to the axle carrier, but don't tighten the nut yet.

14   Place a jack under the carrier and raise it to simulate normal ride height.

15   Tighten the suspension arm bolt(s)/nut(s) and the strut rod bolt/nut to the torque listed in this Chapter's Specifications.

16   On drum brake models, attach the flexible hose to the strut.

17   Reattach the wheel speed sensor to the axle carrier, if equipped.

18   Attach the brake backing plate to the axle carrier, install the hub and tighten the four bolts to the torque listed in this Chapter's Specifications.

19   On models with rear drum brakes, connect the brake line to the wheel cylinder (see Chapter 9). Be careful not to damage the line when bending it back into place.

20   Install the rear brake drum or disc and caliper (see Chapter 9).

21   Install the wheel and lug nuts.

22   Bleed the wheel cylinder (see Chapter 9).

23   Lower the vehicle and tighten the lug nuts to the torque listed in the Chapter 1 Specifications.

15 Steering system - general information

All models are equipped with rack-and-pinion steering. The steering gear is bolted to the engine cradle and operates the steering knuckles via tie-rods. The inner ends of the tie-rods are protected by rubber boots that should be inspected periodically for secure attachment, tears and leaking lubricant.

The power assist system consists of a belt-driven pump and the associated lines and hoses. The fluid level in the power steering pump reservoir should be checked periodically (see Chapter 1).

The steering wheel operates the steering shaft, which actuates the steering gear through universal joints. Looseness in the steering can be caused by wear in the steering shaft universal joints, the steering gear, the tie-rod ends and loose retaining bolts.

16 Steering wheel - removal and installation

※※ WARNING:

The models covered by this manual are equipped with Supplemental Restraint Systems (SRS), more commonly known as airbags. Always disable the airbag system before working in the vicinity of any airbag system component to avoid the possibility of accidental deployment of the airbag(s), which could cause personal injury (see Chapter 12).

REMOVAL

▸ **Refer to illustrations 16.2, 16.3a, 16.3b, 16.4 and 16.6**

1   Turn the ignition key to Off, then disconnect the cable from the negative terminal of the battery (see Chapter 5, Section 1).

2   Turn the steering wheel so that the wheels are pointing straight ahead. Pry off the small covers on either side of the steering wheel and loosen the Torx screws that attach the airbag module to the steering wheel (see illustration). Loosen each screw until the groove in the circumference of the screw catches on the screw case.

➡Note: The screws do not need to be removed completely.

3   Pull the airbag module off the steering wheel and disconnect the module electrical connectors (see illustrations).

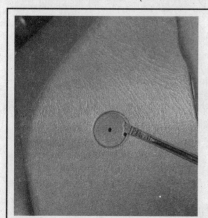

16.2 Pry off the small covers on either side of the steering wheel, then loosen the airbag module Torx screws

※※ WARNING:

Carry the airbag module with the trim side facing away from you and set it down in an isolated area with the trim side facing up.

4   Unplug the electrical connector for the horn and cruise control system (see illustration).

5   Remove the steering wheel retaining nut, then mark the relationship of the steering shaft to the hub (if marks don't already exist or don't line up) to simplify installation and ensure steering wheel alignment.

6   Use a puller to disconnect the steering wheel from the shaft (see illustration).

※※ CAUTION:

Don't hammer on the shaft in an attempt to remove the wheel. If it's necessary to remove the spiral cable, remove the steering column covers (see Chapter 11), unplug the electrical connector and disengage the three claws, then remove it from the column.

16.3a Remove the airbag module . . .

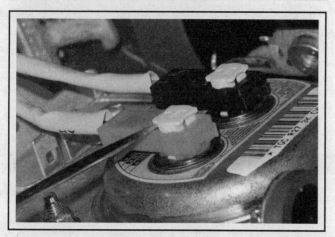

16.3b . . . pry up the locks for the module electrical connectors (black connector is the ground wire), then unplug the electrical connectors

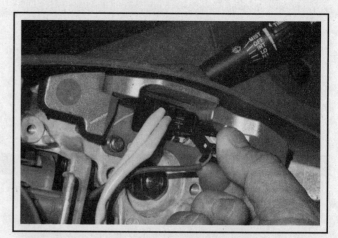

16.4 Unplug the electrical connector for the horn and cruise control

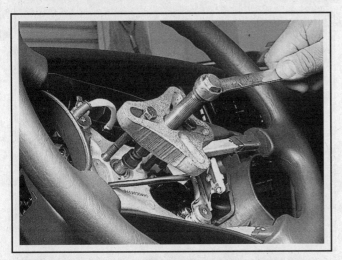

16.6 Use a steering wheel puller to remove the steering wheel

INSTALLATION

▶ **Refer to illustration 16.7**

7   Make sure that the front wheels are facing straight ahead. Turn the spiral cable counterclockwise by hand until it becomes harder to turn the cable. Rotate the cable clockwise about two and a half turns and align the two pointers (see illustration).

8   To install the wheel, align the mark on the steering wheel hub with the mark on the shaft and slip the wheel onto the shaft. Install the

16.7 To center the spiral cable, turn the cable counterclockwise until it's harder to turn, rotate the cable clockwise two and a half turns and align the two red marks (the cable should be able to rotate about two and a half turns in either direction when it's properly centered)

nut and tighten it to the torque listed in this Chapter's Specifications.

9   Plug in the horn and cruise control connector.

10 Plug in the electrical connectors for the airbag module. Make sure the connector locks are pushed back into position.

11 Install the airbag module and tighten the Torx retaining screws to the torque listed in this Chapter's Specifications.

12 Connect the negative battery cable.

17 Tie-rod ends - removal and installation

REMOVAL

▶ **Refer to illustrations 17.2a, 17.2b and 17.4**

1   Loosen the wheel lug nuts. Raise the front of the vehicle, support

it securely on jackstands, block the rear wheels and set the parking brake. Remove the front wheel.

2   Hold the tie-rod with a pair of locking pliers or wrench and loosen the jam nut enough to mark the position of the tie-rod end in relation to the threads (see illustrations).

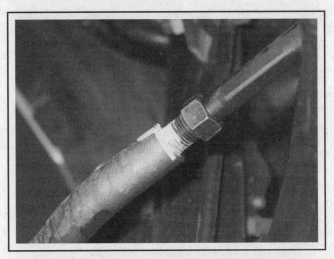

17.2a Hold the tie-rod end with a wrench and break the jam nut loose with another wrench

17.2b Back off the jam nut and mark the exposed threads to ensure that the new tie-rod end is threaded on the same number of turns

3   Remove the cotter pin and loosen the nut on the tie-rod end stud.

4   Disconnect the tie-rod from the steering knuckle arm with a puller (see illustration). Remove the nut and separate the tie-rod.

5   Unscrew the tie-rod end from the tie-rod.

INSTALLATION

6   Thread the tie-rod end on to the marked position and insert the tie-rod stud into the steering knuckle arm. Tighten the jam nut securely.

7   Install the castle nut on the stud and tighten it to the torque listed in this Chapter's Specifications. Install a new cotter pin.

8   Install the wheel and lug nuts. Lower the vehicle and tighten the lug nuts to the torque listed in the Chapter 1 Specifications.

9   Have the alignment checked by a dealer service department or an alignment shop.

17.4 Install a small puller as shown to separate the tie-rod end from the steering knuckle

18 Steering gear boots - replacement

▶ **Refer to illustration 18.3**

1   Loosen the lug nuts, raise the vehicle and support it securely on jackstands. Remove the wheel.

2   Remove the tie-rod end and jam nut (see Section 17).

3   Remove the steering gear boot clamps (see illustration) and slide off the boot.

4   Before installing the new boot, wrap the threads and serrations on the end of the steering rod with a layer of tape so the small end of the new boot isn't damaged.

5   Slide the new boot into position on the steering gear until it seats in the groove in the steering rod and install new clamps.

6   Remove the tape and install the tie-rod end (see Section 17).

7   Install the wheel and lug nuts. Lower the vehicle and tighten the lug nuts to the torque listed in the Chapter 1 Specifications.

18.3 Remove the outer clamp from the steering gear boot with a pair of pliers; the inner clamp (not visible in this photo) must be cut or pried off

19 Steering gear - removal and installation

✳️ WARNING:

Make sure the steering shaft is not turned while the steering gear is removed or you could damage the spiral cable for the airbag system. To prevent the shaft from turning, place the ignition key in the lock position or thread the seat belt through the steering wheel and clip it into place.

REMOVAL

▶ **Refer to illustrations 19.2, 19.3 and 19.6**

1   Park the vehicle with the front wheels pointing straight ahead. Loosen the front wheel lug nuts, raise the front of the vehicle and support it securely on jackstands. Apply the parking brake and remove the wheels. Remove the engine under-covers on models so equipped.

2   Place a drain pan under the steering gear. Detach the power steering pressure and return lines (see illustration) and cap the ends to prevent excessive fluid loss and contamination. Detach the tube-support bracket from the top of the steering gear assembly.

19.2 Disconnect the power steering fluid line fittings from the steering gear, using a crow's-foot wrench and a short extension

19.3 Remove the U-joint pinch bolt (seen here through the fenderwell opening)

3   Mark the relationship of the lower universal joint to the steering gear input shaft. Remove the lower intermediate shaft pinch bolt (see illustration).

4   Separate the tie-rod ends from the steering knuckle arms (see Section 17).

5   Remove the stabilizer bar end links and bushing retainer bolts (see Section 2). (You can't remove the steering gear mounting bolts until the stabilizer bar is lifted up out of the way.)

6   Remove the steering gear mounting nuts (see illustration), lift up the stabilizer bar and knock out the steering gear mounting bolts.

➡**Note: On V6 models, remove the steering gear heat shield.**

7   Separate the intermediate shaft from the steering gear input shaft and pull the steering gear assembly out from the right side.

8   Check the steering gear mounting grommets for excessive wear or deterioration, replacing them if necessary.

19.6 Steering gear mounting nuts

INSTALLATION

9   Raise the steering gear into position and connect the U-joint, aligning the marks.

10 Install the mounting bolts and nuts and tighten them to the torque listed in this Chapter's Specifications.

11 Connect the tie-rod ends to the steering knuckle arms (see Section 17).

12 Install the U-joint pinch bolt and tighten it to the torque listed in this Chapter's Specifications.

13 Connect the power steering pressure and return hoses to the steering gear and fill the power steering pump reservoir with the recommended fluid (see Chapter 1). Reattach the bracket to the top of the steering gear assembly.

14 Install the stabilizer bar bushing retainer bolts and tighten them to the torque listed in this Chapter's Specifications.

15 Lower the vehicle and bleed the steering system (see Section 22).

20 Power steering pump - removal and installation

REMOVAL

▶ **Refer to illustrations 20.4, 20.6 and 20.8**

1   Disconnect the cable from the negative battery terminal (see Chapter 5, Section 1).

2   Using a large syringe or suction gun, suck as much fluid out of the power steering fluid reservoir as possible. Place a drain pan under the vehicle to catch any fluid that spills out when the hoses are disconnected.

3   Loosen the right front wheel lug nuts, raise the vehicle and support it securely on jackstands. Remove the right front wheel.

4   Remove the right front fender apron seal (see illustration).

5   Remove the drivebelt (see Chapter 1).

6   Detach the fluid feed hose from the pump (see illustration). Disconnect the electrical connector from the Power Steering Pressure (PSP) switch (see Section 21).

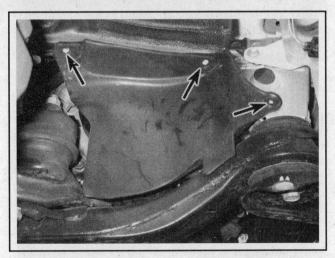

20.4 Remove the three screws and the plastic inner seal from the fenderwell

20.6 Installation details of the power steering pump assembly (four-cylinder engine). Remove the banjo bolt (A) and the feed line fitting bolt (B)

20.8 Power steering pump pivot bolt (four-cylinder engine) - turn the pulley until an opening is over the upper bolt for access

7   Remove the pressure line-to-pump union bolt and separate the line from the pump (see illustration 20.6). Use two wrenches, one to hold the pressure port fitting and one to hold the union bolt. Remove the sealing washers on each side of the fitting - these should be replaced when installing the pump.

8   Remove the pivot, adjuster and any other mounting bolts, and remove the pump (see illustration).

➡**Note: The upper bolt does not come out. Loosen it enough to release it from the engine, and the bolt will come out with the pump.**

INSTALLATION

9   Installation is the reverse of removal. Be sure to tighten the pressure line banjo bolt, the feed line fitting bolt and the adjuster and pivot bolts to the torque listed in this Chapter's Specifications. Adjust the drivebelt tension (see Chapter 1).

10   Top up the fluid level in the reservoir (see Chapter 1) and bleed the system (see Section 22).

21 Power Steering Pressure (PSP) switch - check and replacement

CHECK

▶ **Refer to illustration 21.4**

1   The Power Steering Pressure (PSP) switch is located at the high pressure line outlet fitting of the power steering pump.

2   When steering system pressure reaches a high-pressure setpoint, the PSP switch closes and sends a signal to the PCM that the PCM uses to maintain engine idle speed during parking maneuvers.

3   Check the operation of the PSP switch if the engine stalls during parking or if the engine idles continuously at high rpm.

4   Loosen the right front wheel lug nuts, raise the vehicle and support it securely on jackstands. Remove the right front wheel and the right front fender apron seal (see illustration 20.4). Disconnect the PSP switch connector and connect an ohmmeter to the terminal and the switch body (see illustration).

5   Start the engine and let it idle.

6   Turn the steering wheel to point the front wheels straight ahead and read the ohmmeter. It should indicate no continuity (infinite resistance).

7   Turn the steering wheel to each side and watch the ohmmeter. The PSP switch should close as the wheel nears the steering stop on each side, and the meter should indicate continuity (zero ohms).

8   If the switch fails either test, replace it.

21.4 Location of the Power Steering Pressure (PSP) switch

REPLACEMENT

9   Raise the vehicle and support it securely on jackstands.

10   Disconnect the cable from the negative battery terminal (see Chapter 5, Section 1).

11 Disconnect the electrical connector from the switch and unscrew the switch from the fitting on the steering pump. Remove the old O-ring on the switch and install a new O-ring.

12 Install and connect the new switch and lower the vehicle to the ground.

13 Refer to Section 22 and bleed air from the power steering system. Add fluid as required (see Chapter 1).

22 Power steering system - bleeding

1 Following any operation in which the power steering fluid lines have been disconnected, the power steering system must be bled to remove all air and obtain proper steering performance.

2 With the front wheels in the straight ahead position, check the power steering fluid level and, if low, add fluid until it reaches the Cold mark on the dipstick.

3 Start the engine and allow it to run at fast idle. Recheck the fluid level and add more if necessary to reach the Cold mark on the dipstick.

4 Bleed the system by turning the wheels from side to side, without hitting the stops. This will work the air out of the system. Keep the reservoir full of fluid as this is done.

➡Note: This procedure can be done with the front of the vehicle raised with a jack and supported on jackstands. This makes it easier to turn the wheels back and forth during the bleeding process.

5 When the air is worked out of the system, return the wheels to the straight-ahead position and leave the vehicle running for several more minutes before shutting it off.

6 Road test the vehicle to be sure the steering system is functioning normally and noise free.

7 Recheck the fluid level to be sure it is up to the Hot mark on the dipstick while the engine is at normal operating temperature. Add fluid if necessary (see Chapter 1).

23 Wheels and tires - general information

▶ Refer to illustration 23.1

1 All vehicles covered by this manual are equipped with metric-sized fiberglass or steel belted radial tires (see illustration). Use of other size or type of tires may affect the ride and handling of the vehicle. Don't mix different types of tires, such as radials and bias belted, on the same vehicle as handling may be seriously affected. It's recommended that tires be replaced in pairs on the same axle, but if only one tire is being replaced, be sure it's the same size, structure and tread design as the other.

2 Because tire pressure has a substantial effect on handling and wear, the pressure on all tires should be checked at least once a month or before any extended trips (see Chapter 1).

3 Wheels must be replaced if they are bent, dented, leak air, have elongated bolt holes, are heavily rusted, out of vertical symmetry or if the lug nuts won't stay tight. Wheel repairs that use welding or peening are not recommended.

4 Tire and wheel balance is important in the overall handling, braking and performance of the vehicle. Unbalanced wheels can adversely affect handling and ride characteristics as well as tire life. Whenever a tire is installed on a wheel, the tire and wheel should be balanced by a shop with the proper equipment.

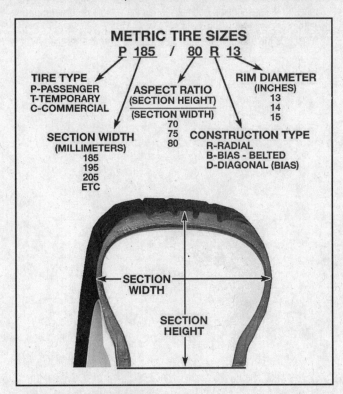

23.1 Metric tire size code

24   Wheel alignment - general information

▶ **Refer to illustration 24.1**

A wheel alignment refers to the adjustments made to the wheels so they are in proper angular relationship to the suspension and the ground. Wheels that are out of proper alignment not only affect vehicle control, but also increase tire wear. The alignment angles normally measured are camber, caster and toe-in (see illustration). Toe-in is the only adjustable angle on the front or the rear. The other angles should be measured to check for bent or worn suspension parts.

Getting the proper wheel alignment is a very exacting process, one in which complicated and expensive machines are necessary to perform the job properly. Because of this, you should have a technician with the proper equipment perform these tasks. We will, however, use this space to give you a basic idea of what is involved with a wheel alignment so you can better understand the process and deal intelligently with the shop that does the work.

Toe-in is the turning in of the wheels. The purpose of a toe specification is to ensure parallel rolling of the wheels. In a vehicle with zero toe-in, the distance between the front edges of the wheels will be the same as the distance between the rear edges of the wheels. The actual amount of toe-in is normally only a fraction of an inch. On the front end, toe-in is controlled by the tie-rod end position on the tie-rod. On the rear end, it's controlled by a threaded adjuster on the rear (number two) suspension arm. Incorrect toe-in will cause the tires to wear improperly by making them scrub against the road surface.

Camber is the tilting of the wheels from vertical when viewed from one end of the vehicle. When the wheels tilt out at the top, the camber is said to be positive (+). When the wheels tilt in at the top the camber is negative (-). The amount of tilt is measured in degrees from vertical and this measurement is called the camber angle. This angle affects the amount of tire tread which contacts the road and compensates for changes in the suspension geometry when the vehicle is cornering or traveling over an undulating surface.

Caster is the tilting of the front steering axis from the vertical. A tilt

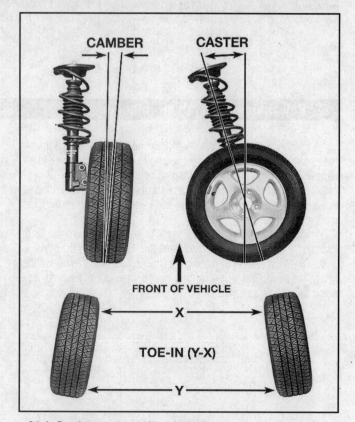

24.1 Camber, caster and toe-in angle

toward the rear is positive caster and a tilt toward the front is negative caster. Too little caster will make the front end wander, while too much caster can make the steering effort higher.

Torque specifications   Ft-lbs (unless otherwise indicated)

➡ Note: One foot-pound (ft-lb) of torque is equivalent to 12 inch-pounds (in-lbs) of torque. Torque values below approximately 15 ft-lbs are expressed in inch-pounds, since most foot-pound torque wrenches are not accurate at these smaller values.

Front suspension

Balljoint	
Balljoint-to-steering knuckle nut	91
Balljoint-to-control arm nuts and bolts	
2002 models	94
2003 models*	
Green bolt and nuts (no strength marks on bolt head)	94
Red bolts and nuts (11 strength mark on bolt head)	55
2004 and later models	55
Control arm-to-cradle bolts	
Front bolts	148
Rear bolts	152
Stabilizer bar	
Stabilizer bar link nuts	55
Stabilizer bushing/retainer bolts	
2002 through 2006	16
2007 and later	20
Strut	
Strut upper mounting nuts	59
Strut-to-suspension support (damper shaft) nut	
2002 through 2006	36
2007 and later	52
Strut-to-steering knuckle bolts/nuts	
Camry, Avalon and Lexus	155
Solara	
2002 and 2003 models	162
2004 and later models	155

* Models built after the following Vehicle Identification Numbers (VIN) have the red bolt and nuts:
   Avalon - 4T1BF28B23U334113
   Camry (including Solara) - 4T1B*32K33U235298, JTDB*32K530239509
   Lexus - JTHBF30G936019295, JTHBF30G930150701

Rear suspension

Crossmember fasteners	41
Hub and bearing assembly-to-axle carrier bolts	59
Strut	
Strut upper mounting nuts	29
Strut-to-suspension support (damper shaft) nut	
2002 through 2006	36
2007 and later	41
Strut-to-axle carrier nuts/bolts	
2002 through 2006	188
2007 and later	133
Stabilizer bar	
Stabilizer bar link-to-strut assembly	29
Stabilizer bushing/retainer bolts	168 in-lbs

Torque specifications   Ft-lbs (unless otherwise indicated)

➡ **Note:** One foot-pound (ft-lb) of torque is equivalent to 12 inch-pounds (in-lbs) of torque. Torque values below approximately 15 ft-lbs are expressed in inch-pounds, since most foot-pound torque wrenches are not accurate at these smaller values.

Rear suspension (continued)

Suspension arms	
Camry	
No. 1/No. 2 arm-to-body	
through-bolt nut	74
No. 1/No. 2 arm-to-axle carrier	
through-bolt nut	74
Solara	
2002 and 2003 models	
No. 1/No. 2 arm-to-body	
through-bolt nut	134
No. 1/No. 2 arm-to-axle carrier	
through-bolt nut	134
2004 and later models	
No. 1/No. 2 arm-to-body	
through-bolt nut	74
No. 1/No. 2 arm-to-axle carrier	
through-bolt nut	74
Avalon	
No. 1/No. 2 arm-to-body	
through-bolt nut	134
No. 1/No. 2 arm-to-axle carrier	
through-bolt nut	134
Lexus	
No. 1/No. 2 arm-to-body	
through-bolt nut	74
No. 1/No. 2 arm-to-axle carrier	
through-bolt nut	74
Strut rod-to-body bolt	83
Strut rod-to-axle carrier bolt	83

Steering system

Airbag module retaining screws	78 in-lbs
Steering wheel nut	37
Steering gear mounting bolts/nuts	52
Steering shaft universal joint pinch bolt	26
Tie-rod end-to-steering knuckle nut	36
Power steering pump	
Adjuster and pivot bolts	32
Pressure line banjo bolt	38
Feed line fitting bolt	120 in-lbs
Wheel lug nuts	See Chapter 1

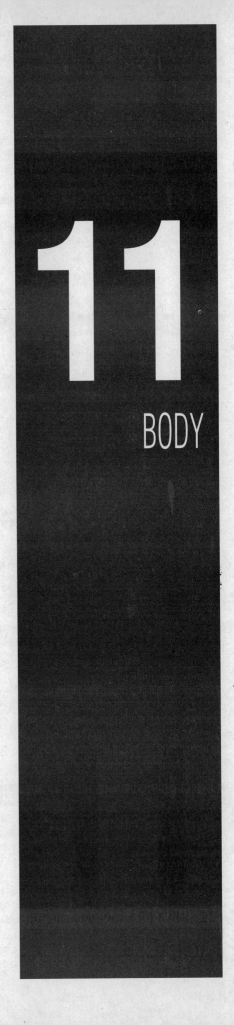

11

BODY

Section

1   General information
2   Body - maintenance
3   Vinyl trim - maintenance
4   Upholstery and carpets - maintenance
5   Body repair - minor damage
6   Body repair - major damage
7   Hinges and locks - maintenance
8   Windshield and fixed glass - replacement
9   Hood - removal, installation and adjustment
10   Hood latch and release cable - removal and installation
11   Bumper covers - removal and installation
12   Front fender - removal and installation
13   Trunk lid - removal, installation and adjustment
14   Trunk lid latch and lock cylinder - removal and installation
15   Trunk release and fuel door cables - removal and installation
16   Door trim panels - removal and installation
17   Door - removal, installation and adjustment
18   Door latch, lock cylinder and handle - removal and installation
19   Door window glass - removal and installation
20   Door window glass regulator - removal and installation
21   Mirrors - removal and installation
22   Center console - removal and installation
23   Dashboard trim panels - removal and installation
24   Steering column covers - removal and installation
25   Instrument panel - removal and installation
26   Cowl cover - removal and installation
27   Seats - removal and installation
28   Rear package shelf - removal and installation

1   General information

These models feature a "unibody" layout, using a floor pan with front and rear frame side rails which support the body components, front and rear suspension systems and other mechanical components.

Certain components are particularly vulnerable to accident damage and can be unbolted and repaired or replaced. Among these parts are the body moldings, bumpers, front fenders, the hood and trunk lid, doors and all glass.

Only general body maintenance practices and body panel repair procedures within the scope of the do-it-yourselfer are included in this Chapter.

> ✳✳ **WARNING:**
>
> The front seat belts on some models are equipped with pre-tensioners, which are pyrotechnic (explosive) devices designed to retract the seat belts in the event of a collision. On models equipped with pre-tensioners, do not remove the front seat belt retractor assemblies, and do not disconnect the electrical connectors leading to the assemblies. Problems with the pre-tensioners will turn on the SRS (airbag) warning light on the dash. If any pre-tensioner problems are suspected, take the vehicle to a dealer service department.

2   Body - maintenance

1   The condition of your vehicle's body is very important, because the resale value depends a great deal on it. It's much more difficult to repair a neglected or damaged body than it is to repair mechanical components. The hidden areas of the body, such as the wheel wells, the frame and the engine compartment, are equally important, although they don't require as frequent attention as the rest of the body.

2   Once a year, or every 12,000 miles, it's a good idea to have the underside of the body steam-cleaned. All traces of dirt and oil will be removed and the area can then be inspected carefully for rust, damaged brake lines, frayed electrical wires, damaged cables and other problems.

3   At the same time, clean the engine and the engine compartment with a steam cleaner or water-soluble degreaser.

4   The wheel wells should be given close attention, since undercoating can peel away and stones and dirt thrown up by the tires can cause the paint to chip and flake, allowing rust to set in. If rust is found, clean down to the bare metal and apply an anti-rust paint.

5   The body should be washed about once a week. Wet the vehicle thoroughly to soften the dirt, then wash it down with a soft sponge and plenty of clean soapy water. If the surplus dirt is not washed off very carefully, it can wear down the paint.

6   Spots of tar or asphalt thrown up from the road should be removed with a cloth soaked in kerosene. Scented lamp oil is available in most hardware stores and the smell is easier to work with than straight kerosene.

7   Once every six months, wax the body and chrome trim. If a chrome cleaner is used to remove rust from any of the vehicle's plated parts, remember that the cleaner also removes part of the chrome, so use it sparingly. On any plated parts where chrome cleaner is used, use a good paste wax over the plating for extra protection.

3   Vinyl trim - maintenance

Don't clean vinyl trim with detergents, caustic soap or petroleum-based cleaners. Plain soap and water works just fine, with a soft brush to clean dirt that may be ingrained. Wash the vinyl as frequently as the rest of the vehicle.

After cleaning, application of a high quality rubber and vinyl protectant will help prevent oxidation and cracks. The protectant can also be applied to weather stripping, vacuum lines and rubber hoses, which often fail as a result of chemical degradation, and to the tires.

4   Upholstery and carpets - maintenance

1   Every three months remove the floormats and clean the interior of the vehicle (more frequently if necessary). Use a stiff whiskbroom to brush the carpeting and loosen dirt and dust, then vacuum the upholstery and carpets thoroughly, especially along seams and crevices.

2   Dirt and stains can be removed from carpeting with basic household or automotive carpet shampoos available in spray cans. Follow the directions and vacuum again, then use a stiff brush to bring back the "nap" of the carpet.

3   Most interiors have cloth or vinyl upholstery, either of which can be cleaned and maintained with a number of material-specific cleaners or shampoos available in auto supply stores. Follow the directions on the product for usage, and always spot-test any upholstery cleaner on an inconspicuous area (bottom edge of a backseat cushion) to ensure that it doesn't cause a color shift in the material.

4   After cleaning, vinyl upholstery should be treated with a protectant.

➡**Note: Make sure the protectant container indicates the product can be used on seats - some products may make a seat too slippery.**

Do not use protectant on steering wheels.

5   Leather upholstery requires special care. It should be cleaned regularly with saddlesoap or leather cleaner. Never use alcohol, gaso-line, nail polish remover or thinner to clean leather upholstery.

6   After cleaning, regularly treat leather upholstery with a leather conditioner, rubbed in with a soft cotton cloth. Never use car wax on leather upholstery.

7   In areas where the interior of the vehicle is subject to bright sun-light, cover leather seating areas of the seats with a sheet if the vehicle is to be left out for any length of time.

5   Body repair - minor damage

FLEXIBLE PLASTIC BODY PANELS (FRONT AND REAR BUMPER FASCIA)

The following repair procedures are for minor scratches and gouges. Repair of more serious damage should be left to a dealer service department or qualified auto body shop. Below is a list of the equipment and materials necessary to perform the following repair procedures on plastic body panels. Although a specific brand of mate-rial may be mentioned, it should be noted that equivalent products from other manufacturers may be used instead.

Wax, grease and silicone removing solvent
Cloth-backed body tape
Sanding discs
Drill motor with three-inch disc holder
Hand sanding block
Rubber squeegees
Sandpaper
Non-porous mixing palette
Wood paddle or putty knife
Curved-tooth body file
Flexible parts repair material

1   Remove the damaged panel, if necessary or desirable. In most cases, repairs can be carried out with the panel installed.

2   Clean the area(s) to be repaired with a wax, grease and silicone removing solvent applied with a water-dampened cloth.

3   If the damage is structural, that is, if it extends through the panel, clean the backside of the panel area to be repaired as well. Wipe dry.

4   Sand the rear surface about 1-1/2 inches beyond the break.

5   Cut two pieces of fiberglass cloth large enough to overlap the break by about 1-1/2 inches. Cut only to the required length.

6   Mix the adhesive from the repair kit according to the instructions included with the kit, and apply a layer of the mixture approximately 1/8-inch thick on the backside of the panel. Overlap the break by at least 1-1/2 inches.

7   Apply one piece of fiberglass cloth to the adhesive and cover the cloth with additional adhesive. Apply a second piece of fiberglass cloth to the adhesive and immediately cover the cloth with additional adhe-sive in sufficient quantity to fill the weave.

8   Allow the repair to cure for 20 to 30 minutes at 60-degrees to 80-degrees F.

9   If necessary, trim the excess repair material at the edge.

10 Remove all of the paint film over and around the area(s) to be repaired. The repair material should not overlap the painted surface.

11 With a drill motor and a sanding disc (or a rotary file), cut a "V" along the break line approximately 1/2-inch wide. Remove all dust and loose particles from the repair area.

12 Mix and apply the repair material. Apply a light coat first over the damaged area; then continue applying material until it reaches a level slightly higher than the surrounding finish.

13 Cure the mixture for 20 to 30 minutes at 60-degrees to 80-degrees F.

14 Roughly establish the contour of the area being repaired with a body file. If low areas or pits remain, mix and apply additional adhe-sive.

15 Block sand the damaged area with sandpaper to establish the actual contour of the surrounding surface.

16 If desired, the repaired area can be temporarily protected with several light coats of primer. Because of the special paints and tech-niques required for flexible body panels, it is recommended that the vehicle be taken to a paint shop for completion of the body repair.

STEEL BODY PANELS

See photo sequence

Repair of minor scratches

17 If the scratch is superficial and does not penetrate to the metal of the body, repair is very simple. Lightly rub the scratched area with a fine rubbing compound to remove loose paint and built up wax. Rinse the area with clean water.

18 Apply touch-up paint to the scratch, using a small brush. Con-tinue to apply thin layers of paint until the surface of the paint in the scratch is level with the surrounding paint. Allow the new paint at least two weeks to harden, then blend it into the surrounding paint by rub-bing with a very fine rubbing compound. Finally, apply a coat of wax to the scratch area.

19 If the scratch has penetrated the paint and exposed the metal of the body, causing the metal to rust, a different repair technique is required. Remove all loose rust from the bottom of the scratch with a pocketknife, then apply rust inhibiting paint to prevent the formation of rust in the future. Using a rubber or nylon applicator, coat the scratched area with glaze-type filler. If required, the filler can be mixed with thinner to provide a very thin paste, which is ideal for filling narrow scratches. Before the glaze filler in the scratch hardens, wrap a piece of smooth cotton cloth around the tip of a finger. Dip the cloth in thin-ner and then quickly wipe it along the surface of the scratch. This will ensure that the surface of the filler is slightly hollow. The scratch can now be painted over as described earlier in this Section.

REPAIR OF DENTS

20 When repairing dents, the first job is to pull the dent out until the affected area is as close as possible to its original shape. There is no point in trying to restore the original shape completely as the metal in the damaged area will have stretched on impact and cannot be restored

These photos illustrate a method of repairing simple dents. They are intended to supplement Body repair - minor damage in this Chapter and should not be used as the sole instructions for body repair on these vehicles.

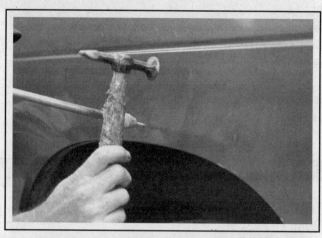

1   If you can't access the backside of the body panel to hammer out the dent, pull it out with a slide-hammer-type dent puller. In the deepest portion of the dent or along the crease line, drill or punch hole(s) at least one inch apart . . .

2   . . . then screw the slide-hammer into the hole and operate it. Tap with a hammer near the edge of the dent to help 'pop' the metal back to its original shape. When you're finished, the dent area should be close to its original contour and about 1/8-inch below the surface of the surrounding metal

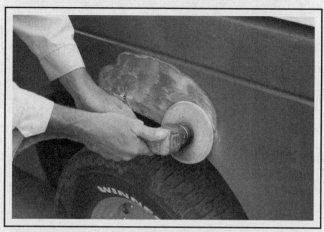

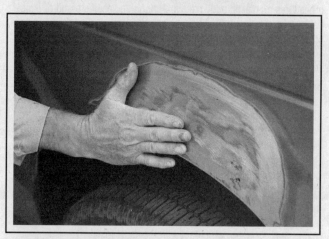

3   Using coarse-grit sandpaper, remove the paint down to the bare metal. Hand sanding works fine, but the disc sander shown here makes the job faster. Use finer (about 320-grit) sandpaper to feather-edge the paint at least one inch around the dent area

4   When the paint is removed, touch will probably be more helpful than sight for telling if the metal is straight. Hammer down the high spots or raise the low spots as necessary. Clean the repair area with wax/silicone remover

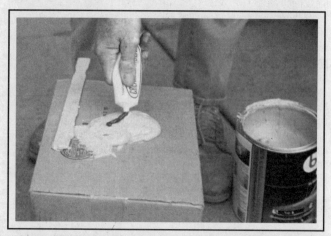

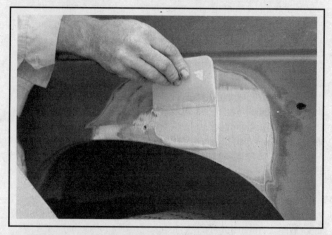

5   Following label instructions, mix up a batch of plastic filler and hardener. The ratio of filler to hardener is critical, and, if you mix it incorrectly, it will either not cure properly or cure too quickly (you won't have time to file and sand it into shape)

6   Working quickly so the filler doesn't harden, use a plastic applicator to press the body filler firmly into the metal, assuring it bonds completely. Work the filler until it matches the original contour and is slightly above the surrounding metal

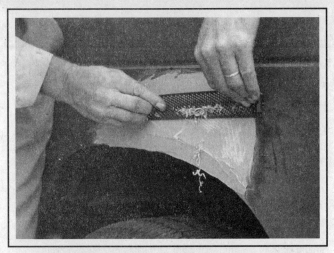

7 Let the filler harden until you can just dent it with your fingernail. Use a body file or Surform tool (shown here) to rough-shape the filler

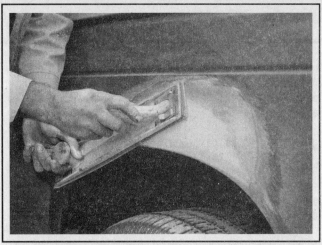

8 Use coarse-grit sandpaper and a sanding board or block to work the filler down until it's smooth and even. Work down to finer grits of sandpaper - always using a board or block - ending up with 360 or 400 grit

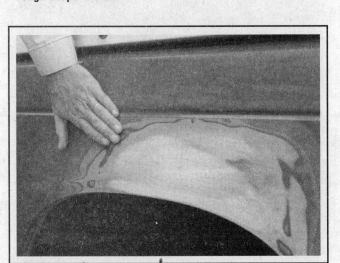

9 You shouldn't be able to feel any ridge at the transition from the filler to the bare metal or from the bare metal to the old paint. As soon as the repair is flat and uniform, remove the dust and mask off the adjacent panels or trim pieces

10 Apply several layers of primer to the area. Don't spray the primer on too heavy, so it sags or runs, and make sure each coat is dry before you spray on the next one. A professional-type spray gun is being used here, but aerosol spray primer is available inexpensively from auto parts stores

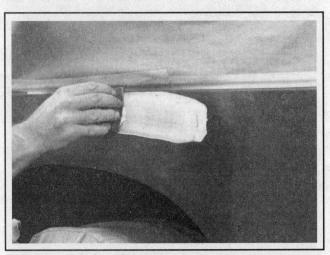

11 The primer will help reveal imperfections or scratches. Fill these with glazing compound. Follow the label instructions and sand it with 360 or 400-grit sandpaper until it's smooth. Repeat the glazing, sanding and respraying until the primer reveals a perfectly smooth surface

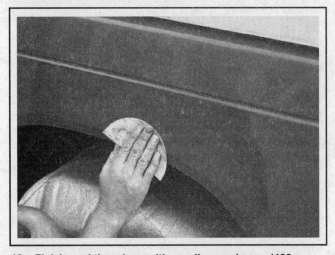

12 Finish sand the primer with very fine sandpaper (400 or 600-grit) to remove the primer overspray. Clean the area with water and allow it to dry. Use a tack rag to remove any dust, then apply the finish coat. Don't attempt to rub out or wax the repair area until the paint has dried completely (at least two weeks)

to its original contours. It is better to bring the level of the dent up to a point that is about 1/8-inch below the level of the surrounding metal. In cases where the dent is very shallow, it is not worth trying to pull it out at all.

21 If the backside of the dent is accessible, it can be hammered out gently from behind using a soft-face hammer. While doing this, hold a block of wood firmly against the opposite side of the metal to absorb the hammer blows and prevent the metal from being stretched.

22 If the dent is in a section of the body which has double layers, or some other factor makes it inaccessible from behind, a different technique is required. Drill several small holes through the metal inside the damaged area, particularly in the deeper sections. Screw long, self-tapping screws into the holes just enough for them to get a good grip in the metal. Now the dent can be pulled out by pulling on the protruding heads of the screws with locking pliers.

23 The next stage of repair is the removal of paint from the damaged area and from an inch or so of the surrounding metal. This is easily done with a wire brush or sanding disk in a drill motor, although it can be done just as effectively by hand with sandpaper. To complete the preparation for filling, score the surface of the bare metal with a screwdriver or the tang of a file or drill small holes in the affected area. This will provide a good grip for the filler material. To complete the repair, see the Section on filling and painting.

REPAIR OF RUST HOLES OR GASHES

24 Remove all paint from the affected area and from an inch or so of the surrounding metal using a sanding disk or wire brush mounted in a drill motor. If these are not available, a few sheets of sandpaper will do the job just as effectively.

25 With the paint removed, you will be able to determine the severity of the corrosion and decide whether to replace the whole panel, if possible, or repair the affected area. New body panels are not as expensive as most people think and it is often quicker to install a new panel than to repair large areas of rust.

26 Remove all trim pieces from the affected area except those which will act as a guide to the original shape of the damaged body, such as headlight shells, etc. Using metal snips or a hacksaw blade, remove all loose metal and any other metal that is badly affected by rust. Hammer the edges of the hole in to create a slight depression for the filler material.

27 Wire brush the affected area to remove the powdery rust from the surface of the metal. If the back of the rusted area is accessible, treat it with rust inhibiting paint.

28 Before filling is done, block the hole in some way. This can be done with sheet metal riveted or screwed into place, or by stuffing the hole with wire mesh.

29 Once the hole is blocked off, the affected area can be filled and painted. See the following subsection on filling and painting.

FILLING AND PAINTING

30 Many types of body fillers are available, but generally speaking, body repair kits which contain filler paste and a tube of resin hardener are best for this type of repair work. A wide, flexible plastic or nylon applicator will be necessary for imparting a smooth and contoured finish to the surface of the filler material. Mix up a small amount of filler on a clean piece of wood or cardboard (use the hardener sparingly). Follow the manufacturer's instructions on the package, otherwise the filler will set incorrectly.

31 Using the applicator, apply the filler paste to the prepared area. Draw the applicator across the surface of the filler to achieve the desired contour and to level the filler surface. As soon as a contour that approximates the original one is achieved, stop working the paste. If you continue, the paste will begin to stick to the applicator. Continue to add thin layers of paste at 20-minute intervals until the level of the filler is just above the surrounding metal.

32 Once the filler has hardened, the excess can be removed with a body file. From then on, progressively finer grades of sandpaper should be used, starting with a 180-grit paper and finishing with 600-grit wet-or-dry paper. Always wrap the sandpaper around a flat rubber or wooden block, otherwise the surface of the filler will not be completely flat. During the sanding of the filler surface, the wet-or-dry paper should be periodically rinsed in water. This will ensure that a very smooth finish is produced in the final stage.

33 At this point, the repair area should be surrounded by a ring of bare metal, which in turn should be encircled by the finely feathered edge of good paint. Rinse the repair area with clean water until all of the dust produced by the sanding operation is gone.

34 Spray the entire area with a light coat of primer. This will reveal any imperfections in the surface of the filler. Repair the imperfections with fresh filler paste or glaze filler and once more smooth the surface with sandpaper. Repeat this spray-and-repair procedure until you are satisfied that the surface of the filler and the feathered edge of the paint are perfect. Rinse the area with clean water and allow it to dry completely.

35 The repair area is now ready for painting. Spray painting must be carried out in a warm, dry, windless and dust free atmosphere. These conditions can be created if you have access to a large indoor work area, but if you are forced to work in the open, you will have to pick the day very carefully. If you are working indoors, dousing the floor in the work area with water will help settle the dust that would otherwise be in the air. If the repair area is confined to one body panel, mask off the surrounding panels. This will help minimize the effects of a slight mismatch in paint color. Trim pieces such as chrome strips, door handles, etc., will also need to be masked off or removed. Use masking tape and several thickness of newspaper for the masking operations.

36 Before spraying, shake the paint can thoroughly, then spray a test area until the spray painting technique is mastered. Cover the repair area with a thick coat of primer. The thickness should be built up using several thin layers of primer rather than one thick one. Using 600-grit wet-or-dry sandpaper, rub down the surface of the primer until it is very smooth. While doing this, the work area should be thoroughly rinsed with water and the wet-or-dry sandpaper periodically rinsed as well. Allow the primer to dry before spraying additional coats.

37 Spray on the top coat, again building up the thickness by using several thin layers of paint. Begin spraying in the center of the repair area and then, using a circular motion, work out until the whole repair area and about two inches of the surrounding original paint is covered. Remove all masking material 10 to 15 minutes after spraying on the final coat of paint. Allow the new paint at least two weeks to harden, then use a very fine rubbing compound to blend the edges of the new paint into the existing paint. Finally, apply a coat of wax.

6   Body repair - major damage

1   Major damage must be repaired by an auto body shop specifically equipped to perform unibody repairs. These shops have the specialized equipment required to do the job properly.
2   If the damage is extensive, the body must be checked for proper alignment or the vehicle's handling characteristics may be adversely affected and other components may wear at an accelerated rate.

3   Due to the fact that some of the major body components (hood, fenders, doors, etc.) are separate and replaceable units, any seriously damaged components should be replaced rather than repaired. Sometimes the components can be found in a wrecking yard that specializes in used vehicle components, often at considerable savings over the cost of new parts.

7   Hinges and locks - maintenance

Once every 3000 miles, or every three months, the hinges and latch assemblies on the doors, hood and trunk should be given a few drops of light oil or lock lubricant. The door latch strikers should also

be lubricated with a thin coat of grease to reduce wear and ensure free movement. Lubricate the door and trunk locks with spray-on graphite lubricant.

8   Windshield and fixed glass - replacement

Replacement of the windshield and fixed glass requires the use of special fast-setting adhesive/caulk materials and some specialized tools

and techniques. These operations should be left to a dealer service department or a shop specializing in glass work.

9   Hood - removal, installation and adjustment

➡Note: The hood is somewhat awkward to remove and install, at least two people should perform this procedure.

REMOVAL AND INSTALLATION

▶ Refer to illustrations 9.3 and 9.4

1   Open the hood, then place blankets or pads over the fenders and cowl area of the body. This will protect the body and paint as the hood is lifted off.

2   Disconnect any cables or wires that will interfere with removal. Disconnect the windshield washer tubing from the nozzles on the hood.
3   Make marks around the hood hinge to ensure proper alignment during installation (see illustration).
4   Have an assistant support the weight of the hood and detach the support struts by prying out the clips at the top (see illustration).
5   Remove the hinge-to-hood bolts and lift off the hood.
6   Installation is the reverse of removal. Align the hinge bolts with the marks made in Step 3.

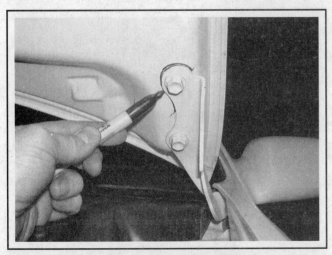

9.3 Draw alignment marks around the hood hinges to ensure proper alignment of the hood when it's reinstalled

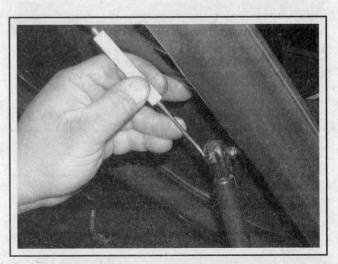

9.4 On models so equipped, detach the hood support struts by prying out the clip and pulling the strut from the stud

9.10 To adjust the hood latch horizontally or vertically, loosen these bolts; the plastic cover must be removed for access to the lower bolt (not visible here)

9.11 To adjust the vertical height of the leading edge of the hood so that it's flush with the fenders, turn each edge cushion clockwise to lower the hood or counter-clockwise to raise the hood

ADJUSTMENT

▶ **Refer to illustrations 9.10 and 9.11**

7   Fore-and-aft and side-to-side adjustment of the hood is done by moving the hinge plate slot after loosening the bolts or nuts.

➡**Note: The factory bolts are "centering" type that will not allow adjustment. To adjust the hood in relation to the hinges, these bolts must be replaced with standard bolts with flat washers and lock washers.**

8   Mark around the entire hinge plate so you can determine the amount of movement.

9   Loosen the bolts and move the hood into correct alignment. Move it only a little at a time. Tighten the hinge bolts and carefully lower the hood to check the position.

10   If necessary after installation, the entire hood latch assembly can be adjusted up-and-down as well as from side-to-side on the radiator support so the hood closes securely and flush with the fenders. Scribe a line or mark around the hood latch mounting bolts to provide a reference point, then loosen them and reposition the latch assembly, as necessary (see illustration). Following adjustment, retighten the mounting bolts.

➡**Note: You will have to remove two clips and a plastic latch cover for access to the lower latch mounting bolt.**

11   Finally, adjust the hood bumpers on the radiator support so the hood, when closed, is flush with the fenders (see illustration).

12   The hood latch assembly, as well as the hinges, should be periodically lubricated with white, lithium-base grease to prevent binding and wear.

10 Hood latch and release cable - removal and installation

✳✳ **WARNING:**

The models covered by this manual are equipped with Supplemental Restraint systems (SRS), more commonly known as airbags. Always disarm the airbag system before working in the vicinity of any airbag system component to avoid the possibility of accidental deployment of the airbag, which could cause personal injury (see Chapter 12).

LATCH

▶ **Refer to illustration 10.2**

1   Scribe a line around the latch to aid alignment when installing, then (on models so equipped) remove the plastic cover over the latch, retained by plastic pins. Remove the retaining bolts securing the hood latch to the radiator support (see illustration 9.10). Remove the latch.

➡**Note: On Solara models, remove the three screws and the radiator grille first for access to the latch.**

10.2 Pry out the cable retainer from the backside of the hood latch assembly, then disengage the cable

2   Disconnect the hood release cable by disengaging the cable from the latch assembly (see illustration).

3   Installation is the reverse of removal.

➡Note: Adjust the latch so the hood engages securely when closed and the hood bumpers are slightly compressed.

CABLE

◆ **Refer to illustration 10.8**

4   Disconnect the hood release cable from the latch assembly as described in Step 2.

5   Attach a piece of thin wire or string to the end of the cable and unclip all remaining cable retaining clips at the radiator support.

6   Refer to Section 12 and remove the plastic inner fenderwell.

7   Working in the passenger compartment, remove the driver's side doorsill cover and kick panel.

8   Refer to Section 23 and remove the driver's knee bolster panel. The hood latch release lever is attached to the panel (see illustration).

9   Pull the cable and grommet rearward into the passenger compartment until you can see the wire or string. Ensure that the new cable has a grommet attached then remove the wire or string from the old cable and fasten it to the new cable.

10 With the new cable attached to the wire or string, pull the wire or string back through the firewall until the new cable reaches the latch assembly.

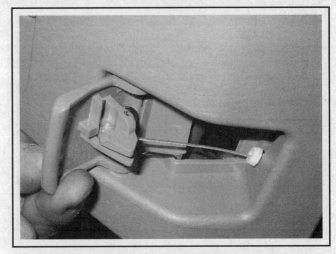

10.8 Remove the knee bolster and remove the cable end from the release lever assembly

11 Working in the passenger compartment, reinstall the new cable into the hood release lever, making sure the cable housing fits snugly into the notch in the handle bracket.

12 The remainder of the installation is the reverse of removal.

➡Note: Push on the grommet with your fingers from the passenger compartment to seat the grommet in the firewall correctly.

11 Bumper covers - removal and installation

✳✳ WARNING:

The models covered by this manual are equipped with Supplemental Restraint systems (SRS), more commonly known as airbags. Always disarm the airbag system before working in the vicinity of any airbag system component to avoid the possibility of accidental deployment of the airbag, which could cause personal injury (see Chapter 12).

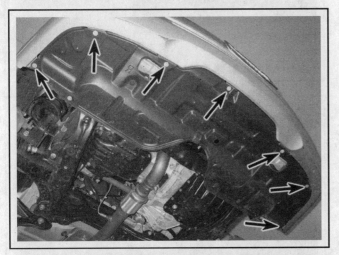

11.3a Remove the screws retaining the splash apron and the bottom edge of the front bumper cover (Camry shown)

FRONT BUMPER

◆ **Refer to illustrations 11.3a, 11.3b and 11.3c**

1   Refer to Section 12 and pull back the front portion of the fenderwell liner. Apply the parking brake, raise the vehicle and support it securely on jackstands.

2   Disconnect the negative cable from the negative terminal of the battery (see Chapter 5, Section 1). On models equipped with fog lights, disconnect the electrical connectors at the fog lights on the back of the bumper fascia.

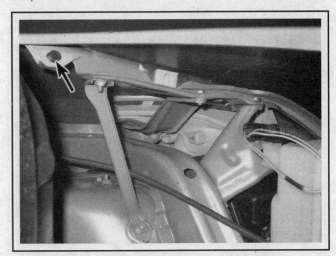

11.3b With the splash shield removed, remove the one fender-to-bumper cover bolt at each side

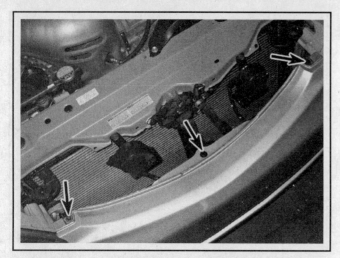

11.3c Remove the screws/pushpins along the top edge of the bumper cover (Camry shown)

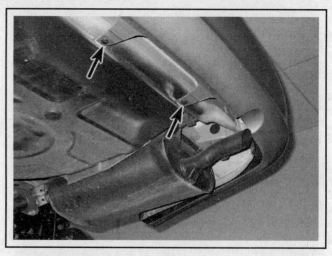

11.7 Remove the pins at the bottom of the rear bumper cover (Camry shown)

3   Detach the screws and/or pushpins securing the top, bottom and sides of the bumper cover (see illustrations).

➡**Note 1: Use a small screwdriver to pop the center button up on the plastic fasteners, but do not try to remove the center buttons. They stay in the ferrules.**

➡**Note 2: The number and location of the fascia screws varies among the different models. Don't try to remove the fascia until all fasteners have been located and removed.**

4   On Solara models, remove the three screws and the radiator grille.

5   Remove the cover. On Lexus models, there are four clips where the fascia meets the front of the fenders. Pull outward on the ends of the fascia to release the clips.

6   Installation is the reverse of removal. Make sure the tabs on the back of the bumper cover fit into the corresponding clips on the body before attaching the bolts and screws. An assistant would be helpful at this point.

REAR BUMPER

▶ **Refer to illustrations 11.7, 11.8, 11.9a and 11.9b**

7   Working under the vehicle, detach the plastic clips and screws

securing the lower edge of the bumper cover (see illustration).

8   In the rear fenderwells, remove the screw(s) securing the front edge of the fascia to the fenderwell. On some models, the plastic fenderwell liner must be released for access (see illustration).

9   Remove the fasteners securing the bumper cover in each corner inside the trunk, and those behind the rear trunk trim panel (see illustrations). To access these fasteners, pull up the trunk mat, then use a trim tool to release the clips securing the rear trunk trim panel and the left and right rear corner panels.

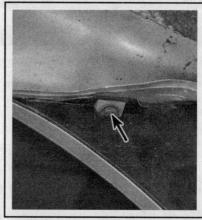

11.8 Remove the fasteners where the rear fascia meets the fenderwell - typical

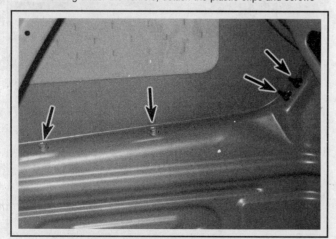

11.9a Inside the trunk with the corner panels removed, remove the two nuts and two bolts (Camry shown)

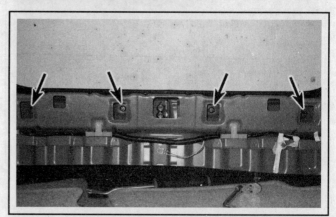

11.9b At the rear of the trunk, remove the four nuts (trim panel removed here)

10 Open the trunk lid and remove the clips or pins securing the upper edge of the bumper cover. Pull the bumper cover out and away from the vehicle.

➡**Note: Use a small screwdriver to pop the center button up on** the plastic fasteners, but do not try to remove the center buttons - they stay in the ferrules. Where studs/bolts stick through the body, use a plastic hammer to tap them out of the body.

11 Installation is the reverse of removal.

12 Front fender - removal and installation

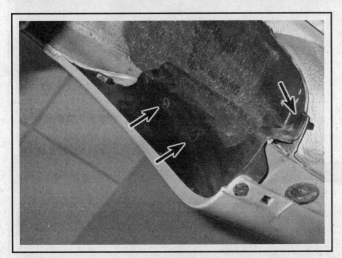

12.3a Remove the bolts at the front lower portion of the inner fenderwell

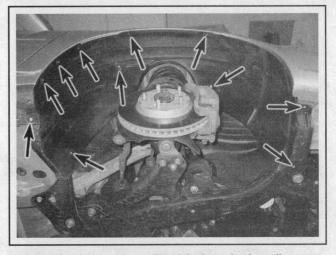

12.3b Detach the main portion of the inner fenderwell, secured by bolts, screws and plastic clips

▶ **Refer to illustrations 12.3a, 12.3b, 12.4, 12.5a, 12.5b and 12.6**

1   Raise the vehicle, support it securely on jackstands and remove the front wheel.

2   On Lexus models, remove the front turn signal light (see Chapter 12).

3   Detach the inner fenderwell screws and clips, then remove the inner fenderwell and mud shield (see illustrations).

4   Open the front door, and remove the upper fender-to-body bolt (see illustration).

5   Unbolt and lower the rocker trim panel to access the lower fender bolt (see illustrations).

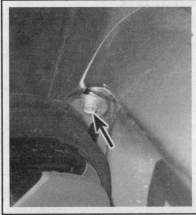

12.4 Remove the upper fender bolt with the door open

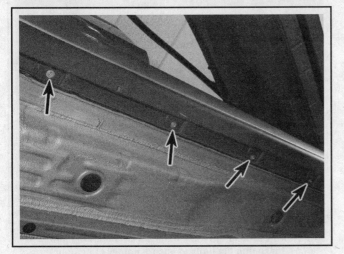

12.5a Remove the bolts securing the rocker trim panel

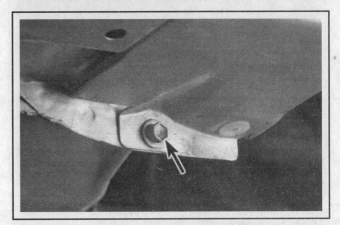

12.5b Remove the lower fender-to-rocker bolt

6   Refer to Section 11 and remove the fascia-to-fender-fasteners. Remove the cowl cover (see Section 26), and the rubber hood sealing strip along the top of the fender, then remove the remaining fender mounting bolts (see illustration).

7   Lift off the fender. It's a good idea to have an assistant support the fender while it's being moved away from the vehicle to prevent damage to the surrounding body panels.

8   Installation is the reverse of removal. Check the alignment of the fender to the hood and front edge of the door before final tightening of the fender fasteners.

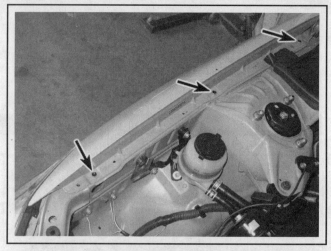

12.6 Remove the three bolts along the top of the fender

13 Trunk lid - removal, installation and adjustment

→Note: The trunk lid is heavy and somewhat awkward to remove and install - at least two people should perform this procedure.

REMOVAL AND INSTALLATION

▶ Refer to illustrations 13.1a, 13.1b and 13.3

1   Open the trunk lid and cover the edges of the trunk compartment with pads or cloths to protect the painted surfaces when the lid is removed. Remove the emergency trunk release handle, then remove the trim fasteners all around the trunk lid trim panel (see illustrations).

2   On Lexus and Avalon models, disconnect the electrical connectors from the backup lights and taillights, then unplug the harness at the front of the trunk lid.

3   Scribe or draw alignment marks around the trunk hinges (see illustration).

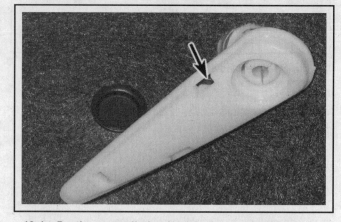

13.1a Pry the cover off, then push in the two tabs (one indicated here) and remove the emergency inside trunk release handle

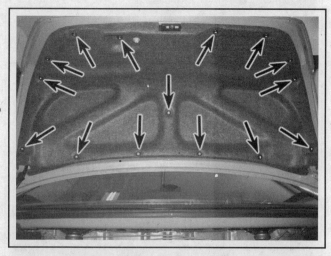

13.1b Remove the plastic fasteners around the perimeter of the trunk lid trim panel

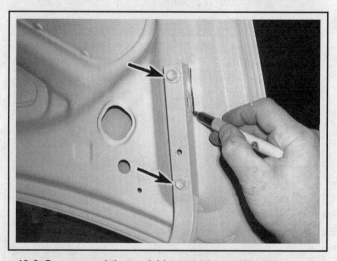

13.3 Draw around the trunk hinges with a marking pen before loosening the bolts to ensure proper alignment of the trunk lid when it's reinstalled

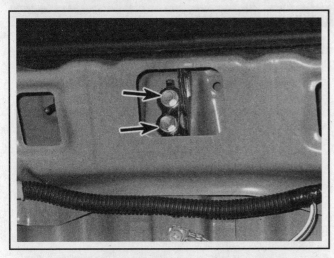

13.7 Loosen the bolts and move the striker as necessary to adjust the trunk lid flush with the body in the closed position

4   Remove the hinge-to-trunk lid bolts from both sides and lift off the trunk lid.

5   Installation is the reverse of removal. Be sure to align the hinge flanges with the marks made on the trunk lid during removal.

ADJUSTMENT

▶ **Refer to illustration 13.7**

6   After installation, close the lid and see if it's in proper alignment with the adjacent body surfaces. Fore-and-aft and side-to-side adjustments of the lid are controlled by the position of the hinge bolts in the slots. To adjust it, loosen the hinge bolts, reposition the lid and retighten the bolts.

7   The height of the rear of the lid in relation to the surrounding body panels when closed can be adjusted by loosening the lock striker bolts, moving the striker up/down or left/right, then re-tightening the bolts (see illustration).

➡**Note: Make a reference mark around the striker before making adjustments.**

---

14   Trunk lid latch and lock cylinder - removal and installation

TRUNK LID LATCH

▶ **Refer to illustration 14.2**

1   Remove the trunk lid trim panel (see illustration 13.1b).

2   Scribe a line around the trunk lid latch assembly for a reference point to aid the installation procedure (see illustration).

3   Detach the two retaining bolts and remove the latch.

4   Disconnect the electrical connector or remove the end of the latch release cable and/or actuator rod(s) from the latch (see illustration 14.2).

5   Installation is the reverse of removal.

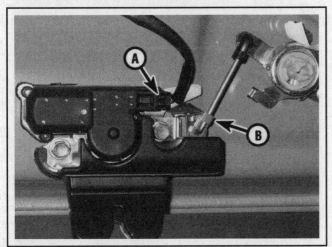

14.2 Scribe around the trunk latch on the trunk lid, then remove the two latch mounting bolts - disconnect the electrical connector (A) and the lock cylinder rod (B)

TRUNK LOCK CYLINDER

▶ **Refer to illustration 14.6**

6   Open the trunk and remove the screws and the trunk lid trim panel. Remove the lock cylinder rod from its clip and remove the lock cylinder mounting bolts (see illustration). On models so equipped, disconnect the electrical connector from the lock.

7   Remove the cylinder from the trunk.

8   Installation is the reverse of removal.

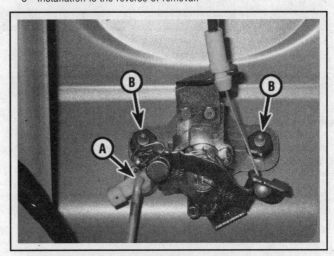

14.6 Pry the rod from its clip (A) and remove the lock cylinder mounting bolts (B)

15 Trunk release and fuel door cables - removal and installation

▶ Refer to illustrations 15.2, 15.6 and 15.7

➡ **Note 1: On Lexus models, the fuel door and trunk releases are both electrically operated - there are no cables.**

➡ **Note 2: The fuel door and trunk release cables are bundled, and are removed/installed together.**

1   Refer to Section 14 for removal of the trunk latch.

2   Inside the trunk, remove the floor mat and left-side panel for access to the fuel door cable end. Push in the tabs of the fuel door latch cable end (white plastic part) and pull it from the fuel door housing (see illustration). To remove the cable end retainer (black plastic) twist it out of the bracket.

3   Remove the rear seat bottom as described in Section 27. On coupe models, both seat back and bottom must be removed.

4   Pry up the driver's side doorsill covers (only one cover on coupe

models). On four-door models, remove the center door pillar's lower trim panel.

5   Peel back the carpeting to access the release cable. Open all of the clips holding the cable to the body.

6   Remove the bolt holding the release handle assembly to the floor (see illustration).

7   Turn the housing over and remove the cable housings from the clips and the eyes from the levers (see illustration).

8   Attach a piece of thin wire to the end of the cable.

9   Working in the trunk compartment, pull the cable towards the rear of the vehicle until you can see the wire.

10 Attach the wire to the front of the new cable and fish it back through the body until it can be attached to the lever. The remainder of the installation is the reverse of removal.

15.2 Twist the fuel door cable end one-quarter turn to remove it from the fuel door housing (Camry models)

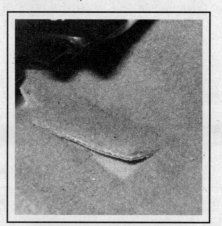

15.6 Open the slit in the carpeting and remove the bolt holding the release mechanism to the floor

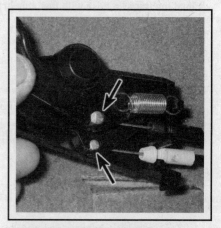

15.7 Remove the cables from the clips and the cable eyes from the slots in the levers

16 Door trim panels - removal and installation

▶ Refer to illustrations 16.2, 16.3, 16.5a, 16.5b and 16.7

❋❋ **WARNING:**

The models covered by this manual are equipped with Supplemental Restraint systems (SRS), more commonly known as airbags. Always disarm the airbag system before working in the vicinity of any airbag system component to avoid the possibility of accidental deployment of the airbag, which could cause personal injury (see Chapter 12).

❋❋ **CAUTION:**

Wear gloves when working inside the door openings to protect against cuts from sharp metal edges.

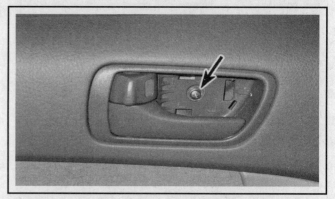

16.2 Remove the decorative cover to reveal the screw, remove the screw and pry the bezel from the door panel

REMOVAL

1   Disconnect the negative battery cable (see Chapter 5, Section 1).

2   Pry out the bezel around the inside door handle, or on some models, remove the setscrew to remove the bezel (see illustration).

3   Pry up the window switch plate to access one panel mounting

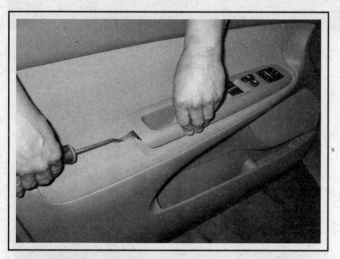

16.3 Pry up the power window switch plate, disconnect the electrical connectors and remove the one screw through the door panel (if present)

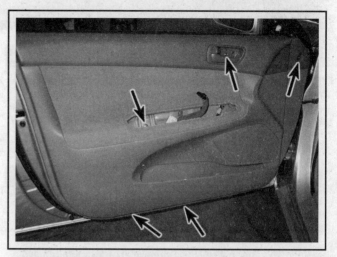

16.5a Remove the mounting screws - the number and location of the screws varies with model (Camry shown)

screw underneath and disconnect the electrical connectors (see illustration).

4   Using a trim tool, pry out the outside mirror trim plate.

5   Remove the door trim panel retaining screws, then carefully pry the panel out until the clips disengage (see illustrations). Work slowly and carefully around the outer edge of the trim panel until it's free.

➡**Note: Most of the screws on the door panel are covered by small plastic discs, which must be pried out before removing the screws.**

6   Once all of the clips are disengaged, pull the trim panel up from the door, unplug any wiring harness connectors, disconnect the inside door handle cables and remove the panel.

7   For access to the door outside handle or the door window regulator inside the door, raise the window fully, remove the power

window control unit (if equipped), the door panel bracket and the speaker assembly (see Chapter 12), then carefully peel back the plastic watershield (see illustration).

INSTALLATION

8   Prior to installation of the door trim panel, be sure to reinstall any clips in the panel which may have come out when you removed the panel.

9   Plug in the wire harness connectors for the power door lock switch and the power window switch, and place the panel in position in the door. Press the door panel into place until the clips are seated. Install the inner door handle and its screw and connect the two cables. Install the power door lock switch assembly, if equipped. Install the power window switch assembly.

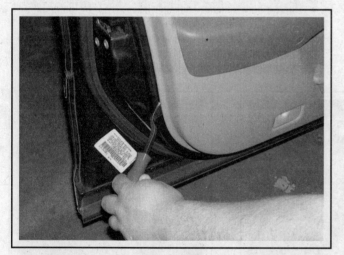

16.5b Carefully use a trim panel tool to pry all around the panel and release the clips

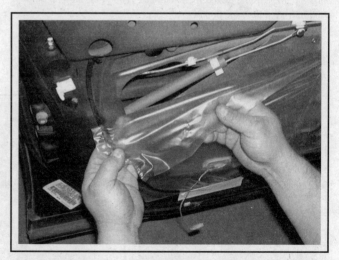

16.7 Carefully peel back the plastic watershield for access to the inner door

17 Door - removal, installation and adjustment

❄❄ WARNING 1:

The models covered by this manual are equipped with Supplemental Restraint systems (SRS), more commonly known as airbags. Always disarm the airbag system before working in the vicinity of any airbag system component to avoid the possibility of accidental deployment of the airbag, which could cause personal injury (see Chapter 12)

❄❄ WARNING 2:

Wear gloves when working inside the door openings to protect against cuts from sharp metal edges.

➡ Note: The door is heavy and somewhat awkward to remove and install - at least two people should perform this procedure.

REMOVAL AND INSTALLATION

⬥ **Refer to illustrations 17.6, 17.8a and 17.8b**

1 Lower the window completely in the door and then disconnect the negative cable from the battery (see Chapter 5, Section 1).

2 Open the door all the way and support it from the ground on jacks or blocks covered with rags to prevent damaging the paint.

3 Remove the door trim panel and watershield as described in Section 16.

4 Disconnect all electrical connections, ground wires and harness retaining clips from the door.

➡ Note: It is a good idea to label all connections to aid the reassembly process.

5 From the door side, detach the rubber conduit between the body and the door. Then pull the wiring harness through the conduit hole and remove it from the door.

6 Remove the doorstop strut bolt (see illustration).

7 Mark around the door hinges with a pen or a scribe to facilitate realignment during reassembly.

8 With an assistant holding the door, remove the hinge-to-door

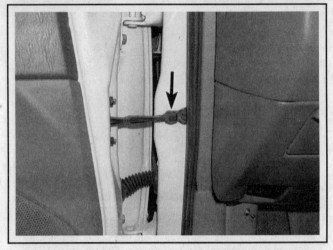

17.6 Remove the bolt retaining the door stop strut

bolts (see illustrations) and lift the door off.

➡ Note: Draw a reference line around the hinges before removing the bolts.

9 Installation is the reverse of removal.

ADJUSTMENT

⬥ **Refer to illustration 17.13**

10 Having proper door-to-body alignment is a critical part of a well-functioning door assembly. First check the door hinge pins for excessive play. Fully open the door and lift up and down on the door without lifting the body. If a door has 1/16-inch or more excessive play, the hinges should be replaced.

11 Door-to-body alignment adjustments are made by loosening the hinge-to-body bolts or hinge-to-door bolts and moving the door. Proper body alignment is achieved when the top of the doors are parallel with the roof section, the front door is flush with the fender, the rear door is flush with the rear quarter panel and the bottom of the doors

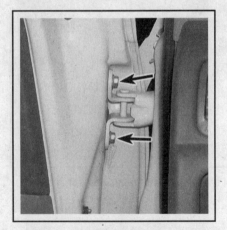

17.8a Remove the door hinge bolts with the door supported (top hinge bolts indicated, bottom hinge similar)

17.8b Open the front door to access the rear door hinge-to-body bolts - the upper hinge has studs going into the B pillar, while the lower hinges are secured by bolts

17.13 Adjust the door lock striker by loosening the mounting screws and gently tapping the striker in the desired direction

are aligned with the lower rocker panel. If these goals can't be reached by adjusting the hinge-to-body or hinge-to-door bolts, body alignment shims may have to be purchased and inserted behind the hinges to achieve correct alignment.

12 To adjust the door-closed position, scribe a line or mark around the striker plate to provide a reference point, then check that the door latch is contacting the center of the latch striker. If not, adjust the up and down position first.

➡Note: On Lexus models, remove the plastic cover over the striker before making adjustments.

13 Finally, adjust the latch striker sideways position, so that the door panel is flush with the center pillar or rear quarter panel and provides positive engagement with the latch mechanism (see illustration).

---

18 Door latch, lock cylinder and handle - removal and installation

✳✳ WARNING:

Wear gloves when working inside the door openings to protect against cuts from sharp metal edges.

DOOR LATCH

▶ **Refer to illustration 18.4**

1 Raise the window, then remove the door trim panel and watershield (see Section 16).

2 Working through the large access hole, disengage the two rods to the outside handle and the lock cylinder.

3 All door lock rods are attached by plastic clips. The plastic clips can be removed by unsnapping the portion engaging the connecting rod and then pulling the rod out of its locating hole. On models with power door locks, disconnect the electrical connectors at the latch.

4 Remove the screws securing the latch to the door (see illustration). Remove the latch assembly through the door opening with the two cables from the inside door handle still attached to the latch.

5 Installation is the reverse of removal.

OUTSIDE HANDLE AND DOOR LOCK CYLINDER

▶ **Refer to illustrations 18.7, 18.8, 18.9, 18.10a and 18.10b**

6 To remove the outside handle and lock cylinder assembly, raise the window and remove the door trim panel and watershield (see Section 16).

✳✳ CAUTION:

Take care not to scratch the paint on the outside of the door. Wide masking tape applied around the handle opening before beginning the procedure can help avoid scratches.

7 Working through the access hole, disengage the plastic clips that secure the outside door lock-to-latch rod (see illustration).

➡Note: The handle can be unbolted and pulled toward the outside of the door to make disconnecting the lock rod easier.

8 Remove an access plug at the rear of the door (jamb side) and use a Torx socket through the hole to loosen the bolt holding the lock cylinder and outside handle cover (see illustration). Slide the handle

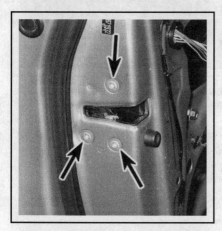

18.4 The latch is secured to the door with three screws

18.7 From inside the door opening, detach the actuating rod

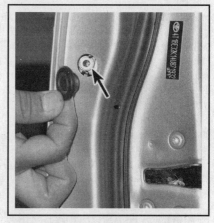

18.8 Remove the rubber plug at the end of the door and use a Torx tool through the hole to loosen the lock cylinder bolt (the bolt does not come out)

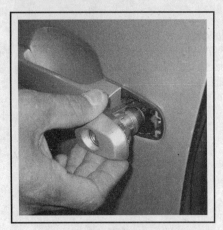

18.9 Slide the lock cylinder out

18.10a From inside the door opening, remove the bolt . . .

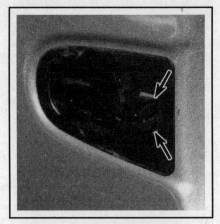

18.10b . . . then squeeze the clip at the outside and remove the door handle assembly from inside the door

rearward and out and the handle will come off.

9   Remove the lock cylinder assembly from the vehicle (see illustration).

10   The lock cylinder can be removed from the handle assembly by removing a clip, or the electrical connector can be unbolted and the cylinder left on the handle assembly (see illustrations).

11   Installation is the reverse of removal.

19 Door window glass - removal and installation

※※ WARNING:

Wear gloves when working inside the door openings to protect against cuts from sharp metal edges.

FRONT DOOR GLASS

▶ **Refer to illustration 19.3**

1   Remove the door trim panel and the plastic watershield (see Section 16).

2   Lower the window glass all the way down into the door.

3   Raise the window just enough to access the window retaining bolts through the holes in the doorframe (see illustration). On Camry models, the two nuts are accessible near the bottom-rear of the door, while on Avalon models the two are accessed near the center of the door, and on Solara and Lexus models there are three nuts accessed with the glass almost all the way up.

4   Place a rag over the glass to help prevent scratching the glass and remove the glass mounting bolts.

5   Remove the glass by pulling it up and out.

6   Installation is the reverse of removal. When installing the glass in Avalon models, make sure the glass is level in the door opening before tightening the bolts.

REAR DOOR GLASS (FOUR-DOOR MODELS)

7   Remove the door panel and watershield (see Section 16). Remove the rear run channel bolt located at the lower portion of the rear jamb on the door.

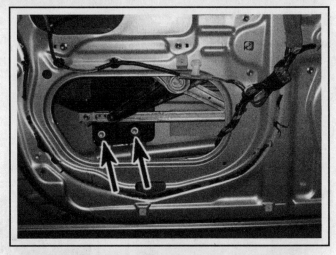

19.3 Raise the window to access the glass retaining bolts through the holes in the doorframe - Camry model shown

8   Lower the window enough to see the bolts on the glass guide bar. Remove the bolts while holding up the glass. Push the glass from the guide bar and remove the glass through the window opening.

9   Installation is the reverse of the removal procedure.

REAR QUARTER GLASS (SOLARA MODELS)

10   Replacement of the fixed quarter glass requires the use of special fast-setting adhesive/caulk materials and some specialized tools and techniques. These operations should be left to a dealer service department or a shop specializing in glass work.

20 Door window glass regulator - removal and installation

☀☀ WARNING:

Wear gloves when working inside the door openings to protect against cuts from sharp metal edges.

FRONT

▶ **Refer to illustration 20.5**

1   Remove the door trim panel and the plastic watershield (see Section 16).

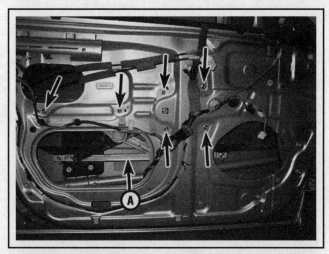

20.5 On Camry and Lexus models, slide the equalizer bar (A) from the bottom rollers, then remove the six mounting screws to remove the regulator/motor from the door

2   Remove the window glass assembly (see Section 19).

3   On power-operated windows, disconnect the electrical connector from the window regulator motor.

4   On Avalon models, remove the regulator/motor assembly mounting fasteners: three nuts at the top, one bolt near the motor, and one nut at the bottom. On Solara models, remove the regulator/motor assembly mounting fasteners: two nuts at the top, three nuts near the motor, and two nuts at the bottom.

5   On Camry and Lexus models, the regulator assembly is a scissors-type. Before removing the bolts, mark the position of the rear bolt of the upper roller guide. Remove the bolts for the lower roller guide (equalizer), then the six screws (nuts on Lexus models) holding the regulator/motor to the door (see illustration).

6   Pull the equalizer arm and regulator assemblies through the service hole in the doorframe to remove it.

7   Installation is the reverse of removal. Lubricate the rollers and wear points on the regulator with white grease before installation.

REAR

8   Remove the door trim panel and the plastic watershield (see Section 16).

9   Remove the window glass assembly (see Section 19).

10 Disconnect the electrical connector from the window regulator motor.

11 Remove the regulator/motor assembly mounting bolts. On all models, the rear regulator/motor assembly is similarly mounted to that model's assembly for the front doors (see above).

12 Remove the equalizer bar and raise the regulator assembly through the service hole in the door frame to remove it.

13 Installation is the reverse of removal. Lubricate the rollers and wear points on the regulator with white grease before installation.

21 Mirrors - removal and installation

OUTSIDE MIRRORS

▶ **Refer to illustration 21.2**

1   Pry off the mirror trim cover on the inside of the door.

2   Disconnect the electrical connector from the mirror (if equipped) (see illustration).

3   Remove the three mirror retaining nuts and detach the mirror from the vehicle.

4   Installation is the reverse of removal.

INSIDE MIRROR

5   To remove/install the mirror, remove/install the screw at the base on the windshield.

6   If the mount plate itself has come off the windshield, adhesive kits are available at auto parts stores to re-secure it. Follow the instructions included with the kit.

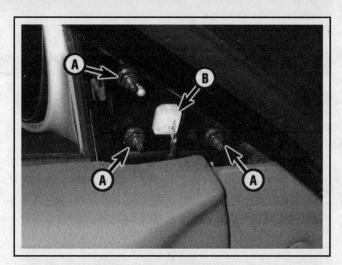

21.2 Remove the three mirror mounting nuts (A) - on electric mirrors, disconnect the connector (B)

22 Center console - removal and installation

▶ Refer to illustrations 22.2 and 22.4

※※ WARNING:

The models covered by this manual are equipped with Supplemental Restraint systems (SRS), more commonly known as airbags. Always disarm the airbag system before working in the vicinity of any airbag system component to avoid the possibility of accidental deployment of the airbag, which could cause personal injury (see Chapter 12).

1   Disconnect the cable from the negative terminal of the battery (see Chapter 5, Section 1).

2   Using a screwdriver with the tip taped to prevent scratching the panels, pry the console upper trim panel off around shifter (see illustration). On Lexus models, there are two trim panels. First remove the small trim panel, then the larger panel beneath it, which is secured by

six clips and two tabs. On manual transaxle models, refer to Chapter 7A and remove the shift knob.

3   On Solara models, disengage the six clips to remove the console upper trim plate, and on Avalon models, pry off a small trim strip at the rear of the shifter trim panel, revealing two screws. Remove the two screws and then pry up the upper trim plate.

4   Lift up the armrest and the cover plate at the floor of the armrest compartment to access the screws for the rear console box (see illustration).

5   Remove the screws at the front of the rear console box and remove the box.

6   Remove the front console screws and lift the console up and over the shift lever. Disconnect any electrical connections and remove the console from the vehicle.

7   Installation is the reverse of removal.

22.2   Use a trim tool to pry up the console upper trim panel

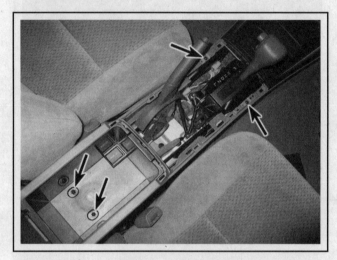

22.4   The rear console box is retained by two bolts in the rear and two screws at the front edge

23 Dashboard trim panels - removal and installation

※※ WARNING:

The models covered by this manual are equipped with Supplemental Restraint systems (SRS), more commonly known as airbags. Always disarm the airbag system before working in the vicinity of any airbag system component to avoid the possibility of accidental deployment of the airbag, which could cause personal injury (see Chapter 12). The yellow wiring harnesses and connectors are for this system. Do not use electrical test equipment on any of the airbag system wiring or tamper with it in any way.

1   Disconnect the cable from the negative terminal of the battery (see Chapter 5, Section 1).

INSTRUMENT CLUSTER BEZEL

▶ Refer to illustration 23.4

2   If equipped with a tilt steering column, tilt the column all the way down.

3   The steering wheel does not need to be removed to access the instrument cluster or bezel.

4   Using a screwdriver with the tip taped with masking tape, carefully pry the lower portion of the bezel away from the instrument panel until the clips are released (see illustration). Take care not to scratch the surrounding trim on the instrument panel.

5   Installation is the reverse of the removal procedure. Make sure

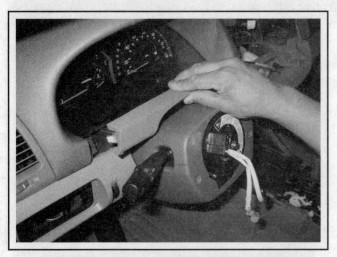

23.4 Carefully pry out the trim panel below the instrument cluster - Camry shown (steering wheel removed for clarity)

the clips are engaged properly before pushing the bezel firmly into place.

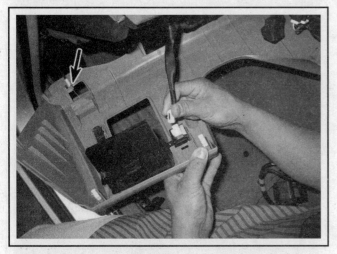

23.8 Once the bolster is pulled away from the instrument panel, disconnect the electrical connector and hood release cable

23.9 Remove the four reinforcement panel bolts

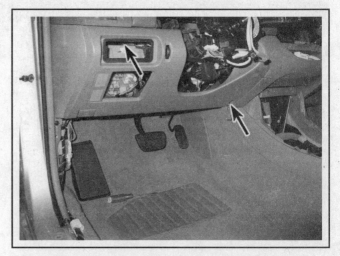

23.7 Remove the knee bolster fasteners - Camry shown

KNEE BOLSTER

▶ **Refer to illustrations 23.7, 23.8 and 23.9**

6 Remove the driver's kick panel for access to one bolster bolt, then remove the change drawer for access to one screw in the change drawer opening.

7 Pry off the small plastic cover over the right-hand bolster screw, remove the bolt at the lower left side and disengage the bolster from four clips (see illustration).

8 Disconnect the electrical connector at the back of the bolster and disconnect the hood release cable (see illustration).

9 Remove the retaining bolts securing the knee bolster reinforcement, if needed for access to components under the dashboard (see illustration). Pull outward on the lower edge of the knee bolster reinforcement panel and detach it from the vehicle.

10 Installation is the reverse of removal.

CENTER TRIM PANEL

▶ **Refer to illustration 23.11**

11 Pry the center instrument panel trim bezel carefully from the dashboard with a taped screwdriver or trim stick, then disconnect the

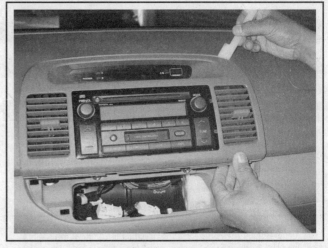

23.11 Pry the center trim bezel away from the clips

clock electrical connector at the back of the panel (see illustration). On Avalon models, pry up the center register panel above the center trim panel and disconnect the electrical connector. On Lexus models, pry off the radio bezel plate to reveal the bolts holding the center trim panel, then remove the bolts and pry the center panel from its clips.

12 Installation is the reverse of removal.

PASSENGER'S SIDE LOWER PANEL AND GLOVE BOX

▶ **Refer to illustration 23.14**

13 Where equipped, the passenger's side lower panel is held in place under the glove box area by clips. Pry and pull it down to release it.

14 Remove the screw securing the glove box strut, then squeeze in the sides and drop the glove box out (see illustration). On Solara models, remove the two lower screws, then open the glove box and remove the upper screws. The glove box comes out with the panel around it.

23.14 Remove the strut screw, then squeeze the sides past their stops and remove the glove box

24 Steering column covers - removal and installation

▶ **Refer to illustration 24.2**

❋❋ WARNING:

The models covered by this manual are equipped with Supplemental Restraint systems (SRS), more commonly known as airbags. Always disarm the airbag system before working in the vicinity of any airbag system component to avoid the possibility of accidental deployment of the airbag, which could cause personal injury (see Chapter 12).

1 Disconnect the cable from the negative terminal of the battery (see Chapter 5, Section 1). On tilt steering columns, move the column to the lowest position. Refer to Chapter 10 and remove the steering wheel.

2 Remove the screws, then separate the halves and remove the upper and lower steering column covers (see illustration).

3 Installation is the reverse of the removal procedure.

24.2 Remove the screws, then remove the steering column covers

25 Instrument panel - removal and installation

▶ **Refer to illustrations 25.7a, 25.7b, 25.8a, 25.8b, 25.9a, 25.9b and 25.9c**

❋❋ WARNING:

The models covered by this manual are equipped with Supplemental Restraint systems (SRS), more commonly known as airbags. Always disarm the airbag system before working in the vicinity of any airbag system component to avoid the possibility of accidental deployment of the airbag, which could cause personal injury (see Chapter 12).

1 Disconnect the cable from the negative terminal of the battery (see Chapter 5, Section 1).

2 Remove the dashboard trim panels (see Section 23) and the center floor console (see Section 22).

3 Remove the instrument cluster (see Chapter 12) and the glove box (see Section 23).

4 Disconnect the passenger's side airbag (if equipped) and remove it (see Chapter 12).

5 Remove the audio unit from the center of the dashboard (see Chapter 12).

6 Remove the air conditioning control panel (see Chapter 3).

7 Remove the driver's knee bolster and reinforcement panel (see Section 23). Then detach the bolts securing the steering column and lower it away from the instrument panel (see illustrations).

8 A number of electrical connectors must be disconnected in

25.7a Remove the lower bolt (A) (and the pinch bolt [B] if removing the column entirely) . . .

25.7b . . . then the two upper bolts

25.8a Label and disconnect the main instrument panel electrical connectors at the left . . .

order to remove the instrument panel. Most are designed so that they will only fit on the matching connector (male or female), but if there is any doubt, mark the connectors with masking tape and a marking pen before disconnecting them (see illustrations).

9 Remove all of the fasteners (bolts, screws and nuts) holding the instrument panel to the body (see illustrations). Once all are removed, lift the panel, pull it away from the windshield and take it out through the driver's door opening.

➡ **Note: This is a two-person job.**

10 Installation is the reverse of removal.

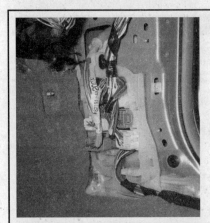

25.8b . . . and the right sides, below the instrument panel

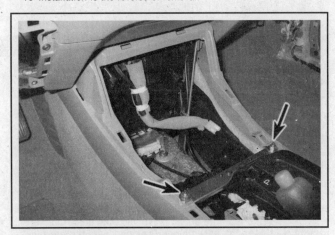

25.9a Remove the lower front portion of the console by removing two nuts, then slide the console to the rear and out (it is held to the instrument panel by clips at the top)

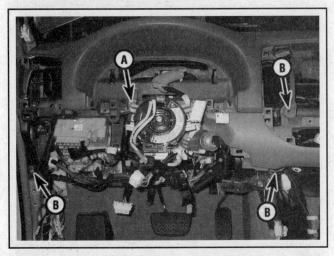

25.9b Remove the nut (A) and bolts (B) holding the instrument panel at the left side

25.9c At the right side of the instrument panel, remove the nut (center arrow) at the cross-cowl tube, then the bolts (outer arrows)

26 Cowl cover - removal and installation

▶ **Refer to illustration 26.2**

1   Remove the wiper arms (see Chapter 12).

2   On most models, remove the two pushpins, one at each end near the fender. Remove the two cowl cover halves by sliding them forward and out (see illustration).

3   On 2002 and 2003 Solara models, the cowl cover is in two halves. Remove the hood seal first, then the two pushpins and the covers. On 2004 and later Solara models, the one-piece cover is retained by 12 clips. All other models have six clips.

4   Installation is the reverse of removal.

26.2 Pry up the plastic pins to remove the hood-seal and cowl cover (LH side shown) and slide the cowl covers forward to remove

27 Seats - removal and installation

FRONT SEAT

▶ **Refer to illustration 27.2**

※※ WARNING 1:

The front seat belts on some models are equipped with pre-tensioners, which are pyrotechnic (explosive) devices designed to retract the seat belts in the event of a collision. On models equipped with pre-tensioners, do not remove the front seat belt retractor assemblies, and do not disconnect the electrical connectors leading to the assemblies. Problems with the pre-tensioners will turn on the SRS (airbag) warning light on the dash. If any pre-tensioner problems are suspected, take the vehicle to a dealer service department.

※※ WARNING 2:

On models with side-impact airbags, be sure to disarm the airbag system before beginning this procedure (see Chapter 12).

1   Pry out the plastic covers to access the seat tracks and their mounting bolts.

2   Remove the retaining bolts (see illustration).

3   Tilt the seat upward to access the underside, then disconnect any electrical connectors and lift the seat from the vehicle.

4   Installation is the reverse of removal.

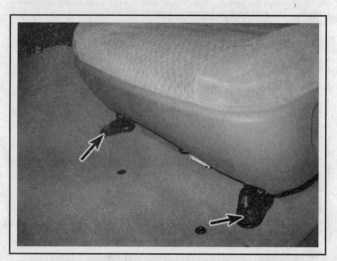

27.2 Typical front seat track retaining bolts, two of the four are indicated here (the track covers have been removed)

27.6a Remove the corner bolts at left and right of the seat back - Camry model left side shown

REAR SEAT

▶ **Refer to illustrations 27.6a and 27.6b**

5   Lift up on the front edge of the rear seat bottom cushion, remove the rear mounting bolt and remove the cushion from the vehicle.

➡**Note: Work the seat belts out of the slits at the back of the cushion.**

6   On Camry and Solara coupe models, pull the seat back locks up and flip the two seat backs down one at a time and remove the mounting bolts (see illustrations). On Avalon, Lexus and Solara convertible models, the four mounting bolts for the one-piece seatback are revealed when the lower cushion is removed.

7   Installation is the reverse of removal.

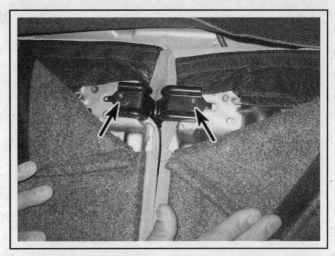

27.6b Flip the seat backs down and remove the two bolts at the center hinges, then remove the seat backs

28 Rear package shelf - removal and installation

▶ **Refer to illustrations 28.3 and 28.4**

1   To remove the package shelf, first remove the high-mounted brake light assembly (see Chapter 12).

2   Unlock and flip forward the seat backs (Camry and Solara coupe) or remove the seat back (Avalon, Lexus and Solara convertible) (see Section 27).

3   Remove the plastic pins retaining the front of the package shelf to the body (see illustration). On some models, the package tray is retained only by clips.

4   To fully remove the package shelf from the vehicle, the bolts must be removed from the bottom ends of the shoulder harness belts, and the belts fed through the holes in the package shelf. Flip up the covers over the child safety belt hooks and unbolt the three hooks (see illustration).

5   Installation is the reverse of the removal procedure. If removed, torque the lower seat belt bolts to 31 ft-lbs.

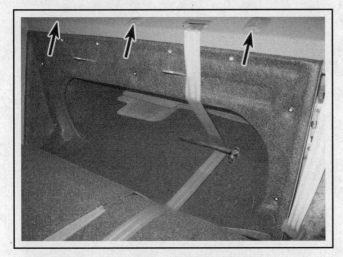

28.3 With the seat back removed (or folded down), remove the plastic pins and the trunk panel

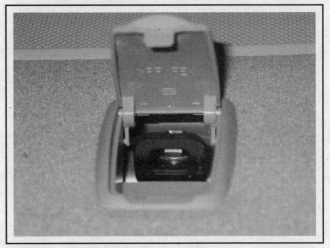

28.4 Flip up the child safety belt covers and remove the bolts securing the child safety belt hooks

Notes

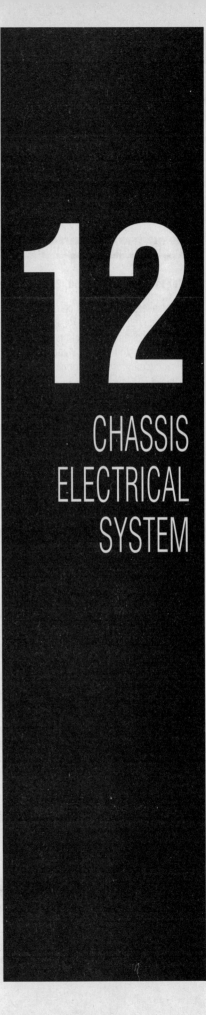

Section

1   General information
2   Electrical troubleshooting - general information
3   Fuses and fusible links - general information
4   Circuit breakers - general information
5   Relays - general information and testing
6   Turn signal and hazard flasher - check and replacement
7   Steering column switches - replacement
8   Ignition switch and lock cylinder - replacement
9   Instrument panel switches - replacement
10 Instrument cluster - removal and installation
11 Wiper motor - check and replacement
12 Radio and speakers - removal and installation
13 Antenna - replacement
14 Rear window defogger - check and repair
15 Headlight bulb - replacement
16 Headlights - adjustment
17 Headlight housing - replacement
18 Horn - check and replacement
19 Bulb replacement
20 Electric side view mirrors - description
21 Cruise control system - description
22 Power window system - description
23 Power door lock system - description
24 Daytime Running Lights (DRL) - general information
25 Airbag system - general information
26 Wiring diagrams - general information

12

CHASSIS
ELECTRICAL
SYSTEM

1 General information

The electrical system is a 12-volt, negative ground type. Power for the lights and all electrical accessories is supplied by a lead/acid-type battery, which is charged by the alternator.

This Chapter covers repair and service procedures for the various electrical components not associated with the engine. Information on the battery, alternator and starter motor can be found in Chapter 5.

It should be noted that when portions of the electrical system are serviced, the cable should be disconnected from the negative battery terminal to prevent electrical shorts and/or fires.

2 Electrical troubleshooting - general information

◆ **Refer to illustrations 2.5a, 2.5b, 2.6 and 2.9**

A typical electrical circuit consists of an electrical component, any switches, relays, motors, fuses, fusible links or circuit breakers related to that component and the wiring and connectors that link the component to both the battery and the chassis. To help you pinpoint an electrical circuit problem, wiring diagrams are included at the end of this Chapter.

Before tackling any troublesome electrical circuit, first study the appropriate wiring diagrams to get a complete understanding of what makes up that individual circuit. Trouble spots, for instance, can often be narrowed down by noting if other components related to the circuit are operating properly. If several components or circuits fail at one time, chances are the problem is in a fuse or ground connection, because several circuits are often routed through the same fuse and ground connections.

Electrical problems usually stem from simple causes, such as loose or corroded connections, a blown fuse, a melted fusible link or a failed relay. Visually inspect the condition of all fuses, wires and connections in a problem circuit before troubleshooting the circuit.

If test equipment and instruments are going to be utilized, use the diagrams to plan ahead of time where you will make the necessary connections in order to accurately pinpoint the trouble spot.

The basic tools needed for electrical troubleshooting include a circuit tester or voltmeter (a 12-volt bulb with a set of test leads can also be used), a continuity tester, which includes a bulb, battery and set of test leads, and a jumper wire, preferably with a circuit breaker incorporated, which can be used to bypass electrical components (see illustra-

tions). Before attempting to locate a problem with test instruments, use the wiring diagram(s) to decide where to make the connections.

VOLTAGE CHECKS

Voltage checks should be performed if a circuit is not functioning properly. Connect one lead of a circuit tester to either the negative battery terminal or a known good ground. Connect the other lead to a connector in the circuit being tested, preferably nearest to the battery or fuse (see illustration). If the bulb of the tester lights, voltage is present, which means that the part of the circuit between the connector and the battery is problem free. Continue checking the rest of the circuit in the same fashion. When you reach a point at which no voltage is present, the problem lies between that point and the last test point with voltage. Most of the time the problem can be traced to a loose connection.

➡**Note: Keep in mind that some circuits receive voltage only when the ignition key is in the Accessory or Run position.**

FINDING A SHORT

One method of finding shorts in a live circuit is to remove the fuse and connect a test light in place of the fuse terminals (fabricate two jumper wires with small spade terminals, plug the jumper wires into the fuse box and connect the test light). There should be voltage present in the circuit. Move the suspected wiring harness from side-to-side while watching the test light. If the bulb goes off, there is a short to ground somewhere in that area, probably where the insulation has rubbed through.

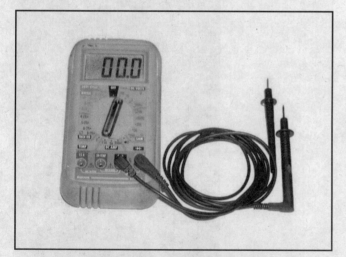

2.5a The most useful tool for electrical troubleshooting is a digital multimeter that can check volts, amps, and test continuity

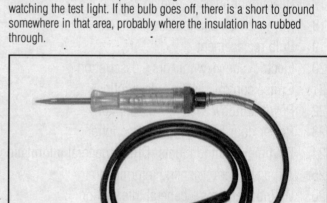

2.5b A simple test light is a very handy tool for testing voltage

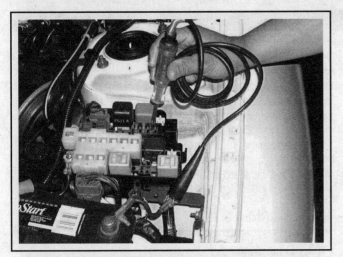

2.6 In use, a basic test light's lead is clipped to a known good ground, then the pointed probe can test connectors, wires or electrical sockets - if the bulb lights, the circuit being tested has battery voltage

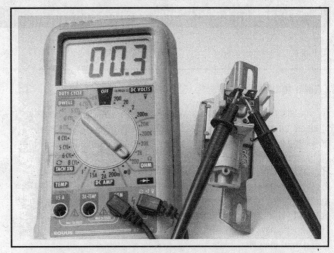

2.9 With a multimeter set to the ohms scale, resistance can be checked across two terminals - when checking for continuity, a low reading indicates continuity, a high reading or infinity indicates lack of continuity

GROUND CHECK

Perform a ground test to check whether a component is properly grounded. Disconnect the battery and connect one lead of a continuity tester or multimeter (set to the ohms scale), to a known good ground. Connect the other lead to the wire or ground connection being tested. If the resistance is low (less than 5 ohms), the ground is good. If the bulb on a self-powered test light does not go on, the ground is not good.

CONTINUITY CHECK

A continuity check is done to determine if there are any breaks in a circuit - if it is passing electricity properly. With the circuit off (no power in the circuit), a self-powered continuity tester or multimeter can be used to check the circuit. Connect the test leads to both ends of the circuit (or to the "power" end and a good ground), and if the test light comes on the circuit is passing current properly (see illustration). If the resistance is low (less than 5 ohms), there is continuity; if the reading is 10,000 ohms or higher, there is a break somewhere in the circuit. The same procedure can be used to test a switch, by connecting the continuity tester to the switch terminals. With the switch turned On, the test light should come on (or low resistance should be indicated on a meter).

FINDING AN OPEN CIRCUIT

When diagnosing for possible open circuits, it is often difficult to locate them by sight because the connectors hide oxidation or terminal misalignment. Merely wiggling a connector on a sensor or in the wiring harness may correct the open circuit condition. Remember this when an open circuit is indicated when troubleshooting a circuit. Intermittent problems may also be caused by oxidized or loose connections.

Electrical troubleshooting is simple if you keep in mind that all electrical circuits are basically electricity running from the battery, through the wires, switches, relays, fuses and fusible links to each electrical component (light bulb, motor, etc.) and to ground, from which it is passed back to the battery. Any electrical problem is an interruption in the flow of electricity to and from the battery.

CONNECTORS

Most electrical connections on these vehicles are made with multi-wire plastic connectors. The mating halves of many connectors are secured with locking clips molded into the plastic connector shells. The mating halves of large connectors, such as some of those under the instrument panel, are held together by a bolt through the center of the connector.

To separate a connector with locking clips, use a small screwdriver to pry the clips apart carefully, then separate the connector halves. Pull only on the shell, never pull on the wiring harness as you may damage the individual wires and terminals inside the connectors. Look at the connector closely before trying to separate the halves. Often the locking clips are engaged in a way that is not immediately clear. Additionally, many connectors have more than one set of clips.

Each pair of connector terminals has a male half and a female half. When you look at the end view of a connector in a diagram, be sure to understand whether the view shows the harness side or the component side of the connector. Connector halves are mirror images of each other, and a terminal shown on the right side end-view of one half will be on the left side end view of the other half.

3 Fuses and fusible links - general information

FUSES

▶ **Refer to illustrations 3.1a, 3.1b and 3.3**

The electrical circuits of the vehicle are protected by a combination of fuses, circuit breakers and fusible links. Fuse blocks are located under the instrument panel and in the engine compartment depending on the model year of the vehicle (see illustrations). On Camry, 2004 and later Solara and all Lexus ES330 models, engine compartment fuses are in the main fuse/relay box at the left front fender. Some Solara models have additional fuses in two smaller boxes to the left and right of the radiator. On Avalon models, a few additional fuses are located in the relay box at the right fender area.

Each of the fuses is designed to protect a specific circuit, and the various circuits are identified on the fuse panel cover.

Miniaturized fuses are employed in the fuse blocks. These compact fuses, with blade terminal design, allow fingertip removal and replacement. If an electrical component fails, always check the fuse first. The best way to check a fuse is with a test light. Check for power at the exposed terminal tips of each fuse. If power is present on one side of the fuse but not the other, the fuse is blown. A blown fuse can also be confirmed by visually inspecting it (see illustration).

Be sure to replace blown fuses with the correct type. Fuses of different ratings are physically interchangeable, but only fuses of the proper rating should be used. Replacing a fuse with one of a higher or lower value than specified is not recommended. Each electrical circuit needs a specific amount of protection. The amperage value of each fuse is molded into the fuse body.

If the replacement fuse immediately fails, don't replace it again until the cause of the problem is isolated and corrected. In most cases, this will be a short circuit in the wiring caused by a broken or deteriorated wire.

FUSIBLE LINKS

▶ **Refer to illustration 3.7**

Some circuits are protected by fusible links. The links are used in circuits which are not ordinarily fused, such as the ignition circuit, or which carry high current.

Cartridge type fusible links are located in the engine compartment fusible link box and are similar to a large fuse (see illustration). After disconnecting the negative battery cable, simply unplug and replace with a fusible link of the same amperage.

3.1a The interior fuse box is located on the dashboard, to the left of the steering column - cover shown removed

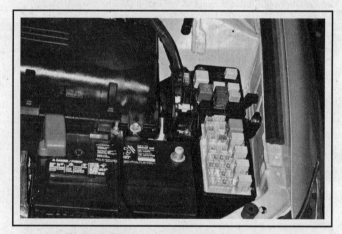

3.1b The main engine compartment fuse/relay box (Camry model shown)

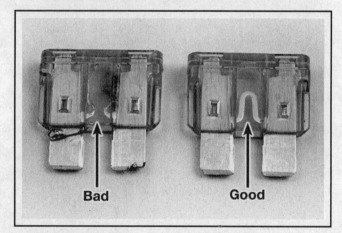

3.3 When a fuse blows, the element between the terminals melts

3.7 Cartridge-type fusible links for high-current applications are found in this area of the main engine compartment fuse/relay box

4 Circuit breakers - general information

Circuit breakers protect certain circuits, such as the power windows or heated seats. Depending on the vehicle's accessories, there may be one or two circuit breakers, located in the fuse/relay box in the engine compartment (see illustration 3.1b).

Because the circuit breakers reset automatically, an electrical overload in a circuit-breaker-protected system will cause the circuit to fail momentarily, then come back on. If the circuit does not come back on, check it immediately.

For a basic check, pull the circuit breaker up out of its socket on the fuse panel, but just far enough to probe with a voltmeter. The breaker should still contact the sockets.

With the voltmeter negative lead on a good chassis ground, touch each end prong of the circuit breaker with the positive meter probe. There should be battery voltage at each end. If there is battery voltage only at one end, the circuit breaker must be replaced.

Some circuit breakers must be reset manually.

5 Relays - general information and testing

GENERAL INFORMATION

1 Several electrical accessories in the vehicle, such as the fuel injection system, horns, starter, and fog lamps use relays to transmit the electrical signal to the component. Relays use a low-current circuit (the control circuit) to open and close a high-current circuit (the power circuit). If the relay is defective, that component will not operate properly. Most relays are mounted in the engine compartment fuse/relay box, with some specialized relays located in the underhood box at the right fender. On some models, the ABS relays are located in a separate underhood relay box at the left side of the radiator. If a faulty relay is suspected, it can be removed and tested using the procedure below or by a dealer service department or a repair shop. Defective relays must be replaced as a unit. Identification of the circuit the relay controls is often marked on the top of the relay, but the decal or imprint inside the cover of the relay box should also indicate which circuits they control.

TESTING

▶ **Refer to illustrations 5.3a, 5.3b and 5.6**

2 Refer to the wiring diagrams for the circuit to determine the proper connections for the relay you're testing. If you can't determine the correct connection from the wiring diagrams, however, you may be able to determine the test connections from the information that follows.

3 There are four basic types of relays used on these models (see illustrations). Some are normally open type and some normally closed, while others include a circuit of each type.

4 On most relays, two of the terminals are the relay control circuit (they connect to the relay coil which, when energized, closes the large contacts to complete the circuit). The other terminals are the power circuit (they are connected together within the relay when the control-circuit coil is energized).

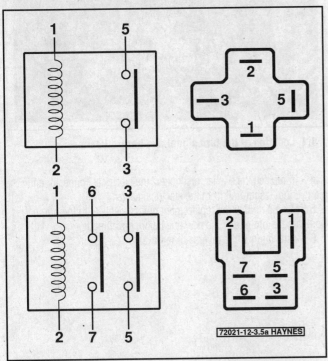

5.3a These two relays are typical normally open types; the one above completes a single circuit (terminal 5 to terminal 3) when energized - the lower relay type completes two circuits (6 and 7, and 3 and 5) when energized

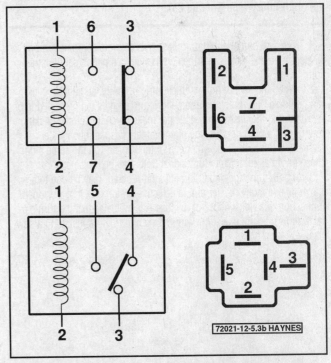

5.3b These relays are normally closed types, where current flows though one circuit until the relay is energized, which interrupts that circuit and completes the second circuit

5   Some relays may be marked as an aid to help you determine which terminals make up the control circuit and which make up the power circuit. If the relay is not marked, refer to the wiring diagrams at the end of this Chapter to determine the proper hook-ups for the relay you're testing.

6   To test a relay, connect an ohmmeter across the two terminals of the power circuit, continuity should not be indicated (see illustration). Now connect a fused jumper wire between one of the two control circuit terminals and the positive battery terminal. Connect another jumper wire between the other control circuit terminal and ground. When the connections are made, the relay should click and continuity should be indicated on the meter. On some relays, polarity may be critical, so, if the relay doesn't click, try swapping the jumper wires on the control circuit terminals.

7   If the relay fails the above test, replace it.

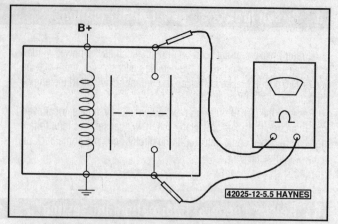

5.6 To test a typical four-terminal normally open relay, connect an ohmmeter to the two terminals of the power circuit - the meter should indicate continuity with the relay energized and no continuity with the relay not energized

6   Turn signal and hazard flasher - check and replacement

▶ **Refer to illustration 6.1**

❊❊ WARNING:

The models covered by this manual are equipped with Supplemental Restraint Systems (SRS), more commonly known as airbags. Always disable the airbag system before working in the vicinity of any airbag system components to avoid the possibility of accidental deployment of the airbags, which could cause personal injury (see Section 25).

1   The turn signal and hazard flasher is a single combination unit, located in an electrical center behind the left kick panel (see illustration).

2   When the flasher unit is functioning properly, an audible click can be heard during its operation. If the turn signals fail on one side or the other and the flasher unit does not make its characteristic clicking sound, or if a bulb on one side of the vehicle flashes much faster than normal but the bulb at the other end of the vehicle (on the same side) doesn't light at all, a faulty turn signal bulb may be indicated.

3   If both turn signals fail to blink, the problem may be due to a blown fuse, a faulty flasher unit, a defective switch or a loose or open connection. If a quick check of the fuse box indicates that the turn signal fuse has blown, check the wiring for a short before installing a new fuse.

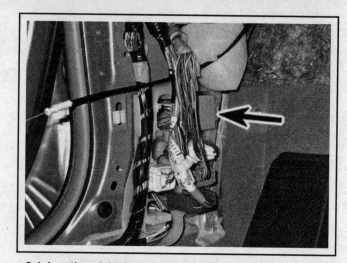

6.1 Location of the turn signal and hazard flasher

4   To replace the flasher, disconnect the electrical connector and remove the flasher unit from the electrical center.

5   Make sure that the replacement unit is identical to the original. Compare the old one to the new one before installing it.

6   Installation is the reverse of removal.

7   Steering column switches - replacement

▶ **Refer to illustrations 7.5a and 7.5b**

✳✳ WARNING:

The models covered by this manual are equipped with Supplemental Restraint Systems (SRS), more commonly known as airbags. Always disable the airbag system before working in the vicinity of any airbag system components to avoid the possibility of accidental deployment of the airbag(s), which could cause personal injury (see Section 25).

1   Disconnect the cable from the negative terminal of the battery (see Chapter 5, Section 1).

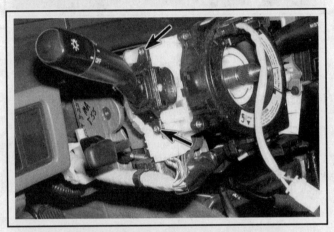

7.5a On some models the steering column switches are retained by screws

2   Remove the steering wheel (see Chapter 10).
3   Remove the steering column covers (see Chapter 11).
4   The steering column switches (combination switch) on these models are two separate switch units connected to a central plastic housing. The left-side switch is for the headlight and turn signal control, while the right-side switch is for the washer/wiper control. Either switch can be replaced separately. Unplug the electrical connectors from the combination switch.
5   Remove the retaining screws (early models) or depress the retaining clips (later models) and pull the combination switch from the column (see illustrations).
6   Installation is the reverse of removal.

7.5b On other models the steering column switches are retained by clips; release the clips by pushing in with a screwdriver (but be careful not to break it)

8   Ignition switch and key lock cylinder - replacement

✳✳ WARNING:

The models covered by this manual are equipped with Supplemental Restraint Systems (SRS), more commonly known as airbags. Always disable the airbag system before working in the vicinity of any airbag system components to avoid the possibility of accidental deployment of the airbag(s), which could cause personal injury (see Section 25).

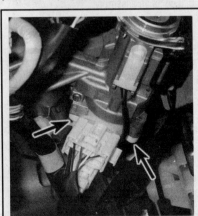

8.6 Unscrew the retaining screws to remove the electrical portion of the ignition switch from the lock cylinder housing

➡Note: These models are equipped with an integration relay. The integration relay works in conjunction with the ignition switch to activate the key unlock warning system and anti-theft system.

1   Disconnect the cable from the negative terminal of the battery (see Chapter 5, Section 1).
2   Place the ignition key in the ACC position.
3   Remove the steering wheel (see Chapter 10).
4   Remove the steering column covers (see Chapter 11).

IGNITION SWITCH

▶ **Refer to illustration 8.6**

5   Unplug the ignition switch electrical connectors.
6   Remove the switch retaining screws (see illustration) then pull the switch from the lock cylinder housing.
7   Installation is reverse of the removal.

8.8 Pry off the illumination ring, then remove the unlock warning switch connector

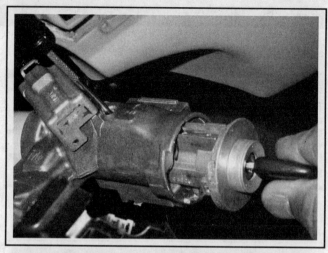

8.9 With the lock cylinder in the ACC position, depress the retaining pin with a small screwdriver, then pull the cylinder straight out

LOCK CYLINDER

▶ **Refer to illustrations 8.8 and 8.9**

8 Disconnect the electrical connector from the key-lock warning switch. On models equipped with the engine immobilizer system, gently pry off the plastic shroud around the key-lock cylinder and disconnect the electrical connector. Lift the shroud edge from the locating tab only enough to slip the shroud off. The shroud houses the amplifier for the special transponder keys. Pry lightly to remove the key lock illumination ring, then remove the unlock warning switch (see illustration).

9 Use a small screwdriver or punch to depress the lock cylinder retaining pin (see illustration).

10 To install the lock cylinder, depress the retaining pin and guide the lock cylinder into the housing until the retaining pin extends itself back into the locating hole in the housing.

11 The remainder of the installation is the reverse of removal.

---

9 Instrument panel switches - replacement

✳✳ WARNING:

The models covered by this manual are equipped with Supplemental Restraint Systems (SRS), more commonly known as airbags. Always disable the airbag system before working in the vicinity of any airbag system components to avoid the possibility of accidental deployment of the airbag(s), which could cause personal injury (see Section 25).

9.5 Use a screwdriver or trim tool to pry the mirror switch from the door panel (Camry models)

HAZARD WARNING SWITCH

1 Disconnect the negative battery cable (see Chapter 5, Section 1).

2 Carefully remove the center cluster finish panel (see Chapter 11) from the instrument panel and pull the assembly out until you can disconnect the electrical connector at the rear of the switch.

➡**Note: On Camry models, the hazard switch is located in the heating/air conditioning control panel, while on other models it's located in the center vent panel.**

3 Depress the tab and remove the switch from the bezel. On Camry models, the hazard switch is integral to the heat/AC controls and the controls and switches are replaced as an assembly.

4 Installation is the reverse of the removal procedure.

POWER MIRROR CONTROL SWITCH

▶ **Refer to illustration 9.5**

5 On Solara, Lexus and Avalon models, the switch is located in a small panel to the left of the steering column. On Camry models, the switch is in the driver's door panel. Carefully pry the panel from the dash with a trim tool, or pry the switch from the door panel (see illustration).

6 Disconnect the electrical connector and remove the switch.

7 Installation is the reverse of the removal procedure.

DEFOGGER CONTROL SWITCH

8   The rear window defogger switch (and on some models the rearview mirror defogger) is located in the heating and air conditioning control panel.

9   Refer to Chapter 3 and remove the control panel, then pull the assembly out until you can disconnect the electrical connector at the rear of the switch. Depress the tab and remove the switch from the bezel.

10 Installation is the reverse of the removal procedure.

INSTRUMENT PANEL LIGHT CONTROL SWITCH

▶ **Refer to illustration 9.12**

11 On Solara models, the switch is in the instrument cluster. See Section 10 and remove the instrument cluster, then disconnect the electrical connector to the switch and squeeze the clips to remove the switch.

12 On Camry models, the switch is in the instrument panel, just to the left of the steering column. From the back of the instrument panel, disconnect the electrical connector and remove the switch (see illustration).

13 On Lexus models, the switch is in a small removable panel

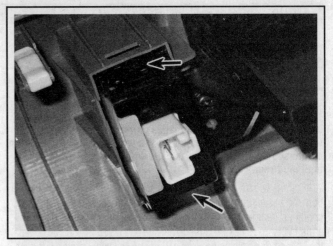

9.12 Disconnect the electrical connector and release the two clips securing the light control switch

to the left of the steering column, and on Avalon models it is in the driver's vent bezel. Use a taped screwdriver or trim tool to release the panel, then disconnect the electrical connector and squeeze the clips to remove the switch.

14 Installation is the reverse of the removal procedure.

10 Instrument cluster - removal and installation

▶ **Refer to illustration 10.3**

✳✳ WARNING:

The models covered by this manual are equipped with Supplemental Restraint Systems (SRS), more commonly known as airbags. Always disable the airbag system before working in the vicinity of any airbag system components to avoid the possibility of accidental deployment of the airbag(s), which could cause personal injury (see Section 25).

1   Disconnect the negative battery cable (see Chapter 5, Section 1).

2   Remove the instrument cluster trim panel (see Chapter 11).

3   Remove the cluster mounting screws (see illustration) and pull the instrument cluster towards the steering wheel.

4   Disconnect any electrical connectors that would interfere with removal.

5   Cover the steering column with a cloth to protect the trim covers, then remove the instrument cluster from the vehicle.

6   Installation is the reverse of removal.

10.3 Remove the instrument cluster mounting screws

11 Wiper motor - check and replacement

WIPER MOTOR CIRCUIT CHECK

➡**Note: Refer to the wiring diagrams for wire colors and locations in the following checks. When checking for voltage, probe a grounded 12-volt test light to each terminal at a connector until it lights; this verifies voltage (power) at the terminal. If the following checks fail to locate the problem, have the system diagnosed by a dealer service department or other properly equipped repair facility.**

1 If the wipers work slowly, make sure the battery is in good condition and has a strong charge (see Chapter 5). If the battery is in good condition, remove the wiper motor (see below) and operate the wiper arms by hand. Check for binding linkage and pivots. Lubricate or repair the linkage or pivots as necessary. Reinstall the wiper motor. If the wipers still operate slowly, check for loose or corroded connections, especially the ground connection. If all connections look OK, replace the motor.

2 If the wipers fail to operate when activated, check the fuse in the driver's side interior fuse panel. If the fuse is OK, connect a jumper wire

between the wiper motor's ground terminal and ground, then retest. If the motor works now, repair the ground connection. If the motor still doesn't work, turn the wiper switch to the HI position and check for voltage at the motor.

➡**Note: The cowl cover will have to be removed (see Chapter 11) to access the electrical connector.**

3 If there's voltage at the connector, remove the motor and check it off the vehicle with fused jumper wires from the battery. If the motor now works, check for binding linkage (see Step 1). If the motor still doesn't work, replace it. If there's no voltage to the motor, check for voltage at the wiper control relays. If there's voltage at the wiper control relays and no voltage at the wiper motor, have the switch tested. If the switch is OK, the wiper control relay is probably bad. See Section 5 for relay testing.

4 If the interval (delay) function is inoperative, check the continuity of all the wiring between the switch and wiper control module.

5 If the wipers stop at the position they're in when the switch is turned off (fail to park), check for voltage at the park feed wire of the wiper motor connector when the wiper switch is OFF but the ignition is ON. If no voltage is present, check for an open circuit between the wiper motor and the fuse panel.

REPLACEMENT

▸ **Refer to illustrations 11.7, 11.9 and 11.11**

6 Disconnect the negative cable from the battery (see Chapter 5, Section 1).

7 Remove the covers over the wiper arm mounting nuts, then remove the wiper arm nuts. Mark the position of each wiper arm to its shaft, then remove the arms (see illustration).

8 Remove the windshield cowl cover (see Chapter 11).

9 Disconnect the wiper motor harness connector and remove the windshield wiper motor/linkage assembly mounting bolts (see illustration).

10 Lift the windshield wiper motor assembly from the cowl area.

11 Use a screwdriver to pry the linkage rod from the motor. Remove the wiper motor mounting bolts and separate the motor from the assembly (see illustration).

12 Installation is the reverse of removal.

11.7 Lift the end cap to access the wiper arm nut, then make a reference mark before removing the arm

11.9 Location of the wiper linkage mounting bolts

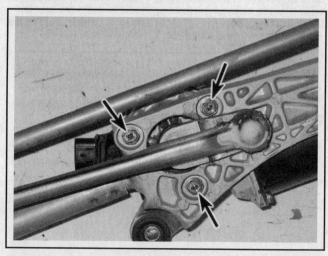

11.11 Location of the wiper motor mounting bolts

12 Radio and speakers - removal and installation

✳✳ WARNING:

The models covered by this manual are equipped with Supplemental Restraint Systems (SRS), more commonly known as airbags. Always disable the airbag system before working in the vicinity of any airbag system components to avoid the possibility of accidental deployment of the airbag(s), which could cause personal injury (see Section 25).

1   Disconnect the negative battery cable (see Chapter 5, Section 1).

RADIO

▶ **Refer to illustrations 12.3a and 12.3b**

2   Access the radio by removing the dash panel surrounding the

12.3a   Remove the radio mounting bolts

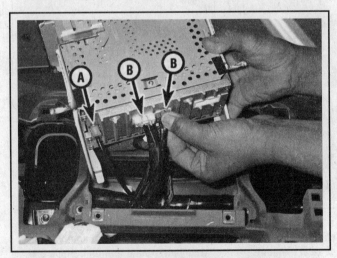

12.3b   Pull the radio forward, then disconnect the antenna lead (A) and the electrical connectors (B)

radio (see Chapter 11). On some models, the air conditioning control panel must be removed before the radio mounting screws can be accessed. On those models, the front console trim must be removed to access the screws at the bottom of the heating/air conditioning control panel.

3   Remove the mounting bolts and pull the radio outward to access the backside, then disconnect the electrical connectors and the antenna lead (see illustrations).

4   Installation is the reverse of removal.

DOOR SPEAKERS

▶ **Refer to illustration 12.6**

5   Remove the door trim panel (see Chapter 11). All models have speakers in both front and rear doors. Rear door speakers are mounted similarly to the front door speakers.

6   Remove the speaker mounting screws (see illustration). Disconnect the electrical connector and remove the speaker from the vehicle

7   Installation is the reverse of removal.

TWEETERS

8   In addition to the standard door and rear speakers, some models are equipped with small tweeters for improved high-range sound.

9   On most models with tweeters, remove the door trim panels to access the screws mounting the tweeters to the door (see Chapter 11). Pull the tweeter out and disconnect the electrical connector. On rear speakers, the package tray must be removed (see Chapter 11).

10   On Solara models, use a taped screwdriver tip or trim tool to pry up the left and right speaker grilles at the top corners of the instrument panel, then unbolt the tweeters.

11   Installation is the reverse of removal.

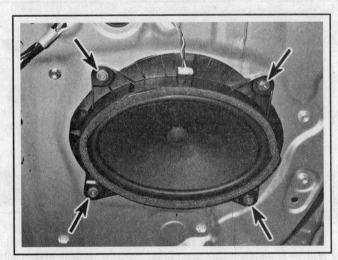

12.6   Remove the speaker mounting screws and disconnect the electrical connector to remove the speaker from the vehicle

13 Antenna - replacement

1   The vehicles covered by this manual are equipped with a wire grid-type antenna attached to the rear window glass.

2   If there is a problem with radio reception, examine the antenna wires by checking for continuity with an ohmmeter.

3   Wrap small pieces of aluminum foil around the tips of your ohm-meter probes and touch them to the wires of the antenna grid. With one probe at one of the antenna terminals, move the other probe along the wire, checking for continuity until a break is found.

4   If a break is found, the wire can be repaired in the same manner as a rear window defogger wire (see Section 14).

14 Rear window defogger - check and repair

1   The rear window defogger consists of a number of horizontal elements baked onto the glass surface.

2   Small breaks in the element can be repaired without removing the rear window.

CHECK

▶ **Refer to illustrations 14.4, 14.5 and 14.7**

3   Turn the ignition switch and defogger system switches to the ON position. Using a voltmeter, place the positive probe against the defogger grid positive terminal and the negative probe against the ground terminal. If battery voltage is not indicated, check the fuse, defogger switch and related wiring. If voltage is indicated, but all or part of the defogger doesn't heat, proceed with the following tests.

4   When measuring voltage during the next two tests, wrap a piece of aluminum foil around the tip of the voltmeter positive probe and press the foil against the heating element with your finger (see illustration). Place the negative probe on the defogger grid ground terminal.

5   Check the voltage at the center of each heating element (see illustration). If the voltage is 5 or 6-volts, the element is okay (there is no break). If the voltage is 0-volts, the element is broken between the center of the element and the positive end. If the voltage is 10 to 12-volts the element is broken between the center of the element and ground. Check each heating element.

6   Connect the negative lead to a good body ground. The reading should stay the same. If it doesn't, the ground connection is bad.

7   To find the break, place the voltmeter negative probe against the defogger ground terminal. Place the voltmeter positive probe with the foil strip against the heating element at the positive terminal end and slide it toward the negative terminal end. The point at which the voltmeter deflects from several volts to zero is the point at which the heating element is broken (see illustration).

REPAIR

▶ **Refer to illustration 14.13**

8   Repair the break in the element using a repair kit specifically recommended for this purpose, available at most auto parts stores.

14.4 When measuring the voltage at the rear window defogger grid, wrap a piece of aluminum foil around the positive probe of the voltmeter and press the foil against the wire with your finger

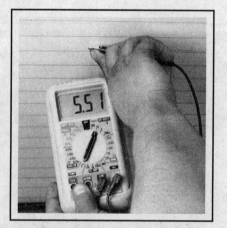

14.5 To determine if a heating element has broken, check the voltage at the center of each element - if the voltage is 5 or 6-volts, the element is unbroken - if the voltage is 10 or 12-volts, the element is broken between the center and the ground side - if there is no voltage, the element is broken between the center and the positive side

14.7 To find the break, place the voltmeter negative lead against the defogger ground terminal, place the voltmeter positive lead with the foil strip against the heating element at the positive terminal end and slide it toward the negative terminal end - the point at which the voltmeter reading changes abruptly is the point at which the element is broken

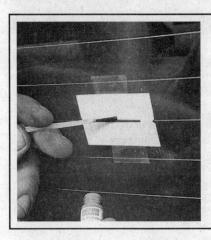

14.13 To use a defogger repair kit, apply masking tape to the inside of the window at the damaged area, then brush on the special conductive coating

Included in this kit is plastic conductive epoxy.

9 Prior to repairing a break, turn off the system and allow it to cool off for a few minutes.

10 Lightly buff the element area with fine steel wool, then clean it thoroughly with rubbing alcohol.

11 Use masking tape to mask off the area being repaired.

12 Thoroughly mix the epoxy, following the instructions provided with the repair kit.

13 Apply the epoxy material to the slit in the masking tape, overlapping the undamaged area about 3/4-inch on either end (see illustration).

14 Allow the repair to cure for 24 hours before removing the tape and using the system.

15 Headlight bulb - replacement

▶ **Refer to illustrations 15.1 and 15.2**

❄❄ WARNING:

Gas filled bulbs are under pressure and may shatter if the surface is scratched or the bulb is dropped. Wear eye protection and handle the bulbs carefully, grasping only the base whenever possible. Do not touch the surface of the bulb with your fingers because the oil from your skin could cause it to overheat and fail prematurely. If you do touch the bulb surface, clean it with rubbing alcohol.

1 Open the hood. Reach behind the headlight assembly, grasp the bulb holder securely and rotate it counterclockwise to remove it from the housing (see illustration). On Lexus and Solara models, remove the headlight housing screws and pull the housing out to access the bulb connections. The low-beam bulb on Lexus models with high-intensity discharge headlights is accessible after unscrewing a large round cover over the bulb. Squeeze the spring-clip to remove the bulb.

2 Unplug the electrical connector from the bulb and holder assembly (see illustration).

3 Without touching the bulb glass with your bare fingers, plug in the electrical connector and insert the new bulb assembly into the headlight housing. Twist it clockwise to lock it in place.

4 On Lexus models, reinstall the round cover over the low-beam bulb and reinstall the headlight housing.

15.1 Location of the two headlight bulbs (Camry shown)

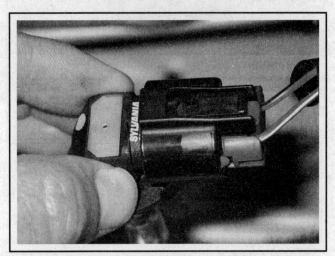

15.2 Push in on the center of the clip, then pull down on the headlight bulb electrical connector

16 Headlights - adjustment

▶ **Refer to illustrations 16.2 and 16.5**

➡**Note: The headlights must be aimed correctly. If adjusted incorrectly they could blind the driver of an oncoming vehicle and cause a serious accident or seriously reduce your ability to see the road. The headlights should be checked for proper aim every 12 months and any time a new headlight is installed or front-end bodywork is performed. It should be emphasized that the following procedure is only an interim step, which will provide temporary adjustment until the headlights can be adjusted by a properly equipped shop.**

1   There are several methods of adjusting the headlights. The simplest method requires masking tape, a blank wall and a level floor.

2   Position masking tape vertically on the wall in reference to the vehicle centerline and the centerlines of both headlights (see illustration).

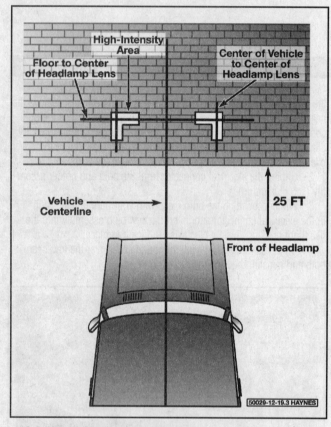

16.2 Headlight adjustment details

3   Position a horizontal tape line in reference to the centerline of all the headlights.

➡**Note: It may be easier to position the tape on the wall with the vehicle parked only a few inches away.**

4   Adjustment should be made with the vehicle parked 25 feet from the wall, sitting level, the gas tank half-full and no unusually heavy load in the vehicle.

5   Starting with the low beam adjustment, position the high intensity zone so it is two inches below the horizontal line and two inches to the side of the headlight vertical line, away from oncoming traffic. Adjustment is made by turning the vertical adjusting screw to raise or lower the beam (see illustration).

➡**Note: Although there are some 2002 models that have a horizontal adjustment screw, later models offer no adjustment for the horizontal plane.**

6   With the high beams on, the high intensity zone should be vertically centered with the exact center just below the horizontal line.

➡**Note: It may not be possible to position the headlight aim exactly for both high and low beams. If a compromise must be made, keep in mind that the low beams are the most used and have the greatest effect on driver safety.**

7   Have the headlights adjusted by a dealer service department or service station at the earliest opportunity.

16.5 You can use a wrench on the bolt head (A) for vertical headlight adjustment, or engage a screwdriver with the adjuster teeth (B) to turn it

17 Headlight housing - replacement

▸ **Refer to illustration 17.2**

❊❊ WARNING:

These vehicles are equipped with gas-filled headlight bulbs that are under pressure and may shatter if the surface is damaged or the bulb is dropped. Wear eye protection and handle the bulbs carefully, grasping only the base whenever possible. Do not touch the surface of the bulb with your fingers because the oil from your skin could cause it to overheat and fail prematurely. If you do touch the bulb surface, clean it with rubbing alcohol.

➡Note: Headlight housings are expensive to replace, but repair kits are available for most models at Toyota dealerships that can save a headlight housing that has broken mounting tabs.

1 Remove the headlight bulbs (see Section 15). On Lexus and Solara models, the headlight housing must be pulled out first to disconnect the bulbs.

2 The front bumper cover must be removed to access one of the headlight housing fasteners (see Chapter 11). Remove the retaining bolts, detach the housing and withdraw it from the vehicle (see illustration).

17.2 Headlight housing mounting bolts - Camry models

3 Installation is the reverse of removal. Be sure to check headlight adjustment (see Section 16).

18 Horn - check and replacement

❊❊ WARNING:

The models covered by this manual are equipped with Supplemental Restraint Systems (SRS), more commonly known as airbags. Always disable the airbag system before working in the vicinity of any airbag system components to avoid the possibility of accidental deployment of the airbag(s), which could cause personal injury (see Section 25).

CHECK

➡Note: Check the fuses before beginning electrical diagnosis.

1 Disconnect the electrical connector from the horn.

2 To test the horn, connect battery voltage to the horn terminal with a jumper wire. If the horn doesn't sound, replace it.

3 If the horn does sound, check for voltage at the terminal when the horn button is depressed. If there's voltage at the terminal, check for a bad ground at the horn.

4 If there's no voltage at the horn, check the relay (see Section 5).

5 If the relay is OK, check for voltage to the relay power and control circuits. If either of the circuits is not receiving voltage, inspect the wiring between the relay and the fuse panel.

6 If both relay circuits are receiving voltage, depress the horn button and check the circuit from the relay to the horn button for continuity to ground. If there's no continuity, check the circuit for an open. If there's no open circuit, replace the horn button.

7 If there's continuity to ground through the horn button, check for an open or short in the circuit from the relay to the horn.

18.9 Location of the horn mounting bolts

REPLACEMENT

▸ **Refer to illustration 18.9**

8 To access the horns, open the hood. The horns are located in front of the radiator.

9 To replace the horns, disconnect the electrical connectors and remove the bracket bolts (see illustration).

10 Installation is the reverse of removal.

19 Bulb replacement

FRONT PARK/TURN SIGNAL LIGHTS

▶ **Refer to illustration 19.2**

1   The park/turn signal lights are part of the headlight housing, and on some models the side-marker light bulbs are also in the headlight housing. These bulbs are accessible from behind the headlight housing (in place), except for Lexus and Solara models, on which the headlight housings must be removed for access to the bulbs (see Section 17).

2   Rotate the bulb holder counterclockwise and pull the bulb out (see illustration). Remove the bulb from the holder. On some models, the side marker light is a separate unit mounted in the front fender. On these models, access to the bulb is from underneath the fender.

3   Installation is the reverse of removal.

REAR TAILLIGHT/BRAKE LIGHT/TURN SIGNAL

▶ **Refer to illustration 19.4**

4   The taillight/brake/turn signal bulbs can be accessed on Camry and Avalon models by swinging out or removing access panels in the trunk (see illustration).

5   Rotate the bulb holders counterclockwise and pull the bulbs out to remove them. Remove the bulb from the holder.

6   On Lexus models, there are rear lights on the body and on the trunk lid. The bulbs in the body-side housings can be accessed by pulling up the floor mat in the trunk and removing the plastic finish panel at the rear of the trunk opening. The lights in the trunk lid are accessible only after removing the trunk lid inner trim panel, using a trim tool to pry up around the edges to release the clips.

7   On Solara models, the taillights are mounted on the body, and the backup lights are on the trunk lid. The taillight bulbs are accessed on 2002 and 2003 models by removing a corner trim panel inside the trunk that is retained by plastic pushpins, while 2004 and later models have swing-open access panels. The backup lights in the trunk lid are accessible only after removing the trunk lid inner trim panel, using a trim tool to pry up around the edges to release the clips.

8   Installation is the reverse of removal.

19.2 Rotate the bulb holder counterclockwise to remove the park/turn signal bulb from the headlight housing

CENTER HIGH-MOUNTED STOP LIGHT (CHMSL)

▶ **Refer to illustration 19.9**

9   Open the trunk and crawl in enough to see the underside of the rear package shelf. Reach the bulb through the opening under the CHMSL housing. You can also access the bulb from inside the car by squeezing the forward edge of the CHMSL housing until it comes free of the package tray, then rotate it upward to see the bulb and connector (see illustration).

10   Twist the bulb holder counterclockwise to remove it, then pull the bulb straight out of the holder.

11   Installation is the reverse of removal.

INSTRUMENT CLUSTER LIGHTS

▶ **Refer to illustration 19.13**

12   To gain access to the instrument cluster illumination bulbs, the instrument cluster will have to be removed (see Section 10). The bulbs can then be removed and replaced from the rear of the cluster.

13   Rotate the bulb counterclockwise to remove it (see illustration).

14   Installation is the reverse of removal.

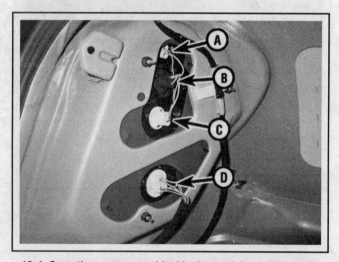

19.4 Open the access panel inside the trunk (panel removed in this photo) to access the following bulbs: taillight and rear side marker bulb (A); turn signal bulb (B); back-up light bulb (C); stop/tail light bulb (D)

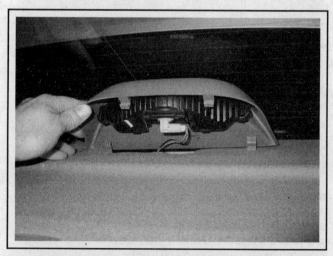

19.9 Rotate the bulb holder and remove it from the high-mounted brake light assembly

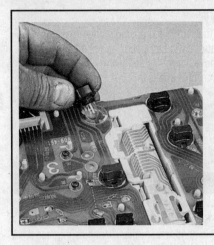

19.13 Remove the instrument cluster bulbs by rotating them 1/4-turn counter-clockwise and pulling straight out

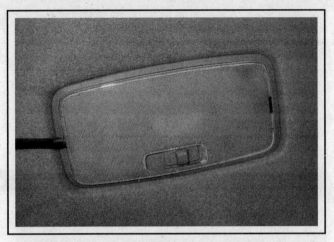

19.15 Carefully pry off the dome light lens using a flat-bladed screwdriver

INTERIOR LIGHT

▸ **Refer to illustration 19.15**

15 Pry the interior lens off the interior light housing (see illustration).

16 Detach the bulb from the terminals. It may be necessary to pry the bulb out - if this is the case, pry only on the ends of the bulb (otherwise the glass may shatter).

17 Installation is the reverse of removal.

LICENSE PLATE LIGHT

▸ **Refer to illustration 19.18**

18 Refer to Chapter 11 and remove the trunk lid liner. Twist out the license plate bulb sockets and replace the bulbs (see illustration).

19 Installation is the reverse of removal.

FOG LIGHT

20 Loosen the front wheel lug nuts, raise the front of the vehicle and secure it on jackstands.

21 Remove the front wheels and remove the inner fender covers to access the fog light assembly. On Lexus models, the front bumper

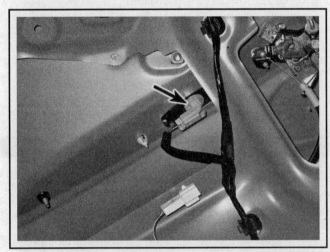

19.18 Location of a license plate light bulb holder inside the trunk lid (right bulb shown, left similar)

fascia must be removed to access the fog lights and their bulbs (see Chapter 11).

22 Twist the bulb holder from the housing and replace the bulb.

23 Installation is the reverse of removal. Be sure to tighten the wheel lug nuts to the torque listed in the Chapter 1 Specifications.

20 Electric side view mirrors - description

1 Most electric rear view mirrors use two motors to move the glass; one for up and down adjustments and one for left-right adjustments.

2 The control switch has a selector portion that sends voltage to the left or right side mirror. With the ignition ON but the engine OFF, roll down the windows and operate the mirror control switch through all functions (left-right and up-down) for both the left and right side mirrors.

3 Listen carefully for the sound of the electric motors running in the mirrors.

4 If the motors can be heard but the mirror glass doesn't move, there's a problem with the drive mechanism inside the mirror. Remove and disassemble the mirror to locate the problem.

5 If the mirrors do not operate and no sound comes from the mirrors, check the fuse (see Chapter 1).

6   If the fuse is OK, remove the mirror control switch from the dashboard. Have the switch continuity checked by a dealership service department or other qualified automobile repair facility.

7   Test the ground connections. Refer to the wiring diagrams at the end of this Chapter.

8   If the mirror still doesn't work, remove the mirror and check the wires at the mirror for voltage.

9   If there's not voltage in each switch position, check the circuit between the mirror and control switch for opens and shorts.

10 If there's voltage, remove the mirror and test it off the vehicle with jumper wires. Replace the mirror if it fails this test.

21   Cruise control system - description

1   The covered vehicles all have an electrically controlled throttle body (no mechanical linkage or cable). The accelerator pedal is linked to the throttle body with wires, and the ECM communicates between them. This aspect also interfaces with the cruise control system, which is also entirely electronic. Listed below are some general procedures that may be used to locate common problems.

2   With the ignition switch turned to the On position, turn the cruise control main switch On. The CRUISE light on the instrument panel should light up, and turn off when you turn the cruise control main switch back to Off.

3   Check the fuses (see Section 3).

4   If the check in Step 2 is abnormal, further diagnosis requires a scan tool to read diagnostic trouble codes for the cruise control system. For more information on diagnostic code retrieval, see Chapter 6.

5   The cruise control system uses inputs from the Vehicle Speed Sensor (VSS). Refer to Chapter 6 for more information on the VSS.

6   Test-drive the vehicle to determine if the cruise control is now working. If it isn't, take it to a dealer service department or an automotive electrical specialist for further diagnosis.

22   Power window system - description

1   The power window system operates electric motors, mounted in the doors, which lower and raise the windows. The system consists of the control switches, relays, the motors, regulators, glass mechanisms and associated wiring.

2   The power windows can be lowered and raised from the master control switch by the driver or by remote switches located at the individual windows. Each window has a separate motor that is reversible. The position of the control switch determines the polarity and therefore the direction of operation.

3   The circuit is protected by a fuse and a circuit breaker. Each motor is also equipped with an internal circuit breaker; this prevents one stuck window from disabling the whole system.

4   The power window system will only operate when the ignition switch is ON. In addition, many models have a window lockout switch at the master control switch that, when activated, disables the switches at the rear windows and, sometimes, the switch at the passenger's window also. Always check these items before troubleshooting a window problem.

5   These procedures are general in nature, so if you can't find the problem using them, take the vehicle to a dealer service department or other properly equipped repair facility.

6   If the power windows won't operate, always check the fuse and circuit breaker first.

7   If only the rear windows are inoperative, or if the windows only operate from the master control switch, check the rear window lockout switch for continuity in the unlocked position. Replace it if it doesn't have continuity.

8   Check the wiring between the switches and fuse panel for continuity. Repair the wiring, if necessary.

9   If only one window is inoperative from the master control switch, try the other control switch at the window.

➡**Note: This doesn't apply to the driver's door window.**

10 If the same window works from one switch, but not the other, check the switch for continuity. Have the switch checked at a dealer service department or other qualified automobile repair facility.

11 If the switch tests OK, check for a short or open in the circuit between the affected switch and the window motor.

12 If one window is inoperative from both switches, remove the trim panel from the affected door and check for voltage at the switch and at the motor while the switch is operated.

13 If voltage is reaching the motor, disconnect the glass from the regulator (see Chapter 11). Move the window up and down by hand while checking for binding and damage. Also check for binding and damage to the regulator. If the regulator is not damaged and the window moves up and down smoothly, replace the motor. If there's binding or damage, lubricate, repair or replace parts, as necessary.

14 If voltage isn't reaching the motor, check the wiring in the circuit for continuity between the switches and motors. You'll need to consult the wiring diagram for the vehicle. If the circuit is equipped with a relay, check that the relay is grounded properly and receiving voltage.

15 Test the windows after you are done to confirm proper repairs.

23 Power door lock system - description

1   A power door lock system operates the door lock actuators mounted in each door. The system consists of the switches, actuators, a control unit and associated wiring. Diagnosis can usually be limited to simple checks of the wiring connections and actuators for minor faults that can be easily repaired.

2   Power door lock systems are operated by bi-directional solenoids located in the doors. The lock switches have two operating positions: Lock and Unlock. When activated, the switch sends a ground signal to the door lock control unit to lock or unlock the doors. Depending on which way the switch is activated, the control unit reverses polarity to the solenoids, allowing the two sides of the circuit to be used alternately as the feed (positive) and ground side.

3   Some vehicles may have an anti-theft system incorporated into the power locks. If you are unable to locate the trouble using the following general Steps, consult a dealer service department or other qualified repair shop.

4   Always check the circuit protection first. Some vehicles use a combination of circuit breakers and fuses.

5   Operate the door lock switches in both directions (Lock and Unlock) with the engine off. Listen for the click of the solenoids operating.

6   Test the switches for continuity. Remove the switches and have them checked by a dealer service department or other qualified automobile repair facility.

7   Check the wiring between the switches, control unit and solenoids for continuity. Repair the wiring if there's no continuity.

8   Check for a bad ground at the switches or the control unit.

9   If all but one lock solenoids operate, remove the trim panel from the affected door (see Chapter 11) and check for voltage at the solenoid while the lock switch is operated. One of the wires should have voltage in the Lock position; the other should have voltage in the Unlock position.

10 If the inoperative solenoid is receiving voltage, replace the solenoid.

11 If the inoperative solenoid isn't receiving voltage, check the relay for an open or short in the wire between the lock solenoid and the control unit.

→**Note: It's common for wires to break in the portion of the harness between the body and door (opening and closing the door fatigues and eventually breaks the wires).**

KEYLESS ENTRY SYSTEM

▶ **Refer to illustrations 23.14 and 23.15**

12 The keyless entry system consists of a remote control transmitter that sends a coded infrared signal to a receiver which then operates the door lock system. On models so equipped, the transmitter may also engage the alarm system and provide a "panic" button that flashes the lights and blows the horn for emergencies.

13 Replace the transmitter batteries when the red LED light on the case doesn't light when the button is pushed. As the batteries deteriorate with age, the distance at which the remote transmitter operates will diminish.

14 Use a coin or small screwdriver to carefully separate the case halves for battery replacement (see illustration).

15 Replace the two lithium batteries with the same type as originally installed, observing the polarity diagram on the case (see illustration).

16 Snap the case halves together.

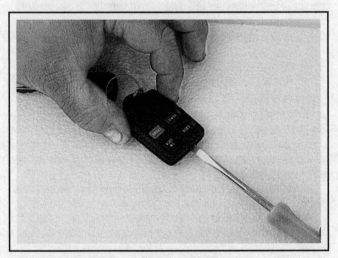

23.14 Use a small screwdriver or coin to separate the transmitter halves

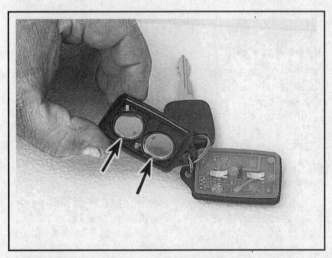

23.15 Replace the lithium batteries with the same type as used originally

24 Daytime Running Lights (DRL) - general information

The Daytime Running Lights (DRL) system used on Canadian models illuminates the headlights whenever the engine is running. The only exception is with the engine running and the parking brake engaged. Once the parking brake is released, the lights will remain on as long as the ignition switch is on, even if the parking brake is later applied.

The DRL system supplies reduced power to the headlights so they won't be too bright for daytime use, while prolonging headlight life.

25 Airbag system - general information

All models are equipped with a Supplemental Restraint System (SRS), more commonly known as an airbag. This system is designed to protect the driver, and the front seat passenger, from serious injury in the event of a head-on or frontal collision. It consists of two impact sensors behind the front bumper, an airbag module in the center of the steering wheel and the right side of the instrument panel and a sensing/diagnostic module mounted in the center of the vehicle, ahead of the floor console. Additionally, some models are equipped with side impact airbags and side curtain airbags.

AIRBAG MODULE

Driver's side

The airbag inflator module contains a housing incorporating the cushion (airbag) and inflator unit, mounted in the center of the steering wheel The inflator assembly is mounted on the back of the housing over a hole through which gas is expelled, inflating the bag almost instantaneously when an electrical signal is sent from the system. A spiral cable assembly on the steering column under the steering wheel carries this signal to the module.

This spiral cable assembly can transmit an electrical signal regardless of steering wheel position. The igniter in the airbag converts the electrical signal to heat and ignites the powder, which inflates the bag.

Passenger's side

The airbag is mounted above the glove compartment. It consists of an inflator containing an igniter, a bag assembly, a reaction housing and a trim cover.

The airbag is considerably larger than the steering wheel mounted unit and is supported by the steel reaction housing. The trim cover is textured and colored to match the instrument panel and has a molded seam that splits when the bag inflates.

Side impact airbags

Extra protection is provided on most models with the addition of side-impact airbags (in earlier covered years the side-impact airbags were an option). These are smaller devices located in the seat backs on the side toward the exterior of the vehicle. The impact sensors for the side-impact airbags are located at the bottom of the door pillars in the body, in the bottom of the driver and passenger seats, or in the driver and passenger doors.

Side curtain airbags

Extra side-impact protection is provided on later models with the addition of side-curtain airbags (in addition to the side-impact airbags in the seatbacks). These are long airbags that, in the event of a side impact, come out of the headliner at each side of the car and come down between the side windows and the seats. They are designed to protect the heads of both front seat and rear seat passengers.

SENSING AND DIAGNOSTIC MODULE

The sensing and diagnostic module supplies the current to the airbag system in the event of the collision, even if battery power is cut off. It checks this system every time the vehicle is started, causing the "AIR BAG" light to go on then off, if the system is operating properly. If there is a fault in the system, the light will go on and stay on, flash, or the dash will make a beeping sound. If this happens, the vehicle should be taken to your dealer immediately for service.

DISARMING THE SYSTEM AND OTHER PRECAUTIONS

✳✳ WARNING:

Failure to follow these precautions could result in accidental deployment of the airbag and personal injury.

Whenever working in the vicinity of the steering wheel, steering column or any of the other SRS system components, the system must be disarmed. To disarm the system:
  a) *Point the wheels straight ahead and turn the key to the Lock position.*
  b) *Disconnect the cable from the negative battery terminal.*
  c) *Wait at least two minutes for the back-up power supply to be depleted.*

Whenever handling an airbag module, always keep the airbag opening (the trim side) pointed away from your body. Never place the airbag module on a bench of other surface with the airbag opening facing the surface. Always place the airbag module in a safe location with the airbag opening facing up.

Never measure the resistance of any SRS component. An ohmmeter has a built-in battery supply that could accidentally deploy the airbag.

Never use electrical welding equipment on a vehicle equipped with an airbag without first disconnecting the electrical connector for each airbag.

Never dispose of a live airbag module. Return it to a dealer service department or other qualified repair shop for safe deployment and disposal.

COMPONENT REMOVAL AND INSTALLATION

Driver's side airbag module and spiral cable

Refer to Chapter 10, *Steering wheel - removal and installation*, for the driver's side airbag module and spiral cable removal and installation procedures.

Passenger's side airbag module

> ⁂ **CAUTION:**
>
> **This procedure requires the removal of the instrument panel and is considered a very difficult job for the home mechanic.**

1 Disarm the airbag system as described previously in this Section.

Under the right side of the instrument panel, disconnect the yellow connectors for the passenger airbag.

2 Remove the instrument panel (see Chapter 11). The airbag is bolted to the underside of the instrument panel. Remove the fasteners and detach the airbag module from the instrument panel. Be sure to heed the precautions outlined previously in this Section.

3 Installation is the reverse of the removal procedure. Tighten the airbag module mounting fasteners to 15 ft-lbs (20 Nm).

26 Wiring diagrams - general information

Since it isn't possible to include all wiring diagrams for every year covered by this manual, the following diagrams are those that are typical and most commonly needed.

Prior to troubleshooting any circuits, check the fuse and circuit breakers (if equipped) to make sure they're in good condition. Make sure the battery is properly charged and check the cable connections (see Chapter 1).

When checking a circuit, make sure that all connectors are clean, with no broken or loose terminals. When unplugging a connector, do not pull on the wires. Pull only on the connector housings themselves.

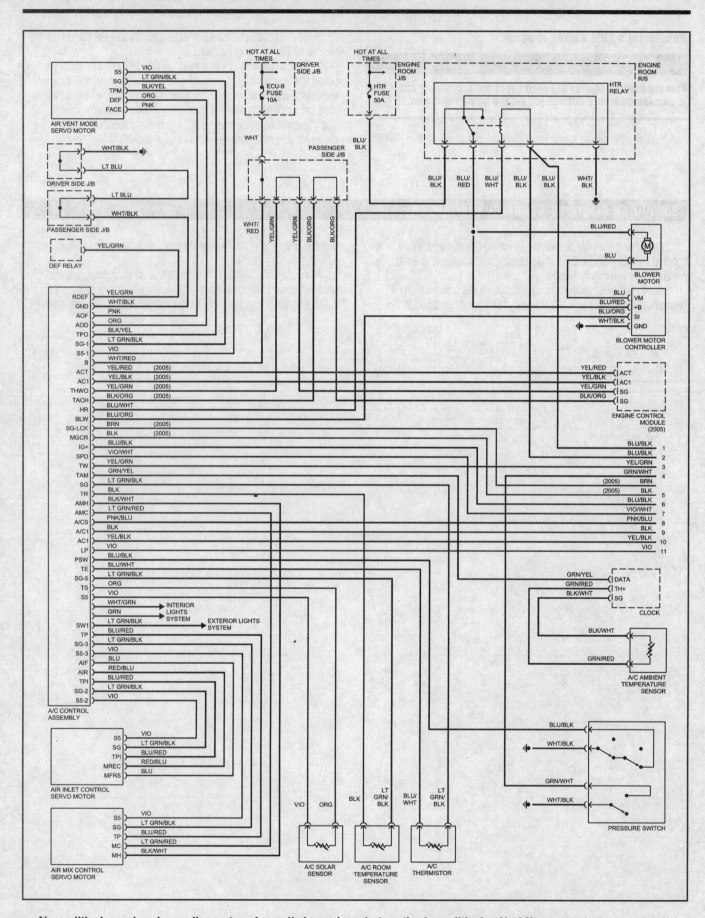

Air conditioning and engine cooling system, four-cylinder engine w/automatic air conditioning (1 of 2)

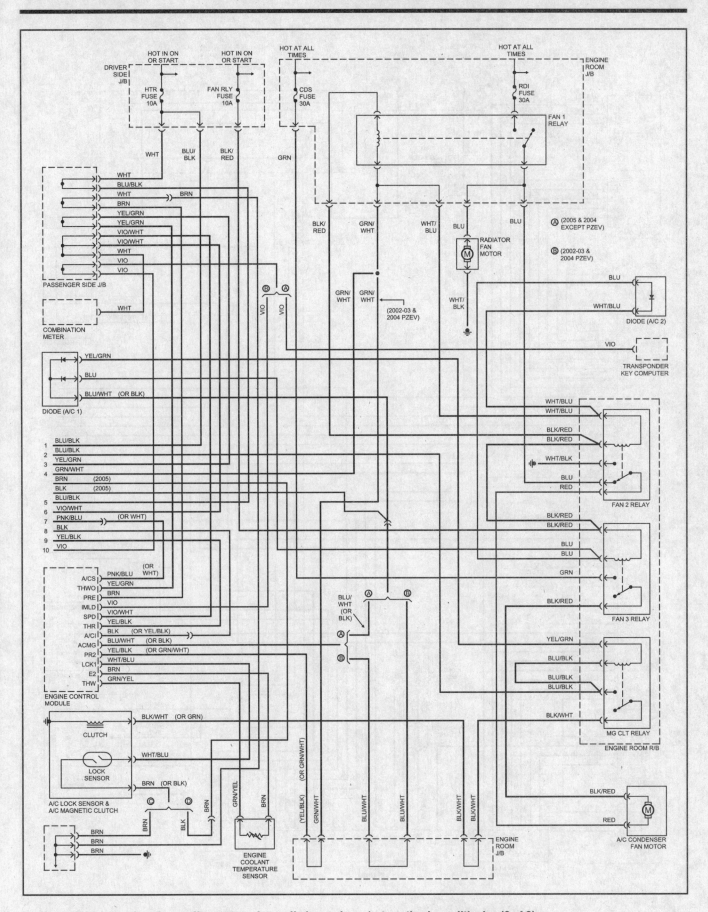

Air conditioning and engine cooling system, four-cylinder engine w/automatic air conditioning (2 of 2)

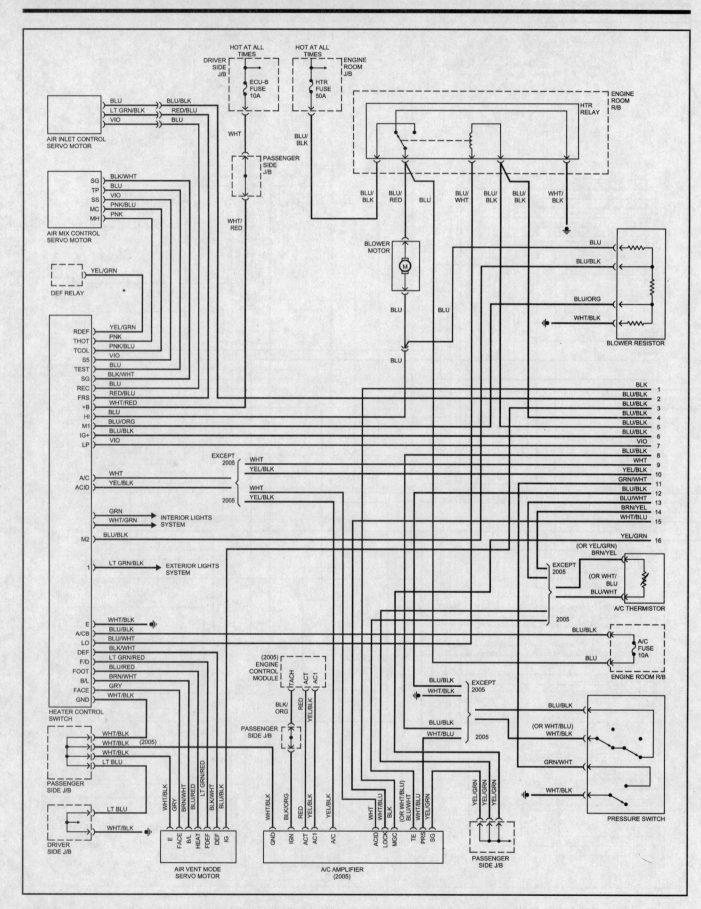

Air conditioning and engine cooling system, four-cylinder engine w/manual air conditioning (1 of 2)

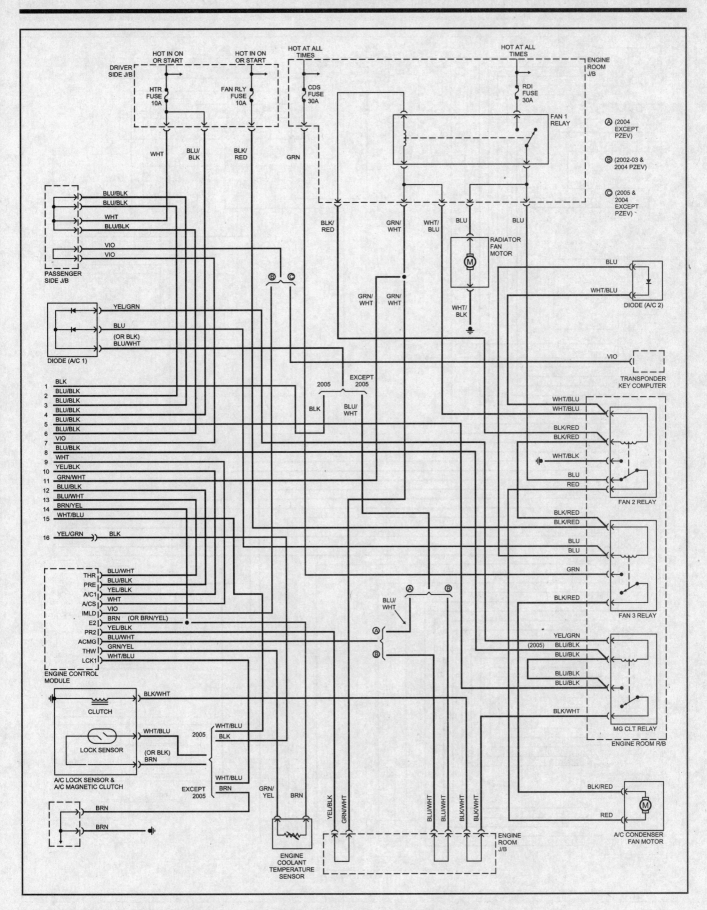

Air conditioning and engine cooling system, four-cylinder engine w/manual air conditioning (2 of 2)

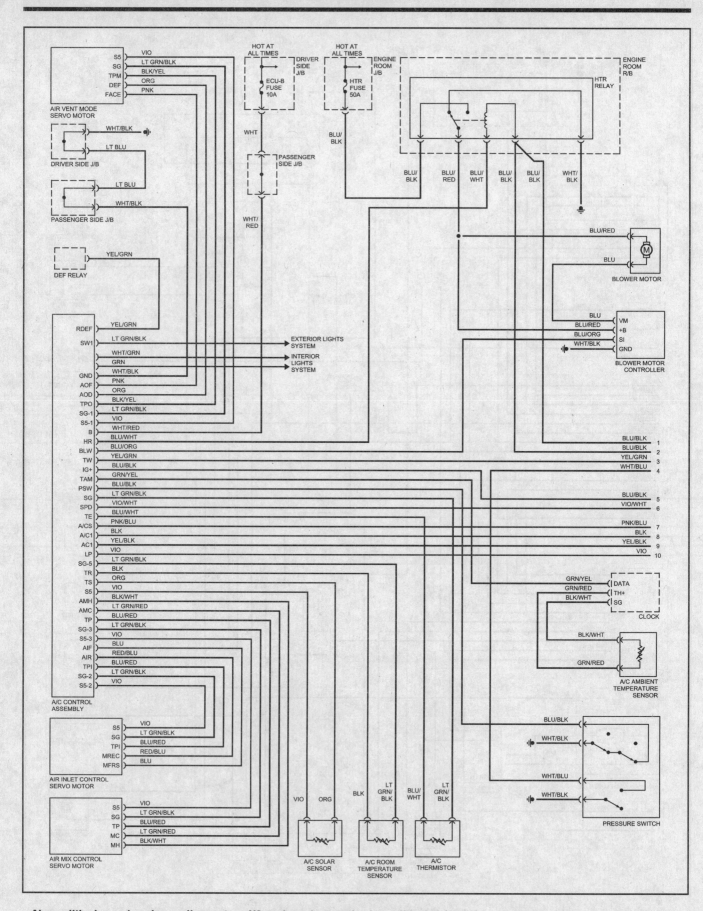

Air conditioning and engine cooling system, V6 engine w/automatic air conditioning (1 of 2)

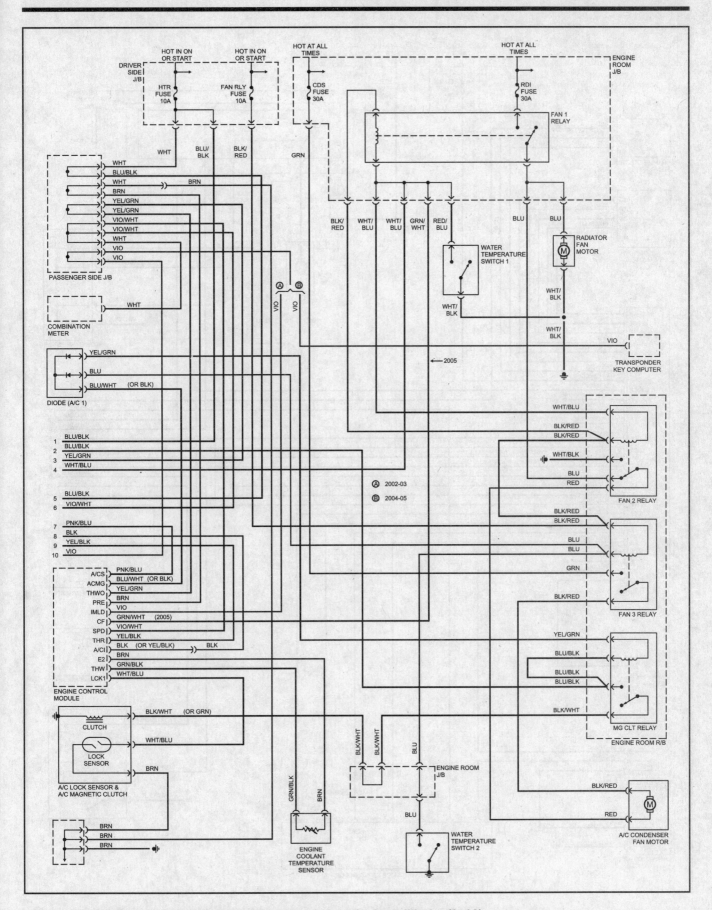

Air conditioning and engine cooling system, V6 engine w/automatic air conditioning (2 of 2)

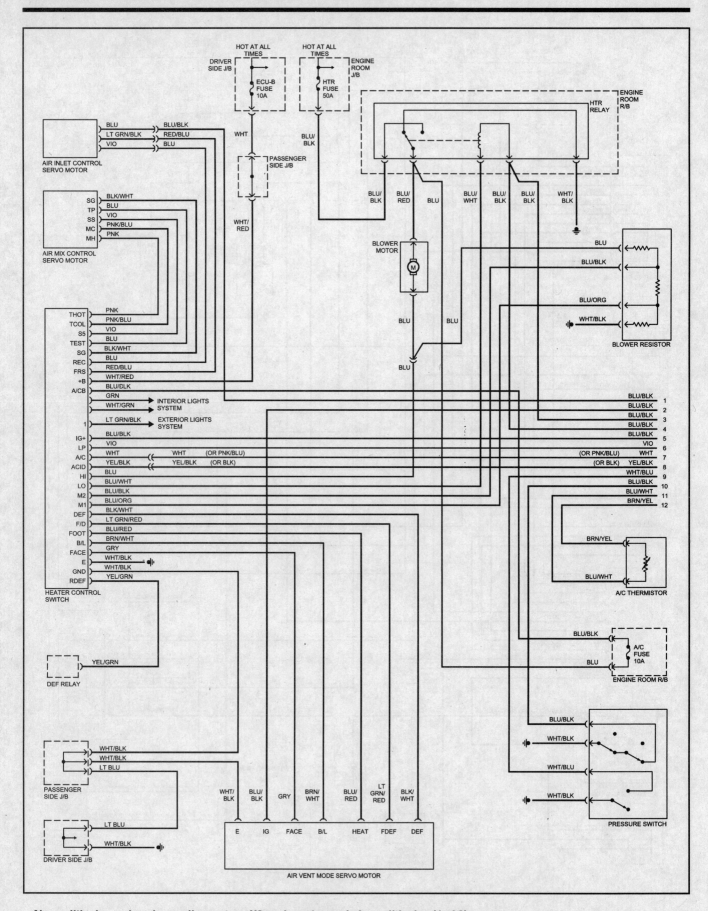

Air conditioning and engine cooling system, V6 engine w/manual air conditioning (1 of 2)

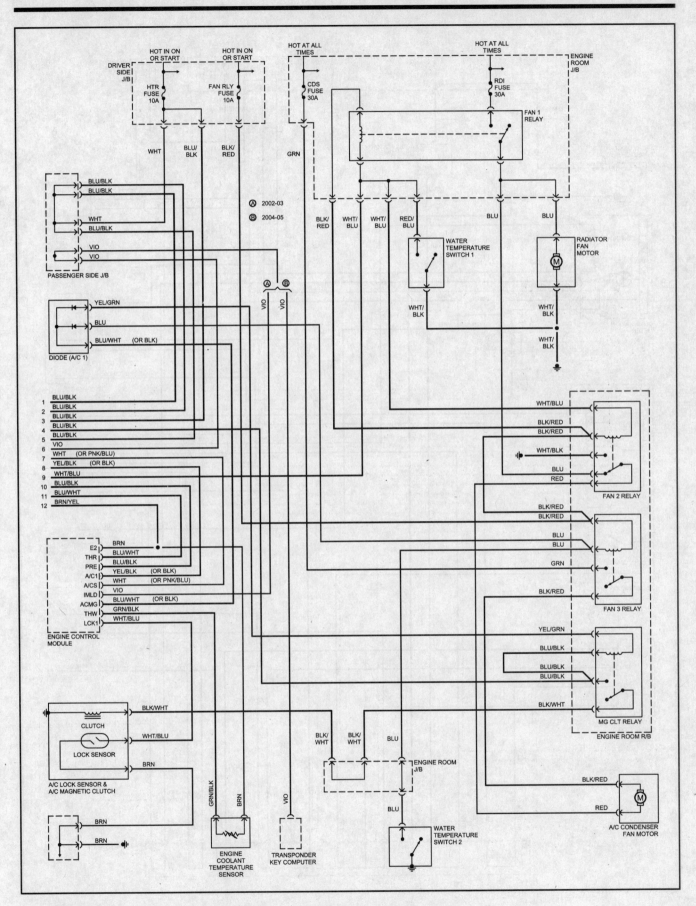

Air conditioning and engine cooling system, V6 engine w/manual air conditioning (2 of 2)

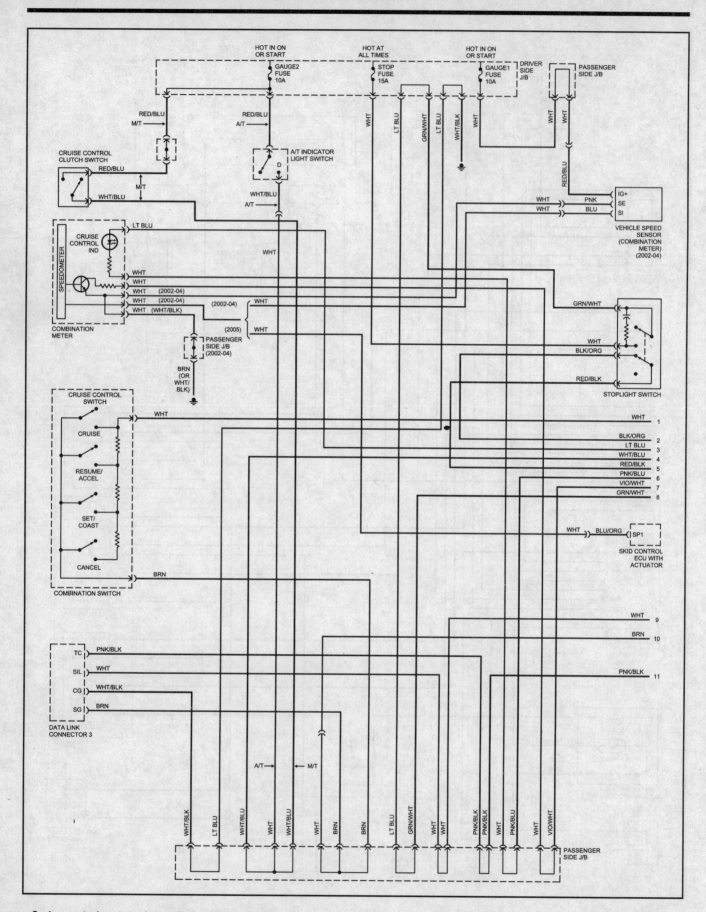

Cruise control system, four-cylinder engine (1 of 2)

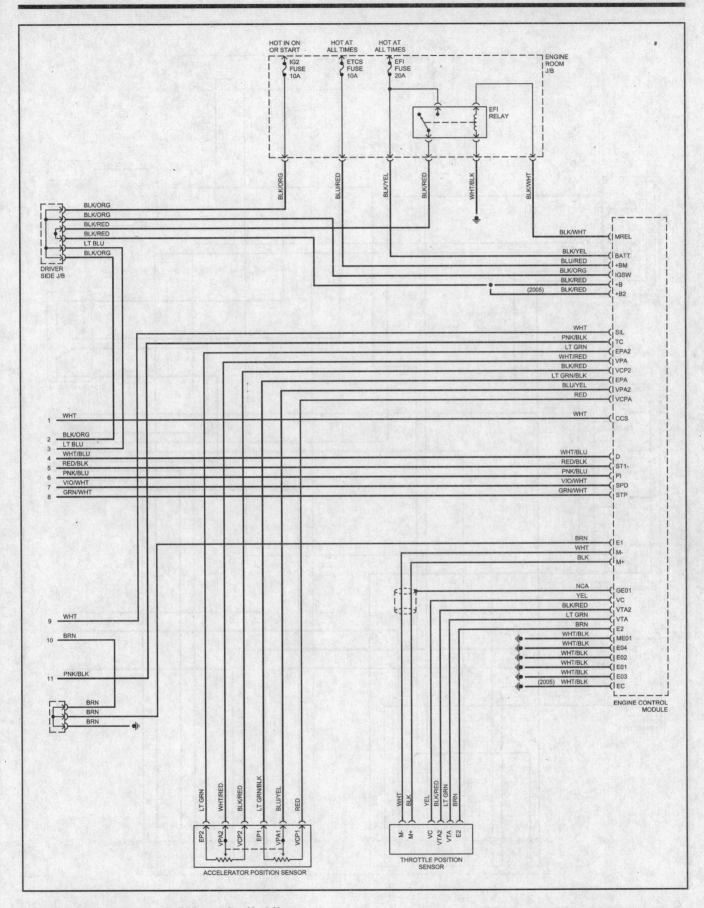

Cruise control system, four-cylinder engine (2 of 2)

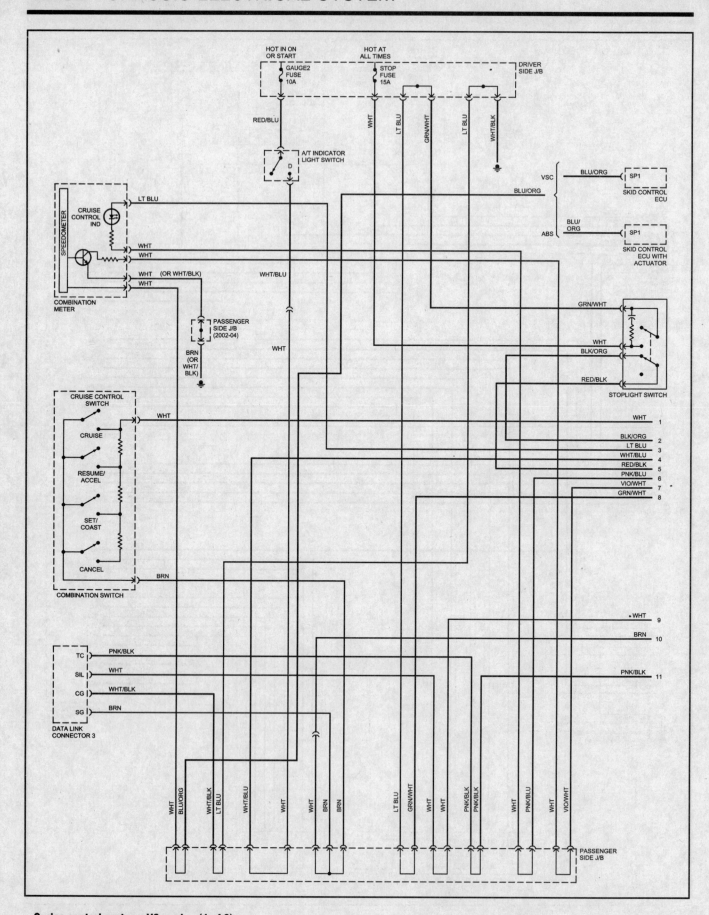

Cruise control system, V6 engine (1 of 2)

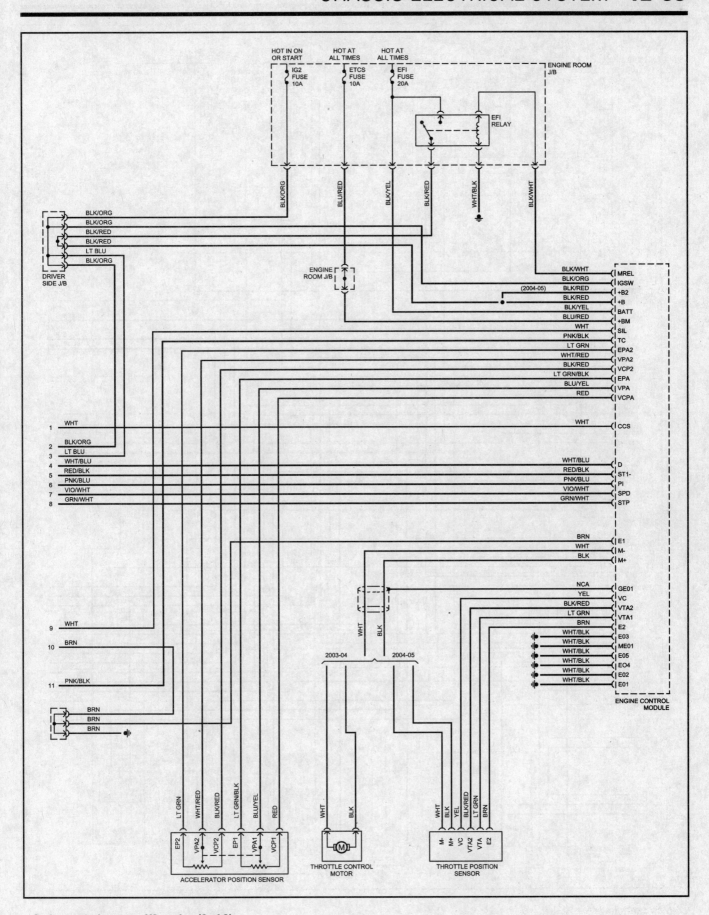

Cruise control system, V6 engine (2 of 2)

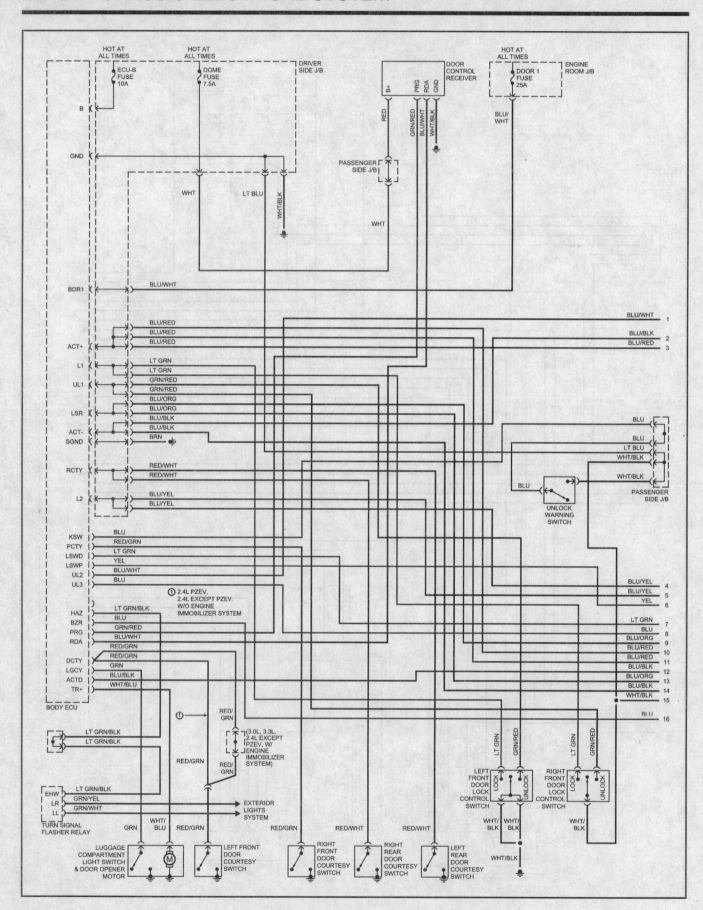

Power door lock system (with keyless entry) (1 of 2)

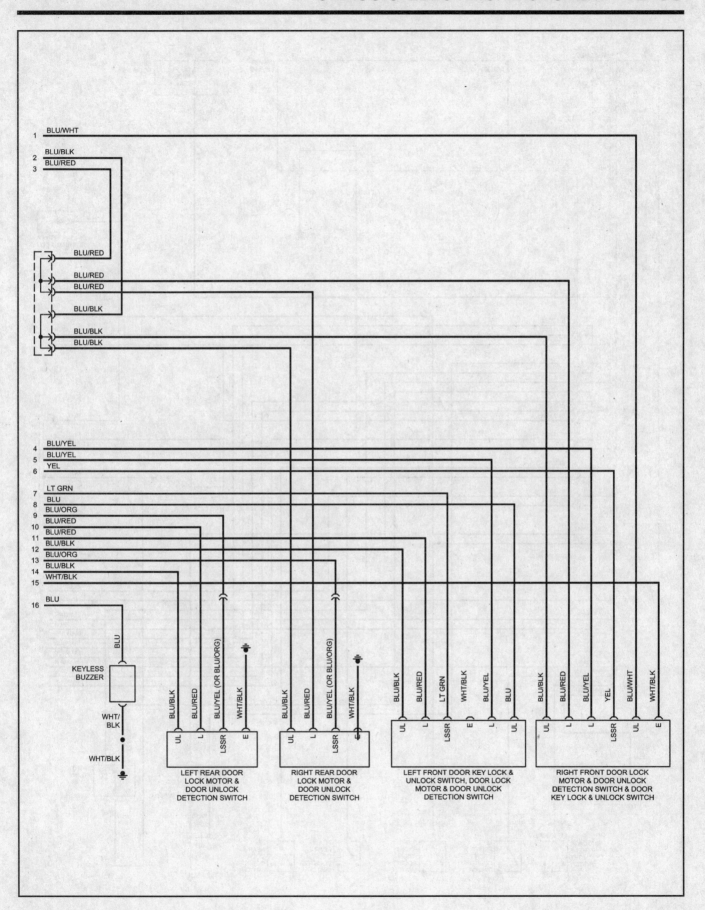

Power door lock system (with keyless entry) (2 of 2)

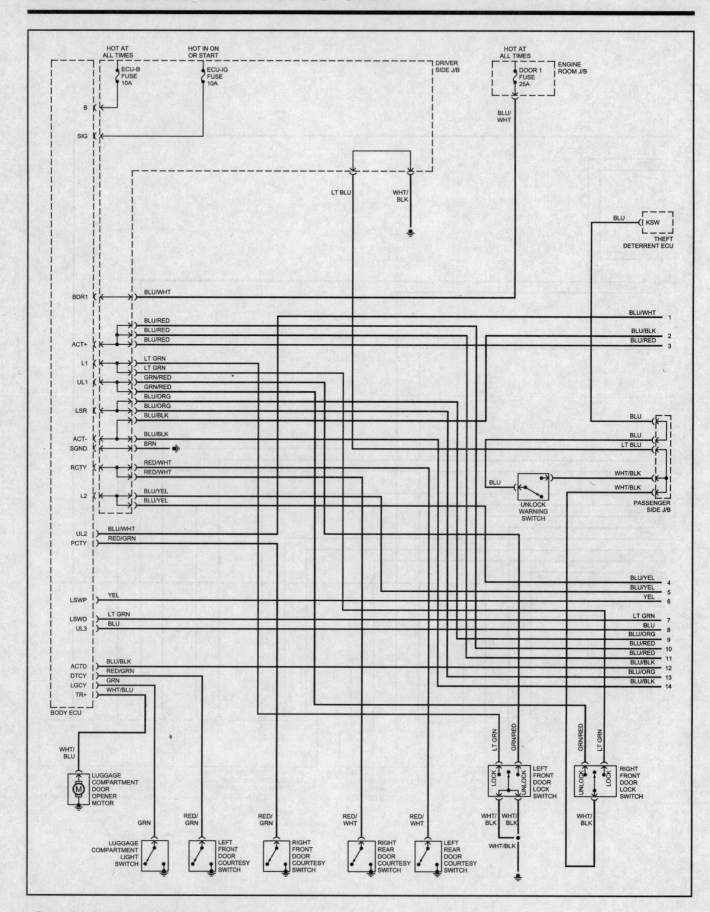

Power door lock system (without keyless entry) (1 of 2)

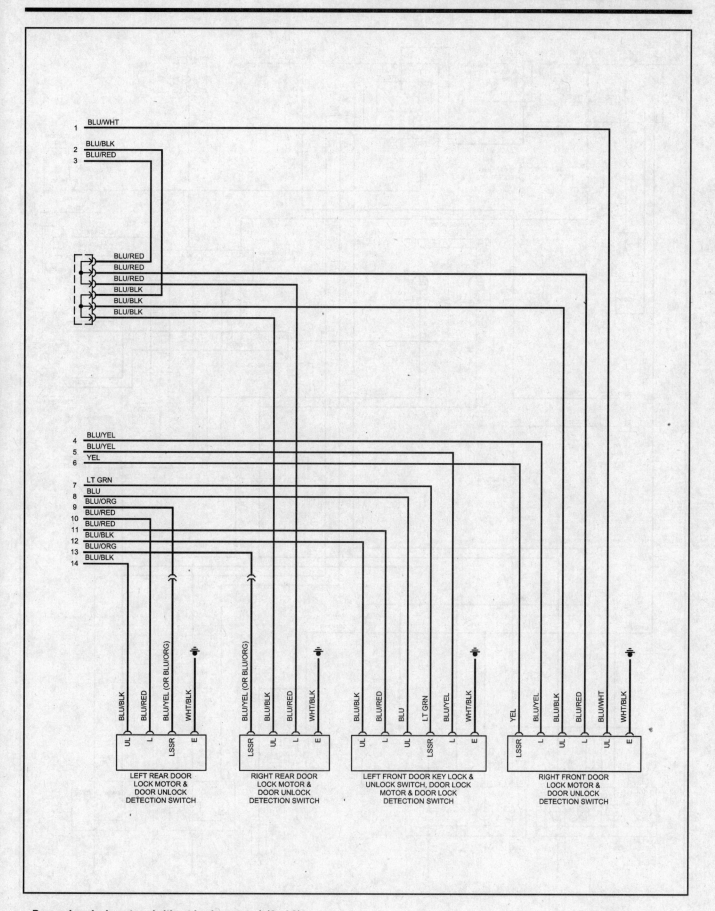

Power door lock system (without keyless entry) (2 of 2)

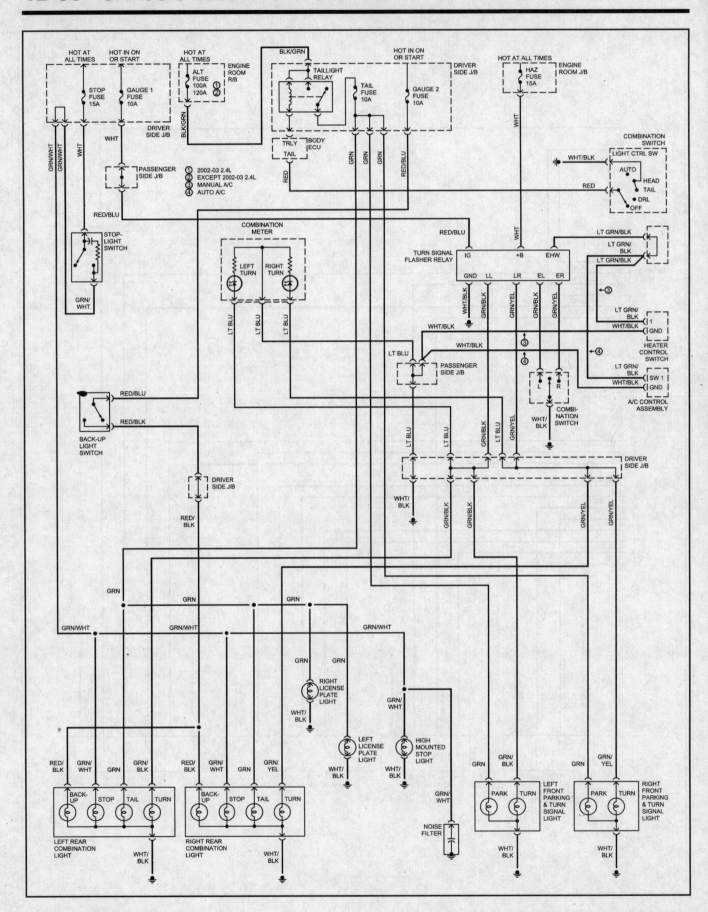

Exterior lighting system (except headlights)

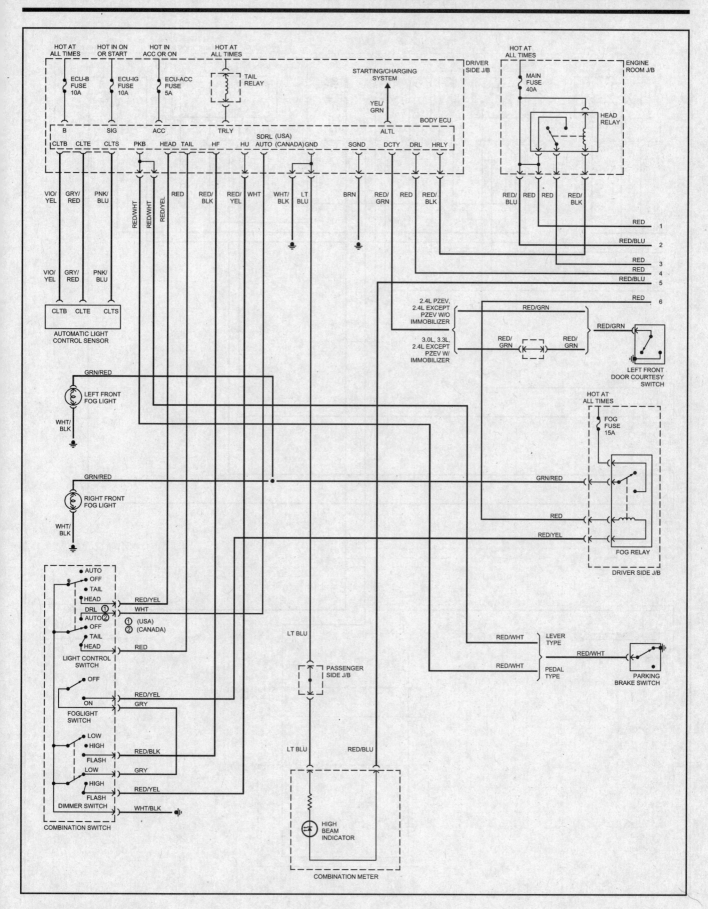

Headlight system (1 of 2)

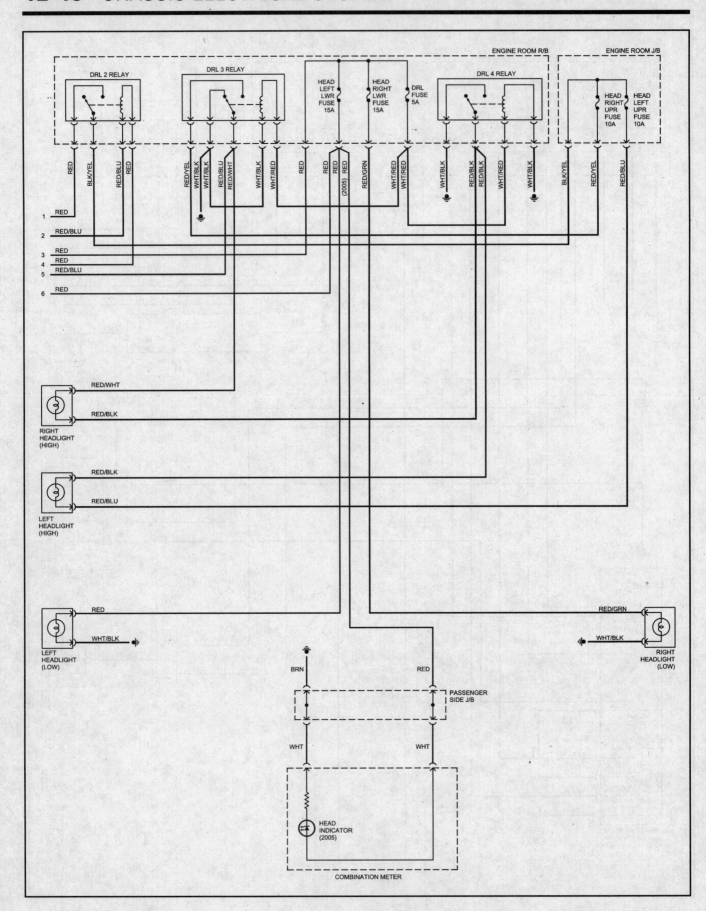

Headlight system (2 of 2)

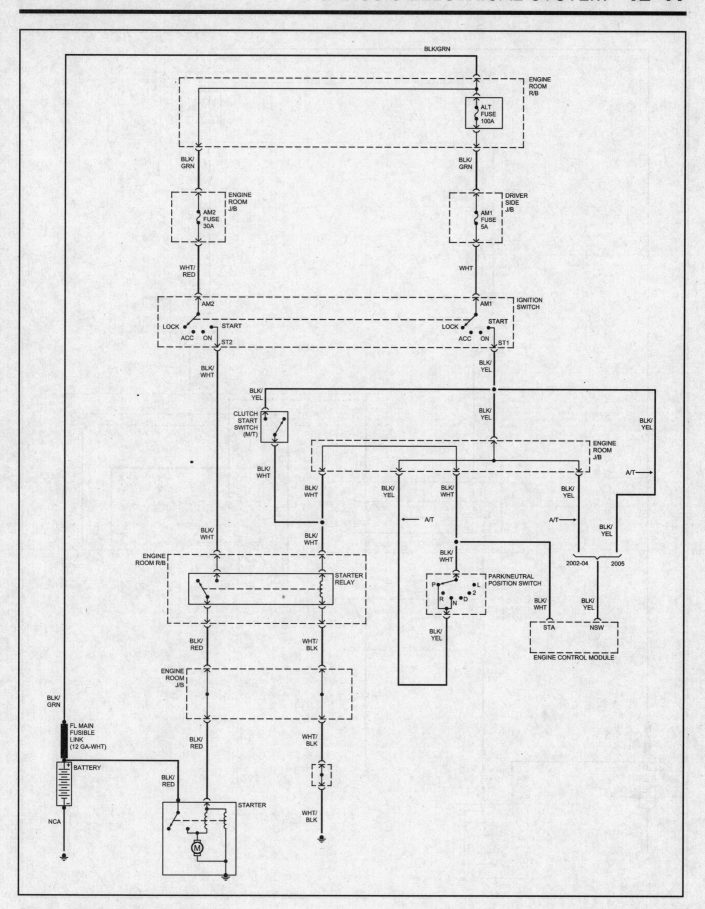

Starting system, four-cylinder engine

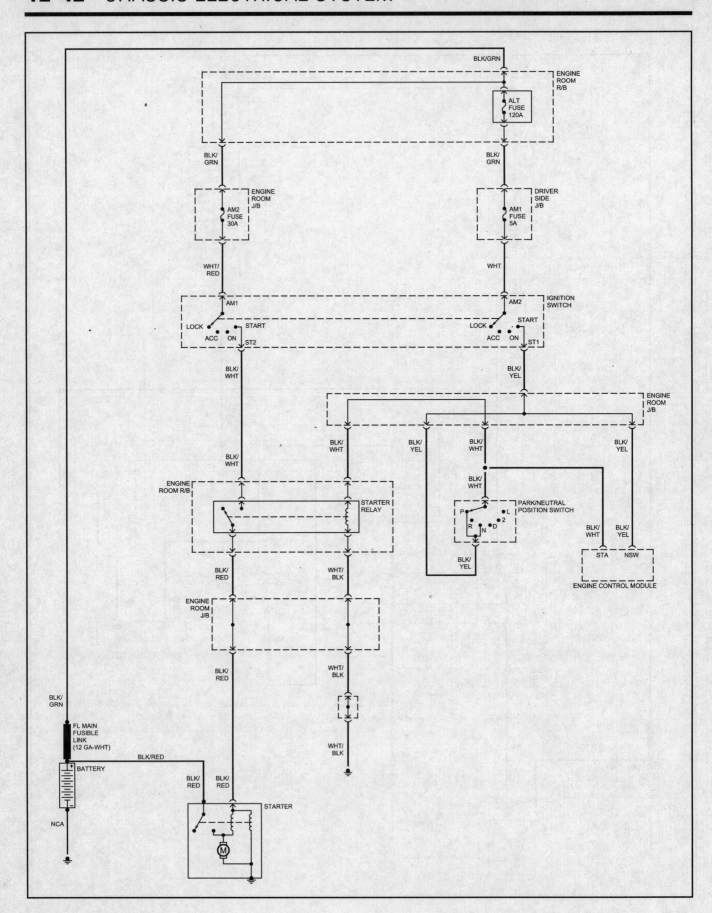

Starting system, V6 engine

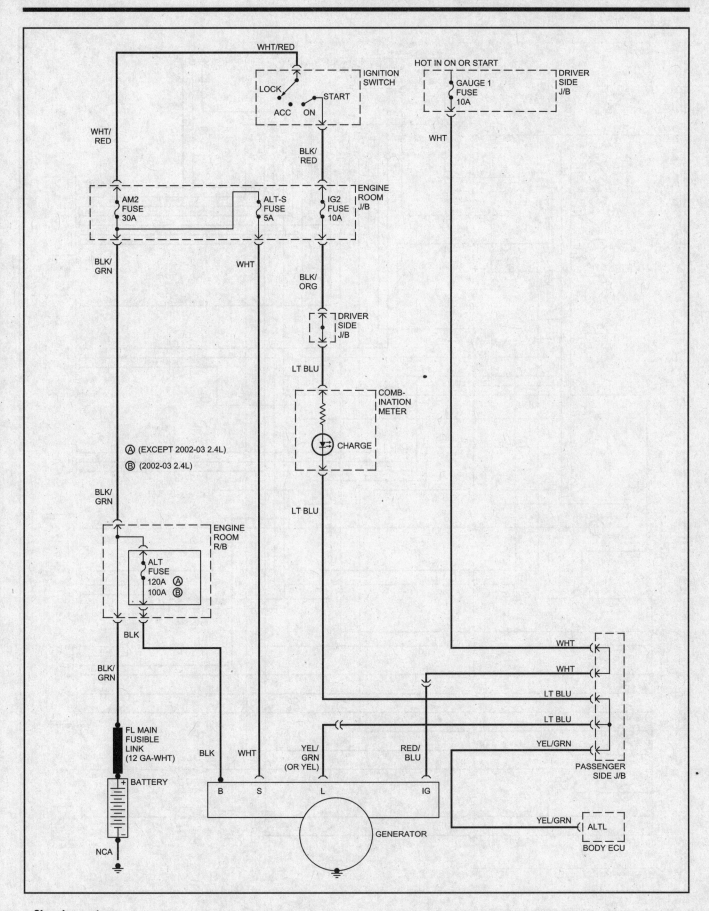

Charging system

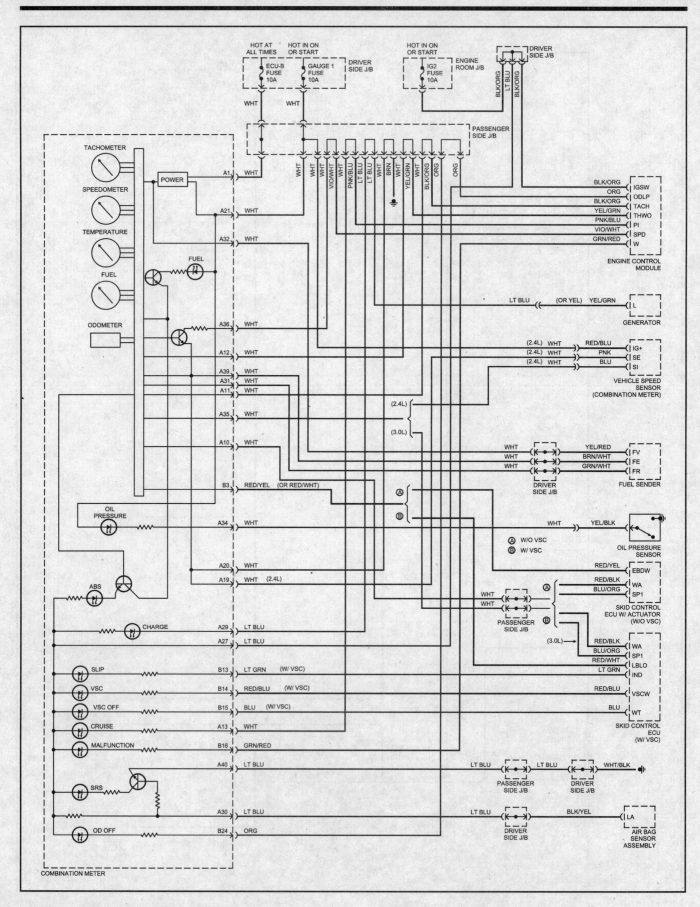

Warning lights system, 2002 and 2003 models

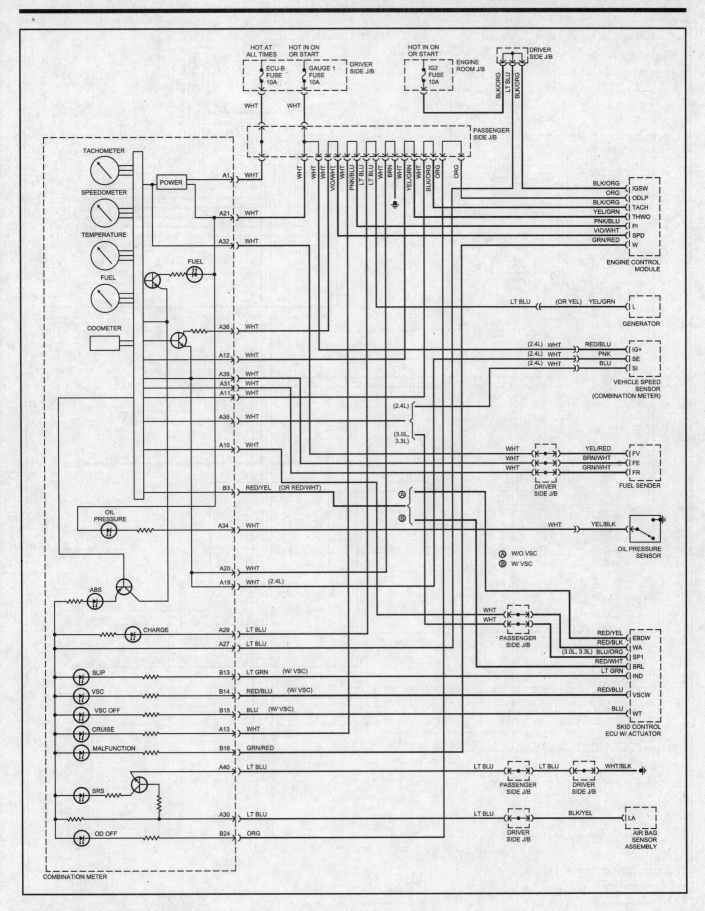

Warning lights system, 2004 models

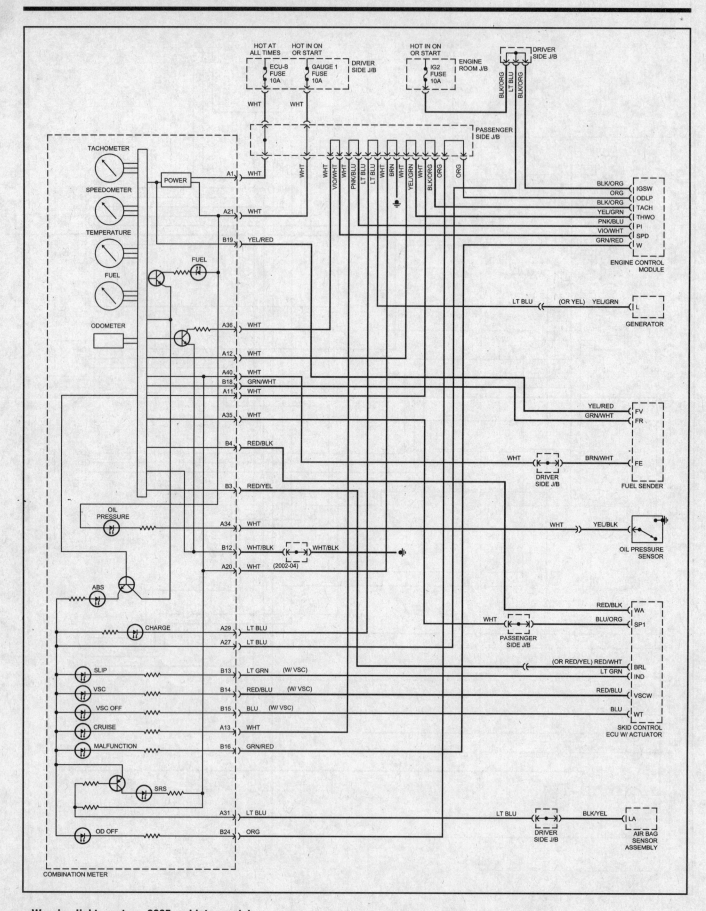

Warning lights system, 2005 and later models

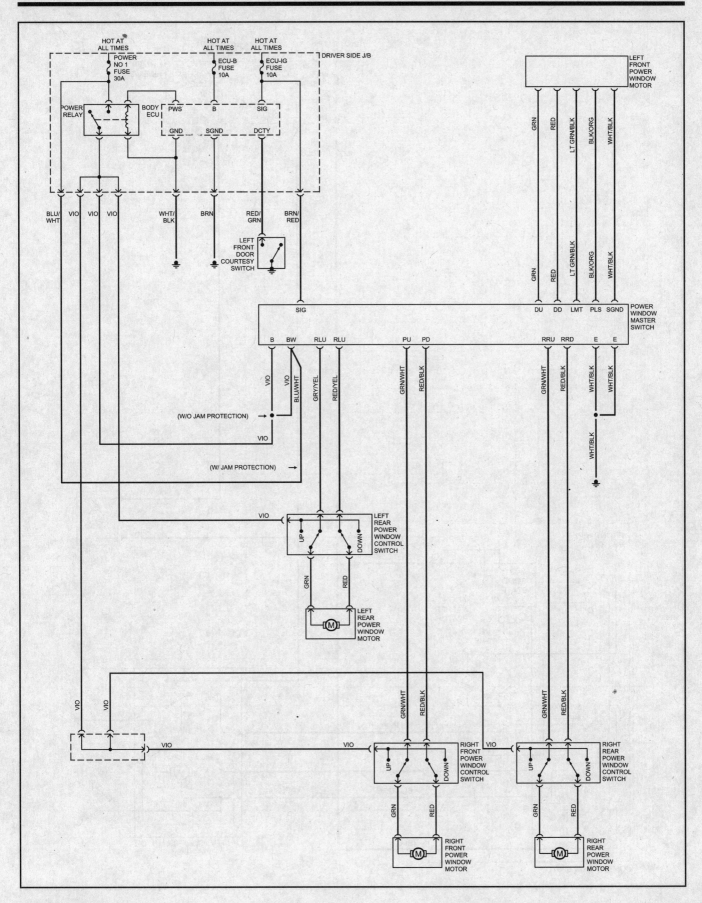

Power window system

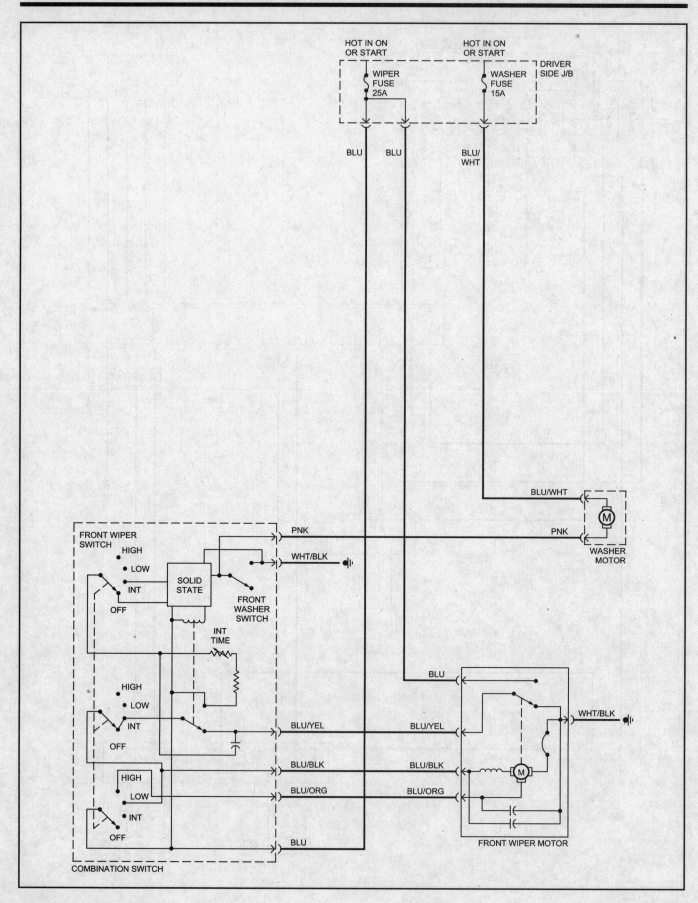

Wiper and washer system

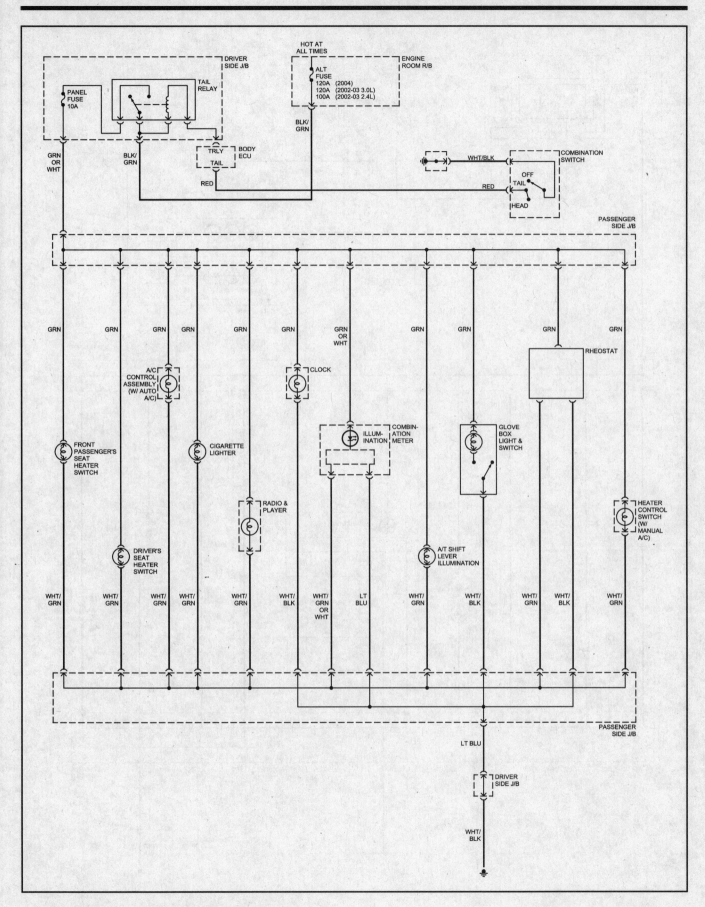

Interior lighting system, 2002 through 2004 models

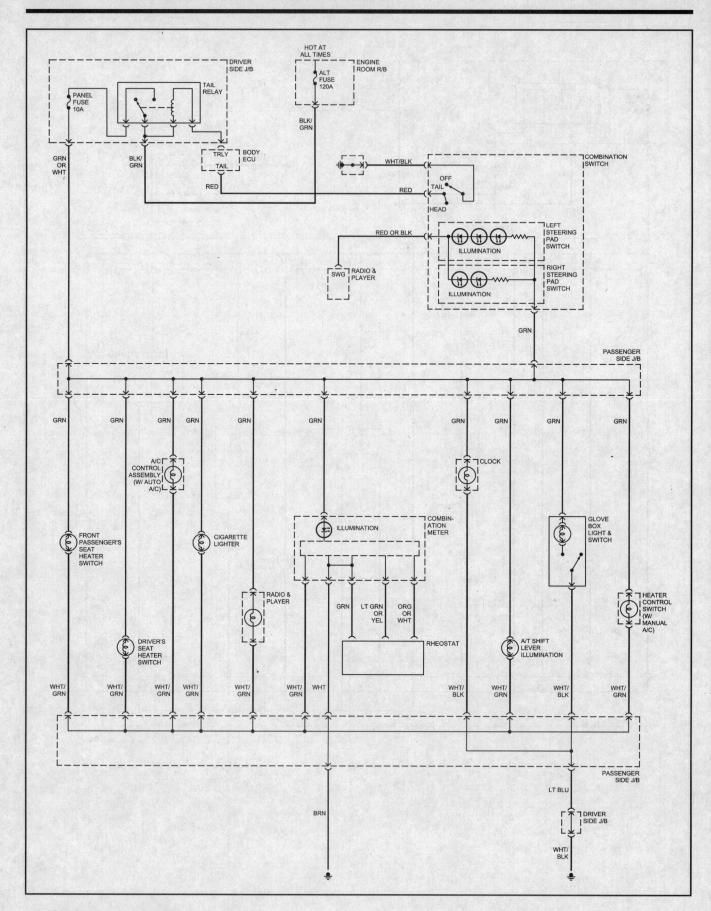

Interior lighting system, 2005 and later models

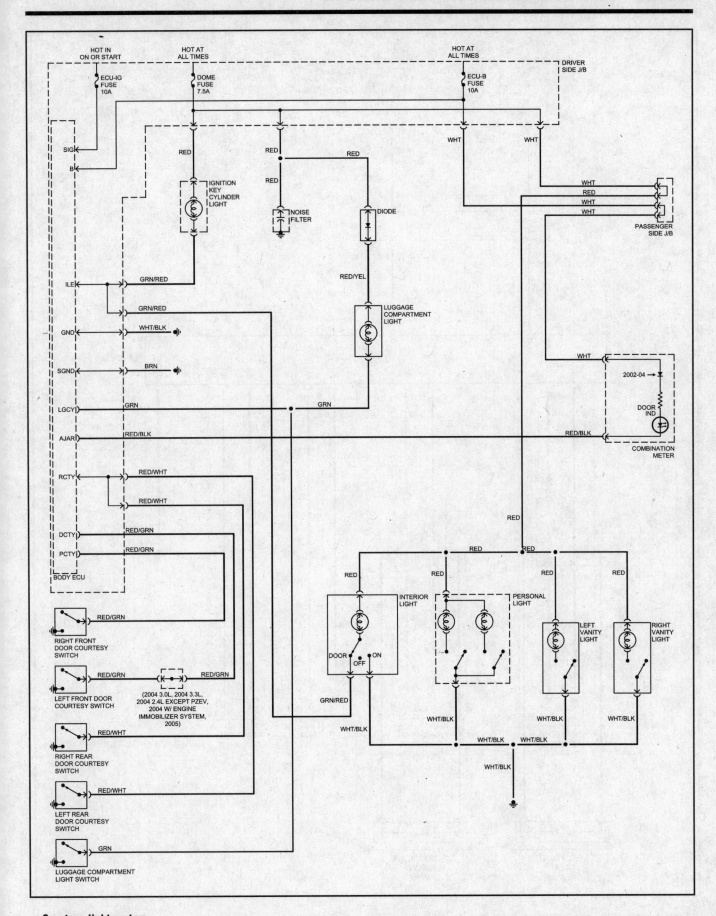

Courtesy light system

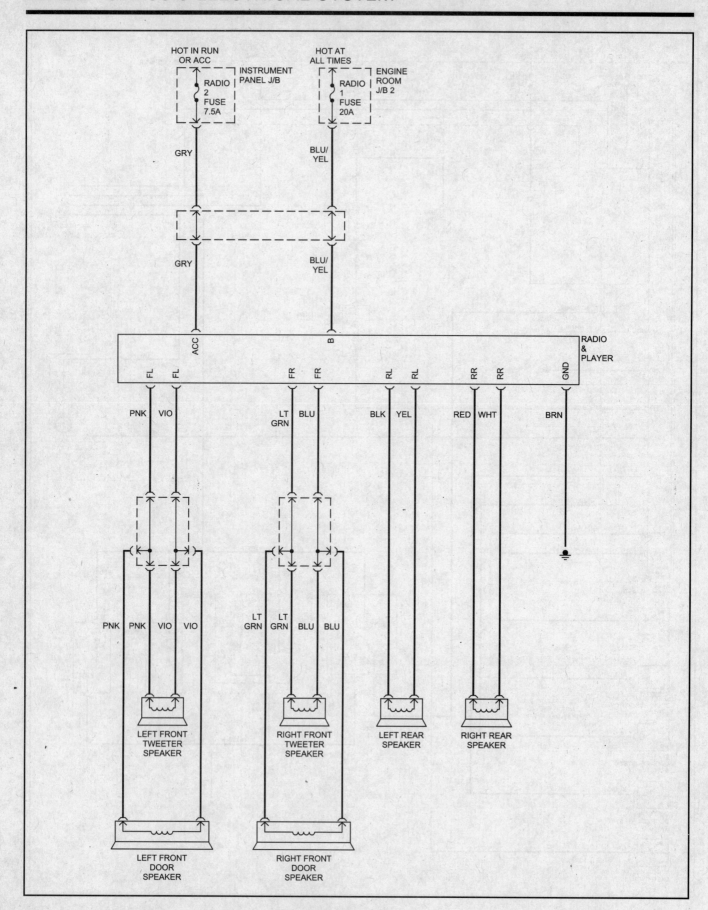

Audio system, 2002 and 2003 models (Camry shown, Solara and Lexus similar)

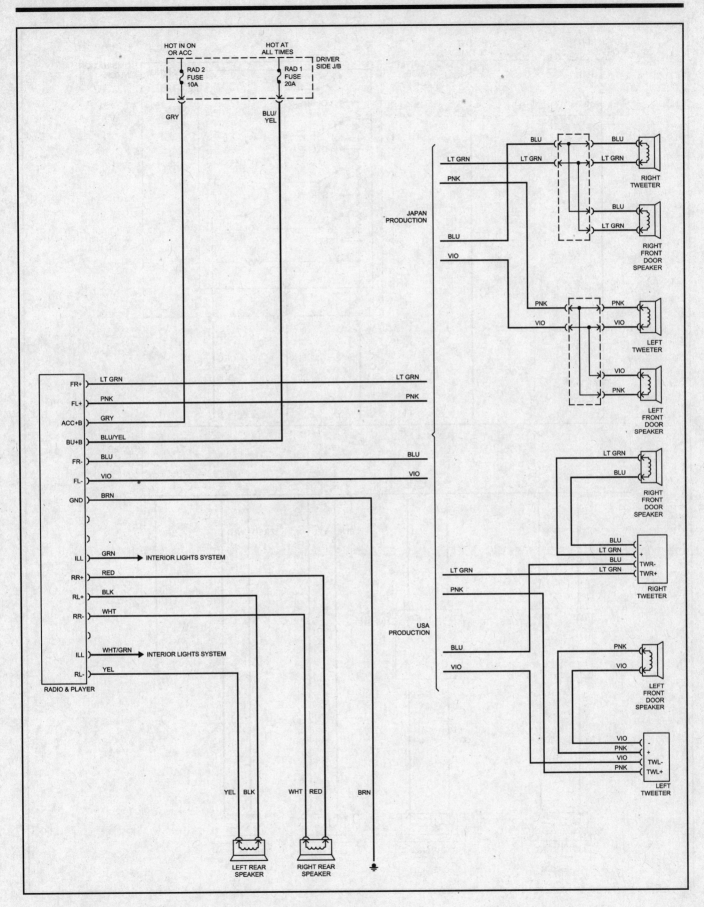

Audio system, 2004 models (Camry shown, Solara and Lexus similar)

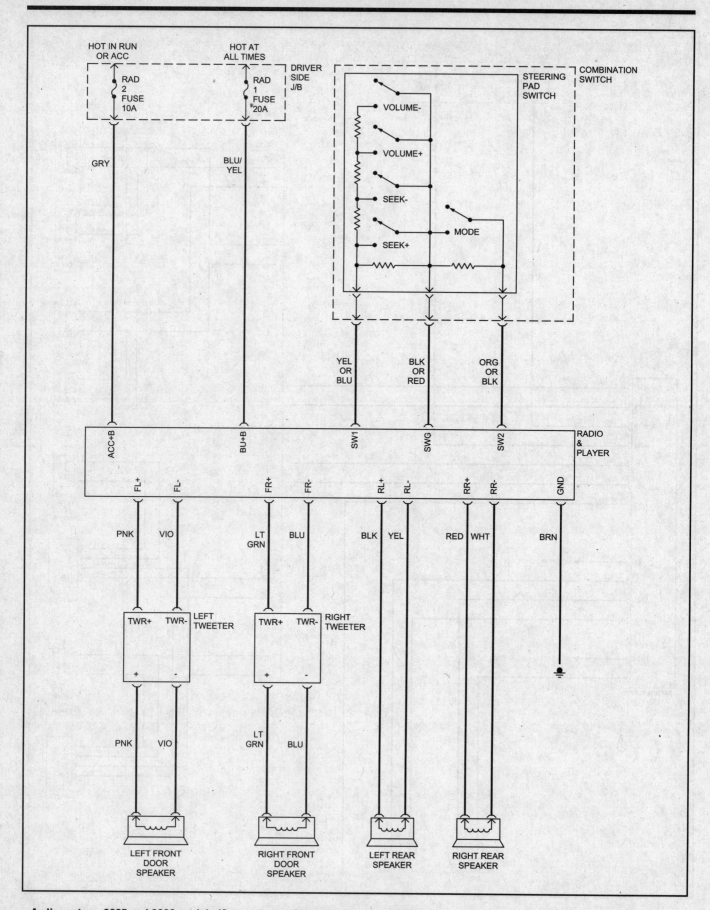

Audio system, 2005 and 2006 models (Camry shown, Solara and Lexus similar)

GLOSSARY

AIR/FUEL RATIO: The ratio of air-to-gasoline by weight in the fuel mixture drawn into the engine.

AIR INJECTION: One method of reducing harmful exhaust emissions by injecting air into each of the exhaust ports of an engine. The fresh air entering the hot exhaust manifold causes any remaining fuel to be burned before it can exit the tailpipe.

ALTERNATOR: A device used for converting mechanical energy into electrical energy.

AMMETER: An instrument, calibrated in amperes, used to measure the flow of an electrical current in a circuit. Ammeters are always connected in series with the circuit being tested.

AMPERE: The rate of flow of electrical current present when one volt of electrical pressure is applied against one ohm of electrical resistance.

ANALOG COMPUTER: Any microprocessor that uses similar (analogous) electrical signals to make its calculations.

ARMATURE: A laminated, soft iron core wrapped by a wire that converts electrical energy to mechanical energy as in a motor or relay. When rotated in a magnetic field, it changes mechanical energy into electrical energy as in a generator.

ATMOSPHERIC PRESSURE: The pressure on the Earth's surface caused by the weight of the air in the atmosphere. At sea level, this pressure is 14.7 psi at 32°F (101 kPa at 0°C).

ATOMIZATION: The breaking down of a liquid into a fine mist that can be suspended in air.

AXIAL PLAY: Movement parallel to a shaft or bearing bore.

BACKFIRE: The sudden combustion of gases in the intake or exhaust system that results in a loud explosion.

BACKLASH: The clearance or play between two parts, such as meshed gears.

BACKPRESSURE: Restrictions in the exhaust system that slow the exit of exhaust gases from the combustion chamber.

BAKELITE: A heat resistant, plastic insulator material commonly used in printed circuit boards and transistorized components.

BALL BEARING: A bearing made up of hardened inner and outer races between which hardened steel balls roll.

BALLAST RESISTOR: A resistor in the primary ignition circuit that lowers voltage after the engine is started to reduce wear on ignition components.

BEARING: A friction reducing, supportive device usually located between a stationary part and a moving part.

BIMETAL TEMPERATURE SENSOR: Any sensor or switch made of two dissimilar types of metal that bend when heated or cooled due to the different expansion rates of the alloys. These types of sensors usually function as an on/off switch.

BLOWBY: Combustion gases, composed of water vapor and unburned fuel, that leak past the piston rings into the crankcase during normal engine operation. These gases are removed by the PCV system to prevent the buildup of harmful acids in the crankcase.

BRAKE PAD: A brake shoe and lining assembly used with disc brakes.

BRAKE SHOE: The backing for the brake lining. The term is, however, usually applied to the assembly of the brake backing and lining.

BUSHING: A liner, usually removable, for a bearing; an anti-friction liner used in place of a bearing.

CALIPER: A hydraulically activated device in a disc brake system, which is mounted straddling the brake rotor (disc). The caliper contains at least one piston and two brake pads. Hydraulic pressure on the piston(s) forces the pads against the rotor.

CAMSHAFT: A shaft in the engine on which are the lobes (cams) which operate the valves. The camshaft is driven by the crankshaft, via a belt, chain or gears, at one half the crankshaft speed.

CAPACITOR: A device which stores an electrical charge.

CARBON MONOXIDE (CO): A colorless, odorless gas given off as a normal byproduct of combustion. It is poisonous and extremely dangerous in confined areas, building up slowly to toxic levels without warning if adequate ventilation is not available.

CARBURETOR: A device, usually mounted on the intake manifold of an engine, which mixes the air and fuel in the proper proportion to allow even combustion.

CATALYTIC CONVERTER: A device installed in the exhaust system, like a muffler, that converts harmful byproducts of combustion into carbon dioxide and water vapor by means of a heat-producing chemical reaction.

CENTRIFUGAL ADVANCE: A mechanical method of advancing the spark timing by using flyweights in the distributor that react to centrifugal force generated by the distributor shaft rotation.

CHECK VALVE: Any one-way valve installed to permit the flow of air, fuel or vacuum in one direction only.

CHOKE: A device, usually a moveable valve, placed in the intake path of a carburetor to restrict the flow of air.

CIRCUIT: Any unbroken path through which an electrical current can flow. Also used to describe fuel flow in some instances.

CIRCUIT BREAKER: A switch which protects an electrical circuit from overload by opening the circuit when the current flow exceeds a predetermined level. Some circuit breakers must be reset manually, while most reset automatically.

COIL (IGNITION): A transformer in the ignition circuit which steps up the voltage provided to the spark plugs.

COMBINATION MANIFOLD: An assembly which includes both the intake and exhaust manifolds in one casting.

COMBINATION VALVE: A device used in some fuel systems that routes fuel vapors to a charcoal storage canister instead of venting them into the atmosphere. The valve relieves fuel tank pressure and allows fresh air into the tank as the fuel level drops to prevent a vapor lock situation.

COMPRESSION RATIO: The comparison of the total volume of the cylinder and combustion chamber with the piston at BDC and the piston at TDC.

CONDENSER: 1. An electrical device which acts to store an electrical charge, preventing voltage surges. 2. A radiator-like device in the air conditioning system in which refrigerant gas condenses into a liquid, giving off heat.

CONDUCTOR: Any material through which an electrical current can be transmitted easily.

CONTINUITY: Continuous or complete circuit. Can be checked with an ohmmeter.

COUNTERSHAFT: An intermediate shaft which is rotated by a mainshaft and transmits, in turn, that rotation to a working part.

CRANKCASE: The lower part of an engine in which the crankshaft and related parts operate.

CRANKSHAFT: The main driving shaft of an engine which receives reciprocating motion from the pistons and converts it to rotary motion.

CYLINDER: In an engine, the round hole in the engine block in which the piston(s) ride.

CYLINDER BLOCK: The main structural member of an engine in which is found the cylinders, crankshaft and other principal parts.

CYLINDER HEAD: The detachable portion of the engine, usually fastened to the top of the cylinder block and containing all or most of the combustion chambers. On overhead valve engines, it contains the valves and their operating parts. On overhead cam engines, it contains the camshaft as well.

DEAD CENTER: The extreme top or bottom of the piston stroke.

DETONATION: An unwanted explosion of the air/fuel mixture in the combustion chamber caused by excess heat and compression, advanced timing, or an overly lean mixture. Also referred to as "ping".

DIAPHRAGM: A thin, flexible wall separating two cavities, such as in a vacuum advance unit.

DIESELING: A condition in which hot spots in the combustion chamber cause the engine to run on after the key is turned off.

DIFFERENTIAL: A geared assembly which allows the transmission of motion between drive axles, giving one axle the ability to turn faster than the other.

DIODE: An electrical device that will allow current to flow in one direction only.

DISC BRAKE: A hydraulic braking assembly consisting of a brake disc, or rotor, mounted on an axle, and a caliper assembly containing, usually two brake pads which are activated by hydraulic pressure. The pads are forced against the sides of the disc, creating friction which slows the vehicle.

DISTRIBUTOR: A mechanically driven device on an engine which is responsible for electrically firing the spark plug at a predetermined point of the piston stroke.

DOWEL PIN: A pin, inserted in mating holes in two different parts allowing those parts to maintain a fixed relationship.

DRUM BRAKE: A braking system which consists of two brake shoes and one or two wheel cylinders, mounted on a fixed backing plate, and a brake drum, mounted on an axle, which revolves around the assembly.

DWELL: The rate, measured in degrees of shaft rotation, at which an electrical circuit cycles on and off.

ELECTRONIC CONTROL UNIT (ECU): Ignition module, module, amplifier or igniter. See Module for definition.

ELECTRONIC IGNITION: A system in which the timing and firing of the spark plugs is controlled by an electronic control unit, usually called a module. These systems have no points or condenser.

END-PLAY: The measured amount of axial movement in a shaft.

ENGINE: A device that converts heat into mechanical energy.

EXHAUST MANIFOLD: A set of cast passages or pipes which conduct exhaust gases from the engine.

FEELER GAUGE: A blade, usually metal, or precisely predetermined thickness, used to measure the clearance between two parts.

FIRING ORDER: The order in which combustion occurs in the cylinders of an engine. Also the order in which spark is distributed to the plugs by the distributor.

FLOODING: The presence of too much fuel in the intake manifold and combustion chamber which prevents the air/fuel mixture from firing, thereby causing a no-start situation.

FLYWHEEL: A disc shaped part bolted to the rear end of the crankshaft. Around the outer perimeter is affixed the ring gear. The starter drive engages the ring gear, turning the flywheel, which rotates the crankshaft, imparting the initial starting motion to the engine.

FOOT POUND (ft. lbs. or sometimes, ft.lb.): The amount of energy or work needed to raise an item weighing one pound, a distance of one foot.

FUSE: A protective device in a circuit which prevents circuit overload by breaking the circuit when a specific amperage is present. The device is constructed around a strip or wire of a lower amperage rating than the circuit it is designed to protect. When an amperage higher than that stamped on the fuse is present in the circuit, the strip or wire melts, opening the circuit.

GEAR RATIO: The ratio between the number of teeth on meshing gears.

GENERATOR: A device which converts mechanical energy into electrical energy.

HEAT RANGE: The measure of a spark plug's ability to dissipate heat from its firing end. The higher the heat range, the hotter the plug fires.

HUB: The center part of a wheel or gear.

HYDROCARBON (HC): Any chemical compound made up of hydrogen and carbon. A major pollutant formed by the engine as a byproduct of combustion.

HYDROMETER: An instrument used to measure the specific gravity of a solution.

INCH POUND (inch lbs.; sometimes in.lb. or in. lbs.): One twelfth of a foot pound.

INDUCTION: A means of transferring electrical energy in the form of a magnetic field. Principle used in the ignition coil to increase voltage.

INJECTOR: A device which receives metered fuel under relatively low pressure and is activated to inject the fuel into the engine under relatively high pressure at a predetermined time.

INPUT SHAFT: The shaft to which torque is applied, usually carrying the driving gear or gears.

INTAKE MANIFOLD: A casting of passages or pipes used to conduct air or a fuel/air mixture to the cylinders.

JOURNAL: The bearing surface within which a shaft operates.

KEY: A small block usually fitted in a notch between a shaft and a hub to prevent slippage of the two parts.

MANIFOLD: A casting of passages or set of pipes which connect the cylinders to an inlet or outlet source.

MANIFOLD VACUUM: Low pressure in an engine intake manifold formed just below the throttle plates. Manifold vacuum is highest at idle and drops under acceleration.

MASTER CYLINDER: The primary fluid pressurizing device in a hydraulic system. In automotive use, it is found in brake and hydraulic clutch systems and is pedal activated, either directly or, in a power brake system, through the power booster.

MODULE: Electronic control unit, amplifier or igniter of solid state or integrated design which controls the current flow in the ignition

primary circuit based on input from the pick-up coil. When the module opens the primary circuit, high secondary voltage is induced in the coil.

NEEDLE BEARING: A bearing which consists of a number (usually a large number) of long, thin rollers.

OHM: (Ω) The unit used to measure the resistance of conductor-to-electrical flow. One ohm is the amount of resistance that limits current flow to one ampere in a circuit with one volt of pressure.

OHMMETER: An instrument used for measuring the resistance, in ohms, in an electrical circuit.

OUTPUT SHAFT: The shaft which transmits torque from a device, such as a transmission.

OVERDRIVE: A gear assembly which produces more shaft revolutions than that transmitted to it.

OVERHEAD CAMSHAFT (OHC): An engine configuration in which the camshaft is mounted on top of the cylinder head and operates the valve either directly or by means of rocker arms.

OVERHEAD VALVE (OHV): An engine configuration in which all of the valves are located in the cylinder head and the camshaft is located in the cylinder block. The camshaft operates the valves via lifters and pushrods.

OXIDES OF NITROGEN (NOx): Chemical compounds of nitrogen produced as a byproduct of combustion. They combine with hydrocarbons to produce smog.

OXYGEN SENSOR: Use with the feedback system to sense the presence of oxygen in the exhaust gas and signal the computer which can reference the voltage signal to an air/fuel ratio.

PINION: The smaller of two meshing gears.

PISTON RING: An open-ended ring with fits into a groove on the outer diameter of the piston. Its chief function is to form a seal between the piston and cylinder wall. Most automotive pistons have three rings: two for compression sealing; one for oil sealing.

PRELOAD: A predetermined load placed on a bearing during assembly or by adjustment.

PRIMARY CIRCUIT: the low voltage side of the ignition system which consists of the ignition switch, ballast resistor or resistance wire, bypass, coil, electronic control unit and pick-up coil as well as the connecting wires and harnesses.

PRESS FIT: The mating of two parts under pressure, due to the inner diameter of one being smaller than the outer diameter of the other, or vice versa; an interference fit.

RACE: The surface on the inner or outer ring of a bearing on which the balls, needles or rollers move.

REGULATOR: A device which maintains the amperage and/or voltage levels of a circuit at predetermined values.

RELAY: A switch which automatically opens and/or closes a circuit.

RESISTANCE: The opposition to the flow of current through a circuit or electrical device, and is measured in ohms. Resistance is equal to the voltage divided by the amperage.

RESISTOR: A device, usually made of wire, which offers a preset amount of resistance in an electrical circuit.

RING GEAR: The name given to a ring-shaped gear attached to a differential case, or affixed to a flywheel or as part of a planetary gear set.

ROLLER BEARING: A bearing made up of hardened inner and outer races between which hardened steel rollers move.

ROTOR: 1. The disc-shaped part of a disc brake assembly, upon which the brake pads bear; also called, brake disc. 2. The device mounted atop the distributor shaft, which passes current to the distributor cap tower contacts.

SECONDARY CIRCUIT: The high voltage side of the ignition system, usually above 20,000 volts. The secondary includes the ignition coil, coil wire, distributor cap and rotor, spark plug wires and spark plugs.

SENDING UNIT: A mechanical, electrical, hydraulic or electro-magnetic device which transmits information to a gauge.

SENSOR: Any device designed to measure engine operating conditions or ambient pressures and temperatures. Usually electronic in nature and designed to send a voltage signal to an on-board computer, some sensors may operate as a simple on/off switch or they may provide a variable voltage signal (like a potentiometer) as conditions or measured parameters change.

SHIM: Spacers of precise, predetermined thickness used between parts to establish a proper working relationship.

SLAVE CYLINDER: In automotive use, a device in the hydraulic clutch system which is activated by hydraulic force, disengaging the clutch.

SOLENOID: A coil used to produce a magnetic field, the effect of which is to produce work.

SPARK PLUG: A device screwed into the combustion chamber of a spark ignition engine. The basic construction is a conductive core inside of a ceramic insulator, mounted in an outer conductive base. An electrical charge from the spark plug wire travels along the conductive core and jumps a preset air gap to a grounding point or points at the end of the conductive base. The resultant spark ignites the fuel/air mixture in the combustion chamber.

SPLINES: Ridges machined or cast onto the outer diameter of a shaft or inner diameter of a bore to enable parts to mate without rotation.

TACHOMETER: A device used to measure the rotary speed of an engine, shaft, gear, etc., usually in rotations per minute.

THERMOSTAT: A valve, located in the cooling system of an engine, which is closed when cold and opens gradually in response to engine heating, controlling the temperature of the coolant and rate of coolant flow.

TOP DEAD CENTER (TDC): The point at which the piston reaches the top of its travel on the compression stroke.

TORQUE: The twisting force applied to an object.

TORQUE CONVERTER: A turbine used to transmit power from a driving member to a driven member via hydraulic action, providing changes in drive ratio and torque. In automotive use, it links the driveplate at the rear of the engine to the automatic transmission.

TRANSDUCER: A device used to change a force into an electrical signal.

TRANSISTOR: A semi-conductor component which can be actuated by a small voltage to perform an electrical switching function.

TUNE-UP: A regular maintenance function, usually associated with the replacement and adjustment of parts and components in the electrical and fuel systems of a vehicle for the purpose of attaining optimum performance.

TURBOCHARGER: An exhaust driven pump which compresses intake air and forces it into the combustion chambers at higher than atmospheric pressures. The increased air pressure allows more fuel to be burned and results in increased horsepower being produced.

VACUUM ADVANCE: A device which advances the ignition timing in response to increased engine vacuum.

VACUUM GAUGE: An instrument used to measure the presence of vacuum in a chamber.

VALVE: A device which control the pressure, direction of flow or rate of flow of a liquid or gas.

VALVE CLEARANCE: The measured gap between the end of the valve stem and the rocker arm, cam lobe or follower that activates the valve.

VISCOSITY: The rating of a liquid's internal resistance to flow.

VOLTMETER: An instrument used for measuring electrical force in units called volts. Voltmeters are always connected parallel with the circuit being tested.

WHEEL CYLINDER: Found in the automotive drum brake assembly, it is a device, actuated by hydraulic pressure, which, through internal pistons, pushes the brake shoes outward against the drums.

A

ABOUT THIS MANUAL, 0-5

ACKNOWLEDGEMENTS, 0-4

AIR CLEANER ASSEMBLY, REMOVAL AND INSTALLATION, 4-8

AIR CONDITIONING

and heating system, check and maintenance, 3-13

compressor, removal and installation, 3-16

condenser, removal and installation, 3-17

control assembly, removal and installation, 3-9

receiver/drier, removal and installation, 3-15

AIR FILTER REPLACEMENT, 1-23

AIR/FUEL SENSOR, GENERAL INFORMATION AND REPLACEMENT, 6-11

AIRBAG SYSTEM, GENERAL INFORMATION, 12-20

ALIGNMENT, WHEEL, GENERAL INFORMATION, 10-20

ALTERNATOR, REMOVAL AND INSTALLATION, 5-7

ANTENNA, REPLACEMENT, 12-12

ANTIFREEZE, GENERAL INFORMATION, 3-3

ANTI-LOCK BRAKE SYSTEM (ABS), GENERAL INFORMATION, 9-2

AUTOMATIC TRANSAXLE, 7B-1

diagnosis, general, 7B-2

differential lubricant level check, 1-24

electronic control system, 7B-10

fluid

    change, 1-27

    level check, 1-12

oil seal replacement, 7B-6

removal and installation, 7B-7

shift cable, adjustment and replacement, 7B-3

shift lock system, description, check and component replacement, 7B-5

Throttle valve (TV) cable, adjustment and replacement (Avalon and Solara models), 7B-4

transmission position switch, replacement and adjustment, 7B-5

trouble codes, 7B-8

AUTOMOTIVE CHEMICALS AND LUBRICANTS, 0-17

B

BACK-UP LIGHT SWITCH, MANUAL TRANSAXLE, CHECK AND REPLACEMENT, 7A-2

BALANCER ASSEMBLY, FOUR-CYLINDER ENGINE, REMOVAL AND INSTALLATION, 2A-21

BALLJOINTS, REPLACEMENT, 10-8

BATTERY

cables, check and replacement, 5-4

check and replacement, 5-3

check, maintenance and charging, 1-15

general information, precautions and disconnection, 5-2

BLOWER MOTOR, REMOVAL AND INSTALLATION, 3-9

BODY REPAIR

major damage, 11-7

minor damage, 11-3

BODY, 11-1

BODY, MAINTENANCE, 11-2

BOOSTER BATTERY (JUMP) STARTING, 0-15

BRAKES, 9-1

Anti-lock Brake System (ABS), general information, 9-2

caliper, removal and installation, 9-10

check, 1-20

disc, inspection, removal and installation, 9-11

fluid level check, 1-9

hoses and lines, inspection and replacement, 9-18

hydraulic system, bleeding, 9-19

light switch, removal, installation and adjustment, 9-26

master cylinder, removal and installation, 9-17

pads, disc brake, replacement, 9-6

parking brake

adjustment, 9-24

cables, replacement, 9-25

shoes (rear disc brakes only), inspection and replacement, 9-21

pedal height and freeplay, check and adjustment, 1-25

power brake booster, check, removal and installation, 9-20

shoes, drum brake, replacement, 9-13

wheel cylinder, removal and installation, 9-16

BULB REPLACEMENT, 12-10

BUMPER COVERS, REMOVAL AND INSTALLATION, 11-9

BUYING PARTS, 0-7

C

CABLE REPLACEMENT

battery, 5-4

fuel filler door, 11-14

hood release, 11-8

parking brake, 9-25

trunk lid release, 11-14

CALIPER, DISC BRAKE, REMOVAL AND INSTALLATION, 9-10

CAMSHAFT POSITION (CMP) SENSOR, REPLACEMENT, 6-10

CAMSHAFTS AND LIFTERS, REMOVAL, INSPECTION AND INSTALLATION

four-cylinder engine, 2A-10

V6 engine, 2B-11

CATALYTIC CONVERTERS, 6-15

CENTER CONSOLE, REMOVAL AND INSTALLATION, 11-20

CHARGING SYSTEM

alternator, removal and installation, 5-7

check, 5-7

general information and precautions, 5-6

CHASSIS AND BODY FASTENER CHECK, 1-29

CHASSIS ELECTRICAL SYSTEM, 12-1

CHEMICALS AND LUBRICANTS, 0-17

CIRCUIT BREAKERS, GENERAL INFORMATION, 12-5

CLUTCH

components, removal, inspection and installation, 8-2

description and check, 8-2

fluid level check, 1-9

hydraulic system, bleeding, 8-6

master cylinder, removal and installation, 8-5

pedal height and freeplay, check and adjustment, 1-25

release bearing and lever, removal, inspection and installation, 8-4

release cylinder and accumulator, removal and installation, 8-6

start switch, replacement, 8-6

CLUTCH AND DRIVEAXLES, 8-1

COIL(S), IGNITION, REPLACEMENT, 5-6

COMPRESSOR, AIR CONDITIONING, REMOVAL AND INSTALLATION, 3-16

CONDENSER, AIR CONDITIONING, REMOVAL AND INSTALLATION, 3-17

CONTROL ARM, REMOVAL, INSPECTION AND INSTALLATION, 10-7

CONVERSION FACTORS, 0-18

COOLANT TEMPERATURE (ECT) SENSOR, REPLACEMENT, 6-9

COOLANT TEMPERATURE SENDING UNIT, REPLACEMENT, 3-8

COOLING SYSTEM

check, 1-18

general information, 3-2

servicing (draining, flushing and refilling), 1-35

COOLING, HEATING AND AIR CONDITIONING SYSTEMS, 3-1

COWL COVER, REMOVAL AND INSTALLATION, 11-24

CRANKSHAFT FRONT OIL SEAL, REPLACEMENT

four-cylinder engine, 2A-16

V6 engine, 2B-11

CRANKSHAFT POSITION (CKP) SENSOR, REPLACEMENT, 6-10

CRANKSHAFT PULLEY/VIBRATION DAMPER, REMOVAL AND INSTALLATION, 2A-16

CRANKSHAFT, REMOVAL AND INSTALLATION, 2C-16

CRUISE CONTROL SYSTEM, DESCRIPTION, 12-18

CYLINDER COMPRESSION CHECK, 2C-4

CYLINDER HEAD, REMOVAL AND INSTALLATION

four-cylinder engine, 2A-15

V6 engine, 2B-13

D

DASHBOARD TRIM PANELS, REMOVAL AND INSTALLATION, 11-20

DAYTIME RUNNING LIGHTS (DRL), GENERAL INFORMATION, 12-20

DEFOGGER, REAR WINDOW, CHECK AND REPAIR, 12-12

DIAGNOSIS, 0-21

DIFFERENTIAL LUBRICANT

change, 1-27

level check, 1-24

DISC BRAKE

caliper, removal and installation, 9-10

disc, inspection, removal and installation, 9-11

pads, replacement, 9-6

DOOR

latch, lock cylinder and handle, removal and installation, 11-17

power lock system, description, 12-19

removal, installation and adjustment, 11-16

trim panels, removal and installation, 11-14

window glass regulator, removal and installation, 11-19

window glass, removal and installation, 11-18

DRIVEAXLE(S)

boot check, 1-22

boot replacement, 8-9

general information and inspection, 8-7

removal and installation, 8-7

DRIVEBELT CHECK, ADJUSTMENT AND REPLACEMENT, 1-30

DRIVEBELT TENSIONER, 2A-5

DRUM BRAKE

shoes, replacement, 9-13

wheel cylinder, removal and installation, 9-16

E

ELECTRIC SIDE VIEW MIRRORS, DESCRIPTION, 12-17

ELECTRICAL TROUBLESHOOTING, GENERAL INFORMATION, 12-2

ELECTRONIC FUEL INJECTION SYSTEM

check, 4-9

general information, 4-8

EMISSIONS AND ENGINE CONTROL SYSTEMS, 6-1

ENGINE, GENERAL OVERHAUL PROCEDURES, 2C-1

crankshaft, removal and installation, 2C-16

cylinder compression check, 2C-4

engine

overhaul

disassembly sequence, 2C-9

reassembly sequence, 2C-18

rebuilding alternatives, 2C-6

removal and installation, 2C-8

removal, methods and precautions, 2C-6

general information, 2C-2

initial start-up and break-in after overhaul, 2C-19

oil pressure check, 2C-3

pistons and connecting rods, removal and installation, 2C-10

vacuum gauge diagnostic checks, 2C-5

ENGINE, IN-VEHICLE REPAIR PROCEDURES

Four-cylinder engine, 2A-1

camshafts and lifters, removal, inspection and installation, 2A-10

crankshaft front oil seal, replacement, 2A-16

crankshaft pulley/vibration damper, removal and installation, 2A-16

cylinder head, removal and installation, 2A-15

engine balancer, removal and installation, 2A-21

exhaust manifold, removal and installation, 2A-14

flywheel/driveplate, removal and installation, 2A-19

intake manifold, removal and installation, 2A-13

oil pan, removal and installation, 2A-17

oil pump, removal and installation, 2A-18

powertrain mounts, check and replacement, 2A-20

rear main oil seal, replacement, 2A-20

repair operations possible with the engine in the vehicle, 2A-2

timing chain and sprockets, removal, inspection and installation, 2A-5

Top Dead Center (TDC) for number one piston, locating, 2A-2

valve cover, removal and installation, 2A-3

Variable Valve Timing (VVT) system, description, 2A-4

V6 engine, 2B-1

camshafts and lifters, removal, inspection and installation, 2B-11

cylinder head, removal and installation, 2B-13

exhaust manifolds, removal and installation, 2B-7

flywheel/driveplate, removal and installation, 2B-18

intake manifold, removal and installation, 2B-6

oil pan, removal and installation, 2B-15

oil pump, removal, inspection and installation, 2B-16

oil seals, replacement, 2B-11

powertrain mounts, check and replacement, 2B-18

rear main oil seal, replacement, 2B-18

repair operations possible with the engine in the vehicle, 2B-2

timing belt and sprockets, removal, inspection and installation, 2B-8

Top Dead Center (TDC) for number one piston, locating, 2B-2

valve covers, removal and installation, 2B-4

Variable Valve Timing (VVT) system, description, check and component replacement, 2B-3

ENGINE COOLANT TEMPERATURE (ECT) SENSOR, REPLACEMENT, 6-9

ENGINE COOLANT, LEVEL CHECK, 1-8

ENGINE COOLING FANS, REMOVAL AND INSTALLATION, 3-5

ENGINE ELECTRICAL SYSTEMS, 5-1

ENGINE OIL AND OIL FILTER CHANGE, 1-13

ENGINE OIL, LEVEL CHECK, 1-8

ENGINE REBUILDING ALTERNATIVES, 2C-6

ENGINE, REMOVAL AND INSTALLATION, 2C-8

EVAPORATIVE EMISSIONS CONTROL (EVAP) SYSTEM, 6-14

EVAPORATIVE EMISSIONS CONTROL SYSTEM CHECK, 1-27

EXHAUST GAS RECIRCULATION (EGR) SYSTEM, 6-13

EXHAUST MANIFOLD, REMOVAL AND INSTALLATION

four-cylinder engine, 2A-14

V6 engine, 2B-7

EXHAUST SYSTEM

check, 1-23

servicing, general information, 4-12

F

FANS, ENGINE COOLING, REMOVAL AND INSTALLATION, 3-5

FAULT FINDING, 0-21

FENDER, FRONT, REMOVAL AND INSTALLATION, 11-11

FILTER REPLACEMENT

engine air, 1-23

engine oil, 1-13

interior ventilation, 1-25

FLAT TIRE, CHANGING, 0-16

FLUID LEVEL CHECKS

automatic transaxle, 1-12

brake fluid, 1-9

clutch fluid, 1-9

engine coolant, 1-8

engine oil, 1-8

manual transaxle, 1-25

power steering, 1-11

windshield washer fluid, 1-9

FLUIDS AND LUBRICANTS

capacities, 1-39

recommended, 1-39

FLYWHEEL/DRIVEPLATE, REMOVAL AND INSTALLATION

four-cylinder engine, 2A-19

V6 engine, 2B-18

FOUR-CYLINDER ENGINE, 2A-1

camshafts and lifters, removal, inspection and installation, 2A-10

crankshaft front oil seal, replacement, 2A-16

crankshaft pulley/vibration damper, removal and installation, 2A-16

cylinder head, removal and installation, 2A-15

engine balancer, removal and installation, 2A-21

exhaust manifold, removal and installation, 2A-14

flywheel/driveplate, removal and installation, 2A-19

intake manifold, removal and installation, 2A-13

oil pan, removal and installation, 2A-17

oil pump, removal and installation, 2A-18

powertrain mounts, check and replacement, 2A-20

rear main oil seal, replacement, 2A-20

repair operations possible with the engine in the vehicle, 2A-2

timing chain and sprockets, removal, inspection and installation, 2A-5

Top Dead Center (TDC) for number one piston, locating, 2A-2

valve cover, removal and installation, 2A-3

Variable Valve Timing (VVT) system, description, 2A-4

FRACTION/DECIMAL/MILLIMETER EQUIVALENTS, 0-19

FUEL AND EXHAUST SYSTEMS, 4-1

air cleaner assembly, removal and installation, 4-8

electronic fuel injection system
    check, 4-9
    general information, 4-8

exhaust system servicing, general information, 4-12

filler door release cable, removal and installation, 11-14

level sending unit, replacement, 4-7

lines and fittings, general information, 4-4

pressure regulator, removal and installation, 4-6

pressure relief, 4-3

pulsation damper, replacement, 4-11

pump, removal and installation, 4-5

pump/fuel pressure, check, 4-3

rail and injectors, removal and installation, 4-11

system check, 1-24

tank
    cap gasket inspection and replacement, 1-26
    cleaning and repair, general information, 4-8
    removal and installation, 4-7
    throttle body, check, removal and installation, 4-10

FUSES AND FUSIBLE LINKS, GENERAL INFORMATION, 12-4

G

GENERAL ENGINE OVERHAUL PROCEDURES, 2C-1

crankshaft, removal and installation, 2C-16

cylinder compression check, 2C-4

engine
    overhaul
        disassembly sequence, 2C-9
        reassembly sequence, 2C-18
    removal and installation, 2C-6
    removal, methods and precautions, 2C-8

engine rebuilding alternatives, 2C-5

general information, 2C-2

initial start-up and break-in after overhaul, 2C-19

oil pressure check, 2C-3

pistons and connecting rods, removal and installation, 2C-10

vacuum gauge diagnostic checks, 2C-5

H

HAZARD FLASHER, CHECK AND REPLACEMENT, 12-6

HEADLIGHTS

adjustment, 12-14

bulb, replacement, 12-13

housing, replacement, 12-15

HEATER AND AIR CONDITIONING CONTROL ASSEMBLY, REMOVAL AND INSTALLATION, 3-9

HEATER CORE, REMOVAL AND INSTALLATION, 3-10

HINGES AND LOCKS, MAINTENANCE, 11-7

HOOD

latch and release cable, removal and installation, 11-8

removal, installation and adjustment, 11-7

HORN, CHECK AND REPLACEMENT, 12-15

HUB AND BEARING ASSEMBLY, REMOVAL AND INSTALLATION

front, 10-9

rear, 10-12

I

IGNITION SYSTEM

check, 5-5

coil(s), replacement, 5-6

general information and precautions, 5-5

switch and key lock cylinder, replacement, 12-7

INITIAL START-UP AND BREAK-IN AFTER OVERHAUL, 2C-19

INJECTORS, FUEL, REMOVAL AND INSTALLATION, 4-11

INSTRUMENT CLUSTER, REMOVAL AND INSTALLATION, 12-9

INSTRUMENT PANEL
switches, replacement, 12-8
removal and installation, 11-22

INTAKE MANIFOLD, REMOVAL AND INSTALLATION
four-cylinder engine, 2A-13
V6 engine, 2B-6

INTERIOR VENTILATION FILTER REPLACEMENT, 1-25

INTRODUCTION TO THE TOYOTA CAMRY, AVALON, SOLARA AND LEXUS ES 300/330, 0-5

J

JACKING AND TOWING, 0-16
JUMP STARTING, 0-15

K

KNOCK SENSOR, REPLACEMENT, 6-12
KNUCKLE AND HUB, STEERING, REMOVAL AND INSTALLATION, 10-9

L

LOCK CYLINDER, REPLACEMENT
door, 11-17
ignition, 12-7
trunk lid, 11-13

LUBRICANTS AND CHEMICALS, 0-17

LUBRICANTS AND FLUIDS
capacities, 1-39
recommended, 1-39

M

MAINTENANCE SCHEDULE, 1-6
MAINTENANCE TECHNIQUES, TOOLS AND WORKING FACILITIES, 0-7

MAINTENANCE, ROUTINE, 1-1

MANUAL TRANSAXLE, 7A-1
back-up light switch, check and replacement, 7A-2
lubricant
    change, when vehicle used for towing, 1-29
    level check, 1-25
overhaul, general information, 7A-3
removal and installation, 7A-3
shift and select cables, replacement, 7A-2
shift lever assembly, removal and installation, 7A-2

MASS AIRFLOW (MAF) SENSOR, REPLACEMENT, 6-9

MASTER CYLINDER, REMOVAL AND INSTALLATION
brake, 9-17
clutch, 8-5

MIRRORS, ELECTRIC SIDE VIEW, DESCRIPTION, 12-17

MIRRORS, REMOVAL AND INSTALLATION, 11-19

O

OIL PAN, REMOVAL AND INSTALLATION
four-cylinder engine, 2A-17
V6 engine, 2B-15

OIL PRESSURE CHECK, 2C-3

OIL PUMP, REMOVAL AND INSTALLATION
four-cylinder engine, 2A-18
V6 engine, 2B-16

OIL, ENGINE, CHANGE, 1-13

ON BOARD DIAGNOSTIC (OBD) SYSTEM AND TROUBLE CODES, 6-2

OXYGEN SENSOR AND AIR/FUEL SENSOR, GENERAL INFORMATION AND REPLACEMENT, 6-11

P

PADS, DISC BRAKE, REPLACEMENT, 9-6

PARKING BRAKE
adjustment, 9-24
cables, replacement, 9-25
shoes (rear disc brakes only), inspection and replacement, 9-21

PISTONS AND CONNECTING RODS, REMOVAL AND INSTALLATION, 2C-10

POSITIVE CRANKCASE VENTILATION (PCV) SYSTEM, 6-13

POSITIVE CRANKCASE VENTILATION (PCV) VALVE CHECK AND REPLACEMENT, 1-27

POWER BRAKE BOOSTER, CHECK, REMOVAL AND INSTALLATION, 9-20

POWER DOOR LOCK SYSTEM, DESCRIPTION, 12-19

POWER STEERING

fluid level check, 1-11

Power Steering Pressure (PSP) switch, check and replacement, 10-18

pump, removal and installation, 10-17

system, bleeding, 10-19

POWER WINDOW SYSTEM, DESCRIPTION, 12-18

POWERTRAIN CONTROL MODULE (PCM), REMOVAL AND INSTALLATION, 6-8

POWERTRAIN MOUNTS, CHECK AND REPLACEMENT

four-cylinder engine, 2A-20

V6 engine, 2B-18

R

RADIATOR AND COOLANT RESERVOIR, REMOVAL AND INSTALLATION, 3-5

RADIO AND SPEAKERS, REMOVAL AND INSTALLATION, 12-11

REAR AXLE CARRIER, REMOVAL AND INSTALLATION, 10-13

REAR MAIN OIL SEAL, REPLACEMENT

four-cylinder engine, 2A-20

V6 engine, 2B-18

REAR PACKAGE SHELF, REMOVAL AND INSTALLATION, 11-25

REAR WINDOW DEFOGGER, CHECK AND REPAIR, 12-12

RECEIVER/DRIER, REMOVAL AND INSTALLATION, 3-15

RECOMMENDED LUBRICANTS AND FLUIDS, 1-39

RELAYS, GENERAL INFORMATION AND TESTING, 12-5

REPAIR OPERATIONS POSSIBLE WITH THE ENGINE IN THE VEHICLE

four-cylinder engine, 2A-2

V6 engine, 2B-2

REPLACEMENT PARTS, BUYING, 0-7

ROTOR, BRAKE, INSPECTION, REMOVAL AND INSTALLATION, 9-11

ROUTINE MAINTENANCE, 1-1

S

SAFETY FIRST!, 0-20

SCHEDULED MAINTENANCE, 1-6

SEATS, REMOVAL AND INSTALLATION, 11-24

SHIFT (AND SELECT) CABLE(S), REPLACEMENT

automatic transaxle, 7B-3

manual transaxle, 7A-2

SHIFT LEVER ASSEMBLY, MANUAL TRANSAXLE, REMOVAL AND INSTALLATION, 7A-2

SHIFT LOCK SYSTEM, AUTOMATIC TRANSAXLE, DESCRIPTION, CHECK AND COMPONENT REPLACEMENT, 7B-5

SHOES, DRUM BRAKE, REPLACEMENT, 9-13

SHOES, PARKING BRAKE (REAR DISC BRAKES ONLY), INSPECTION AND REPLACEMENT, 9-21

SPARE TIRE, INSTALLING, 0-16

SPARK PLUG

check and replacement, 1-36

torque, 1-42

type and gap, 1-40

SPEAKERS, REMOVAL AND INSTALLATION, 12-11

STABILIZER BAR AND BUSHINGS, REMOVAL AND INSTALLATION

front, 10-3

rear, 10-9

STARTER MOTOR AND CIRCUIT, CHECK, 5-8

STARTER MOTOR, REMOVAL AND INSTALLATION, 5-9

STARTING SYSTEM, GENERAL INFORMATION AND PRECAUTIONS, 5-8

STEERING

column covers, removal and installation, 11-22

column switches, replacement, 12-7

gear boots, replacement, 10-16

gear, removal and installation, 10-16

knuckle and hub, removal and installation, 10-9

system, general information, 10-13

wheel, removal and installation, 10-14

STEERING, SUSPENSION AND DRIVEAXLE BOOT CHECK, 1-22

STRUT ASSEMBLY, REMOVAL, INSPECTION AND INSTALLATION
front, 10-4
rear, 10-10
STRUT ROD, REMOVAL AND INSTALLATION, 10-11
STRUT/COIL SPRING ASSEMBLY, REPLACEMENT, 10-5
SUSPENSION AND STEERING SYSTEMS, 10-1
SUSPENSION ARMS (REAR), REMOVAL AND INSTALLATION, 10-1

T

THERMOSTAT, CHECK AND REPLACEMENT, 3-3
THROTTLE BODY, CHECK, REMOVAL AND INSTALLATION, 4-10
THROTTLE POSITION SENSOR (TPS) AND THROTTLE CONTROL MOTOR, REPLACEMENT, 6-8
THROTTLE VALVE (TV) CABLE (AVALON AND SOLARA MODELS), ADJUSTMENT AND REPLACEMENT, 7B-4
TIE-ROD ENDS, REMOVAL AND INSTALLATION, 10-15
TIMING BELT AND SPROCKETS, V6 ENGINE, REMOVAL, INSPECTION AND INSTALLATION, 2B-8
TIMING CHAIN AND SPROCKETS, FOUR-CYLINDER ENGINE, REMOVAL, INSPECTION AND INSTALLATION, 2A-5
TIRE AND TIRE PRESSURE CHECKS, 1-10
TIRE ROTATION, 1-19
TIRE, SPARE, INSTALLING, 0-16
TOOLS AND WORKING FACILITIES, 0-7
TOP DEAD CENTER (TDC) FOR NUMBER ONE PISTON, LOCATING
four-cylinder engine, 2A-2
V6 engine, 2B-2
TORQUE SPECIFICATIONS
brake caliper mounting bolts, 9-27
cylinder head bolts
four-cylinder engine, 2A-23
V6 engine, 2B-20
spark plugs, 1-42

thermostat housing bolts, 3-18
water pump bolts/nuts, 3-18
wheel lug nuts, 1-42
Other torque specifications can be found in the Chapter that deals with the component being serviced
TOWING, 0-16
TRANSAXLE, AUTOMATIC, 7B-1
diagnosis, general, 7B-2
differential lubricant level check, 1-24
electronic control system, 7B-10
fluid
change, 1-27
level check, 1-12
oil seal replacement, 7B-6
removal and installation, 7B-7
shift cable, adjustment and replacement, 7B-3
shift lock system, description, check and component replacement, 7B-5
Throttle valve (TV) cable (Avalon and Solara models), adjustment and replacement, 7B-4
transmission position switch, replacement and adjustment, 7B-5
trouble codes, 7B-8
TRANSAXLE, MANUAL, 7A-1
back-up light switch, check and replacement, 7A-2
lubricant
change, when vehicle used for towing, 1-29
level check, 1-25
overhaul, general information, 7A-3
removal and installation, 7A-3
shift and select cable(s), replacement, 7A-2
shift lever assembly, removal and installation, 7A-2
TROUBLE CODES, ACCESSING, 6-2
TROUBLESHOOTING, 0-21
TRUNK LID
release cable, removal and installation, 11-14
removal, installation and adjustment, 11-12
TRUNK LID LATCH AND LOCK CYLINDER, REMOVAL AND INSTALLATION, 11-13
TRUNK RELEASE AND FUEL DOOR CABLES, REMOVAL AND INSTALLATION, 11-14
TUNE-UP AND ROUTINE MAINTENANCE, 1-1
TUNE-UP GENERAL INFORMATION, 1-7
TURN SIGNAL AND HAZARD FLASHER, CHECK AND REPLACEMENT, 12-6

U

UNDERHOOD HOSE CHECK AND
   REPLACEMENT, 1-18
UPHOLSTERY AND CARPETS, MAINTENANCE, 11-2

V

V6 ENGINE, 2B-1
camshafts and lifters, removal, inspection and
   installation, 2B-11
cylinder head, removal and installation, 2B-13
exhaust manifolds, removal and installation, 2B-7
flywheel/driveplate, removal and installation, 2B-18
intake manifold, removal and installation, 2B-6
oil pan, removal and installation, 2B-15
oil pump, removal, inspection and installation, 2B-16
oil seals, replacement, 2B-11
powertrain mounts, check and replacement, 2B-18
rear main oil seal, replacement, 2B-18
repair operations possible with the engine in the
   vehicle, 2B-2
timing belt and sprockets, removal, inspection and
   installation, 2B-8
Top Dead Center (TDC) for number one piston,
   locating, 2B-2
valve covers, removal and installation, 2B-4
Variable Valve Timing (VVT) system, description, check and
   component replacement, 2B-3
VACUUM GAUGE DIAGNOSTIC CHECKS, 2C-5
VALVE CLEARANCE CHECK AND
   ADJUSTMENT, 1-31
VALVE COVER, REMOVAL AND INSTALLATION
four-cylinder engine, 2A-3
V6 engine, 2B-5
VARIABLE VALVE TIMING (VVT) SYSTEM,
   DESCRIPTION
four-cylinder engine, 2A-4
V6 engine, 2B-3

VEHICLE IDENTIFICATION NUMBERS, 0-6
VEHICLE SPEED SENSOR (VSS),
   REPLACEMENT, 6-12
VINYL TRIM, MAINTENANCE, 11-2

W

WATER PUMP
check, 3-6
removal and installation, 3-7
WHEEL ALIGNMENT, GENERAL
   INFORMATION, 10-20
WHEEL BEARING, REMOVAL AND INSTALLATION
front, 10-9
rear, 10-12
WHEEL CYLINDER, REMOVAL AND
   INSTALLATION, 9-16
WHEELS AND TIRES, GENERAL
   INFORMATION, 10-19
WINDOW DEFOGGER, CHECK AND REPAIR, 12-12
WINDOW GLASS, REMOVAL AND
   INSTALLATION, 11-18
WINDOW REGULATOR, REMOVAL AND
   INSTALLATION, 11-19
WINDOWS, POWER, DESCRIPTION, 12-18
WINDSHIELD AND FIXED GLASS,
   REPLACEMENT, 11-7
WINDSHIELD WASHER FLUID, LEVEL CHECK, 1-9
WINDSHIELD WIPER BLADE INSPECTION AND
   REPLACEMENT, 1-14
WIPER MOTOR, CHECK AND REPLACEMENT, 12-10
WIRING DIAGRAMS, GENERAL
   INFORMATION, 12-21
WORKING FACILITIES, 0-7

Notes